M000238184

Democracy, Bureaucracy, and the Study of Administration

ASPA Classics

Conceived and sponsored by the American Society for Public Administration (ASPA), the ASPA Classics series will publish volumes on topics that have been, and continue to be, central to the contemporary development of public administration. The ASPA Classics are intended for classroom use and may be quite suitable for libraries and general reference collections. Drawing from the Public Administration Review and other journals related to the ASPA sections, each volume in the series is edited by a scholar who is charged with presenting a thorough and balanced perspective on an enduring issue. These journals now represent some six decades of collective wisdom. Yet, many of the writings collected in the ASPA Classics might not otherwise easily come to the attention of future public managers. Given the explosion in research and writing on all aspects of public administration in recent decades, these ASPA Classics anthologies should point readers to definitive or groundbreaking authors whose voices should not be lost in the cacophony of the newest administrative technique or invention.

Public servants carry out their responsibilities in a complex, multidimensional environment. The mission of ASPA Classics is to provide the reader with a historical and firsthand view of the development of the topic at hand. As such, each ASPA Classics volume presents the most enduring scholarship, often in complete, or nearly complete, original form on the given topic. Each volume will be devoted to a specific continuing concern to the administration of all public sector programs. Early volumes in the series address public sector performance, public service as commitment, and diversity and affirmative action in public service. Future volumes will include equally important dialogues on reinventing government and public service ethics.

The volume editors are to be commended for volunteering for the substantial task of compiling and editing these unique collections of articles that might not otherwise be readily available to scholars, teachers, and students.

ASPA Classics Editorial Board

Marc Holzer, Editor-in-Chief
Rutgers University, Campus at Newark

Walter Broadnax, University of Maryland
Beverly Cigler, Pennsylvania State University
Patricia Ingraham, Syracuse University
Richard C. Kearney, East Carolina University
Don Kettl, University of Wisconsin
Camilla Stivers, Cleveland State University

Books in This Series

Democracy, Bureaucracy, and the Study of Administration

edited by

Camilla Stivers

Cleveland State University

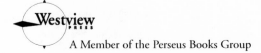

A Member of the Perseus Books Group

ASPA Classics series

All rights reserved. Printed in the United States of America. No part of this publication may be reproduced or transmitted in any form or by any means, electronic or mechanical, including photocopy, recording, or any information storage and retrieval system, without permission in writing from the publisher.

Copyright © 2001 by Westview Press, A Member of the Perseus Books Group

Published in 2001 in the United States of America by Westview Press, 5500 Central Avenue, Boulder, Colorado 80301-2877, and in the United Kingdom by Westview Press, 12 Hid's Copse Road, Cumnor Hill, Oxford OX2 9JJ

Find us on the World Wide Web at www.westviewpress.com

Library of Congress Cataloging-in-Publication Data
Democracy, bureaucracy, and the study of administration / edited by Camilla Stivers.
        p.   cm. — (ASPA classics)
    ISBN 0-8133-9809-6
    1. Public administration.   2. Bureaucracy.   3. Democracy.   I. Stivers, Camilla.
II. Series.

JF1351.D447   2000
351—dc21

                                                                                00-05-357

The paper used in this publication meets the requirements of the American National Standard for Permanence of Paper for Printed Library Materials Z39.48-1984.

10   9   8   7   6   5   4   3   2   1

PERSEUS
POD
ON DEMAND

CONTENTS

TABLES AND ILLUSTRATIONS

INTRODUCTION

The essays collected in this volume address several of the most central and enduring ideas in the field of public administration. All appeared originally either in *Public Administration Review* or another of the journals sponsored by the American Society for Public Administration. This volume focuses on themes that cross subdisciplinary and topical boundaries in the field of public administration. They are as relevant to public budgeting as they are to performance measurement, human resource management, and issues of diversity. They are what Dwight Waldo, a former editor of *Public Administration Review,* referred to as "political theories," that is, they deal with issues that are ultimately unresolvable yet crucial to a sound understanding of the nature of public administration and to good practice. In a real sense, the existence of this volume constitutes a tribute to Waldo, whose vision of public administration as both a set of practical techniques and a political philosophy contributed so much to the subsequent development of the field.

Waldo (1948) argued that the tension between democracy and efficiency was the central question in the field of public administration. He believed that it was a tension fated never to be resolved, since administrators are required not only to try to do their work as efficiently and effectively as possible but also to try to conduct themselves in a way that is consistent with democratic values. The idea of "most efficient" or "most effective" practice suggests that administrators, at least over time, can figure out the best way to practice. Yet ideas of democratic administration suggest that, since citizens and their representatives are rarely unanimous about governmental purposes and practices, the single-minded search for a best way is both inappropriate and doomed to failure. As Waldo's view implies, most administrative actions have political implications, because of the power administrators exercise when they make decisions. Thus no matter how hard they search for a best way, their actions will raise debatable political questions. Out of this paradox have grown some of the most important and lasting debates in the field.

Beginning with an examination of the tension between *politics* and *administration* (another way of stating the tension between democracy and efficiency), the volume moves to consider:

- whether there can be or should be a *science of administration*, as the search for one best way suggests;
- ways of thinking about administrative *accountability*, which ideas of democratic administration demand;
- relationships between *citizens and the administrative state*;
- the question of whether *professionalism* is an adequate mechanism for ensuring accountability;
- several issues surrounding the idea of *bureaucracy*, a key means by which efficiency is promoted; and
- *leadership*, as it should be practiced by administrators hoping to address, if not to reconcile, issues of political democracy and issues of administrative effectiveness.

The introduction to each section explores in more detail the dimensions of each issue and how it relates to the overall theme of tension between democracy and bureaucracy.

It is hoped that by collecting together in one place a number of significant and lasting contributions to these fundamental debates, this volume will encourage readers to reflect on the political implications of the work they do. Through such reflection they may come to see the study of administration not as a search for final answers or nuts-and-bolts techniques but rather as a framework within which to consider the larger implications of administration in a representative democracy. The articles have been selected to illustrate major positions taken on these important issues over the course of the field's development since the founding of *Public Administration Review* in 1940. One testimony to the enduring quality of these debates is their persistence through more than half a century and the extent to which ideas expressed thirty, forty, or sixty years ago are still fresh. Readers are invited to join in these debates and to consider for themselves their applicability to public administration today.

Camilla Stivers

Part One
Politics and Administration

In his famous 1887 essay "The Study of Administration," Woodrow Wilson advocated systematic examination of administrative processes, so that administrators could do the best possible, most efficient and businesslike job of carrying out orders issued by legislatures. Wilson (1887) argued in much the same vein as Alexander Hamilton had in the Federalist Papers: Running the nation required an administration with large powers and unhampered discretion, yet susceptible to serious public criticism. Wilson's views were somewhat more complex and sophisticated than the simplistic "politics-administration dichotomy" he has been credited with (or accused of). In any case, his article established the relationship between politics and administration as a—perhaps the—central question in the emerging field, and set in motion a long-lasting debate.

By now it is widely accepted that politics permeates administrative processes; but a fundamental divide still exists between two views. One sees administration, despite the undeniable presence of politics, as basically concerned with questions that appear to have right answers, such as: Given particular circumstances, how can administrators get the most bang for the buck? Or, What is the most effective way to motivate employees? Or, What managerial control system is most likely to ensure results? In this view, politics is treated as, in a sense, a contaminant of what would otherwise be rational administrative processes. The other perspective sees administration not as polluted by politics but as itself fundamentally political because of the power wielded by tenured, unelected bureaucrats in the exercise of dis-

1

cretionary authority. In this view, public administration is as much about wrestling with questions to which there are no final answers, such as What is the public interest in this situation? as it is with questions of efficiency or results.

These two perspectives have contrasting implications for the relationship between politics and administration. You may believe that all or nearly all the important administrative questions have right answers, though we may not know what they are yet. If so, you are more likely to see administration as a search for those answers. This could be through drawing on the results of rigorous scientific study or on a blend of research findings and judgment. On the other hand, you may believe that many important administrative questions have no final *right* answers, though they may have *good* answers in the sense that solid arguments can be made in defense of them. In this case you are more likely to see administration as encompassing a great deal of systematic reflection in addition to relying on empirical analysis. The two landmark essays in this section explore the tension between politics and administration; in the following section, we expand the discussion by considering various views of how to study administration.

David M. Levitan's "Political Ends and Administrative Means" appeared in *Public Administration Review (PAR)* in mid–1943. While it would count in any context as an important contribution to the ongoing dialogue about the relationship between politics and administration, this essay has a special resonance in that it was written by a practitioner during the thick of World War II. As he and his colleagues struggled to find effective ways of carrying on the work of the War Production Board, Levitan evidently sensed the utterly practical implications of a rather theoretical-sounding question: Can public administration be confined to a scientific study of techniques? His answer is a resounding "no."

The central point of the essay is that "democratic government means democracy in administration, as well as in the original legislation." This insight, Levitan argues, was shared by the field's founders, including Woodrow Wilson, Frank Goodnow, Leonard White, and William Willoughby, but has been lost sight of in the quest for a science of administration. Levitan suggests that administrative techniques must not only be consistent with the political philosophy on which a government is based but also with contemporary social and economic conditions. The search for proper techniques must entail a search for ways to saturate administrative machinery with democratic philosophy.

Barry D. Karl's "The American Bureaucrat: A History of a Sheep in Wolves' Clothing," was published in a 1987 issue of *PAR* commemorating the centennial of Woodrow Wilson's essay. Karl provides broad historical context for the question of the relationship between politics and administration, particularly the extent to which bureaucratic efficiency and democratic government can be reconciled or harmonized. He sees Americans as fundamentally suspicious of bureaucratic power and willing to tolerate considerable inefficiency in order to control it. This complicates the quest for "best ways" of administration, since best solutions are determined by experts, such as scientists or other professionals, rather than through democratic processes. Karl thinks of American negativism toward bureaucracy as a reaction against the views of the framers of the U. S. Constitution, who deplored party politics and sought to keep government in the hands of an educated elite. This goal was later adopted in modified form by civil service reformers, Progressives, and advocates of professionalism in administration. But it has always sat uneasily in the context of American devotion to democratically accountable government. The result, Karl argues, is that citizens will always be likely to judge efforts to improve the efficiency of the bureaucracy on political rather than administrative grounds.

The issue of the relationship between administrative methods and political goals permeates most of the essays in this collection. As Wallace Sayre pointed out in a 1950 *PAR* essay (not included here because of space limitations), the central question in the field of public administration is "whether it shall strive to be primarily a non-normative science divorced from values, or whether it shall aspire toward a theory of governance which embraces the political and social values of a democratic society as well as the 'facts' of administrative behavior" (Sayre 1950, 5).[1]

Note

1. Editor's references are on page 498.

1

POLITICAL ENDS AND ADMINISTRATIVE MEANS

David M. Levitan

I

More than half a century has elapsed since Woodrow Wilson published his essay on "The Study of Administration."[1] This marked the first effort, in America, at a systematic delineation of the scope and meaning of the field of administration. The essay was soon followed by Goodnow's *Politics and Administration,* in which the subject matter of administration was again emphasized. Great progress has since been made in the clarification and systematization of the discipline brought to light by these earlier works. In fact, the outstanding development during the twentieth century in the field of public administration has been the evolution of a separate discipline concerned with the execution of public policy, as distinguished from the function of policy determination. The study of administration has become a study of techniques, a study of the "means" as distinguished from the "ends"—a concept aptly summarized in White's statement that "administration is a process."

This identification of administration with techniques, most elaborately developed by Willoughby, has been called the "institutional" approach, perhaps because of its resemblance to the approach of institutional eco-

Source: *Public Administration Review* 3(1943): 353–359.

nomics. Whatever the origin of the term, the attention focused on administrative techniques, processes, and procedures has contributed much to the improvement of administration in the modern state.

But, valuable as the institutional approach has been for the development of administration, it has also led to the appearance of some dangerous tendencies in modern administrative theory. It is easy to advance from the concept of "administration is a process" to the view that its principles can be scientifically stated, that it can be developed as a separate science, and that, once discovered, administrative principles have universal applicability.

In regarding administration as a separate discipline no one, of course, claims that administration exists in a vacuum; it is generally recognized as a tool for putting into effect policy decisions—for carrying out the purposes of the state. But it is in the tendency to regard it as a tool which, once perfected, can be used for the effectuation of *any* policy decisions, for carrying out *any* purposes, that the danger lies.

Two specific instances may be cited of trends resulting from this view which have highly dangerous potentialities. The first is its effect on administrative personnel, present and future. If sound administrative principles and techniques are equally applicable in any situation, it follows logically that a good administrator need know only these principles and techniques in order to fulfill his functions adequately. And, in fact, the emphasis on administration as concerned only with techniques fosters among some present administrative employees the development of a bureaucratic point of view and a total unconcern with the broader implications of administrative action or, in the case of those with broader training, a deep feeling of resentment as to the lack of importance of their work. Almost every day in Washington one encounters some friend of college or school days who bemoans his plight with red tape, his total frustration as a result of his preoccupation with "administrivia." Most of these people have simply failed to see the fundamental nature of their work and its relation to the broader aspects of government and public policy, because it has so often been emphasized to them that their job is to deal with techniques and that broad questions of policy and theory are outside the scope of administration. They no longer search for the more fundamental. They see only a "paper-shuffling" job.

The same emphasis portends some serious shortcomings as to the training of future administrative officials. The tendency is clear. The growth of schools of public administration with their type of program is indicative of the trend with respect to the scope of the training of the administrative official of the future. The emphasis is on courses dealing with "Introduction to Administration," "Principles of Personnel Administration," "Techniques of Classification," "Principles of Budgeting," Principles of Overhead Management," and the like. This type of training, unless founded on a broad theoretical and historical background, will greatly influence the type of students who turn to the study of administration and as a result will greatly influence the type of administration. The administration of the modern service state places a premium upon administrative officials with imagination and insight; yet students with a flair for the broad and endowed with a faculty for assimilating the general will view askance the study of administration. There is a very real concern among many administrators regarding the supply of younger administrators—men with broad vision and understanding. Mr. Paul Appleby, Undersecretary of the Department of Agriculture, emphasized this problem in a paper read before the Washington Chapter of the American Society for Public Administration in the fall of 1942, stressing the importance for higher administrative work of broad training, imagination, and capacity for abstract thinking.

The second unfortunate tendency which has its genesis in the view of administration as a tool which can be used for the effectuation of any policy is the (again logical) extension of this idea to include the belief that administrative machinery can be transplanted from one system of government to another; if it works well in the one, it will work well in the other. Wilson has stated this belief succinctly:

> If I see a murderous fellow sharpening a knife cleverly, I can borrow his way of sharpening the knife without borrowing his probable intention to commit murder with it; and so, if I see a monarchist dyed in the wool managing a public bureau well, I can learn his business methods without changing one of my republican spots.[2]

The dangerous fallacy implicit in this view needs to be clearly understood in order to avoid transplanting into this country from other governments administrative techniques intrinsically incompatible with the underlying philosophy of democratic government.

It should be pointed out that the men who were responsible for the development of the institutional approach themselves realized the importance of the relation between the administration and the broad underlying philosophy of a government. The emphasis on administration as concerned with techniques and means rather than with ends has been so great that sight is often lost of an equally definite aspect of their philosophy of administration. Wilson, after stating the value of a comparative study of techniques of administration, showed that he fully realized the dangers inherent in transmitting systems of administration without regard to the local philosophy:

> By keeping this distinction in view—that is, by studying administration as a means of putting our own politics into convenient practice, as a means of making what is democratically politic towards all administratively possible towards each—we are on perfectly safe ground, and can learn without error what foreign systems have to teach us.[3]

Even more pointed is his admonition that "the principles on which to base a science of administration for America must be principles which have democratic policy very much at heart."

Similarly, Goodnow recognized the close relation between administration and the underlying philosophy of the government. He stated clearly that the nature of the state is as much influenced by the administrative system as by the underlying philosophical principles, that "a system of government" refers to both its principles and its administrative system. "The administrative system has, however, as great influence in giving its tone to the general governmental system as has the form of government set forth in the constitution."[4] And he refers with approval to the view of the German jurist and administrator, Gneist, that "English parliamentary government could not be understood apart from the administrative system."

Other students of the administrative process have also emphasized the closeness of the relationship between administration and political and social philosophy. For example, White, writing in the *Encyclopaedia of the Social Sciences*, says:

> The general character of administration has always been governed by the physical basis of state organization, by the prevailing level of social and cultural organization, by the development of technology, by theories of the function of the state and by more immediate governmental and political traditions and ideals.

There is, therefore, nothing new in the recognition of an organic relationship between the basic principles of a system of government and its administration. In view of the dangerous tendencies already noticed, however, it would seem to be necessary to reemphasize and to clarify this concept. That a need for such reemphasis and clarification exists is made further evident by such statements as that of Schuyler C. Wallace in his *Federal Departmentalization* (pp. 231–33):

> There exists a tendency on the part of many of those who deal with administration to concentrate upon some particular aspect of the general field and to ignore or neglect its relations to the process of government as a whole. . . . Those who deal with administration generally do not look upon the study of that subject as requiring the study of government as a whole—much less as necessitating a broad consideration of the economic, social, and psychological characteristics of the society in which they are operating.

At this time, when many are turning their attention to the solution of the problems related to the establishment of a postwar world order, a genuine understanding of the significance of the administrative and procedural is especially important.

II

Administrative procedural machinery is much more than a *tool* for the implementation of a political ideology. Administrative procedural machinery is an integral *part* of each political ideology—it is a part of a system of government.

Any system of government is composed of the sum total of its political and philosophical principles and the administrative procedural machinery established for their effectuation. The democratic system of government includes not only such principles as that government is based on the consent of the governed, that the individual is the basis of all legitimate governmental authority, and that the dignity of the individual must be preserved, but also the fundamental administrative procedural machinery to implement these principles. It follows that a system of government cannot be considered as a democratic system, even though its theoretical foundation be the principles included by political theorists in their statement of the democratic dogma, if it is not accompanied by administrative machinery for the realization of the principles.

A striking example is found in the Middle Ages. Recent studies, such as McIlwain's brilliant volume, *Growth of Political Thought in the West*, have done much to clarify our thinking about the political philosophy of the Middle Ages. It had been customary to speak of that era as a period of supreme absolutism. Even now one sometimes hears the statement that Hitlerism or fascism marks a return to the philosophy of the Middle Ages. Nothing could be further from the truth. The truth is that the notion of unlimited government—government not subject to a higher law—is foreign to the Middle Ages. The modern doctrine of sovereignty was first enunciated by the apologists for papal authority and church supremacy at the beginning of the fourteenth century. Much of the democratic philosophy was part of the tradition of the Middle Ages, finding expression in the writings of both students and rulers. Yet no one would include the system of government of the Middle Ages in a list of democratic governments, even if the concept include states espousing democratic principles but formally headed by a monarch, as is the case with Great Britain today.

The distinguishing feature between modern democratic government and governments of the past apparently based on democratic principles is the establishment of procedures, of administrative machinery for the effectuation of the basic democratic tenets. The real contribution of modern democracy is not in the development of new principles, or what the lawyer calls "substantive" law, but rather in the development of "procedural" law—the implementation of broad philosophical principles with concrete administrative machinery. The "due process of law" concept, in its true historical sense, is at the very foundation of democratic government.

The fact that in the mind of the average man Hitlerism, barbarism, unfettered government are associated with the idea of the Middle Ages is itself illustrative of this point. Since it is clearly established that no adequate procedural guarantees for checking the authority of the ruler were in existence during the Middle Ages, the system of government has become identified in the popular mind with absolutism; and rightly so. It is a gross error for a student of theory to identify fascism with the philosophy of the Middle Ages, but it is natural for the common man to identify one with the other, for with regard to the things that concern him—his actual rights and liberties—Hitlerism and the governments of the Middle Ages have much in common.

The importance of the administrative and procedural was eloquently summarized by Quincy Wright at the time of the Munich settlement:

> The fundamental legal criticism of the settlement rests on the fact that the statesmen responsible for it placed the substance of the settlement ahead of the procedure by which it was achieved. They thus duplicated the error of the statesmen at Versailles twenty years earlier. . . .
>
> Constitutional government consists in a determination of the citizens of the state that adherence to the procedures set forth in the constitution shall be treated as more important than any specific grievance, demand, or reform. Until the people of the world are similarly determined to place procedures ahead of substance, we may expect the world to alternate between dictates of Versailles and dictates of Munich, with little respite from wars and rumors of wars.[5]

Students of American foreign affairs will need little prodding to realize the role of procedural machinery. The fate of the Versailles Treaty is still too fresh in our minds.

What is true with regard to basic procedures in relation to the basic structure and constitutional framework of the state is equally true with regard to procedures and administrative machinery for the effectuation of the day-by-day decisions and legislation. Social legislation, whether dealing with minimum wages, maximum hours, social security, or labor relations, can have little significance to the citizen; it begets meaning only when supported by detailed "administrivia." A liberal government has value only when based on liberal legislation supported by administrative machinery.

The nature of the administrative procedural machinery is thus seen to be as important as, if not more important than, the nature of the philosophical principles of government. Democratic government means democracy in administration, as well as in the original legislation. It is of supreme importance that the administrative machinery established for the execution of legislation be permeated with democratic spirit and ideology, with respect for the dignity of man.

Few would gainsay the truth of Wilson's warning: "Liberty cannot live apart from constitutional principle; and no administration, however perfect and liberal its methods, can give men more than a poor counterfeit of liberty if it rest upon illiberal principles of government." But it is apparently not so generally recognized that the converse is likewise true—that no principles of government, however perfect and liberal, can give men more than a poor counterfeit of liberty if they are not implemented by democratic administrative machinery. Administrative authoritarianism, officiousness, and arbitrariness are much more serious threats to the rights and liberties of the individual than arbitrary legislation. The German historian, Niebuhr, summarized this view in his statement that "liberty depends incomparably more upon administration than upon constitutions." Unwise legislation may be mitigated somewhat by considerate and humane administration, but the citizen has no "cushion" against arbitrary officialdom, often hidden behind the cloak of "administrative necessity." The real protection of the citizen lies in the development of a high degree of democratic consciousness among the administrative hierarchy.

Continued emphasis on the universal applicability of administrative principles tends to obfuscate this organic relationship between the political and social theory of the government as a whole and the political and social theory underlying its administration. There is little real basis for a comparative study of the administrative machinery in Nazi Germany and in democratic America. The fact that German administrative machinery is geared to effectuate a philosophy which recognizes no rights of the individual, which denies the very dignity of the human personality—either of the citizen or of the public servant—while the American system is based on the very opposite philosophy makes the German experience of little value, so far as the United States is concerned, not only as to methods and machinery for dealing with the citizen, but even as to internal management. Administrative procedures cannot be transplanted from one system of government to another, but must have their roots in the political and social philosophy underlying their own system of government.

All this is not to deny the existence of any general applicable principles of administration, but to affirm that such principles must be interpreted and applied in a manner consistent with the basic philosophy of the state, and that as so interpreted and applied they exhibit fundamental differences from the same principles applied elsewhere. For example, the concept of "unity of command" has assumed different meanings in Germany and in America. It is one thing to say that in the administration of any program someone must be empowered to make final decisions, after a genuine exchange of ideas up and down the hierarchy. It is a totally different thing to say that in the administration of any program there must be one man to give orders and issue commands. The *Fuehrerschaft* principle denies that all men have the capacity to make some contribution; consequently it is useless to establish channels for the exchange of ideas up and down the hierarchy. In the American system a public servant is not only an employee but also a citizen and, above all, a human being, who retains his basic rights and is therefore entitled to dignity and respect.

The natural human tendency to emulate what others have done is so great, especially if it has appeared successful, that unless the limited aspect of "transplantable administration" is constantly emphasized and the importance of the frame of reference reiterated, much that is contrary to the fundamental spirit of the forum will be transplanted. The danger is especially great where some are interested in changing the spirit of the forum, and the advocated measures carry the blessings of the god of "efficiency." Only maximum vigilance by the administrative hierarchy, based upon a clear understanding and acceptance of the philosophy of the state, will effectively check such efforts.

III

Up TO this point, stress has been laid on the prime importance of procedural machinery in effectuating the ends of government and on the necessity for gearing administrative machinery to the basic philosophy of the state. It is also important to realize that, while the existence of such machinery is basic, the machinery itself may be modified from time to time; in fact, must be modified if it is to continue to implement the fundamental principles of the government under changing social and economic conditions.

One of the discouraging symptoms of the myopic condition prevailing among some students of administration is manifested in their failure to see the relation between administrative techniques and social and political environment. On more than one occasion I have heard such students decry the Jacksonian system of administration—the spoils system—without the slightest indication of any realization on their part that the spoils system was based on a very genuine theory of democracy. The technique may be a bad one by our standards; but it was in tune with the social and political philosophy of its day.

Those desiring the *status quo ante* or a return to "normalcy" inevitably rely on old established procedural safeguards, though under the new conditions they are only legal fictions, no longer serving the purposes which they were intended to serve. Students of American constitutional and administrative law will readily recall the "sham" of the due process doctrine. This doctrine, long a bulwark of individual freedom, became under changed conditions an instrument for the miscarriage of justice.

The administrator, whether in a court of law or executive department, must at all times ask himself: "Is the established administrative machinery effectuating the policy—the end which the law sought to accomplish?" Ends broadly and adequately conceived will remain valid for long periods of time, if there are no fundamental changes in the basic philosophy of the government. Such is not the case, however, with regard to the detailed machinery of government. Whereas the ends of a just government have changed little from the days of Plato and Aristotle to our own, the machinery and the specific legal enactments necessary for the realization of these ends have completely changed and will continue to change with the modifications of the physical, technological, social, and economic world about us.

Administrative machinery, then, as an important—perhaps the most important—part of a system of government, must be constantly reexamined in terms of the ends it is intended to serve—in terms of the results which are to be accomplished. Further, the maintenance in this manner of procedural machinery which is in accord with the basic philosophy of the state is, in the long run, more important for the achievement of those ends than is the enactment of substantive law.

This last generalization should, of course, be understood as referring to such broad and intangible ends as liberty of the individual or a just world order. When we are dealing with specific and clearly defined ends, we must not permit ourselves to get so involved in the administrative machinery as to lose sight of the ends; policy decisions will necessarily come before administrative considerations in realizing the ends in view. But even then the importance of the administrative machinery should always be kept in mind and, in connection with the broader, long-term ends, it should be recognized as paramount.

IV

An outstanding government administrator once remarked that "administration must have a soul." That, in a way, magnificently summarizes the thesis I have been developing. It needs to be added, however, that administration should contribute to the fuller development of the soul of the state. I have tried to point out that the administrative machinery and the political and philosophical principles together determine the system of government; that a democratic state must be not only based on democratic principles but also democratically administered, the democratic philosophy permeating its administrative machinery and being manifested in its relations both with the citizen outside the government and with the citizen inside the government, the public servant; that administrative procedures are even more important in effectuating the basic principles of government than in substantive law; and that these procedures must therefore be constantly reexamined in terms of the ends they serve and changed when the changing social and economic milieu requires different means to attain these ends.

The institutional approach has contributed greatly to the development of administrative theory and practice, but if we so misinterpret it as to regard administration as concern with "means" and nothing more, we shall be dealing a serious blow not only to administration itself, but to the democratic principles which we are striving to put into effect. The administrators of tomorrow must be men with a clear understanding and acceptance of the philosophy of the state and with the broad vision and imaginative power to gear the administrative machinery to that philosophy.

Notes

1. 2 *Political Science Quarterly* 197–222 (1887).
2. *Ibid.*, p. 220.
3. *Ibid.*, p. 220.
4. *Politics and Administration*, p. 5.
5. "The Munich Settlement and International Law," 33 *American Journal of International Law* 31–32 (1939).

2

THE AMERICAN BUREAUCRAT: A HISTORY OF A SHEEP IN WOLVES' CLOTHING

Barry D. Karl

For most of American history the terms "bureaucrat" and "bureaucracy" have been used in popular discourse as epithets, when they have been used at all. Although both terms have achieved a certain amount of academic credibility in American social science over the last 30 or 40 years, it is an acceptance which is grudging. That is true, in many respects, even in the worlds of political science and public administration where the influence of European theory since the end of World War II has brought about a broader understanding of comparative administrative practices. Nonetheless, in the sophisticated professions that now constitute the complex fields of journalism and political commentary the terms are part of a political language that has evolved in American political life. They evoke negative images. Even when they appear in debates that are ostensibly about deregulation and the role of the state in the life of the citizen, they are in fact expressions of an American suspicion of government that goes back to our national origins. Americans believed that power was essentially

Source: *Public Administration Review* 47(1987): 26–34.

corrupting long before Lord Acton articulated the idea for them; and "bureaucracy" is a term that can easily be used to describe the inherent corruption of power.

Revolutionary Origins: The Two Revolutions

The framers of the Constitution of 1787 and the authors of the *Federalist Papers* had already adopted British attitudes toward reform politics that lumped political parties, patronage, and self-interest together as enemies of the public virtues which they defined as Republican. Their revolution had been a rebellion against George III's failure to become the hero of their Republican ideal, the monarch who could see through the factionalism of his parliament and his ministers and restore virtue to the state. The subsequent development of political parties in the new nation was thus an unwanted consequence of their state building, not simply an unintended one. The fact that the framers' ultimate acceptance of the grim reality of party difference required a major constitutional change in the method of selecting the President and Vice-President is often lost in the now familiar experience with partisan political contests.[1]

The election of Andrew Jackson in 1828 signified a major reshaping of politics and an acceptance of party practices. As Matthew Crenson has pointed out so effectively, the Jacksonian administrators were indeed a newer breed than Leonard White had believed them to be. They objected to the personal control which Federalist and Jeffersonian bureaucrats had used to maintain and justify their sense of their own public virtue. They sought a definition of Republican virtue that could be verified by public records and made accountable, in every sense of the term, to public judgment.[2]

In time even the new system would be perceived as corrupt, in the standard sense of the term. Rotation in office, or spoils, depending on where one stood on the democratic reform spectrum, formalized the establishment of a two-tiered system of political management. One tier used party organization and the distribution of offices as its base, while the other depended on elite figures chosen from traditional elite families, as well as the newer elites of business, banking, the law, and the emerging professions. In some parts of the country, notably New England and the coastal South where the traditions of politics allowed for the selection of individuals from the old elite to run for office, the two merged. But by the middle of the nineteenth century one could see in most parts of the country—and particularly in the rapidly expanding cities of the nation—a growing distinction between politicians who controlled political offices and business and professional elites who alternated between cautious support of candidates who met their standards and the angry organizing of reform opposition to defeat those who did not. The distinction between politics and administration rested on social and economic realities that went back to the beginning of the nation's partisan political organization.

The profound character of that distinction is part of what makes the idea of bureaucracy in the United States so complexly different from European conceptions of bureaucracy. On the continent bureaucracy developed prior to and independent of the growth of mass democracy. In England the emergence of a civil service elite which shared and supported upper class values reflected a different tradition of parliamentary control that was both Republican and elitist before mass democracy entered the scene. Without going through the complex distinctions that mark debates about the development of British politics in the eighteenth century, it is still important to point out again that such debates were part of the background of the framers of early American governments. It is just as important to remind ourselves of the changes produced by Jacksonian democracy, for the embedding of the conflict between mass democracy and elite professionalism in the American political structure is what really shapes the American meaning of bureaucracy and American attitudes toward it.

Hostility to the term itself has distinctive Anglo-American roots. Thomas Carlyle's reference to it as "the continental nuisance" became the often-repeated source quotation in definitions in English dictionaries and encyclopedias.[3] The substitution of the term "civil servant" was probably an attempt to articulate the sense of public control which made it possible to argue that such service was the fulfillment of a public trust, not an opportunity for independent, self-serving aggrandizement.

For American reformers the term "administration" served to focus a kind of pragmatic attention on the governing process. The term became part of an elite reform vocabulary, however, one which appealed primarily to the post-Civil War reformers who had begun to designate efficient government as the opposite of partisan political government. The Civil Service reform movement adopted the rhetoric of public service to attack, in effect, the basic party structure that had developed. Designations like "stalwart" and "regular" were used by reformers as criticisms of the party machinery which, from their perspective, violated the logic of good government, if not the practice, even if party adherents rejected their criticisms. Adherence to party for committed party regulars was not simply the recognition of the personal benefits bought by party loyalty but an acknowledgment of the function which party membership had played in supporting and maintaining the national union.

Administration and the Progressives

Woodrow Wilson's essay, "The Study of Administration," appeared in 1887 and established not only the field but the clear articulation of conern world, democratic governments must find ways of adopting methods associated with despotic governments, and they must do it within the rhetorical frameworks defined by the democratic revolutions of the eighteenth and early nineteenth centuries. That might not have been so difficult had those frameworks stayed the same through the nineteenth century. Democratic theory, in its eighteenth century guise, had also accepted the classical theorists' view of democracy as a potentially dangerous force and had established a complex range of limits on participatory democracy.

By the end of the nineteenth century the progress of democratic thought had produced a wide range of populist and socialist conceptions that were far more radical. Whether or not one chooses to think of it as a paradox, it seems nonetheless true that the pressures of technological, scientific advance on conceptions of participatory democracy and self-government produced the confrontation with which we are now familiar: mass democracy versus class leadership. The use of the term "class" is itself open to controversy in American life where the relation among intellectual leadership, wealth, and the educational institutions that tend to provide the states and the nation with its leaders is far more complex an issue than it is elsewhere in the world.[9]

The fact that the potential class confrontation has always been clearer in Europe than it is for Americans has made it difficult for American theorists to cope with it. Bureaucracy and bureaucrats were familiar figures in European government. Every revolution against the traditional state has raised the question of the role of the bureaucracy, whether it be in the administration of the Nazi regime or the structure of revolutionary Marxist states of Eastern Europe and the Soviet Union. Americans have coped with the introduction of the bureacratic state by castigating it all the while and attempting to place upon it every limitation of which they could think.

Wilson's identification of what he was now calling the "science" of administration with despotic European governments was going to haunt many of his followers in the years after World War I, when the identification of efficiency with totalitarianism plagued efforts at administrative reform and governmental planning. Yet it is clear in Wilson's writings that he recognizes the necessity of strong leadership, that he requires of leaders an unswerving commitment to their ideals and a force of character which makes them less the followers of public opinion than the creators of it. His essay, "Leaders of Men," is, in some respects, a shocking document, filled with what generations today would consider "macho" images of leaders and leadership, but images which historians would clearly identify with Nietzschean and Hegelian categories understood by Wilson's generation.[10]

Wilson and his generation of Progressive leaders were trying to create a British-like, upper-middle class elite, to put themselves in control of it, and to co-opt others into it as a means of stabilizing the wildly growing American society of the late nineteenth century. One can trace the careers of men and women from upper class backgrounds who adopt careers in politics or reform management as their method of using family wealth. At the same time, there is an expansion of voting publics, a transformation in attitudes toward party loyalty, and a whole raft of changes in politics traceable to urbanization, industrialization, communication, rapid technological change, and the uses of the educational system from kindergarten through graduate school as a route of access to power. The question is, what does the period say about attitudes toward bureaucracy, and I summarize my points here to make that clear.

First, the identification of administration with continental despotism may have turned out to be an unfortunate way to introduce the topic. Although other writers on administrative reform continued to look admiringly toward Germany and the management of German cities, some, like Herbert Croly, rejected both the British and the German models entirely. World War I, the Russian Revolution of 1917, and the development of fascism in the 1920s and 1930s gave those whose interests would be threatened by efficient administration an effective weapon to use, namely, that it was foreign and that it represented what was increasingly being called "totalitarian rule."

Secondly, the inability of American proponents of effective administration to cope with the fact that American definitions of democracy excluded sophisticated conceptions of a public interest elite capable of being responsible to the national interest as a whole was bound to give reformers difficulty. In the years after World War I men like Walter Lippmann would attempt to use ideas current in British politics and formulated there by Graham Wallas to talk about the public's limited focus, its preoccupation with self-interest, and its lack of profound contact with all of the issues involved in governing a nation state to avoid as far as they could the more pessimistic continental approach to public psychology exemplified by Sorel. British and American publics were neither neurotic, animalistic, nor stupid. They were busy with their own interests. John Dewey's *The Public and Its Problems* became the American description of the potentiality of popular reform politics.[11]

Thirdly, even enthusiasts like Wilson, who saw the need for new administrative forms, were profoundly committed to what they felt were the origins of American democracy in the country's state and local governments, not in the federal government in Washington. The generation that still celebrated the Fourth of July as a secular holiday and revered the Constitution of 1787 as a biblical document had also experienced the hard reality of the Civil War and accepted the compromises that concluded it. Wilson looked on the disenfranchisement of Negro voters as a good thing, not simply as an expedient. His New Freedom in 1912 was a virtual glorification of localism, politically as well as economically.

ment in American society that began with Woodrow Wilson and his generation of academicians in economics and political science who deliberately began working to formulate ideas that would influence policy makers in government.[16] Richard Ely, E. R. A. Seligman, and John R. Commons spent
their careers struggling with what often seemed, at least to some of them, an
endless battle of educating the nation's leaders in politics and business not
only to use their services but to follow their plans and programs. Thorstein
Veblen spent his time castigating those same leaders but seeded the profession with students whose influence carried through the New Deal.

Even before the seeming collapse of traditional business practices in the
Crash of 1929 and the Depression, business leaders like Owen D. Young.
Samuel Insull, and Herbert Hoover were searching for ways of establishing
a new and larger conception of business responsibility for guiding the social order and utilizing the new academicians to provide ideas.[17] Through
the New Deal and into the Truman Administration the notion of "on tap
but not on top" was accepted by academicians and political leaders as a
way of restating the staff-line distinction in American terms; but by the
Eisenhower Administration the distinction had begun to blur under the
pressure, chiefly of scientists moving into government as both administrators and advisers. While we are more familiar with the famous warning
against the industrial-military complex in Eisenhower's farewell address,
we should also note the next sentence in which he warned of the influence
of scientists and academicians. Within a matter of months the Kennedy
Administration appeared to obliterate the distinction entirely as academicians took over the management of programs. The group that later critics
would come to label "the best and the brightest" had taken over.

From the historical perspective of the present, it seems clear that the
United States was developing its own version of that cadre of trained officialdom designated by European theorists as "bureaucrats," yet the refusal
to label them as such and the continuing use of the term as a pejorative
continued. In the years before World War II, academicians interested in
public administration carried on the American tradition of British disdain
of bureaucracy. Leonard White's article on Public Administration for the
1930 edition of the *Encyclopedia of the Social Sciences* was both the high
point of the Anglo-American establishment of concepts of democratic administration and the watershed moment in what even White was prepared
to see as a momentous transition. White acknowledged responsibility to
Wilson, as well as to German methodological influences and those of
American industrial management; but his references to the emergence of
fascism in Italy—Hitler was still a year away and Mussolini was still
viewed as an interesting experiment—indicated that even with all of its efficiency, it was still "at the opposite pole from the American," and he went
on to spell out the differences.

"On the one hand are centralized systems in which administrative authority is concentrated in the hands of national officials, in whom is vested the responsibility for all administrative action, central or local, who appoint, supervise, and at will remove local agents to execute orders issuing from above. . . . On the other hand are decentralized systems, inherent in the structure of federal states and characteristic of Anglo-Saxon civilization, in which local autonomy prevails over the demands of central control, yielding in the face of modern economic problems but retaining a powerful vitality well displayed in the home rule movement for cities in the American commonwealths." Also, White made the basic and traditional distinction between "[T]he centralized type of administration which is related to the bureaucratic (i.e., the professional), and the decentralized type to the self-governmental (i.e., the amateur)." "Fascist Italy," he explained, "has eliminated the amateur from her administrative system in favor of a politico-professional bureaucracy; the United States, in spite of the technical nature of many aspects of administration, is still powerfully influenced by preference for amateur self-governmental forms."[18]

It is important to remember that White was writing while Hoover was still President. Both were still committed—as Franklin Roosevelt would continue to be—to Wilson's faith in the compromise between methods and ideology. White's identification of bureaucracy with non-democratic forms of government is precisely the sort of argument Hoover would make when he began his public criticisms of the New Deal.[19] Part of White's argument was made for him, too, by the editors' selection of Harold Laski to write the article on Bureaucracy for the *Encyclopedia*. Laski's brief essay goes not one step beyond the tone of the 11th edition of the *Britannica* two decades earlier, uses the same pejorative quotes, and assures us that the bureaucratic state is just as anti-democratic as it always was.

The editors also suggest another important distinction for us, one that relates importantly to their grudging confirmation of the role of industrial management theory. Public Administration as an entry is alphabetized under A, not under P, while the entry for Business Administration is under B. Misguided searchers who look for it under A are referred to the next letter in the alphabet, conveniently just above the reference to "Administration, Public," which gives them the correct reference. The distinction between business administration and public administration was one which the post-Progressive generation wanted to make clear, although in other parts of the world, including the admired Great Britain, the distinction provoked less disturbance. Like White's assertion of the difference between "professionals" and "amateurs," it was one to which Americans were peculiarly sensitive. White's generation of reformers was promoting professionalism in government, training experts, and trying to create a science of politics, even while they were agreeing that the replacement of their democratic amateurs by the new professionals might—just might, mind you—suggest that some important changes were underway.

They protected their faith in democracy by assuming that the values which held them together as a reforming community of scholars were values shared by all Americans, regardless of their professional interests. They assumed, too, that administrative skills and procedures, like social values, were common, more or less, to all professions, not specific to professions. The possibility that their commitment to neutrality and objectivity might contain some threatening flaws appears not to have occurred to them, at least as a serious issue, until well after World War II.

The closest they came to understanding the possibility of real conflict had always been in their relation to the business community. Whether administration designed to produce services differed significantly from administration designed to produce profits became a question that generations of Americans answered differently just as political-pendulum swings alternately defined business and industry as the model of innovation and opportunity which the rest of the world would do well to imitate and the chief stumbling block on the road to prosperity. Samuel Insull was the hero of the Twenties and the villain of the Thirties. Henry Ford was the focus of similar ambivalence. Ida Tarbell could censure John D. Rockefeller and Standard Oil in the Progressive era and idolize Owen D. Young and RCA a decade-and-a-half later. Thorstein Veblen could castigate and caricature the business leaders of the turn of the century and call upon the industrial engineers of the 1920s to take responsibility for reforming the nation's industrial system. Historians now tend to view Herbert Hoover as the era's victim, the man trapped by the paradoxes of the American view of management in an industrial society committed to preserving capitalism and free enterprise yet free to blame it for its inabilities to realize the American dream every time for everyone.

In the decades that followed the New Deal both its defenders and its critics distorted the picture by claiming either that it was an era of effective reform to which one could return by finding an attractive and compassionate leader or that it was a threatening period of dictatorial centralization or national management in Washington. It was, in fact, neither one. Both of the pictures have at their center conceptions of bureaucracy which, for better or for worse, bear little relation to the actual role of bureaucracies in American history.

The good New Deal bureaucrat is a trained and benevolent public servant dutifully carrying out the programs of a popularly elected American philanthropist. The bad New Deal bureaucrat is a tyrannical ideologue attempting to impose a narrow intellectual elite's standard of well-being on a complex, pluralist society. The real New Deal bureaucrat was, by and large, something quite different. "He," and the surprising number of "shes" among them, were administering politically designed programs with the expressed intention of maintaining intact the political system that had designed them.[20] While their distaste for partisan politics matched that of their Progressive forebears, their commitment to the two-party political debate was profound. While they were aware of the academic distinction between politics and administration, they were never fooled by it. The civil servant called for by their civil service reforms was a servant of political interests backed by the voters, not an administrative neuter fulfilling scientific objectives rationally defined. The protection of civil service was a protection from the mindless victimization produced by partisan politics, not a protection from the responsibility of serving the political aims signified by such changes. It was certainly never intended to certify scientifically defined policies believed by adherents to be above political judgment and control.

Bureaucratic agencies established by the New Deal took it from both sides. They were, on the one hand, evidence of the radical takeover of authority by a suspect elite. They were, on the other hand, partisan boondoggles writ large. Critics and supporters alike would, for half a century after the New Deal, continue to enjoy the parks, roadways, waterways, and public buildings built by the New Deal without ever associating them with the work of a federal bureaucracy.

Both labels stuck. Bureaucracy was radical and wasteful, revolutionary, tyrannical, and dishonest. Abolishing it would remain the most attractive and popular remedy, while making it more efficient and effective would gradually drift toward a private professional preserve where political scientists, teachers of public administration, and, by the 1950s a new group of sociologically oriented social scientists interested in bureaucratic theory would debate a curious historical reality only they seemed able to understand.

Modern technology, post-industrialism, and the ideas of Max Weber and Talcott Parsons were now ways of describing the consciousness that had emerged. When by 1962 the *New International Encyclopedia of the Social Sciences* appeared, its article on bureaucracy marked the essential transformation. Reinhard Bendix quickly swept past the pejoratives of the Anglo-American tradition and presented his readers with a brilliant panoramic view of the new Euro-American social thought. The American bureaucrat had come of age, or so it seemed.

The fact that by 1976 the Democratic Party could support a winning candidate whose campaign could be directed against the bureaucracy in Washington was certainly not envisaged by the proud academicians of the *Encyclopedia*. Nor was the fact that the argument would be sustained successfully by the Republicans as well, to become by the 1980s a major movement that could be defined not only as bipartisan but as a return to democracy, the recapture of a lost heritage. Sweeping aside a century of regulatory idealism built on the dream of a federal government that would protect its citizens from predatory interests, leaders in both parties extolled a new freedom, the freedom from bureaucratic dictation. Even the Supreme Court in its recent attack on Gramm-Rudman could call on the tradition by criticizing the power of an appointed bureaucrat, the Comptroller General, rather than raising the issue of separation of powers.

Bureaucracy, the Threat to Democracy: The Real Battle

Americans make no distinction, in political terms, between public needs and popular desires. Their refusal to accept such a distinction and to agree to an objective standard of public need defined by rationally determined considerations may distinguish Americans from members of societies where the state defines needs and debates only the degree and the timing of their fulfillment. Americans charge their government with the responsibility of meeting their individual needs in accordance with the shifting moods and perceptions that determine exactly what those needs are. The public will accept decisions that seem plausible if they are defended as expansions of democratic opportunity. But as the consequences of those decisions unfold, the American public will assume no responsibility for its own role in the process. The mood swings are percipitous and the penalties severe. Americans who elect leaders who reflect a current consensus on their attitudes toward political issues of the day will turn against those same leaders if and when that consensus changes.

Men who are elected for their administrative skills rather than their presence as popular public figures may find themselves sorely taxed by an unexpected public need for drama and charismatic leadership. The public wanted what Herbert Hoover represented in 1928. By 1931 it was clear that they sensed a need for something else, qualities which Hoover himself considered objectionable. He was never forgiven for his inability, in fact his refusal, to transform himself into the new, and needed, public image.

In an important sense the problem is not a new one. The debates that began in the Progressive Era used the terms "politics" and "administration" as the way of defining what has variously been viewed as a Manichaean opposition, a pair of correlative terms, or a necessary, if not altogether happy, partnership in the management of the democratic state. What seems clear, however, is that the dynamics of the relationship are and have continued to be historically volatile, more so, perhaps, than in any of the familiar cultures of western society where the growth of the administrative state and its relation to the social order are traced by students of administrative history. It might be useful to try to suggest some reasons for that volatility.

First, as Tocqueville suggested, Americans may be more committed believers in the essential politics of self-government than any other people on earth. As he pointed out, the belief that the passage of a law will solve every problem tends to be at the root of the American reform impulse. Even the most popular presidents have been forced to subject their administrative judgment to Congress and the courts. The Supreme Court has been pressed to respond to political judgments, at times to forestall legislative punishment.

Secondly, Americans have tended to look on government, and the federal government in particular, as the distributor of resources and the opportunities for advancement which such resources represent. Such distribution has always been subjected to the rule that benefits must be available to all, not just to the needy, and that there be as little administrative intervention as possible in what is essentially a process of democratic redistribution. That was as true of public lands in the nineteenth century as it is of educational opportunities, social security, medical benefits, and jobs today. Americans do not want to think of themselves as dependent upon state managers whose jobs they cannot threaten by the casting of a ballot or the rewriting of a law. The attractiveness of the short ballot and the growth of appointed rather than elected officialdom in American government has always been limited by the public's sense that it could find substitute controls and the legislature's sense that its threatened rebellions would elicit appropriate responses. Control over jobs and resources remains the basis of the cry of corruption, whether the target be a lowly ward heeler whose living depends on the voters he drags to the polls on election day or the management of a high level technology industry supplying the armed services with absurdly expensive screwdrivers.

Thirdly, Americans hold their elected administrators responsible for serving them and accept patronage as part of the process. The justice meted out to political and administrative decision makers has no equivalent of the legal distinction between involuntary manslaughter and premeditated murder. This ruthlessness of public judgment leads politicians and administrators alike to at least two recourses. They can try to please every one a little, thereby lessening the impact of criticism even though the end result may be the equivalent of doing nothing at all; or they can set up an opponent, one enemy who is preventing the action they really want to take, thereby directing attention away from themselves.

Nothing has done more to strengthen the role of administrative courts and the battles over the use of the legislative veto than the confusion of the political and administrative processes and the resulting conflicts among administrators charged with managing the programs. Frustrated presidents resort to the invention of new methods, the questionable use of old ones, and the inevitable force of public exhortation, which in itself may become a highly questionable theater in the world of public affairs. Presidential candidates running against incumbents, presidents seeking reelection, second-term presidents fighting unresponsive congresses, and vice-presidents hoping to succeed to candidacy, if not to office, all face the problem of attempting to turn administrative problems into political theater. The situation is an open invitation to irresponsibility, if not, under certain circumstances, a guarantee of it. Suggestions that there be a single term for presidents are all built on the belief that such a restriction would separate the office from the politics of reelection; but that, in a way, is too close to the logic that dictated the mischievous twenty-second amendment in the first place. A president without political clout ceases to be a political leader. From a historical point of view, the only real answer to the problem of maintaining administrative power in the presidency would be to remove the limitation on reelection entirely, thereby giving the political public the only kind of leader it feels it can control.

The dream of removing partisanship from American politics is essentially an elite dream that has no place in the American public's most profound conception of its own political power. Part of the hostility to bureaucracy stems from the fact that Americans see it as an inhibiting force, blocking their access to political power. Part of the inherent inefficiency of bureaucracy in the American administrative tradition is a result of that hostility, a consciousness on the part of even the most committed administrator that meeting the public's perception of need is the bottom line.

John Kennedy's *Profiles in Courage* may be the clearest expression of the paradox. Each of his courageous figures sacrifices a political career in the interest of some principle. They do not stay in Congress, or win the presidency, or succeed in gaining whatever career prize they set out to win. Most of them are martyrs: and while martyrs may be useful models for developing certain kinds of character, losing, as our Kennedys were raised to understand, is not the name of the game.

The threat of some kind of administrative tyranny is the oldest threat to democracy in our 200 years of independent history. It is the menace in twentieth century communism, just as it was in nineteenth century monarchy. The inefficiency, irrationality, and corruption we are willing to sustain in order to protect ourselves from it have succeeded, perhaps, in creating bureaucratic forms that are uniquely ours. We demand a bureaucracy we can control, by our votes, our bribes, our capacity for public wrath, and, if necessary, by the price we are willing to pay for inefficiency.

This is not to argue the impossibility of administratively efficient democracy, only its fragility. For our commitment to individual autonomy, to self-interest, and to material well-being as the touchstones of American democracy places limits on the definitions of efficiency that are acceptable to us, particularly in times of economic stringency. Politics remains our method of requiring the state to serve us.

The growth of the bureaucratic state may be the single most unintended consequence of the Constitution of 1787, in a sense, perhaps, the heart of the partisanship the framers thought they could avoid. What may be the most consistent with their intention, however, is the hostility to bureaucracy we inherited from them, and that we have continued to preserve. It is a reality with which we have learned to live, albeit somewhat uncomfortably; but it is a reality that should give pause to those who believe that there is in the intentions of the framers of the Constitution of 1787 a world to which we can return. All of the current interest in deregulation cannot obliterate the existence of the bureaucratic state or relieve us of the responsibility of adjusting our democracy to it. The battle between bureaucracy and democracy is written into our history. So is the fact that democracy must win. All we have left to debate is the cost.

Notes

1. Ralph Ketcham, *Presidents Above Party: The First American Presidency, 1789 to 1829* (Chapel Hill: University of North Carolina Press, 1984).

2. Matthew A. Crenson, *The Federal Machine: Beginnings of Bureaucracy in Jacksonian America* (Baltimore: Johns Hopkins University Press, 1975).

3. The reference is used by the author of the article on Bureaucracy in the famous 11th edition of the *Encyclopedia Britannica* and is dutifully repeated even today in the *Oxford English Dictionary.* When Harold Laski covered the topic for the *Encyclopedia of the Social Sciences,* he again repeated it.

4. Arthur S. Link, ed., *The Papers of Woodrow Wilson,* vol. 5 (Princeton, NJ: Princeton University Press, 1968).

5. *Ibid.,* p. 366.

6. *Ibid.,* p. 367.

7. *Ibid.,* pp. 367–68.

8. William Graham Sumner, *Andrew Jackson,* in the American Statesman series, edited by J. T. Morse (New York: AMS Press, Inc., repr. of 1899 ed.).

9. The late Joseph Ben David was being particularly acute in his efforts to mark the distinction between the development of American educational institutions and those in other parts of the world. He, however, has concentrated on the issue of intellectual development rather than political power. *Fundamental Research and the Universities* (Paris: OECD, 1968).

10. Although the essay was not published until 1954 (Princeton University Press), it was apparently delivered on several occasions as a graduate address.

11. Woodrow Wilson, *Leaders of Men* (Princeton, NJ: Princeton University Press, 1954); Walter Lippmann, *Public Opinion* (New York: Harcourt, Brace and Co., 1922); Graham Wallas, *Human Nature in Politics* (London: A. Constable and

Co., Ltd., 1908); John Dewey, *The Public and Its Problems* (Denver: A. Swallow, c1927, 1954, 3d ed.).

12. Stephen Skowronek, *Building a New American State: The Expansion of National Administrative Capacities, 1877–1920* (Cambridge: Cambridge University Press, 1982).

13. Charles Maier, "Between Taylorism and Technology: European Ideologies and the Vision of Industrial Productivity in the 1920's." *Journal of Contemporary History*, vol. 5 (No. 2, 1969), pp. 27–61.

14. Judith A. Merkle, *Management and Ideology: The Legacy of the International Scientific Management Movement* (Berkeley: University of California Press, 1980).

15. Max Weber, *General Economic History*, translated by Frank H. Knight (New York: Greenberg, 1927). Hans H. Gerth and C. Wright Mills, *From Max Weber: Essays in Sociology* (New York: Oxford University Press, 1946); and Talcott Parsons' translation of *The Theory of Social and Economic Organization* (New York: Free Press, 1947).

16. Edward Shils, in Daniel Lerner and Harold D. Lasswell, eds., *The Policy Sciences* (Stanford, CA: Stanford University Press, 1951). The volume is a kind of monument to the emergence of a distinction between policy science and behavioral scientific research.

17. Guy Alchon, *The Invisible Hand of Planning: Capitalism, Social Science, and the State of the 1920's* (Princeton, NJ: Princeton University Press, 1985).

18. Leonard White, "Public Administration," *Encyclopedia of the Social Sciences*, vol. 1 (New York: MacMillan Company, January 1930), p. 444.

19. Herbert Hoover, *The Challenge to Liberty* (New York and London: C. Scribner's Sons, 1934).

20. The presence of women is traceable not to any premonitions of the liberation movement that followed the era but to the fact that women were represented in such overwhelming numbers among the managers and providers of social services at the state and local levels, services now being transferred to the federal government.

Part Two

The Study of Administration

As early as the first decade of the twentieth century, municipal government reformers declared that there is a right way to manage a public agency. Municipal research bureaus were established, first in New York City, then elsewhere, to study administrative processes and recommend improvements (Stivers 2000, Schachter 1998, Waldo 1948). Municipal researchers firmly believed that there was a right way (the scientific way) and a wrong way (the machine politics way) to run city governments. They established the idea that systematic study could yield answers to administrative questions, solutions that would be applicable in every agency regardless of the nature of its work. These answers could be expressed in the form of administrative principles. The classic volume illustrating this frame of mind is Luther Gulick and Lyndall Urwick's collection, *Papers on the Science of Administration* (1937). Gulick was trained at the New York Bureau of Municipal Research, the hub of the municipal research movement, and served for many years as director of its successor organization, the New York Institute of Public Administration.

Perhaps the most famous clarion call for the scientific approach to public administration came with the 1946 publication in *Public Administration Review (PAR)* of Herbert A. Simon's "The Proverbs of Administration." By the time of Simon's essay, what became known as the behavioral revolution in social science was imposing a demanding form of empiricism on the study of administration. Behavioralists insisted on the use of natural science-based principles such as hypothesis testing, the restriction of research to quantifiable phenomena, and the elimination of values from the research process. Simon led the behavioralist charge in public administration. In the classic article included here, he accuses research in the field of being too descriptive and insufficiently explanatory or predictive. He is scornful of the administrative maxims relied on by Luther Gulick and others. Simon shifts attention from the administrative situation, where Gulick believed principles could serve as guides, to logic (specifically the logical principle of noncontradiction). He characterizes administrative maxims (for example, "Limit the number of people any one person supervises," or "Group people according to specialized tasks") as ambiguous proverbs that can be interpreted in contradictory ways. Simon calls for the scientific study of administration, meaning the careful testing of hypotheses to determine causal relationships among variables, so findings are valid for all situations of the same type. From Simon's position, while democratic values should not—or at least cannot—be eliminated from the practice of public administration, they should and must be eliminated from the search for the lasting administrative truths from which practice should be deduced.

In 1947, Robert A. Dahl presented in *PAR* a critique of the effort to find a science of public administration. Targeting the work of Lyndall Urwick, coeditor with Gulick of *Papers on the Science of Administration*, Dahl argues that a value-free science is impossible, because there is no way of insulating it from conflicts among values; even efficiency itself is a value. He points out that *public* administration inevitably involves "the toils of ethical consideration." Furthermore, a science of administration entails a study of human behavior in its complex interpersonal/organizational context; as such, it cannot feasibly be experimental. The attempt to make administrative processes rational, such as by coming up with "laws" of administration, will only work if human beings can be counted on to be rational. "The science of organization," comments Dahl, has "learned too much from industry and not enough from Freud." Dahl concludes that a science of public administration requires clarifying the place of values, gaining a better understanding of human nature, and doing comparative studies to determine the impact of social and economic factors, the prerequisite to generalizing across national boundaries.

A decade later, Lyndall Urwick (*PAR* 1957) offered a rejoinder to Dahl's critique. Interestingly, Urwick defends the principles of administration (the same ones Simon dismissed as proverbs) as scientific. Although he maintains that by "science" he means no more than an organized body of knowledge, Urwick insists that "there is a vast amount of human experience about all kinds of administrative and managerial problems. If we will organize it, measure it where we can, and generalize from it, we can build up a body of knowledge about managing which can be taught and learned." The alternatives, Urwick believes, are the "accidents of practical apprenticeship and 'trial and error.'" Yet he defends the idea that practitioners ought not to have to wait for perfect scientific findings. Rather they should "fill in" where they must, using approximations derived from their experience. Where the situation calls for it, they may well need to use the very principles like span of control derided by Simon and others for their lack of rigor.

Despite their centrality in the emergence of public administration as a field of study, the maxims promulgated by Gulick and others, the so-called "proverbs of administration," came to seem more and more questionable as an adequate basis for practice and as a legitimate foundation for systematic knowledge. But observers differed about the nature of the problem. Some, like Simon, argued for more empiricism and greater rigor. In this view, facts and values, administration and politics, should remain in distinct camps, the one susceptible to rational scientific study, the other consigned to nonrational forms of decision-making, such as elections, pressure tactics, or at best, administrative "art." On the other hand, observers such as Levitan, Dahl, and Sayre insisted that there is a normative element in public administration, both as practice and as a field of study, that cannot be brought under the umbrella of science, but neither should it be relegated to the realm of the irrational.

During the time when public administrationists were arguing about whether the field could be confined to scientific investigation, a parallel development in social science raised new questions that eventually found their way into the field. These questions revolved around the issue of whether, as a practical discipline devoted not just to knowledge for its own sake but to its application in administrative situations, public administration needed to broaden its menu of research approaches to include interpretive techniques. In the interpretive framework, the goal is not to mimic natural science, with its emphasis on objectivity, control, and prediction. Rather the aim is to tap the knowledge that administrators and firing line workers develop on the job. Interpretivists argued that difficulties in applying scientific studies to actual situations stemmed from an inappropriate effort to study agencies objectively rather than bringing to light the learning gained from experience and making it more widely available.

Two essays are presented here that reflect the interpretive approach. The first, Ralph P. Hummel's "Stories Managers Tell: Why They Are as Valid as Science," appeared in *PAR* in 1991. Hummel argues that instead of trying ever harder to be objective, the study of administration should turn its attention to the stories managers tell about their experiences. Rather than dismissing such stories as anecdotal, Hummel says, public administrationists should see them as a valid means of producing and accumulating knowledge. Scientific standards of validity are inappropriate to this type of study of administrative practices, which have validity standards of their own. Stories include listeners in the storyteller's world, engaging them in helping to define a problem and "winning their commitment to its solution." Stories also enable listeners to broaden their worlds, by juxtaposing the storyteller's situation with their own and enabling them to see both what is familiar and what is strange. The validity standards for stories include relevance ("Does this ring true?" "Does it open up possibilities of action for me?"), believability, and coherence. Hummel argues that the biggest problem for managers is gaining access to what people in their shop think is going on. To meet this need, stories are an irreplaceable resource, not only for managers but for researchers as well.

The second interpretive essay is Mary R. Schmidt's "Grout: Alternative Kinds of Knowledge and Why They Are Ignored," which won *Public Administration Review*'s 1993 Louis Brownlow Award for the best article by a practitioner. Schmidt studied records from the investigation of the 1975 collapse of the Teton River Dam in Idaho. Investigators attributed the disaster to an inadequate design and to overconfidence on the part of the sponsoring agency, the U. S. Bureau of Reclamation. Schmidt found, however, that an entire batch of potential testimony had gone untapped: the testimony of grouters, the workers who used cement slurry to fill holes and caves in the bedrock on which the dam was to rest. The grouters' hands-on knowledge, Schmidt argues, could have anticipated the dam collapse if attention had been paid to it. But their protests about engineering decisions were ignored. Schmidt points out that hands-on knowledge can only be learned in practice, not in classrooms or through scientific studies. Such knowledge is not inferior to the knowledge of managers or engineers, it is simply different. Over time, hands-on workers build up a repertoire of strategies, but each situation is unique. Therefore a worker cannot rely on abstract models or recipes but must be "constantly alert to the 'back talk' of the specific situation."

Readers must judge for themselves the respective roles of scientific study versus the interpretive approach, as well as the tension between normative and factual dimensions. The last essay in this section, a comparatively recent one, brings many of these issues together. It has been included because the "public management" perspective it illustrates has, over the last several decades, become the most significant effort at an empirical science of administration. As such it may be the severest challenge to the idea that the study and practice of public administration is constitutively normative as well as factual. In fact, the term "public management" was coined to connote rigorous research in contrast to scholarship under the rubric of "public administration," the latter seen as traditional, value-laden, and anecdotal. Robert Behn's "Public Management: Should It Strive to be Art, Science, or Engineering?" which appeared in 1996 in the *Journal of Public Administration Research and Theory,* is a notably thoughtful statement on the study and practice of public management. Behn's framework is clearly empirical rather than normative. But, recognizing the difficulties that lie in wait for any effort to make public management a pure science, Behn insists that we should conceive of public management as engineering—that is, as a combination of art and science.

The big question Behn poses is how managers can increase the organization's ability to produce results. This is clearly a causal question, one that appears to lend itself to empirical study. Behn turns to engineering on the grounds that public managers, like engineers, have to use judgment because there is never one clear "best way."

Management, like engineering, does not consist of the simple application of demonstrated scientific findings. The manager, knowing what he or she wants to accomplish, "gropes along," trying out different approaches and discarding what doesn't work (compare the Urwick essay in this section on that point). For this reason, the case study is as useful as the results of more rigorous research, because practical lessons and tentative theories can emerge from reflecting on actual situations. (How does Hummel's argument differ from Behn's in this respect?) Management, like engineering, does not consist of the simple application of demonstrated scientific findings. Behn concludes that public management scholarship ought to aim toward measuring what it can measure, but more importantly it must link research results with managers' accomplishments in a way that can provide guidance to others. Normative theorists would add that even an approach as eminently pragmatic as Behn's could be strengthened by greater consciousness that the questions public managers are called upon to address are not purely managerial, that is, not just about achieving results, but also political, that is, about the public interest.

3

THE PROVERBS OF ADMINISTRATION

Herbert A. Simon

A fact about proverbs that greatly enhances their quotability is that they almost always occur in mutually contradictory pairs. "Look before you leap!"—but "He who hesitates is lost."

This is both a great convenience and a serious defect—depending on the use to which one wishes to put the proverbs in question. If it is a matter of rationalizing behavior that has already taken place or justifying action that has already been decided upon, proverbs are ideal. Since one is never at a loss to find one that will prove his point—or the precisely contradictory point, for that matter—they are a great help in persuasion, political debate, and all forms of rhetoric.

But when one seeks to use proverbs as the basis of a scientific theory, the situation is less happy. It is not that the propositions expressed by the proverbs are insufficient; it is rather that they prove too much. A scientific theory should tell what is true but also what is false. If Newton had announced to the world that particles of matter exert either an attraction or a repulsion on each other, he would not have added much to scientific knowledge. His contribution consisted in showing that an attraction was exercised and in announcing the precise law governing its operation.

Source: *Public Administration Review* 6(1946): 53–67.

Most of the propositions that make up the body of administrative theory today share, unfortunately, this defect of proverbs. For almost every principle one can find an equally plausible and acceptable contradictory principle. Although the two principles of the pair will lead to exactly opposite organizational recommendations, there is nothing in the theory to indicate which is the proper one to apply.[1]

It is the purpose of this paper to substantiate this sweeping criticism of administrative theory, and to present some suggestions—perhaps less concrete than they should be—as to how the existing dilemma can be solved.

Some Accepted Administrative Principles

Among the more common "principles" that occur in the literature of administration are these:

1. Administrative efficiency is increased by a specialization of the task among the group.
2. Administrative efficiency is increased by arranging the members of the group in a determinate hierarchy of authority.
3. Administrative efficiency is increased by limiting the span of control at any point in the hierarchy to a small number.
4. Administrative efficiency is increased by grouping the workers, for purposes of control, according to (*a*) purpose, (*b*) process, (*c*) clientele, or (*d*) place. (This is really an elaboration of the first principle but deserves separate discussion.)

Since these principles appear relatively simple and clear, it would seem that their application to concrete problems of administrative organization would be unambiguous and that their validity would be easily submitted to empirical test. Such, however, seems not to be the case. To show why it is not, each of the four principles just listed will be considered in turn.

Specialization

Administrative efficiency is supposed to increase with an increase in specialization. But is this intended to mean that *any* increase in specialization will increase efficiency? If so, which of the following alternatives is the correct application of the principle in a particular case?

1. A plan of nursing should be put into effect by which nurses will be assigned to districts and do all nursing within that district, including school examinations, visits to homes or school children, and tuberculosis nursing.

2. A functional plan of nursing should be put into effect by which different nurses will be assigned to school examinations, visits to homes of school children, and tuberculosis nursing. The present method of generalized nursing by districts impedes the development of specialized skills in the three very diverse programs.

Both of these administrative arrangements satisfy the requirement of specialization—the first provides specialization by place; the second, specialization by function. The principle of specialization is of no help at all in choosing between the two alternatives.

It appears that the simplicity of the principle of specialization is a deceptive simplicity—a simplicity which conceals fundamental ambiguities. For "specialization" is not a condition of efficient administration; it is an inevitable characteristic of all group effort, however efficient or inefficient that effort may be. Specialization merely means that different persons are doing different things—and since it is physically impossible for two persons to be doing the same thing in the same place at the same time, two persons are always doing different things.

The real problem of administration, then, is not to "specialize," but to specialize in that particular manner and along those particular lines which will lead to administrative efficiency. But, in thus rephrasing this "principle" of administration, there has been brought clearly into the open its fundamental ambiguity: "Administrative efficiency is increased by a specialization of the task among the group in the direction which will lead to greater efficiency."

Further discussion of the choice between competing bases of specialization will be undertaken after two other principles of administration have been examined.

Unity of Command

Administrative efficiency is supposed to be enhanced by arranging the members of the organization in a determinate hierarchy of authority in order to preserve "unity of command."

Analysis of this "principle" requires a clear understanding of what is meant by the term "authority." A subordinate may be said to accept authority whenever he permits his behavior to be guided by a decision reached by another, irrespective of his own judgment as to the merits of that decision.

In one sense the principle of unity of command, like the principle of specialization, cannot be violated; for it is physically impossible for a man to obey two contradictory commands—that is what is meant by "contradictory commands." Presumably, if unity of command is a principle of administration, it must assert something more than this physical impossibility. Perhaps it asserts this: that it is undesirable to place a member of an organization in a position where he receives orders from more than one superior. This is evidently the meaning that Gulick attaches to the principle when he says,

> The significance of this principle in the process of co-ordination and organization must not be lost sight of. In building a structure of co-ordination, it is often tempting to set up more than one boss for a man who is doing work which has more than one relationship. Even as great a philosopher of management as Taylor fell into this error in setting up separate foremen to deal with machinery, with materials, with speed, etc., each with the power of giving orders directly to the individual workman. The rigid adherence to the principle of unity of command may have its absurdities; these are, however, unimportant in comparison with the certainty of confusion, inefficiency and irresponsibility which arise from the violation of the principle.[2]

Certainly the principle of unity of command, thus interpreted, cannot be criticized for any lack of clarity or any ambiguity. The definition of authority given above should provide a clear test whether, in any concrete situation, the principle is observed. The real fault that must be found with this principle is that it is incompatible with the principle of specialization. One of the most important uses to which authority is put in organization is to bring about specialization in the work of making decisions, so that each decision is made at a point in the organization where it can be made most expertly. As a result, the use of authority permits a greater degree of expertness to be achieved in decision-making than would be possible if each operative employee had himself to make all the decisions upon which his activity is predicated. The individual fireman does not decide whether to use a two-inch hose or a fire extinguisher; that is decided for him by his officers, and the decision is communicated to him in the form of a command.

However, if unity of command, in Gulick's sense, is observed, the decisions of a person at any point in the administrative hierarchy are subject to influence through only one channel of authority; and if his decisions are of a kind that require expertise in more than one field of knowledge, then advisory and informational services must be relied upon to supply those premises which lie in a field not recognized by the mode of specialization in the organization. For example, if an accountant in a school department is subordinate to an educator, and if unity of command is observed, then the finance department cannot issue direct orders to him regarding the technical, accounting aspects of his work. Similarly, the director of motor vehicles in the public works department will be unable to issue direct orders on care of motor equipment to the fire-truck driver.[3]

Gulick, in the statement quoted above, clearly indicates the difficulties to be faced if unity of command is not observed. A certain amount of irresponsibility and confusion are almost certain to ensue. But perhaps this is not too great a price to pay for the increased expertise that can be applied to decisions. What is needed to decide the issue is a principle of administration that would enable one to weigh the relative advantages of the two courses of action. But neither the principle of unity of command nor the principle of specialization is helpful in adjudicating the controversy. They merely contradict each other without indicating any procedure for resolving the contradiction.

If this were merely an academic controversy—if it were generally agreed and had been generally demonstrated that unity of command must be preserved in all cases, even with a loss in expertise—one could assert that in case of conflict between the two principles, unity of command should prevail. But the issue is far from clear, and experts can be ranged on both sides of the controversy. On the side of unity of command there may be cited the dictums of Gulick and others.[4] On the side of specialization there are Taylor's theory of functional supervision, Macmahon and Millett's idea of "dual supervision," and the practice of technical supervision in military organization.[5]

It may be, as Gulick asserts, that the notion of Taylor and these others is an "error." If so, the evidence that it is an error has never been marshalled or published—apart from loose heuristic arguments like that quoted above. One is left with a choice between equally eminent theorists of administration and without any evidential basis for making that choice.

What evidence there is of actual administrative practice would seem to indicate that the need for specialization is to a very large degree given priority over the need for unity of command. As a matter of fact, it does not go too far to say that unity of command, in Gulick's sense, never has existed in any administrative organization. If a line officer accepts the regulations of an accounting department with regard to the procedure for making requisitions, can it be said that, in this sphere, he is not subject to the authority of the accounting department? In any actual administrative situation authority is zoned, and to maintain that this zoning does not contradict the principle of unity of command requires a very different definition of authority from that used here. This subjection of the line officer to the accounting department is no different, in principle, from Taylor's recommendation that in the matter of work programming a workman be subject to one foreman, in the matter of machine operation to another.

The principle of unity of comand is perhaps more defensible if narrowed down to the following. In case two authoritative commands conflict, there should be a single determinate person whom the subordinate is expected to obey; and the sanctions of authority should be applied against the subordinate only to enforce his obedience to that one person.

If the principle of unity of command is more defensible when stated in this limited form, it also solves fewer problems. In the first place, it no longer requires, except for settling conflicts of authority, a single hierarchy of authority. Consequently, it leaves unsettled the very important question of how authority should be zoned in a particular organization (i.e., the modes of specialization) and through what channels it should be exercised. Finally, even this narrower concept of unity of command conflicts with the principle of specialization, for whenever disagreement does occur and the organization members revert to the formal lines of authority, then only those types of specialization which are represented in the hierarchy of authority can impress themselves on decision. If the training officer of a city exercises only functional supervision over the police training officer, then in case of disagreement with the police chief, specialized knowledge of police problems will determine the outcome while specialized knowledge of training problems will be subordinated or ignored. That this actually occurs is shown by the frustration so commonly expressed by functional supervisors at their lack of authority to apply sanctions.

Span of Control

Administrative efficiency is supposed to be enhanced by limiting the number of subordinates who report directly to any one administrator to a small number—say six. This notion that the "span of control" should be narrow is confidently asserted as a third incontrovertible principle of administration. The usual common-sense arguments for restricting the span of control are familiar and need not be repeated here. What is not so generally recognized is that a contradictory proverb of administration can be stated which, though it is not so familiar as the principle of span of control, can be supported by arguments of equal plausibility. The proverb in question is the following: Administrative efficiency is enhanced by keeping at a minimum the number of organizational levels through which a matter must pass before it is acted upon.

This latter proverb is one of the fundamental criteria that guide administrative analysts in procedures simplification work. Yet in many situations the results to which this principle leads are in direct contradiction to the requirements of the principle of span of control, the principle of unity of command, and the principle of specialization. The present discussion is concerned with the first of these conflicts. To illustrate the difficulty, two alternative proposals for the organization of a small health department will be presented—one based on the restriction of span of control, the other on the limitation of number of organization levels:

1. The present organization of the department places an administrative over-load on the health officer by reason of the fact that all eleven employees of the department report directly to him and the further fact that some of the staff lack adequate technical training. Consequently, venereal disease clinic treatments and other details require an undue amount of the health officer's personal attention.

It has previously been recommended that the proposed medical officer be placed in charge of the venereal disease and chest clinics and all child hygiene work. It is further recommended that one of the inspectors be designated chief inspector and placed in charge of all the department's inspectional activities and that one of the nurses be designated as head nurse. This will relieve the health commissioner of considerable detail and will leave him greater freedom to plan and supervise the health program as a whole, to conduct health education, and to coordinate the work of the department with that of other community agencies. If the department were thus organized, the effectiveness of all employees could be substantially increased.

2. The present organization of the department leads to inefficiency and excessive red tape by reason of the fact that an unnecessary supervisory level intervenes between the health officer and the operative employees, and that those four of the twelve employees who are best trained technically are engaged largely in "overhead" administrative duties. Consequently, unnecessary delays occur in securing the approval of the health officer on matters requiring his attention, and too many matters require review and re-review.

The medical officer should be left in charge of the venereal disease and chest clinics and child hygiene work. It is recommended, however, that the position of chief inspector and head nurse be abolished and that the employees now filling these positions perform regular inspectional and nursing duties. The details of work scheduling now handled by these two employees can be taken care of more economically by the secretary to the health officer, and, since broader matters of policy have, in any event, always required the personal attention of the health officer, the abolition of these two positions will eliminate a wholly unnecessary step in review, will allow an expansion of inspectional and nursing services, and will permit at least a beginning to be made in the recommended program of health education. The number of persons reporting directly to the health officer will be increased to nine, but since there are few matters requiring the coordination of these employees, other than the work schedules and policy questions referred to above, this change will not materially increase his work load.

The dilemma is this: in a large organization with complex interrelations between members, a restricted span of control inevitably produces excessive red tape, for each contact between organization members must be carried upward until a common superior is found. If the organization is at all large, this will involve carrying all such matters upward through several levels of officials for decision and then downward again in the form of orders and instructions—a cumbersome and time-consuming process.

The alternative is to increase the number of persons who are under the command of each officer, so that the pyramid will come more rapidly to a peak, with fewer intervening levels. But this, too, leads to difficulty, for if an officer is required to supervise too many employees, his control over them is weakened.

If it is granted, then, that both the increase and the decrease in span of control have some undesirable consequences, what is the optimum point? Proponents of a restricted span of control have suggested three, five, even eleven, as suitable numbers, but nowhere have they explained the reasoning which led them to the particular number they selected. The principle as stated casts no light on this very crucial question. One is reminded of current arguments about the proper size of the national debt.

Organization by Purpose, Process, Clientele, Place

Administrative efficiency is supposed to be increased by grouping workers according to (*a*) purpose, (*b*) process, (*c*) clientele, or (*d*) place. But from the discussion of specialization it is clear that this principle is internally inconsistent; for purpose, process, clientele, and place are competing bases of organization, and at any given point of division the advantages of three must be sacrificed to secure the advantages of the fourth. If the major departments of a city, for example, are organized on the basis of major purpose, then it follows that all the physicians, all the lawyers, all the engineers, all the statisticians will not be located in a single department exclusively composed of members of their profession but will be distributed among the various city departments needing their services. The advantages of organization by process will thereby be partly lost.

Some of these advantages can be regained by organizing on the basis of process *within* the major departments. Thus there may be an engineering bureau within the public works department, or the board of education may have a school health service as a major division of its work. Similarly, within smaller units there may be division by area or by clientele: e.g., a fire department will have separate companies located throughout the city, while a welfare department may have intake and case work agencies in various locations. Again, however, these major types of specialization cannot be simultaneously achieved, for at any point in the organization it must be decided whether specialization at the next level will be accomplished by distinction of major purpose, major process, clientele, or area.

The conflict may be illustrated by showing how the principle of specialization according to purpose would lead to a different result from specialization according to clientele in the organization of a health department.

1. Public health administration consists of the following activities for the prevention of disease and the maintenance of healthful conditions: (1) vital statis-

tics; (2) child hygiene—prenatal, maternity, postnatal, infant, preschool, and school health programs; (3) communicable disease control; (4) inspection of milk, foods, and drugs; (5) sanitary inspection; (6) laboratory service; (7) health education.

One of the handicaps under which the health department labors is the fact that the department has no control over school health, that being an activity of the county board of education, and there is little or no coordination between that highly important part of the community health program and the balance of the program which is conducted by the city-county health unit. It is recommended that the city and county open negotiations with the board of education for the transfer of all school health work and the appropriation therefor to the joint health unit. . . .

2. To the modern school department is entrusted the care of children during almost the entire period that they are absent from the parental home. It has three principal responsibilities toward them: (1) to provide for their education in useful skills and knowledge and in character; (2) to provide them with wholesome play activities outside school hours; (3) to care for their health and to assure the attainment of minimum standards of nutrition.

One of the handicaps under which the school board labors is the fact that, except for school lunches, the board has no control over child health and nutrition, and there is little or no coordination between that highly important part of the child development program and the balance of the program which is conducted by the board of education. It is recommended that the city and county open negotiations for the transfer of all health work for children of school age to the board of education.

Here again is posed the dilemma of choosing between alternative, equally plausible, administrative principles. But this is not the only difficulty in the present case, for a closer study of the situation shows there are fundamental ambiguities in the meanings of the key terms—"purpose," "process," "clientele," and "place."

"Purpose" may be roughly defined as the objective or end for which an activity is carried on; "process" as a means for accomplishing a purpose. Processes, then, are carried on in order to achieve purposes. But purposes themselves may generally be arranged in some sort of hierarchy. A typist moves her fingers in order to type; types in order to reproduce a letter; reproduces a letter in order that an inquiry may be answered. Writing a letter is then the purpose for which the typing is performed; while writing a letter is also the process whereby the purpose of replying to an inquiry is achieved. It follows that the same activity may be described as purpose or as process.

This ambiguity is easily illustrated for the case of an administrative organization. A health department conceived as a unit whose task it is to care for the health of the community is a purpose organization; the same department conceived as a unit which makes use of the medical arts to carry on its work is a process organization. In the same way, an education department may be viewed as a purpose (to educate) organization, or a clientele (children) organization; the forest service as a purpose (forest conservation), process (forest management), clientele (lumbermen and cattlemen utilizing public forests), or area (publicly owned forest lands) organization. When concrete illustrations of this sort are selected, the lines of demarcation between these categories become very hazy and unclear indeed.

"Organization by major purpose," says Gulick, ". . . serves to bring together in a single large department all of those who are at work endeavoring to render a particular service."[6] But what is a particular service? Is fire protection a single purpose, or is it merely a part of the purpose of public safety?—or is it a combination of purposes including fire prevention and fire fighting? It must be concluded that there is no such thing as a purpose, or a unifunctional (single-purpose) organization. What is to be considered a single function depends entirely on language and techniques.[7] If the English language has a comprehensive term which covers both of two subpurposes it is natural to think of the two together as a single purpose. If such a term is lacking, the two subpurposes become purposes in their own right. On the other hand, a single activity may contribute to several objectives, but since they are technically (procedurally) inseparable, the activity is considered a single function or purpose.

The fact, mentioned previously, that purposes form a hierarchy, each subpurpose contributing to some more final and comprehensive end, helps to make clear the relation between purpose and process. "Organization by major process," says Gulick, ". . . tends to bring together in a single department all of those who are at work making use of a given special skill or technology, or are members of a given profession."[8] Consider a simple skill of this kind—typing. Typing is a skill which brings about a means-end coordination of muscular movements, but at a very low level in the means-end hierarchy. The content of the typewritten letter is indifferent to the skill that produces it. The skill consists merely in the ability to hit the letter "*t*" quickly whenever the letter "*t*" is required by the content and to hit the letter "*a*" whenever the letter "*a*" is required by the content.

There is, then, no essential difference between a "purpose" and a "process," but only a distinction of degree. A "process" is an activity whose immediate purpose is at a low level in the hierarchy of means and ends, while a "purpose" is a collection of activities whose orienting value or aim is at a high level in the means-end hierarchy.

Next consider "clientele" and "place" as bases of organization. These categories are really not separate from purpose, but a part of it. A complete statement of the purpose of a fire department would have to include the area served by it: "to reduce fire losses on property in the city of X." Objectives of an administrative organization are phrased in terms of a service to be provided and an area for which it is provided. Usually, the term "purpose" is meant to refer only to the first element, but the second is just as le-

gitimately an aspect of purpose. Area of service, of course, may be a specified clientele quite as well as a geographical area. In the case of an agency
which works on "shifts," time will be a third dimension of purpose—to
provide a given service in a given area (or to a given clientele) during a
given time period.

With this clarification of terminology, the next task is to reconsider the
problem of specializing the work of an organization. It is no longer legitimate to speak of a "purpose" organization, a "process" organization, a
"clientele" organization, or an "area" organization. The same unit might
fall into any one of these four categories, depending on the nature of the
larger organizational unit of which it was a part. A unit providing public
health and medical services for school-age children in Multnomah County
might be considered (1) an "area" organization if it were part of a unit
providing the same service for the state of Oregon; (2) a "clientele" organization if it were part of a unit providing similar services for children of all
ages; (3) a "purpose" or a "process" organization (it would be impossible
to say which) if it were part of an education department.

It is incorrect to say that Bureau A is a process bureau; the correct statement is that Bureau A is a process bureau *within* Department X.[9] This latter statement would mean that Bureau A incorporates all the processes of a
certain kind in Department X, without reference to any special subpurposes, subareas, or subclientele of Department X. Now it is conceivable
that a particular unit might incorporate all processes of a certain kind but
that these processes might relate to only certain particular subpurposes of
the department purpose. In this case, which corresponds to the health unit
in an education department mentioned above, the unit would be specialized by both purpose and process. The health unit would be the only one in
the education department using the medical art (process) and concerned
with health (subpurpose).

Even when the problem is solved of proper usage for the terms "purpose," "process," "clientele," and "area," the principles of administration
give no guide as to which of these four competing bases of specialization is
applicable in any particular situation. The British Machinery of Government Committee had no doubts about the matter. It considered purpose
and clientele as the two possible bases of organization and put its faith entirely in the former. Others have had equal assurance in choosing between
purpose and process. The reasoning which leads to these unequivocal conclusions leaves something to be desired. The Machinery of Government
Committee gives this sole argument for its choice:

> Now the inevitable outcome of this method of organization [by clientele] is a
> tendency to Lilliputian administration. It is impossible that the specialized ser-
> vice which each Department has to render to the community can be of as high

a standard when its work is at the same time limited to a particular class of persons and extended to every variety of provision for them, as when the Department concentrates itself on the provision of the particular service only by whomsoever required, and looks beyond the interest of comparatively small classes.[10]

The faults in this analysis are obvious. First, there is no attempt to determine how *a* service is to be recognized. Second, there is a bald assumption, absolutely without proof, that a child health unit, for example, in a department of child welfare could not offer services of "as high a standard" as the same unit if it were located in a department of health. Just how the shifting of the unit from one department to another would improve or damage the quality of its work is not explained. Third, no basis is set forth for adjudicating the competing claims of purpose and process—the two are merged in the ambiguous term "service." It is not necessary here to decide whether the committee was right or wrong in its recommendation; the important point is that the recommendation represented a choice, without any apparent logical or empirical grounds, between contradictory principles of administration.

Even more remarkable illustrations of illogic can be found in most discussions of purpose *vs.* process. They would be too ridiculous to cite if they were not commonly used in serious political and administrative debate.

> For instance, where should agricultural education come: in the Ministry of Education, or of Agriculture? That depends on whether we want to see the best farming taught, though possibly by old methods, or a possibly out-of-date style of farming, taught in the most modern and compelling manner. The question answers itself.[11]

But does the question really answer itself? Suppose a bureau of agricultural education were set up, headed, for example, by a man who had had extensive experience in agricultural research or as administrator of an agricultural school, and staffed by men of similarly appropriate background. What reason is there to believe that if attached to a Ministry of Education they would teach old-fashioned farming by new-fashioned methods, while if attached to a Ministry of Agriculture they would teach new-fashioned farming by old-fashioned methods? The administrative problem of such a bureau would be to teach new-fashioned farming by new-fashioned methods, and it is a little difficult to see how the departmental location of the unit would affect this result. "The question answers itself" only if one has a rather mystical faith in the potency of bureau-shuffling as a means for redirecting the activities of an agency.

These contradictions and competitions have received increasing attention from students of administration during the past few years. For example, Gulick, Wallace, and Benson have stated certain advantages and disadvantages of the several modes of specialization, and have considered the conditions under which one or the other mode might best be adopted.[12] All this analysis has been at a theoretical level—in the sense that data have not been employed to demonstrate the superior effectiveness claimed for the different modes. But though theoretical, the analysis has lacked a theory. Since no comprehensive framework has been constructed within which the discussion could take place, the analysis has tended either to the logical one-sidedness which characterizes the examples quoted above or to inconclusiveness.

The Impasse of Administrative Theory

The four "principles of administration that were set forth at the beginning of this paper have now been subjected to critical analysis. None of the four survived in very good shape, for in each case there was found, instead of an unequivocal principle, a set of two or more mutually incompatible principles apparently equally applicable to the administrative situation.

Moreover, the reader will see that the very same objections can be urged against the customary discussions of "centralization" *vs*. "decentralization," which usually conclude, in effect, that "on the one hand, centralization of decision-making functions is desirable; on the other hand, there are definite advantages in decentralization."

Can anything be salvaged which will be useful in the construction of an administrative theory? As a matter of fact, almost everything can be salvaged. The difficulty has arisen from treating as "principles of administration" what are really only criteria for describing and diagnosing administrative situations. Closet space is certainly an important item in the design of a successful house; yet a house designed entirely with a view to securing a maximum of closet space—all other considerations being forgotten—would be considered, to say the least, somewhat unbalanced. Similarly, unity of command, specialization by purpose, decentralization are all items to be considered in the design of an efficient administrative organization. No single one of these items is of sufficient importance to suffice as a guiding principle for the administrative analyst. In the design of administrative organizations, as in their operation, over-all efficiency must be the guiding criterion. Mutually incompatible advantages must be balanced against each other, just as an architect weighs the advantages of additional closet space against the advantages of a larger living room.

This position, if it is a valid one, constitutes an indictment of much current writing about administrative matters. As the examples cited in this chapter amply demonstrate, much administrative analysis proceeds by selecting a single criterion and applying it to an administrative situation to reach a recommendation; while the fact that equally valid, but contradictory, criteria exist which could be applied with equal reason, but with a different result, is conveniently ignored. A valid approach to the study of administration requires that *all* the relevant diagnostic criteria be identified; that each administrative situation be analyzed in terms of the entire set of criteria; and that research be instituted to determine how weights can be assigned to the several criteria when they are, as they usually will be, mutually incompatible.

An Approach to Administrative Theory

This program needs to be considered step by step. First, what is included in the description of administrative situations for purposes of such an analysis? Second, how can weights be assigned to the various criteria to give them their proper place in the total picture?

The Description of Administrative Situations

Before a science can develop principles, it must possess concepts. Before a law of gravitation could be formulated, it was necessary to have the notions of "acceleration" and "weight." The first task of administrative theory is to develop a set of concepts that will permit the description, in terms relevant to the theory, of administrative situations. These concepts, to be scientifically useful, must be operational; that is, their meanings must correspond to empirically observable facts or situations. The definition of "authority" given earlier in this paper is an example of an operational definition.

What is a scientifically relevant description of an organization? It is a description that, so far as possible, designates for each person in the organization what decisions that person makes and the influences to which he is subject in making each of these decisions. Current descriptions of administrative organizations fall far short of this standard. For the most part, they confine themselves to the allocation of *functions* and the formal structure of *authority*. They give little attention to the other types of organizational influence or to the system of communication.[13]

What does it mean, for example to say: "The department is made up of three bureaus. The first has the function of ____, the second the function of ____, and the third the function of ____?" What can be learned from such a description about the workability of the organizational arrangement? Very little, indeed. For from the description there is obtained no idea of the degree to which decisions are centralized at the bureau level or at the departmental level. No notion is given as to the extent to which the (presumably unlimited) authority of the department over the bureau is actually exercised or by what mechanisms. There is no indication of the extent to which systems of communication assist the coordination of the three bureaus or, for that matter, to what extent coordination is required by the nature of their work. There is no description of the kinds of training the members of the bureau have undergone or of the extent to which this training permits decentralization at the bureau level. In sum, a description of administrative organizations in terms almost exclusively of functions and lines of authority is completely inadequate for purposes of administrative analysis.

Consider the term "centralization." How is it determined whether the operations of a particular organization are "centralized" or "decentralized"? Does the fact that field offices exist prove anything about decentralization? Might not the same decentralization take place in the bureaus of a centrally located office? A realistic analysis of centralization must include a study of the allocation of decisions in the organization and the methods of influence that are employed by the higher levels to affect the decisions at the lower levels. Such an analysis would reveal a much more complex picture of the decision-making process than any enumeration of the geographical locations of organizational units at the different levels.

Administrative description suffers currently from superficiality, oversimplification, lack of realism. It has confined itself too closely to the mechanism of authority and has failed to bring within its orbit the other, equally important, modes of influence on organizational behavior. It has refused to undertake the tiresome task of studying the actual allocation of decision-making functions. It has been satisfied to speak of "authority," "centralization," "span of control," "function," without seeking operational definitions of these terms. Until administrative description reaches a higher level of sophistication, there is little reason to hope that rapid progress will be made toward the identification and verification of valid administrative principles.

Does this mean that a purely formal description of an administrative organization is impossible—that a relevant description must include an account of the content of the organization's decisions? This is a question that is almost impossible to answer in the present state of knowledge of administrative theory. One thing seems certain: content plays a greater role in the application of administrative principles than is allowed for in the formal administrative theory of the present time. This is a fact that is beginning to be recognized in the literature of administration. If one examines the chain of publications extending from Mooney and Reilley, through Gulick and the President's Committee controversy, to Schuyler Wallace and Benson, he sees a steady shift of emphasis from the "principles of administration" themselves to a study of the *conditions* under which competing principles are respectively applicable. Recent publications seldom say that "organization should be by purpose," but rather that "under such and such conditions purpose organization is desirable." It is to these conditions which underlie the application of the proverbs of administration that administrative theory and analysis must turn in their search for really valid principles to replace the proverbs.

The Diagnosis of Administrative Situations

Before any positive suggestions can be made, it is necessary to digress a bit and to consider more closely the exact nature of the propositions of administrative theory. The theory of administration is concerned with how an organization should be constructed and operated in order to accomplish its work efficiently. A fundamental principle of administration, which follows almost immediately from the rational character of "good" administration, is that among several alternatives involving the same expenditure that one should always be selected which leads to the greatest accomplishment of administrative objectives; and among several alternatives that lead to the same accomplishment that one should be selected which involves the least expenditure. Since this "principle of efficiency" is characteristic of any activity that attempts rationally to maximize the attainment of certain ends with the use of scarce means, it is as characteristic of economic theory as it is of administrative theory. The "administrative man" takes his place alongside the classical "economic man."[14]

Actually, the "principle" of efficiency should be considered a definition rather than a principle: it is a definition of what is meant by "good" or "correct" administrative behavior. It does not tell *how* accomplishments are to be maximized, but merely states that this maximization is the aim of administrative activity, and that administrative theory must disclose under what conditions the maximization takes place.

Now what are the factors that determine the level of efficiency which is achieved by an administrative organization? It is not possible to make an exhaustive list of these, but the principal categories can be enumerated. Perhaps the simplest method of approach is to consider the single member of the administrative organization and ask what the limits are to the quantity and quality of his output. These limits include (*a*) limits on his ability to perform and (*b*) limits on his ability to make correct decisions. To the extent that these limits are removed, the administrative organization approaches its goal of high efficiency. Two persons, given the same skills, the same objectives and values, the same knowledge and information, can rationally decide only upon the same course of action. Hence, administrative theory must be interested in the factors that will determine with what skills, values, and knowledge the organization member undertakes his work. These are the "limits" to rationality with which the principles of administration must deal.

On one side, the individual is limited by those skills, habits, and reflexes which are no longer in the realm of the conscious. His performance, for example, may be limited by his manual dexterity or his reaction time or his strength. His decision-making processes may be limited by the speed of his mental processes, his skill in elementary arithmetic, and so forth. In this area, the principles of administration must be concerned with the physiology of the human body and with the laws of skill-training and of habit. This is the field that has been most successfully cultivated by the followers of Taylor and in which has been developed time-and-motion study and the therblig.

On a second side, the individual is limited by his values and those conceptions of purpose which influence him in making his decisions. If his loyalty to the organization is high, his decisions may evidence sincere acceptance of the objectives set for the organization; if that loyalty is lacking, personal motives may interfere with his administrative efficiency. If his loyalties are attached to the bureau by which he is employed, he may sometimes make decisions that are inimical to the larger unit of which the bureau is a part. In this area the principles of administration must be concerned with the determinants of loyalty and morale, with leadership and initiative, and with the influences that determine where the individual's organizational loyalties will be attached.

On a third side, the individual is limited by the extent of his knowledge of things relevant to his job. This applies both to the basic knowledge required in decision-making—a bridge designer must know the fundamentals of mechanics—and to the information that is required to make his decisions appropriate to the given situation. In this area, administrative theory is concerned with such fundamental questions as these: What are the limits on the mass of knowledge that human minds can accumulate and apply? How rapidly can knowledge be assimilated? How is specialization in the administrative organization to be related to the specializations of knowledge that are prevalent in the community's occupational structure? How is the system of communication to channel knowledge and information to the appropriate decision-points? What types of knowledge can, and what types cannot, be easily transmitted? How is the need for intercommunication of information affected by the modes of specialization in the organization? This is perhaps the *terra incognita* of administrative theory, and undoubtedly its careful exploration will cast great light on the proper application of the proverbs of administration.

Perhaps this triangle of limits does not completely bound the area of rationality, and other sides need to be added to the figure. In any case, this enumeration will serve to indicate the kinds of considerations that must go into the construction of valid and noncontradictory principles of administration.

An important fact to be kept in mind is that the limits of rationality are variable limits. Most important of all, consciousness of the limits may in itself alter them. Suppose it were discovered in a particular organization, for example, that organizational loyalties attached to small units had frequently led to a harmful degree of intraorganizational competition. Then, a program which trained members of the organization to be conscious of their loyalties, and to subordinate loyalties to the smaller group to those of the large, might lead to a very considerable alteration of the limits in that organization.[15]

A related point is that the term "rational behavior," as employed here, refers to rationality when that behavior is evaluated in terms of the objectives of the larger organization; for, as just pointed out, the difference in direction of the individual's aims from those of the larger organization is just one of those elements of nonrationality with which the theory must deal.

A final observation is that, since administrative theory is concerned with the non-rational limits of the rational, it follows that the larger the area in which rationality has been achieved the less important is the exact form of the administrative organization. For example, the function of plan preparation, or design, if it results in a written plan that can be communicated interpersonally without difficulty, can be located almost anywhere in the organization without affecting results. All that is needed is a procedure whereby the plan can be given authoritative status, and this can be provided in a number of ways. A discussion, then, of the proper location for a planning or designing unit is apt to be highly inconclusive and is apt to hinge on the personalities in the organization and their relative enthusiasm, or lack of it, toward the planning function rather than upon any abstract principles of good administration.[16]

On the other hand, when factors of communication or faiths or loyalty are crucial to the making of a decision, the location of the decision in the organization is of great importance. The method of allocating decisions in the army, for instance, automatically provides (at least in the period prior to the actual battle) that each decision will be made where the knowledge is available for coordinating it with other decisions.

Assigning Weights to the Criteria

A first step, then, in the overhauling of the proverbs of administration is to develop a vocabulary, along the lines just suggested, for the description of administrative organization. A second step, which has also been outlined, is to study the limits of rationality in order to develop a complete and comprehensive enumeration of the criteria that must be weighed in evaluating an administrative organization. The current proverbs represent only a fragmentary and unsystematized portion of these criteria.

When these two tasks have been carried out, it remains to assign weights to the criteria. Since the criteria, or "proverbs," are often mutually competitive or contradictory, it is not sufficient merely to identify them. Merely to know, for example, that a specified change in organization will reduce the span of control is not enough to justify the change. This gain must be balanced against the possible resulting loss of contact between the higher and lower ranks of the hierarchy.

Hence, administrative theory must also be concerned with the question of the weights that are to be applied to these criteria—to the problems of their relative importance in any concrete situation. This question is not one that can be solved in a vacuum. Arm-chair philosophizing about administration—of which the present paper is an example—has gone about as far as it can profitably go in this particular direction. What is needed now is empirical research and experimentation to determine the relative desirability of alternative administrative arrangements.

The methodological framework for this research is already at hand in the principle of efficiency. If an administrative organization whose activities are susceptible to objective evaluation be subjected to study, then the actual change in accomplishment that results from modifying administrative arrangements in these organizations can be observed and analyzed.

There are two indispensable conditions to successful research along these lines. First, it is necessary that the objectives of the administrative organization under study be defined in concrete terms so that results, expressed in terms of these objectives, can be accurately measured. Second, it is necessary that sufficient experimental control be exercised to make possible the isolation of the particular effect under study from other disturbing factors that might be operating on the organization at the same time.

These two conditions have seldom been even partially fulfilled in so-called "administrative experiments." The mere fact that a legislature passes a law creating an administrative agency, that the agency operates for five years, that the agency is finally abolished, and that a historical study is then made of the agency's operations is not sufficient to make of that agency's history an "administrative experiment." Modern American legislation is full of such "experiments" which furnish orators in neighboring states with abundant ammunition when similar issues arise in their bailiwicks, but which provide the scientific investigator with little or nothing in the way of objective evidence, one way or the other.

In the literature of administration, there are only a handful of research studies that satisfy these fundamental conditions of methodology—and these are, for the most part, on the periphery of the problem of organization. There are, first of all, the studies of the Taylor group which sought to determine the technological conditions of efficiency. Perhaps none of these is a better example of the painstaking methods of science than Taylor's own studies of the cutting of metals.[17]

Studies dealing with the human and social aspects of administration are even rarer than the technological studies. Among the more important are the whole series of studies on fatigue, starting in Great Britain during World War I and culminating in the Westinghouse experiments.[18]

In the field of public administration, almost the sole example of such experimentation is the series of studies that have been conducted in the public welfare field to determine the proper case loads for social workers.[19]

Because, apart from these scattered examples, studies of administrative agencies have been carried out without benefit of control or of objective measurements of results, they have had to depend for their recommendations and conclusions upon *a priori* reasoning proceeding from "principles of administration." The reasons have already been stated why the "principles" derived in this way cannot be more than "proverbs."

Perhaps the program outlined here will appear an ambitious or even a quixotic one. There should certainly be no illusions, in undertaking it, as to the length and deviousness of the path. It is hard to see, however, what alternative remains open. Certainly neither the practitioner of administration nor the theoretician can be satisfied with the poor analytic tools that the proverbs provide him. Nor is there any reason to believe that a less drastic reconversion than that outlined here will rebuild those tools to usefulness.

It may be objected that administration cannot aspire to be a "science"; that by the nature of its subject it cannot be more than an "art." Whether true or false, this objection is irrelevant to the present discussion. The question of how "exact" the principles of administration can be made is one that only experience can answer. But as to whether they should be logical or illogical there can be no debate. Even an "art" cannot be founded on proverbs.

Notes

1. Lest it be thought that this deficiency is peculiar to the science—or "art"—of administration, it should be pointed out that the same trouble is shared by most Freudian psychological theories, as well as by some sociological theories.

2. Luther Gulick, "Notes on the Theory of Organization," in Luther Gulick and L. Urwick (eds.), *Papers on the Science of Administration* (Institute of Public Administration, Columbia University, 1937), p. 9.

3. This point is discussed in Herbert A. Simon, "Decision-Making and Administrative Organization," 4 *Public Administration Review* 20–21 (Winter, 1944).

4. Gulick, "Notes on the Theory of Organization," p. 9; L. D. White, *Introduction to the Study of Public Administration* (Macmillan Co., 1939), p. 45.

5. Frederick W. Taylor, *Shop Management* (Harper & Bros., 1911). p. 99; Macmahon, Millett, and Ogden *The Administration of Federal Work Relief* (Public Administration Service, 1941), pp. 265–68; and L. Urwick, who describes British army practice in "Organization as a Technical Problem," Gulick and Urwick (eds.), *op. cit.,* pp. 67–69.

6. *Op. cit.,* p 21.

7. If this is correct, then any attempt to prove that certain activities belong in a single department because they relate to a single purpose is doomed to fail. See, for example, John M. Gaus and Leon Wolcott, *Public Administration and the U.S. Department of Agriculture* (Public Administration Service, 1940).

8. *Op. cit.,* p. 23.

9. This distinction is implicit in most of Gulick's analysis of specialization. However, since he cites as examples single departments within a city, and since he usually speaks of "grouping activities" rather than "dividing work," the relative character of these categories is not always apparent in this discussion (*op. cit.,* pp. 15–30).

10. *Report of the Machinery of Government Committee* (H. M. Stationery Office, 1918).

11. Sir Charles Harris, "Decentralization," 3 *Journal of Public Administration* 117–33 (April, 1925).

12. Gulick, "Notes on the Theory of Organization," pp. 21–30; Schuyler Wallace, *Federal Departmentalization* (Columbia University Press, 1941); George C. S. Benson, "International Administrative Organization," 1 *Public Administration Review* 473–86 (Autumn, 1941).

13. The monograph by Macmahon, Millett, and Ogden, *op. cit.,* perhaps approaches nearer than any other published administrative study to the sophistication required in administrative description. See, for example, the discussion on pp. 233–36 of headquarters-field relationships.

14. For an elaboration of the principle of efficiency and its place in administrative theory see Clarence E. Ridley and Herbert A. Simon, *Measuring Municipal Activities* (International City Managers' Association, 2nd ed., 1943), particularly Chapter I and the preface to the second edition.

15. For an example of the use of such training, see Herbert A. Simon and William Divine, "Controlling Human Factors in an Administrative Experiment," 1 *Public Administration Review* 487–92 (Autumn, 1941).

16. See, for instance, Robert A. Walker, *The Planning Function in Urban Government* (University of Chicago Press, 1941), pp. 166–75. Walker makes out a strong case for attaching the planning agency to the chief executive. But he rests his entire case on the rather slender reed that "as long as the planning agency is outside the governmental structure . . . planning will tend to encounter resistance from public officials as an invasion of their responsibility and jurisdiction." This "resistance" is precisely the type of non-rational loyalty which has been referred to previously, and which is certainly a variable.

17. F. W. Taylor, *On the Art of Cutting Metals* (American Society of Mechanical Engineers, 1907).

18. Great Britain, Ministry of Munitions, Health of Munitions Workers Committee, *Final Report* (H.M. Stationery Office, 1918); F. J. Roethlisberger and

William J. Dickson, *Management and the Worker* (Harvard University Press, 1939).

19. Ellery F. Reed, *An Experiment in Reducing the Cost of Relief* (American Public Welfare Administration, 1937); Rebecca Staman, "What Is the Most Economical Case Load in Public Relief Administration?" 4 *Social Work Technique* 117–21 (May-June, 1938); Chicago Relief Administration, *Adequate Staff Brings Economy* (American Public Welfare Association, 1939); Constance Hastings and Saya S. Schwartz, *Size of Visitor's Caseload as a Factor in Efficient Administration of Public Assistance* (Philadelphia County Board of Assistance, 1939); Simon *et al.*, *Determining Work Loads for Professional Staff in a Public Welfare Agency* (Bureau of Public Administration, University of California, 1941).

4

THE SCIENCE OF PUBLIC ADMINISTRATION: THREE PROBLEMS

Robert A. Dahl

The effort to create a science of public administration has often led to the formulation of universal laws or, more commonly, to the assertion that such universal laws *could* be formulated for public administration.[1] In an attempt to make the science of public administration analogous to the natural sciences, the laws or putative laws are stripped of normative values, of the distortions caused by the incorrigible individual psyche, and of the presumably irrelevant effects of the cultural environment. It is often implied that "principles of public administration" have a universal validity independent not only of moral and political ends, but of the frequently nonconformist personality of the individual, and the social and cultural setting as well.

Perhaps the best known expression of this kind is that of W. F. Willoughby. Although he refused to commit himself as to the propriety of designating administration as a science, Willoughby nevertheless asserted that "in administration, there are certain fundamental principles of general application analogous to those characterizing any science. . . ."[2] A more recent statement, and evidently an equally influential one, is L. Urwick's con-

Source: *Public Administration Review* 7(1947): 1–11.

tention that "there are certain principles which govern the association of human beings *for any purpose,* just as there are certain engineering principles which govern the building of a bridge."[3]

Others argue merely that it is possible to discover general principles of wide, although not necessarily of universal validity.[4] Surely this more modest assessment of the role of public administration as a study is not, as an abstract statement, open to controversy. Yet even the discovery of these more limited principles is handicapped by the three basic problems of values, the individual personality, and the social framework.

Public Administration and Normative Values

The first difficulty of constructing a science of public administration stems from the frequent impossibility of excluding normative considerations from the problems of public administration. Science as such is not concerned with the discovery or elucidation of normative values; indeed, the doctrine is generally, if not quite universally, accepted that science *cannot* demonstrate moral values, that science cannot construct a bridge across the great gap from "is" to "ought." So long as the naturalistic fallacy is a stumbling block to philosophers, it must likewise impede the progress of social scientists.

Much could be gained if the clandestine smuggling of moral values into the social sciences could be converted into open and honest commerce. Writers on public administration often assume that they are snugly insulated from the storms of clashing values; usually, however, they are most concerned with ends at the very moment that they profess to be least concerned with them. The doctrine of efficiency is a case in point; it runs like a half-visible thread through the fabric of public administration literature as a dominant goal of administration. Harvey Walker has stated that "the objective of administration is to secure the maximum beneficial result contemplated by the law with the minimum expenditure of the social resources."[5] The term "social resources" is sufficiently ambiguous to allow for almost any interpretation, but it suggests that the general concept involved is one of maximizing "output" and minimizing "cost." Likewise, many of the promised benefits of administrative reorganization in state governments are presumed to follow from proposed improvements in "efficiency in operation." And yet, as Charles Hyneman has so trenchantly observed, there are in a democratic society other criteria than simple efficiency in operation.[6]

Luther Gulick concedes that the goal of efficiency is limited by other values.

> In the science of administration, whether public or private, the basic "good" is efficiency. The fundamental objective of the science of administration is the

accomplishment of the work in hand with the least expenditure of man-power and materials. Efficiency is thus axiom number one in the value scale of administration. This brings administration into apparent conflict with certain elements of the value scale of politics, whether we use that term in its scientific or in its popular sense. But both public administration and politics are branches of political science, so that we are in the end compelled to mitigate the pure concept of efficiency in the light of the value scale of politics and the social order.[7]

He concludes, nevertheless, "that these interferences with efficiency [do not] in any way eliminate efficiency as the fundamental value upon which the science of administration may be erected. They serve to condition and to complicate, but not to change the single ultimate test of value in administration."[8]

It is far from clear what Gulick means to imply in saying that "interferences with efficiency" caused by ultimate political values may "condition" and "complicate" but do not "change" the "single ultimate test" of efficiency as the goal of administration. Is efficiency the supreme goal not only of private administration, but also of public administration, as Gulick contends? If so, how can one say, as Gulick does, that "there are . . . highly inefficient arrangements like citizen boards and small local governments which *may* be necessary in a democracy as educational devices"? Why speak of efficiency as the "single ultimate test of value in administration" if it is not ultimate at all—if, that is to say, in a conflict between efficiency and "the democratic dogma" (to use Gulick's expression) the latter must prevail? Must this dogma prevail only because it has greater political and social force behind it than the dogma of efficiency; or ought it to prevail because it has, in some sense, greater value? How can administrators and students of public administration discriminate between those parts of the democratic dogma that are so strategic they ought to prevail in any conflict with efficiency and those that are essentially subordinate, irrelevant, or even false intrusions into the democratic hypothesis? What *is* efficiency? Belsen and Dachau were "efficient" by one scale of values. And in any case, why is efficiency the ultimate test? According to what and whose scale of values is efficiency placed on the highest pedestal? Is not the worship of efficiency itself a particular expression of a special value judgment? Does it not stem from a mode of thinking and a special moral hypothesis resting on a sharp distinction between means and ends?

The basic problems of *public* administration as a discipline and as a potential science are much wider than the problems of mere *administration*. The necessarily wider preoccupation of a study of *public* administration, as contrasted with *private* administration, inevitably enmeshes the problems of public administration in the toils of ethical considerations. Thus the tangled question of the right of public employees to strike can scarcely be answered without a tacit normative assumption of some kind. A pragmatic answer is satisfactory only so long as no one raises the question of the "rights" involved. And to resolve the question of rights merely by reciting *legal* norms is to beg the whole issue; it is to confess that an answer to this vital problem of public personnel must be sought elsewhere than with students of public administration. Moreover, if one were content to rest one's case on legal rights, it would be impossible to reconcile in a single "science of public administration" the diverse legal and institutional aspects of the right to strike in France, Great Britain, and the United States.

The great question of responsibility, certainly a central one to the study of public administration once it is raised above the level of academic disquisitions on office management, hinges ultimately on some definition of ends, purposes, and values in society. The sharp conflict of views on responsibility expressed several years ago by Carl Friedrich and Herman Finer resulted from basically different interpretations of the nature and purposes of democratic government. Friedrich tacitly assumed certain values in his discussion of the importance of the bureaucrat's "inner check" as an instrument of control. Finer brought Friedrich's unexpressed values into sharp focus and in a warm criticism challenged their compatibility with the democratic faith.[9]

It is difficult, moreover, to escape the conclusion that much of the debate over delegated legislation and administrative adjudication, both in this country and in England, actually arises from a concealed conflict in objectives. Those to whom economic regulation and control are anathema have with considerable consistency opposed the growth of delegated legislation and the expansion of the powers of administrative tribunals—no doubt from a conviction that previously existing economic rights and privileges are safer in the courts than in administrative tribunals; whereas those who support this expansion of administrative power and techniques generally also favor a larger measure of economic regulation and control. Much of the debate that has been phrased in terms of means ought more properly to be evaluated as a conflict over general social goals.

One might justifiably contend that it is the function of a science of public administration, not to determine ends, but to devise the best means to the ends established by those agencies entrusted with the setting of social policy. The science of public administration, it might be argued, would be totally nonnormative, and its doctrines would apply with equal validity to any regime, democratic or totalitarian, once the ends were made clear. "Tell me what you wish to achieve," the public administration scientist might say, "and I will tell you what administrative means are best designed for your purposes." Yet even this view has difficulties, for in most societies, and particularly in democratic ones, ends are often in dispute; rarely are they clearly and unequivocally determined. Nor can ends and means ever be sharply distinguished, since ends determine means and often means ultimately determine ends.[10]

The student of public administration cannot avoid a concern with ends. What he *ought* to avoid is the failure to make explicit the ends or values that form the groundwork of his doctrine. If purposes and normative considerations were consistently made plain, a net gain to the science of public administration would result. But to refuse to recognize that the study of public administration must be founded on some clarification of ends is to perpetuate the gobbledygook of science in the area of moral purposes.

A science of public administration might proceed, then, along these lines:

1. *Establishing a basic hypothesis.* A nonnormative science of public administration might rest on a basic hypothesis that removed ethical problems from the area covered by the science. The *science* of public administration would begin where the *basic hypothesis* leaves off. One could quarrel with the moral or metaphysical assumptions in the basic hypothesis; but all normative argument would have to be carried on at that level, and not at the level of the science. The science, as such, would have no ethical content.

Can such a basic hypothesis be created? To this writer the problem appears loaded with enormous and perhaps insuperable difficulties; yet it is unlikely that a science of public administration will ever be possible until this initial step is taken.

2. *Stating ends honestly.* Some problems of the public services, like that of responsibility, evidently cannot be divorced from certain ends implied in the society served by the public services. If this is true, there can never be a universal science of public administration so long as societies and states vary in their objectives. In all cases where problems of public administration are inherently related to specific social ends and purposes, the most that can be done is to force all normative assumptions into the open, and not let them lie half concealed in the jungle of fact and inference to slaughter the unwary.

Public Administration and Human Behavior

A second major problem stems from the inescapable fact that a science of public administration must be a study of certain aspects of human behavior. To be sure, there are parts of public administration in which man's behavior can safely be ignored; perhaps it is possible to discuss the question of governmental accounting and auditing without much consideration of the behavior patterns of governmental accountants and auditors. But most problems of public administration revolve around human beings; and the study of public administration is therefore essentially a study of human beings as they have behaved, and as they may be expected or predicted to behave, under certain special circumstances. What marks off the field of public administration from psychology or sociology or political institutions is its concern with *human behavior in the area of services performed by governmental agencies.*[11]

This concern with human behavior greatly limits the immediate potentialities of a science of public administration. First, it diminishes the possibility of using experimental procedures; and experiment, though perhaps not indispensable to the scientific method, is of enormous aid. Second, concern with human behavior seriously limits the uniformity of data, since the datum is the discrete and highly variable man or woman. Third, because the data concerning human behavior constitute an incredibly vast and complex mass, the part played by the preferences of the observer is exaggerated, and possibilities of independent verification are diminished. Fourth, concern with human action weakens the reliability of all "laws of public administration," since too little is known of the mainsprings of human action to insure certitude, or even high probability, in predictions about man's conduct.

All these weaknesses have been pointed out so often in discussing the problems of the social sciences that it should be unnecessary to repeat them here. And yet many of the supposed laws of public administration and much of the claim to a science of public administration derive from assumptions about the nature of man that are scarcely tenable at this late date.

The field of organizational theory serves as an extreme example, for it is there particularly that the nature of man is often lost sight of in the interminable discussions over idealized and abstract organizational forms. In this development, writers on public administration have been heavily influenced by the rational character that capitalism has imposed on the organization of production, and have ignored the irrational qualities of man himself.

Capitalism, especially in its industrial form, was essentially an attempt to organize production along rational lines. In the organization of the productive process, the capitalistic entrepreneur sought to destroy the old restrictive practices and standards of feudalism and mercantilism; to rid the productive process of the inherited cluster of methods and technics that characterized the guilds and medieval craftsmen; in short, to organize production according to rational rather than traditional concepts. Combined with a new acquisitive ideal, this rational approach to production transformed not only the whole economic process but society itself. The rapid growth of mechanization, routine, and specialization of labor further increased the technically rational quality of capitalist production. It was perhaps inevitable that concepts should arise which subordinated individual vagaries and differences to the ordered requirements of the productive process: for it was this very subordination that the replacement of feudal and mercantilist institutions by capitalism had accomplished. The organization (though not the control) of production became the concern of the engineer; and because the restrictive practices authorized by tradition, the protective standards of the guilds, the benevolent regulations of a mercantilist monarchy, and even the non-acquisitive ideals of the individual had all been swept away, it was actually feasible to organize production without much regard for the varying individual personalities of those in the productive process. The productive process, which to the medieval craftsman was both a means and an end in itself, became wholly a means.

Ultimately, of course, men like Taylor provided an imposing theoretical basis for regarding function, based on a logical distribution and specialization of labor, as the true basis of organization. Men like Urwick modified and carried forward. Taylor's work, and in the process have tremendously influenced writers on public administration. Urwick, so it must have appeared, provided a basis for a genuine science of administration. "There are principles," he wrote, *"which should govern arrangements for human association of any kind.* These principles can be studied as a technical question, *irrespective of the purpose of the enterprise, the personnel composing it, or any constitutional, political, or social theory underlying its creation."*[12] And again, "Whatever the motive underlying persistence in bad structure it is always more hurtful to the greatest number than good structure."[13]

Sweeping generalizations such as these gave promise of a set of "universal principles": i.e., a science. American students of public administration could not fail to be impressed.

Aside from the fact that Urwick ignored the whole question of ends, it is clear that he also presupposed (though he nowhere stated what sort of human personality he *did* presuppose) an essentially rational, amenable individual; he presupposed, that is to say, individuals who would accept logical organization and would not (for irrelevant and irrational reasons) rebel against it or silently supersede it with an informal organization better suited to their personality needs. Urwick must have supposed this. For if there is a large measure of irrationality in human behavior, then an organizational structure formed on "logical" lines may in practice frustrate, anger, and embitter its personnel. By contrast, an organization not based on the logic of organizational principles may better utilize the peculiar and varying personalities of its members. Is there any evidence to suggest that in such a case the "logical" organization will achieve its purposes in some sense "better" or more efficiently than the organization that adapts personality needs to the purposes of the organization?[14] On what kind of evidence are we compelled to assume that the rationality of organizational structure will prevail over the irrationality of man?

Patently the contention that one system of organization is more rational than another, *and therefore better,* is valid only (a) if individuals are dominated by reason or (b) if they are so thoroughly dominated by the technical process (as on the assembly line, perhaps) that their individual preferences may safely be ignored. However much the latter assumption might apply to industry (a matter of considerable doubt), clearly it has little application to public administration, where technical processes are, on the whole, of quite subordinate importance. As for the first assumption, it has been discredited by all the findings of modern psychology. The science of organization had learned too much from industry and not enough from Freud.

The more that writers on public administration have moved from the classroom to the administrator's office, the more Urwick's universal principles have receded. As early as 1930, in a pioneering work, Harold Lasswell described the irrational and unconscious elements in the successful and unsuccessful administrator.[15] Meanwhile, experiments in the Hawthorne plant of Western Electric Company were indicating beyond doubt that individual personalities and social relationships had great effects even on routinized work in industry. Increased output was the result of "the organization of human relations, rather than the organization of technics."[16] Urwick had said (with little or no supporting evidence): "The idea that organizations should be built up round and adjusted to individual idiosyncracies, rather than that individuals should be adapted to the requirements of sound principles of organization, is . . . foolish. . . ." The Hawthorne experiment demonstrated, on the contrary, that ". . . no study of human situations which fails to take account of the non-logical social routines can hope for practical success."[17]

In 1939, Leonard White seriously qualified the principle of subordinating individuals to structure by adding the saving phrase of the neo-classical economists: "in the long run." "To what extent," he said, "it is desirable to rearrange structure in preference to replacing personnel is a practical matter to be determined in the light of special cases. In the long run, the demands of sound organization require the fitting of personnel to it, rather than sacrificing normal organizational relationships to the needs or whims of individuals."[18] In the same year, Macmahon and Millett went far beyond the customary deductive principles of public administration theory by making an actual biographical study of a number of federal administrators.[19] In the most recent text on public administration, the importance of personality is frankly admitted. ". . . administrative research," say the authors, "does not seek its goal in the formulation of mechanical rules or equations, into which human behavior must be molded. Rather, it looks toward the systematic ordering of functions *and human relationships* so that organizational decisions can and will be based upon the certainty that each step taken will actually serve the purpose of the organization as a whole."[20] And one whole chapter of this text is devoted to informal organizations— the shadow relationships that frequently dominate the formal structure of the organization.

Thus by a lengthy and circumspect route, man has been led through the back door and readmitted to respectability. It is convenient to exile man from the science of public administration; it is simpler to forget man and write with "scientific" precision than to remember him and be cursed with his maddening unpredictability. Yet his exclusion is certain to make the study of public administration sterile, unrewarding, and essentially unreal.

If there is ever to be a science of public administration it must derive from an understanding of man's behavior in the area marked off by the boundaries of public administration. This area, to be sure, can never be clearly separated from man's behavior in other fields; all the social sciences are interdependent and all are limited by the basic lack of understanding of man's motivations and responses. Yet the ground of peculiar concern for a prospective science of public administration is that broad region of services administered by the government; until the manifold motivations and actions in this broad region have been explored and rendered predictable, there can be no science of public administration.

It is easier to define this area in space than in depth. One can arbitrarily restrict the prospective science of public administration to a certain region of human activity; but one cannot say with certainty how deeply one must mine this region in order to uncover its secrets. Does concern with human behavior mean that the researcher in public administration must be a psychiatrist and a sociologist? Or does it mean rather that in plumbing human behavior the researcher must be capable of using the investigations of the psychiatrist and sociologist? The need for specialization—a need, incidentally, which science itself seems to impose on human inquiry—suggests that the latter alternative must be the pragmatic answer.

Development of a science of public administration implies the development of a science of man in the area of services administered by the public. No such development can be brought about merely by the constantly reiterated assertion that public administration is already a science. We cannot achieve a science by creating in a mechanized "administrative man" a modern descendant of the eighteenth century's rational man, whose only existence is in books on public administration and whose only activity is strict obedience to "universal laws of the science of administration."

Public Administration and the Social Setting

If we know precious little about "administrative man" as an individual, perhaps we know even less about him as a social animal. Yet we cannot afford to ignore the relationship between public administration and its social setting.

No anthropologist would suggest that a social principle drawn from one distinct culture is likely to be transmitted unchanged to another culture; Ruth Benedict's descriptions of the Pueblo Indians of Zuñi, the Melanesians of Dobu, and the Kwakiutl Indians of Vancouver Island leave little doubt that cultures can be integrated on such distinctly different lines as to be almost noncomparable.[21] If the nation-states of western civilization by no means possess such wholly contrasting cultures as the natives of Zuñi, Dobu, and Vancouver Island, nevertheless few political scientists would contend that a principle of political organization drawn from one nation could be adopted with equal success by another; one would scarcely argue that federalism has everywhere the same utility or that the unitary state would be equally viable in Britain and the United States or that the American presidential system would operate unchanged in France or Germany.

There should be no reason for supposing, then, that a principle of public administration has equal validity in every nation-state, or that successful public administration practices in one country will necessarily prove successful in a different social, economic, and political environment. A particular nation-state embodies the results of many historical episodes, traumas, failures, and successes which have in turn created peculiar habits, mores, institutionalized patterns of behaviour, *Weltanschauungen,* and even "national psychologies."[22] One cannot assume that public administration can escape the effects of this conditioning; or that it is somehow independent of and isolated from the culture or social setting in which it develops. At the same time, as value can be gained by a comparative study of government based upon a due respect for differences in the political, social, and economic environment of nation-states, so too the comparative study of public administration ought to be rewarding. Yet the comparative aspects of public administration have largely been ignored; and as long as the study of public administration is not comparative, claims for "a science of public administration" sound rather hollow. Conceivably there might be a science of American public administration and a science of British public administration and a science of French public administration; but can there be "a science of public administration" in the sense of a body of generalized principles independent of their peculiar national setting?

Today we stand in almost total ignorance of the relationship between "principles of public administration" and their general setting. Can it be safely affirmed, on the basis of existing knowledge of comparative public administration, that there are *any* principles independent of their special environment?

The discussion over an administrative class in the civil service furnishes a useful example of the difficulties of any approach that does not rest on a thorough examination of developmental and environmental differences. The manifest benefits and merits of the British administrative class have sometimes led American students of public administration to suggest the development of an administrative class in the American civil service; but proposals of this kind have rarely depended on a thorough comparison of the historical factors that made the administrative class a successful achievement in Britain, and may or may not be duplicated here. Thus Wilmerding has virtually proposed the transfer to the United States of all the detailed elements in the British civil service; although he does not explicitly base his proposals on British experience except in a few instances, they follow British practices with almost complete fidelity.[23] White has likewise argued for the creation of an "administrative corps" along the lines of the British administrative class. He has suggested that reform of the civil service in Britain and creation of an administrative class were accomplished in little more than two generations; profiting by British experience, he argues, we ought to be able to accomplish such a reform in even shorter time.[24] Since the question of an administrative class is perhaps the outstanding case where American writers on public administration have employed the comparative method to the extent of borrowing from foreign experience, it is worthy of a brief analysis to uncover some of the problems of a comparative "science of public administration." For it throws into stark perspective the fundamental difficulties of drawing universal conclusions from the institutions of any one country, and at the same time sharply outlines the correlative problem of comparing the institutions of several nations in order to derive general principles out of the greater range of experiences.

The central difficulty of universal generalizations may be indicated in this way: An administrative class based on merit rests upon four conditions. All of these prerequisites were present coincidentally in Britain in the mid-nineteenth century; and none of them is present in quite the same way here.

First of all, an administrative class of the British type rests upon a general political acceptance of the hierarchical idea. This acceptance in Britain was not the product of forty years; it was the outcome of four centuries. It is not too much to say that it was the four centuries during which the public service was the particular prerogative of the upper classes that made a hierarchical civil service structure feasible in Britain. The Tudor monarchy had rested upon a combination of crown power administered under the King by representatives of the upper middle and professional classes in the towns and newly created members of the gentry in the country; Tudor authority was in effect derived from an alliance of King and upper middle classes against the aristocracy. From the Revolution of 1688 until 1832, public service was the special domain of an increasingly functionless aristocracy whose monopoly of public office was tacitly supported by the upper middle classes of the cities. Whatever the Reform Bill of 1832 accomplished in terms of placing the urban oligarchy overtly in office, no one in Britain had many illusions that a change in the hierarchical structure of politics and public service was entailed. The upper middle classes were no more keen than were the landed gentry of the eighteenth century to throw

open the doors of public service and politics to "the rabble." Out of this
long historic background the idea of an administrative class emerged. The
unspoken political premises of the dominant groups in the nation reflected
an acceptance of hierarchy in the social, economic, and political structure
of Britain; the contention, common in the American scene, that an administrative class is "undemocratic" played no real part in mid-nineteenth century Britain. One may well question whether it would be so easy to create
an administrative class in any society, like the American, where egalitarian-
ism is so firmly rooted as a political dogma; however desirable such a class
may be, and however little it may actually violate the democratic ideal, one
is entitled to doubt that the overt creation of an administrative elite is a
practical possibility in American politics.[25] In any case, the idea must be fitted into the peculiar mores and the special ethos of the United States, and
cannot be lightly transferred from Britain to this country.[26]

Second, the administrative class idea rests upon a scholastic system that
creates the educated nonspecialist, and a recruiting system that selects him.
Too often, the proposal has been made to recruit persons of general rather
than specialized training for an "administrative corps" without solving the
prior problem of producing such "generalists" in the universities. The
British public school system and the universities have long been dominated
by the ideal of the educated gentleman; and for centuries they have succeeded admirably in producing the "generalist" mind, even when that
mind is nourished on apparently specialized subjects. It is a peculiarly
British paradox that persons of high general ability are recruited into the
civil service by means of examinations that heavily weight such specialities
as classical languages and mathematics. In so far as this country has an educational ideal (a question on which this writer speaks with considerable
trepidation), it appears to be, or to have been, the ideal of the specialist.
Much more is involved, too, than a question of education; at base the
problem is one of social mores that give the specialist a prestige and a social utility that no person of general education is likely to attain. That the
recruiting process has been forced to adapt itself to the educational specialization characteristic of American universities (indeed, one might say of
American life) is scarcely astonishing. It would be more astonishing if the
Civil Service Commission were able to recruit nonexistent "generalists" to
perform unrecognized functions within a corps of practitioners where almost everyone regards himself as a subject-matter specialist.[27]

In the third place, the administrative class idea rests upon the acceptance
of merit as the criterion of selection. In Britain this acceptance was no mere
accident of an inexplicable twenty-year change in public standards of
morality. If patronage disappeared in Britain, it was partly because patronage had ceased to have any real function, whereas efficiency had acquired a
new social and political utility. Prior to the nineteenth century, patronage
had two vital functions: it provided a place for the sons of the aristocracy

who were excluded from inheritance by primogeniture; and it placed in the hands of the King and his ministers a device for guaranteeing, under the limited franchise of the eighteenth century, a favorable House of Commons. Both these factors disappeared during the first decades of the nineteenth century. With the expansion of the electorate after 1832, the monarchy was forced to withdraw from politics, or risk the chance of a serious loss of prestige in an electorate that was now too large to control.[28] Meanwhile, the development of dissolution as a power available to the Prime Minister upon his request from the Crown gave the executive a means of party discipline and control far more effective than the promise of office. Finally, the accession to power of the manufacturing and trading classes by the reforms of 1832 placed a new emphasis on efficiency, both as a means of cutting down public expenses and insuring economies in government, and (especially after 1848) of warding off the revolutionary threat that might develop out of governmental incompetence.[29] All these conditions made possible, and perhaps inevitable, the substitution of merit for patronage. To talk as if reform arose out of some change in public morality, obscure and mysterious in origin but laudable in character, is to miss the whole significance of British reforms. In the present-day politics of the United States, it is not so clear that the utility of patronage has disappeared; under the American system of separation of powers, patronage remains almost as useful as it was under the British constitution of the eighteenth century. And in any case, it is self-evident that the problem here lies in a distinctly different political and social setting from that of Victorian England.

Last, a successful administrative class rests upon the condition that such a group possesses the prestige of an elite; for unless the class has an elite status, it is in a poor position to compete against any other elite for the brains and abilities of the nation. It is one thing to *offer* a career in a merit service; it is quite another to insure that such a service has enough prestige to acquire the best of the nation's competence. The argument that the mere creation of an administrative class would be sufficient to endow that group with prestige in the United States may or may not be valid; it is certainly invalid to argue that this was the causal sequence in Britain. In assessing the ability of the British civil service to recruit the best products of the universities, one can scarcely overlook the profound significance of the fact that for centuries the public service was one of the few careers into which a member of the aristocracy could enter without loss of prestige. Like the church, the army, and politics, and unlike trade and commerce, public service was a profession in which the aristocracy could engage without violating the mores of the class. Even during the eighteenth century and the first half of the nineteenth, when the burden of incompetence and patronage in the public service was at its heaviest, government was a field into which the social elite could enter without a diminution of prestige, and often enough without even a loss in leisure. Throughout the age of patronage, the British public service succeeded in obtaining some of the best of Britain's abilities.[30] The effect of the reforms after 1853 was to make more attractive a profession that already outranked business and industry in prestige values. In Britain, as in Germany, the psychic income accruing from a career in the civil service more than compensates for the smaller economic income. Contrast this with the United States, where since the Civil War prestige has largely accrued to acquisitive successes. It is small wonder that in the United States the problem of government competition with business for the abilities of the community should be much more acute.

If these remarks about the British administrative class are well founded, then these conclusions suggest themselves:

> 1. Generalizations derived from the operation of public administration in the environment of one nation-state cannot be universalized and applied to public administration in a different environment. A principle *may* be applicable in a different framework. But its applicability can be determined only after a study of that particular framework.
>
> 2. There can be no truly universal generalizations about public administration without a profound study of varying national and social characteristics impinging on public administration, to determine what aspects of public administration, if any, are truly independent of the national and social setting. Are there discoverable principles of *universal* validity, or are all principles valid only in terms of a special environment?
>
> 3. It follows that the study of public administration inevitably must become a much more broadly based discipline, resting not on a narrowly defined knowledge of techniques and processes, but rather extending to the varying historical, sociological, economic, and other conditioning factors that give public administration its peculiar stamp in each country.

The relation of public administration to its peculiar environment has not been altogether ignored.[31] Unhappily, however, comparative studies are all too infrequent; and at best they provide only the groundwork. We need many more studies of comparative administration before it will be possible to argue that there are any universal principles of public administration.

In Conclusion

We are a long way from a science of public administration. No science of public administration is possible unless: (1) the place of normative values is made clear; (2) the nature of man in the area of public administration is better understood and his conduct is more predictable; and (3) there is a body of comparative studies from which it may be possible to discover principles and generalities that transcend national boundaries and peculiar historical experiences.

Notes

1. See, for example, F. Merson, "Public Administration: A Science," 1 *Public Administration* 220 (1923); B. W. Walker Watson, "The Elements of Public Administration, A Dogmatic Introduction," 10 *Public Administration* 397 (1932); L. Gulick, "Science, Values and Public Administration," *Papers on the Science of Administration,* ed. by Gulick & Urwick, (Institute of Public Administration, 1937); Cyril Renwick, "Public Administration: Towards a Science," *The Australian Quarterly* (March 1944), p. 73.

2. *Principles of Public Administration* (The Brookings Institution, 1927), Preface, p. ix.

3. See fn. 12, *infra,* for the full quotation and citation.

4. This I take to be Professor Leonard D. White's position. See his "The Meaning of Principles in Public Administration," in *The Frontiers of Public Administration* (University of Chicago Press, 1936), pp. 13–25.

5. *Public Administration* (Farrar & Rinehart, 1937), p. 8.

6. "Administrative Reorganization," 1 *The Journal of Politics* 62–65 (1939).

7. *Op. cit.,* pp. 192–93.

8. *Op. cit.,* p. 193.

9. C. J. Friedrich, "Public Policy and the Nature of Administrative Responsibility," in *Public Policy* (Harvard University Press, 1940); Herman Finer, "Administrative Responsibility in Democratic Government," 1 *Public Administration Review* 335 (1940–41). See also Friedrich's earlier formulation, which touched off the dispute, "Responsible Government Service under the American Constitution," in *Problems of the American Public Service* (McGraw-Hill Book Co., 1935); and Finer's answer to Friedrich in 51 *Political Science Quarterly* 582 (1936).

10. See Aldous Huxley's discussion in *Ends and Means* (Harper & Bros., 1937), and Arthur Koestler, *The Yogi and the Commissar* (Macmillan Co., 1945).

11. See Ernest Barker's excellent and useful distinctions between state, government, and administration, in *The Development of Public Services in Western Europe, 1660–1930* (Oxford University Press, 1944), p. 3. Administration "is the sum of persons and bodies who are engaged, under the direction of government, in discharging the ordinary public services which must be rendered daily if the system of law and duties and rights is to be duly 'served.' Every right and duty implies a corresponding 'service'; and the more the State multiplies rights and duties, the more it multiplies the necessary services of its ministering officials." See also Leon Duguit, *Law in the Modern State* (B. W. Huebsch, 1919), Ch. II.

12. L. Urwick, "Organization as a Technical Problem," *Papers on the Science of Administration,* p. 49. (Italics added.) See also his "Executive Decentralisation with Functional Co-ordination," 13 *Public Administration* 344 (1935), in which he sets forth "some axioms of organisation," among others that "there are certain principles which govern the association of human beings *for any purpose,* just as there are certain engineering principles which govern the building of a bridge. Such principles should take priority *of all traditional, personal or political considerations.* If

they are not observed, co-operation between those concerned will be less effective than it should be in realising the purpose for which they have decided to co-operate. There will be waste of effort." (Italics added.) See also his criticisms of the "practical man fallacy," p. 346.

13. *Ibid.,* p. 85.

14. See John M. Gaus's excellent definitions: "Organization is the arrangement of personnel for facilitating the accomplishment of some agreed purpose through the allocation of functions and responsibilities. It is the relating of efforts and capacities of individuals and groups engaged upon a common task in such a way as to secure the desired objective with the least friction and the most satisfaction to those for whom the task is done and those engaged in the enterprise. . . . Since organization consists of people brought into a certain relationship because of a humanly evolved purpose, it is clear that it should be flexible rather than rigid. There will be constant readjustments necessary because of personalities and other natural forces and because of the unpredicted and unpredictable situations confronted in its operations." "A Theory of Organization in Public Administration," in *The Frontiers of Public Administration,* pp. 66–67.

15. *Psychopathology and Politics* (University of Chicago Press, 1930), Ch. 8 "Political Administrators."

16. L. J. Henderson, T. N. Whitehead, and Elton Mayo, "The Effects of Social Environment," in *Papers on the Science of Administration, op. cit.,* p. 149. It is worth noting that this essay properly interpreted contradicts the implicit assumptions of virtually every other essay in that volume; and it is, incidentally, the only wholly empirical study in the entire volume.

17. Urwick, *op. cit.,* p. 85, and Henderson, *et al.,* p. 155. Urwick has set up a false dilemma that makes his choice more persuasive. Actually, the choice is not between (a) wholly subordinating organizational structure to individual personalities, which obviously might lead to chaos or (b) forcing all personalities into an abstractly correct organizational structure which might (and often does) lead to waste and friction. There is a third choice, (c) employing organizational structure and personalities to the achievement of a purpose. By excluding purpose, Urwick has, in effect, set up organization as an end in itself. An army may be organized more efficiently (according to abstract organizational principles) than the political structure of a democratic state, but no one except an authoritarian is likely to contend that it is a *superior* organization—*except for the purposes it is designed to achieve.* Yet once one admits the element of purpose, easy generalizations about organizational principles become difficult if not impossible; and the admission presupposes, particularly in the case of public organizations, a clear statement of ends and purposes.

18. Leonard White, *Introduction to the Study of Public Administration* (Macmillan Co., 1939), p. 38.

19. A. W. Macmahon and J. D. Millett, *Federal Administrators* (Columbia University Press, 1939).

20. Fritz Morstein Marx, ed., *Elements of Public Administration* (Prentice-Hall, 1946), p. 49. (Italics added.)

21. *Patterns of Culture* (Houghton Mifflin Co., 1934).

22. See the fragmentary but revealing discussion on national differences in *Human Nature and Enduring Peace* (Third Yearbook of the Society for the Psychological Study of Social Issues) Gardner Murphy, ed. (Houghton Mifflin, 1945).

23. Lucius Wilmerding, Jr., *Government by Merit* (McGraw-Hill Book Co., 1935).

24. "The British civil service, which the whole world now admires, went through nearly twenty years of transition before its foundations even were properly laid. It went through another twenty years of gradual adjustment before the modern service as we know it today was fully in operation. . . . In the light of British experience, and by taking advantage of modern knowledge about large-scale organization, we can easily save the twenty years in which the British were experimenting to find the proper basis for their splendid service. We shall, however, need ten years of steady growth, consciously guided and planned, to put a new administrative corps into operation, and probably another ten years before it is completely installed." *Government Career Service* (University of Chicago Press, 1935), p. 8.

25. Significantly, the most recent study of reform of the American civil service states, "We do not recommend the formation of a specially organized administrative corps for which a special type of selection and training is proposed." *Report of President's Committee on Civil Service Improvement* (Government Printing Office, 1941), p. 57. Instead, the Committee recommends that "all positions whose duties are administrative in nature, in grades CAF–11, P–4, and higher . . . be identified as an occupational group within the existing classification structure." This is a noteworthy step in an attempt to achieve the advantages of an administrative class within the framework of American mores and institutions. It is therefore a great advance over the earlier proposal in the Report of the Commission of Inquiry on Public Service Personnel, *Better Government Personnel* (McGraw-Hill Book Co., 1935), which recommended the outright creation of a distinct administrative class (p. 30).

26. This was the essential point, stated in more specific terms, of Lewis Meriam's criticism of the administrative corps idea. See his excellent *Public Service and Special Training* (University of Chicago Press, 1936).

27. It is noteworthy that the latest U. S. Civil Service Commission announcement for the junior professional assistant examination (November, 1946) follows the subject-matter specialist concept; junior professional assistants will be recruited in terms of specialities unthinkable in the British administrative class examinations for university graduates. See, by comparison, *Specimen Question Papers for the Reconstruction Competition for Recruitment to* (1) *The Administrative Class of the Home Civil Service,* (2) *The Senior Branch of the Foreign Service,* (C.S.C. 18) (H.M. Stationery Office 1946).

28. See D. Lindsay Keir, *The Constitutional History of Modern Britain 1485–1937* (A. & C. Black, 1943), p. 405.

29. See J. Donald Kingsley, *Representative Bureaucracy, An Interpretation of the British Civil Service* (Antioch Press, 1944), Ch. III.

30. Hiram Stout, *Public Service in Great Britain* (University of North Carolina Press, 1938), pp. 25–26, 82–83.

31. See, for example, Walter Dorn, "The Prussian Bureaucracy in the Eighteenth Century," 46 *Political Science Quarterly* 403–23 (1931) and 47 *Ibid.,* 75–94, 259–73 (1932); Fritz Morstein Marx, "Civil Service in Germany," in *Civil Service Abroad* (McGraw-Hill Book Co., 1935); John M. Gaus, "American Society and Public Administration," *The Frontiers of Public Administration* (University of Chicago Press, 1936).

5

PUBLIC ADMINISTRATION
AND BUSINESS MANAGEMENT

L. Urwick

Some ten years ago Professor Dahl in an article in the *Public Administration Review,* "The Science of Public Administration: Three Problems," took me very severely to task for the statement that "there are principles . . . which should govern arrangements for human association of any kind. These principles can be studied as a technical question, irrespective of the purpose of the enterprise, the personnel composing it, or any constitutional, political, or social theory underlying its creation."[1]

"Sweeping generalizations such as these," he commented, "gave promise of a set of 'universal principles': i.e. a science. American students of public administration could not fail to be impressed." He then proceeded to take me to task on the ground, *inter alia,* that I had "presupposed an essentially rational, amenable individual . . . who would accept logical organization. . . ." (p. 5)

Source: *Public Administration Review* 17(1957): 77–82.

Note: This article was a luncheon address at the Annual Conference of the American Society for Public Administration, March 21, 1957.

Meaning of a "Science"

It is not my purpose here this afternoon to enter into debate with Professor Dahl. Though I must confess that some of his dicta at that time made me chuckle.

For instance, "Development of a science of public administration implies the development of a science of man in the area of services administered by the public" (p. 7). Why not just "a science of man"? Admittedly the genus *homo* was somewhat optimistically classified *sapiens*. But are his behavior and his habits really so frozen into the ice pack of his calling that we can detect no common rules, no human qualities and tendencies, that transcend these occupational categories? Is this suggestion more than the ancient alibi which so long handicapped the development of a body of knowledge about business management—"my business is different"—implying that the maker of soap had nothing to learn from the vendor of sausages. Are we really condemned to a biology of bureaucrats, a physiology of professors, and a psychopathology of politicians? Are these occupational distinctions valid?

The trouble, of course, centers round the phrase "a science." But it was Professor Dahl, not I, who stated that my "generalizations gave promise of a science." The article from which the quotations are drawn made no such claim. It was entitled, with intention, "Organization as a *Technical* Problem."

Personally I believe that an *exact* science of human social behavior is many centuries away. Individual psychology has been an inductive study for little more than half-a-century. Our knowledge of the biochemistry of the nervous system is as yet insufficient to provide an adequate physical foundation for an exact science of individual psychology. The prospects of a reliable group psychology are much more remote. Indeed it seems to me that altogether too much ink and paper are being expended on discussing whether this or that body of knowledge is or is not a science, as though there were no two meanings to the word.

A "science" can mean a body of knowledge like the knowledge found in the physical sciences. Or it can mean an organized body of knowledge of any kind. The argument about this ambiguity is at least half-a-century old. It started with the phrase "scientific management" adopted by Frederick Winslow Taylor, though with misgivings.

But that Taylor ever meant by the phrase that management is "a science" in the first sense is contrary to the record. He said precisely the opposite— "management is also destined to become more of an art."[2] And he also made it quite clear that in using the adjective "scientific" he merely intended to imply the possibility of an organized body of knowledge about the subject.[3]

There is a vast amount of human experience about all kinds' of administrative and managerial problems. If we will organize it, measure it where we can, and generalize from it, we can build up a body of knowledge about managing which can be taught and learned. And that will be a much better plan than leaving people to learn merely by the accidents of practical apprenticeship and "trial and error." Before supporting too enthusiastically the old empirical method of learning, critics would be wise to remember that in the activity of managing the learner's errors are other peoples' trials.

What Taylor did say very definitely, however, and I think very rightly, was that the only way out of the conflict between employers and employed which has crystallized since the industrial revolution is for both sides (1) to recognize that they are engaged in a common activity and (2) to approach the problems created by that common activity in the scientific temper and spirit. That seems to me incontestable. We cannot live within a culture dominated and shaped by advances in our control over material things, advances which have placed a great strain on our capacity to cooperate with each other, without modifications in our political and social arrangements. And if we are to arrive at such changes without endless strife and confusion we must agree on a common mental approach to our problems. That it should be the same approach as has created the problems, the scientific approach, is merely an example of the traditional remedy for another form of excess "the hair of the dog."

A similar lack of semantic sophistication is found in the use of the word "principle." In the same article Professor Dahl refers to the "supposed laws of public administration" (p. 4). And it is obvious that he regards my "principles" not as provisional generalizations which have, so far, been found useful in practice, but as statements of an invariable relation between cause and effect. The same mistake was made by Professor Simon, in his chapter on "Some Problems of Administrative Theory," in his otherwise invaluable *Administrative Behavior.*[4]

I find it necessary to make the point because there is obviously a reaction under way, especially among academic people, against the proposition that there are very great similarities about the way human beings react to similar organizational and administrative arrangements whether in the public service, in business, or anywhere else. I am convinced that by the study of those similarities we can arrive at important generalizations which are of the greatest value both as a diagnostic instrument and as a guide to correcting difficulties encountered in practice.

A more hopeful note was sounded recently by Chancellor Edward Litchfield of the University of Pittsburgh:

> Actually our practice is years ahead of our thought. There is abundant evidence to demonstrate our unexpressed conviction that there is much that is common in administration. . . . The constant movement of executive personnel from business to government, from the military forces into large business,

from both government and business into education, is emphatic testimony supporting our conviction . . . of an essential universality in the administrative process itself. Again, it is a commonplace to observe that management consulting firms find their knowledges and skills applicable in the department store, on the one hand, and in the government bureau or the university, on the other. . . . As theorists we have not yet established generalized concepts which keep pace with the facts of contemporary administration.[5]

Surely the discovery of such similarities and their use as a guide in our perplexities and confusions is a more hopeful and constructive task than endless logic-chopping directed to proving that a particular principle is not universal or that this or that presentation is not truly scientific. Criticism let there be in plenty. That is healthy and invigorating. But let the critics from the academic world remember that they are professionals in inky warfare. The practical man trying to describe his experiences and to generalize from them is not. They may well lose the advantage of that experience if they try to make the practical man compete with them on their own professional terms.

Personally, I infinitely prefer the homespun philosophy of the late Ortega y Gasset:

Life cannot wait until the sciences may have explained the universe scientifically. We cannot put off living until we are ready. The most salient characteristic of life is its coerciveness: it is always urgent, "here and now" without any possible postponement. . . . If the physicist had to *live* by the ideas of his science, you may rest assured he would not be so finicky as to wait for some other investigator to complete his research a century or so later. He would renounce the hope of a complete scientific solution, and fill in, with approximate or probable anticipations, what the rigorous corpus of physical doctrine lacks at present, and in part, always will lack.[6]

It is to such "approximate or probable anticipations" that I attach the title "principle." We use them all the time in our practical work as management consultants.

The Span of Control

Take, for instance, the principle described as "the span of control," about which there has been much verbal disputation on the ground that it is supposed to conflict with the principle of reducing administrative levels to a minimum. To be sure, when the doctor tells you not to eat too much your wife is apt to invoke the opposite principle and to tell you that you will make yourself ill if you starve yourself so. But that doesn't prove your doctor wrong.

Men have an appetite for power and self-importance, just as they have an appetite for good food. It is an appetite which feeds on having rows of subordinates waiting on their doormat. And where it is not restrained by recognition of the limits imposed by the span of control, there will always be some managers in every kind of undertaking driving their subordinates scatty and themselves into the ground by ignoring the human limitation of a restricted span of attention.

Literally hundreds of times in the course of professional practice our consultants have encountered cases of managers and foremen who were "falling down on the job" for no other reason save failure to recognize the importance of that principle. A simple adjustment, grouping up independent subordinate units or appointing an assistant who could take direct responsibility for half his too numerous brood, and both the man (they were often good men: merely ignorant) and the situation were saved.

And yet, only the other day, there was a young assistant professor from an American School of Business Administration arguing at great length in *Advanced Management* that the principle has no validity.[7] He even quoted a soldier who had admitted that in peacetime, and especially in Washington, the Army often neglects the principle because of personal ambitions, status hunting, and similar sinister motives, to prove that the principle had no application to business.

What I am pleading for is a more open-minded approach to the whole problem of administration, a more thorough exchange of experience and knowledge, a determination to hang, draw, and quarter the ancient fallacy that "my business is different."

I am also arguing that there is a vast fund of experience on which we all can and should draw. I am pleading with the academic people not to get in the light of that process of cross-infiltration of knowledge by verbal campaigns aimed at proving that this or that "possible or probable anticipation" is not "scientific." I am arguing on the same lines as my old and deeply-mourned friend Mary Parker Follett when she explained why she had transferred her attention and her researches from the field of government to the field of business management.

> the principles of organization and administration which are discovered as best for business can be applied to government or international relations. Indeed, the solution of world problems must eventually be built up from all the little bits of experience wherever people are consciously trying to solve problems of relation. And this attempt is being made more consciously and deliberately in industry than anywhere else.[8]

The Clearinghouse Principle

Take another example of a principle which I have encountered practically both in business and in government. Let us call it the clearinghouse principle. "Communication" is currently somewhat of a "blessed word" in the study of management and of administration. We all know Chester Barnard's dictum that a chief executive is really the center of a system of communication.

If communication is important it is essential that the mechanics of the process should run smoothly and easily *and quickly.* On the other hand, we all believe in decentralization. And in any large complex of offices constituting the government of a country or the headquarters of a business, decentralization tends to run along functional lines. The heads of functional departments are often jealous of their authority and independence. They all manage their own communications with each other. The consequence is a sea anchor on routine communications. They take an inordinate time to pass from the desk of one official in one department to the desk of the addressee in another department. It follows that, since many communications are reasonably urgent, there is an excessive use of "special messengers."

I don't know how it is in Washington. It is so in Whitehall. There are more than 100 offices within two or three square miles each running its own post office to all the others. There is no clearinghouse. Any document which calls for an answer within, say, twenty-four hours tends to go by "special messenger." If the chief executive is really the center of a process of communication, there is one quite routine responsibility which he cannot, with safety, delegate away from his central control, the actual routine of communication. It is quite secondary in importance, but critical to effectiveness. Of course, in Whitehall there is at the executive level no chief, only a vestigial anachronism, a committee which never meets, called The Lords of the Treasury.

The same clearinghouse principle indicates that, whether in business or in government, specialized advice and direction should never flow directly downward to lower echelons. If they do you are bound to get clashes about competence and authority between specialists and those with general responsibility at lower echelons. The specialist always expects the man with general responsibility to devote more time and attention to his "ewe lamb" than the "generalist" thinks either suitable or convenient. That's the way of specialists.

Specialized advice and direction should always move *upward* so that they can be incorporated in the "chain of command." I know the word "command" is not liked in this country. But the use of the term here merely implies a particular channel of communication. This has two advantages. It enables specialist requirements to be coordinated with the other demands on those responsible for lower echelons *before* instructions are issued. This saves much friction and subsequent recrimination. It also ensures that specialized communications are "authenticated" before reaching subordinates.

If this is done, however, it means that there is quite a large volume of "paper work" passing over the chief's desk. The number of specialists who have to be integrated in the overall plan tends to increase. The chief will have insufficient time to visit his subordinates. They will lose confidence in central direction and tend to kick at "paper" instructions.

The General Staff Relationship

This makes it virtually mandatory that in any large organization the chief should have an assistant or assistants in a "general staff" relation to himself. The *general* should be distinguished from the *special* staff relation. The special staff officer looks after and advises on his special function: the general staff assistant advises the chief and assists him with all *his*, the chief's, functions of direction. He is his *alter ego*. He should also relieve him of at least 90 per cent of his paper work. Paper work is really quite secondary at the level of the chief. His main function is personal leadership. If he is so desk bound with paper work that he has insufficient time for it, the organization will suffer.

The paper work, the records, are essential. Some men lie and all men die. The record becomes critical where these accidents occur. It is also essential in all large-scale organization because men change posts and forget. But it is only a record, an *aide memoire*. The big decisions get taken not on paper, but by individuals meeting face to face who trust each other. The paper is like the drains in a house: it carries off the waste matter of poor human relations. Far too many people in responsible positions try to live in their drains.

This general staff relationship is not very well understood in civil life. Many mistakes are being made in using it. It is a direction in which both business and the public services can learn from the experience of the combat services.[9] All these questions flow from an acceptance of the clearinghouse principle. No chief can be an effective center of a system of communication unless he is equipped with the apparatus and the assistance which being such a center postulates.

The Need for a Chief Executive

In discussing the clearinghouse principle I have, of course, made an assumption that is not generally accepted, though it is a part of the Constitution and of the general business practice of this country. That is that there must be in all organizations which aim to *do* something, rather than at deciding what is to be done, a chief executive.

This executive principle was clearly laid down by the President's Committee on Administrative Management in 1937:

the foundations of effective management in public affairs, no less than in private, are well known. . . . Stated in simple terms these canons of efficiency require the establishment of a responsible and effective chief executive as the center of energy, direction, and administrative management. . . .[10]

It is F. W. Taylor's distinction between planning and performance carried to a higher level.

Fear of this principle is undoubtedly at the root of much of the confusion in the ordering of our affairs. It is felt to be undemocratic, arbitrary. The President's Committee on Administrative Management recognized this fear and gave the answer:

> It may be said that there is danger that management itself will grow too great and forget where it came from or what it is for—in the old and recurring insolence of office. [But] a weak administration can neither advance nor retreat successfully—it can merely muddle. Those who waver at the sight of needed power are false friends of modern democracy. . . . (p. 53)

If this principle, this distinction, between the legislative, the policy-making, and the executive function is clearly admitted the pattern begins to fall into shape. Because management today is nine-tenths a technical, a scientific job. The dream in many men's minds that it can be submitted to mechanisms of control modeled on those devised for political purposes is "a moonbeam from the larger lunacy." Attempts to impose such mechanisms are as crazy as the requirement that the captain of a ship should call a meeting of the crew every time he wished to change course. Such a requirement would not only greatly increase the hazards of the crew: it ignores completely the rights of another party to the transaction—the passengers, the consumers.

To say this in no way absolves the captain from his responsibility so to discharge the duties of his office that his leadership is acceptable to the members of the crew. Indeed that is the first of those duties.

Will Rationality Prevail?

Professor Dahl posed the rhetorical question "On what kind of evidence are we compelled to assume that the rationality of organizational structure will prevail over the irrationality of man?" We are not compelled to assume it. We can only hope that it will be so. For this hope we have two grounds:

1. Men when they engage in some common activity for a defined end prefer to "know where they are" and "what is expected of them." Rational organization tells them this. It does not leave the issue vague and at the mercy of those who are stronger or less scrupulous than their fellows. In

other words, rational organization creates positions in which the necessary leadership can be developed and is expected. It is acceptable leadership which identifies the social sentiments and social living of those under authority with the purpose that authority was created to fulfill and the methods it adopts in doing so.

2. Men, where their lives are at stake, are usually fairly quick at grasping the realities of a situation. I have heard of ships' crews mutinying: I have yet to hear of a ship's crew electing a committee to do the steering. They know, being sailors, that safe steering isn't done that way.

In the same way we are assimilating, albeit all too slowly, the lesson that a civilization dependent on modern science and power-driven machinery for its material necessities must observe the imperatives underlying the design and utilization of these facilities if it is to avoid total disruption. To be sure, our old folkways and superstitions die hard. But we do learn. I doubt if there is a citizen in this country today who would try to make a stalled automobile start again by kissing its radiator or kicking its differential. He knows that he can only make the thing go by understanding how it works, or by finding someone else who does and trusting him.

We may not learn this simple lesson in time. In the words of an American thinker of the first order, Thorstein Veblen:

> History records more frequent and more spectacular instances of the triumph of imbecile institutions over life and culture than of peoples who have by the force of instinctive insight saved themselves alive out of a desperately precarious institutional situation, such, for instance, as now faces the peoples of Christendom.[11]

It is not without significance that that somber passage was written two world wars away—in March, 1914.

Notes

1. Robert A. Dahl, "The Science of Public Administration: Three Problems," 7 *Public Administration Review* 5 (Winter, 1947), quoting from L. Urwick, "Organization as a Technical Problem," in Luther Gulick and L. Urwick, eds., *Papers on the Science of Administration* (Institute of Public Administration, Columbia University, 1937), p. 49.

2. F. W. Taylor, "Shop Management" in *Scientific Management* (Harper & Bros., 1947), p. 63.

3. *Ibid.*, "Testimony," p. 41.

4. Herbert A. Simon, *Administrative Behavior* (Macmillan Co., 1947), Chap. II, "Some Problems in Administrative Theory."

5. Edward H. Litchfield, "Notes on a General Theory of Administration," 1 *Administrative Science Quarterly* 8–9 (June, 1956).

6. José Ortega y Gasset, *Mission of the University* H. L. Nostrand, tr., (Princeton University Press, 1944), p. 84. Italics added.

7. Waino W. Suojanen, "The Span of Control—Fact or Fable?," 20 *Advanced Management* 5 (November, 1955). See also, L. Urwick, "The Manager's Span of Control," 34 *Harvard Business Review* 39 (May-June, 1956), and "The Span of Control—Some Facts about the Fables," 21 *Advanced Management* 5 (November, 1956).

8. Henry C. Metcalf and L. Urwick, eds. *Dynamic Administration* (Harper & Bros., 1941), p. 19, quoting from a paper, "Leadership," by Mary Parker Follett, read to the Rowntree Oxford Conference, 1928.

9. For a fuller discussion of this question, see L. Urwick and Ernest Dale, *Profitably Using the General Staff Position in Business* (American Management Association, 1953), General Management Series No. 165.

10. President's Committee on Administrative Management, *Report* (U. S. Government Printing Office, 1937), p. 3.

11. Thorstein Veblen, *The Instinct of Workmanship* (Macmillan Co., 1914), p. 25.

6

STORIES MANAGERS TELL: WHY THEY ARE AS VALID AS SCIENCE

Ralph P. Hummel

Public administration is dying. It is dying because people in the field are not producing enough scholars capable of producing significant research.

Scientist[1]

I suspect that public administration is not going to disappear. Whether you call it a profession or not is maybe a semantic term more involved with our egos than what is going to be happening. Since people do act, either explicitly or implicitly, on the basis of theory part of the time or most of the time, the job of the theorist is in large part to ascertain first of all what is it that we're operating on and how can it be improved.

Ambassador, 1989

In the last seven years, a small but vociferous group of critical scientists has conducted a concerted attack on how public managers acquire knowledge.[2] In addition, they condemn how public administration professors guide research, and how students write dissertations. The upshot of this criticism is that neither practitioners nor academicians know what they are doing be-

Source: *Public Administration Review* 51(1991): 31–41.

cause they are not scientific enough. The implication is that more use of science among managers and in public administration curricula can cure what ails public administration: namely an alleged deficit of valid knowledge. The extreme penalty for failure to comply is, in the words of one scientist, the supposed fact that "Public Administration is dying."[3]

There is, however, another possibility besides epidemic stupidity among public administrationists: It is that public managers and teachers and students know what they are doing. This article explores that possibility.

Until scientific critics do what they themselves have never done—explore the possibility that the prevailing form of knowledge acquisition is basically healthy and functional for public administrators' own purposes—it may be time to declare a moratorium on further attacks.

The defense of knowledge acquisition in public administration is possible on several grounds:

1. On the grounds that managers live and work in an environment different from that of scientists.
2. On the grounds that managers need knowledge for purposes different from those of scientists.
3. On the grounds that scientists themselves have uncovered an alternate way that managers use to obtain knowledge, one that critical scientists have deprecated but have failed to investigate.
4. On the grounds that managers themselves, far from being naive, can consciously question whether the assumptions of science apply to their situation.
5. On the grounds that managers themselves are concerned with and utilize validity standards for their own preferred way of communicating and acquiring knowledge; that, in other words, their form of knowledge acquisition is for their purposes as valid as science.

The major alternate means of acquiring knowledge that managers use is story-telling, in written form: the case study and descriptive narratives. The critics themselves admit this when they note that most of the field's research, as reflected in studies of its leading journal, relies on deductive reasoning, recalled experience, or case studies.[4] A similar tendency was observed by critics of dissertation research: "Case studies were frequently used, but not as often as purely descriptive studies and more porous alternatives to social science research which outnumbered case studies in our study of dissertation work two to one."[5]

In the private sector, we have known since the studies of Aguilar[6] and Mintzberg[7] that managers "favor verbal channels—face-to-face contact and the telephone and, to a lesser extent, direct observation as means of supplementing (and often replacing) formal sources of information."[8] In addition, Kanter found that managers spent about half their time in face-to-face communication, concluding that the manager's ability to win acceptance and to communicate was often more important than their substantive knowledge of the business.[9] Aguilar found that personal sources exceeded impersonal sources in perceived importance for providing information by 71% to 29%.[10] Further, Mintzberg reports that managers seldom spend more than a few minutes on any given event, making it problematic that a manager can engage in lengthy scientific analysis before needing to come to a judgment of what is going on and what can be done about it.[11] In the public sector, much of the evidence on managers' preference for personal communications over scientific reports comes from the utilization literature in policy analysis. For example, the most recent study of four agency heads in each of the fifty states found that they rely more on talking with the people they deal with and make little direct use of scientific policy analysis.[12]

The trouble that critics have with formal written echoes of such communications, for example case studies, is that these generally did not meet scientific validity standards. For example, one pair of critics posed the test question "Did the author set up the study in such a way so a reader could have confidence in the findings and infer their applicability to similar situations?" (McCurdy and Cleary, 1984:50). This general criterion already begs the question of what managers are supposed to learn from case studies; it begs the question because it predefines knowledge in an analytic scientific way.

In contrast, in-depth conversations with managers show that they are quite capable of defining their reality, judging what kind of knowledge is useful to them, and developing validity standards relevant to their world. Even initial research into the appropriateness of science and scientific validity standards for managerial knowledge acquisition shows that both analytic science and its standards may not be appropriate for providing the fundamental kind of knowledge and confidence in it that managers need. The knowledge they seek must answer the question "What is going on here?" before any scientific attempt at measuring what goes on where and when.

The following two sections explore how managers see their world differently from the way scientists see it and how managers rely on stories to provide them with what is in their context valid knowledge.

How Managers Define Their World

When managers are asked how they determine what is going on in their world, they refer to "intuition," "judgment," "flying by the seat of your pants." Typical is the comment of an Apollo moon astronaut, who said this about selecting facts for a report: "You choose only by drawing on the most intuitive and most deeply buried recesses of your mind."[13] In the past, testimony of this kind has been the terminal point of inquiry about how managers think.[14]

However, conversations with managers can show that they can critically think about their own thinking. They can judge the utility of basic assumptions of science and rationalistic inquiry for their work world. Managers can be engaged not only in counterposing their own assumptions against those of science and pure reason but to suggest valid alternatives to these forms of inquiry. To the surprise of their critics perhaps, their responses are as profound as—and fit with—similar fundamental propositions about what is real and how it can be known in the philosophy of science itself. For example, in problem formulation, managers seem to operate in a world that is often quite different from the kind of world to which analytic science can apply but a world not much different from that of the great original scientists who set up paradigms that define the research paths of their successors. Like the original scientist's world, the manager's world seems to be a world founded on synthesis, not analysis.

But managers' needs also differ from those of paradigm-setting scientists. Managers question the need for all-pervasive objectivity; to them a reality is constituted not by consensus of all imaginable detached observers but by the present community of those involved in a problem who must be brought along to constitute a solution. They question the relevance of the analytic scientific tenet that experiences pile up into an aggregate about which rules then can be formed; to the manager this still leaves the problem of judging whether a rule about by-gone experiences applies to a new situation at hand. They question the principle of the separation of reality and observer; that the observer is separate from what is observed, can usefully be detached from what is observed, and can leave the observed undisturbed. In short, managers who were engaged in conversations about the foundations of knowledge—about what is real (ontology) and how we get to know it (epistemology)—juxtaposed tenets of their experience against the tenets of science and pure reason. To get knowledge about what is real:

- Managers question the value of mere objectivity. Managers prefer hearing from participants in a problem rather than from an objective outsider, such as a consultant. They find they can work better with intersubjectivity rather than mere objectivity.
- Managers question the direct relevance of mere science and pure reason in problem solving. They express a concern for the difficulty of judgment. To them aggregated facts or rules drawn

from these do not directly address a new problem but must be
judged for their applicability.
* Managers question the value of scientific or rationalist
  detachment. They value the skill of sensibility that comes from
  being in touch with events rather than being detached from them.

Intersubjectivity vs. Objectivity

A manager is challenged to explain why she would accept five different reports on an event rather than a single scientific report.[15] The manager's response: "By us, by each one of the five of us, by each one of the five of us
coming up with a different thing and listening to each other, it would actually be better" (A military contracts manager, 1989). What can explain this
answer?

Managers find themselves in social situations in which they do not have
the power to set up a way of looking at a problem so that the problem will
appear the same to all involved, what scientists would call objectivity. Instead, when the problem is created by the interactions of people, it exists in
a work group and different participants in it will look at it differently. The
practical solution for the manager is to permit and encourage participants
to help define the problem—not in an objective way in which all can agree
on the same objective definition of the problem but in an inter-subjective
way. In intersubjectivity, all agree to respect each other's definition of the
problem and, by respecting this, puzzle out a synthesis that leads to a solution. To do otherwise would often mean to ask participants to surrender
their position, of professional standing or of power or of entitlement, that
sets the perspectives from which each views a problem.[16]

In asserting that "coming up with different things and listening to each
other would actually be better" than waiting for a scientific report with a
single viewpoint, the manager confronts directly analytic science's claim
that what she needs is "objectivity." "Objectivity" may be won—that is,
an object is grasped with accuracy and certainty—when an investigation is
so designed that different observers will agree, not disagree. But the point
here is that a problem in management often arises exactly because different
people involved in a situation cannot agree. This is not because they are
people of ill will, irrational, or anti-scientific, but because they are so
placed in the organization that their roles give them specific perspectives
and responsibilities that are not necessarily compatible. The division of labor, for example, or position in hierarchy, divides work and the approach
to work; such design assumes that different roles' approach to and role inhabitants' knowledge of the work ought to differ. In short, organization

design is also the design of conditions of knowledge, or in Frederick Thayer's words: ". . . any epistemology is an organization theory, and vice versa."[17]

The manager is, by structural impact of the institution as knowledge system, precisely not in that situation which the scientist makes a precondition for establishing the nature of an event; the manager cannot become the "author" of a single method for establishing reality. She has some authority and some discretion. But the institutional framework does not provide the total latitude necessary to permit her the scientific freedom to "set up"[18] a way of looking at the problematic event that would, according to scientific analytic method, guarantee one way of seeing it. She does not control the variables of observation that might guarantee seeing an event in an objective sense according to a single standpoint to which all viewers would previously have agreed. Rather, she is caught in an organization structure involving hierarchy and division of labor which, by design and for the original purpose of the specialization of work and of control, guarantees that people see the same event from different perspectives. Given the shortness of time for dealing with most events, the manager must deal with perceptions as they are structured by the institutional environment.[19]

Uniqueness vs. Replicability

Another manager took on another assumption of science. It is assumed that aggregate data analysis produces rules governing a type of event. It is then assumed that users can directly benefit from established scientific knowledge because they will be ready to apply the scientific rule governing an event when the event comes along again in the future. Asked whether she believed that things that happened in the past ever repeat themselves in just that way in the future, she at first tried to be accommodating. "Yes . . . ," she said, but there was an ellipsis in her words. "But?" asked the interviewer. "Things are always different," she said. "There's different people. There's different mindsets," (Office manager, 1987).

Even if an event—and we by now know how varied these can be in real life—should repeat itself, the manager would still have to make a judgment as to the degree to which past scientifically established variables could be used to affect the situation today. An astute manager might ask: If the problem is patterned enough for science to study it, what is it doing on my desk? Clearly, for patterned problems there are organizational routines that can be installed to handle them.

What makes an event a problem is that it does not fit into existing routines. This is true even and especially in the context of institutionalized routines of a bureaucratic structure. If an event does not fit into established routines it is in that context unique. Even if a general pattern of scientific findings is available about this kind of problem from research elsewhere, the manager must still make a judgment as to how the general and repeated pattern of the past fits *this* event of the present with an opening toward a future solution. As Robert Denhardt and Jay White put it: "Effective public administration requires not only technique but balanced judgment, broad understanding, and a good sense of future possibilities."[20] The world of problems that surrounds the manager is not one of routines but of particular events—this event or that. About each event, judgments must be made as to how general knowledge can fit it—and, if not, what kind of knowledge can help. "We are not paid for doing what we are told to do . . . but for doing rightly that part of our job which is left to our discretion."[21]

Involvement vs. Detachment

Another manager questioned the scientific assumption that the observer can be detached from what is observed. An engineer by training, he referred to the engineering concept of the undisturbed sample: "What I'm saying: The civil engineer knows there is no such thing as an undisturbed sample" when a core sample is pulled out of the ground. Pointing to an organization chart, he then drew this analogy: ". . . the practitioner up here being part of the problem, therefore being part of the solution." So you carry this over to management, he was asked. "Hell, yes," he said. "You assume that people are shaken by your presence?" "Disturbed," he answered, ". . . or, uh, varied or wavered or somewhat deviated from their original course just by the fact that I'm there" (Former city manager, 1987).

In bringing this description of the managerial world to light, the manager simply reflects the practical fact that a manager is never an individual by and for him- or herself but is an individual who lives in an already preexisting context. In that context, subordinates are as aware of the manager as he or she is of them. They are not objects to be moved around; they are sentient subjects who respond to the mere presence of the manager, to say nothing of his or her subliminal signals or expressed words and actions. The manager does not have the luxury of detachment that the scientist tries to gain. Even doing nothing or not appearing will be interpreted by the members of the managers' organization, and responses will result from unintended and unexpressed positions of the manager.

Managerial World Definition and Philosophers of Science

Survey research will still have to show to what extent these findings can be generalized.[22] But assume that managers find themselves in a world in which they are participants rather than detached observers. Grant, for the moment, that their knowledge is intersubjective rather than objective when it comes to problem-definition. Stipulate that even where there are rules summarizing past experience, a judgment must still be made as to whether *those* rules apply in *this* situation. If all this is true about managers in general, not just those we have talked with, then does this not add up to a picture of a world deficient in every crucial aspect of any capacity for producing the certain knowledge that analytic science or rational calculation can produce? What, then, can make any managerial claim to knowledge, much less valid knowledge, legitimate?

Here managers find a perhaps unexpected ally, and analytic scientists a long-ignored foe, among those who have thought as deeply as human reason can about knowledge and how it can be acquired: philosophers and theoreticians of science.

Kant

How can we know when to apply a scientific finding to a new situation? This is one problem posed by managers. In the philosophy of science, Immanuel Kant, who thought through the operations of science down to their basic assumptions, said an answer to this question requires a prior operation of synthesis, not analysis. Before any empirical research can be applied, before any "fact" can be fitted into problem, a "concept" must be developed for the mind to catch in the abstract an event that occurs in the concrete.[23] Concept and event relate to each other the way a hand shapes itself to grasp a stone. The stone must be small enough to fit the hand; but for the hand to grasp it, the hand itself must take on a shape that will fit the contours of the stone. This sounds surprisingly like what managers do. As in synthesis they try to determine *what* is going on before analyzing it. For them as for Kant, "the synthesis (the making) of concepts always precedes," in the words of one commentator, "their analytic relationships. Concept *formation* always precedes the analysis of already formed concepts."[24]

Now, what analytic scientists do is to take apart already formed concepts and operationalize the testing of elements of them against reality. They do not spend much time studying how a concept comes together, and even less on validating concept formation prior to empirical testing.[25] Yet judging rightly how a concept comes together within which the facts of a problem can be captured and brought to a solution is everything to the manager. The office manager cited above recognizes the priority of concept formation over analysis when she says, "Things are always different. There's different people. There's different mindsets" (Office manager, 1987). She implies that different mindsets have to be taken into account before a judgment can be made as to whether findings about past situations can be fitted, along with other knowledge, to a present situation that may constitute a problem.

Kant himself calls such concern for the combination of factors in the consciousness of the observing individual the "supreme"[26] and "first"[27] principle of human understanding, "[f]or without such combination nothing can be thought or known . . . "[28]

Heidegger

Kant also opens up science's position on objectivity to subsequent criticism. He warns that all knowledge, even knowledge under the categories of space and time, depends on the presence of the human observer. For example, "If we depart from the subjective condition under which alone we can have outer intuition . . . the representation of space stands for *nothing whatsoever.*"[29] Under the influence of subsequent philosophy of science, Kant can be taken as a point of departure for the city manager (above) who noted that ". . . the practititioner up here [is] part of the problem . . ." What is out there must already, in Kant's words, become "an object for me."[30] The philosopher Martin Heidegger takes up the suggestion that scientific laws may be universal but whether they apply to specific situations depends on the presence of an acting and perceiving subject and the approach he or she takes toward the object.

Further, Heidegger, following Edmund Husserl,[31] proposes that, when we are at the point of approaching an object, knowledge is never knowledge apart from an object but is always "knowledge of . . ." something. An object shows itself, but only if properly addressed. To properly address an object a subject must become attuned to it with a certain concern or care. As the approach changes, the object changes also, yet there is a limit to approaches; the approach must be adequate to the object. Again, a manager is legitimated by the philosopher of science when, as in the case of the former city manager (1987), he suspects that his mere presence in the field constructed by himself and his subordinates alters their relationship: People are "varied or wavered or somewhat deviated from their original course just by the fact that I'm there" (Former city manager, 1987). Heidegger calls this process the constitution of "the thing." By this he means the field within which subjects and objects, managers and colleagues or subordinates find themselves.[32]

A military contracts manager (1989) suggests that a better sense of what is going on is mutually constructed by participants in a reality: ". . . by each one of the five of us coming up with a different thing and listening to each other . . ." Her philosophy of how reality is constructed parallels that of Heidegger's premise that a thing, or state of affairs, is constructed by mutual attunement between subject and object. Only if their views are taken into account, is it possible to construct a thing that is held in common. Beginning with the initial premise that even physical objects must be so approached that they can reveal themselves in their own terms,[33] Heidegger leads us to the definition of a social object: things as they stand between us are created when we so address our partner in a social relationship that he or she can freely take part in defining what is to be talked about.[34]

Weber

On the level of method, Max Weber offers perhaps the most easily understood solution to the problem of the relative place of analysis and synthesis. As one of the founders of social science, he placed at the center of his investigations what things mean to people. This move addresses the experience of managers who find themselves in situations in which their colleagues or subordinates exercise the freedom to define what is going on. This is the familiar problem that in real life things are defined by talk among different subjects in different positions—intersubjectively—rather than by scientists conveniently able to take the same position. Weber shows how such inter-subjectivity can be achieved with an explicit set of methods that refer the action of a fellow social actor to core values of a situation or culture to establish their meaning. Weber concludes that until the definition of what is going on is undertaken all further analysis or statistical operation is meaningless: ". . . wherever there exists the possibility of interpretation in principle, there it should be completed; that is, the mere relating of human 'action' to a rule of experience that is simply empirically observed, be it ever so strict, does not suffice us in the interpretation of human 'action.'"[35]

In this conclusion, Weber develops on the methodological level and in the realm of culture Kant's tenet that our seeing is blind without concepts and anticipates Heidegger's tenet that objects held in common—things as they stand between us—are mutually constructed.

An End to an Embarrassment

All three thinkers concerned with how knowledge is acquired, and what can make it valid, stand critically opposed to the corps of critical scientists that argues that all knowledge acquisition must meet analytic validity standards.

The question of "Why can't we resolve the research issue in public administration?" has an embarrassingly simple answer. It is because some analytic scientists confuse two operations: the analytic operation of taking a reality apart and the synthesizing operation of putting a reality together.

It is to the eternal credit of managers that despite the pressures of a scientific culture and a rationalist/scientist education, they have stayed realistic. The best of them—those with the longest track record and those most highly educated[36]—explicitly rely on sources of knowledge other than the mere scientific. They thus resist the importuning of scientists that managers need to get in line with analytic validity standards when managers are well and appropriately engaged in their prior task of putting and keeping the world of work together.

The question remains: Are there validity standards for synthesis? It can be argued there are. If there are, and to the extent that managers exercise them, their knowledge of how a world is put together must be considered as potentially as valid for its purpose as analytic scientists' knowledge of how a world can be taken apart.

There is at least some evidence—much of it unintentionally gathered by those who criticize public administration research for not following the canons of analytic science—that managers care first and foremost about putting a problem together, in a way that makes sense to those concerned, before taking it apart. In the synthesis of construction, immediate concern for objective determination of scientific facts takes a back seat. In the driver's seat is the need to construct intersubjective agreements defining particular events in which self and others are, and remain, involved. To steer their work group in the right direction, managers talk to each other and their subordinates; the story and story-telling emerge as the prime means of orienting oneself.[37] Stories can take many forms, including the recalled experiences, case studies, or purely descriptive studies so decried by analytic scientists.

It is not possible to give an account of all kinds of stories available as sources of knowledge to the manager. Here, only two types of story are used to illustrate how stories work: the engaging anecdote and a biographical anecdote. The engaging anecdote directly invites the listener to practice reality construction by taking an active part in the story. Second, the biographical anecdote—a "recalled experience"—serves the function of making a new situation part of the listener's previously experienced world, broadening the parameters of his or her world and deepening or intensifying the meaning of its contents. Examining the story can show how it works to do at least two things:

1. Including listeners in a story-teller's world; i.e., engaging them in helping define a situation or problem and winning their commitment to its solution.
2. Expanding the listener's own world, or definition of reality, by allowing him or her to tentatively include the story-teller's different and even strange experience.

The Story as a Tool of Engagement

Jay White, in the original draft of his research on the growth of knowledge in public administration, told a story about a manager. As reproduced elsewhere,[38] what happened went like this:

> A middle manager is called upon to "do something quick" by her executive assistant who bursts into her office announcing: "Your people are killing each other on the fifth floor."
>
> The manager rushes into the elevator, takes it down to the fifth floor, flings open the door to the claims bureau and finds a fist fight in progress among ten of her employees.
>
> What is the first thing the manager says?

She might say, "Get me a consultant to do a scientific study to explain what happened here!" though this is unlikely. Or she might say, "Get the operations research unit to do a trend projection on how long this is going to go on." Unlikely also. More likely, perhaps: "What the hell is going on here?" Or, as many practitioners in our classes have said: "Stop!" Or, from those at the more advanced levels of administrative sophistication: "Who's in charge here?"—thereby both allocating blame and distancing oneself from the problem.

What function does this kind of story serve? Note that no matter what the manager says, the events are not given their managerial meaning until she says it, and the story is not complete until she says it.[39] Further, as we hear the story, the events are not meaningful for us *until we have read ourselves into the story.* This is how a story, and the telling of it, functions in a fundamentally different way for us than does analytic science. Analytic science gives us events that are objective fragments of reality and leaves us detached from them; the story always gives us events that are intended to be coherent and meaningful *to* us, something that cannot happen unless we become involved with them.

The story is a tool of engagement. But engagement in what? Engagement in this context means participating with others—the story-teller as well as those about whom the story is told—in the construction of the reality that the story opens up. In the case of the open-ended anecdote, the invitation to become involved in "making up" a reality is explicit.

For the manager there is no "right answer" to the problem posed by the story until she has committed herself to participating in the co-definition of the event in question. Only the commitment of the individual to both the perception of the problem and possible efforts directed at a solution can bring about an answer that "fits"—fits not merely the past "facts" of the situation but its future resolution. Any validity standard applied to this active synthesis will have to answer the question: Can the story so engage the listener so that he or she will contribute to co-defining what the story is about—the problem—and work on solving it? The ultimate test is that a new and desired reality is jointly created. Clearly managers are first in the creation business not the analysis business.

For us as listeners, the best we can do with such a story is to judge this: given who the manager is, did he or she do the right thing by him/herself, by the situation, by others involved as these were coherently involved in the situation?

The case of the engaging anecdote is our first occasion for showing how the structure of a story appeals and draws in the listener by its congruence with the structure of the world of practice. The story is a report about an event, a situation, a little world, as seen through the eyes of the story-teller who reports about his relations with an object or objects in that world. In the case of the engaging anecdote, the listener is literally asked to step into the manager's shoes and provide a point of contact between the story world and his or her own. This point of congruence gives the listener who has now become a participant in the story a vantage point into a larger reality. From it, he or she can see that the structural characteristics of his or her own world and the story world are the same. Both will be marked by an observing subject, at least one object, and the relations between the two; and these markers will constitute a coherent field. What this experience minimally tells the listener is that the story-teller's world is essentially just like your world—even though the story content is different—as you prove to yourself by being able to feel at home in either. Managers are able to understand this quite well when pressed on the point. In the words of one manager asked about what could be learned from the story of another dealing with an entirely different work situation: "You're looking for somebody that has the, that shares—this is a contradiction in terms—that shares a unique experience" (Parks and recreation manager, 1989). Pictorially the point of contact and the congruence that becomes visible from it is depicted in Figure 6.1.

As the listener steps into the position of the manager and faces the task of how to deal with the fight, the fight becomes thematic to him or her and moves into the foreground of his or her concern. Meanwhile, the objects of his or her own world become temporarily hazy and move out of focus. In putting him- or herself in the manager's position, the listener not only construes what the manager's world would mean to him or her but in fact is enabled to reenact the structural steps of world constructing that the manager in the original story would have had to go through. Even though the listener's solution might be different, the listener touches base with the same structural elements in the story that construct his or her own world: *subject* involved in *relationship* with an *object* and through this relationship constituting a *field*.[40]

FIGURE 6.1   Listeners and Story Tellers: Worlds Apart

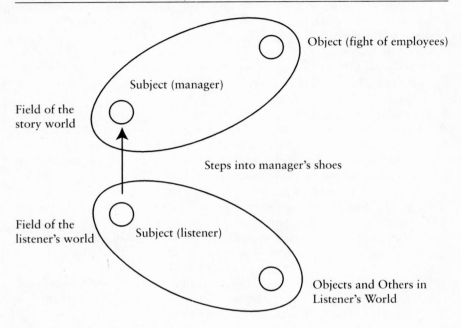

In short the structure of the story, because it is congruent with the structural elements of the world described above by managers as the elements of their world, inspires a trust in being able to move back and forth between one's own experienced world and the world represented by story-tellers.

This moves us already to the question of validity. The reference points for any questions of validity applying to a story told do not lie originally in the facts of the story; rather, they are constituted by its structure. Each structural element of the story must stand up to scrutiny: subject, object, relationships between subject and object. Ultimately, the question is raised whether all of these together constitute a coherent and therefore plausible field for action. By referring to the structures of subject, object, relationships, and field, the unfamiliar can become familiar because it can be assigned to structural categories already mutually understood between two subjects, each belonging to different worlds.

Contrary to the analytic scientist, who takes for granted the existence of a shared world that has relevance to all who use his approach, the manager listening to a story is concerned with the prior problem of establishing the relevance of the world told about to his own world and his interests in it.[41]

The fundamental criterion of validity for a story is therefore the ability of the listener to literally "re-cognize"—in the original sense of knowing again—the familiar even in an unfamiliar story. On the level of practice there is no mystery in this; this is simply how human beings expand their horizons of knowledge.

But, what can be familiar in what is strange?—except the structures of the storied world when compared to the structures of one's own. The validity the listener seeks is a structural validity. Its key question is: Are there those structures in the story told that the listener needs to orient himself or herself in the new world the story announces? Structure by structure, the subordinate questions can be formulated like this:

- Is there a subject, and can I identify with him or her?
- Is there an object, and is it likely that *such* an object as is told about could exist? If the object is a person, or persons, a recognizable bit of personality will help make the connection to the newly involved listener. If the object is a physical substance, the question is whether there is something whose familiarity or even contradiction to familiarity provides a hand-hold.
- Is there a relationship between subject and object that is likely between such a subject and such an object? Practically this may simply mean referring the relationship between subject and object to a previous similar or contrasting experience the listener has had.
- Does the field of the story told hold together? This is a question of whether the story makes sense as a totality.

The validity standards applied to a story are relevance standards first, and factual standards second. This is not to say that relevance standards are not epistemological standards, just as scientists claim factual standards are. In fact, relevance standards are epistemological standards of the first order, because they ask the question: "Does this ring true?"

The emerging relevance standards test both the relevance of all parts of the story to each other and to me and my world. They are further distinct from factual standards in that they open up a world, when they are met, while factual standards can only foreclose what is not fact and thereby close worlds. Beyond ringing true, a story well and properly told opens up possibilities of action for me, rather than foreclosing them; it broadens and deepens my world.

The primacy of structural elements of the story as points of contact between worlds experienced by different subjects and their primacy as referents for validity questions becomes explicit in the words of a senior foreign service manager recounting a biographical anecdote.

Parallel Experience and Structural
Congruence in a Biographical Anecdote

All stories invite us to become engaged with the reality they represent. But why should we believe in anything that is represented in the story being told? Beyond the very fact that the story engages our attention and concern, do we apply validity standards or criteria that give the story strength and command us to believe it? And what is it that we are being asked to believe?

A high-ranking foreign service manager (Ambassador, 1989) tells a story about Colonel X in a foreign army who, instead of prosecuting two soldiers who had mistreated civilians, "had them drop their trousers and their underwear. He removed his Sam Brown belt, ordered them to lean over and grab his desk, and he beat them til they had welts on them. He gave them more verbal hell, telling them that he would apply the law if they ever repeated such behavior, and he sent them to their quarters.

"Now those men went out and they told that story. They *loved* Colonel X. The adoration was shared by all other men in the unit who heard the story. . . ."

While there is no space to report this story in full, it can be used to point out two things. First, the manager considered the story a tool not only to widen understanding of Colonel X by his men but also to widen understanding back home of the nature of the forces allied with the United States in its foreign policy. He had begun his story with the comment, "Colonel X, whom everyone accuses or alleges to be someone who at least turns his head to human rights abuses by his men, if he does not in fact encourage them, is important politically and in the conduct of the war. It is important that American policy makers and diplomats understand him. Now, by the time I get through I won't be able to articulate to you all that I learned from the story, but you will have learned something and I will have learned something." Second, the manager expressed concern for validity standards and was able to produce at least two:

"The story had a particular relevance to me because when I was a brand new Marine lieutenant with my first platoon, one of my Marines came in drunk and took a poke at the Company First Sergeant. Believe me, that is *not* acceptable behavior in the Marine Corps. The First Sergeant wanted to bring charges under the Uniform Code of Military Justice. I did not let it happen. Instead I took that Marine on an all-night training exercise, I made him carry that 54-pound radio plus all his 782 gear, and made him run up and down mountains until he was vomiting between lamentations that he would never drink whiskey again. But I did not permit my Marine to be thrown in jail. As things ended up, he became one of my most loyal supporters and as a shave-tail lieutenant I won the admiration of my men.

"I could empathize with Colonel X, and I understood him better. When I heard that story about Colonel X it meant something to me. I had a certain amount of empathy for him and his situation."

Why would he believe that story?

"Well, I believed that story because of the person who told me, who was present. But, without my having had my own experience—I've told that story to other people in trying to help them understand Colonel X, and it added to their understanding, certainly."

What the manager has done here is build himself a framework within which the personality or the actions of the individual in question can be understood. Clearly reliable tests for the further analysis of the individual's character can be applied through science. But it is only once a previous framework exists, and is validated as reflecting events in reality according to its own validity standards, that any kind of action, including scientific investigation, can proceed.

Are there such criteria for the frameworks that stories become and is the person who hears a story aware of them? In the words of the same manager: "Sure there are. Criteria of coherence: whether it's credible in terms of your previous experience, whether it's comparable to other experience. There are all kinds of standards." Interviewer: "Is the person a notorious truth-teller or a notorious liar?" Manager: "What is his previous history? . . ." Interviewer: "Things like that. So there are standards." Manager: "Sure there are."

It is interesting to see how the manager here paints a picture of points of validation that correspond to the structural reference points of reality developed above. Managers can think not only about the structure of their world but about validity standards.

Summary

In sum, managers first and foremost communicate through stories that constitute or construct their world. How could it be otherwise? When problems arise in life or at work, people tell each other what is going on. Lois High of the Department of Veterans Affairs says in a pointed way what most managers know: "As managers, our people are our *only* resource. We must know our people."[42]

Getting access to what people in their shop think is going on is the first, and perhaps the biggest, problem for the manager. Judging the validity of stories about what is going on is perhaps the toughest. When the manager at Morton-Thiokol ignored an engineer's warning that the space shuttle's O-rings might fail at low launch temperatures, the resulting disaster was not directly caused by scientific or technical faults. It was mediated by a failure of interpretation, a failure of a previous problem formulation to include scientific facts as one source of reality definition. The manager simply did not believe the engineer's story, so scientific analysis could find no place in the construction of reality.

People in management everywhere—including public management—could do worse than hone their skills in story-telling and in story-validating. In a highly technical workplace, science and rational calculations have their place. But the manager must also develop a felt sense for what it is that his or her subordinates and coworkers are talking about. It has been argued that this requires developing a special aesthetic sensibility that reaches beyond the confines of the manager's desk,[43] and may involve occasional re-apprenticeships in which managers develop a feel for how the work gets done at the physical or hands-on level.

But ultimately what managers must judge is not what has been scientifically calculated in the past or even what trends a computer can project into the future. They must judge whether the data of science and rational calculation fit into a future no one has yet seen.

In the words of the secretary of state of a southwestern state, who was asked about whether science can drive policy: "That's not how we operate in a cabinet meeting. Sure we hand the [scientific] reports around, but then we have to see if they fit with what we can do" (Secretary of State, 1989). This means not only puzzle-solving that requires hearing from many sources—technical, scientific, rationalist, interpersonal, psychological, political, ideological, cultural, etc.—but the art of feeling one's way with all one knows across a great divide to open up the potential of an unknowable future.

The questions closest to the manager are what constitutes good work and what constitutes good management. With their eyes firmly fixed on the hands-on or street-level knowledge that comes from knowing one's workers and the integrative knowledge that is the synthesis of management itself, managers have been founding and re-founding the practice of public service every day while academicians have been fighting over the definition of a discipline that can teach future managers. There is no doubt that, as our foreign service manager interviewed said, "Public administration is not going to disappear," (Ambassador, 1989). But the academician's task, as this manager said, "[is] to ascertain first of all what is it that we're operating on and how can it be improved."

Whether public administration in the tradition of Franklin Delano Roosevelt can survive is not the issue here, though that survival faces a challenge and a crisis. Public choice or privatization may or may not appeal to the efficiency- and economy-oriented and may succeed traditional public administration or not. Implementation studies and policy analysis with their focus on outcomes rather than administrative processes may appeal to those concerned with whether what emerges is in tune with the law's intent. Top administrators may continue to spread the literature of their lofty experience. Excellence or quality management may be the future, with more lessons from the private sector, or an entirely new concern for the public enterprise may develop out of disappointment with deregulation and the failure of controls.

Whoever legislates the delivery of public goods and services with whatever means, there will still be those who manage and those who work. We could do worse than study and give full credence to the knowledge of those who manage and work to maintain not so much public administration but public service. They and their realities are the only possible foundation for a renewed or new discipline.

Notes

The sources for citations from conversations with managers include: military contracts manager, 1989; former city manager, 1987; parks and recreation manager, 1989; office manager, 1987; secretary of state, 1989; and ambassador (career foreign service officer of ambassadorial rank), 1989. Interviews reported as 1987 were conducted in the period 1986–1987. Interviews reported as 1989 were conducted beginning 1989.

1. Howard E. McCurdy, "The Dismal Quality of Public Administration Research," Discussion Pieces of the Bamard Society, U.S.A., no.4, undated, p. 1.

2. My rebuttal to this attack has, I believe, been greatly helped by comments on earlier versions of this paper from members of the Project on Reviving the Case Study (Mary Timney Bailey, Richard Mayer, and Robert Zinke) as well as the many questioners at meetings of the Public Administration Theory Network which spawned the project. I was also helped by concurrent studies on how managers think undertaken by Richard Herzog, on how city managers newly perceive their relation to policy and politics by John Nalbandian, and by the usual critical support of Dwight Waldo. Anonymous managers gave freely of their time and and deeply of their thought. Gregory Brunk, David Carnevale, C. Kenneth Meyer and Richard Wells, in my own department, provided the kind of collegial support that the academic enterprise demands. I consider Professor Brunk, in his role as scientific methodologist, the moral co-author of my current position between scientific-analytic and synthesizing thought. Finally, my thanks to analytic scientists who made it all possible. Their critical writings include: Howard E. McCurdy and Robert E. Cleary, "Why Can't We Resolve the Research Issue in Public Administration?" *Public Administration Review,* vol. 44, no. 1 (January/February 1984), pp. 49–55; James L. Perry and Kenneth L. Kraemer, "Research Methodology in *The Public Administration Review,* 1975–1984," *Public Administration Review,* vol. 46, no. 3 (May/June 1986), pp. 215–226; Robert A. Stallings "Doctoral Programs in Public Administration: An Outsider's Perspective," *Public Administration Review,* vol. 46, no. 3 (May/June 1986), pp. 235–240; Robert A. Stallings and James M. Ferris, "Public Administration Research: Work in *PAR,* 1940–1984," *Public Administration Review,* vol. 48, no. 1 (January/February 1988), pp. 580–586.

3. H. McCurdy, *op. cit.* p. 1.

4. Perry and Kraemer, "Research Methodology in *The Public Administration Review*, 1975–1984," *op. cit.*

5. H. McCurdy, *op. cit.* p. 4.

6. F. J. Aguilar, *Scanning the Business Environment* (New York: Macmillan, 1967).

7. Henry Mintzberg, *The Nature of Managerial Work* (New York: Harper & Row, 1973).

8. Mintzberg's own summary in Henry Mintzberg, "Impediments to the Use of Management Information," a study carried out on behalf of the National Association of Accountants and the Society of Industrial Accountants of Canada (New York: National Association of Accountants, 1975), p. 3.

9. Rosabeth Moss Kanter, *Men and Women of the Corporation* (New York: Basic Books, 1977).

10. Cited in Mintzberg, *op. cit.*, p. 4.

11. Mintzberg, *op. cit.* (1973), pp. 51–52.

12. For a forthcoming review of utilization literature: James P. Lester and Leah J. Wilds, "The Utilization of Public Policy Analysis—A Conceptual Framework," *Evaluation and Program Planning*, vol. 13 (1990). Lester and Wilds conclude that "early utilization research suggests that governmental decision makers make little direct use of this [policy analysis] research . . ." though "More recent trends are somewhat more optimistic about the utilization of policy analysis by decision makers . . ." However, for the data on the heads of four agencies in each of the fifty states in a more pessimistic study, see James P. Lester and David J. Webber, "The Utilization of Policy Analysis by State Agency Officials: A Comparative Analysis," paper presented at the 1990 annual meeting of the Southwestern Political Science Association, March 28–31, at Ft. Worth, Texas, for additional evidence of low utilization.

13. Ian I. Mitroff, *The Subjective Side of Science: A Philosophical Inquiry into the Psychology of the Apollo Moon Scientists* (New York: American Elsevier Publishing Co., 1975), cited in Frederick Thayer, "Organization Theory as Epistemology: Transcending Hierarchy and Objectivity," in Carl J. Bellone, ed., *Organization Theory and Public Administration* (Boston: Allyn and Bacon, Inc., 1980), pp. 113–139; citation from p. 135.

14. For an alternate path of inquiry, see the work of Weston H. Agor, for example: Agor, ed., *Intuition in Organizations: Leading and Managing Productively* (Newbury Park, CA: 1989). I would like to thank Patricia Ingraham for bringing this work to my attention.

15. The following three sections are based on exchanges with managers that I would like to describe as exploratory conversations rather than interviews. In these conversations the author challenged managers to agree or disagree with assumptions underlying science and rationalist inquiry and to judge whether these could be accepted in the management world. They were also pressed to admit to and assert other ways of knowledge acquisition they might be using. The use of stories was explicitly brought up and, if managers admitted to their use, they were asked about validity standards for these stories. In the conversations, the author made a special effort to engage those he talked with in full partnership of dialogue pushing his

points as hard as he could and encouraging or even provoking managers to push theirs as hard as they could. The references to the conversations are listed at the end of the paper.

16. Accepting here a general principle of the sociology of knowledge.

17. Thayer, *op. cit.*, p. 113.

18. McCurdy and Cleary, *op. cit.* (1984), p. 50.

19. It may be argued that different locations in an organization may give different people different power to insist their view of reality is the correct one, and that therefore power becomes a determinant of knowledge among managers while among scientists this does not happen. Thayer, *op. cit.*, pp. 119–121, refers to the literature that establishes that power is also a factor in the determination of which scientific paradigms or methods become official standards.

20. Robert B. Denhardt and Jay D. White, "Integrating Theory and Practice in Public Administration," in Donald J. Calista, ed., *Bureaucratic and Governmental Reform* (Greenwich, CT: JAI Press, 1986), pp. 311–320; citation from p. 316.

21. Geoffrey Vickers, "The Art of Judgment," in D. S. Pugh, ed.; *Organization Theory*, 2d ed, (New York: Viking Penguin, 1984), pp. 183–201; paraphrase from Elliott Jacques by Sir Geoffrey Vickers, p. 200.

22. Any survey instrument, however, will have to be open to offering respondents a choice between defining problems and procedures of knowledge acquisition according to at least three paradigms: that of science, that of pure rationalism, and that of story-telling.

23. The best known Kantian comment on concepts is perhaps this: "Without sensibility no object would be given to us, without understanding no object would be thought. Thoughts without content are empty, intuitions without concepts are blind. It is, therefore, just as necessary to make our concepts sensible, that is, to add the object to them in intuition, as to make our intuitions intelligible, that is, to bring them under concepts. . . . We therefore distinguish the science of the rules of sensibility in general, that is, aesthetic, from the science of the rules of the understanding in general, that is, logic." [Immanuel Kant, *Critique of Pure Reason*, Norman Kemp Smith, tr. (New York: St. Martin's Press, 1965). Original editions: 1781 referred to as "A"; 1787 referred to as "B."] A51–52; B 75–76. The application here is that managers are more concerned with the rules of sensibility that govern the problem of how to get access to reality, while scientists are more concerned with the rules of logic that govern the problem of how to get clarity about that which one has previously gotten access to.

24. Eugene T. Gendlin, "Analysis," in Martin Heidegger, *What Is a Thing?*, W. B. Barton and Vera Deutsch, trs. (South Bend, IN.: Regnery/Gateway, 1967), p. 278. Similarly, another commentator observes that "Kant has made the discovery that there are judgments which are both a priori and synthetic, and that they are the presuppositions of science." In synthesis, putting the case in philosophical terms, ". . . the predicate was not got by analysis of the subject, but by somehow going out of or beyond the subject and coming to connect it with what it had not hitherto been seen to be connected with." Even in mathematical discovery, previously held to be the result of analysis, Kant insists that discovery is not a mere matter of analysis: "It always involves a synthetical element: even the result of a simple sum is not got by analysis, but by counting or some kind of construction." A. D.

Lindsay, *Kant* (London: Oxford University Press—Humphrey Milford, 1936), pp. 57–58.

25. For example, one current textbook on research methods gives two paragraphs to the heading of "Ideas" and where they come from ("insight," "experience, knowledge or opinions") out of 450 pages of text. See Elizabeth O'Sullivan and Gary R. Rassel, *Research Methods for Public Administrators* (New York: Longman, 1989), p. 6.

26. Kant, *op. cit.*, B135.

27. *Ibid.*, B139.

28. *Ibid.*, B137.

29. *Ibid.*, A46, B42; my italics for emphasis.

30. *Ibid.*, B138.

31. For example, Husserl suggests that most of our propositions about the nature of reality in daily life are "occasional propositions" whose meaning depends on the occasion, the person speaking, and his situation. Edmund Husserl, *The Crisis of European Sciences and Transcendental Phenomenology*, David Carr, tr., (Evanstown, IL: Northwestern University Press, 1970), p. 122. Knowledge based on these, Husserl adds, constitute "a realm of good verification and, based on this, of well-verified predicative cognitions and of truths which are just as secure as is necessary for the practical projects of life that determine their sense." *Ibid.*, p. 125.

32. Martin Heidegger, *What Is a Thing?*, p. 5.

33. Martin Heidegger, *Sein und Zeit* (Tuebingen: Max Niemeyer, 1976 [originally 1927]), pp. 28, 34.

34. The guiding principle to the conversations with managers here reported.

35. Max Weber, "Roscher und Knies und die logischen Probleme der historischen Nationaloekonomie," in *Gesammelte Aufsaetze zur Wissenschafislebre*, ed. Johannes Winckelmann (Tuebingen: J.C.B. Mohr, 1968 [originally 1922]), pp. 1–145; my translation from p. 69.

36. Lester and Webber, *op. cit.*

37. See Martin Rein, *Social Science and Public Policy* (New York: Penguin Books, 1976), Ian I. Mitroff and Robert Kilman, "Stories Managers Tell," *Management Review* (1975), pp. 18–28, and Jay White, "Action Theory and Literary Interpretation," *Administration and Society*, vol. 19, no. 3 (November 1987), pp. 346–366.

38. Ralph P. Hummel, *The Bureaucratic Experience*, 3d ed., (New York: St. Martin's Press, 1987), p. 83.

39. John R. Searle, *Speech Acts: An Essay in the Philosophy of Language* (London: Cambridge University Press, 1969), p. 47.

40. Donald A. Schoen, *The Reflective Practitioner: How Professionals Think in Action* (New York: Basic Books, 1983), pp. 150–151; Max Weber, *Economy and Society: Introduction to Interpretive Sociology*, Guenther Roth and Claus Wittich, eds., (New York: Bedminster Press, 1968), pp. 4, 22, 26. The idea of a managerial reality as a field, dating back to Kurt Lewin, has been most fully developed in the organization development consulting movement and its resulting action research approach.

41. Up to a point, my model here parallels the work of Alfred Schutz. For the contrast between science's and managers' constructs of the world, see Schutz,

"Common-Sense and Scientific Interpretation of Human Action," in *Collected Works*, I: *The Problem of Social Reality* (The Hague: Martinus Nijhoff, 1967), pp. 3–47; specifically pp. 38–44: "3) Differences between common-sense and scientific constructs of action patterns." On relevance structures, see also Peter L. Berger and Thomas Luckmann, *The Social Construction of Reality: A Treatise in the Sociology of Knowledge* (Garden City, NY: Doubleday—Anchor, 1967), p. 45. See also, for a later update of relevance into interests: Juergen Habermas. *Knowledge and Human Interests* (Boston: Beacon Press, 1971), p. 212: "interest is attached to actions that both establish the conditions of possible knowledge and depend on cognitive processes. . . ."

42. Lois A. High, "What Are You Going to Be When You Grow Up?" *The Bureaucrat,* vol. 19, no.1 (spring, 1990), pp. 68–71; citation from p. 70; my italics for emphasis.

43. The exercise of such sensibility is advocated in concepts like that of "managing by walking about" in Tom Peters and Gary Waterman, *In Search of Excellence: Lessons from America's Best-Run Companies* (New York: Warner Books, 1982). For empirical evidence that mental operations establishing a "felt sense" for things can be distinguished from other mental operations: Eugene T. Gendlin, "Existential Phenomenology," in Maurice Natanson, ed., *Phenomenology and the Social Sciences* (Evanstown, IL: Northwestern University Press, 1973). On executive apprenticeships, see Ralph P. Hummel, "Behind Quality Management: What Workers and a Few Philosophers Have Always Known and How It Adds Up to Excellence in Production," *Organizational Dynamics,* vol. 16, no. 1 (summer, 1987), pp. 71–78.

7

GROUT: ALTERNATIVE KINDS OF KNOWLEDGE AND WHY THEY ARE IGNORED

Mary R. Schmidt

In 1975, as the federal Bureau of Reclamation was filling the reservoir behind an earthen dam just completed on the Teton River in Idaho, the structure unexpectedly collapsed. Eleven people died, 3,000 homes were damaged, 16,000 head of cattle drowned, and 100,000 acres of newly planted farmland were flooded. The property damage was estimated at over a billion dollars (U.S. Congress, 1976, p. 8).

What had gone wrong? Several blue ribbon committees investigated the causes—just as was later done after the accident at Three Mile Island and the explosion of the shuttle Challenger. The investigators concluded that the failure was due to inadequacies in the engineers' design and to overconfidence in the bureau, both ignoring safety factors. The remedy was a set of general administrative guidelines (Interagency Committee on Dam Safety, 1979) to govern all facets of work on dams in a dozen federal agencies.

Everyone acknowledged that the site was poor; the rock on which the dam was built was highly fractured, crisscrossed with narrow cracks, and

---

Source: *Public Administration Review* (53)1993: 525–530.

peppered with larger holes. The project engineer had been confident that extensive use of grout—a mixture of cement and water—could seal these holes. However, the bureau's own grouting expert testified before Congress after the failure that grouting is not an exact science and that absolute certainty is impossible. Grouting is more like an art and requires a certain "feel" for the work (U.S. Congress, 1976, p. 24).

A Feel for the Hole

To appreciate the grouters' feel, one must understand the context and details of their work. Grouters are often expected to stabilize the material under the foundation of a structure. On this particular project, they worked 450 feet down at the bottom of a steep, walled canyon more than 3,000 feet across. Their job was to pump grout under pressure into closely spaced holes drilled 300 feet farther down in the bedrock to create a subsurface "curtain." This solid underground wall was to prevent water from undermining the dam. As a clue to subsurface conditions, before they grouted each hole, the workmen first measured the amount of water they could pump under pressure to fill these holes to overflowing. However, the rock was so porous that the water often disappeared as into a bottomless pit, only to surface later far downstream.

To prevent wasting grout flowing too far through narrow cracks, the bureau specified that salt be added to harden it more rapidly, a fairly common procedure. If the grouters suspected larger holes, they were to add sand instead. The bureau had made preliminary tests to analyze how fast the grout would set with various proportions of salt but could not discover a formula relating salt to setting time because of the complex interactions among many variables (U.S.Department of Interior, 1976, Appendix G). So the decision on whether to add salt or sand, and how much of each, was left to the grouters and their mysterious "feel for the hole."

What kind of knowledge is this? Obviously these workers could not directly observe conditions deep below the surface nor know with any certainty where the grout had traveled, how soon it had set, or what voids remained. Unlike most artisans and skilled craftspersons, whose work can be judged by others, they alone could evaluate their work. Yet the integrity of the dam depended on it. Their knowledge seems more like that of an old-time doctor who diagnoses an illness by palpating the patient, listening to his heart and breathing, and asking about his life and family.

The grouter's knowledge in practice is difficult to put into words. It cannot be measured and represented by formulas nor subjected to rules or standards. It cannot be taught in a classroom, but only learned in the field, by direct hands-on experience in specific situations, under the guidance of a master craftsperson.

The art of grouting appears to require continuous attention to a host of subtle qualities, such as the resistance of the rock to drilling, the color and even the smell of the water flowing back, the pressure of water and grout at the pump, and the humidity in the air. These data cannot be treated as independent nor separate from the context nor subjected to analysis, as the bureau discovered.

Instead, the grouter must combine data from many senses, including kinesthetic ones. These senses may be sharpened with time, as the newly blind learn to hear sounds that sighted people miss. This synthesis, the essence of art as opposed to science, must be further understood in the context of particular local conditions.

I posit that over time grouters build up a repertoire of strategies for treating various kinds of rocks in specific situations and acquire a kind of general knowledge. Because, as was said, each site, each hole, and even different stages of a single hole, are unique, they can never rely upon formal models or general rules of thumb or recipes. If they settle into a mindless routine, they will jeopardize the quality of the work. They must constantly be alert to the "back talk" of the specific situation.

Ralph Hummel addressed such issues in a short paper entitled "Bottom-up Knowledge in Organizations" (Hummel, 1985). He too posited that craftspersons working directly with their hands have a special kind of knowledge in their mundane understanding of their tools and material. A sensitive worker without preconceptions or *a priori* notions may acquire a feel for the object of his or her work, apprehend its unique qualities, and come to know it "in its own terms" and "how it wants to be handled." Such workers become attuned to the qualitative phenomena that seem to emanate from an object and thereby overcome the subject/object dichotomy typical of the scientific attitude.

Underlying this kind of knowledge, Hummel wrote, is an assumption that reality is *more* than what is known through analysis, under a unilateral approach with the intent to control materials. This richer view of reality requires a worker to interact with an object, understand it in the context of the work, and synthesize that understanding with a feel for and receptiveness to the back talk of the object and the opportunities it presents. This description captures the grouters' knowledge. But there is more.

A Feel for the Whole

The grouters' feel for the hole is not the only kind of knowledge essential in securing a dam's foundation. In this case, the cracks and holes in the surface of the foundation also had to be tightly sealed with a thin slurry grout to prevent the hard-packed fill, which would form the core of the dam, from sinking into fissures, leaving voids through which water could later tunnel. A larger and less professional crew worked, on three shifts around the clock, on the irregular surface of the base and then up the steep slopes. Each shift encountered unique conditions; sometimes workers could fill ten holes in eight hours, at other times, barely one. These surface crews worked under pressure to avoid delaying the laying of fill. But several times they had to stop work and flee swarms of bats emerging from caves through narrow holes (U.S. Department of the Interior, Appendix D, p. 6).

Although these workers might sense the extent of a hole by the feel of cold dank air—or bats—coming out, they had more superficial knowledge than the grouters. As they worked on the irregular surface, they would each have observed details of individual fissures and areas around them. Over time, these workers collectively must have acquired a more complete knowledge of the heterogeneous surface than anyone had before or would be able to ever have again.

The designers had known local conditions only indirectly from core samples taken before the site was excavated. The project engineer, high in an office on one bank, had largely second-hand knowledge from formal reports filed by supervisors after each shift. Indeed no one person on these grouting crews observed all the surface conditions. During the four years of construction, each worker acquired only a fraction of the knowledge that they collectively possessed. Communication was limited by the organization of crews into separate shifts and, on any one crew, by the noise from heavy trucks and compression equipment echoing off the canyon walls. The only time and place these workers might have shared their individual knowledge was in a local bar on weekends.

From a social perspective, this collective knowledge can be called a "feel for the whole," but it was disaggregated by the formal organization and working conditions. Moreover, this fine-scaled knowledge was ephemeral: it would soon be forgotten. It would also become obsolete as tons of fill covered the surface, settled into cracks, and shifted with the inevitable seepage of water through the dam. Such knowledge is like that of witnesses of an automobile accident; no one sees it all, but each may contribute to a fuller picture.

Passive/Critical Knowledge

A third kind of knowledge emerged as these same workers were finishing surface treatment high on one bank. They received "orders from above" to stop their work. They were at first bewildered, because the rocks there were as fractured as those below. They tried to construct an explanation and finally accepted a plausible one that was "floating around." The pressure of water at the bottom of the reservoir is always greater than at the top, where the water pressure "would be low enough to allow quitting"

(U.S. Department of the Interior, 1976, Appendix C, p. 15). Although these workers lacked formal training in dam engineering, they understood this hydrological principle. They attributed its use to their superiors as a valid basis for stopping work. They were right in principle, but wrong in giving credit for such reasoning to those above. Bureau officials far off in Denver were unaware of these site conditions; they were simply in a hurry to complete the dam (Independent Panel, 1976, pp. 10–12).

These workers demonstrated a kind of passive knowledge, as when one understands a language but cannot speak it or appreciates a good design but cannot create it. An interested amateur may have the critical ability to distinguish between a masterful and sloppy performance and offer evidence in valid arguments as sound as any expert's to support his or her judgment.

Top engineers were unaware of the critical knowledge of these lowly workers, who stopped sealing the surface where the water later tunneled and undermined the dam. The investigators never spoke with the grouters or other workers but took statements from supervisors, made tests at the site, and reviewed formal records on construction. Based on these, they absolved the contractor and crews from responsibility because they had faithfully adhered to the specifications (U.S. Department of the Interior, 1976, p. v).

Why were these three kinds of knowledge ignored? (A fourth kind will be given later.) A simple explanation might lie in the lowly status of these workers, both physically at the bottom of the site and organizationally at the bottom of the hierarchies of engineering practice and the bureaucracy in which that practice took place. A complex explanation seems more valid. For it is science that dismisses knowledge expressed as feelings, engineering that scorns the knowledge of uneducated laborers, and bureaucracy that disaggregates such knowledge. Thus the reasons seem to lie in the context of these three overlapping institutions.

The Institutions of Science, Engineering, and Bureaucracy

These institutions interact in complex ways. Engineering is said to depend upon science, drawing on and applying scientific principles in its practice. It uses bureaucratic forms of organization for large projects and also works within the federal bureaucracy. The government in turn builds and supports large, engineered public works as a matter of public policy. It also depends upon technical experts for analyses and advice in making rational decisions on policy matters. It sponsors scientific research and development, which usually requires engineering. Science, with its freedom to do pure research, seems to be at the top of a hierarchy among these institutions. I will describe the stereotypical characteristics of each one, starting with science, its structure, view of the physical reality, goals, way of acquiring knowledge, and concept of valid knowledge.

The structure of science itself is hierarchical, headed by an elite corps, notably theoretical physicists. As a model for other sciences, physics has claimed to know and represent the physical reality directly with general theories couched in abstract terms. Observed regularities have been expressed as deterministic causal "laws of nature"; physicists seek one unifying law (Keller, 1985). These laws act as structuring principles to describe the material reality below in ways that differ radically from the flux of heterogeneous phenomena we perceive in everyday life.

Science suggests a universe unfolding progressively over time, in causal sequence, under uniform laws that governed the past and will continue eternally. The past is assumed to be a reliable guide to the future and the basis for making predictions. Indeed, a goal of science is to make reliable predictions, eliminate uncertainty, and through technology, bring nature under control.

Science has claimed that the only reliable knowledge is obtained by the scientific method, which involves deduction, pulling hypotheses down from theories, and testing them in experiments under controlled conditions. Such experiments generally utilize analysis, removing objects from contexts and dividing them into independent parts, which are then manipulated to test hypotheses and strengthen theories. Here the assumption is that the whole is nothing more than the sum of the parts, and that partial knowledge will add up to reliable knowledge of the whole. Thus the everyday world of our senses is transformed, reduced to abstract forces and unobservable essences.

Engineering, in turn, is said to derive its knowledge from science and to apply scientific principles. However, many competent and forthright civil engineers admit that their practice also involves a kind of artistry. They are artists in the sense that they must closely attend to the unique characteristics of a specific site and also consider economic, social, and even political factors before they design a project. Such a synthesis transcends scientific principles (Office of Science and Technology Policy, 1978).

Top engineers then send the design down to less-seasoned specialists, who flesh it out with details of components that worked well in projects at other locations, on the assumption that various kinds of sites are basically alike, all salient features are known, and again that the parts will add up to a reliable whole. Mid-level engineers write specifications for these details and make schedules so that construction can adhere to a predetermined causal-like sequence. A contractor with the lowest bid will then apportion parts of the job to specialized subcontractors. Such institutional arrangements create constraints of time and money, which preclude attention to any new information available after excavation and during construction, and inhibit costly changes in the design, which acquires an almost sacred status. Thus artistry remains at the top, the exclusive property of the chief engineers.

Bureaucratic organizations have their own kinds of knowledge and ways of distributing it. Ideally, top leaders use complete information from analysis of problems to make rational decisions on the best means to achieve clear ends, much as causes determine effects. In this way, they produce general policies, which serve as a kind of reality to those at the top. These broad statements are sent down through stratified layers to lesser officials in specialized offices, who subdivide them and spell them out with written rules and regulations and transform them into standard operating procedures, the "how to" knowledge of bureaucracy. Lowly workers can then be trained and held accountable to perform these tasks by rote.

Communication flows down but little flows up unless it is written on proper forms that confirm that work has conformed to specifications. These forms have no place for the sensory knowledge, aggregate observations, or critical judgments that were found among the workers at the dam. Bureaucracies thus rationally structure and suppress information and disaggregate knowledge of the whole.

All three institutions are led by artists, in a sense, who express reality in the form of general theories, designs, and policies. Such elites tend to act like disembodied heads, sending down hypotheses, specifications, or procedural rules to control the specialized functions below. This division of head from body is reflected in the split of theory from practice, design from construction, and policy from programs of implementation, and in other dualities. These reified entities take on a temporal dimension, a life of their own, to make things orderly at the bottom and predictable over time, through the control of nature or of public life. However, they greatly oversimplify reality, as will be illustrated next by an example from science.

Another Model of Science and Reality

The kinds of knowledge found in engineering can also be found in science. Many competent scientists develop a feel for the phenomena they study, building on the collective observations of their peers and sometimes drawing on a passive critical understand of other fields; such practices are rarely discussed. They were most evident in the work of Barbara McClintock, a geneticist who won a Nobel prize, who offers an alternative view of the physical reality (Keller, 1983).

McClintock's style of research contrasted with that of her peers. When most geneticists were interested in the mechanism and structure of genes, she wanted to understand their organization and functions in relation to the rest of the cell, within the organism as a whole; she sought a kind of feel for the whole. Rather than dismissing exceptional cases as irrelevant to general theory, she focused on anomalous pigmentation of individual plants. Instead of starting with an hypothesis prescribing what she expected and framing the questions for the material to answer, as in most controlled experiments, she felt the need to "let the experiment tell you what it wants to do" and to "listen to the material" (Keller, 1985, p. 162).

She followed each unique seedling through its life in the field, relating to it as a friend and ally. At times, she became so engrossed in examining individual cells in a grain of corn through her microscope that she felt as if she were down there within the cell, the same size as the chromosomes, and could see how they were interacting (p. 164). In such ways, she developed what she called a "feeling for the organism," akin to the grouter's "feel for the hole."

Her unique understanding led her to question the genetic theory of Watson and Crick: the DNA contained a cell's vital information, which was copied onto the RNA and acted as a blueprint for genetic traits. She thought that this "master molecule theory" claimed to explain too much and did not acknowledge the differences between small simple organisms and large complex multicellular ones. More important, it treated DNA as a central autonomous actor, sending out information one way, through a genetic organization structured hierarchically, like a classic bureaucracy (p. 170). McClintock showed that genetic organization is more complex and interdependent. The DNA itself adapts to outside factors and can be reprogrammed by signals from the environment to meet the survival needs of the organism. In essence, information flows both ways.

These findings confirmed what McClintock viewed as "the resourcefulness of nature" (p. 171). For her, nature is not simple and deterministic. The universe is richer, more bountiful and abundant than can be captured in formulas or put into words, than we can describe or prescribe. Within that *a priori* complexity is a "natural order" of patterns, regularities, and rhythms, with a kind of facticity that challenges scientists to go on. The complexity of this order transcends our capacity for ordering and dwarfs our scientific intelligence (p. 162).

This view of science shifts the focus from an hierarchical model of a relatively simple static system to more interactive models of complex dynamic systems. Picturing nature as generative and resourceful also allows it to become an active partner in reciprocal relationships with an equally active observer. That observer, however, must assume an attitude of humility, patience, and open attentiveness that allows one to listen to the material in an inquiry based on respect rather than on domination (p. 135).

Keller draws out the implications of such a view. Science has fostered dichotomies: knowledge/belief, objective/subjective, reason/feeling, eternal truth/ transient phenomena. The search for universal laws and consistency imposes a rank order on these transforming differences into otherness, inequalities, and ultimately into exclusion (p. 163), such as many women in science, engineering, and public administration have experienced. This new view of reality, which respects differences and interactive relationships without hierarchy, threatens the authority of a particular form of science, and, by extension, of engineering that depends on the laws and principles of science, and of bureaucracy as the organizational expression of the rational scientific approach.

Rather than pursue epistemological and ontological questions, I emphasize only that this new picture of the physical reality allows for great diversity in local expressions of nature, in particular places and specific objects, and is even more relevant to the social and cultural reality. Such diversity seems to require alternative ways of knowing. I now suggest a fourth kind of knowledge drawn from dam engineering, which was also evident in McClintock's science.

Intimate Knowledge

After construction, a dam must be monitored for signs of damage or aging. In the hills of California, forest rangers often monitor dams within their territories and are said to develop an "intimate knowledge" of each one over time. It takes time to acquire this kind of knowledge (which McClintock displayed in her patient study of individual plants). After a heavy rain or hard winter, rangers would look for signs of weakening. If they spotted something unusual, they would discuss it with their supervisor in the central office to determine if it merited a more extensive field check.

When the U.S. Corps of Army Engineers (1976) was considering a national dam inspection program in the 1970s, few engineers were competent to inspect the 10,000 dams across the country in a timely manner. Yet no one set of uniform guidelines would be adequate for less competent people inspecting the details of a wide variety of dams. So a decentralized bottom-up approach was devised. Each state received a brief set of general guidelines with a checklist for earthen and less-common concrete structures (Appendix D). Dam safety officers should use discretion and refine the guidelines for large or particularly hazardous structures. Other dams would be inspected in stages, by reviewing written records, then through field surveys by low-level people, like the forest rangers, and then with detailed sophisticated analyses by top engineers, if warranted. Few of these were needed.

Translating the checklist into simple English reveals that almost anyone could recognize signs of weakness in an earthen dam, such as an irregular alignment, surface cracks, or fresh springs at the base. Ordinary people who regularly fish or hike around a dam may, like the rangers, acquire a familiarity or intimate knowledge of it over time. They would know it in the way one knows a spouse or fellow worker, well enough to recognize when something is amiss and even how to cope with it.

People who live in a floodplain below a dam should be motivated to act on such knowledge, since a failure could destroy their homes or even their lives. They may fail to act for many reasons: they do not understand the significance of what they see, or do not feel responsible, or even know who is. More likely, they will assume, like those who quit work at Teton, that the people in charge already know about these conditions. Outside amateurs may also rightly fear that if they voice their concerns, the people in charge will dismiss them as unqualified meddlers. Those at the bottom of an organization who speak out on the basis of intimate knowledge or other information risk more than humiliation; like "whistleblowers," they risk being fired.

On the other hand, if people in organizations would listen and check and then deem such observations valid, they could prevent a disaster. Even if no cause for concern existed, they could at least commend laymen for their sense of responsibility and tell them what to look for in the future. In this way, local people would acquire critical knowledge to assist officials in watching over potentially hazardous structures, transforming rare and costly national inspection programs into continuous monitoring.

Social Rationality

After studying Teton and other disasters, Charles Perrow concluded that some kinds of accidents may become so common that they should be treated as normal, especially in certain types of systems, both technological and organizational. The very nature of some systems transforms minor incidents into major accidents. For instance, in complex interactive systems with tightly coupled components, small unexpected failures can occur in invisible ways and proliferate before they can be contained (Perrow, 1984). Components could be decoupled in some systems, but Perrow would eliminate others, like nuclear power plants, altogether. In a few, greater top-down control is needed, but many should be decentralized so that those closest to anomalies can stop work, move about, ask questions of others, reflect, and make unauthorized changes to contain the errors. This exemplifies the value of alternative kinds of knowledge.

Perrow recognizes that the reality of many man-made organizations and technologies, like nature itself, is more complex than can be imagined. The knowledge and action of lowly workers is often vital in coping with unforeseeable events. Such a bottom-up approach horrifies the technical elite, who deem the public, and lowly workers, irrational. Nonexperts do not use logic and statistics to make rational decisions about risks the way experts do. On the other hand, studies show that ordinary people consider many technologies in a larger context, with a sense of "dread," which combines their feelings of limited control and fears about the long-term future with skepticism about the ability of experts or institutions to avoid potential catastrophes (Perrow, 1984, p. 328). Such studies aggregate the feel for the unknown, the hole, and passive critical knowledge and even intimate knowledge into a kind of knowledge of the whole, to provide an understanding of the context of public dread.

Perrow also points out that choosing a context, framing a problem, is a predecision process, which experts also do, but usually within the limited framework of their specialized disciplines, selecting solutions to fit their methods. Indeed everyone has cognitive limits and special skills, some with numbers, others with words, still others in visualization. Because of our different perspectives and limited abilities, we need each other. In working together, we enrich our view of the world and increase the possibilities of solving problems. For such reasons, Perrow sees the limits of rationality in decision making not as a liability but as an asset, for it points to our need for interdependence and suggests a broader concept, which he labels "social rationality" (p. 321).

Social rationality acknowledges the limits of human understanding and the value of people's feelings, such as fear of the unknown and unknowable. It transforms both reason and feelings from dichotomies, divisions contending as opposites, into a synthesis that respects and retains the differences and gives them equal voice. Thus it seems rational to take account of alternative kinds of bottom-up knowledge, to supplement and complement, but not necessarily replace, the top-down knowledge of science, engineering, and bureaucracy.

Conclusions

Certain general characteristics or family resemblances link these alternative kinds of knowledge, and set them apart from the traditional view of scientific knowledge. One characteristic is that this knowledge is usually of specific phenomena, as opposed to the general knowledge about abstract classes of objects in science. Another is the need for direct, bodily involvement in acquiring such knowledge, in contrast to the tendency of science to use impersonal instruments to acquire objective data. Related to this characteristic is the need for a synthesis of data from several senses, for a feel for the hole, over time in the case of intimate knowledge, or from several individuals for knowledge of the whole; this contrasts with the analytical approach attributed to science. The qualitative nature of such knowledge is another characteristic that sets it apart from science, which seeks to reduce its knowledge to quantitative terms. Finally, although verbal communication may contribute to the acquisition or expression of alternative kinds of knowledge, these are often difficult to describe completely in words; "we know more than we can say."[1]

The value of such kinds of knowledge to public administration may be illustrated by a hypothetical case. An unfamiliar male field worker unexpectedly staggers into a central office, raving incoherently about a local program. Using a kind of feel for the hole, or a person, the administrator looks him over, helps him into a chair, and even sniffs his breath for alcohol. The administrator telephones his local supervisor, who has intimate knowledge of this employee but cannot explain his bizarre behavior and denies his story. The administrator then calls the regional office, which only has indirect passive knowledge of the local program but a plausible hypothesis to explain the story, based on experiences with unrelated programs. Sending the man to a hotel, the administrator flies to his city, talks with caseworkers and clients there to gain a bottom-up knowledge of the whole situation, and confirms the regional office's hypothesis. The administrator is then able to prevent a scandal that could have undermined a national program.

To conclude, such kinds of knowledge are not necessarily mutually exclusive, the list all-inclusive, nor the characteristics complete. As our awareness of global diversity expands, we need to be alert for and respect other ways of seeing the world and other kinds of knowledge, such as that of rainforest inhabitants on the medicinal value of plants. We need to remember that all kinds and sources of knowledge are not superior nor inferior but simply different ways of perceiving and organizing our limited understandings of a rich and complex reality.

Note

1. The author wishes to express her thanks to Donald A. Schön for his quote and his critical research support.

References

Hummel, Ralph, 1985. "Bottom-Up Knowledge in Organizations." Paper delivered at Conference on Critical Perspectives in Organization Theory, Baruch College, September 6.

Independent Panel to Review the Causes of the Teton Dam Failure, 1976. *Report to the U.S. Department of the Interior and the State of Idaho.* Washington, DC, December.

Interagency Committee on Dam Safety, 1979. *Federal Guidelines on Dam Safety.* Washington, DC: Federal Coordinating Committee for Science, Engineering and Technology. June 25.

Keller, Evelyn Fox, 1983. *A Feeling for the Organism: The Life and Work of Barbara McClintock.* New York: W. H. Freeman and Company.

_____, 1985. *Reflections on Science and Gender.* New Haven: Yale University Press.

Office of Science and Technology Policy, 1978. *Federal Dam Safety; Report of the Independent Review Panel.* Washington, DC: Executive Office of the President.

Perrow, Charles, 1984. *Normal Accidents: Living with High-Risk Technologies.* New York: Basic Books.

U.S. Congress, 1976. House Committee on Government Operations. *Teton Dam Disaster.* Report of Hearings of Subcommittee, August 5, 6, and 31.

U.S. Corps of Army Engineers, 1976. *National Program of Inspection of Dams.* Washington, DC.

U.S. Department of the Interior, 1976. Teton Dam Failure Review Group. *Failure of Teton Dam: A Report of Findings.* Washington, DC.

8

PUBLIC MANAGEMENT: SHOULD IT STRIVE TO BE ART, SCIENCE, OR ENGINEERING?

Robert Behn

My purpose in pursuing public-management research is to help improve public-management practice. I seek to answer the big question:[1]

What do the managers of large (and small) public (and nonprofit) agencies need to do to increase the ability of their organizations to produce results?

This is, of course, a personal choice.[2] Other scholars can and do choose other purposes. They may seek to understand how public managers think and make decisions. They may choose to examine how public agencies behave. They may decide to analyze the differences between public and private organizations. They may wish to focus on the kind of results that public managers do and/or should produce. Or, they may wish to determine what we do or should mean by public-management success. All of these are important questions; all are worthy of serious research. There are, of course, other questions that public-management scholars have sought to answer.

Source: *Journal of Public Administration Research and Theory* 6(1996): 91–123.

Although the choice of a research question may be personal or even arbitrary, it is not without consequence. For this choice predetermines, in many ways, the strategy of research. The macro research strategy has to fit the macro research question, and different questions clearly require different strategies.

In an effort to help improve the practice of public management, I have chosen to examine several subordinate questions—questions that I hope will help answer the larger question.

- What do public managers actually do? What do successful public managers actually do?
- What is it that successful public managers do that makes them successful?
- How do public managers think and learn?

To answer the first subordinate question, I undertake a variety of case studies (Behn 1991 and 1992a). To answer the second question, I seek some kind of syntheses of these case studies (Behn 1994); this is, of course, a risky undertaking. Finally, I am interested in the third question because I wish to present the answers to the second question in a way that will be convincing to practicing public managers.[3]

Motivational Management

To illustrate this macro research strategy and to examine whether this is art, science, or engineering, I will focus on a set of ideas that I will call *motivational management*. I present these ideas in a prescriptive format, but they could be presented descriptively as well.[4] These ideas are drawn explicitly from three different case studies.[5]

- In New York City, Gordon Chase used motivational management to organize an effort to test 120,000 children for lead poisoning in one year (Neustadt 1975).
- At Homestead Air Force Base, Col. William Gorton, the base commander, used these ideas to achieve his wing's goal of flying 17,000 sorties in one year (Behn 1992a).
- At the Massachusetts Department of Public Welfare, Commissioner Charles Atkins and his leadership team used these ideas to place 50,000 welfare recipients in jobs over five years (Behn 1991).

None of these three public managers did precisely the same thing. In fact, the specifics of what they did are, predictably, quite different; after all, each was dealing with a different public-policy problem and, thus, with

TABLE 8.1   The Seven Components of Motivational Management

Establishing the basis for motivation:
   (1)   Articulate a clear mission.
   (2)   Define operational goals.
Achieving the purposes:
   (3)   Monitor results personally.
   (4)   Provide adequate resources.
   (5)   Reward success visibly.
Rethinking and revising purposes and means:
   (6)   Be vigilant for distortions.
   (7)   Be prepared to change mission, goals, monitoring, resources, or rewards.

Sources: Behn 1991, chapter 4; Behn 1994.

different political and managerial problems. At the same time, the underlying principles that each employed—while shaped by the specifics of his own environment—possess some fundamental commonalities. The following seven ideas are a model—an abstraction drawn from all three of these cases and not a perfect description of any one.

When faced with the task of getting a large public agency to produce some specific results within a limited period of time, a public manager can motivate the people in (and associated with) that agency to invent and carry out the complicated tasks necessary to accomplish the desired result by doing seven general things (grouped into three categories). These seven things are summarized in exhibit 1, and, although they are numbered, this does not imply that they are actions to be carried out in sequential order. Rather, there is much iteration among them, with numerous activities undertaken simultaneously.

This model for motivational management raises a number of research questions: Is this really what Chase, Gorton, and Atkins did? If so, does this really work? Does it guarantee results? Have I left out something important? Did I capture the right things? Or is something else responsible for any success that these managers achieved? Indeed, are these three cases really examples of public-management successes?

But, here I want to raise a particularly scholarly question: Is this science?

The Science in Public-Management Research

What does it mean to say that research in public management is scientific? What exactly would science look like when applied to public management? Let me offer five criteria for what we mean by science and use them to test whether the above research is scientific. These five tests are:

- Is the research asking a big question?
- Does this research build on existing theory?

- Are the results falsifiable?
- Does the research employ operational definitions that permit easy replication?
- Are the data-collection methods designed to eliminate potential bias?

A Big Question

Science (or at least Big Science) seeks the answers to big questions (Behn 1995). And I would certainly classify this question—How can public managers motivate the people in (and associated with) large agencies to invent and carry out the complicated tasks necessary to produce some specific results within a limited period of time?—as a big one for the scholarly field of public management. It is certainly not the only big question, but it fits within that overall category.[6]

Existing Theory

This model of motivational management is certainly not consistent with the economic theories of motivation developed by the rational-choice school embodied by principal-agent theory. Rather, it builds directly on the psychological theories of motivation (Maslow 1943; McGregor 1960; Herzberg 1968; Ouchi 1981). In particular, several components of the model—articulate a clear mission; define operational goals; monitor results personally; reward success visibly—create those symbols and rituals that create the shared values of Ouchi's clans (1980). Although the three cases and the model deduced from them can be attacked as ad hoc research (Lynn 1994), the underlying principles have a distinguished scholarly pedigree (though not one based on traditional theories of economics). Motivational management draws on the management strategies of public managers who were—explicitly or implicitly, knowingly or unknowingly—adapting a number of the well-established ideas about human motivation to the task of getting large public agencies to produce results.

Falsifiable

For centuries, this has been one of the fundamental tests of true science. It is a legacy of Newtonian physics, codified in this century by Karl Popper: The criterion is not *verifiability* but *falsifiability*; "it must be possible for an empirical scientific system to be refuted by experience" (1959, 40–41). Yet much of modern science—particularly the big science of physics—does not meet this test. It is not possible to refute by experience the current thinking about the formation of the universe or the composition of matter. There exists no experiment that can—even in theory—falsify the big-bang theory or the idea that six quarks are some of the smallest building-blocks of matter. (Rather, argues Adams [1991, 43], "Mathematical models that are consistent with observed astrophysical phenomena are the basis for cosmologists' beliefs about the design of the universe.") And how can we define a test to falsify Stephen Jay Gould's idea (1989, 293–99; 1994) that if we were to re-run the evolutionary clock we would get a very different result?[7]

The physical theories of the Newtonian era were indeed experimentally falsifiable. Today, however, much of big science must rely on less potent tests. Physicists and paleontologists offer theories, then they and others seek data that might be consistent with these theories:[8] Can the theory generate predictions that can be verified?[9]

The concept of motivational management is no more falsifiable than is the big bang. Nevertheless, it is possible to verify it by examining whether other public managers who employ its concepts are able to produce significant results.

Operational Definitions

Even this effort at verification encounters some significant problems. To employ the concepts of motivational management, a manager must articulate a mission and define operational goals. But what exactly does this mean? How would we know whether a public manager really had articulated a mission for his or her agency? How would we know if an agency's leadership team really had defined a set of operational goals to achieve? Scholars of public management might be able to construct a widely acceptable operational definition of *goals*. But how would we know whether the manager had articulated a clear mission? Is hanging a mission statement in the lobby of every branch of the agency enough? Or could a manager do this and still not achieve the real purpose underlying the idea of articulating a mission? Furthermore, how visibly must success be rewarded? Indeed, how significant must a reward be to count as a real reward?

Operational definitions permit precision in measurement. That is one reason physics was the first real science; the things that really mattered to answer the first big questions of physics—distance, mass, time, speed, acceleration—are (relatively) easy to measure. This is also why economics has made the most progress as a social science; to answer the original big questions of economics, economists need to be able to measure some important things like price and quantity—things that, again, are (relatively) easy to measure.

Data-Collection Methods

In seeking to test any theory—in physics, paleontology, or public management—scholars need some systematic methods of collecting data. After all, if the data are corrupted, the conclusions will be too. To cope with this problem, social science has developed the idea of the randomized, controlled experiment. And yet the limitations of this (or any) method of collecting data restrict the kind of theories to which it can be applied. Physics could not test the theory that light traveled at a constant speed regardless of the nature of the source until it developed data-collection tools more sophisticated than the yardstick. Similarly, the controlled experiment of social science has its limitations (Behn 1991, chapters 8 and 9). In particular, controlled experiments are not well adapted to the task of testing a seven-component theory such as motivational management.[10]

At the same time, the data-collection methods of case-study research are quite crude. Specifically, how do you select the cases to be studied? If you start by looking for successes, you may end up with cases about people who simply got lucky.[11] Peters and Waterman (1982) were widely criticized for deriving their eight characteristics of excellent business firms by examining only firms that satisfied their operational definition of excellence. Maybe, said the critics, nonexcellent firms followed the same eight prescriptions (Carroll 1983; Golembiewski 1987). For case-study research, the strategy for collecting data is at best haphazard. At worse, it is systematically biased toward finding what the researcher is looking for.

That is another reason the falsification test is better than the verification test. It can help eliminate this bias. If the only real test for a theory is whether it has failed numerous efforts to falsify it (rather than passing a variety of efforts to verify it), scholars will have to devote themselves to looking for what they do not want to find.[12]

And yet, what do we really want from a managerial concept like motivational management? Suppose we never will be able to conduct an experiment or collect any data that might (somehow) falsify it? Does this make the theory completely useless? Suppose we only could verify that it worked in a wider and wider variety of circumstances. Would this have any value?

Certainly. Public managers are not sitting around idly waiting for some scholar to come up with a management theory that has passed the falsification test. They are working—right now—to get their agencies to motivate their people to produce results. And they constantly are looking for ideas that can help them do precisely that. (Why do you think they are spending so much money in Barnes & Noble purchasing all those books on private-sector management?) They will be happy to experiment with any ideas that have helped other public managers do their (similar) jobs.

Public managers do not behave like scientists. In their daily work, they are much more like engineers.

Is This Really Engineering?

Really? What do engineers actually do? What does it mean to say that public managers behave like engineers? Let me offer five characteristics of engineering and then compare the practice of public management with the practice of engineering.[13] In going about their job, engineers do five things:

- concentrate on a big picture;
- recognize multiple means;
- employ personal judgment;
- undertake multiple iterations; and
- focus on shipping a product.

A Big Picture

Engineers start with a big picture, a conception of something that they want to create. This may be a bridge, a sports car, or a personal computer. Engineers want to do something—to literally *build* something.

When discussing science, I was talking implicitly about big science. Now I am talking about big engineering—about the engineers such as Imhotep who invented the pyramid and Khufu who designed and built the Great Pyramid, not those subordinates who created the hammers, trowels, chisels, and drills required to build them (de Camp 1960, 20–27). I am interested in the engineering team that designed, developed, and produced the Boeing 777, not those who designed, fabricated, and tested the bracket that holds the jet engines to the fuselage. This, however, is completely consistent. When I talk about public management, I mean big public management. I am not interested in how to reorganize a local welfare office; I want to focus on how the entire welfare department can produce some well-specified and socially desirable results.

Big engineering can mean what Walter Vincenti, professor emeritus of aeronautical engineering at Stanford University, calls *radical design*. An engineer working on a problem in "normal design," writes Vincenti, "knows at the outset how the device in question works, what are its customary features, and that, if properly designed along such lines, it has good likelihood of accomplishing the desired task. A designer of a normal aircraft engine prior to the turbojet," explains Vincenti in *What Engineers Know and How They Know It,* "took it for granted that the engine should be piston driven by a gasoline-fueled, four-stroke, internal-combustion cycle." In contrast, "the initiators of the turbojet revolution," he continues, "had little to take for granted in the way that designers of normal engines could. In radical design, how the device should be arranged or even how it works is largely unknown. The designer has never seen such a device before and has no presumption of success" (1990, 7–8).[14]

"Both the artisan and the engineer start with visions of the complete machine, structure, or device," writes Eugene Ferguson, professor of history emeritus at the University of Delaware, in *Engineering and the Mind's Eye,* his analysis of the nature of engineering knowledge. "Before a thing is made, it exists as an idea" (1992, 3, 5). Indeed, it is this initial vision, this original idea that shapes the rest of the design—predetermining some features and precluding others:

> Usually, the 'big,' significant, governing decisions regarding an artisan's or an engineer's design have been made before the artisan picks up his tools or the engineer turns to his drawing board. Those big decisions have to be made first so that there will be something to criticize and analyze. Thus, far from starting with elements and putting them together systematically to produce a finished design, both the artisan and the engineer start with visions of the complete machine, structure, or device. (1992, 3, 5)

Henry Petroski, professor of civil engineering at Duke University, writes of "the unique engineering problem of designing what has not existed before" (1985, 10). Similarly, the unique public-management problem is getting a public agency to do what none has done before. In both cases, however, this requires a big picture—a vision of that never-existed-before design or that never-done-before accomplishment.

Thus, like engineers, public managers also start with the big picture of that new thing—at least big public management does. Gordon Chase started with the major (if general) assignment given to him by New York's Mayor John Lindsay: Do something about the lead poisoning that was infecting thousands of the city's children. He quickly converted that into the challenge of testing all of the 120,000 vulnerable children in the city for lead poisoning. Colonel Gorton was charged by his boss, General William Creech, the head of the Tactical Air Command, with increasing to 17,000 the number of sorties flown by the TAC wing at Homestead Air Force Base. Charles Atkins was not given the task of placing 50,000 welfare recipients in jobs; rather, in discussing with his future boss the possibility of becoming welfare commissioner, Atkins proposed this specific challenge. Chase, Gorton, and Atkins each started off with his own big picture of what he wanted to accomplish.

Moreover, the chief engineer and the public agency's leadership team not only create a big picture, they constantly keep focused on it and are not distracted from their vision.

In the age of the individual inventor—Alexander Graham Bell, Thomas Alva Edison, George Westinghouse—keeping focused might not have been too difficult. But today, engineers rarely work alone. They are part of a large design team. And, Ferguson explains, this gives the chief engineer a particular responsibility:

> A complex modern device such as an internal-combustion engine is usually designed by a team of engineers, the specialized knowledge of each one contributing to meeting the various requirements of the overall problem. The [design] team is invariably led by an engineer who keeps the overall design constantly in mind, even as unanticipated problems force its modification. (1992, 5)

Ferguson offers an example:

> Although the planning of a large engineering project such as the Tarbela dam [on the Indus River in Pakistan] may employ hundreds of engineers, many of whom will have detailed knowledge and skills not possessed by the engineer in charge, to be successful the entire design must be always held in the chief engineer's mind. That image should include sufficient detail to ensure that the various components perform harmoniously and that crucial features and details will not drop through the cracks. (1992, 29)

Hundreds of engineers worry about the different details. The chief engineer does not—indeed, cannot—understand them all. As an example, Louis Bucciarelli of M.I.T. notes in his book, *Designing Engineers,* that "there is no single individual alone who knows how all the ingredients that constitute a telephone system work together to keep each of our phones functioning" (1994, 3). Certainly the chief engineer does not understand all the details. But it is not his or her job to know how all the individual ingredients work together. The chief engineer's job is to keep everyone on the design team focused on the big picture.

Similarly, a public agency has numerous managers who are responsible for different details. The agency's leader, however, cannot—and should not try to—understand how all the ingredients work together. Rather, the responsibility of the agency's leadership is to keep everyone in the agency focused on the big picture.

"Inventors, not infrequently, fall in love with their own inventions," observes Gordon L. Glegg, a lecturer in engineering at the University of Cambridge, in his book, *The Design of Design.* "This is actually a good thing if it gives you that relentless determination to overcome all obstacles which has been the hall-mark of all the great inventors" (1981, 62).[15] Management analyst Peter Drucker offers a similar view: "Whenever anything is being accomplished, it is being done, I have learned, by a monomaniac with a mission" (1979, 255). This focus on the big picture, it would appear, applies to art, science, engineering, private management, and public management.

Multiple Means

Engineers recognize that there is not just one way to build a bridge across a specific river or an automobile for a particular market niche. For a personal computer, it is reasonable to have both the Apple and the IBM architectures.[16] "Every technical problem has alternative solutions—often several," writes Ferguson. "The diversity that is found in a particular [design] style again points up the wide range of acceptable solutions that a given design problem can elicit." To illustrate this diversity, Ferguson notes that the docking mechanisms for the American Apollo and the Russian Soyuz spacecrafts were "radically different" (1992, 13, 17, 29).

When "designing a bridge or any other large structure," Petroski writes, "the end may be clear and simple. . . . But the means may be limited only by our imagination. . . . Each opportunity to design something new, either bridge or airplane or skyscraper, presents the engineer with choices that may appear countless" (1985, 64, 73). Indeed, the abundance of approaches does not necessarily simplify the engineering task. As Glegg observes, "The main complication arises when you are faced with not one but a variety of proposed solutions" (1981, 63).

This dilemma arises because all approaches have both advantages and disadvantages. Thus, Ferguson argues, the task of the engineer is to "solve an ill-defined problem that has no single 'right' answer but has many better or worse solutions" (1992, 2–3). Indeed, he continues, "engineering design is surprisingly open-ended. A goal may be reached by many, many different paths, some of which are better than others but none of which is in all respects the one best way" (1992, 2–3, 23).

Indeed, in engineering, there is no "one best way." Similarly, in management—despite the claims of Frederick Winslow Taylor, Henry Gantt, and Lillian M. and Frank B. Gilbreth—there is no "one best way." In science there is only one answer.[17] But in engineering, there are many. "Scientific management"[18] was not engineering management. If there had been a few true engineers in the scientific-management movement, they might not have devoted themselves to the futile search for the one best way.

Similarly, I make no claims that this outline of "motivational management" is the only way to get large public agencies to achieve public purposes. In some situations, a bureaucratic, command-and-control system might work just fine. Rather, motivational management is simply one way. It has both advantages and disadvantages. In some situations, it will work acceptably; in others it won't.[19]

Often the various means to accomplish a particular engineering task come from different approaches that had been employed successfully to solve prior engineering problems. "In designing a new machine, an engineer employs familiar components, often in rearranged configurations and occasionally in radically modified ones," writes Ferguson. "Although we pay attention chiefly to new and showy technical marvels, at least 80 percent of engineers work with technologies that have been around for decades or even centuries." When Thomas Newcomen created his steam engine—which Ferguson calls "an inspired tour de force of engineering design"—he borrowed liberally from the works of others (1992, 13, 15, 60, 64). Similarly, motivational management contains a lot of familiar components, though perhaps (for some) in rearranged configurations.

Even when engineers are engaged in Vincenti's "radical design," they are employing a large number of components from "normal design." The Wright brothers did not invent the airfoil wing or the propeller or the rudder or the elevator; they borrowed and adapted these components from the designs employed by others. In order to solve the six problems that were necessary to sustain powered flight in a heavier-than-air craft, they employed their mechanical and analytical skills to borrow and adapt these components from the designs employed by others—adding their own unique components, such as the concept of wing warping (Combs 1979, 63, 70).

"Inventors and designers nearly always devise new combinations of familiar elements to accomplish novel results," writes Ferguson. "The limits of any design are culture-bound: all successful designs rest solidly on specific precedents" (1992, 15, 22). The historian Reese Jenkins has observed, for example, the stylistic continuity among many of Edison's inventions and concluded that "a creative technologist possesses a mental set of stock solutions from which he draws in addressing problems" (1984). Similarly, public managers possess a mental set of stock solutions—their own management repertoires (Behn 1987)—one item of which could be the concepts of motivational management.

For both engineers and public managers, when solving problems of "normal design" the task is to figure out what old ideas to incorporate in what configurations. Both professions are culture bound; they incorporate components from previous successes they have experienced or witnessed. Even when the task involves "radical design," both engineers and public managers still need to figure out what few new ideas to configure in what combinations with what old ideas. For both professions, there will be no single right answer. Like engineers, public managers can and do choose different means to achieve similar (even identical) ends.

Personal Judgment

Engineering is not science. Precisely because there is no one best way—no single right answer—engineers are constantly using their judgment.[20] Science—particularly mathematics and physics—may be a business in which the young excel, perhaps because their minds are not constrained by a lifetime's accumulation of implicit assumptions. Engineering, in contrast, is a business in which experience matters—in which a lifetime of practice produces not constraints but insights. Experienced engineers have accumulated the wisdom necessary to make the personal judgments that their profession requires. "Sometimes," Petroski writes, engineers "learn more from experience than calculations" (1985, 31).

The most obvious form of such personal judgment comes in the engineers' rules of thumb—those ratios and ranges that provide the engineer with practical guidance.[21] Sometimes such rules of thumb have been established and codified by the profession and used by everyone from the pros to the neophytes. Glegg, for example, analyzed the work of engineers in an effort "to find general and helpful maxims" (1969, 92). Sometimes these rules of thumb are derived solely from an individual's personal experience; thus they reflect the limited range of problems on which that engineer has worked and may mesh only with that engineer's stylistic approach and stock solutions. Regardless, such rules of thumb, Vincenti emphasizes, have two important characteristics: They are "derived from design experience," and they "show up in all branches of engineering" (1990, 219). (The concepts of motivational management might be viewed as one effort to codify some rules of thumb that have proven successful for some public managers in some situations.)

A much more subtle form of personal judgment comes from the assumptions that "will always be present in engineering design" (Ferguson 1992). Because engineers start with a big picture that precludes some possibilities, they start by making assumptions. Because they cannot check out every possibility—even within that overall design framework shaped by their big picture—they must continue to make assumptions. Because they cannot calculate everything that remains, they make even more assumptions. And behind every one of these assumptions lies the engineer's personal judgment: "Because not all assumptions can be made explicit—there is too much tacit knowledge and too many inarticulate (and inarticulable) judgments to make that possible—it is important to put the assumptions, judgments, and decisions (big, small, and tiny) in the hands of designers who have studied reality as well as the engineering sciences" (Ferguson 1992, 39–40). In making the assumptions required by engineering, judgment—and thus experience—is important.

Engineers require judgment, because they do not have engineering answers to all the questions; indeed, they do not even know what all the questions might be. As Petroski observes, "No matter how well today's engineer understands the behavior of cracks," in, for example, aircraft or nuclear power plants, "he cannot factor in the unknown human element, including that of his own limitations of prescience, into all his calculations." Thus, the engineer must build in an extra margin of safety. Yet even this requires judgment: "No designers want their structures to fail, and no structure is deliberately underdesigned when safety is an issue. Yet designer, client, and user must inevitably confront the unpleasant questions of 'How much redundancy is enough?' and 'What cost is too great?'" (1985, 120). That, too, requires judgment.

In his book, *To Engineer is Human,* Petroski focuses on the failures of engineering because, "engineering design has as its first and foremost objective the obviation of failure." Citing such engineering failures as the collapse of numerous bridges—the Tay Bridge in Scotland in 1879, the Quebec Bridge in 1907, the Tacoma Narrows bridge in 1940, and the Mianus

River Bridge in Connecticut in 1983—he writes that "the history of structural engineering, indeed the history of engineering in general, may be told in its failures as well as in its triumphs" (1985, viii, 9).

Furthermore, argues Ferguson, such structural failures reflect judgment failures: "Nearly all engineering failures result from faulty judgments rather than faulty calculations." He notes, for example, that at the Three Mile Island nuclear plant, operators were given erroneous information on the control panel because of the faulty design of an indicator. This design failure, Ferguson concludes, reflected "not a failure of calculation but a failure of judgment" (1992, 183).

Like other scholars of engineering practice, Petroski takes "design and engineering to be virtually synonymous" and argues that "design is the obviation of failure" and that "to obviate failure, a designer must anticipate it." Thus, for engineering, declares Petroski, "success is foreseeing failure" and then eliminating it (1985, vii, 53, 104, 209). Even the analysis of failure requires judgment—judgment about what possible failures to analyze and what to ignore, as well as the judgment about what factor of safety to incorporate into a structural component that might break. Unfortunately, Glegg admonishes engineers, "there is no one normally there to warn you that there is something wrong somewhere and so you must develop a critical attitude to your own work" (1969, 92). Such a critical attitude requires personal judgment that can be developed only through experience.

Furthermore, the creation of new analytical techniques does not eliminate the need for engineering judgment. Instead, it requires a new kind of judgment: Which analytical tools should be used to design this new product, and how? First, there is the step of deciding what the computer will be used to analyze; this requires judgment. In a critique of the use of the computer as a substitute for engineering judgment, Petroski writes, "Since it could take years of nonstop computing and millions of dollars to examine every conceivable location, size, and type of crack in every conceived piece of pipe [in a nuclear reactor], the human engineer must make a judgment just as in the old days as to which is the most likely situation to occur and which is the most likely way in which the pipe can fail." Next there is the task of designing the computer analysis; this too requires judgment:

> Should there be an oversimplification or an outright error in translating the designer's structural concept to the numerical model that will be analyzed through the automatic and unthinking calculations of the computer, then the results of the analysis might have very little relation to reality. And since the engineer himself presumably has no feel for the structure he is designing, he is not likely to notice anything suspicious about any numbers the computer produces for the design. (Petroski 1985, 194–95, 196)

This is the old computer warning: Garbage in; garbage out.

Thus, Petroski defines the dilemma created by the engineer's expanded computational capacity: "The computer is both blessing and curse for it makes possible calculations once beyond the reach of human endurance while at the same time also making them virtually beyond the hope of human verification" (1985, 197). Indeed, he argues that some contemporary engineering failures—such as the collapse of both the Tacoma Bridge and the roof of the Hartford Coliseum—resulted from an attempt to replace engineering judgment with sophisticated (but limited) analytical techniques.

To Ferguson, there is another important source of engineering judgment: "the mechanics and others who use tools and skills and judgment to give life to the visions of engineers." Unfortunately, Ferguson argues, engineers often ignore their front-line workers:

> Those workers—machinists, millwrights, carpenters, welders, tinsmiths, electricians, riggers, and all the rest—supply all made things with a crucial component that the engineer can never fully specify. Their work involves the laying on of knowing hands. It is sad that engineering schools teach contempt, not admiration, for those hands. It apparently seems more important to maintain the engineers' status and control than to acknowledge the indispensability of the hands and to welcome workers' warnings and insights when (or, preferably, before) things go wrong. (1992, 58)

Similarly, public managers often have had contempt for their own "mechanics," though managers are beginning to understand that these hands are also an important source of valuable judgment.

Scientific management made, of course, the opposite assumption. "Scientific managers," Taylor told Congress, would take "the great mass of traditional knowledge, which in the past has been in the heads of the workmen . . . recording it, tabulating it, and, in many cases, finally reducing it to laws, rules, and even to mathematical formulae" (1912). The purpose, Taylor explained, was "to replace the judgment of individual workmen" with "absolute uniformity" (1911, 36).

Yet, management—as Taylor proved—is not a science.[22] Rather, like engineering, management depends upon judgment. Consequently, those scholars who seek to improve the actual practice of public management ought to look for ways that can better inform those necessary managerial judgments.

Multiple Iterations

Engineers don't just design something. They design it, create it, test it, modify it, test it again, redesign it. . . . Engineers are constantly experimenting, constantly making modifications, constantly redesigning. Sometimes these are minor improvements. Sometimes these modifications are necessary to fix fundamental problems. Regardless, the process of engineering is one of multiple iterations.

For example, in his "catalogue of the great inventions," Gerald Messadié devotes "particular attention . . . to chains of inventions, showing the process of trial and error involved in the development of inventions by humankind" (1991, 6). "The cathedrals [of medieval Europe] evolved through a process of experimentation and trial and error," writes Petroski. "One builder's structural and aesthetic successes and failures were challenges and lessons to others." The engineers who were designing cathedrals learned from the best practice of their peers. Similarly, Petroski observes, "The evolution of bridges can be traced back to primitive man felling a log across a brook, and the proud history includes Roman aqueducts" (1985, 55, 67). There is no such thing as good engineering design, only good engineering redesign.

"In the development of an engineering design," Glegg concludes, there are three stages: "the basic idea," which is the responsibility of the inventor; "the first embodiment" of the idea, which is usually called a *prototype;* and "the contemporary embodiment," or what might otherwise be called "the state of the art." Glegg calls these three stages "a castle in the air," "a castle on the ground," and "a castle in the market place" (1981, 2–3).

This engineering process does not, however, move smoothly from one stage to the next. "While a new idea in principle is normally positive and exciting, the first embodiment inevitably appears negative and frustrating, often plagued by irritating delays," observes Glegg, for the prototypes rarely work as designed. Glegg calls this "the phase of failures." In fact, he continues, "Prototypes justify their existence by not working the first time." Yet this might not be the fault of the original, basic idea: "Often detail design features, not directly dependent on the new idea itself, make things grind to a halt, blow up or fall down." To make it to the third, market-place stage, Glegg concludes, "Prototypes need a clear head, a stout heart, and about three times as much money as you originally thought" (1981, 50).

Echoing Glegg, Ferguson describes the engineering process of designing an internal-combustion engine:

> The design of the engine will inevitably have been modified as the engineer wrestled with unanticipated difficulties that appeared only when the 'paper parts' were converted to metal ones. Myriad design choices will have been made to orchestrate the operation of the various components of the engine. Some of the choices will have been wrong. Yet making wrong choices is the same kind of game as making right choices; there is often no *a priori* reason to do one thing rather than another, particularly when neither has been done before.

To Ferguson (as to Glegg), "[e]ngineering design is always a contingent process, subject to unforeseen complications and influences as the design develops" (1992, 9, 37).

Moreover, to Ferguson, the process of coping with these "unanticipated difficulties" and "unforeseen complications" necessarily requires engineering judgment:

> No bell rings when the optimum design appears. The principles and techniques of engineering design can never be fully articulated, however much those promoting a 'design science' may believe that a designer's judgment can be incorporated in a general-purpose computer program. Design is not, as some textbooks would have us believe, a formal, sequential process that can be summarized in a block diagram.

"Although many designers believe that design" can be divided "into discrete segments, each of which can be 'processed' before one turns to the next," Ferguson argues that "any orderly pattern is quite unlike the usual chaotic growth of a design." Indeed, "the steps in the design process may all be going on at once" (1992, 9, 37).

To Bucciarelli, "design is a social process" that is "full of uncertainty and ambiguity." Indeed, "the sometimes chaotic workings of real people within the R&D laboratory or the engineering firm" help to make it clear that "there is no science of design process." Engineering design, Bucciarelli concludes, is like "going up a down staircase in an Escher engraving rather than neatly traversing an engineering textbook's block diagram." Furthermore, the design process is highly informal. "Small groups are talking and laughing," reports Bucciarelli, and "not all the important exchanges occur during the official hours of the meeting; the coffee break can be the most critical time—a time when an irksome question gets answered or a fiat is proclaimed one-on-one" (1994, 17, 18, 29, 35, 47, 199). Indeed, Bucciarelli's untidy characterization of engineering is remarkably similar to the descriptions of management offered by John Kotter (1982), Henry Mintzberg (1975), and Thomas Peters (1979).

Petroski describes engineering "design as revision" and compares it with writing. The writer goes through multiple drafts, developing ideas, keeping some and discarding others. For the engineer, observes Petroski, the process is similar:

> Some designs survive longer than others on paper. Eventually one evolves as *the* design, and it will be checked part by part for soundness, much as the writer checks his manuscript word by word. When a part is discovered that fails to perform the function it is supposed to, it is replaced with another member from the mind's catalog, much as the writer searches the thesaurus in his own mind to locate a word that will not fail as he imagines the former choice has. Eventually, the engineer, like the writer, will reach a version of his

design that he believes to be as free of flaws as he thinks he can make it, and the design is submitted to other engineers who serve much as editors in assessing the success or failure of the design.

Of the bridge designer Robert Maillart, Petroski writes, "His practice of self-criticism and revision was not unlike the writer's" (1985, 78–79, 82).[23]

In creating the first airplane, Combs reports, the Wright brothers "groped in the dark, even about such simple things as the leading edges of their wings, running the gamut from strangely shaped and awkward surfaces to flat areas, all of which contributed to the subsequent control problems that sorely bedeviled them." Moreover, after their first flight, the Wright brothers continued (for years) to improve their planes. For example, they modified their original propeller blades only to discover that they failed to perform as their calculations predicted. So, reports Combs, "they guessed quickly that a new element affected the propellers—perhaps under the pressures of actual flight, the blades twisted away from their shape at rest." They tested this possibility, found it to be correct, and modified their propellers so that they possessed the desired shape when twisted during flight (1979, 115, 246).

Significantly, however, the Wright brothers did not grope *around;* rather, they groped *along* toward the clear goal that they shared: to design, build, and fly the first airplane. They began with some basic ideas, experimented with them, learned from them, and based their new groping on their new knowledge. The process is similar to what I have called "Management by Groping Along" (Behn 1988; Behn 1991, chapter 7). The public manager knows *what* he or she wants to achieve but not *how* to achieve it. The big picture of the final accomplishment is clear, but the means to that end is not at all obvious. Consequently, the manager gropes along: Starting with some basic ideas, the manager experiments with different approaches, learns what works, discards what doesn't, and constantly modifies what does.

This is what Gordon Chase did at the New York City Health Services Administration, what Col. William Gorton did at Homestead Air Force Base, and what Charles Atkins and his leadership team did at the Massachusetts Department of Public Welfare. Each possessed a big picture of what his organization could accomplish; each had some idea of how to start motivating that organization. Then, each groped along. In the process, each also created his own particular version of motivational management.

But when does the process of management by groping along end? Petroski calls this "the nagging question": "Does this iterative process of design by failure ever end? Will there be a day when the designers will be able to say with assurance and finality, This is a flawless design? Yes, the process can converge on a design as reliable as it is reasonable; but, no, it can never be guaranteed to produce a perfectly flawless product" (1985, 219).

Shipping the Product

Engineers understand that there is no one best way to design, build, and manufacture any product. They also understand that their product will never be flawless.[24] Finally, they understand that the product is useless unless they can get it "out the door."

In *The Soul of a New Machine*, Tracy Kidder recounts how the Eclipse Group at Data General designed and built the Eagle computer. But they also had to, in the words of the team's leader, Tom West, get it "out the door." Such understanding comes from engineering experience. Kidder reports that one of the young engineers "would concede that the managers had probably known something he hadn't yet learned: that there's no such thing as a perfect design." Further, reported Kidder: "Most experienced computer engineers I talked to agree that absorbing this simple lesson constitutes the first step in learning how to get machines out the door." He continued, "[i]t is the most talented engineers who have the hardest time learning when to stop striving for perfection"; they are the ones who have to learn when it is time to ship the product. It is the engineers turned managers, the ones with the big picture in their heads, who keep the team focused on getting the product out the door. At Data General, "West was the voice," observed Kidder, who kept people focused: "Okay. It's right. Ship it" (1981, 120).

Engineers solve problems. They build bridges, airplanes, and computers not because these objects are nice in the abstract. They build these products because they solve problems for people. Glegg writes that "the engineer's job is to design an objective solution to an objective problem. He should not be expected to solve a purely abstract one and would be wise not to attempt it. He may be presented with a general problem and have some general ideas on how to tackle it, but he cannot design the particular without boundary particulars" (1969, 16–17). That is, the engineer solves the problem within the constraints of dollars, people, skills, and support. The public manager does the same.

In *The Civilized Engineer*, Samuel Florman offers a similar perspective:

> Although we [engineers] are committed to scientific truth, there comes a point where this truth is not enough, where the application of truth to human objectives comes into play. Once we start to think in terms of utility, we must leave the placid environment of the laboratory, take off our white coats, and roll up our sleeves. We are no longer considering theoretical forces and ideal substances. We are now obliged to work with materials that are real, impure, and sometimes unpredictable. Our aim is no longer to discern absolute truth, but rather to create a product that will perform a function. And suddenly we find ourselves under constraints of time and money. To a practicing engineer the search for perfection becomes self-defeating. (1987, 70)

For eventually—indeed, sooner rather than later—the practicing engineer has to ship a product.

Glegg admonishes his fellow engineers to "remember that what is normally required is not the best possible design but the cheapest that will work. The temptation to design something that is new or sophisticated merely for the fun of doing it is a very real one and the more interested a man is in design the harder he may find it to resist" (1969, 70–71).

Engineers create a product that will perform a function. Public managers have to create an organization that will do the same. They have to work under the constraints of time and money. They have to create not the best possible organization but the cheapest that will work. They have to work with the available resources—the people, the administrative systems, the political environment. Public managers can influence their resources, just as engineers can influence theirs. But in engineering, as in public management, resources are scarce. Tom West and the Eclipse Group designed, built, and shipped the Eagle with extremely limited resources; another design team, which had been designated by the Data General's hierarchy as the group to actually produce the corporation's next computer, got the real resources. Yet it was West's group that eventually got to ship their product.

Gordon Chase in New York, William Gorton at Homestead, and Charles Atkins in Massachusetts all had limited resources. They had to work with existing resources—real, impure, and unpredictable. None attempted to design the perfect public agency. Rather, each sought to produce an organization that could get a real public service out the door.

Science and Engineering

In 1959, C. P. Snow gave his famous two-cultures lecture in which he talked about the "gulf of mutual incomprehension" between literary intellectuals and scientists. "The intellectual life of the whole of Western society is increasingly being split into two polar groups," said Snow, and these two poles have "almost ceased to communicate at all." Moreover, he warned, the gulf was impoverishing our intellectual development (1971, 14–15). Nevertheless, thirty-five years later, the gulf still exists. And those who grew up in the scientific tradition—who have come to worship science as the basis of all scholarship and knowledge—may be widening that gulf.

But the cultural divide between the literati and the scientists was not the only intellectual division that Snow identified. We ought not to forget that he also found a gulf between pure scientists and engineers. "The gaps are wide," Snow said, and the two groups "often totally misunderstand each other." In particular, he argued, the "pure scientists" have been "dim-witted about engineers." The "instinct" of the scientist, Snow continued, "was to take it for granted that applied science was an occupation for second-rate minds" (1971, 23, 32).

It is customary to think of engineering and science as related, with engineering being a subdiscipline of science and, as Snow noted, an inferior one at that. James Adams, at Stanford University's Department of Values, Technology, Science, and Society, argues that this "intellectual stereotyping associated with engineering" is derived from the "attitude of the influential Greeks toward technology." In ancient Greece, he writes, "the activities associated with technology were considered to be properly done by slaves and foreigners, while citizens involved themselves in more disembodied mental activities." Thus, "the ideal of ancient Greece," Adams continues, is hardly compatible with the task of "choosing the proper ball bearing or worrying about defects in the coating of a reflective surface" (1991, 12). Florman is more specific, attributing the Greeks' disrespect for technology to "Plato and his cronies." While "mathematics and pure science . . . were admired, Platonic scorn for technology has been transmitted along with 'classical' education and has plagued engineers in every age" (1987, 34–36).

Still, science and engineering appear to be closely related. After all, scientists and engineers are educated at the same or similar institutions, studying the same fundamental laws of physics and chemistry and building upon common intellectual traditions. As undergraduates, for example, those majoring in physics and those majoring in mechanical engineering both take a basic course in thermodynamics. Scientists and engineers both use mathematics to do their work and (today, at least) both employ what we commonly call "the scientific method."

Moreover, engineers often employ theories developed by scientists to solve their problems. Indeed, we think of science as developing new theoretical ideas that engineers later employ to make practical products. At least as often, however, the engineers have produced the practical products first and left it to the scientists to figure out later why they actually work. Long before Charles Darwin was born, genetic engineers (i.e., animal breeders) understood that the species were not immutable—that they were, in fact, evolving or at least could be evolved. These "engineers" were consciously creating new breeds through artificial (rather than natural) selection, and Darwin reported that their practices helped shape his theory of natural selection (Mayr 1991, 71, 81–82). Similarly, Florman reports on "the tenacious work of the engineering experimenter—the tinkerer, if you will—that often turns up new facts and relationships long before they are scientifically understood. Aircraft, rocketry, turbines, and semiconductors are just a few of the many fields in which engineering has led and science follows" (1987, 46–47).

Thus engineering cannot be merely "the application of science," for often the science is not there for the engineers to apply in solving their problems. In such cases, the engineer develops a solution based on formal engineering knowledge, professional experience, guesswork, and instinct, and leaves it to the scientists to (later) figure out *why* it works. In Vincenti's search for an "epistemology of engineering," he found that "technology appears, not as a derivative from science, but as an autonomous body of knowledge, identifiably different from the scientific knowledge with which it interacts." This conclusion differs from the "hierarchical model", in which "the knowledge content of technology is seen as coming entirely from science"—a view that, Vincenti argues, "is summarized in the discredited statement that 'technology is applied science'" (1990, 3–5). The "assumption" that "whatever knowledge may be incorporated in the artifacts of technology must be derived from science," writes Ferguson, "is a bit of folklore that ignores the many nonscientific decisions, both large and small, made by technologists as they design the world we inhabit" (1992, xi). In fact, throughout most of history, engineering and science have led disconnected lives (Adams 1991, 5–30, 39).[25]

If engineering is not applied science, if it is not second-class science, if it is not even derived from science, what exactly is it? How should we, to use Vincenti's phrase, sort out "the notoriously troublesome problem of distinguishing between science and engineering" (1990, 225)? Observers from the engineering perspective, at least, find the answer in the difference between intellectual puzzles that engineers and scientists each try to solve. These writers each use distinctive words and unique metaphors, but the message is the same:

- "An engineer can make something. . . . A scientist can discover a new star but he cannot make one. He would have to ask an engineer to do it for him." Gordon L. Glegg, *The Design of Design* (1969, 1).
- An engineer's "invention causes things to come into existence from ideas, makes world conform to thought; whereas science, by deriving ideas from observation makes thought conform to existence." Carl Mitcham, "Types of Technology" (1978, 244).
- "The scientist discovers a new type of material or energy and the engineer discovers a new use for it." Gordon L. Glegg, *The Development of Design* (1981, 19).
- "Engineering or technology is the making of things that did not previously exist, whereas science is the discovering of things that have long existed." David Billington, *The Tower and the Bridge* (1983).

- "Engineers use knowledge primarily to design, produce, and operate artifacts. . . . Scientists, by contrast, use knowledge primarily to generate more knowledge." Walter Vincenti, *What Engineers Know and How They Know It* (1990, 226)

The scientists and engineers ask different questions: scientists care about *why;* engineers want to know *how.*[26] "The essential difference" between science and engineering, argues Vincenti, "is one between intellectual understanding and practical utility" (1990, 254). Scientists seek new knowledge—and strictly for the sake of that knowledge. Engineers solve problems—because overcoming those problems permits the engineer to create something that is useful. Vincenti offers a criterion for value of new knowledge in engineering: "Does it help in designing something that works in solution of some practical problem?" In contrast, he writes (borrowing a phrase from Keller [1984, 169]) that the parallel criterion for science is: "Does it help in understanding 'some peculiar features of the universe'?" To illustrate the difference, Vincenti notes that "theoretical tools useful in engineering are even known to be wrong—they explain nothing. These items are retained in the engineering box [of knowledge] because they help with design" (1990, 254–55). Scientific knowledge needs to be true, but it does not have to be practical. In contrast, engineering knowledge does not need to be scientifically correct, but it must be useful.[27]

A difference between the focus and style of the scientist and the engineer can be found, perhaps, in the different approaches taken by Octave Chanute and the Wright brothers in their experiments with gliders. Both were designing and flying gliders, but Chanute emphasized experiments that collected data, while the Wright brothers attempted to develop experience flying. In one exchange of correspondence, reports Combs, "Chanute insisted the brothers must reduce all glides to computable data, a notion that struck Wilbur as preposterous. He stressed this to Chanute, explaining it was impossible to do, since the conditions between any two glides could vary so greatly" (1979, 187).[28] Although Chanute was an accomplished engineer, by his sixties his contribution to flying consisted primarily of collecting data on the behavior of his and other gliders and seeking an answer to the question: Why do gliders behave the way they do? The Wright brothers also collected data, but only when they found it directly helpful in answering the question: How can we build an airplane that will fly?

"Engineering knowledge," says Vincenti, is "knowledge used by engineers. Scientific knowledge, by contrast, usually means the knowledge generated by scientists. This practice probably reflects the fact that scientists are perceived mainly as producers of knowledge and engineers as users" (1990, 228). And the parallel with public management is obvious: The scholars of public management are the scientists; the practitioners of public management are the engineers. Scholarly knowledge is the knowledge *created* by the scholars of public management. Practical knowledge is the knowledge *used* by practicing public managers.

Indeed, in the pursuit of a science of public management, we ought not to forget that management itself is like engineering: engineers don't discover things; they create things. Similarly, public managers don't discover things; they too create things. And the things that public managers create can be valuable indeed.

Thus, scholars of public management ought to take public managers seriously. We ought not to be seduced by the intellectual snobbery of ancient Greece and conclude that only our own "disembodied mental activities" are truly worthy of our time and talent. We ought to recognize that just as engineers possess engineering knowledge that is distinct from science and valuable in its own right, so public managers possess their own knowledge that also has unique value. And we ought to see if we can somehow ensure that such knowledge is specified and classified, codified and disseminated.

Scholarship About Engineering and About Public Management

Of course, the actual process of engineering and the process of generating engineering knowledge go on simultaneously. Engineers learn from doing. And much engineering knowledge is taught by doing. As Vincenti explains, "[E]ngineering knowledge cannot—and should not—be separated from engineering practice. The nature of engineering knowledge, the process of its generation, and the engineering activity it serves form an inseparable whole" (1990, 257). Many scholars who are concerned not only with engineering science but also with engineering practice (e.g., Bucciarelli, Ferguson, Florman, Glegg, Petroski, and Vincenti) are not only teachers and writers, they are also practicing engineers. They have a mechanism for testing their ideas against reality.

Why are engineering practice and engineering scholarship so closely linked? Certainly this is not the case in public management. One possible explanation is that both practicing engineers and academic engineers have gone to the same schools, taken the same courses, and thus possess the same intellectual tradition. They speak the same language. These characteristics do not, however, hold true for public management. Those who actually manage the largest public agencies may have no formal and little informal training in management (many are, unfortunately, lawyers) and may have no one to even provide them with on-the-job training. They do not share a common language with the scholars of public management; indeed, they may not even share a common definition of the task of public management.

So how do engineers organize their knowledge about their profession? How is knowledge about engineering practice specified and codified, classified and disseminated? One way that the scholars of engineering knowledge do all this is by examining engineering cases.

"Historical case studies contain a wealth of wisdom about the nature of design and the engineering method," writes Petroski. "The use of pithy and classic anecdotes set in familiar design situations is an excellent means for abstracting general principles while at the same time providing unifying themes and useful lessons that will be remembered" (1994, ix–x). Indeed, the work of the scholars of engineering cited here is usually built around cases.

Petroski also notes, however, "that collections of examples, no matter how vivid, no more make an explanation than do piles of beams and girders make a bridge" (1985, 2). Someone has to provide the analytical framework to turn the beams and girders into a bridge or the examples into an explanation. Both tasks are necessarily selective and thus subjective. The engineer chooses a framework—that initial big picture—and the materials to be employed; indeed, turning beams and girders into a bridge requires, first, the decision to build a bridge (rather than a tower) and then the decision to use beams and girders rather than, say, stones and mortar.[29] Similarly, the engineering scholar is selective—choosing which cases to examine and then what framework to use in examining them.

In both cases, however, all these choices are open to review and critique. The engineer faces challenges from those who think no bridge should be built—there is certainly no science that predetermines whether a bridge is socially desirable—and those who think it should not be built with beams and girders. Those with other social or engineering frameworks can easily criticize the engineer's design. Similarly, a case analysis is open to criticism: This example is hardly worthy of serious analysis; this case is significant but the engineering scholar used the wrong tools and thus drew the wrong lessons. Engineers can be (and are) criticized for the artifacts and the knowledge they create. Maybe that is why engineers are so comfortable using cases. The process looks similar to their other professional tasks.

In public management, we think that any case that is not about today's problems (or at least last year's problems) is obsolete. For engineering, however, Petroski makes the exact opposite argument: "[T]here is no obsolescence in individual case studies that reveal flaws in the logic or practice of design; indeed, the more distant the case study in time, the more objective our analysis and interpretation of it can often be" (1985, 232). Petroski (1994) draws his cases from ancient Rome and the work of Galileo, as well as from bridges constructed in the nineteenth and twentieth centuries. For example, he argues that "The value of a paradigm like that of Galileo's story of the marble column is not in its literal telling but in its power to evoke analogies that lead to the drawing of generalized caveats" (1994, 63). Amazing! If ancient cases can be informative in a field that is constantly developing new technological concepts, cases from a decade or two ago ought to be informative for a field that is changing as slowly as public management.

Focusing on case studies of failure because "we learn much more from failures that from successes" (1994, 1), Petroski makes the rationale behind the two components of his research strategy clear.[30] First, he argues that understanding the sources of failure is important:

> The history of engineering is full of examples of dramatic failures that were once considered confident extrapolations of successful designs; it was the failures that ultimately revealed the latent flaws in design logic that were initially masked by large factors of safety and a design conservatism that became relaxed with time. (1994, 1)

He explains why building a large mental library of cases is important for the development of the engineer's professional repertoire:

> Understanding from case histories how and why errors were made in the past cannot but help eliminate errors in designs. And the more case histories a designer is familiar with or the more general the lessons he or she can draw from the cases, the more likely are patterns of erroneous thinking to be recognized and generalizations reached about what to avoid. (1994, 6)

Cases about engineering failure are important, writes Petroski, because of "the generality of lessons to be learned from failures" (1994, 5).

Should scholars of public management follow those of engineering and seek lessons from failures rather than successes? I would argue no. Public management does not have enough "successful designs" from which to extrapolate—confidently or even tentatively. At the current stage of intellectual development, the search ought to be for successful designs. (Then, we could attempt to learn under what situations those designs are successful.) But the real issue is not whether cases should focus on successes or failures but what we ought to learn from them.

The first thing that a case can reveal is the public manager's rules of thumb.[31] Like every engineer, every public manager has them. Some have only a few. Others, like Gordon Chase, have a complete catalogue of personal bromides (1980). These can be helpful, but only in a limited way. They can suggest general lessons that public managers ought not to overlook, but they will rarely contain the quantitative ratios or ranges of engineering's rules of thumb. Moreover, all rules of thumb—for both engineers and managers—only apply in specific contexts. Consequently, someone (either practitioner or scholar) will have to attempt to identify the range of circumstances under which the rule of thumb is applicable, let alone important.

A more challenging intellectual task for those analyzing cases is to link the *why* with the *how*. The public-manager practitioner can explain how he or she did it—how the agency pulled off the success or botched the failure. But even that task requires an analytical framework; a description of *how* does not include what the manager had for breakfast. Someone—either the practitioner or the scholar, usually both of them together—has to filter out the extraneous from the consequential. Finally, someone—again, either practitioner, or scholar, or both—has to provide the linkages among the consequential. Someone has to link circumstances and actions to consequences.

That is what Petroski tries to do in his studies of engineering failures (1984; 1990). That is what Vincenti (1990) tries to do in his studies of developments in aeronautical engineering. It is what Adams (1991), Bucciarelli (1994), Combs (1979), Ferguson (1992), and Glegg (1969 and 1981) all try to do.

It is what I try to do with the cases about Chase, Gordon, and Atkins and the concept of motivational management. As with engineering design and engineering cases, this process is open to criticism. But it does attempt to do more than merely report on the rules of thumb of individual managers. The ideas of motivational management attempt to link what we know about human motivation with what some specific public managers have successfully accomplished and do so in a way that can provide guidance to others.

Even if these concepts are basically correct, there well may be some latent flaws in the concept of motivational management that have been masked in these cases by, for example, either the perseverance of the managers or the fortuitousness of the circumstances. Consequently, as other managers confidently extrapolate from what Chase, Gorton, and Atkins did (and from any attempt to codify what they did), they will reveal these flaws and provide new cases about failures (maybe even dramatic ones). If the scholarly analysis of cases can help engineers to understand and improve the practice of their profession—if they can provide (to use Petroski's word) useful *paradigms* for engineers—perhaps they can do the same for public managers.

Art, Science, and Engineering

If engineering is not science, what is it? The answer is that engineering is a unique blend of science and art. The reinforced-concrete bridges designed at the turn of the century by Robert Maillart, writes David Billington of Princeton University's Department of Civil Engineering, are "structural art." Maillart's 1905 bridge over the Rhine River at Tavanasa was, says Billington, "a new form with unprecedented visual power, increased material efficiency, and decreased cost for construction and maintenance—in short, a better bridge" (1983, 4, 155, 158). Ferguson observes that "Maillart's bridges exhibit the personal 'style' of their designer" (1992, 26).

"Engineering does share traits with both art and science, for engineering is a human endeavor that is both creative and analytical," Petroski writes. "The process of design divorces engineering from science and marries it to art" (1985, 80, 8). Glegg also emphasizes the artistic component of engineering design. "The mind of the designer has three realms of activity: the inventive, the artistic, and the logical or rational" (1969, 18). Florman offers a similar description: "Although engineering is serious and methodical, it contains elements of spontaneity. Engineering is an art as well as a science, and good engineering depends upon leaps of imagination as well as painstaking care. Creativity and ingenuity, the playfulness of original ideas—these are also a part of the engineering view" (1987, 75). Writing about "the art of the engineer," Vincenti notes that "[t]he creative, constructive knowledge of the engineer is the knowledge needed to implement that art. Technological knowledge in this view appears enormously richer and more interesting than it does as applied science" (1990, 4).

Ferguson argues that when doing their design work, engineers make "many nonscientific decisions" and use "nonscientific modes of thought." Much of engineering thinking is not verbal but visual, he argues; engineers work through "the mind's eye." "Visual thinking can be successful to the extent that the thinker possesses an adequate array of sensual experience, converted by the mind's eye to usable visual information." For example, Ferguson notes that engineers James Watt (steam engine), James Nasmyth (steam pile driver), and Elmer Sperry (gyrocompass and gyroscopic stabilizers) all report having first visualized key components, and even their entire invention, in their own mind's eye. Concludes Ferguson, "most of an engineer's deep understanding is by nature nonverbal, the kind of intuitive knowledge that experts accumulate." (1992, xi, xii, 42, 47–51).

Many of these observers, however, worry that, in an attempt to become more scientific, engineering is losing the benefits gained from its artistic side. According to Ferguson:

> Since World War II, the dominant trend in engineering has been away from knowledge that cannot be expressed as mathematical relationships. The art of engineering has been pushed aside in favor of the analytical 'engineering sciences,' which are higher in status and easier to teach. The underlying argument of this book is that an engineering education that ignores its rich heritage of nonverbal learning will produce graduates who are dangerously ignorant of the myriad subtle ways in which the real world differs from the mathematical world their professors teach them. (1992, xii)

It is not merely that the scientific engineers may fail to build bridges with Robert Maillart's aesthetic touch. The real worry is that in the haste to build bridges scientifically, these engineers will build bridges that fall down.

Nevertheless, at the end of the twentieth century, the scientific side of engineering is seen as—well—more scientific. As Ferguson observes, "Most engineers today are happy to be called scientists but resist being called artists. Art, as it is understood in engineering schools, is effete, marginal, and perhaps useless. It is a 'soft' subject, lacking the rigor of the hard sciences and the supposed objectivity of engineering" (1992, 22–23).

All professionals, regardless of their fields, would like to declare that in their work they strictly employ the science of their professions. Indeed, many do make this claim. Yet, the analysis of the real work of any profession reveals a variety of decisions that can only be called judgments. Ferguson writes about engineering: "Design engineers have recourse to analytical calculations to assist them in making decisions, but the number of decisions that are based on intuition, a sense of fitness, and personal preference made in the course of working out a particular design is probably equal to the number of artists' decisions that engineers call arbitrary, whimsical, and undisciplined" (1992, 23).

Good public managers—like good engineers—have to be both scientists and artists. Effective public managers are both creative and analytical. They can be serious and methodical—but also inventive and spontaneous. In our haste to make public management more scientific, we ought not to get rid of the art.

To ensure the proper balance—to get the right blend of science and art—we need a research agenda and a pedagogical strategy that can produce both. We should reduce to equations what can be reduced to equations. But we ought to remember that not everything can. Consequently, we ought to specify and codify, classify and disseminate those activities of experienced, effective public managers that produce significant results. The result will be knowledge about public management that is enormously richer and more interesting than anything ever envisioned by scientific management.

To the extent that some scholars of public management may wish to devote some of their time to helping improve the practice of public management, they might find it useful to think of this work as neither art nor science but that blend we call engineering.

Notes

1. Elsewhere (Behn 1995), I have argued that the three big questions of public-management research are:

- The micromanagement question: How can public managers break the micromanagement cycle—rules, poor results, more rules, more poor results . . .?
- The motivation question: How can public managers motivate people to work energetically and intelligently toward public purposes?

- The measurement question: How can public managers measure achievements to increase achievements?

Obviously, in answering these three big questions, public management scholars will directly assist in answering this overarching larger question.

2. My implicit choice from among the possible macro questions has an autobiographical explanation. As an undergraduate, I went to engineering school in Massachusetts. But before you jump to any conclusions, I should report that I went not to M.I.T. but to W.P.I. Worcester Polytechnic Institute is located in New England's second largest city—a city built around its large industrial base. W.P.I. was created not as a school of science but as one for the industrial arts; its original purpose was to produce the engineers needed by the city's manufacturing firms, and that legacy remains. Thus, although I was an undergraduate science major, spending four years at a very practical place encouraged me to focus on very practical questions. (Or, you can assume that it is not my education while there but my prior self-selection in choosing that kind of college that explains my interest in practical questions.) I suspect that scholars who choose other questions can point to similar experiences that can help explain the research focus they have chosen.

3. In my writing, I seek to do one more thing—to influence the scholarly field of public management and thus what questions public-management scholars study and how they conduct their research. This article is directed toward that purpose.

4. I have noted elsewhere (Behn 1991, 137–38) that descriptive conclusions about management are also prescriptive—though the descriptive format has more scholarly acceptance. Thus, when Peters and Waterman advocate "management by walking around," that is mere anecdote. But when Mintzberg describes managers as "adaptive information manipulators who prefer a stimulus-response milieu," he is being quite scholarly.

5. My colleague Frederick Mayer points out that my base for these ideas is much larger than these three specific cases—that, in addition to the detailed cases referenced here, I have, in developing these ideas about motivational management, obviously drawn (implicitly, at least) on a large number of other, less formally analyzed examples. Similarly, although Vincenti (1990) built his book—and his analysis of the nature of engineering knowledge—around five case studies (chapters two through six), his conclusions (chapters seven and eight) drew upon a much broader base of experience and knowledge.

6. Of my three big questions of public management (Behn 1995; see note 1 on p. 91), this question directly addresses the second one about motivation. How can public managers motivate people to work energetically and intelligently toward public purposes? It also engages directly the third question about measurement and indirectly the first question about micromanagement.

7. Gould himself makes this point: "In all these speculations about replaying life's tape [and getting different results], we lament our lack of any controlled experiment. We cannot instigate the actual replay, and our planet provided only one run-through." Nevertheless, Gould does find some confirming evidence in the different evolutionary patterns in South America, which was for a long period completely separated from other land masses (1989, 297–99).

8. For example, to *verify* the existence of the neutrino, which physicists invented to solve some tricky problems about the conservation of energy, other physicists de-

signed experiments to observe phenomena that would exist if neutrinos existed. Because the neutrino, as originally conceived, has no electrical charge and no (or very little) mass, it is impossible to detect by ordinary means. Consequently, physicists have had to resort to a second-best research strategy (Behn 1992b).

9. Similarly, Glegg suggests that in engineering "the usefulness of a new principle is best judged by its ability to predict the future" (1981, 8).

10. The controlled experiment in social science is the equivalent of what, in engineering, Glegg calls "competitive research": essentially the technique consists of making constants identical and the relevant variable either common or cancelling. And competitive research in engineering has the same disadvantage as the controlled experiment has in social science. Writes Glegg, "You cannot play squash and tennis at the same time, nor compare both common load and common deflection [of two different concrete slabs] in the same experiment. You can only answer one question at a time." Moreover, as Glegg points out, how do you decide what it is appropriate to compare? When attempting to decide what kind of concrete to use for highways or runways, how do you know whether you should compare the concrete slabs under a common load, or common deflection, or something else? Glegg asks, "How can you be certain why the variables you have chosen are, in fact, the relevant ones?" (1981, 41–43).

11. This problem also occurs when engineers test an idea directly by building the prototype. As Glegg explains, "The direct test method tells you what works but not why it works. It tells you something in particular but nothing in general. . . . It is all practice and no theory . . . [T]he basic problem of direct testing . . . is its inability to unscramble right from wrong." In one investigation into why the production version of an idea failed while the prototype performed quite satisfactorily, Glegg discovered that "the original model only worked because of some remarkable dimensional coincidences." Indeed, this original model well illustrates the point that Glegg makes when he writes that "the direct test has the advantage of being convincing and the disadvantage of being too convincing." Thus, concludes Glegg, "No idea should be accepted or rejected on the basis of a single test for that would put you at the mercy of coincidences" (1981, 6–10).

12. There is a bias here, too. Scholars can make their reputations by falsifying the well-established theories of others. Indeed, in social science, argues Aaron (1978), this is a significant bias.

13. The reader will notice that I have cheated—that in moving from science to engineering, I have made a subtle but important shift in frameworks. When comparing public management to science, I ask if public management scholarship in general (and one specific example of it in particular) possesses five well-established characteristics that we have come to expect from science. I compare a specific example of (perhaps questionable) scholarship about public management with the traditional scholarship of the natural sciences. When comparing public management to engineering, however, I compare public managers directly to engineers. I ask if the practice of public management (not the research about it) is similar to the practice of engineering.

14. In public management, it might be that we have too much radical design—that we ought to be in the business of establishing a variety of normal designs that managers can use in a variety of normal circumstances, rather than approaching

each management task as if it required a completely new, radical design. Radical design, as defined by Vincenti, is "revolutionary," while normal design is "evolutionary"; public management needs a basis from which it can do more evolutionary design. After all, even for normal design, argues Vincenti, "the kinds of knowledge required are enormously diverse and complex. [Moreover] the activities that produce the knowledge, unlike the activity it is intended to support, are also sometimes far from normal and day-to-day" (1990, 8–9).

15. Glegg does note, however, that falling in love can have a downside "if your enthusiasm biases your judgement" (1981, 62).

16. In the marketplace, however, there is often a battle to decide which design for a video cassette recorder or high-definition television will dominate consumer preferences.

17. This is not completely true. To physicists, light can be *both* a wave and a particle. This is the "dual theory" of light (Behn 1992b, 412).

18. The phrase *scientific management* was coined by neither a scientist nor an engineer, but by a lawyer—Louis D. Brandeis in arguing before the Interstate Commerce Commission in 1910.

19. For a description of the circumstances necessary for it to work, see Behn (1984).

20. The kind of judgments examined in this section concern *how* engineers do their work—not *what* kind of work they choose to do. Yet such *what* decisions involve another—and important—form of engineering judgment: *What* should engineers build? *What* should they not build?

Florman argues that engineers ought not to make these kinds of judgments: "I do not believe that it is up to the engineering profession to decide what is good for society, to decide, for example, whether we should favor mass transit or individual automobiles, allow drilling for oil off our coasts, authorize the use of public lands for mining, or determine how much of our national product should be devoted to armaments. In other words, I do not believe in technocracy" (1987, 72). Unless society is very explicit about these choices, however, engineers will end up making them by default. Society never told the engineers that it wanted personal computers or e-mail. Engineers made these *what* decisions.

The same applies to public management. Wilson's theory of public administration cleanly separated politics and administration. The choice of *what* to do was the responsibility of elected officials; the choice of *how* to do that was the responsibility of public managers. That theory is, however, no more connected to reality than is the idea that engineers make all their decisions based on scientific calculations. If society gives ambiguous or conflicting instructions (or fails to give any instructions at all), the engineers and the public managers will be left with no alternative but to choose.

21. For example, "the design community," Vincenti writes, "knows from years of experience that for successful jet airplanes the ratio of thrust of the engines to weight of the loaded aircraft always comes out somewhere between about 0.2 and 0.3. This knowledge supplies a rough check as a new design proceeds; if the calculated ratio falls outside this range, the designer suspects a misjudgment or miscalculation" (1990, 218–19).

22. Actually, you could argue that the concepts of scientific management were disproved scientifically. That is, through repeated experiments they were falsified;

they were proven not to work. Today, no one really professes to believe in scientific management. And yet, the practice of scientific management still lives.

23. My previous comment, "There is no such thing as good engineering design, only good engineering redesign," is actually derived from a comment that I often make to students about writing: "There is no such thing as good writing, only good rewriting."

24. Petroski again draws this parallel between writers and engineers. "Some writers," he notes, "recognize that they will never reach perfection and will eventually have to choose the least imperfect from among all the tries" (1985, 77).

25. Obviously, there exists some synergism between science and engineering. For example, Adams writes, "The development of solid-state electronics is an excellent example where scientific knowledge is essential to the engineering and where engineering activities tend to focus and direct scientific investigations" (1991, 41).

26. Engineers are, of course, intellectually curious as to why their new designs work, though they are much more concerned that they actually do work. Engineers care about the *why* because it will help them do a better job with the *how*. Knowing why the design works is very helpful when translating a specific design to one that will work in a different environment, for knowing the *why* can help the engineer adapt the original design to the new circumstances. If the original design is robust enough, the design can easily be adapted to a variety of new circumstances. But eventually someone will push the envelope, and, if that engineer does not understand the *why* of the original design, the result may be disaster.

When an engineer figures out a *why* he or she is behaving—if only momentarily—as a scientist. Richard T. Whitcomb was an engineer working on the design of supersonic aircraft for which air resistance was unacceptably large. As an engineer, Whitcomb invented the *wasp waist* design that reduced the cross-section area where the wings meet the aircraft and thus air resistance. As a scientist, Whitcomb discovered the *area rule:* the air resistance created by part of an aircraft is a function of the cross-sectional area at that point. Moreover, although he spent years doing engineering science—conducting wind-tunnel experiments measuring drag as a function of a variety of variables—a fellow aeronautical engineer described him as "a guy who just has a sense of intuition about these kinds of aerodynamic problems. He sort of feels what the air wants to do" (Ferguson 1992, 51–54).

27. Glegg offers another way to understand the difference between the engineer and the scientist: "The engineer is concerned to travel from the abstract to the concrete. He begins with an idea and ends with an objective. He journeys from theory to practice. The scientist's job is the precise opposite. He explores nature with his telescopes or microscopes, or much more sophisticated techniques, and feeds into a computer what he finds or sees in an attempt to define mathematically its significance and relationships. He travels from the real to the symbolic, from the concrete to the abstract. The scientist and the engineer are the mirror image of each other" (1981, 19–20).

28. This is the same problem that afflicts the collection of public-management data. The conditions between any two public-management situations "vary so greatly" that it is impossible to hold some conditions constant while others are systematically varied. Moreover, it also may be impossible to figure out what data

ought to be collected. What data are relevant? Compared with the data collection challenge facing public managers, the Wright brothers had it easy.

29. Although this task is subjective, it need not be ad hoc. Vincenti contrasts the Wright brothers' research and experimentation to construct the first airplane with the strategy employed by "the French [who] proceeded mostly by direct trial and error, that is, by building various types of machines and trying them by proof test in flight. They did little systematic research and development. . . . Since the French were not inclined toward theoretical analysis, variations could be selected for retention and refinement only by trials in flight" (1990, 243–44). Piles of beams and girders do not make a bridge. Neither do machines and test flights create a functioning airplane. Both require a conscious strategy—an explicit framework—from which to undertake design and research.

30. Petroski does not, however, completely ignore cases of success. For example, he calls John A. Roebling, the designer of the Brooklyn Bridge, "a paradigmatic designer" while at the same time noting that Roebling achieved his success by concentrating his design judgment on how his bridge might fail (1994, 135).

31. For a discussion of the role of rules of thumb in public management, see Bardach (1987).

References

Aaron, Henry J.
1978   *Politics and the Professors.* Washington, D.C.: Brookings Institution.
Adams, James L.
1991   *Flying Buttresses, Entropy, and O-Rings. The World of an Engineer.* Cambridge, Mass.: Harvard University Press.
Bardach, Eugene.
1987   "From Practitioner Wisdom to Scholarly Knowledge and Back Again." *Journal of Policy Analysis and Management* 7:1:188–99.
Behn, Robert D.
1987   "The Nature of Knowledge About Public Management: Lessons for Research and Teaching from Our Knowledge about Chess and Warfare." *Journal of Policy Analysis and Management* 7:1:200–12.
1988   "Management by Groping Along." *Journal of Policy Analysis and Management* 7:3:643–63.
1991   *Leadership Counts: Lessons for Public Managers.* Cambridge. Mass.: Harvard University Press.
1992a   "Homestead Air Force Base" (a public management teaching case and sequel). The Governors Center, Terry Sanford Institute of Public Policy, Duke University.
1992b   "Management and the Neutrino: The Search for Meaningful Metaphors." *Public Administration Review* 52:5:409–19.
1994   "Bottom-Line Government." The Governors Center, Terry Sanford Institute of Public Policy, Duke University. Unpublished manuscript.
1995   "The Big Questions of Public Management." *Public Administration Review* 55:4:313–24.

Billington, David P.
1983   *The Tower and the Bridge: The New Art of Structural Engineering.* New York: Basic Books.

Bucciarelli, Louis L.
1994   *Designing Engineers.* Cambridge, Mass.: MIT Press.

Carroll, David T.
1983   "A Disappointing Search for Excellence." *Harvard Business Review* 61:6:78–79 ff.

Chase, Gordon.
1980   "Bromides for Public Managers." Cambridge, Mass.: Kennedy School of Government, Harvard University.

Combs, Harry.
1979   *Kill Devil Hill: Discovering the Secret of the Wright Brothers.* Boston: Houghton Mifflin.

de Camp, L. Sprague.
1960   *The Ancient Engineers.* New York: Ballantine.

Drucker, Peter F.
1979   *Adventures of a Bystander.* New York: Harper & Row.

Ferguson, Eugene S.
1992   *Engineering and the Mind's Eye.* Cambridge, Mass.: MIT Press.

Florman, Samuel C.
1987   *The Civilized Engineer.* New York: St. Martin's.

Glegg, Gordon L.
1969   *The Design of Design.* Cambridge: Cambridge University Press.
1981   *The Development of Design.* Cambridge: Cambridge University Press.

Golembiewski, Robert T.
1987   "Toward Excellence in Public Management: Constraints on Emulating America's Best-Run Companies." In Robert B. Denhardt and Edward T. Jennings, Jr., eds. *The Revitalization of the Public Service.* Columbia: University of Missouri, Department of Public Administration, 177–98.

Gould, Stephen Jay.
1989   *Wonderful Life: The Burgess Shale and the Nature of History.* New York: Norton.
1994   "The Evolution of Life on Earth." *Scientific American* 271:10:85–91.

Herzberg, Frederick.
1968   "One More Time: How Do You Motivate Employees." *Harvard Business Review* 46:1:53–62.

Jenkins, Reese V.
1984   "Elements of Style: Continuities in Edison's Thinking." In Margaret Latimer, Brooke Hindle, and Melvin Kranzberg, eds. *Bridge to the Future: A Centennial Celebration of the Brooklyn Bridge.* New York: New York Academy of Sciences.

Keller, Alexander.
1984   "Has Science Created Technology?" *Minerva* 22: (summer): 160–82.

Kidder, Tracy.
1981   *The Soul of a New Machine.* Boston: Little, Brown.

Kotter, John P.
1982   "What Effective General Managers Really Do." *Harvard Business Review* 60:6:156–67.

Lynn, Laurence E. Jr.
1994   "Public Management Research: The Triumph of Art Over Science." *Journal of Policy Analysis and Management* 13:2:231–59.

McGregor, Douglas M.
1960   *The Human Side of Enterprise.* New York: McGraw-Hill.

Maslow, Abraham H.
1943   "A Theory of Human Motivation." *Psychological Review* 50:(July): 370–96.

Mayr, Ernst.
1991   *One Long Argument: Charles Darwin and the Genesis of Modern Evolutionary Thought.* Cambridge, Mass.: Harvard University Press.

Messadié, Gerald.
1991   *Great Inventions Through History.* Edinburg: Chambers.

Mintzberg, Henry.
1975   "The Manager's Job: Folklore and Fact." *Harvard Business Review* 53:4: 49–61.

Mitcham, Carl.
1978   "Types of Technology." *Research in Philosophy and Technology* 1: 229–94.

Neustadt, Richard.
1975   "Lead Poisoning" (A) & (B) (a public management teaching case). Cambridge, Mass.: Kennedy School of Government, Harvard University.

Ouchi, William G.
1981   *Theory 2: How American Business Can Meet the Japanese Challenge.* Reading, Mass: Addison-Wesley.

Peters, Thomas J.
1979   "Leadership: Sad Facts and Silver Linings." *Harvard Business Review* 57:6:164–72.

Peters, Thomas J., and Waterman, Robert H. Jr.
1982   *In Search of Excellence: Lessons from America's Best-Run Companies.* New York: Harper & Row.

Petroski, Henry.
1985   *To Engineer is Human: The Role of Failure in Successful Design.* New York: St. Martin's.
1994   *Design Paradigms: Case Histories of Error and Judgment in Engineering.* New York: Cambridge University Press.

Popper, Karl R.
1959   *The Logic of Scientific Discovery.* London: Hutchinson.

Snow, C. P.
1971   *Public Affairs.* New York: Scribner's.

Taylor, Frederick W.
1911   [1967] *The Principles of Scientific Management.* New York: Norton.
1912   "Scientific Management." Testimony before the U.S. House of Representatives (January 25). Reprinted in Hay M. Shafritz and Albert C. Hyde, eds. *Classics of Public Administration,* 3d ed. Chicago: Dorsey, 1987, 29–32.

Vincenti, Walter G.
1990   *What Engineers Know and How They Know It: Analytical Studies from Aeronautical History.* Baltimore: Johns Hopkins University Press.

Part Three

Responsibility, Accountability, Responsiveness

Essays in the two preceding sections illustrated how central to the study of administration is the tension between democratic governance and bureaucratic effectiveness. This tension has made important topics of debate out of questions of bureaucratic accountability, responsibility, and responsiveness. Unfortunately, the dual meaning of "responsible" (as in, responsible *to* and responsible *for*) can lead to confusion. But the key questions are clear: (1) *To whom* are bureaucrats *accountable* (or responsible)? To whom should they have to answer? (2) *For what* functions are they *responsible?* Specifically, are bureaucrats policy makers as well as policy implementers? (3) How *responsive* should they be to particular constituencies? In other words, to what extent should bureaucrats gear their actions to the needs and demands of interest groups, political parties, or the public at large? Beneath these questions is the even more fundamental issue we encountered in the first section, that is, how to make the power exercised by career bureaucrats consistent with democratic government. It is assumed that modern government needs the expert and efficient action that bureaucracy makes possible. But a basic tenet of democracy, enshrined in the U.S. Constitution, is that public power ultimately comes from the people. How, then, does the bureaucracy make itself answerable to the people?

The terms of the debate over this issue were set back around 1940 in a famous exchange between Carl J. Friedrich and Herman Finer. Friedrich (1940) argued that professionalism would ensure bureaucratic responsibility—that is, would make bureaucrats answerable in the sense that they would be able to give an account of their actions. Professional administrators would have technical expertise and an ingrained sense of the public interest, both of which would discourage them from using their power irresponsibly. The anticipated disapproval of professional colleagues and important stakeholders would act as an inner check to encourage accountability. This argument put a premium on professional training of public administrators, which would socialize them into the appropriate frame of mind as well as impart specific knowledge and skills. Finer (1941) distrusted the idea that requiring bureaucrats to give an explanation of their actions was enough to ensure responsible behavior. His position was that accountability/responsibility would never be adequate unless bureaucratic action was restricted to the specific terms of applicable statutes and regulations and bureaucrats were punished if they stepped outside these boundaries.

Arthur A. Maass and Laurence I. Radway explored these issues in their 1959 *Public Administration Review (PAR)* article, "Gauging Administrative Responsibility." Maass and Radway assume that constitutional government needs an efficient administration but must find ways to restrain it. They ask two basic questions. The first is rather quickly answered: "For what are bureaucrats responsible?" Administrative agencies are responsible both for formulating and executing policy. Bureaucrats formulate policy not only by means of specific proposals to the legislature but also in the day-to-day exercise of discretionary powers, an exercise shaped by their expertise, by the agency mandate, and by the need to mediate among conflicting interests.

The second question is "To whom are bureaucrats responsible?" The answer is more complex. Maass and Radway were writing in a time dominated by pluralist views of American politics that stressed the influence of organized interest groups. They rather quickly dismiss the idea that administrative agencies should have to answer directly to the people at large. Instead they defend accountability to pressure groups, on the grounds that such groups represent important interests, are sources of knowledge necessary to the successful accomplishment of agency mandates, and provide crucial political support for agency programs. Maass and Radway argue that, in addition, administrative agencies should be accountable to the legislature, but only through the chief executive. They reject the notion that agencies should be independently responsible to political parties, as is the case in a parliamentary system, but they support Friedrich's idea that professionalism is an important check on the inappropriate use of bureaucratic power.

A landmark 1987 *PAR* article by Barbara S. Romzek and Melvin J. Dubnick used the *Challenger* disaster to call into question previous treatments of accountability. The space shuttle *Challenger* exploded in January, 1986, shortly after take-off, killing all seven crew members. Romzek and Dubnick argue that the causes of the accident were not simply technical and managerial but can also be traced to unsuccessful efforts by the National Aeronautics and Space Administration (NASA) to manage diverse and conflicting forms of accountability. The authors emphasize that equating accountability with simple answerability (as do Maass and Radway in the preceding article) is too narrow. In practice, accountability also involves a more complex and less formalized effort to "manage expections" inside and outside the agency. Romzek and Dubnick argue that NASA's attempts to manage political and bureaucratic expectations interfered with professional accountability. As the space program became increasingly politicized, responsiveness to key external constituencies and to internal demands of hierarchy and cost-reduction weakened the agency's earlier commitment to professional expertise and judgment. Romzek and Dubnick argue that such heavy reliance on political and bureaucratic accountability was inappropriate to the nature of NASA's work. They suggest that giving equal weight to professional judgment might have prevented the launch of the *Challenger* on that fateful, too-cold January day.

In his 1992 *PAR* article, "Responsiveness and Neutral Competence in American Bureaucracy," Francis E. Rourke maintains that pressures from the White House and Congress for greater political responsiveness on the part of administrative agencies have had pernicious results. They have diminished long-standing faith in bureaucrats' neutral competence and undermined the legitimacy of bureaucratic participation in national policy-making. Rourke writes that it is now widely assumed that bureaucrats are biased rather than disinterested when it comes to making programmatic decisions. (Readers must judge for themselves whether this is still the case.) Skepticism about the technical competence of administrative agencies has led to greater reliance on contracting-out and other forms of privatization. Presidents and Congress have resorted to various strategies to increase their control over bureaucratic action, that is, to make bureaucracy more responsive to political goals set legislatively or by the chief executive. The result, in Rourke's view, is a bureaucracy too caught up in political responsiveness and insufficiently driven by professional competence, dedication, and indifference to political pressure.

The final essay in this section, Camilla Stivers's 1994 *PAR* article "The Listening Bureaucrat: Responsiveness in Public Administration," takes a somewhat different view of responsiveness. The article's theme is that, while professional norms that rely for accountability on the bureaucrat's "inner check" are obviously important, responsiveness implies more than inappropriate bias or political influence. Autonomous professional judgment is in tension with democratic accountability; it leaves too much up to the unpredictable administrative conscience and trusts too much in professional skills and worldviews, which have their limits. The author argues that public administrators can learn to be appropriately responsive by developing their listening skills. Listening bureaucrats can be open, able and willing to take into consideration diverse points of view, including those of ordinary citizens, but still remain judicious and uncorrupted. Skillful listening promotes accountability by helping administrators hear neglected voices, engage in reciprocal communication with stakeholders, and remain open to new perspectives. It promotes administrative effectiveness by helping bureaucrats deepen their understanding of complex situations and develop more complete definitions of problems. From this perspective, being responsive entails actively listening to what citizens say and taking it into account rather than being inappropriately swayed by it.

Since professionalism has been such a central element in ideas about how to hold administrators accountable, readers may want to compare the views expressed by authors in this section with those in the section on professionalism (Part V).

9

GAUGING ADMINISTRATIVE RESPONSIBILITY

Arthur A. Maass
Laurence I. Radway

Method of Approach

The following discussion is an effort, albeit tentative and incomplete, to establish criteria which will be useful in determining the extent to which any administrative agency conducts itself as a responsible instrument of government. It is not primarily addressed to the related problem of how best to sustain the state of mind that issues in responsible administrative conduct. The emphasis here is rather on appraising degrees of responsibility on the basis of criteria applicable to particular functioning agencies.

Much has been written on the "principles" of administrative responsibility. Students have engaged in lively controversy over their nature and validity. But these principles are frequently equivocal; and though mutually incompatible, they are often equally applicable to the same administrative situation. It is therefore believed desirable to use the more modest language of "criteria" of responsibility, some of which may indeed conflict with others, but all of which must be weighted and applied together in any attempt to gauge the responsibility of a specific administrative agency.

Of course, these criteria have not been formulated *in vacuo*. They rest on certain points of view or biases which must be made explicit. Necessarily

Source: *Public Administration Review* 19(1959):182–193.

these biases are cast in normative terms. But they are held as tools for the task, not as dogma for the ages. In particular, the analysis assumes large-scale federal organization in the context of contemporary American society; and this context is taken to include both constitutional government in its presidential form and prevailing democratic ideology.

Responsibility—A General and Historical View

To appreciate the general nature and importance of administrative responsibility it is necessary to understand the significance of bureaucracy in the modern state. Logically, of course, constitutional government presupposes a functioning bureaucracy; for until an administrative machine exists there cannot be efforts to subject it to popular influence and control. But more than this, bureaucracy is the very core of constitutional democracy in the sense that no modern government can long survive without an efficient administrative organization. "It is . . . not a question of *either* democracy *or* bureaucracy, of *either* constitutionalism *or* efficient administration," but of "a combination of the two, of a working balance between them, in short, of a responsible bureaucracy."

Historically, the responsibility of officials has been enforced more often, and perhaps more easily, through religious than through secular sanctions. The only way to escape religious responsibility and its restraints is to emancipate oneself from religious faith itself. This is what happened in Renaissance Italy. Deviations from the religious norm seemed necessary to meet the practical requirements of government. They were made in the name of *raison d'état*. The Christian mind, still clinging to its ideological traditions, attempted to rationalize such conduct by deifying the political order. In the seventeenth century, government by and responsible to divine law thus became government by and responsible to kings ruling by divine right. But ultimately the religious sanction lost its force, and modern government has on the whole been obliged to seek other means for enforcing responsibility. These means are summed up in the term "modern constitutionalism," which is essentially "an effort to produce responsible conduct of public affairs without religious sanctions."

Constitutional democracy thus seeks to restrain bureaucracy by secular devices. And administrative responsibility under such a regime has been termed the sum total of the constitutional, statutory, administrative, judicial, and professional practices by which public officers are restrained and controlled in their official actions. But it is not possible to identify the *criteria* for gauging administrative responsibility by relying on such general language. It becomes necessary, therefore, to relate the general concept of responsibility to the specific functions of power (i.e. responsibility to whom?) and purpose (i.e. responsibility for what?).

Responsibility for What?

Working Bias: An administrative agency should be responsible for formulating as well as executing public policy.

It has been popular in the past for American political scientists to assume that administrative officials are responsible only for the execution of policy and not at all for the formulation of policy. The distinction between policy making and policy execution may have a great deal of practical value as a relative matter. By accepting such a distinction, we have been enabled, for example, to develop many of the detailed techniques for the conduct of personnel, budget, and related functions in government. But as an absolute form, any such distinction between politics (the making of policy) and administration (the execution of policy) is unrealistic and leads to incomplete, if not incorrect, analyses of the conduct of responsible government. Public policy is being formed as it is being executed, and it is being executed as it is being formed. Politics and administration are not two mutually exclusive processes; they are, rather, two closely linked aspects of the same process.

Administrative hierarchies have a profound influence on public policy formulation in two ways: (1) in the exercise of the discretionary powers allowed in everyday operations; (2) in the process of developing specific proposals for legislative consideration.

With respect to everyday operations, the extent to which an administrative agency determines policy depends largely on the nature of the discretionary powers which the legislature has assigned to the agency. These powers may be classified according to the legislature's disposition regarding its mandate:

a. Technical discretion. Here the legislature states the desired results or assumes that the administrator knows them. Its mandate is clear, and the administrator plays the role of a technical expert in fulfilling it.

b. Discretion in social planning. Here the legislature does not know in fine detail what results it seeks. Its mandate is vague or general, and the administrator is authorized both to work out definite rules for action and to plan goals for government activities.

c. Discretion in reconciliation of interests. Here the legislature in effect asks the administrator to break a political deadlock. Its mandate is in dispute, and the administrator acquires a certain discretion to mediate and to facilitate negotiations between pressure groups.

Administrative hierarchies may also formulate specific proposals for legislative approval, amendment, or rejection. That they do in fact play such a role has been established by careful studies of the origin of legislation in both federal and state governments. That they should play such a role is coming to be accepted by most political scientists and practitioners, though the ritual of partisan politics often appears to require denunciation of bureaucratic influence on legislation. Accordingly the administrator has a responsibility to seek a legislative policy that is clear, consistent, feasible, and consonant with basic community values.[1] It is his obligation to anticipate problems, to devise alternative policies for meeting them, to estimate the probable consequences of each alternative, and, through the chief executive, to transmit this information to the legislature along with his own recommendations.

The bureaucrat is peculiarly well equipped for this task by virtue of his opportunity to develop professionally accepted techniques and standards; his opportunity to observe at first hand how policies work out in practice; his capacity for tempering enthusiasm for theory with a shrewd appreciation of what is practical and what is not; and his ability to represent interests which are not well represented by organized pressure groups, for example, the consumers.

Responsibility to the People at Large

Working Bias: An administrative agency cannot and should not normally be held directly responsible to the people at large.

In the last century direct official responsibility to the entire electorate was encouraged by requiring that many administrative officials be elected at the polls. But the long ballot secured hardly more than an ill-defined and intermittent responsibility to the general public at the expense of an unfortunate dispersion of authority and an undue responsiveness to private interests. Popular election has given way therefore to an integrated administration governed by the power of appointment and the principle of hierarchical subordination. Other devices for holding the bureaucracy directly accountable to the electorate, such as the recall, the initiative, and the referendum, have not been conspicuously successful, and none is used in the federal government. In general it is becoming clear that direct control by the public at large cannot insure administrative responsibility and that the influence of John Doe can be exerted effectively only through the legislature, the executive, and special interest associations.

More recently, some governmental programs have come to depend significantly on voluntary cooperation of the general public for their administration. Good examples are selective service and consumer rationing. In such cases the information function of the government agency becomes of central importance. The people at large need to be informed of available administrative services. They must also be notified of what is expected of them in conformance to government rules and regulations. The agency's intelligence service must in turn pick up from the public the attitudes and information necessary to the successful development and execution of policy—"where the shoe pinches," how it can be made to fit better, what is felt to be unnecessary red tape, and so on. Thus it is possible to state one criterion for gauging administrative responsibility to the people at large—the extent to which the voluntary cooperation of the general public is sought for programs whose success depends significantly on such cooperation. Application of this criterion requires an evaluation of methods for disseminating, collecting, and utilizing the type of information discussed above.

Responsibility to the People—Pressure Groups

Working Bias: An administrative agency should be responsible to pressure groups so far as necessary to equalize opportunities for safeguarding interests, to acquire specialized knowledge, and to secure consent for its own program.

It has been argued that the responsibility of all government is the free and effective adjustment of group interests. Certainly the administrator as well as the legislator operates within a context of intense intergroup activity. Indeed, the legislator often confers upon the administrator a specific responsibility for consulting with groups and reconciling their respective interests. He may do this either because group conflict is so intense that he is unable or unwilling to make the necessary reconciliation, or because the issues are so complex that he lacks the time and information to resolve them and has, therefore, to delegate to administrators the authority to make the necessary rules and regulations. In either case the responsibility of the administrator is clear: to recognize what the legislature has required of him and to conduct his operations accordingly. The extent to which he does this is, then, the first of the possible criteria of responsibility which relates the administrator to pressure groups.

But the administrator will undoubtedly have to work with special interests even in the absence of a specific legislative mandate. His agency and the laws which he administers are usually the product of the pressures and rivalries of organized groups. Naturally, these groups will continue to seek a voice in the development of programs which affect them; and as the scope of the administrator's activities continues to increase, group attention will tend to shift from legislator to bureaucrat in conformity to the adage, "where power rests, there influence will be brought to bear."

This growing tendency for interest groups to participate in the formulation and execution of policy, irrespective of legislative provision, can be supported on at least three grounds: first, that such group representation is desirable to equalize opportunities for protecting and promoting respective interests; second, that the preparation of detailed regulations on complicated matters requires exact knowledge which even the best informed official may not possess and which interest groups can supply; third, that group participation in policy decisions makes possible the winning of consent for the agency's program. This last proposition is not, of course, intended to imply that the agency should attempt to win consent at any price. The desires of the legislature, the chief executive, and other agencies, relevant professional standards, and the dictates of ordinary morality set limits which must be respected in any program which pretends to further the public interest. But within these limits there is ample margin for the agency to seek consent by anticipating the reaction of affected interest groups, by keeping them informed of agency activities, and by permitting them to be notified in advance, to be heard, and to be informed of the basis of emerging policy.[2] In this manner the official can avoid foolish mistakes; he can resolve differences with less "loss of face" on the part of all; and he can impart to the people organized as pressure groups both a sense that they are respected and a conviction that they are playing a valuable role in the process by which they are governed.

The effectiveness with which an agency discharges the aforementioned obligations to special interests furnishes the three criteria of responsibility which follow:

a. The extent to which an agency equalizes opportunities to safeguard interests. Do the groups dealt with represent all major interests allected by the program? Is each given equitable treatment? Have steps been taken to assure that group spokesmen fairly reflect the views of those whom they claim to represent?

b. The adequacy of the means employed and the results achieved in securing from interest groups technical knowledge necessary to policy decisions.

c. The extent to which an agency succeeds in winning group consent in the sense discussed above. This includes an appraisal of its methods and its effectiveness in forecasting the reaction of interested groups to contemplated measures and in exchanging with these groups factual data and attitudes of mutual concern.[3]

Application of these criteria, so far as they involve an appraisal of the methods by which an agency maintains contact with interest groups, requires some study of the precise *form* of the relationship between agency and interest group. Often, groups are represented in the very structure of government, as when an organization is created to benefit a special category of citizens. The Veterans Administration, Women's Bureau, and Bureau of Indian Affairs are generally cited as examples of such clientele agencies. When a number of different interest groups is involved, resort is sometimes made to "staffing for point of view," i.e. appointing officials on the basis of special vocational affiliation or experience. A more direct device is interest representation on multiheaded boards; and occasionally interest groups are even authorized to nominate members of such boards. Finally, public power may actually be delegated to private organizations, although this practice is not generally in accord with our constitutional traditions.[4]

Perhaps more often, however, interest groups maintain merely an advisory or consultative status in their relations to administrative agencies. They present their views in the process of legal or less formal procedures of investigation, notice, and hearing. Some agencies create special staff units to maintain contact with outside groups and present their grievances and suggestions. A common technique is to establish advisory committees composed of the relevant special interests. Wartime experience with such advisory bodies, particularly in the War Production Board and the Office of Price Administration, was on the whole successful, and from that experience improved techniques for the utilization of advisory bodies have been developed.

A general bias is here stated in favor of the advisory devices. An incentive should be placed upon the administrator to win group assent; and group representatives should be free to withdraw or criticize as they see fit. To build interest representation into the governmental structure, at least on a piecemeal basis, is to invite the extremes of hierarchical suppression of group demands or of undue responsiveness thereto. Furthermore, the advisory relationship should be formalized or legalized, since an informal relationship opens the way to invisible exertion of pressure with consequent danger of action that is irresponsible in the eyes of all third parties. It is conceded, however, that these results need not necessarily follow in each situation; that a general preference for formalized consultation may derive from an uncritical acceptance of traditional democratic ideology; and that each case must be examined on its own merits. With this approach, a finding that pressure groups have been directly integrated into the administrative structure, or at the other extreme, that complete informality exists in the relationship between bureaucrat and group spokesman, should be regarded only as a red flag indicating possible lack of responsibility ahead.

Responsibility to the Legislature

Working Bias: An administrative agency should be responsible to the legislature, but only through the chief executive, and primarily for broad issues of public policy and general administrative performance.

Representative bodies are the institutional embodiment of democratic theory, and an administration responsible to the legislature is of the very essence of democratic government. Yet many political scientists fear that representative bodies are losing both power and prestige because of the compelling necessity to delegate to administrators broad discretion in the initiation and execution of public policy. There is no reason, however, why delegation of power need necessarily result in loss of power provided the legislature devises techniques for holding the administration responsible for the exercise of its discretion. If it is true that Congress has lost power and prestige, that is because Congress has not adapted its organization and procedures to the needs of the time, not because such adaptation is inherently impossible within our present form of government.[5]

Moreover, it has been pointed out that the problem of responsible government today is not so much that of legislative-executive relations as of the relationships between the legislature and chief executive on the one hand, and the administrative agency, often allied with pressure groups and legislative blocs, on the other. The administrative agency must be answerable in some sense to *both* the chief executive and the legislature. The real question is how to structure such dual responsibility under our present constitutional system. Should the agency be responsible directly to the legislature, or should it be responsible to the legislature through the chief executive?

The advocates of direct responsibility point out that the legislature creates, defines the powers of, and appropriates the money for each administrative agency. Also, they note that many agencies exercise sublegislative and quasi-judicial functions which they feel should be supervised by legislature and courts respectively. And perhaps most important, they argue that the direct responsibility of an agency cannot end with the chief executive because the chief executive himself cannot be made answerable to the legislature in quite the same sense as under parliamentary government. In its relationships with the President, Congress lacks the ultimate sanction: authority to force resignation when the President no longer commands the confidence of the Congress.

Advocates of indirect responsibility argue that it is of supreme importance to focus responsibility sharply, and that if the legislature attempts to hold each agency directly accountable, responsibility for the coordinated conduct of government programs in broad areas of public policy will become too diffused to be made effective. It is contended: (1) that there must be unity of ultimate command and clearly formulated lines of authority in any such hierarchical organization as a public bureaucracy. Lack of clarity gives rise to uncertainty, conflict, and irresolution, making it difficult to enforce responsible conduct. It is asserted that this can best be prevented by running the line of authority from agency to chief executive to legislature. (2) That careful coordination of the often conflicting programs of different agencies is required if the official is to be kept from an unduly narrow view of the public interest. The legislature alone cannot accomplish such coordination, particularly if it attempts to hold each single agency directly responsible. However, the chief executive, if assisted by adequate staff, is in a position to develop clear and balanced programs for areas of public policy which cut across organizational lines. He is also in a better position to insure effective execution of such programs. (3) That legislators must have balanced programs responsibly placed before them if they are to be able to make intelligent policy decisions. It is the chief executive who is best equipped to prepare such programs and assume responsibility for placing them before the elective body. (4) That the legislature is not equipped to hold the many individual officers and agencies of government to a detailed responsibility. On the other hand, the interposition of the chief executive can reduce the pressure on the legislature. He can devise procedures for settling matters too trivial for legislative attention, for eradicating administrative parochialism, and for controlling the executive agencies in such a manner as to simplify the task of legislative surveillance. (5) That direct responsibility to the legislature nearly always means direct responsibility to individual members of particular legislative committees which happen to have jurisdiction. In such cases the legislature often finds it difficult to check its own entrenched and uncoordinated minorities. This is less likely to occur when the legislature considers integrated policies submitted by the chief executive. (6) That the difficulties of executive-legislative relationships under a system of separated powers are reduced by the presentation, through the chief executive, of an internally consistent and coherent legislative program. (7) That sublegislative powers are really similar to the policy making powers of regular executive agencies, and as such should be exercised under direct responsibility to the chief executive, while judicial functions should be independent of both legislature and executive. (8) That a single responsible chief executive to manage the departments in accordance with statute is an essential part of our republican system and was clearly intended by the framers of the Constitution.

On balance, it is believed that the advocates of indirect responsibility have the better of the argument. Of course, there is no question but that a determined legislature can in fact control individual agencies directly if it wishes to pay the price; the general position taken here requires rather the evolution of a custom of legislative self-restraint where direct controls are concerned. Nor is it meant to imply that the legislature should be denied the *authority* to prescribe the duties and procedures of administrative agencies in detail. No more is meant than that the requirements for a truly effective responsibility today will call for sparing use of such authority.[6] The legislature can neither determine a national policy nor maintain effective supervision over the executive branch unless it focuses on the great issues and rests content with having laid out general lines of policy for the executive branch. To impose mandatory and minute specifications for the organization and operation of the administrative machine is to absolve "first the bureau chief, then the Secretary of the department, and then the

President . . . from part of his executive responsibility, and in consequence the Congress is foreclosed from adequately criticizing the conduct of the business." Accordingly, administrative agencies should be responsible to the legislature, but only through the chief executive, and primarily for the broader questions which arise in formulating and executing policy.

If an agency can be controlled effectively only when Congress focuses on major issues of integrated policy, a major criterion of its responsibility is the success with which that agency, in reporting to Congress through the President, points up the broad policy questions which require legislative determination and plays down administrative details. The remaining criteria of indirect responsibility to the legislature can be derived in the process of examining the nature of the business which draws legislator and bureaucrat together.

First, agencies give legislative committees professional assistance and advice that leads to the drafting of statutes. Here the criterion of their responsibility is the effort which they make, by producing competent advice, to encourage the passage of laws containing a careful definition of the agencies' obligations and authorities. An official cannot proceed to a wise and democratic use of his discretion unless the legislature has indicated the general nature of the standards which should guide his action: and it is his responsibility to present the professional information available to him to the legislature, through the chief executive, in a way to insure the writing of competent standards into law. A corollary of this criterion is the extent to which the agency presses for revision of vague or overly ambitious statutes when it has access to technical information for the determination of more satisfactory standards. Yet another corollary is the response of legislative committees to the agency's recommendations. However, this last criterion does not have wide application. It is based on the assumption that committees generally respond more favorably to recommended legislation that incorporates professionally determined standards than to other recommendations. Though this may be true, there are so many other factors which enter into legislative response that it will usually be difficult to isolate this one.

Second, agencies are required to come before appropriation committees annually to present their plans for the ensuing year, to account for activities and expenditures for the current and past years, and generally to satisfy these committees that the legislature's purposes are actually guiding their operations. Review of the budget is the most important of the regular legislative controls over the executive branch. Even though changes in items may be relatively small, it should not be thought that this review is ineffective. Departments and budget officers are keenly aware of legislative attitudes and prepare their budgets to meet them.[7] In this activity, the criterion of responsibility is the effectiveness with which the agency (a) reports and justifies projected work, and (b) reports and accounts for accomplishments. A corollary measure is the treatment accorded the agency's budget by the appropriations committees, but here again there are too many other factors conditioning legislative response to permit any but extremely guarded conclusions.

Third, an agency is constantly subject to legislative investigations; and though it may never have undergone such an investigation, the threat of one is a continued sanction by which the legislature insures conformity to its own policies and safeguards against abuses which run counter to community values. The agency must always be prepared to answer; its record must be good; and it must be prepared to spread that record before the legislature. The criterion of responsibility is thus the willingness and ability of an agency to provide investigating committees with a complete, accurate, and clear record of its activities. A corollary, again to be used with extreme care because of the vagaries of "politics," is the extent to which an investigating committee indicates satisfaction with its findings.

Fourth, the accounts of agencies are regularly audited by an independent instrumentality of the legislature. The criterion of responsibility is here self-evident.

Fifth, agencies conduct business with the legislature which involves the appointment and removal of personnel, both personnel whom the agency appoints directly and personnel whom it recommends to the President to be confirmed with the consent of the Senate. The criteria of responsibility here are also difficult to apply because of the supervention of "political" factors, but they can be enumerated as the success of the agency in obtaining confirmation of appointments which it has in fact initiated, absence of legislative efforts to impeach or by other means remove or place obstacles on the removal of agency personnel, and general evidence of legislative satisfaction with the agency's staff.

Finally, agencies often maintain a network of informal contacts with individual legislators and committees. In some form such relationships are inevitable, and in fact indispensable. But in their pathological form, a single legislator or committee may occupy a position of influence so commanding in matters affecting the agency that responsibility to the remainder of the legislature is prevented. Accordingly, a final criterion of responsibility to the legislature is whether an agency conducts its relationships therewith in a manner to prevent minority control over its affairs.

Responsibility to the Chief Executive[8]

Working Bias: An administrative agency should be directly responsible for conforming to the general program of the chief executive and for coordinating its activities with other agencies of the executive branch.

To the extent that the chief executive is held responsible by the legislature and by the public for the administration of a government-wide program, he will in turn try to establish the responsibility of administrative agencies to himself.[9] In so doing he must define the duties for which they are held accountable and the means by which this accountability is to be effectuated.

Both in formulating and in executing programs, agencies usually operate under the general policies or philosophy of the Administration. The broad lines of such policy are normally laid down by the chief executive. But he cannot be expected to provide detailed direction on all matters. He is entitled to expect that, within the limitations of specific legislative determinations, agencies will adapt their activities to his general policy directives and to the broad philosophy of his Administration.[10] The extent to which such adaptations are made is one major criterion of an agency's responsibility to the chief executive.

Moreover, nearly all agencies operate in fields in which they also affect the programs and interests of other organizations immediately subordinate to the chief executive. If the purposes set by the President are to be achieved with maximum effectiveness, it is essential that these agencies act in concert. To be sure, it is becoming fashionable to observe that a sophisticated executive may prefer something less than complete coordination of his establishment on the ground that occasional conflict between subordinates enables him to keep posted and insures that policy conflicts will be brought before him for resolution. But a decision to adopt this strange substitute for an effective intelligence service should rest with the superior, not with the subordinate. Generally, an agency subordinate to the chief executive has an obligation not to take action which has not been carefully checked with other interested agencies through the established means for coordination. Thus, a second major criterion of responsibility to the chief executive is the extent to which an agency coordinates its work with that of other agencies. A closely related criterion is the extent to which controversial matters of detail, unworthy of legislative attention, are settled within the executive branch.

The remaining criteria of responsibility to the chief executive relate to the means for attaining concerted conformance to his program. They involve techniques for departmental and overhead organization designed to provide public leadership. These techniques include not only unity of ultimate command and clearly formulated lines of authority, but also the existence of effective staff organs at appropriate levels in the administrative hierarchy. Some progress has been made in recent years in securing such staff organs, especially for administrative staff services (budget and personnel) and long-term planning. The development of policy general staff has lagged behind. By direction of the President, the Bureau of the Budget performs a central clearance function for the programs of executive agencies. But though central clearance has proved effective in a large number of instances, the procedure is notoriously less adequate for those important cases which involve highly controversial subjects. On broader issues inter-departmental committees have been used to eliminate conflicts in policy. Such committees, however, especially when unsupported by secretariat, are too often stultified by the "veto power" and by the presence of members more concerned with defending their positions than with reaching genuine agreement.

More recently, there has grown a general awareness that negative and piecemeal review of individual proposals flowing up from agencies to the chief executive cannot produce an integrated governmental program at the time it is required. It is becoming clear that top level executives require policy staff organs to formulate general programs which subordinate units cannot evolve because of limited terms of reference, inertia, organizational or professional bias, or inadequate factual information. Such a policy general staff, by supplying common premises for action, can help insure coordination "before the event," that is, by prior indoctrination.

From this discussion it is possible to derive the following additional criteria of responsibility to the chief executive: (1) the existence of unity of ultimate command and clearly formulated lines of authority within an agency; (2) the availability and effectiveness of administrative staff organs, intra-agency committees, and liaison or other devices for insuring concerted conformance with the chief executive's policies: (3) the extent and genuine sincerity of agency cooperation with staff, liaison, interdepartmental, or other coordinating mechanisms established by the chief executive; (4) the extent to which an agency conforms to the chief executive's program in information transmitted to the legislature or to the public;[11] (5) as a measure of successful adjustment of program conflicts, the extent to which evidence of such conflicts with other agencies fails to appear in information transmitted to the legislature or to the public;[12] (6) so far as can be ascertained by rough estimate, the extent to which an agency demonstrates a "sense of administrative discipline" in its conduct.[13]

Responsibility to Political Parties

Working Bias: An administrative agency cannot be held independently responsible to the organization or policies of political parties.

If responsibility to political parties exists at all in the federal government, it is largely indirect and can be included within the criteria already developed. For example, for some purposes the political party can be considered an interest group. Furthermore, political parties dictate the organization of the legislature and the selection of the chief executive and his top aides, so that the manner in which responsibility to the legislature and chief executive is effectuated will reflect whatever responsibility to political parties exists. In contrast to cabinet government and to British society, the structure of American government and of American society has not encouraged the development of party organization or policy to which administrative agencies can be held responsible.

Responsibility to Profession

Working Bias: An administrative agency should be responsible for maintaining, developing, and applying such professional standards as may be relevant to its activities.

An administrative agency can be held responsible for adherence to the standards of technical knowledge, craftsmanship, and professionalism applicable to the function administered. In other words, it can be said that objective standards of professional performance are one technique for insuring responsible conduct. Where such standards exist, the official often sacrifices his personal preference to the compulsion of professional group opinion. Should he fail to do so, he faces a loss of professional status or possibly affirmative action by executive, legislative, or judicial agents based on use of professional standards as a measure of conduct.

It is generally agreed that the professional sanction does not of itself provide an adequate guarantee of responsibility in our society. Some students have even emphasized the special dangers of any heavy reliance on professional standards. It is held that there can be no real responsibility unless it is an obligation to someone else (X being responsible to Y for Z), and that this condition cannot be fulfilled by the relationship of a man and a science or by an inward personal sense of moral obligation. It is also feared that professional responsibility leads to group introversion, undue emphasis on technique, and inflexibility. It is felt that agency traditions based on a sense of narrow monopoly of expertness often harden into a pattern that resists alteration. Finally, there is the traditional democratic aversion to the efficiency which is one of the objectives of professional standards. The maxim that "men who think first and foremost of efficiency are seldom democrats" is of hoary, if not wholly palatable, vintage.

But most of the objections cited above are not really objections to reliance on professional standards. They are objections to the fact that the bureaucracy often has a monopoly of skill in modern government, and that the indispensability of skilled administrators tends to make such a bureaucracy autonomous. Professionalization may actually play an important role in transforming the quasi-autonomous bureaucracy into a subservient tool. Conversely, responsibility is often most conspicuously absent where objective professional standards either do not exist or are not applied.

For present purposes it is enough that the professional responsibility recognized by an agency must be supplemented by responsibility to interest groups, legislature, and chief executive, and that it must be convincing to persons not associated with the profession or agency concerned. Whether or not it will be convincing depends in part on the status of the profession involved, i.e. the extent to which the profession has developed or can be made to develop objective standards which are generally recognized and respected, and in part on evidence that the agency recognizes and has taken steps to insure fidelity to such standards by its personnel.

Accordingly the criteria for gauging the responsibility of an agency to professional standards includes: (1) the extent to which it recognizes such generally accepted standards and utilizes them to formulate policies and to anticipate problems which a technically qualified man knows will arise; (2) the extent to which it makes an effort to develop additional standards, especially when it possesses a near monopoly of skill in its field; and the extent to which such standards gain the respect of competent professional personnel outside the agency; (3) the extent to which it takes into account the professional education and experience of personnel in its recruitment, advancement, and separation policies; (4) the nature and extent of in-service training programs designed to improve professional skills; and (5) the nature and extent of its cooperation with outside organizations which attempt to keep their members up-to-date on professional developments and to promote devotion to the highest professional standards.

Beyond the standards of any one profession or craft, there are also standards common to the whole body of public servants considered as a distinctive social group—i.e. as "bureaucracy." These standards usually reflect (a) the fiduciary relationship in which bureaucracy generally stands to political authority and (b) the norms of the wider social order. Consequently in a democracy they will include the demand for honesty, efficiency, courtesy, and impartiality in public acts, and an insistence that administration, both as to policy and procedure, be conducted in accordance with the prevailing democratic values.[14] The extent to which these requirements are met furnishes the major criteria of the responsibility of public officials regarded as a single identifiable profession.

Responsibility to the Courts

Administrative responsibility to the courts will not be discussed in any detail, nor will criteria for this type of responsibility be developed. Administrative law has recently been the subject of so many specialized studies that the limited examination that might be made here would add nothing.

Failure to develop criteria for judicial responsibility is not intended to detract from its importance. All responsibility of public officials is, of course, responsibility under law; and in the United States it is generally to the regular courts that administrative agencies must prove, when challenged, that they have not abused their discretion, overstepped their jurisdiction, or committed an error of law, fact, or procedure. It should be noted, however, that such administrative abuses as excessive red tape or offensive conduct toward the public are beyond the reach of the courts. Moreover, judicial review is largely a negative, *post hoc*, and unduly ritualized check addressed to errors of commission, whereas administrative irresponsibility in the modern state is just as likely to arise from errors of omission.

For these reasons it is necessary to supplement the legal accountability of administrative agencies with responsibility to the people organized as interest groups, to the legislature, to the chief executive, and to relevant professional standards. Ordinarily, the analysis of a genuinely responsible agency will reveal a high positive correlation on all the criteria developed in connection with these relationships. But such a multiplicity of responsibilities may occasionally impose mutually contradictory obligations on an agency; and in such cases, as was suggested at the outset, the criteria of responsibility herein developed may well conflict. In this event there is a residual responsibility for the agency to evidence rational policy and good faith in seeking a resolution of the impasse, primarily through the chief executive.

Bibliographical Note

Method of Approach: The general approach is suggested by Herbert A. Simon, *Administrative Behavior; A Study of Decision-making Processes in Administrative Organization* (Macmillan, 1947), especially chapter 2.

Responsibility—A General and Historical View: Friedrich's analysis of bureaucracy forms the basis of the discussion. See Carl J. Friedrich, *Constitutional Government and Democracy* (Little, Brown & Co., 1941), especially chapters 2, 18, 19. The citations are from this text.

See also Max Weber on bureaucracy in H. H. Gerth and C. Wright Mills (translators), *From Max Weber* (Oxford University Press, 1946), chapter 8; and in Talcott Parsons (ed.), *Max Weber: The Theory of Social and Economic Organization* (Oxford University Press 1917), chapter 3.

Responsibility for What? The following deal with responsibility for formulating as well as executing public policy: Carl J. Friedrich, "Public Policy and the Nature of Administrative Responsibility," in Friedrich and Edward S. Mason (eds.), *Public Policy, 1940* (Harvard University Press, 1940); V. O. Key, "Politics and Administration," in Leonard D. White (ed.), *The Future of Government in the United States* (University of Chicago Press, 1942); Don K. Price, "Democratic Administration," in Fritz Morstein Marx (ed.), *Elements of Public Administration* (Prentice-Hall, 1946); Wayne A. R. Leys, "Ethics and Administrative Discretion," 3 *Public Administration Review* 10 (1943); Edwin E. Witte, "Adminis-

trative Agencies and Statute Law Making," 2 *PAR* 116 (1942); Elisabeth McK.
Scott and Belle Zeller, "State Agencies and Lawmaking," 2 *PAR* 205 (1942).

Responsibility to the People—Pressure Groups: The need for such responsibility is
seen and defended by E. Pendleton Herring, *Public Administration and the Public Interest* (McGraw-Hill Book Co., 1936); John Dickinson, "Democratic Realities in Democratic Dogma," 24 *American Political Science Review* 283 (1930);
Avery Leiserson, "Interest Groups in Administration," in Morstein Marx, *op. cit.;* V. O. Key, *Politics, Parties, and Pressure Groups* (Thomas Y. Crowell Co., 1947), chapter 7.

The role of advisory groups in recent administration is discussed by William H.
Newman, "Government-Industry Cooperation That Works," 6 *PAR* 240 (1946).

Responsibility to the Legislature: The argument for indirect responsibility is taken
from Friedrich, "Public Policy and the Nature of Administrative Responsibility,"
op. cit.; Price, "Democratic Administration," *op. cit.;* John M. Gaus, *Reflections on Public Administration* (University of Alabama Press, 1947); V. O. Key, *Politics, Parties . . . , op. cit.,* and "Politics and Administration," *op. cit.;* Leonard D. White, "Legislative Responsibility for the Public Service," in *New Horizons in Public Administration* (University of Alabama Press, 1945); President's Committee on Administrative Management, *Report . . . with Studies . . .* (Government Printing Office, 1937). The quotation on page 188 is from this last report.

Some of the forms of responsibility to legislature are discussed by Joseph P. Harris,
"The Future of Administrative Management," in White (ed.), *The Future of Government, op. cit.*

Responsibility to the Chief Executive: Problems of staffing the presidency are analyzed in Don K. Price, "Staffing the Presidency," in Fritz Morstein Marx (ed.),
"Federal Executive Reorganization Re-examined: A Symposium I," 40 *American Political Science Review* 1154–68 (1946); and V. O. Key, "Politics and Administration," *op. cit.*

Responsibility to Profession: Friedrich in particular has emphasized this aspect of
administration. See "Public Policy and the Nature of Administrative Responsibility" and *Constitutional Government and Democracy,* especially chapter 19. In this connection, see also Fritz Morstein Marx, "Administrative Responsibility," in Morstein Marx (ed.), *Public Management in the New Democracy,* (Harper & Bros., 1940); and Reinhard Bendix, "Bureaucracy and the Problem of Power," 5 *PAR* 194 (1945).

The dangers of heavy reliance on professional responsibility are pointed up by Herman Finer, "Administrative Responsibility in Democratic Government," 1 *PAR* 335 (1941); Marshall Dimock, "Bureaucracy Self-Examined," 4 *PAR* 197 (1944); Key, "Politics and Administration," *op. cit.*

Notes

1. "Many of the most severe breakdowns in contemporary administration, accompanied by violent public reactions against irresponsible bureaucracy, will be found to trace back to contradictory and ill-defined policy. . . ." Carl J. Friedrich, "Public Policy and the Nature of Administrative Responsibility," p. 4.

2. Leiserson also observes cogently that the administrator may endanger his whole program by too meticulous an effort to resist group pressures. Both the agency and the pressure group are part of the same community, and legislative support for the achievement of the agency's aims depends on its ability to get the support of vocal groups. See his "Interest Groups in Administration."

3. This is merely one form of what Friedrich has termed "the rule of anticipated reactions." See *Constitutional Government and Democracy*, p. 589 ff. It is impossible to overestimate the general importance of this "rule" as a restraint on power of all types.

4. There are some exceptions, notably those relating to professional groups. Appleby vigorously opposes any tendency to delegate public power to private groups since it is difficult to hold them responsible. See Paul H. Appleby, *Big Democracy* (Knopf, 1945).

5. General analysis of the broader questions of the relative effectiveness of cabinet and presidential government is beyond the scope of this paper. Similarly, proposals to establish other types of executive-legislative relations, e.g., the interpellation and the joint legislative-executive council, are not analyzed since they cannot provide criteria for gauging administrative responsibility in the United States today. For a convenient summary of such proposals see George B. Galloway, *Congress at the Crossroads* (Thomas Y. Crowell Co., 1946), especially chapter 7.

6. ". . . in the future, legislatures perforce must deal with administration on the basis of principle and generality if they are to deal with it effectively and in the public interest." Leonard D. White, "Legislative Responsibility for the Public Service," p. 6.

7. Too often, alas, the "rule of anticipated reactions" here dictates that an agency request more money than it really wants in order that it will not be granted less than it actually needs. But though this practice is common, and to some extent inevitable, astute officials are aware that it may "backfire" with disastrous consequences.

8. No effort is made to establish a separate set of criteria for measuring the responsibility of subordinate officials to the heads of their own agencies. However, these will not differ substantially, *mutatis mutandis*, from the criteria for measuring the responsibility of agency heads to the chief executive.

9. In this connection, Pendleton Herring has questioned whether too close a responsibility of the chief executive for the actions of administrative agencies is desirable. He raises practical arguments against pushing the current shibboleths too far. "If the President were held to a closer accountability, he would inevitably become laden with an accumulation of grievances. Is this compatible with an official elected for a fixed term of years?" If the President is to remain effective, he must to some extent be guarded "from the frictions that his administration creates." *Presidential Leadership* (Farrar and Rinehart, 1940), p. 114 ff.

10. Failure to make such adaptation should be an occasion for disciplinary action, but direct political ties between the offending agency and individual legislators often prevent the required measures. This points up the importance of the final criterion of responsibility set forth in the preceding section.

11. Deviations can, of course, be justified when the legislature demands information which may be contrary to the chief executive's program.

12. It is realized that information concerning a conflict may be suppressed and that such suppression should not be considered evidence that the conflict has been resolved. However, unless the chief executive purposefully presents the conflict to the legislature or to the people for their determination, or unless the legislature demands the facts in the case, the administrative agencies should not publicize the unresolved issues.

13. For many reasons, such a sense is "not a firm part of the American heritage of public administration. . . . Not even the literature of public administration has yet described what are respectable standards of administrative discipline. . . ." Leonard D. White, "Field Coordination in Liberated Areas," 3 *PAR* 192–3 (1943).

14. This does not imply that an official may sabotage a legislative or executive policy simply because *he* happens to deem it undemocratic. The remedy must be sought "through channels," and, should this fail, outside of channels, i.e. by severing his official relationship with the authority which promulgated the policy he condemns and indulging his passion for "higher law" from another vantage point.

10

ACCOUNTABILITY IN THE PUBLIC SECTOR: LESSONS FROM THE CHALLENGER TRAGEDY

Barbara S. Romzek
Melvin J. Dubnick

On January 28, 1986, the space shuttle Challenger exploded in mid-flight and seven crew members lost their lives. The widely known details of that tragic event need not be retraced here. Opinion is growing, however, that the official explanations offered by the Presidential Commission on the Space Shuttle Challenger Accident (the Rogers Commission) fail to provide full answers to why the disaster occurred. We offer an alternative explanation which addresses institutional factors contributing to the shuttle accident.

I. Seeking an Institutional Perspective

Two common threads ran through public discussions of the Challenger incident. First was the urge to pinpoint the technical problems contributing directly to the booster rocket explosion on the shuttle. Second was the de-

Source: *Public Administration Review* 47(1987): 227–238.

sire to uncover human and managerial errors that might have caused National Aeronautics and Space Administration (NASA) officials to overlook or ignore those technical flaws. By the time the Rogers Commission issued its findings on June 9, 1986, those technical and managerial issues dominated its conclusions.

On the first point, the verdict of the Commission was unequivocal:

> The consensus of the commission . . . is that the loss of the space shuttle Challenger was caused by a failure in the joint between the lower segments of the right solid rocket motor. The specific failure was the destruction of the seals that are intended to prevent hot gases from leaking through the joint during the propellant burn of the rocket motor. The evidence assembled . . . indicates that no other element of the space shuttle system contributed to this failure.[1]

The Commission was equally explicit about managerial problems at NASA being a "contributing cause" of the accident:

> The decision to launch the Challenger was flawed. Those who made the decision were unaware of the recent history of problems concerning the O rings [seals] and the joint and were unaware of the initial written recommendation of the contractor advising against the launch at temperatures below 53 degrees Fahrenheit and the continuing opposition of engineers at [Morton] Thiokol after the management had reversed its position. . . . If the decision-makers had known all the facts, it is highly unlikely that they would have decided to launch [the shuttle] on January 28, 1986.[2]

The Commission's report was notable for its conclusive tone regarding these specific findings. More interesting, however, is the untravelled investigative path which asks if the problems at NASA and in the space shuttle program were institutional as well as technical or managerial. The institutional perspective is familiar to students of organizational theory who, following the lead of Talcott Parsons and James D. Thompson, note three levels of organizational responsibility and control: technical, managerial, and institutional.[3]

At the *technical level,* organizations focus on the effective performance of specialized and detailed functions. At the *managerial level,* an organization provides for mediation among its technical components and between its technical functionaries and those "customers" and "suppliers" in the organization's "task environment." At the *institutional level,* the organization deals with the need for being part of the "wider social system which is the source of the 'meaning,' legitimation, or higher-level support which makes implementation of the organization's goals possible."[4]

Applying this framework to the study of specific program or project failures such as the Challenger, one can argue that critical problems can arise at any or all three levels. Thus, an investigation of such events would be incomplete without considering the possible implications of activity at each level. The fact that NASA and other public agencies must constantly contend with the institutional forces that surround them (i.e., the "wider social system" of which they are part) is worthy of attention because agency efforts to deal with those forces may contribute to shaping the outcomes of agency action.

Investigators might ignore the role of institutional factors for several reasons. Attention to such factors might raise questions that are too basic and too dangerous for the organization or its supporters. Thus, a commission composed of individuals committed to the enterprise under investigation[5] and to the political system in general[6] is unlikely to open up the Pandora's Box of institutional factors. In contrast, institutional factors might be overlooked because analysts lack a conceptual framework that facilitates such considerations. Assuming the latter explanation, we offer a framework useful for highlighting the institutional factors that might have contributed to the Challenger disaster.

II. An "Accountability" Perspective

While often regarded as a unique public organization,[7] NASA has institutional characteristics similar in very important respects to other public sector agencies. As such, NASA has to deal with the diversity of legitimate and occasionally conflicting expectations emanating from the democratic political system of which it is a part (its institutional context). In the following pages we present a framework of public accountability as a means for examining NASA's management of its institutional pressures and its implications.

Managing Expectations

Accountability is a fundamental but underdeveloped concept in American public administration. Scholars and practitioners freely use the term to refer to answerability for one's actions or behavior. Administrators and agencies are accountable to the extent that they are required to answer for their actions. Beyond this basic notion of answerability, there has been little refinement of the term. Most of the discussion in the literature centers on the "best" strategy for achieving accountability, with the Friedrich-Finer exchange of the 1940s being the most cited example.[8]

From an alternative perspective, accountability plays a greater role in the processes of public administration than indicated by the idea of answerability. In its simplest form, answerability implies that accountability involves limited, direct, and mostly formalistic responses to demands generated by specific institutions or groups in the public agency's task

FIGURE 10.1 Types of Accountability Systems

		Source of Agency Control	
		Internal	External
Degree of Control Over Agency Actions	High	1. Bureaucratic	2. Legal
	Low	3. Professional	4. Political

environment. More broadly conceived, *public administration accountability involves the means by which public agencies and their workers manage the diverse expectations generated within and outside the organization.*[9]

Viewed as a strategy for managing expectations, public administration accountability takes a variety of forms. The focus here is on four alternative systems of public accountability, each based on variations involving two critical factors: (1) whether the ability to define and control expectations is held by some specified entity inside or outside the agency; and (2) the degree of control that entity is given over defining those agency's expectations. The interplay of these two dimensions generates the four types of accountability systems illustrated in Figure 10.1.

Regarding the first dimension, the management of agency expectations through accountability mechanisms calls for the establishment of some authoritative source of control. Internal sources of control rely on the authority inherent in either formal hierarchical relationships or informal social relationships within the agency. External sources of control reflect a similar distinction, for their authority can be derived from either formalized arrangements set forth in laws or legal contracts or the informal exercise of power by interests located outside the agency.

A second ingredient in any accountability system is the degree of control over agency choices and operations exercised by those sources of control. A high degree of control reflects the controller's ability to determine both the range and depth of actions which a public agency and its members can take. A low degree of control, in contrast, provides for considerable discretion on the part of agency operatives.

Bureaucratic Accountability Systems (cell 1) are widely used mechanisms for managing public agency expectations.[10] Under this approach, the expectations of public administrators are managed through focusing attention on the priorities of those at the top of the bureaucratic hierarchy. At the same time, supervisory control is applied intensively to a wide range of agency activities. The functioning of a bureaucratic accountability system involves two simple ingredients: an organized and legitimate relationship between a superior and a subordinate in which the need to follow "orders" is unquestioned; and close supervision or a surrogate system of standard operating procedures or clearly stated rules and regulations.[11]

Legal Accountability[12] (cell 2) is similar to the bureaucratic form in that it involves the frequent application of control to a wide range of public administration activities. In contrast to bureaucratic accountability, however, legal accountability is based on relationships between a controlling party outside the agency and members of the organization. That outside party is not just anyone; it is the individual or group in a position to impose legal sanctions or assert formal contractual obligations. Typically, these outsiders make the laws and other policy mandates which the public administrator is obligated to enforce or implement. In policymaking terms, the outsider is the "lawmaker" while the public administrator has the role of "executor."

The legal accountability relationship between controller and the controlled also differs from that found between supervisor and subordinate in bureaucratic accountability forms. In the bureaucratic system, the relationship is hierarchical and based on the ability of supervisors to reward or punish subordinates. In legal accountability, however, the relationship is between two relatively autonomous parties and involves a formal or implied fiduciary (principal/agent) agreement between the public agency and its legal overseer.[13] For example, Congress passes laws and monitors a federal agency's implementation of those laws; a federal district court orders a school board to desegregate its classrooms and oversees the implementation of that order; the local city commission contracts with a private firm to operate the city refuse dump. In each case the implementors are legally or contractually obliged to carry out their duties, and the enforcement of such obligations are very different from those found in situations where bureaucratic accountability systems are applied.[14]

Professional Accountability[15] (cell 3) occurs with greater frequency as governments deal increasingly with technically difficult and complex problems. Under those circumstances, public officials must rely on skilled and expert employees to provide appropriate solutions. Those employees expect to be held fully accountable for their actions and insist that agency leaders trust them to do the best job possible. If they fail to meet job performance expectations, it is assumed they can be reprimanded or fired. Otherwise they expect to be given sufficient discretion to get the job done. Thus, professional accountability is characterized by placement of control over organizational activities in the hands of the employee with the expertise or special skills to get the job done. The key to the professional accountability system, therefore, is deference to expertise within the agency. While outside professional associations may indirectly influence the decision making of the in-house expert (through education and professional standards), the source of authority is essentially internal to the agency.

Typically the professional accountability organization will look like any other public agency with a manager in charge of a set of workers, but the relationships among them are much different. Under a bureaucratic accountability system, the key relationship would be that of close supervision. In contrast, under professional accountability the central relationship is similar to that found between a layperson and an expert, with the agency manager taking the role of the layperson and the workers making the important decisions that require their expertise.[16]

Political Accountability (cell 4) is central to the democratic pressures imposed on American public administrators. If "deference" characterizes professional accountability, "responsiveness" characterizes political accountability systems (cell 4).[17] The key relationship under these systems resembles that between a representative (in this case, the public administrator) and his or her constituents (those to whom he or she is accountable). Under political accountability, the primary question becomes, "Whom does the public administrator represent?" The potential constituencies include the general public, elected officials, agency heads, agency clientele, other special interest groups, and future generations. Regardless of which definition of constituency is adopted, the administrator is expected to be responsive to their policy priorities and programmatic needs.

While political accountability systems might seem to promote favoritism and even corruption in the administration of government programs, they also serve as the basis for a more open and representative government. The urge for political accountability, for example, is reflected in open meetings laws, freedom of information acts, and "government in the sunshine" statutes passed by many state and local governments.

Table 10.1 summarizes the principal features of the four general types of accountability systems. Under the bureaucratic system, expectations are managed through a hierarchical arrangement based on supervisory relationships; the legal accountability system manages agency expectations through a contractual relationship; the professional system relies on deference to expertise; while the political accountability system promotes responsiveness to constituents as the central means of managing the multiple expectations.

TABLE 10.1   Relationships Within Accountability Systems

Type of Accountability System	*Analogous Relationship (Controller/Administrator)*	*Basis of Relationship*
1. Bureaucratic	Superior/subordinate	Supervision
2. Legal	Lawmaker/law executor	Fiduciary
	Principal/agent	
3. Professional	Layperson/expert	Deference to expertise
4. Political	Constituent/representative	Responsiveness to constituents

Preferences for Accountability Systems

Given these alternative means for managing expectations, what determines the preference for one accountability approach over others in any particular situation? The appropriateness of a specific accountability system to an agency is linked to three factors: the nature of the agency's tasks (technical level accountability); the management strategy adopted by those heading the agency (management level accountability); and the institutional context of agency operations (institutional level accountability).[18] Ideally, a public sector organization should establish accountability mechanisms which "fit" at all three levels simultaneously.

In the American political system, all four accountability types offer potentially legitimate means for managing *institutional level* expectations.[19] Under current institutional norms, no single type of accountability system is inherently more acceptable or legitimate than another. *In theory,* each of the four accountability systems can insure agency responsibility at the institutional level. Thus, in theory an agency might manage its expectations using the accountability system most appropriate in light of relevant institutional considerations. The same potential flexibility may not exist at the technical or managerial levels where the appropriateness of accountability mechanisms is more closely tied to specific tasks or the strategic orientations or idiosyncrasies of individual managers.

In reality, most U.S. public agencies tend to adopt two or more types of accountability systems at any time depending on the nature of existing environmental (institutional) conditions as well as their technical tasks and management orientations. We argue, however, that institutional pressures generated by the American political system are often the salient factor and frequently take precedence over technical and managerial considerations.[20] If this is the case, the challenge of managing expectations changes as institutional conditions change. If the environmental changes are drastic enough, they may trigger a different type of accountability system, one which attempts to reflect those new institutional conditions.

III. Accountability Under Different Challenges: The Case of NASA

NASA was an organizational initiative born in the midst of a national crisis and nurtured in the relatively protective shelter of an institutional consensus that lasted until at least 1970. That nurturing consensus focused attention on President Kennedy's mandate to land an American on the moon by the end of the 1960s. In addition, it fostered the belief that achieving that objective required complete deference to those experts who could get the job done. In short, it was a consensus which supported a professional accountability system.

Over time, the pressures to develop a politically responsive agency strategy became dominant. Even before the successful lunar landing of Apollo 11, changing institutional conditions were creating an organizational setting that encouraged more reliance on bureaucratic and political accountability mechanisms. This reliance on bureaucratic and political accountability systems produced circumstances which made the agency ill-equipped to contend with the problems that eventually led to the Challenger disaster. Furthermore, institutional reactions to the Challenger tragedy itself may be creating new pressures that are moving the agency toward a greater reliance on legal and bureaucratic accountability methods for managing expectations.

The Professionalization of the Space Program

NASA's earliest programs had three important characteristics: they involved clearly defined outcome objectives, highly technical methodologies for achieving those goals, and almost unqualified political (and therefore budgetary) support.[21] The task of overcoming the technical barriers to space exploration was central to the agency's mission, and NASA was able to invest its expenditures primarily in research and development projects associated with its missions.[22]

Those early conditions had a significant impact on the development and management of NASA. The agency's structure and recruiting practices reflected an institutional willingness to respect the technical nature of NASA's programmatic tasks. NASA's form of organization emphasized deference to expertise and minimized the number of political appointments at the top of the administrative structure (in this case, two political appointees with extensive professional expertise in public management).[23]

NASA's initial staff consisted almost entirely of individuals with the relevant substantive knowledge, primarily aeronautical engineers.

These circumstances afforded NASA the opportunity to become among the most innovative organizations (public or private) in recent American history and a classic example of an agency operating under a professional accountability system. The locus of control over agency activities was internal; NASA's relationship to outside sources (including Congress, the President, and the general public) was that of expert to layperson. Internally, NASA developed a matrix structure in which managers and technicians were assigned to project teams based on the expertise they could offer to the particular task at hand. Technical experts in NASA were expected to make decisions based upon their expertise. Thus, within the agency the degree of control exercised over NASA technical personnel was relatively low. Much of this deference to NASA's technical experts was based on trust in their judgment as well as their expertise. The early managers at NASA "were highly technical people, who knew the spacecraft from the ground up, and they were all very conservative." If "an order to launch came down from on high, they wouldn't do it without first giving everybody the bottom line."[24]

The professional accountability system was evident in the three centers under the Office of Manned Space Flight (OMSF): the Marshall Space Flight Center (Alabama), the Manned Spacecraft Center (Texas; later renamed the Johnson Space Center), and Kennedy Space Center (Florida). During the early 1960s, OMSF and its subunits acted with considerable autonomy. NASA's top management in Washington did occasionally pull in the organizational reins. In several cases (1961, 1963, and 1965), reorganizations were intended to redirect several key units toward new program goals as NASA moved from Project Mercury toward Project Apollo. Each of these changes led to a short-term centralization of control which was intentionally relaxed once programmatic arrangements were in place. In 1967, however, a major long-term effort was made to reduce the autonomy of the manned space flight centers in light of the agency's first major budget constraints and the launch pad fire that killed three astronauts.[25]

The Politicization and Bureaucratization of Accountability

Although many of the technical tasks facing NASA did not change significantly over the past 30 years, institutional pressures on the agency have undergone considerable change. In the late 1960s, NASA faced a leveling off of both its political and financial support. Beginning in the early 1970s there was more concern about the managerial challenges inherent in making NASA into an operational agency—a concern arising from pressures to make the shuttle system a fully operational program.[26] The result of these pressures was a reconfiguration of the accountability systems used by some of the agency's key units. Ironically, the very success of NASA's early programs generated those changes.

NASA's apparent victory in the "space race" coincided with an end to the nurturing consensus that permitted the agency to rely almost exclusively on professional accountability for managing expectations. With America's attention turned increasingly toward Vietnam and economic issues, the space program no longer took priority. A new consensus had to be constructed around some new programmatic mission, and in the late 1960s the idea of a space shuttle began to take form. According to its proponents, the shuttle would represent "a whole new way of space flight," one that would transform NASA from an agency committed to accomplishing specific and discrete program goals within given time constraints (e.g., Apollo) to an agency obligated to the continuous operation of a commercial-like enterprise.[27]

The effort to gain presidential endorsement for the space shuttle program made NASA more aware of and responsive to key actors in the political system. Building the necessary consensus was not easy in the highly volatile and competitive institutional context of the early 1970s. James Fletcher, NASA's Administrator from 1971 to 1977 (and the individual President Reagan brought back to head the agency after the Challenger disaster), needed to sell the space shuttle effort to Congress and the American public as well as the White House. Most of the opposition to the shuttle came from the Office of Management and Budget which was supported by negative assessments of the program by a presidential scientific advisory committee and the RAND Corporation.[28]

During this period NASA entered into political coalitions with groups that it had previously ignored or fought in the policy-making arena, as well as with its traditional supporters in government and among its contractors. The shuttle program, for example, was designed to attract the support of those who might take advantage of its capacity to launch satellites and conduct unique scientific and technological experiments in space. Aided by the military, the scientific community, and parts of the business community, NASA was able to get President Nixon's backing for the program in 1972 despite OMB's opposition. Political accountability was no longer secondary or peripheral to NASA.[29] It became a critical ingredient in guaranteeing its maintenance as a viable agency. In more recent years, that urge for public and political support was implicit in NASA's widely publicized efforts to include members of Congress and non-agency civilians on its shuttle flights. These programs represented NASA's efforts to cultivate or maintain general support for its activities.

Another important (and related) set of institutional constraints emerged in the form of major budget cutbacks and (in the late 1970s) greater pressures for privatization. From the height of its support in the late 1960s to the mid–1970s, NASA's budget was cut in half (in constant dollars). Recent estimates indicate that NASA went through a staff cut of 40 percent from the big-budget days of Apollo and that NASA's safety and quality control staff alone were cut by 71 percent between 1970 and 1986.[30] Operating with fewer resources, the agency had to economize; it became just like most other agencies in Washington. NASA experienced a new-found interest in efficiency and thus became more willing to use bureaucratic means for dealing with its financial problems.

NASA officials intended to accommodate these new institutional pressures by reducing the organizational costs that characterized NASA in the "old days" when external support and availability of resources were not major concerns. NASA has "had to pinch pennies to protect the shuttle, accepting lower-cost technologies and making what seem to have been extravagant claims for its economic potential."[31] Agency decentralization and field center specializations continued, and decentralization brought with it increasing reliance on bureaucratic accountability mechanisms. The shift allowed for economies due to a careful division of labor and compartmentalization of authority based on position. While professional accountability systems survived *within* some of the field centers, for the agency as a whole professional accountability patterns characteristic of the early NASA nearly disappeared. With decentralization in NASA came an isolation and competition among field centers.[32]

NASA's use of contractors was, to a certain extent, a manifestation of its efforts to manage changing institutional expectations. In addition to any technical and financial benefits they provided NASA, contractors had always proved very helpful politically in establishing support for the agency's programs and annual funding requests. During the 1970s the link between contract decision and political support became increasingly critical to NASA.[33]

Bureaucratically, contracting out established the ultimate superordinate/subordinate relationship between NASA's top managers and those carrying out the specific parts of the shuttle program. A contract establishes clear responsibilities and gives top management considerable leverage to apply pressures for better performance. It also allows top management to avoid the problems and costs associated with directly maintaining professional accountability mechanisms. Thus, contracting out not only enhanced the bureaucratization process at NASA; it also reduced reliance on deference to expertise characteristic of professional accountability systems.

Changing institutional conditions altered the locus of control over NASA's activities as well as the degree of control over agency activities. The result was a shift in the types of accountability systems relevant to

NASA's operations. In place of the dominant professional accountability systems of the pre-Apollo 11 era, NASA created an elaborate mixture of accountability mechanisms that stressed the political and bureaucratic. It was under these conditions that decisions regarding the general schedule of space shuttle flights and specific launch times were being made when the Challenger lifted from its Kennedy Space Center pad on January 28, 1986.

The Case of the Challenger

Evidence gathered by the Rogers Commission Report and through the mass media illustrate the various forms of accountability in operation in NASA before the launch of the Challenger. The principal question is whether (and to what extent) the Challenger accident resulted from the efforts by NASA's leadership to manage changing institutional expectations through political and bureaucratic forms of accountability. Did NASA's emphasis on these accountability mechanism to eventually take precedence over the professional system of accountability that characterized NASA in the early 1960s? Were the problems that eventually led to the Challenger accident linked at all to the poor fit between agency tasks and agency accountability mechanisms? In our view, the answer to both questions is "yes."

Political pressures.   The contention that NASA was feeling considerable political pressure to launch the Challenger on January 28 was widely rumored just after the Challenger accident, particularly stories about direct pressure emanating from the White House. The Rogers Commission emphatically denied the truth of those rumors.[34] Nonetheless, similar pressures existed and came from a variety of sources outside of NASA, including the White House.

On the official policy level, President Reagan announced in July 1982 that the first priority of the shuttle program was "to make the system fully operational." Given the costs involved in supporting the program, additional pressures emanated from an increasingly budget-conscious Congress.[35] Other pressures on NASA were due to widespread reporting of shuttle delays in the mass media. One top agency official argued that the press, in giving major coverage to numerous shuttle delays over the previous year, had "pressured" the agency to jeopardize flight safety. "I don't think it caused us to do anything foolish," he said. "But that's where the pressure is. It's not from anywhere else."[36]

These external pressures were easily translated into internal decisions that set an overly ambitious launch schedule.[37] In short, NASA set that schedule for the purposes of reducing the program's cost factors and appeasing various attentive publics, including the White House, Congress, the media, and the agency's military and private sector "customers" who were important actors in NASA's supportive political coalition.

These political pressures may not have been specifically addressed to the Challenger launch, but there is little doubt they were felt throughout the agency. The increasing emphasis on political accountability was bound to cause attitudinal as well as operational problems. "The pressure on NASA to achieve planned flight rates was so pervasive," concluded a congressional report, "that it undoubtedly adversely affected attitudes regarding safety."[38] An agency official noted that NASA's organization culture changed "when NASA felt itself under pressure to demonstrate that the shuttles were operational vehicles in a 'routine' transportation system."[39] Part of that "routinization" took the form of "streamlining" the reporting requirements for safety concerns. Less documentation and fewer reporting requirements replaced previous directives that all safety problems and responses were to be reported to higher levels in NASA's hierarchy. The "old requirements," it was argued, "were not productive for the operational phase of the Shuttle program."[40]

The same political accountability pressures had an impact on NASA's key shuttle program contractor, Morton Thiokol. The assent of Morton Thiokol management (and the silence of their engineers) to the Challenger launch recommendation was influenced in part by NASA's importance as a primary customer—a customer who was in the process of reviewing its contracts with the firm. The company's management did not want to jeopardize their relationships with NASA. As a result, rather than emphasizing deference to the experts who worked for them, Morton Thiokol deferred to the demands of NASA's top managers who, in turn, were under a self-imposed, politically derived launch schedule.

Bureaucratic Pressures.   Indications of preference for bureaucratic rather than professional forms of accountability in NASA are evident in the agency's shuttle program operations. By the early 1980s, NASA's managers were having difficulty coordinating their projects.[41] They came to rely increasingly on hierarchical reporting relationships, a clear manifestation of bureaucratic accountability. This had two effects. First, it increased the potential for "bureaupathological" behavior which the professional accountability system attempted to minimize.[42] Second, it reduced the cross-cutting communications channels which once characterized the less hierarchical and flexible matrix structure at NASA.

The failure of NASA's management system is a fundamental theme of the Rogers Commission. Supervisors were criticized for not passing on up the hierarchy their subordinates' recommendations. Managers were criticized for judgments that were contrary to those suggested by the available data. The Commission reported that its investigation revealed "failures in communication that resulted in a decision to launch [the Challenger] based on incomplete and sometimes misleading information, a conflict between engineering data and management judgments, and a NASA management structure that permitted internal flight safety problems to bypass key Shuttle managers."[43] But what the Rogers Commission perceived as a failure of the agency's management system was, in fact, an inherent characteristic of the bureaucratic accountability system adopted by NASA in order to meet the institutional expectations of the post-Apollo 11 era.

Under NASA's shuttle program, responsibility for specific aspects of the overall program was allocated to supervisors at lower levels in the reporting hierarchy, and the burden for giving the go-ahead to launch decision makers shifted from the engineers and experts toward those supervisory personnel. As scheduling and other pressures increased, so did the reluctance of those supervisors to be the individual who threw a monkey wrench into the shuttle program machinery. Thus it is not surprising that lower-level managers tried to cope on their own instead of communicating their problems upward.[44]

The relevance of this problem to the Challenger disaster was illustrated time and time again in the testimony given before the Rogers Commission. NASA officials noted that individuals higher up in the agency had not been informed about the Rockwell engineers' reservations about ice on the launch pad nor the concerns of Morton Thiokol's personnel about weather conditions and the O-rings.[45] In another instance, when asked why he had not communicated the Thiokol engineers' concerns about the O-ring seals to the Program Manager of the National Space Transportation System, the manager of the Solid Rocket Booster Project (based at the Marshall center) answered that he believed it was an issue that had been resolved at his level in the organization.[46] As one reporter observed, "no one at Marshall saw any reason to bother the managers at the top of NASA's chain of command—the normal procedure in the face of disturbing new evidence." This bureaupathological behavior reflects an attitude among employees at Marshall who feel they are competing with Johnson and the other centers. "Nothing [sic] was ever allowed to leave Marshall that would suggest that Marshall was not doing its job. . . ."[47]

The impact of the bureaucratic accountability system is also evident in testimony about discussions between NASA representatives and Thiokol engineers on the night before the Challenger launch. During an "off-line" caucus between Morton Thiokol management and their engineers (while NASA prelaunch review officials were "on hold"), a member of management asked one of his colleagues

> *to take off his engineering hat and put on his management hat.* From that point on, management formulated the points to base their decision on. There

was never one comment in favor . . . of launching by any engineer or other nonmanagement person in the room before or after the caucus. . . . [The engineers were] never asked nor polled, and it was clearly a management decision from that point. . . . This was a meeting where the determination was to launch, and it was up to [the Thiokol engineers] to prove beyond a shadow of a doubt [to Thiokol management and NASA] that it was not safe to do so. This is in total reverse to what the position usually is in a preflight conversation or a flight readiness review. It is usually exactly opposite that.[48] (emphasis added)

A final example of the bureaucratic accountability system's relevance to the failure of the Challenger focuses on an incident occurring in 1984. Problems with the O-rings were noticed and noted by Morton Thiokol engineers in February that year after the tenth Shuttle mission had been completed, and a report on the problem was ordered by the Office of the Associate Administrator for Space Flight before the launch of the eleventh flight in late March. A decision was made to launch the shuttle, but not before it was determined by the Associate Administrator, James Abrahamson, and NASA's Deputy Administrator, Hans Mark, that the O-ring problem had to be solved. A meeting to discuss the problem with relevant officials from the different NASA centers was called for May 30. It was a meeting that would have drawn attention to the technical factor that would later cause the shuttle tragedy; it was a meeting that never took place. By May 30, Abrahamson had left the agency to work on President Reagan's Strategic Defense Initiative, and Deputy Administrator Mark cancelled the meeting to visit Austin, Texas, where he was being considered for the position of University Chancellor. Abrahamson's successor, Jesse A. Moore, was never informed of the problem, and Mark's successor was not appointed for a full year. Thus, the O-ring problem was never communicated to the relevant experts for action. In Mark's words, it was "a classic example of having something fall between the 'cracks.'"[49] In our terms, it was another instance of bureaucratic accountability applied in inappropriate circumstances.

IV. A Post-Commission Era:
The New Institutional Pressures

Given the technical and managerial focus of the Rogers Commission Report and other investigations of the Challenger accident, it is not surprising that calls for changes in the space program tend to favor two objectives: punishing those in NASA who were to blame for the tragedy and instituting reforms that would guarantee that a similar event would not occur in the future. In both form and content, these efforts represented increased in-

stitutional pressures for NASA, pressures likely to lead the agency to develop new legal accountability mechanisms as well as increase its reliance
on bureaucratic accountability mechanisms.

The search for scapegoats and legal responsibility for the Challenger accident are unsavory but perhaps unavoidable by-products of the Rogers
Commission's focus on technical and managerial problems. If a technical
problem existed, why was it not discovered in time; and if it was discovered in time, why was it not taken seriously by those in charge?[50] These are
the questions which have led to personnel actions within NASA (and
Thiokol) ranging from reassignments and resignations to early retirements.
Beyond these actions, the families of most Challenger crew members either
filed lawsuits or accepted legal settlements from the government and its
subcontractors.[51]

On less personal levels, suggestions for reforms in the space agency have
proliferated. On the surface many of these seem to signal a return to professional accountability. Some recommendations call for improving the
role and voice of certain classes of individuals within NASA with special or
unique insight into the risks associated with space exploration. There is,
for example, a proposal for placing ex-astronauts in management positions
at NASA.[52] At first glance, this looks like an attempt to reinvigorate the
role of experts and professionals in the agency, but bringing former astronauts into NASA does not guarantee improvement in technical expertise
and actually looks more like a thinly veiled attempt to use highly visible
symbols of the space program to enhance the agency's damaged credibility.

Another proposal that at first seems to involve a return to professional
accountability calls for establishment of explicit guidelines and criteria for
use in making launch decisions. Supposedly these criteria would represent
the accumulated wisdom of many experts in the field, but they can just as
easily be regarded as another step away from deference to professional engineering judgments and toward imposing accountability that carries with
it threats of legal liability if such checklists are not properly followed.

Legal accountability mechanisms are also manifested in the emphases in
many other proposed reforms on establishing independent or external
oversight bodies capable of vetoing decisions by agency personnel regarding safety issues. For example, the Rogers Commission called for the creation of an independent Solid Rocket Motor design oversight committee to
review the rocket design and make recommendations to the Administrator
or NASA.[53] Similarly, the Commission called for creation of a separate Office of Safety, Reliability and Quality Assurance outside the normal lines of
the agency hierarchy to report directly to the NASA Administrator.[54] In
both instances, actors outside the normal lines of the agency hierarchy
would oversee key decision-making points within NASA dealing with the

design and launch of future manned space flights.[55] While these bodies are not intended to exercise direct control over the day-to-day operations of NASA's space shuttle program, such bodies would have jurisdiction over a wide range of agency actions.

It is also evident that congressional oversight of NASA activities is likely to focus a great deal more on details of technical and managerial matters than in the past.[56] In the past, Congress' role regarding NASA was that of patron rather than overseer. For the most part, congressional concerns about NASA were limited to the general priorities of the agency and its potential as a source of pork-barrel projects. In the near future, at least, members of relevant congressional committees and their staffs will become more involved in the details of NASA's operations.[57]

Other suggested reforms (some already being implemented) attempt internal changes in NASA that would complement this movement toward changing accountability. For example, recommendations for reorganizing the shuttle management structure include redefining the program manager's responsibilities to enhance that official's decision-making role. In addition, units within NASA are being reorganized to improve intraorganizational communications. Operationally, suggested reforms include a call for refinement of decision criteria used in equipment maintenance, landing safety, and launch abort procedures. These changes reinforce or legitimize the influence of bureaucratic structures within NASA by formalizing organizational relationships and operational procedures. In form and function, they attempt to move the bureaucratic structures of NASA closer to a centralized system more easily held legally accountable for the agency's future actions.

It was inevitable that the Challenger disaster would generate strong institutional pressures for NASA, and those pressures are creating new demands and expectations for the agency. Ironically, the direction of those pressures has been toward enhanced bureaucratic structures and growing reliance on legal accountability mechanisms which stress NASA's formal responsibilities for the safety of its astronauts. Since President Reagan ordered NASA to terminate its commercial operations temporarily, a major source of political pressure and support has been removed. Thus, we might expect a decline of political accountability in the space agency's operations. Nevertheless, political factors have not disappeared. At present, NASA lacks a clear sense of direction and faces programmatic competition from the military and commercial sectors. At the end of 1986, Dr. Fletcher's view was reported as follows: "the policy-making process is not so straightforward because there are 'so many players.'"[58] In addition, there is little likelihood that Challenger-related reforms will reflect the need for NASA to reestablish the priority of professional accountability systems which held sway in the agency during pre-Apollo 11 heydays.

V. Conclusion

The primary contention of this paper is that the Rogers Commission was shortsighted in focusing exclusively on the failure of NASA's technological or management systems. The problem was not necessarily in the *failure* of those systems, but rather in the *inappropriateness* of the political and bureaucratic accountability mechanisms which characterized NASA's management approach in recent years. The agency's emphasis on political and bureaucratic accountability was a relevant response to changing institutional expectations in NASA's environment, but they were inappropriate for the technical tasks at hand. To the extent that these accountability mechanisms were ill-suited to the technical nature of NASA's agency task, they comprised a major factor in the Challenger tragedy.

In more prescriptive terms, if the professional accountability system had been given at least equal weight in the decision-making process, the decision to launch would probably not have been made on that cold January morning. Had NASA relied exclusively on a professional system of accountability in making the decision to launch the Challenger space shuttle, perhaps deference would have been given to the technical expertise of the engineers. Their recommendation against launch might never have been challenged by the Project Manager for the Solid Rocket Booster.[59] Instead, the Thiokol engineers' initial recommendation against launch was ignored by their hierarchical superiors. Decision makers relied upon supervisors to make the decision rather than deferring to professional experts.

Will the post-accident push for greater emphases on the legal and bureaucratic accountability systems improve NASA's ability to successfully pursue its mission? If this assessment of the role of institutional factors in the success and failure of NASA's programs is correct, then the proposals for reform increase the chances of other failures. This conclusion is consistent with the thesis that adding safety mechanisms to already complex systems in fact may increase the chances that something can go wrong.[60] As NASA gets drawn further away from what it can do best—namely, mobilizing the expert resources needed to solve the technical challenges of space exploration—its chances for organizational success are diluted. Ideally, NASA needs to return to what it does best, using the form of accountability that best suits its organizational mission, i.e., a professional accountability based on deference to expertise.[61] The reality of NASA's institutional context, however, makes achievement of this ideal highly improbable. NASA no longer enjoys a nurturing institutional context; instead it faces increased environmental pressures calling for the adoption of political, bureaucratic, and legal accountability mechanisms. Such is the dilemma facing NASA and the challenge confronting all American public administrators.

Notes

The authors gratefully acknowledge the helpful comments of Dwight Kiel, John Nalbandian, Laurence J. O'Toole, Jr., and anonymous referees.

1. *Report of the Presidential Commission on the Space Shuttle Challenger Accident* (Washington: June 6, 1986), p. 40; hereafter cited as *Rogers Commission Report*.

2. *Rogers Commission Report*, p. 82.

3. See James D. Thompson, *Organizations in Action: Social Science Bases of Administrative Theory* (New York: McGraw-Hill Book Co., 1967), pp. 10–11.

4. Thompson, *Organizations in Action*, p. 11.

5. Besides current astronaut Sally Ride and former astronaut Neil Armstrong, the commission membership included: Eugene Covert, an MIT professor and frequent consultant to NASA who received the agency's "Public Service Award" in 1980; Robert W. Rummel, an aerospace engineer and private consultant who was also a recipient of a NASA public service award; and Major General Donald J. Kutyna, director of the U.S. Air Force's Space Systems program and former manager of the Defense Department's space shuttle program.

6. For example, Commission Chair Rogers was Attorney General for President Eisenhower and Secretary of State for Richard Nixon. David C. Acheson, a well-known Washington lawyer, had previously served as a U.S. Attorney, counsel for the Atomic Energy Commission, and Senior Vice President of COMSAT. Other members of the Commission were: two physicists, Richard P. Feynman and Albert D. Wheelan (Executive Vice President, Hughes Aircraft); astronomer, Arthur B. C. Walker, Jr.; test pilot, Charles E. Yeager; aeronautical engineer, Joseph F. Sutter; and Robert B. Hotz, former editor of *Aviation Week and Space Technology Magazine*.

7. See Paul R. Schulman, *Large-Scale Policy Making* (New York: Elsevier North Holland, Inc., 1980), pp. 22–41; James E. Webb, *Space Age Management* (New York: McGraw-Hill Book Co., 1968); Leonard R. Sayles and Margaret K. Chandler, *Managing Large Systems* (New York: Harper and Row, 1971); and Peter F. Drucker, *Management: Tasks, Responsibilities, and Practices* (New York: Harper and Row, 1974), chapter 47.

8. See discussion in Herbert A. Simon, Donald W. Smithburg, and Victor A. Thompson, *Public Administration* (New York: Alfred A. Knopf, Inc., 1950), especially chapters 24 and 25. Also, Carl Joachim Friedrich, "Public Policy and the Nature of Administrative Responsibility," in C. J. Friedrich and Edward S. Mason, eds., *Public Policy, 1940* (Cambridge: Harvard University Press, 1940), pp. 3–24; and Herman Finer, "Administrative Responsibility and Democratic Government," *Public Administration Review*, vol. 1 (Summer 1941), pp. 335–350.

9. This view of accountability is developed more fully in Barbara Romzek and Mel Dubnick, "Accountability and the Management of Expectations: The Challenger Tragedy and the Costs of Democracy," presented at the annual meeting of the American Political Science Association, the Washington Hilton, August 28–31, 1986.

10. See Max Weber, *Economy and Society; An Outline of Interpretive Sociology*, edited by Guenther Roth and Claus Wittich (Berkeley: University of California Press, 1987), chapter XI.

11. See Alvin Gouldner, *Patterns of Industrial Bureaucracy* (New York: The Free Press, 1954), pp. 159–162.

12. Philosophically and ideologically, the basis of legal accountability is found in the "rule of law" concept; see Friedrich A. Hayek, *The Road to Serfdom* (Chicago: University of Chicago Press, 1944), chapter VI; also see Theodore J. Lowi's call for "juridical democracy" in *The End of Liberalism: The Second Republic of the United States,* 2d ed. (New York: W.W. Norton and Co., 1979), chapter 11.

13. For a comprehensive application of the theory of agency, see Barry M. Mitnick, *The Political Economy of Regulation: Creating, Designing, and Removing Regulatory Forms* (New York: Columbia University Press, 1980).

14. While bureaucratic accountability relies on methods available to members, such as close supervision and rules and regulations, legal accountability is limited to the tools available to outsiders, such as monitoring, investigating, auditing, and other forms of "oversight" and evaluation.

15. See Carl Joachim Friedrich, "Public Policy and the Nature of Administrative Responsibility."

16. For an example of a professional accountability system, see the story of the Manhattan Project offered in Peter Wyden, *Day One: Before Hiroshima and After* (New York: Warner Books, 1985), Book One.

17. See Emmette S. Redford, *Democracy in the Administrative State* (New York: Oxford University Press, 1969); also see works by Paul Appleby and Herman Finer.

18. See James Thompson, *Organizations in Action.*

19. See Robert C. Fried, *Performance in American Bureaucracy* (Boston: Little, Brown and Co., 1976).

20. It is possible (at least theoretically) for different accountability mechanisms to operate within one agency at different levels of the organization. For example, a professional accountability mechanism may be in operation at the technical level of an organization while a legal accountability mechanism may be used to manage external expectations at the institutional or boundary-spanning level. See Thompson, *Organizations in Action.* For an application of this notion in a related area, see Donald Klingner and John Nalbandian, "Values and Conflict in Public Personnel Administration," *Public Administration Quarterly* (forthcoming).

21. See Hans Mark and Arnold Levine, *The Management of Research Institutions: A Look at Government Laboratories* (Washington: National Aeronautics and Space Administration, 1984), pp. 117–118. On the political support for NASA in those early years, see Don K. Price, *The Scientific Estate* (Cambridge, MA: The Belknap Press, 1965), pp. 222–223. On the effects of its budgetary support through 1966, see Paul R. Schulman, *Large-Scale Policy Making* (New York: Elsevier North Holland, Inc., 1980), pp. 87–88.

22. Through the Apollo program, NASA spent over 80 percent of its funding on research and development (R&D) efforts. See Philip N. Whittaker, "Joint Decisions in Aerospace," in Matthew Tuite, Roger Chisolm, and Michael Radnor, eds., *Interorganizational Decision Making* (Chicago: Aldine Publishing Co., 1972), p. 272.

23. On the early history of NASA by an "insider," see John D. Young, "Organizing the Nation's Civilian Space Capabilities: Selected Reflections," in Theodore W. Taylor, ed., *Federal Public Policy: Personal Accounts of Ten Senior Civil Service Executives* (Mt. Airy, MD: Lomond Publications, Inc., 1984), pp. 45–80. Some analysts have defined that "nurturing consensus" as little more than a "political vac-

uum" in which the agency got to define its own programmatic objectives. See John Logsdon, *The Decision to Go to the Moon,* cited in Lambright, *Governing Science and Technology* (New York: Oxford University Press, 1976), pp. 41–42.

24. Henry S. F. Cooper, Jr., "Letter from the Space Center," in *The New Yorker* (November 10, 1986), p. 93.

25. Mark and Levine, *The Management of Research Institutions,* pp. 60, 200–202.

26. Schulman, *Large-Scale Policy Making,* pp. 62–74. Also Cooper, "Letter from the Space Center," p. 99.

27. Schulman, *Large-Scale Policy Making,* pp. 74–76; also Mark and Levine, *The Management of Research Institutions,* pp. 117–118.

28. Lambright, *Governing Science and Technology,* p. 43. Also see Wayne Biddle, "NASA: What's Needed To Put It On Its Feet?" *Discover,* vol. 8 (January 1987), pp. 36, 40.

29. It is incorrect to think that NASA was apolitical even during its early years. Tom Wolfe describes a heated argument between John Glenn and NASA Administrator James Webb when Glenn bitterly complained of the number of trips he had to take at the request of members of Congress or the White House. See Wolfe's *The Right Stuff* (New York: Bantam Books, 1979), p. 331. See also Mark and Levine, *The Management of Research Institutions,* p. 82, for a discussion of the importance of generating "new business" for the agency. The politics surrounding the shuttle are reflected in investigations of the role Fletcher played in awarding contracts for the shuttle project in 1973; see William J. Broad, "NASA Chief Might Not Take Part in Decisions on Booster Contracts," *The New York Times* (December 7, 1986), pp. 1, 14.

30. W. Henry Lambright, *Governing Science and Technology,* pp. 21–22; and U.S. Congress, House, Committee on Science and Technology, *Investigation of the Challenger Accident,* Report, 99th Congress, 2d Session (Washington: U.S. Government Printing Office, 1986), pp. 176–177.

31. John Noble Wilford, "NASA May Be a Victim of Defects in Its Own Bureaucracy," *The New York Times* (February 16, 1986), p. 18E.

32. See Cooper, "Letter from the Space Center," especially pp. 85–96.

33. See Mark and Levine, *The Management of Research Institutions,* pp. 122–123, on NASA contracting. NASA's use of "pork barrel" politics dates to the agency's earliest years; see Amitai Etzioni, *The Moon Doggle* (Garden City, NY: Doubleday and Co., 1964), and Price, *The Scientific Estate,* pp. 21–23. The continuation of political considerations in NASA's contracting practices during the 1970s is demonstrated by the circumstances surrounding the competition for the shuttle's booster rocket contract which was eventually awarded to Thiokol in 1973; see Broad, "NASA Chief May Not Take Part in Decisions on Booster Contracts."

34. *Rogers Commission Report,* p. 176.

35. *Rogers Commission Report,* pp. 176, 201. Also Cooper, "Letter from the Space Center," pp. 99–100, and U.S. Congress, House, *Investigation of the Challenger Accident,* pp. 119–120.

36. William J. Broad, "NASA Aide Assails Panel Investigating Explosion of Shuttle," *The New York Times* (March 16, 1986), p. 23.

37. U.S. Congress, House, *Investigation of the Challenger Accident,* p. 120.

38. U.S. Congress, House, *Investigation of the Challenger Accident*, p. 122. Richard P. Feynman, a member of the Rogers Commission, speculated about agency attitudes regarding safety. He believed the agency might have downplayed the riskiness of the shuttle launching to "assure" Congress of the agency's "perfection and success in order to ensure the supply of funds." See David E. Sanger, "Looking Over NASA's Shoulder," *The New York Times* (September 28, 1986), p. 26E.

39. John Noble Wilford, "NASA Chief Vows to Fix Problems," *The New York Times* (June 10, 1986), p. 22.

40. *Rogers Commission Report*, pp. 153–154.

41. Laurie McGinley and Bryan Burrough, "Backbiting in NASA Worsens the Damage from Shuttle Disaster," *The Wall Street Journal* (April 2, 1986), p. 1.

42. See Victor A. Thompson, *Modern Organization*, 2d ed. (University: University of Alabama Press, 1977), chapter 8.

43. *Rogers Commission Report*, p. 82.

44. On the factors which make it difficult for employees to pass bad news to upper levels of the organization, see Chris Argyris and Donald A. Schon, *Organizational Learning: A Theory of Action Perspective* (Reading, MA: Addison-Wesley Publishing Co., 1978).

45. *Rogers Commission Report*, p. 82.

46. Testimony of Lawrence Mulloy, *Rogers Commission Report*, p. 98.

47. Cooper, "Letter from the Space Center," pp. 89, 96.

48. Testimony of Roger Boisjoly, *Rogers Commission Report*, p. 93. Also see testimony of R. K. Lund, *Rogers Commission Report*, p. 94.

49. David E. Sanger, "Top NASA Aides Knew of Shuttle Flaw in '84," *The New York Times* (December 21, 1986), pp. 1, 2.

50. See William J. Broad, "NASA Had Solution to Key Flaw in Rocket When Shuttle Exploded," *The New York Times* (September 22, 1986), p. 1; and David E. Sanger, "NASA Pressing Shuttle Change Amid Concerns: Fear of Short-Circuiting Safety Search Raised," *The New York Times* (September 23, 1986), p. 1.

51. In July 1986, the family of shuttle pilot Michael Smith filed a "wrongful death" suit against NASA and some of its top managers. Later settlements with other families were announced. See William J. Broad, "4 Families Settle Shuttle Claims," *The New York Times* (December 30, 1986), p. 1.

52. *Rogers Commission Report*, pp. 199–201.

53. *Rogers Commission Report*, p. 198.

54. *Rogers Commission Report*, p. 199.

55. *Rogers Commission Report*, pp. 198–199.

56. Members of Congress criticized the Commission for not going deeply enough into the question of which individuals bore direct responsibility for the accident. See Philip M. Boffey, "Shuttle Panel is Faulted for Not Naming Names," *The New York Times* (June 11, 1986), p. 16.

57. Philip M. Boffey, "NASA Challenged on Modification That Rockets Met Requirements," *The New York Times* (June 12, 1986), p. 18.

58. John Noble Wilford, "Threat to Nation's Lead in Space is Seen in Lack of Guiding Policy," *The New York Times* (December 30, 1986), p. 18.

59. *Rogers Commission Report*, p. 96.

60. See Charles Perrow, *Normal Accidents: Living With High Risk Technologies* (New York: Basic Books, Inc., 1984).

61. Our suggestion that a professional system of accountability is the most appropriate to NASA should not be construed as an endorsement of professional accountability under all circumstances. Rather, our point is to indicate that the type of accountability system needs to suit the agency task.

11

RESPONSIVENESS AND NEUTRAL COMPETENCE IN AMERICAN BUREAUCRACY

Francis E. Rourke

In American politics today, an air of uncertainty surrounds a question that once seemed to have a simple answer. Is there a fundamental element that government bureaucrats bring to the process through which public policy is made in the United States that it would otherwise lack and, even more important, that it cannot do without?

Earlier in this century, the answer to this question seemed clear. Leading figures in the Progressive movement agreed that the distinctive contribution of administrators to national policy making was what Herbert Kaufman (1956) later described as "neutral competence"—a wealth of knowledge and skills available in the corridors of bureaucracy that all elected officials, no matter what their political persuasion, could call upon for both useful information and disinterested advice in designing national policy.

However, recent years have seen a growing inclination to question whether the term neutral competence any longer describes either the role that administrators now play in national policy making or the principal

Source: *Public Administration Review* 52(1992): 539–546.

ideal around which that role should be organized. This declining faith in the neutral competence of civil servants threatens to undermine the legitimacy of bureaucratic participation in national policy making, because the courts have always regarded the professional expertise of bureaucrats as the chief justification that can be given in a democracy for allowing such unelected officials to have a major hand in shaping the country's policy decisions (Freedman, 1978).[1]

Symptomatic of this decline is the current tendency of both the White House and Congress to look upon the bureaucrats working for the national government as being far from neutral in their policy perspective. Much more common in these quarters is the view that bureaucrats are so strongly committed to the programs their agencies administer—or to the career opportunities these programs afford—that they are unable or unwilling to carry out alternative policies that the public might prefer and from which, legislators and White House officials often believe, the American people might derive much greater benefit.

In contemporary American politics, bureaucrats are thus suspected of being biased rather than neutral in their policy perspectives or even of trying to sabotage policy proposals that political leaders want to put into effect. Fear of such sabotage haunted the presidency of Richard M. Nixon, but it has surfaced and has been a source of concern during the tenure of other modern presidents as well.

It is not only the neutrality of bureaucrats that has been increasingly questioned in modern American politics. Also under much more skeptical scrutiny in recent decades has been the assumption that administrative agencies bring any kind of unique or irreplaceable competence to policy discussions within either the legislative or executive branches. This skepticism is reflected in the tendency of national policy makers to turn increasingly to private organizations and groups for technical assistance in designing government programs (Rourke and Schulman, 1989).

In fact, expertise on public policy issues is now commonly seen as flourishing as abundantly in the outside world as it does within government itself. From this perspective, policy expertise has, to a large extent, been "privatized" in modern American politics, especially in vital areas of economic policy and foreign affairs. Former government officials, working in universities, think tanks, or private consulting firms, may now have more opportunity to influence policy development within executive agencies than they once did when they were civil servants.

Moreover, both Congress and the President have greatly expanded their in-house expertise in dealing with policy issues during recent decades, mainly by strengthening their own staff resources. As a result, career officials in the national bureaucracy may find their suggestions drowned out in the general din of expert opinion from all sources that now engulfs virtually every policy debate in contemporary American politics. The neutral competence that once seemed to provide administrative agencies with a distinctive capacity to illuminate the dark corners of policy issues now competes with a "thousand points" of expert light generated in all sectors of American government and society.

How does one explain this growing reluctance to rely upon the expertise of executive bureaucrats in molding national policy—a reliance that is taken for granted in other highly industrialized countries? A close examination of the attitudes toward such expertise that now prevail in the White House and Congress may help yield an answer. The American Constitution never empowered bureaucrats to play a role in the policy process. Bureaucratic involvement in policy making has hinged instead on the willingness of presidents and legislators to draw upon the resources of executive agencies in shaping and carrying out the policy decisions that these officials alone have the constitutional authority to make. When calls for such assistance cease to come from the White House and Congress, bureaucratic influence over policy making is sharply diminished.

Presidential Distrust of Bureaucracy

Presidents have had more than a half-century of interaction with a highly developed administrative apparatus in the national government. Throughout this period, the White House has had recurring difficulty with the notion that the bureaucracy they inherit from their predecessors can be relied upon to provide a reservoir of neutral competence on which they can confidently draw for expertise on policy issues. Such lack of trust in civil servants has been particularly evident when presidents come to office after their political party has endured a long period of lonely and fretful exile from the White House, or when they themselves project a radically new vision of national policy.

Consider, for example, the case of Franklin D. Roosevelt, when he was first elected to the presidency in 1933. A Democrat following in the wake of three Republican presidents, FDR had little reason to trust the neutral competence of the permanent bureaucracy he confronted. For one thing, he knew that, prior to leaving office, his predecessors in the White House had granted many of their own political appointees the tenured status normally reserved for the civil servants recruited on the basis of merit. When the bureaucracy that a President inherits falls short in this way of being a true meritocracy, it loses much of its credibility as a source of neutral competence.

Even if American bureaucrats could lay a legitimate claim to such unbiased expertise, this fact by itself would only seem to provide the White House with the prospect of passive compliance with presidential goals by civil servants throughout the far-flung executive establishment. If new presidents like Roosevelt are contemplating landmark changes in national policy, what they are hoping for is passionate commitment rather than passive neutrality on the part of the bureaucrats on whom they must depend to give life to their bold new policy agenda. Roosevelt's widely celebrated strategy for ensuring such energetic support in the executive bureaucracy was the creation of new organizations to administer New Deal programs, rather than reliance upon the suspect agencies established by his predecessors.

Thus, presidents who regard themselves as trail-blazing innovators (and no self-respecting White House is likely to see itself in any other way today) may look upon neutral competence as having about it an aura of passivity, whereas the hallmark of an administration with path-breaking policy goals is activism. Even a bureaucracy with genuine neutral competence as its outstanding characteristic may thus have little attraction for a White House committed to making dramatic breakthroughs in policy—no more appealing perhaps than a bureaucracy that is perceived to have a deep-seated bias against the President's programs.

When Dwight D. Eisenhower took over the presidency in 1953 as the first Republican in the White House after 20 years of Democratic ascendancy, his administration, like Roosevelt's before him, worried less about the quality of bureaucratic expertise than it did over the possibility that partisans from the other political party had infiltrated the ranks of the executive bureaucracy. In at least its first years in office, the Eisenhower White House suspected that high-level civil servants were primarily loyal to the "free-spending" New Deal and Fair Deal programs they were already administering rather than the more parsimonious objectives of the new chief executive.

This suspicion led Eisenhower to launch the effort presidents have been making ever since to use their appointing power to install political loyalists as far down into the ranks of bureaucracy as they could reach. Eisenhower's own contribution to this effort was the creation of the now familiar category of Schedule C positions within the civil service—a category embracing both middle-level policy making and politically sensitive roles within the bureaucratic establishment. As a result of the changes he initiated, presidents now have the luxury of taking political allegiance into account in making appointments to many more executive posts.

However, Eisenhower's efforts to make the bureaucracy more responsive to the White House were considerably less valuable to him than they eventually proved to be for his successors. Because he was not himself bent on making radical departures in national policy, passive immobility on the part of the bureaucracy was not a great source of frustration for Eisenhower. On the contrary, he had been long schooled in the routines of the military establishment, and he appreciated the valuable role that a formal and deliberate executive process could play in preventing error in government decision making. As Walter Williams describes him (1990, p. 112), "more than any other president, he understood large-scale organizations and the critical place of orderly procedures and high staff morale."

In recent years, revisionist scholars, most notably Fred I. Greenstein (1982), have been highly successful in showing that Eisenhower was far more active in his conduct of the presidency than his contemporaries were inclined to believe. However, in the view of his immediate successors, John F. Kennedy and Lyndon B. Johnson, the Eisenhower presidency was a time of policy stagnation from which they proposed to rescue the nation by, in Kennedy's oft-quoted words, "getting the country moving again." Once again, perceptions may have been more important than reality in shaping the course of political history. Kennedy and Johnson saw Eisenhower's tenure in office as a time of presidential passivity, and their activism took much of its impetus from this perception, however mistaken their view may have been in the eyes of contemporary revisionists.

In any case, as was true of Roosevelt before them, the activism of these latter-day Democratic presidents largely shaped their views of the administrative apparatus. It led them to see a bureaucracy wedded to neutral competence as more of a hindrance than a help to a White House bent on rejuvenating American society. Instead, both Kennedy and Johnson turned to experts from outside the government and from their own White House staff to work on task forces set up to blaze new trails in national policy.

Moreover, some of the major domestic policy initiatives of these presidents, such as the War on Poverty, were handed over to the states and localities to carry out. The national agencies involved in this program were given the task of parceling out the financial resources needed by the state and local organizations—private as well as public—that would actually carry on the specific activities associated with the poverty program. The neutral competence of the national bureaucracy was thus relegated to a secondary role in the execution as well as the design of War on Poverty programs.

It should be noted that a reluctance to rely upon the bureaucracy's neutral competence has had somewhat different roots in Republican and Democratic presidencies. The concern of Republican presidents has usually focused on what they regard as the questionable neutrality of bureaucrats. They are inclined to suspect that civil servants in Washington have hidden Democratic loyalties or liberal policy leanings that will make it difficult for them to carry out the policies of conservative Republican presidents.

Political disloyalty on the part of bureaucracy since the days of Franklin Roosevelt has not been of equal concern to Democratic presidents. They have worried instead about bureaucratic passivity—the apparent inability of career officials to bring sufficient enthusiasm and energy to the task of carrying out the innovative government programs that a new chief executive intends to put in place. At the root of this Democratic concern is the fear that such path-breaking programs will not be vigorously pursued if they threaten the interests of either the established bureaucracies charged with their administration or the outside groups to which these agencies commonly defer.

In short, Republican presidents in recent decades have tended to see bureaucracy as being in the camp of their political enemies, as being perhaps Democrats in disguise—or worse, closet liberals. Democratic presidents, on the other hand, have been inclined to view bureaucrats as having an agenda of their own, which they pursue no matter who occupies the White House. Although the views of the two major political parties may diverge in this way, neither attitude creates a promising atmosphere for bureaucrats looking for opportunities to play a significant role in shaping national policy.

This is true at least as long as neutral competence is the chief credential bureaucrats can offer for entry into the policy making game. It has, of course, always been possible for civil servants to become key players in the policy process by demonstrating a strong sympathy with the political goals of the administration in power, or at least a willingness to accommodate to its objectives. The metamorphosis of executive officials from career to political status is a familiar Washington phenomenon in all political seasons.

The arrival of Richard Nixon in the White House in 1969 ushered in a new era in the relationship between the President and the bureaucracy. Until then, the White House had generally followed what can be described as a defensive strategy in dealing with the so-called permanent government. It had concentrated on protecting itself against the possibility of being taken in by incomplete information or misleading advice from the bureaucratic sector of the executive branch. Pursuit of this strategy brought about a steady expansion of both the White House staff and the Executive Office of the President in the decades following World War II.

Just as his predecessors, Richard Nixon strongly distrusted the bureaucracy, and certainly no president worked harder at developing White House organizations that might forestall bureaucratic efforts to influence administration policies. Nixon also saw something that his predecessors had not. He saw the discretionary power vested in the bureaucracy by the statutes they administered as representing an opportunity as well as a problem for a new president. If the exercise of this discretion could be controlled by the White House, it could be used to advance presidential rather than congressional objectives in the everyday administration of the laws that executive agencies were charged with enforcing.

All that this strategy appeared to require for its success was a significant expansion in the number of appointees at the top echelons of the bureaucracy who would be highly responsive to presidential goals in administering the statutes over which Congress had given them authority. Thus was born what Richard Nathan (1975) was eventually to call the administrative presidency. Under this new regime, responsiveness rather than neutral competence would be the star that would guide administrative behavior. The President had earned the right to govern through an election in which every qualified American citizen had an opportunity to participate. In being responsive to the President and to his political appointees, the bureaucracy would be acting in accord with the basic imperatives of a democratic society, since a presidential election was the chief occasion on which the national electorate had a chance to speak in American democracy. Any bureaucratic failure to carry out White House directives could thus be interpreted as an effort to sabotage the democratic order itself.

This new regime of responsiveness traveled a somewhat rocky path during the Nixon presidency. It sometimes confronted administrators with the unpleasant task of choosing between obeying the President and obeying the law they were supposed to be administering—a dilemma from which only the courts could rescue them. It can be argued that Nixon's use of this strategy was forced upon him by the emergence of "divided government" as a fundamental aspect of American political life in the late 1960s, with Republicans almost completely monopolizing the presidency, while the Democrats maintained an equally firm grip on the House of Representatives, and, for much of the time, the Senate (Mayhew, 1991).

Certainly it is true that when they took office, Nixon and his entourage saw themselves as being confronted by a triad of hostile forces in Congress, the media, and the bureaucracy. They could not capture or control either Congress or the media, though they tried mightily—and often successfully—to neutralize the power of these adversaries. It was the bureaucracy alone that was open to real conquest from the perspective of the Nixon White House. If the strategic heights in the executive structure could be seized and held by presidential appointees who looked to the Oval Office for their policy orientation, then the administration could go a long way toward achieving its programmatic goals, no matter how much hostility it might encounter elsewhere in the political system.

So it is possible that Nixon's use of the administrative presidency was the product of political necessity, and that it was divided government alone that gave rise to a preoccupation with responsiveness on the part of both the White House and Congress. Whether Nixon's hand was forced in this way is arguable, however. A study of bureaucratic attitudes during his administration suggests that career civil servants were far less hostile to the goals of the White House than the Nixon entourage expected (Cole and Caputo, 1979). Moreover, Nixon's distrust of government bureaucrats had been evident long before he arrived in the White House, so reliance upon the neutral competence of administrative officials might not have been in the cards during his presidency even if the Republican party had controlled Congress as well as the White House.

The regime of responsiveness fell more or less into abeyance during the Ford and Carter years. It got a new lease on life with the arrival of Ronald Reagan in the White House in the 1980s. Reagan is widely credited with having been the most successful of all modern presidents in his efforts to place like-minded partisans in high executive posts during his tenure in office and with being able as a result to put together an executive apparatus highly sensitive to directions from the White House on policy issues.

However, in the Reagan as in the Nixon years, the regime of responsiveness initiated by the administrative presidency had its ups and downs. Even true-blue and highly responsive Reaganite appointees could not always help the President achieve his goals when they ran up against the tenacious policy networks that sustain agencies such as the Social Security Administration and the Environmental Protection Agency. Eventually, Reagan found himself using his appointing power at agencies of this sort not to ensure their responsiveness to the White House but to reassure outside groups that his administration was sensitive to their needs and concerns (Rourke, 1990).

What modern political history thus suggests is that the ideal of neutral competence has been least attractive for American presidents during periods of political transition. Such a transition may only take the form of a shift from one political party to another, as was true when both Eisenhower and Nixon were first elected president, or it may also represent a fundamental change in the political climate of the country, as was the case when Roosevelt and Reagan took office.

Neutral competence has been most acceptable as an administrative ideal in the case of presidents with more modest images of themselves as agents of change. Moreover, even in the case of those presidents who see themselves as the authors of great transformations in American public policy, neutral competence may resurface as a viable ideal after such presidents are elected to a second term, when revolutionary ardor has spent itself, and the White House has become preoccupied with keeping the new governmental apparatus spawned by its vision of a brave new world from breaking down (Grossman, *et al.* 1990).

Congress and Neutral Competence

Of the three major institutions of national governance, Congress has always been the most reluctant to accept the claim that executive bureaucrats do indeed have neutral competence as their stock in trade. For one thing, bureaucrats are officials in the executive branch, subordinate to the

President, and legislators in both political parties have a natural inclination to suspect that, rather than being neutral, such administrative experts will tailor their findings and recommendations to suit the political needs of the White House.

Moreover, Congress differs from both the President and the Supreme Court in one salient respect. It derives no strong institutional advantage from accepting the claim that administrative agencies are repositories of neutral competence. Quite the contrary, the institutional rivalry between the President and Congress that is so salient a feature of the American constitutional process has long made it difficult for legislators to defer to executive agency bureaucrats merely because they are supposed to have some special kind of knowledge or skill at their disposal.

In point of fact, institutional incentives push the other way, tempting members of Congress to question whether executive officials can be relied upon to give dispassionate advice on policy issues or to be faithful to the intent of Congress rather than their own preferences in carrying out the legislation that lawmakers enact. Legislators inclined to this skeptical view of the bureaucrats who come before them to testify are unlikely to be overawed by any expertise such officials are alleged to command.

In the White House, on the other hand, the credibility of bureaucrats as neutral experts has frequently been a valuable resource in the policy debates that characterize relations between the President and the national legislature. In foreign affairs, for example, the unique and often secret knowledge of national security agencies gives the President a weapon of great strategic utility in disputes over policy issues with Congress, and from Roosevelt to Bush, Presidents have used this weapon with great success in rallying public support during conflicts with their legislative critics over how to deal with international crises.

The Supreme Court has also had a strong incentive to go along with the assumption that administration is a province of neutral expertise. In the past, this assumption has enabled the Court to defer to the neutral competence of administrative agencies, thus limiting its agenda and simplifying the task it confronts in the modern administrative state of reviewing and passing judgment on innumerable decisions by countless administrators in a wide variety of policy fields. From an institutional perspective at least, the justices have thus had one very practical reason for believing in the neutral competence of administrators—the plain and simple fact that it makes feasible a task that might otherwise be unmanageable.

Over the years, a number of political factors have reinforced the legislature's unwillingness to view the executive bureaucracy as a source of neutral competence. When the modern administrative state first saw the light of day in the 1930s, Congress was controlled by a conservative coalition of Southern Democrats and Northern Republicans. This coalition was strongly opposed to the expanding network of executive agencies created to carry out the liberal agenda of Franklin Roosevelt's New Deal. Consequently, the national legislature at that time was not an environment in which the notion that executive bureaucrats had a special claim to neutral competence could find ready acceptance.

In more recent years, the political tide has turned, as liberal Democrats have become dominant in Congress, while conservative Republicans remain ascendant in the executive branch. Nevertheless, Congress today, or at least the Democratic majority in the national legislature, is no less suspicious of the neutral competence of bureaucrats serving in an executive branch under control of the opposition than were conservative legislators in the 1930s.

This suspicion has opened the door in contemporary politics to what critics often describe as legislative "micromanagement"—an effort on the part of a Congress to monitor executive decision making in areas that the White House regards as lying within its own domain (Fisher, 1991). It has also led Congress to broaden opportunities for ordinary citizens to challenge and for judges to review these administrative decisions.

Perhaps the most important factor contributing to a decline in Congressional deference to executive expertise is the development alluded to earlier: the emergence of a formidable legislative staff system to which members of Congress can turn for information and advice on policy issues. This staff has grown at a much faster pace in the past few years than the executive bureaucracy itself. As Michael Mezey (1989) has noted, "Between 1970 and 1986, the size of committee and subcommittee staff increased by 250 percent, the personal staff of legislators increased by 60 percent, and the staff of support agencies such as the Congressional Research Service, the Government Accounting Office, and the Office of Technology Assessment doubled." (p. 133).

Responsiveness and Competence in American Bureaucracy

The wide-ranging efforts of both the White House and Congress to increase their control over bureaucracy in recent years clearly indicate that the administrative state has come of age in present-day American society. The obsession of political leaders in each of these institutions with the responsiveness of bureaucracy to their policy goals pays unmistakable homage to the fact that governmental power increasingly asserts itself today through the decisions and actions of civil servants. This is as true in a country like the United States characterized by a highly democratic political culture as it has long been in autocratic states in which bureaucratic hierarchies play a dominant role.

Moreover, the current struggle to increase the responsiveness of bureaucrats in the United States to the cues and directions they receive from elected officials is analogous to the earlier efforts made in this country to ensure the continued health of American democracy by expanding the franchise or by amending the Constitution to permit voters to become directly involved in the election of the President and U.S. Senators. It clearly indicates that, in the day of the administrative state, controlling the bureaucracy has become one of the highest imperatives of democratic politics.

Because the presidential office is widely regarded as the instrument through which the democratic impulse in the United States finds its clearest and most legitimate expression, it should not be surprising that the call for greater bureaucratic responsiveness has been heard most loudly and clearly at the White House. Or that, during the battles that have periodically erupted over the attempts of presidents to extend their control over bureaucracy, the White House has been able at various times to draw strong support for its position from virtually every sector of the political spectrum.

This support came mainly from the Left in the 1930s and the 1940s, when the presidents seeking to secure or maintain this hegemonial position were Franklin D. Roosevelt and Harry S. Truman. Since the 1970s and the 1980s, when conservative presidents like Richard Nixon and Ronald Reagan have been trying to rule the bureaucratic roost, new and fervent support for presidential control over bureaucratic decision making has come to the fore on the Right. Even while commanding such broad public support for their position of executive leadership, presidents have encountered real difficulty in trying to translate into administrative practice this theoretical authority over the executive branch that they have been able to win on the political battlefield.

This difficulty stems in large part from the fact that pluralism always seems to find a way of reasserting itself in American politics no matter how much effort is made to suppress it. Despite the valiant attempts of reorganization commissions to increase their power over the executive branch (Arnold, 1986), presidents cannot single-handedly work their will on a vast and complex national bureaucracy. They "need help," in the immortal words of the Brownlow Commission, and so they inevitably turn to a growing number of presidential appointees to assist them in imposing their policy choices on the bureaucracy.

In this fashion presidents have created a new ruling class of presidential surrogates in American politics, who are expected to act and speak on behalf of the White House throughout the length and breadth of the executive branch. All presidents soon discover that these surrogates have minds of their own, and they cannot always be relied upon to remain mere envoys of the White House once they have tasted the pleasures of power themselves in positions of executive authority. Indeed many presidential appointees have been able to build a commanding position for themselves within the executive establishment on the strength of their ability to get along well with Congress rather than the White House.

The hard fact that presidents must also confront is that dutiful responsiveness to administration goals may not actually be the greatest service that appointees in executive agencies can render the White House. Although most presidential aides would like to see all agency appointees demonstrate such blind loyalty to their chief executive, the ultimate success of any administration may depend less on the unswerving allegiance of its appointees to the President than it does on their skill and dexterity in being responsive not only to Congress but also to the configuration of groups that their agency serves.

Indeed, past history would suggest that many of the executive appointees who brought the greatest credit to the administration in which they served were mavericks, individuals who marched to an altogether different tune from the one being played at the White House. So legitimate questions can be raised about the real value of the dutiful responsiveness that recent presidents have tried so ardently to win from both their executive appointees and the agencies for whose policies these presidential surrogates have been given responsibility.

The truth of the matter is that consensus within the executive branch may not always be the highest good as far as presidents are concerned. If it shifts the focus of its concern from the need to maintain an executive consensus in support of presidential decisions to the vigor and vitality of the deliberative process preceding such decisions, the White House will soon discover the real value of neutral competence within the bureaucracy. Not least of all, such independent expertise ensures that an administration's decisions are subject to informed criticism that will help anticipate and avert problems that may arise when the decisions are put into effect.

However, as American bureaucracy has evolved in the twilight of the twentieth century, the need for political responsiveness in executive policy making has been increasingly upgraded, while the value of dispassionate neutral competence in the decision making process has just as steadily receded in importance. Witness, for example, the controversy that arose in 1991 over the nomination of Robert B. Gates to be Director of the Central Intelligence Agency (CIA).

A number of former CIA officials testified that Gates, while serving in senior positions at the agency during the Reagan years, made frequent efforts to bring intelligence findings into line with the needs and goals of White House policy makers. Gates was charged with having "actively suppressed dissent, slanted intelligence conclusions, and intimidated analysts who disagreed with his views in his years as a senior intelligence official" (Sciolino, 1991a). It was alleged that subordinate officials were obliged to "cook" data gathered by the agency so that it lent support to administration policies.

Whether or not these charges represented a fair appraisal of Gates's performance as a CIA official, they do point up the perception that exists within the intelligence community of the ideal role that intelligence analysts should play in the policy process—a role that closely conforms to the traditional administrative ideal of neutral competence. This role obligates such officials to present dispassionate analysis reflecting their honest judgment in communications with their political superiors, even if their reports challenge or even discredit the apparent policy commitments of the administration in power.

However, the final resolution of this dispute suggested that for the Senate as for the White House, it is responsiveness rather than neutral competence that is of paramount importance in the operation of American bureaucracy. In advocating confirmation of the Gates nomination before the Senate, Senator David Boren (D., OK), chair of the Senate Intelligence Committee, stressed the fact that Gates had always been highly responsive to Congress as a senior official at the CIA, and that this aspect of his past performance strongly argued for his confirmation. After much debate on this and other issues, the Senate eventually approved the Gates nomination by a wide margin, although Boren made at least a token gesture in behalf of the ideal of neutral competence by extracting a promise from Gates prior to his confirmation that he would not retaliate against past or present CIA officials who had testified against him during the Senate hearings (Sciolino, 1991b).

The acute form in which the conflict between political responsiveness and neutral competence took shape during the Gates affair reflects the extent to which the intelligence analyst's craft had been professionalized during the Cold War. It also exemplifies the way in which neutral competence tends over time to translate itself into professionalism in modern bureaucracy. The rise of such professionalism greatly enhances the strength of the claims that can be made for civil servants as a source of proven expertise in helping elected officials cope with policy issues.

The emergence of bureaucracy as the chief habitat of professionalism within modern government has another important effect. It strengthens the likelihood that any new demands for political responsiveness will produce conflict within executive agencies. In the case of intelligence analysts, the advent of professionalism brought with it a code of ethics, and a central principle of this code was the injunction that intelligence analyses should not be shaped by political pressure.

In the past, members of more traditional professions employed within the bureaucracy have also confronted demands for political responsiveness

that severely strained their professional conscience. This has been an en-
demic problem for scientists working for the federal government, but it is a
difficulty that other professionals employed in a bureaucratic setting have
had to face. Lawyers in the Justice Department, for example, have sometimes had to choose between their responsibility to serve the President and
their professional obligation to abide by the laws they have sworn to uphold, not least of all the Constitution of the United States.

In the 1970s, the Watergate affair put this dilemma squarely in the public eye, forcing the body politic to confront the fact that there are circumstances in which the bureaucracy cannot in good conscience always look
upon itself as merely an agent, serving the needs of a President who is its
principal.

A decade later, the same issue resurfaced during the Reagan era. Much
to the consternation of many lawyers in the Social Security Administration,
they were compelled to continue to enforce administration policies denying
benefits to disabled beneficiaries on grounds that the courts had repeatedly
found to be in violation of the law (Mezey, 1988). Attorneys in the Civil
Rights Division of the Justice Department found themselves faced with an
equally disquieting dilemma. When Reagan appointees at the agency began
to shift its policies to a more conservative direction, a goodly number of its
career lawyers "held strong convictions that many of the Reagan administration's civil rights policies were seriously misguided, detrimental to the
effective enforcement of civil rights, and in conflict with existing statute
and case law" (Golden, 1992, p. 38). As one such lawyer expressed her dissatisfaction, "[our] ultimate boss is not Reagan or Reynolds but the courts.
They set the law. That's why attorneys disagree. They take an oath to carry
out the law."

All these cases reflect and exemplify both the power and the vulnerabil-
ity of neutral competence in the policy-making process today. For a very
long time, as Brian Balogh (1991) has clearly shown, professional groups
in the United States resisted any involvement in government because of
their fear that it would compromise their professional autonomy. Recent
events suggest that these fears were well-grounded. The growing demand
for responsiveness in government policy making puts the survival of a professional outlook characterized by independence of judgment and indifference to political pressures increasingly at risk in the corridors of American
bureaucracy.

This is not to deny that professionalism poses problems of its own as far
as policy making in this country is concerned. Professional myopia can
sometimes be a serious obstacle to resolving policy questions. Lawyers in
the Office of Legal Counsel of the Justice Department have often advised
recent presidents to hold fast to the legal authority vested in them by the
Constitution during disputes with Congress over executive privilege and

the legislative veto, even when both the White House and congressional leaders were trying to find a compromise that would satisfy the legitimate claims of both sides. In these separation-of-powers controversies, a purely legalistic outlook embittered and prolonged disputes that were otherwise susceptible to a constructive political settlement (Strine, 1992).

Clearly, both responsiveness and professionalism will always remain highly ranked values in the design and operation of a democratic bureaucracy, and each requires constant nurturing. The American public has a strong and well-recognized interest in preserving the responsiveness of its bureaucracy to political control. The varied ways in which the United States has successfully pursued this goal are envied in many parts of the world today, where bureaucracies are commonly seen as being remote organizations wholly indifferent to the needs and concerns of the people dependent upon them.

The American public also has a vital stake in the contribution that neutral competence can make to the policy-making process, especially when such competence matures into more advanced forms of professionalism. For politics only gives government its direction in a democratic order. It is commonly left to highly trained officials within the bureaucracy to provide the knowledge and skill that will enable government policy to arrive safely at its destination. These assets of career administrators have taken on increased importance in an era of divided government, when conflicting directives from Congress and the White House must often be compromised and integrated into effective national policies (Rosenbloom, 1983).

Note

Research on which this article draws was supported by a grant from the Russell Sage Foundation for which the author would like to express his gratitude.

1. Professionalism has attracted a great deal more attention in the modern literature of public administration than neutral competence per se. See, for example, the leading study by Mosher (1982) and more recent work by Young (1985); Ingraham (1987); Kearney and Sinha (1988); Hodges and Durant (1989); Cigler, (1990); and Daniel and Rose (1991).

References

Arnold, Peri E., 1986. *Making the Managerial Presidency: Comprehensive Reorganization Planning, 1905–1980.* Princeton: Princeton University Press.
Balogh, Brian, 1991. "Reorganizing the Organizational Synthesis: Federal-Professional Relations in Modern America." *Studies in American Political Development,* vol. 5 (Spring), pp. 119–172.

Cigler, Beverly A., 1990. "Public Administration and the Paradox of Professional-ization." *Public Administration Review,* vol. 50 (November/December), pp. 637–653.

Cole, Richard L. and David A. Caputo, 1979. "Presidential Control of the Senior Civil Service: Assessing the Strategies of the Nixon Years." *American Political Science Review,* vol. 73 (June), pp. 399–413.

Daniel, Christopher and Bruce J. Rose, 1991. "Blending Professionalism and Polit-ical Acuity: Empirical Support for an Emerging Ideal." *Public Administration Review,* vol. 51 (September/October), pp. 438–441.

Fisher, Louis, 1991. "Congress as Micromanager of the Executive Branch." In James P. Pfiffner, ed., *The Managerial Presidency.* Pacific Grove, CA: Brooks/Cole Publishing Company, pp. 225–237.

Freedman, James O., 1978. *Crisis and Legitimacy.* Cambridge, Eng.: Cambridge University Press.

Golden, Marissa M., 1992. "Exit, Voice, Loyalty, and Neglect: Bureaucratic Re-sponses to Presidential Control During the Reagan Administration." *Journal of Public Administration Research and Theory,* vol. 2 (January, 1992), pp. 29–62.

Greenstein, Fred I., 1982. *The Hidden-Hand Presidency: Eisenhower as Leader.* New York: Basic Books.

Grossman, Michael B., Martha J. Kumar, and Francis E. Rourke, 1990. "Second-Term Presidencies: The Aging of Administrations." In Michael Nelson, ed., *The Presidency and the Political System,* 3d ed. Washington, DC: Congressional Quarterly Press, pp. 213–232.

Hodges, Donald G. and Robert Durant, 1989. "The Professional State Revisited: Twixt Scylla and Charybdis?" *Public Administration Review,* vol. 49 (September/October), pp. 474–485.

Ingraham, Patricia W., 1987. "Building Bridges or Burning Them? The President, the Appointees, and the Bureaucracy." *Public Administration Review,* vol. 47 (September/October), pp. 425–435.

Kaufman, Herbert, 1956. "Emerging Conflicts in the Doctrines of Public Adminis-tration." *American Political Science Review,* vol. 50 (December), pp. 1057–1073.

Kearney, Richard C. and Chandan Sinha, 1988. "Professionalism and Bureaucratic Responsiveness: Conflict or Compatibility?" *Public Administration Review,* vol. 48 (January/February), pp. 571–579.

Mayhew, David R., 1991. *Divided We Govern: Party Control, Lawmaking, and Investigations, 1946–1990.* New Haven: Yale University Press.

Mezey, Michael L., 1989. *Congress, the President, and Public Policy.* Boulder, CO: Westview Press.

Mezey, Susan Gluck., 1988. *No Longer Disabled: The Federal Courts and the Poli-tics of Social Security Disability.* New York: Greenwood Press.

Mosher, Frederick, 1982. *Democracy and the Public Service.* New York: Oxford University Press.

Nathan, Richard P., 1975. *The Plot That Failed: Nixon and the Administrative Presidency.* New York: John Wiley and Sons.

Rosenbloom, David H., 1983. "Public Administrative Theory and the Separation of Powers." *Public Administration Review,* vol. 43 (May/June), pp. 219–227.

Rourke, Francis E., 1990. "Executive Responsiveness to Presidential Policies: The Reagan Presidency." *Congress and the Presidency,* vol. 17 (Spring), pp. 1–11.

Rourke, Francis E. and Paul R. Schulman, 1989. "Adhocracy in Policy Development." *The Social Science Journal,* vol. 26, no. 2, pp. 131–142.

Sciolino, Elaine, 1991a. "Ex-C.I.A. Official Is Said to Testify Gates Cut Dissent." *New York Times* (September 26), pp. A1, A24.

———, 1991b. "Gates Takes Over C.I.A., Challenged to Lift Its Anxious Mood." *New York Times* (November 12), p. A 20.

Strine, J. Michael, 1992. "Principle and Politics: The Office of Legal Counsel and Executive Branch Legal Interpretation." Unpublished Ph.D. dissertation, Johns Hopkins University.

Williams, Walter, 1990. *Mismanaging America: The Rise of the Anti-Analytic Presidency.* Lawrence, Kansas: University Press of Kansas.

Young, John D., 1985. "Institutional Expressions of the Separation of Executive-Legislative Powers." *Public Administration Review,* vol. 45 (May/June), pp. 431–432.

12

THE LISTENING BUREAUCRAT: RESPONSIVENESS IN PUBLIC ADMINISTRATION

Camilla Stivers

Vision is a spectator; hearing is a participation.
(John Dewey in Levin, 1989, p. 29)

In public administration, "responsiveness" is a problematic concept. Democracy would seem to require administrators who are responsive to the popular will, at least through legislatures and elected chief executives if not directly to the people. Yet administrators and scholars alike tend to treat responsiveness as at best a necessary evil that appears to compromise professional effectiveness, and at worst an indication of political expediency if not outright corruption. Rourke's recent assessment is illustrative:

> The growing demand for responsiveness in government policy-making puts the survival of a professional outlook characterized by independence of judgment and indifference to political pressures increasingly at risk in the corridors of American bureaucracy (1992, p. 545).

Source: *Public Administration Review* 54(1994):364–369.

The most common strategy for dealing with the idea of responsiveness is to treat it as an aspect of responsibility. This approach was evident as early as Woodrow Wilson's "The Study of Administration," which advocated "ready docility" on the part of administrators to "all serious, well-sustained public criticism" (1887, p. 222), but argued that, in order to be expert and efficient rather than partisan, the administrator should have a "will of his own in the choice of means for accomplishing his work. He is not and ought not to be a mere passive instrument" (p. 212). Although literal responsiveness was problematic, bureaucrats could be *considered* responsive because in choosing business-like, apolitical methods they were fulfilling their responsibility to the public. Wilson's scheme backed up the individual's sense of responsibility with a structural mechanism: a chain of command with a constitutional officer at the top. In his view, Americans could rest easy about the power of administrative expertise because "clear-cut responsibility" would make it "easily watched and brought to book" (pp. 213–214).

Over the years, emphasis has increased on trust in the administrator's personal sense of responsibility, what Friedrich called "the actual psychic conditions which might predispose any agent toward responsible conduct" (1940, p. 12). Drawing on John Gaus's idea of the administrator's "inner check," Friedrich maintained that bureaucratic responsibility consisted of technical knowledge and responsiveness to popular opinion; the former would be judged by professional colleagues while the latter would become operational as bureaucrats *anticipated* political responses to their actions and crafted strategies accordingly.

In answer, Finer (1941) argued that responsibility was a mirage unless the public and its representatives defined the public interest and punished administrators who defined it differently. In other words, he made responsibility a subset of responsiveness, rather than vice versa. Although a few observers have continued to argue in favor of assuring bureaucratic responsiveness by means of stronger laws and procedures that constrain discretion (e.g., Lowi, 1979), most locate the primary roots of responsibility in the expertise and morality of the individual bureaucrat (e.g., Cooper, 1990; Burke, 1987). This position is clearest in arguments for professionalism in public administration; Rourke's (1992) is only one of a host (e.g., Kearny and Sinha, 1988; Stever, 1988; Nalbandian, 1990).

Dictionary definitions give us a hint as to why there may be so much more overt support for responsibility than for responsiveness. "Responsive" means "quick to respond or react appropriately or sympathetically; sensitive" (*Webster's Ninth New Collegiate Dictionary*, 1986). Synonyms include "sentient, answering, passible [capable of feeling or suffering], respondent, reactive" (*The New Roget's Thesaurus*, 1964). "Responsible," on the other hand, means "liable to be called on to answer, liable to be called to account as the primary cause, motive, or agent; being the cause or explanation; able to answer for one's conduct and obligations; trustworthy; able to choose for oneself between right and wrong; politically answerable" (*Webster's*, 1986). Synonyms are "answerable, accountable, dependable, reliable, stable" (*Roget's*, 1964).

Given the choice, and persuaded that the two ideas meet democracy's need for accountability equally well, what bureaucrat would not rather be "responsible" than "responsive"? The responsible bureaucrat is a proactive agent, one who causes things to happen, in charge of his or her own conduct, trustworthy, capable of moral judgment, reliable, *and* politically answerable to boot. The responsive bureaucrat, in contrast, is reactive, sympathetic, sensitive, and capable of feeling or suffering—worthy qualities, perhaps, but together hardly an image that would draw people to public service or strengthen their commitment to it. When one adds in the partisan taint that appears to color responsive public administration, it is no wonder that responsiveness seems relatively unappealing. For example, to contrast responsibility and responsiveness, Rohr (1989) offers the case of former national security advisor John Poindexter, who during the Iran-Contra hearings acknowledged authorizing an illegal diversion of funds. Rohr comments: "If this is so, he was 'responsive' to the Contras; but he failed to act responsibly because he ignored the chain of command" (p. 51). Responsibility is laudable, grounded in law; responsiveness connotes improper bias.

Yet responsiveness needs defending, if democracy's only alternative is the responsible, professional administrator. Difficulties with too great a reliance on professional norms of responsibility have been noted. Professional autonomy is in fundamental tension with democratic accountability (Mosher, 1968). Fox and Cochran (1990) suggest that professional administrators can even become Platonic guardians who use professional values to justify bureaucratic autonomy and power. They argue that by conceiving of politics as "untrammeled and greedy self-interest" bureaucratic apologists turn the electoral process into "epiphenomenal noise" and rationalize the insulation of administrative governance from "corrupting influences" (p. 106). White and McSwain (1993) warn that the legitimate expert might become a self-effacing manipulator, an "Andy Griffith of Mayberry": one who, like the benign, all-knowing small town sheriff made familiar by television reruns, gives citizens the comforting feeling that the solutions he has implanted in their minds are their own.

Interestingly, White and McSwain worry less about Andy's power or deceptiveness than about the illusory promise he represents. In their view,

there are no Andys in the world, and there is no hope of one arising because the knowledge base required for being one cannot, in principle, be developed. . . . Our strongest knowledge traditions reach us that there are no answers of the sort that Andy always seems to be able to produce: specific, workable, on the point (1993, p. 21).

Along similar lines, Wellman and Tipple (1990) note that professional expertise per se is not enough to enable administrators to cope with changing and turbulent policy environments. For example, in a world that values forests for their beauty, recreational use, and wildlife habitat, professional foresters can no longer afford to focus solely on efficient and skillful harvesting of trees as a crop.

Thus reliance on administrators' sense of responsibility has been faulted because: (1) it tends to put too much emphasis on bureaucratic discretion, leaving judgments about the public interest to the ultimately uncontrollable and unpredictable administrative conscience (individual and/or collective); and (2) it trusts too much in professional skills and world views, which by themselves cannot be counted on to generate workable approaches in an increasingly complex world.

Granted that these propositions are debatable and likely to remain so, the questions they raise are significant enough to warrant reconsideration of that conceptual stepsister, administrative responsiveness. I would like to offer a different idea of responsiveness from the conventional one, with the aim of reducing the tension between administrative effectiveness and democratic accountability, both in theory and in practice. The argument, in essence, will be that *listening*, an embodied ability, way of knowing, moral capacity, and potential administrative practice, can help us shape a revivified responsiveness, one that avoids passivity and partisanship alike. After centuries of neglect in favor of the pervasive Western emphasis on vision, the capacity to listen has recently attracted the attention of a range of scholars, in philosophy (Levin, 1989; Fiumara, 1990), psychology (Brown and Gilligan, 1992), linguistics (Ong, 1982), and planning (Forester, 1989). In one way or another, all argue that the nature of our ability to listen has practical, moral, and societal implications that can teach us much, if we are only willing to open ourselves to these lessons. I will briefly review these arguments and try to show their relevance to the question of responsiveness in public administration.

The Capacity to Listen

Listening "lets be," lets come into presence the unbidden giving of sound.

(Ihde 1976, p. 110)

We have less control over what we hear than over what we see. We can shut our eyes easily, but we have to plug our ears, and even then some sound usually comes through. Therefore we are fundamentally open to sound, as anyone working near a construction site or living with a rock music fan is all too aware. We have the subjective impression that we can fix or pin down objects by means of sight, but sounds cannot be preserved.

> When I listen to auditory events there seems to be no way in which I can escape the sense of a "coming into being" and a "passing from being". . . . I cannot "fix" the note not make it "come to stand" before me . . . (Ihde, 1976, p. 94).

While sight distances the one who sees from the objects of his or her gaze, sound penetrates the listener; as Ong notes, "sight isolates, sound incorporates" (1982, p. 72). Vision objectifies and disembodies; things appear to us as if they existed in an eternal present. Sound, on the other hand, "pours into the hearer. . . . When I hear, . . . I gather sound simultaneously from every direction at once" (Ong, 1982, p. 72). Rather than distancing, listening immerses and engages. The experience of sound, therefore, is an experience of openness. Listening makes us aware that reality, at least as we experience it, has permeable boundaries, and that our understanding of what *is* is relative to what *is not*. Listening calls our attention to emergent aspects of situations and leads us in the direction of contextual rather than eternal (timeless) truth.

In part because of this essential openness and relativity, the act of listening to another person is characterized by reciprocity and a committed letting-be. Fiumara says that in dialogue the listening person is a participant in the speaker's emerging thought, which in fact requires engaged listening in order to attain its fullest expression. The listener evokes that potential, paradoxically, "'by taking leave,' by standing aside and making room" (1990, p. 144). At the same time, in sharing the speaker's language, the listener hears his or her own voice, evoked in and through another, just as a speaker, listening to his or her own words, is always hearing in them the voices of others (Levin, 1989, Lionnet, 1989). In dialogue, we echo and resonate with one another:

> to listen to another is to learn what the world is like from a position that is not one's own; to listen is to reverse position, role, and experience (Levin, 1989, p. 193).

Through speaking and listening, we make room for the voices of others and responsively reshape the dialogue and its context. Listening lets be without passivity, participates without imposition. Listening facilitates communication.

Clearly, not all listening fulfills its potential. At the everyday level of awareness, much of the listening we do is really *hearing*—simply taking in sound, a great deal of which flows through us virtually unnoticed. When we do notice what we hear, particularly when we are in conversation, we tend to listen in an ego-driven way, shaping what comes to us so that it fits our existing ideas, channeling it according to our desires and needs (Levin, 1989). We wait impatiently for another speaker to finish, as we shape our reply in advance, rather than attending to what he or she is really saying. Levin argues that with practice we can move beyond this everyday form of listening to what he calls "skillful listening," which involves slowing down, giving deliberate attention to the experience, and cultivating a welcoming receptivity that accepts others in their uniqueness.

Levin suggests that skillful listening can constitute a practice of the self, that is, a deliberate self-development that also develops society. In contrast to much of the current "self-help" literature, which tends to avoid the economic and political dimensions of social interaction in favor of a focus on "co-dependence" and "getting in touch with your inner child," Levin believes there are practices of the self that make self-development a process of social change. In other words, skillful listening can join self and society, theory and action, in reflexive relationship (see also Forester, 1989). Listening has this potential because of the characteristics we have just reviewed: openness, engagement, letting-be, reflexivity.

Listening as Self-Development

In listening to others, we are gathered into compassion.

(Levin, 1989, p. 89)

Skillful listening promotes the development of moral sensibilities because it models the reciprocity inherent in ideas of justice. Children develop a sense of identity, a sense of self, by hearing themselves echoed and reflected back in the voices of others. To the extent that others give us respectful attention, we eventually learn to respect ourselves and to reciprocate this respect and attention. Thus according to Levin, justice is more than an abstract idea; we literally live its analogue. As we improve our ability to listen, we increasingly understand the extent to which we hear ourselves in others and they in us; this reciprocity is evoked in our theories and practices of justice. Instead of stripping away the qualities of unique individuals in favor of an ideal of universality, listening expands justice to include the details of the situation and the significant differences among human beings.

The openness of listening—the fact that we cannot pin sounds down, that we are in constant touch with the horizons from which sound emerges and beyond which it disappears—encourages our openness to the viewpoints of others and our recognition of the fundamental complexity and unpredictability of the situations in which we find ourselves. Instead of spurring us to reduce every situation to a "type," listening helps us see situations as unfolding stories and trust that, if we remain open, dialogue may eventually convey to us what we do not know or what is necessary for our own self-development (Fiumara, 1990, p. 162). We may also become more open to understanding others: "[B]y taking in the voice of another, we gain the sense of an entry, an opening, a connection with another person's psychic life" (Brown and Gilligan 1992, p. 28). Such connections may encourage the kind of compassion that comes when we relinquish oversimplification and the urge to impose premature diagnoses of our own on complex problems.

The openness and reciprocity of listening promote relationship. Dialogue marked by skilled listening creates a shared reality, a public or common space (Taylor, 1989) that promotes responsiveness ("response-ability") and a sense of mutual obligation or commitment (Levin, 1989; Brown and Gilligan, 1992). Listening responsively may, therefore, help promote accountability on the part of public officials as they begin to see citizens as inhabitants of the same public square they themselves occupy and as they engage them in dialogue.

Relationship based on listening emerges from acknowledgement of the importance of difference. Each human self is shaped through interaction with people who are both similar and different. A community of listeners not only promotes diversity but recognizes that there can be no common space without difference. How we respond to difference "makes up the politics of our everyday lives" (Forester, 1992, p. 107); difference is the essence of democracy rather than a roadblock to it. In the sense that it makes room for every voice, responsiveness enacted through skillful listening is less partisan or biased than more conventional approaches.

In summary, then, listening fosters self-development in certain directions: it vivifies a reciprocal understanding of justice; it encourages open-mindedness, relationship, and acceptance of difference; and it promotes a situation-emergent view of truth, gleaned through the suspension of premature judgment. It has this potential, in Levin's view, because it is a bodily capacity. Levin (1989) argues that reciprocity is "built in," so to speak, and that working for justice is a matter of collaborating with our physical capacity to listen. If Levin is right, then the development of skill in listening can become the starting point for a practice of responsiveness in public administration.

Listening and Responsive Public Administration

Responsibility must begin with attention. To act responsibly we must ask: What is happening? What is calling us to respond?

(Bellah *et al.*, 1991, p. 283)

How can skillful listening help bureaucrats develop responsiveness in their work? Consider what notion of responsiveness we would want as a practical ideal for democratic administrators. Responsive administrators should be open, able, and willing to respond, but also just, that is, judicious, uncorrupted. They should know how to draw on their expertise while seeking diverse viewpoints and remaining open to the unexpected and the unpredictable. They should be receptive to difference and able to help evoke the reciprocal dynamics and expressive potential of dialogue.

One might wonder whether this list of qualities is too demanding: Does it not require responsive bureaucrats who can "leap tall buildings at a single bound?" Does not the complexity and turbulence of current-day public administration require bureaucrats who can "satisfice," who can do more with less in an imperfect world? Surely if we are to promote responsiveness, we must do it in a way that helps hard-pressed administrators rather than expecting them to waste energy trying to live up to an impossible ideal.

The advantage of listening as a practice of responsiveness is that it asks administrators not to try to turn themselves into superpeople but simply to try some rather humble tactics and work on developing fairly modest but significant capacities. Because it promotes openness, respect for difference, and reciprocity, the practice of skillful listening can help administrators evolve toward a form of responsiveness that supports both democratic accountability and administrative effectiveness.

How does skillful listening promote accountability? By helping administrators to hear neglected voices, engage in truly reciprocal communication with stakeholders, and remain open to emerging perspectives. Listening enables us to sense the dream of power behind our hope of a single, transparent voice, with its urge to eliminate diversity, and accept instead the public space as an "interweaving of willings" (Follett, 1965 [1918], p. 69). Skillful listening helps administrators to understand responsiveness as constructive rather than reactive: public institutions take their shape partly as a result of how people at the intercept between agency and environment listen to and respond to one another. In this sense, the challenge for administrators is not whether or not to be responsive, but to whom they will respond and to what ends.

How does skillful listening promote administrative effectiveness? By helping bureaucrats to deepen their understanding of complex situations, distinguish the impossible from the merely difficult, develop more nuanced problem definitions, and synthesize as well as they now analyze. Skillful listening helps us to open ourselves to what we do not understand but might, with time. It helps us construct possibilities for doing and being otherwise, that is, to get a sense of what limits we might be able to go beyond. Korten (1981) has underscored the importance of openness and synthesis in a global environment increasingly pressed toward sustainability and social learning, where in order to avoid costly errors, comprehensive plans and blueprints must give way to tentative, iterative approaches guided by participative processes.

In essence, then, listening helps public administrators to realize the impossibility of the final answers that Andy of Mayberry always seemed to be able to come up with *and* to develop a different ethical ideal than the benign manipulator Andy appeared to be. Listening bureaucrats understand themselves less as manipulators and more as facilitators, sensing the various themes sounding in their worlds, appreciating their harmony and their dissonance, creating occasions for the possibility of their interweaving.

Here and there in public administration, the importance of listening is vividly evoked. One interesting example from the early history of the American administrative state involves the Children's Bureau and the Sheppard-Towner Act of 1921. Established in 1912, the Children's Bureau was a product of lobbying efforts on the part of settlement house leaders. Bureau chief Julia Lathrop deliberately created an organizational culture that valued "responsiveness, individual initiative, and personal relationships" (Muncy, 1991, p. 55) and that established a network of active collaboration with female voluntary associations across the country. Over 3,000 club-women went door-to-door to help the bureau with its project of improving birth registration records, and millions more took part in bureau-sponsored conferences on child welfare.

Bureau chief Lathrop received hundreds of letters each month from poor women about their difficulties in bearing and rearing children; agency staff responded personally to each one. After women gained the national franchise in 1920, organized lobbying by the Women's Joint Congressional Committee, together with the demonstrable need reflected in the poor women's correspondence with the bureau, resulted in passage of the Sheppard-Towner Act providing maternal and infant care services to needy families (Ladd-Taylor, 1993).

The activities and approach of the Children's Bureau show the potential impact of a deliberate resolve to listen to the voices of the public and to involve its members in agency work. The openness and responsiveness instilled by Lathrop from the bureau's earliest days (values carried forward from the settlement houses where Lathrop and others began their careers) not only spurred thousands of middle-class volunteers to support the bureau goals with their intelligent legwork but found their way to poverty-stricken women in rural hamlets, gave them the hope that their cries for help would be heard, and made their pleas telling evidence in the fight for legislation.

A similar but current-day example is the federal community health center program, which funds over 500 community-based organizations to provide health care to residents of urban neighborhoods and rural areas where need is great and existing resources limited. I argue that reciprocal relationships between health center board members and federal officials charged with overseeing the centers, expressed in dialogue that reproduces and carries forward key values, helps all parties to achieve a shared understanding of the program mission and objectives and creates a "public space" in which the views of citizens have real impact on federal priorities and strategies. Working together, bureaucrats and citizens translate program goals into activities geared to particular community needs (Stivers, 1990).

A recent profile of William Ruckelshaus provides another example, one that emphasizes the impact of a single official's commitment to good listening. The effectiveness of Ruckelshaus's leadership began with "a commitment to listen and learn from all sides," particularly by making sure that underrepresented groups were heard, trying to "view the world from the other person's perspective," and having an open mind (Dobel, 1992, p. 250). As head of the Environmental Protection Agency, Ruckelshaus's skillful listening was evident in his response to auto company requests for an extension to the deadlines of the Clean Air Act: after listening carefully to all sides at open hearings, Ruckelshaus had the basis to resist strong White House pressure and deny the request. Thus he was responsive without being inappropriately biased.

Berger (1977) describes similar good listening in the Alaska pipeline hearings in Mackenzie Valley, Canada: in addition to standard formal hearings involving oil company representatives and an array of technical experts, hearing officers traveled to all 35 native communities in the region to hear evidence from residents in their own languages, thus ensuring the presence of neglected voices in the deliberations.

The sense that good listening in the public sector requires adjustment of standard policy processes has been underscored recently by Daniel Kemmis, mayor of Missoula, Montana. Kemmis (1990) argues that not much "public hearing" goes on at the typical public hearing; therefore public officials must create alternative processes in which parties to contested issues can speak directly with, and listen to, one another. He cites several successful examples, including one in which a grass-roots group that wanted to combine a community solar greenhouse with a laundromat (which would provide backup heat and needed revenue) reached an accommodation with owners of existing laundromats. The mayor brought the parties together but required them to negotiate their own settlement. Kemmis comments:

> Once the parties themselves get the idea that they are responsible for coming up with the answer, rather than simply turning it over to a third party, they are very likely to begin to think and behave differently. . . . There seems to be something inherently mutual about the taking of responsibility; it is difficult not to respond to it (1990, p. 113).

Thus public officials can be good listeners (they can be responsive) by encouraging citizens' responsibility to listen to one another and solve disputes.

Wellman and Tipple's (1990) study of the U. S. Forest Service citizen participation processes leads them to argue that, like other bureaucrats, foresters who want to create lasting and effective partnerships with citizens must begin by being good listeners:

> True communication is hard work. It requires persistent effort, since nobody—including foresters—develops wisdom on the basis of one trial. It means stimulating citizens' involvement at times when their interest is not aroused by a perceived crisis. It means continual dialogue, which can lead to seemingly endless meetings. It means listening, sometimes with saintly patience. It means giving reasons for professional judgments. . . . It means being concerned with all the communications between the agency and its environment, including the routine exchanges between citizens and field staff, so that agency leadership at all levels of the organization hears what it needs to hear and misleading messages are not sent (p. 84).

Only foresters who can listen skillfully can hope to facilitate intractable disputes such as the ongoing conflict over the harvesting of old-growth timber in the Pacific Northwest.

In all these contexts, listening is important because it helps administrators glean important information, define situations more carefully, hear neglected aspects and interests, and facilitate just and prudent action in often turbulent environments. Listening offers the possibility for a real "reinvention" of agency policy and management processes, one that vivifies the common space occupied by citizens and bureaucrats and offers prospects of substantive community.

Conclusion

In public administration, as elsewhere, responsiveness begins with listening. If, as Bellah *et al.* argue, "democracy is paying attention" (1991, p. 254), democratically minded public administrators may want to pay attention to their own listening abilities in order to be able better to pay attention—to respond—to the public. Community activist Fran Peavey, who once traveled around the world simply to listen to what people had to say about their lives and how they viewed the United States, found the experience "a kind of tuning-up of my heart to the affairs of the world." She says: "I hear the news in a very different way now, and I act with a larger context in mind" (1986, p. 91). Listening bureaucrats could, too.

References

Bellah, Robert N., Richard Madsen, William M. Sullivan, Ann Swidler, and Steven M. Tipton, 1991. *The Good Society.* New York: Knopf.

Berger, Thomas, 1977. *Northern Frontier, Northern Homeland: The Report of the Mackenzie Valley Pipeline Inquiry* (2 vols.). Toronto: Lorimer.

Brown, Lynn Mikel and Carol Gilligan, 1992. *Meeting at the Crossroads: Women's Psychology and Girls' Development.* Cambridge: Harvard University Press.

Burke, John P., 1986. *Bureaucratic Responsibility.* Baltimore: Johns Hopkins University Press.

Cooper, Terry L., 1990. *The Responsible Administrator: An Approach to Ethics for the Administrative Role* (3d ed). San Francisco: Jossey-Bass.

Dobel, J. Patrick, 1992. "William D. Ruckelshaus: Political Prudence and Public Integrity." In Terry L. Cooper and N. Dale Wright, eds., *Exemplary Public Administrators: Character and Leadership in Government:* San Francisco: Jossey-Bass. pp. 241–269.

Finer, Herman, 1941. "Administrative Responsibility in a Democratic Government." *Public Administration Review,* vol. 1, pp. 335–350.

Fiumara, Gemma Corradi, 1990. *The Other Side of Language: A Philosophy of Listening.* Trans. Charles Lambert. London: Routledge.

Follett, Mary Parker, 1965 [1918]. *The New State.* Gloucester, MA: Peter Smith.

Forester, John, 1989. *Planning in the Face of Power.* Berkeley: University of California Press.

Fox, Charles J. and Clarke E. Cochran, 1990. "Toward a Platonic Guardian Class?" In Henry D. Kass and Bayard L. Carton, eds., *Images and Identities in Public Administration.* Newbury Park, CA: Sage. pp. 87–112.

Friedrich, Carl J., 1940. "Public Policy and the Nature of Administrative Responsibility." In E. S. Mason and C. J. Friedrich, eds., *Public Policy 1940.* Cambridge: Harvard University Press. pp. 3–24.

Ihde, Don, 1976. *Listening and Voice: A Phenomenology of Sound.* Athens, OH: Ohio University Press.

Kearny, R. C. and C. Sinha, 1988. "Professionalism and Bureaucratic Responsiveness: Conflict or Compatibility." *Public Administration Review,* vol. 48, no. 1, pp. 571–579.

Keller, Evelyn Fox and Christine Grontkowski, 1983. "The Mind's Eye." In S. Harding and M. B. Hintikka, eds., *Discovering Reality.* Dordrecht, The Netherlands: Reidel, pp. 207–224.

Kemmis, Daniel, 1990. *Community and the Politics of Place*. Norman, OK: University of Oklahoma Press.

Korten, David F., 1981. "The Management of Social Transformation." *Public Administration Review*, vol. 41., no. 6. 609–618.

Ladd-Taylor, Molly, 1993. "My Work Came out of Agony and Grief: Mothers and the Making of the Sheppard-Towner Act." In Seth Koven and Sonya Michel, eds., *Mothers of a New World: Maternalist Politics and the Origins of Welfare States*. New York: Routledge, pp. 321–342.

Levin, David Michael, 1989. *The Listening Self: Personal Growth, Social Change and the Closure of Metaphysics*. London: Routledge.

Lionnet, Francoise, 1989. *Autobiographical Voices: Race, Gender, Self-Portraiture*. Ithaca, NY: Cornell University Press.

Lowi, Theodore, 1979. *The End of Liberalism: The Second Republic of the United States*. New York: Norton.

Mosher, Frederick C., 1968. *Democracy and the Public Service*. New York: Oxford University Press.

Muncy, Robyn, 1991. *Creating a Female Dominion in American Reform 1890–1935*. New York: Oxford University Press.

Nalbandian, John, 1990. "Tenets of Contemporary Professionalism in Local Government." *Public Administration Review* vol. 50, no. 6, pp. 654–662.

Ong, Walter J., 1982. *Orality and Literary: The Technologizing of the Word*. London: Methuen.

Peavey, Fran, 1986. *Heart Politics*. Philadelphia: New Society, 1986.

Rohr, John A., 1989. *Ethics for Bureaucrats*, 2d ed. New York: Marcel Dekker.

Rourke, Francis E., 1992. "Responsiveness and Neutral Competence in American Bureaucracy." *Public Administration Review*, vol. 52, no. 6, pp. 539–546.

Stever, James A., 1988. *The End of Public Administration: Problems of the Profession in the Post-Progressive Age*. Dobbs Ferry, NY: Transnational.

Stivers, Camilla, 1990. The Public Agency as *Polis:* Active Citizenship in the Administrative State. *Administration and Society*, vol. 22, no. 2, pp. 86–105.

Taylor, Charles, 1989. *Sources of the Self: The Making of the Modern Identity*. Cambridge: Harvard University Press.

Wellman, J. Douglas and Terrence J. Tipple, 1990. "Public Forestry and Direct Democracy." *The Environmental Professional*, vol. 12, pp. 76–85.

White, Orion F. and Cynthia J. McSwain, 1993. "The Semiotic Way of Knowing and Public Administration." *Administrative Theory and Praxis,* vol. 15, no. 1, pp. 18–35.

Wilson, Woodrow, 1887. "The Study of Administration." *Political Science Quarterly,* vol. 2, no. 2 (June), pp. 197–222.

Part Four

Citizens and the Administrative State

In this section we move from broad concerns of accountability and responsiveness to one particular aspect of the tension between administrative effectiveness and democratic government. During the field's first half century, the dialogue surrounding this issue widely assumed that if administrative agencies were effective, democracy would have been well served. Alexander Hamilton had declared as much in the Federalist Papers. Defending a constitution that afforded only limited opportunities for direct citizen involvement with government, Hamilton argued that what citizens really want from their government is not the chance to participate but sound administration—a government that works (Cooke 1961). Up until the end of World War II, when the Administrative Procedures Act of 1946 installed a few basic rules of bureaucratic answerability directly to the public, few public administrationists questioned the idea that giving citizens what they wanted, effective government, could be equated with democratizing administration. Not until the 1960s "war on poverty" was this consensus upset. At that point came the clear call for greater direct citizen participation in governance. This call is still heard today.

Most proponents of more direct forms of citizen–administrator interaction argue that reliance on professionalism leaves too much up to the indi-

235

vidual administrator's conscience or the dictates of technical expertise. Similarly, they believe that the bureaucratic chain of command, up the line to a politically appointed agency head and thence to the elected chief executive, is not an adequate way of answering to the people. While many still adhere to notions of professionalism and the chain of command as accountability mechanisms, advocates of direct involvement by citizens in the workings of administrative agencies have raised important new questions. (Compare the articles in this section with those in the following section on professionalism.)

The first selection is almost unique in the literature of citizen participation: It is a direct expression of the voices of citizen activists. Although the contents were set down on paper by Sherry R. Arnstein, a planning professional, the real authors of "Maximum Feasible Manipulation" (*Public Administration Review* 1973) were the members of an areawide council in Philadelphia created under the terms of the federal Model Cities Program. The goal of Model Cities was to maximize the impact of federal antipoverty dollars by concentrating them on target areas in selected cities. The citizens tell the story of their attempt to use the federal program to change the balance of power between themselves and City Hall.

The steep decline over the last several decades in federal support for programs aimed at ameliorating poverty and its effects may make this article read at first like a period piece. Yet the story is worth remembering for at least two reasons. Many students and others who study administration today are too young to remember the days of activist government. They hear little about the 1960s and 1970s except the unchallenged opinion that the war on poverty "failed." To them, the story from Philadelphia gives a direct taste of what the struggle to democratize administration was like from the citizens' perspective. Such unfiltered views are rare enough in the study of administration to be worth rescuing from obscurity. In a related way, while the context has changed, many criticisms of government–citizen interaction voiced in this article are still applicable in today's quite different public arena. (For example, excluding citizens from the initial stages of a project, or holding meetings when people have to take time off from work to attend.) But the fundamental issue is power. The citizen authors conclude that citizens cannot expect governments to hand them real power; they must develop their own agendas and be able to retain technical experts who work for them rather than for government. They must also be prepared to "deliver the goods"—not just plans—to their communities. Even today, in a time when raw confrontations between disadvantaged citizens and their governments seem like ancient history, the areawide council's story remains fresh.

The next article is a classic in a different way. Terry Cooper's "Citizenship and Professionalism in Public Administration" appeared in *PAR* in

1984, as part of a special issue on citizenship in the administrative state. Cooper explores the role of citizen as a model for administrative action. Moving away from reliance on professionalism untempered by more direct forms of accountability, Cooper argues that the ethical obligations of the administrator can be derived from the obligations of citizenship in a democratic political community. The implications for the practice of administration include transitioning from a hierarchical model of accountability to a horizontal model that entails "power with" citizens rather than "power over" them. Cooper writes that the power of technical expertise and specialized knowledge has encouraged administrators to think of members of the public not as citizens but as "consumers" whose only relationship to government is to receive services. (Note that today's "customer" role also puts citizens in a similarly passive position vis-à-vis government.) Observing that "the source of our authority is the citizenry," Cooper urges public administrators to act as fellow citizens, not as remote authority figures, exercising their expertise on behalf of their citizen peers, and under their sovereignty.

Another important essay from the same special issue of *PAR* is Charles H. Levine's "Citizenship and Service Delivery: The Promise of Coproduction." Levine was writing in light of the anti-government atmosphere generated not only by the Vietnam War and the Watergate scandal but more specifically by the taxpayer revolt of the late 1970s. This movement produced California's Proposition 13 and a host of other measures to limit government activity by imposing automatic controls on public expenditures. As current-day readers will be aware, this trend has only grown stronger over the intervening years since the article appeared.

Levine writes that, in the face of public negativism, "aggressive professionalism" is doomed to failure. Administrators can no longer hope to hunker down in enclaves protected from citizens; they must find ways to work with them. Levine argues that the very reality of fiscal stress produced by reductions in public budgets affords an opportunity. Coproduction, the joint provision of public services by public agencies and service consumers, "lays the foundation for a positive relationship between government and citizens by making citizens an integral part of the service delivery process." Levine stresses that coproduction will not work, either as an effective service delivery mechanism or as a way of improving citizen-government relationships, unless agencies view it not as marginal but as central to their responsibilities.

The final essay in this section is "The Question of Participation: Toward Authentic Public Participation in Public Administration," by Cheryl Simrell King, Kathryn M. Feltey, and Bridget O'Neill Susel (*PAR* 1998). The authors address the question of how to make participation itself more effective and satisfying. In their framework, good participation is an end in itself rather than a means to managerial success. Given citizen skepticism with government in general and the bureaucracy in particular, the authors argue that ineffective participation may be as bad as none at all.

By good participation, King, Feltey, and Susel mean "authentic participation," that is, "deep and continuous involvement in administrative processes with the potential for all involved to have an effect on the situation." They maintain that citizens want their views to be listened to and heeded. They want to know that they have made a difference. Furthermore, participation should be not a one-shot affair but a real continuing dialogue with administrators, one in which citizens not only "judge" but "decide." Given these requirements for authenticity, public hearings, surveys, and most advisory groups prove to be poor mechanisms. The authors present a host of suggestions for achieving authentic participation, grouped into strategies for (1) educating and empowering citizens, (2) reeducating administrators, and (3) creating enabling administrative structures and processes. Their overall message: Authentic participation is possible.

13

MAXIMUM FEASIBLE MANIPULATION

as told to Sherry R. Arnstein

Introduction

We, the North City Area Wide Council, Inc., believe this is a unique case study. It has been put together *by* community people *for the benefit of other community people*. Although it will be widely read by policy makers and politicians, it is addressed only to people like ourselves who are struggling against impossible odds to make public programs relevant to poor and powerless people.

Most case studies are written by social scientists whose biases are just like those of the traditional power structure. For years they have been invading our communities and diagnosing what ails us Blacks, Puerto Ricans, Chicanos, Indians, and by-passed whites. For years they have been analyzing us as apathetic, stupid, and lazy. Until now, action-oriented community groups like the Area Wide Council (AWC) have been unable to fight back. We have had neither the journals, the dollars, nor the luxury of time to put together the six-syllable words and the technical jargon to tell our side of the story.

This community case study is different! It is our analysis of what happened here in North Philadelphia as we struggled to use our Model Cities Program to create a new balance of power between ourselves and City Hall.

Source: *Public Administration Review* 33(1973):377–390.

This study was made possible by the National Academy of Public Administration (NAPA). Mrs. Sherry Arnstein was asked to write it with the clear understanding that she would write *only what we told her to write!*

We gave her access to all our records, including newspaper clippings, minutes of meetings, and correspondence—even a daily personal diary kept by one of our staff technicians. We talked to her for many days and many nights, individually and in groups. We made appointments for her to interview other community people in Philadelphia, and established her credibility so that people would share sensitive information with her.

We did this because she and NAPA guaranteed that every word in this case study could be edited in or out by us. In putting her technical skills at our disposal, she had the right to read everything available and to argue with any of us. But we retained full veto power over every comma, word, and phrase. What Mrs. Arnstein agrees or disagrees with in this document is completely irrelevant *to us and to her* since her objective was to *help us do our thing*—not hers, not HUD's, and not the Academy's!

When we started on this unique assignment, we intended to tell what the courts call the truth, the whole truth, and nothing but the truth. As we traveled down that road, however, we discovered that it would be better to deliberately leave out some of the hang-ups that are internal to our community.

Such hang-ups are pretty well known to most community leaders. They are not so well known to the establishment types who will also be reading this document. It would be foolish to let them in on such information, because they would use it to hurt the poor and the powerless.

Our case study, therefore, emphasizes what the power structure did to us, and excludes some of those things that we now realize we did to ourselves.

In the interest of community development, however, we pledge to share this sensitive information with any legitimate community leader in the country who wishes to call, write, or come to North Philadelphia.

Rev. J. Jerome Cooper, *President*
Mr. Salvador Barragan, *1st Vice President*
Rev. David Weeks, Jr., *2nd Vice President*
Rev. Michael H. Jordan, S.J., *Treasurer*
Mrs. Verna E. Watson, *Secretary*
Mrs. Laura Evans, *Corresponding Secretary*
Mr. Frank Garcia, *AWC Board*
Mr. Benjamin James, *AWC Board*
Mr. Japhers Parks, *AWC Board*
Mr. William Meek, *Volunteer Director*
Miss Virginia Treherne, *Volunteer Staff*

North City Area Wide Council Inc.
P.O. Box 3255
1700 W. Thompson St.
Philadelphia, Pennsylvania 19121

Month-by-Month Frustration

We want to tell you right off that the AWC is no longer recognized by the power structure as being in the Model Cities business. HUD and the city foreclosed on us in May 1969 because they got up-tight about the degree of power we managed to achieve over the program.

If only we knew two years ago what we now know about city and federal politics, it might have been a different story. But we were political novices, and they[1] were experts in political chicanery. We were trying to change things, and they were trying to keep us boxed in. It's so much harder to bring about change than it is to sit there and resist it. They had the upper hand, particularly the money and the sophisticated methods for maximum feasible manipulation.

As long as we were able to centralize the community's demands for change, the city feared us, and we were able to achieve stunning victories. When they finally managed to splinter us, we lost the only real power we had—people power. Here's how it happened day-by-day, month-by-month:

Fall 1966

Knowing nothing about the possibility of a Model Cities Program, four professional people who worked for different agencies in the community were meeting quietly to talk about the dire need for creating a new community coalition in North Philadelphia. Representing a community group, a settlement house, and a church group, these four staffers discussed how their agencies might support such a new coalition to do three things: (1) to identify issues, (2) to mobilize the community, and (3) to articulate community-defined plans.

November–December 1966

Philadelphia officials knew about the Model Cities Program long before most other cities. Inside information from Washington, D.C., was that Philadelphia would be awarded a planning grant of $750,000. Like every city in the country we know about, Philadelphia was planning to submit its application to HUD with no input from the residents of the neighborhood, or with some last-minute public hearings engineered to result in a rubber-stamp approval from the residents.

The mayor appointed a task force to prepare the required bulky application and a policy committee to review it before it was sent to Washington in March. Sitting on that policy committee, the task force, and its several subcommittees were officials from city agencies and a few silk-stocking civic leaders. No grass-roots people from the Model Cities neighborhood even knew about their meetings in November and December.

January 1967

The mayor announced to his policy committee that he had named his Washington, D.C., lobbyist as development coordinator and head of the Model Cities Program. One of the first products of the new director was an administrative structure chart for the Model Cities Program. The chart confirmed that all policy decisions would be made by him, and that city officials and establishment leaders would be advisory to him. Residents like us were to have no role at all except as the passive dumping ground for the program.

At this same meeting, a few members of the policy committee persuaded the mayor to invite at least one community leader from the Model Cities neighborhood to sit with them during the remaining weeks before the application was sent to Washington. Little did most of them realize that the token representative they had invited was no token man. That he really knew the historic games being run down on the community under urban renewal and the antipoverty program. That he was one of the four staff people who were already planning to create a community coalition to speak up and speak out for the people's interests. When he heard that the city's Human Relations Commission was trying to open the door for community input by holding an open meeting on those parts of the application that fell in its bailiwick, he put the word out for community volunteers to attend the meeting.

January 20, 1967

Representatives from approximately 30 community groups took time off from work to go to that afternoon meeting. At first, we listened quietly as city officials described three parts of the application: citizen participation, administrative structure, and equal opportunity in employment and housing. Then, having done our homework, we zeroed in with hard-hitting questions. Like, how come they were describing our community organizations and churches as historically ineffectual? Like, what proportion of the policy committee would be neighborhood residents? We argued that the first failure had already occurred because proposals were coming down the pipe from them with no grass-roots participation.

Our temporary spokesman stated that his organization was preparing an alternate proposal for citizen participation which would see to it that policy would come up the pipe from citizens instead of down. We demanded that several mass meetings be held in the community at night so that the grass-roots people could find out what was in the works and have an opportunity to suggest alternatives. It was futile, because the Human Relations Commission did not have the power to agree or disagree with us. All we got was a promise to circulate minutes of the meeting around City Hall. We knew then that it was up to us to mobilize the community and get our views directly to the mayor.

January 25, 1967

When the mayor's policy committee met again, a couple of its members supported our demands for real representation on their committee. Most of them, including the mayor, put the idea down. Instead, two new task force subcommittees were created—a subcommittee on citizen participation and a subcommittee on administrative machinery. The administrative machinery group had only one community representative, but the citizen participation group had 14 of our people, including the four community staff people who had been meeting in the fall to talk about the community's powerlessness before they even knew about the Model Cities Program.

January 30, 1967

At the first meeting of the subcommittee on citizen participation, the development coordinator apologized for the lack of citizen involvement in drawing up the application. He invited us to send representatives to sit in on the remaining meetings of all the task force subcommittees. We told him that we probably could get a few people to volunteer to join these task forces. But on such short notice and at such a late date, we wanted to put our real efforts into developing a community-defined approach to citizen participation. We told him that we had called a meeting in the community for January 31 to discuss our tentative definition and mechanism.

January 31, 1967

More than 70 people attended the first meeting as representatives of block clubs, settlement house groups, civil rights groups, and church groups. We laid out our sketchy proposal for what we called an "equal partnership" with the city and talked late into the night about what structure, what ground rules, and what resources could be put together to achieve a real community definition of citizen participation. We appointed a temporary steering committee to put our ideas on paper and to present them to a still larger mass meeting of community leaders.

February 2, 1967

When the city's participation subcommittee met again, we told them about our plans for a second mass meeting. Again the city invited us to send representatives to the remaining meetings of the other task force subcommittees. Again we reminded the city that while about 12 people had volunteered to attend those meetings, our real concern at this late date was not to argue over the details of 350 pages that they had already written. Instead we wanted to focus on our partnership model for citizen participation plus a complete rewrite of their first chapter, which outlined the city's warped and paternalistic view of our neighborhood.

Late February 1967

By late February, our temporary steering committee had worked out the details of the partnership proposal. It called for the creation of a broad-based coalition of all active community organizations that would call itself the Area Wide Council (AWC). The AWC would have partnership status at City Hall to represent the community's interests in the Model Cities Program. To make the partnership real, the city would contract $117,000 of the HUD planning grant to the AWC. The funds would be used by the AWC to hire its own community planners, organizers, lawyers, etc., to help the community react to plans prepared by the city and to enable the community to develop plans of its own for the city's reaction. The proposal spelled out guarantees that whenever there were disagreements over plans or policies between the city and the AWC, those disagreements would be negotiated until a solution acceptable to both parties was reached. It asked for six out of 15 seats on the policy committee of the Model Cities Program and for AWC representation on all of the city's task forces. In short, the AWC would be the legally constituted citizen structure for the program. It would have the authority, the financial resources, and the independence to bargain with the city on behalf of the community.

More than 140 representatives from community groups helped work out the details of that proposal. It was the first time that so many groups with such diverse and competing interests had gotten together. We were Black, Puerto Rican, and white organizations. We were conservatives and militants. We were from both sides of Broad Street, which had always been an organizational dividing line in the community. It was beautiful!

March 1967

The mayor knew that we were prepared to send a delegation to Washington to protest his application, and since he desperately needed the votes from our neighborhood to get re-elected, he agreed to our partnership proposal. The application that went to Washington included our proposal almost word for word and said in plain English:

> Recognizing that the quality of citizen participation in government programs has often fallen short of the mark, even when it was sincerely sought, the MCP in Philadelphia will strive to incorporate *within its very core guarantees of citizens' authority to determine basic goals and policies for planning and implementing the program* [emphasis added].

April 1967

Since insiders knew that Philadelphia was definitely going to be named a Model City, we moved ahead without HUD funds to develop the internal structure of the AWC. After many evening meetings, we came up with a structure which would assure that the AWC remained accountable and responsive to the total community. On April 20, more than 500 people showed up at a mass meeting and voted unanimously to "formally establish the AWC" and to adopt the recommendations of our hard-working temporary committee on structure.

The AWC structure was designed to strengthen existing community organizations and interest groups in the community. It called for the creation of 16 "hubs" located throughout the model neighborhood. Each "hub" would build itself on whatever community groups already existed and would locate itself in offices volunteered by friendly neighborhood settlement houses, churches, or community agencies.

The AWC Board would have 92 members: 12 of the 14 original organizers who had negotiated the partnership arrangement with the city, plus the elected chairman of each of the 16 hubs, plus the four representatives selected by each hub to serve on the four AWC standing committees. (These committees were created to correspond to the city's four task forces on physical environment, human resources, employment and manpower, and education.) The AWC structure also called for a 27-man staff which would be responsible to the AWC Board. Sixteen of the AWC staff would be field workers assigned to work with the 16 hubs.

May–July 1967

By June, when HUD was supposed to have awarded the planning grants to the winning Model Cities, we had already begun to organize the 16 neighborhood hubs, and had started working within each of our newly created standing committees.

In July, when HUD still had not announced the winning cities and we heard that Congress might cut some of the Model Cities appropriation, various community leaders were urged to write their congressmen and senators to demand full support for the program.

We also used the waiting period to support various happenings in the community. In July, for example, we organized a mass meeting to introduce the new school superintendent to the community. We begged poster paper, borrowed sound trucks, and did everything we could to get a mass turnout for him.

During that waiting period, we learned that if we were going to organize the community, we would have to respond to all kinds of community demands to deal with existing problems. We could not tell the woman whose child had just been bitten by a rat that she should join us in a year-long Model Cities planning process. We would have to begin to help people with today's problems today, or they would not believe that the Model Cities planning process would affect their lives tomorrow.

We began to digest thick reports and evaluations written by various public and private agencies—in short, to educate ourselves on what was happening and who was doing what to whom.

August 1967

We held an emergency session to discuss the governor's announcement that the state might get the Model Cities Program rolling by making state funds available immediately to each of the Pennsylvania cities waiting for federal funds. On the one hand, we were delighted. On the other, we were worried that the state might not respect the partnership we had worked out with the city. We talked about sending a delegation to Washington to find out why HUD was still holding back on its promised announcement.

Finally, we were advised that the mayor would advance the AWC $57,000 of city funds so that we would not lose the Model Cities momentum built up in the community. Finally, we could hire staff, rent office space, install telephones, and buy typewriters. Finally, we could hire an executive director. Our first move was to call a mass meeting to let the community know we were really in business. Someone figured out by then that we had already put in more than 100,000 hours of volunteer time. Calculated at the rate of $2.50 per hour, the community had already contributed the equivalent of $250,000 to get the Model Cities Program rolling.

In August, more residents started attending AWC Board meetings and raising new issues that needed immediate responses. For example, one of our hubs pointed out that Temple University had held a hearing to expand its campus into the community, but residents had not attended because they didn't know about it and didn't understand its importance. It was agreed that the AWC would be ineffective if it limited itself to future planning and ignored immediate issues like informing and mobilizing the community to protect itself at such hearings.

Again we voted to write to our congressmen to protest the continuing delay in launching the Model Cities Program.

November 16, 1967

HUD finally announced that out of 194 contestants, Philadelphia was indeed one of the 63 winners. However, instead of the expected $750,000 planning grant, HUD gave the city only $278,000.

November 17, 1967

More than 3,500 Black students turned out for a demonstration at the school administration building downtown. They were demanding 14 major changes in the high schools, including recognition of the Black student movement and the right to have Black studies, Black values, and Black principals. Inside the school superintendent's office, adults from the community were discussing the legitimacy of the students' demands. All of a sudden, without provocation, police attacked the youths and turned a street demonstration into a scene of violence in which 57 people were injured and 29 arrested.

This incident became a major turning point in the life of the AWC when police jailed two Black community leaders who had helped the students organize the demonstration. One of the jailed organizers was an AWC community organizer! From this point on, the city was bent on destroying the power of the AWC.

November 18, 1967

News headlines the following day were mixed—some blamed the police; others blamed the students. News accounts revealed that the leaflets for the demonstration had been mimeographed at AWC offices. Our executive director immediately acknowledged that the students had asked to use the AWC mimeograph. He felt it was a legitimate request from a community group (and he later argued in court that AWC's first responsibility had to be the community).

The two Black community leaders were released from jail; their bail, which had been set at $50,000, was reduced to $5,000. This action was prompted by a five-man interdenominational clergy group which petitioned the judge on the grounds that the two men weren't even present when "the police began their brutal attack on the students, nor did the defendants do anything whatsoever to incite a riot." The clergymen stated that they considered the high bail a "ransom," and one of their group wryly pointed out "it's a strange system of justice indeed that Father _____ who is white and wears a collar . . . is released on $1 bail, while _____ who is black and wears a beard is held on $50,000 bail."

November 21, 1967

The city development coordinator demanded that the AWC redefine its role and stick "simply and solely to planning." Trying to intimidate us, he sent an auditor to review our books for improper use of the $39,000 advanced to us by the city. At least two federal agencies, including the FBI, did character investigations on several AWC staff to determine what should be done about the "troublemakers."

November 24, 1967

We refused to be intimidated and behave like a bunch of apologetic children caught stealing from the cookie jar. Instead, we reaffirmed our rights by issuing a policy statement that outlined the AWC's view of self-dignity, self-expression, and self-determination. The statement underscored the basic principle of community organization by pointing out that AWC's "acceptance in the community hinges on meaningful involvement in dealing with immediate problems while planning for longer-range solutions."

Some of our members at first objected to the proposed policy statement. There was lengthy debate on the issue. Finally, there was rousing support for the students' demonstration and the AWC's support for their demands.

December 7, 1967

Close to 600 people turned out for a special meeting called by the AWC to explain the role it had played in the students' street demonstration.

Also at the meeting was the city development coordinator. He made it clear that City Hall and HUD were planning to punish the AWC by cutting back on the city's firm commitment to fund AWC operations at a level of $21,000 a month. He refused to see our point that when constituents who had helped to build the AWC demanded legitimate help in expressing their discontent, the AWC could not turn its back on that demand. To do so would reduce the AWC to nothing more than a tool of the power structure.

It was a noisy meeting with heated debate among community people who ranged all the way from conservative citizens to militant youth. Though some objected the AWC's position, the overwhelming number backed us all the way. They approved an AWC policy statement that residents of North Philadelphia would "determine their own capacity for participation" and endorsed a resolution "extending our support to all students who participated in the demonstration, in their struggle to get a better education."

December 10, 1967

Later in the week, the AWC's "punishment" was announced. The city used the cutback in HUD planning funds as an excuse to cut us back to $13,000 a month to force us to fire several AWC staff. Though the city was planning to accept state funds and add $187,000 from its own coffers to make up for some of the reduced HUD grant, it would not give us any of that money. The development coordinator announced that unless we agreed to the cutback, he would not sign any contract with us—even though he knew that we didn't have enough money left to meet the next AWC payroll.

December 12, 1967

We demanded a meeting with the mayor, who refused to see us. The development coordinator threatened to find another community organization in North Philadelphia to unseat the AWC if we didn't agree to a $13,000 contract. Still we insisted that we had done nothing wrong in supporting a request from the community and would not be demeaned by accepting the cutback. The city admitted that the auditors had found no discrepancies in our books and nothing which indicated dishonesty in our use of the $39,000 advanced to us by the city.

December 14, 1967

Our Board announced formally that it would reject the $13,000 and try to meet our payroll by raising funds in the community. The Philadelphia Crisis Committee supported our appeal to the mayor.

January 15, 1968

The mayor appointed a new development coordinator to head the Model Cities Program. Still we were without funds!

Late January 1968

To dramatize our stalemate with the city and to help some of our employees get money to meet emergency food and rent problems, 10 of our staff were escorted to the Welfare Department by the Welfare Rights Organization to apply for public assistance grants. By then, some of the staff had not received paychecks for more than seven weeks, even though the community came to our rescue with contributions of $7,500! (Contributions the city has never repaid despite its public promise to reimburse us so that we, in turn, could offer to give the money back to the donors.)

January 22, 1968

Finally our determined campaign paid off. The city signed a contract with us for $18,000 a month. We remained committed to our position that planning and action go hand-in-hand or neither are meaningful.

February 22, 1968

One of our hubs reported that residents in the Simon Gratz High School neighborhood were furious because the planned expansion of the overcrowded school had been stalemated by the city's refusal to condemn 14 homes occupied by white families. The hub asked the AWC to support a neighborhood demonstration at the board of education. In keeping with our committment to combine planning with social action, we, of course, supported their request. We felt it was both an educational and moral crisis. More than 40,000 Black people had been kicked out of their homes in North Philadelphia for the benefit of urban renewal and Temple University. But now that 14 white families were objecting, it looked as if the desperately needed expansion of the Gratz School might go down the drain. (The issue was ultimately settled, but unlike the thousands of dislocated Black families, the white people got paid off handsomely for their homes.)

February 26, 1968

We objected to the city's unilateral deadline of March 15 for developing a joint work program for HUD. We pointed out that our AWC standing committees had to take their proposals back to the hubs for approval before the AWC could commit itself as an organization. We proposed an alternate schedule which showed how the community's voice could be built in by adding two weeks to the schedule. Finally they agreed, but it was typical of the many incidents between us when we emphasized the AWC's interest in honest involvement as opposed to the development coordinator's interest in using the community as a rubber stamp.

March–April–May 1968

Though we won our battle with the city and HUD over the November 17 incident, the battle had significant side effects. Some white liberal and conservative Negro leaders dropped away from the AWC. On the other hand, the more militant sectors of the community became more active in AWC affairs. It was a turning point: AWC became more militant, more angry, and more determined.

Meanwhile, back at City Hall, the development coordinator was violating our partnership agreement left and right. He didn't even send us copies of correspondence on his wheeling and dealing. His task forces were meeting regularly, but only the Welfare Task Force notified us of its meetings so that we could attend. He hired a man to work directly with the hubs to try to divide and conquer the hub structure. His Physical Planning Task Force was emphasizing lots of new public housing, while our committee endorsed strategies of subsidized home ownership for poor people. He was ramrodding plans through that would improve the city's image with HUD, while we were struggling for major constructive change in our neighborhood's quality of life.

The final blow came when we learned that instead of submitting to HUD the joint work program that we had so carefully negotiated with him, he had sent in three different work programs: ours, his, and that of the individual city agencies. We considered the pro's and con's of demanding his resignation on the grounds that he couldn't relate to the community in even an elementary way, to say nothing of an honest partnership.

May 9, 1968

Instead, we asked for a meeting with HUD officials. That's how we learned that while HUD was requiring the city to submit the finished comprehensive demonstration plan by January 1969, he was pushing to finish a plan within *one month* (so that Philadelphia could get Model Cities action money for pacification programs to "cool the hot summer"). That's when we realized that after all the meetings we had gone to, and all the listening we had done, and all the negotiating we had engaged in, *that he was quietly moving ahead on his own to violate every one of those agreements!* How's that for a guaranteed partnership between community and City Hall!

Late May 1968

Another major clash between the city and the community arose over the use of open space money which HUD was making available to Model Cities in order to get some quick, visible results. We looked at the program and saw in it all kinds of opportunities for construction jobs for community people, planner and architectural jobs for Black and Puerto Rican professionals, plus linkages with new and exciting recreation programs planned by the youth themselves. The city, on the other hand, wanted us to concentrate solely on site selection and leave all those "minor details" to the Recreation Department.

June 1968

Having uncovered just how dishonest our second Model Cities director was, we called a mass meeting to demand that he be replaced by a Black director screened by the Black community. But we knew by then that his dishonest dealing with us were really a reflection of the city's callousness toward the community. Our distrust of the mayor had zoomed sky high.

Though we knew the development coordinator was on his way out of his job, he did not. His next move, therefore, was to throw still another ball down the street for us to go chasing after. He gleefully reminded us that our contract with the city was again expiring on June 30, and he imposed a whole set of unreasonable conditions on its renewal. He wanted a copy of our by-laws, which he knew well that we had not yet managed to put together because of all the other balls we had been chasing. He wanted copies of all our minutes, which he knew we wouldn't entrust to him since those carefully kept minutes revealed our strategies for dealing with him. He wanted the names and addresses of our leaders, which we knew he would use to harass them since many of them held jobs in government agencies. Though he sent us late notices of official task force meetings, he demanded advance notice of all hub meetings. This he wanted so that he could try to drive wedges between us and the hubs by manipulating them.

We set up a contract negotiating committee. We instructed it to take a hard line to be sure that the community's interests were not sold down the river. We also voted to negotiate for a larger contract. We wanted more money to strengthen the hubs—to pay for their office expenses and to pay stipends of $7 per meeting to hub chairmen and other community leaders who were by then sacrificing three or four evenings almost every week for the program.

In late June our efforts to oust the second development coordinator paid off. Though the mayor did not allow us to join him in selecting a new man, he did at least appoint a Black man as the Model Cities administrator.

July–August 1968

This move created a temporary truce between us and the city. First we resolved the contract dispute. We came out of those negotiations with an AWC contract for $46,000 per month! Next we worked out a new structure for joint city-community planning.

We all agreed that the Model Cities Executive Committee which had formerly been like a secret society would now include the city's task force chairmen and city staff, the AWC's standing committee chairmen and AWC staff, the Model Cities and the AWC directors. We also agreed that the Executive Committee would meet every two weeks to review the work of the city's task forces and the AWC standing committees.

We further agreed on the composition of a policy committee to mediate disputes which might arise between the city and AWC; and if that mediation failed, the disputes would be referred to the mayor who would decide the issue. Finally, we agreed to a new work program under which an interim report would be sent HUD by September 15 and the first-year action proposal would be ready by January 15, 1970.

September–December 1968

What a wild period! To meet that January deadline for getting a plan to HUD, both the AWC and the city had to hire many new people, orient them to what it was all about, and let them sink or swim! By November (when the Republicans got elected) we were advised to get the plan in by December 31, because once the Republicans took over, they might hold up funding of all first-year action programs from all cities.

We worked night and day, weekends, and holidays to put together our ideas and the city's ideas. We had many differences in approach, but with our partnership arrangement, we were able to trade off so that they got some of their priorities, but so did we. At the end, it was literally a last-minute cut-and-paste job which reflected our agreements on how Philadelphia would move ahead with $49 million for the first year of action.

The significance of our struggle for partnership status is best seen in the Model Cities administrator's page of acknowledgements: "Most rewarding was the destruction of the myth that a Model Cities community and a governmental body politic cannot enjoy a successful partnership." In addition the application said:

> This joint planning relationship between the City and the community, as could have been anticipated, has not been without its share of conflict. . . . There is every indication that with time, Philadelphia will become a model for the country of what form joint planning with citizens should assume. It must be understood, however, that this relationship will never be static or conflict-free.

Rather, the basic realities of life in America today insure that some conflict will be inevitable. It is the opinion here, however, that this residual conflict may provide the kind of dynamism that is necessary to make government truly responsive to the needs of its citizens and to further the realization of an ever-elusive democratic society.

January–February 1969

Can you believe that after having managed to achieve this level of interaction, that right after the application went to Washington we were again betrayed by City Hall?

What happened was that HUD decided that the $49 million plan had to be revised and scaled down to projects totalling $25 million. HUD said that the revisions and paring process should be done during what it called a hiatus period. HUD offered the city a Letter to Proceed, which meant that if HUD accepted the revised plan for $25 million, the city would be reimbursed for its operating expenses during the hiatus period.

We had known about this hiatus thing back in December, and had been assured verbally by the city and by HUD that the promised Letter to Proceed would include the AWC at its $46,000 per month level of operations. But because our legal guard was down, we did not ask for this in writing. Well, the city arbitrarily decided in January not to renew our contract unless we would agree to slash our 52-man staff down to 22.

We were outraged! All of our "partners" were drawing their full pay during the damned hiatus period, but we were expected to fend for ourselves unless we were willing to fire more than half of our staff. It took nine weeks, a mass meeting, and two marches down to the mayor's office to turn him around.

During the nine nasty weeks, the city played real dirty pool. Trying to split the AWC staff, it offered city paychecks to the 22 AWC staff people whose jobs were not at stake. It even tried to buy some of them off with offers of permanent city jobs. Nevertheless, the staff stayed together. Again, the Welfare Rights Organization helped them get emergency welfare checks, and somehow they managed to survive. Finally, the mayor asked the City Council to approve city funds being advanced, and finally our whole staff got retroactive paychecks. But it was hell, and during the controversy some community factions and staff factions began to turn on each other.

March 1969

In early March we got our fourth Model Cities administrator, because the third one decided to seek election as a judge. Once again, the community was not consulted. We all learned about the changeover by reading the morning newspaper. This time the mayor picked a Black woman from the community who knew the AWC from her personal experience with a hub.

Despite the unexpected changeover, we and the city managed to continue to work together to complete the revised $25 million plan. Strangely enough, despite all the double-dealing, our partnership was really beginning to make an impression. Some of the city and private power structure had actually learned to swing with us. Some of them really were able to appreciate what we were fighting for and to agree that our demands for drastic changes in the system were more than legitimate.

The revised comprehensive plan is a testimonial to that learning. It stated boldly on page one that the two basic problems in the Model Neighborhood were poverty and powerlessness. It therefore promised that Philadelphia would use the $25 million to deal with those twin problems by:

1. assisting Model Cities residents to assume some control over their own economic resources and providing effective mechanisms for participating in the policy making system of the City
2. providing programs and services which are developed by, and (are) therefore more capable of meeting the needs of the . . . residents.

Page three showed the agreed-upon priorities: 50 per cent for economic development, 23 per cent for comprehensive community education, 21 per cent for physical environment, and only 6 per cent for social service delivery systems.

Later pages showed how some of these priorities would be realized by creating seven new corporations, four of which were to be community controlled in that the majority of their board of directors would be chosen by the AWC.

There it was, right out in the open for everyone to see that this was a radically different proposal from any that the politicians would have come up with if they had not been forced to bargain with the community. Among the many innovative projects proposed were:

—an economic development corporation with the power to buy land, machinery, and buildings, and borrow and lend money
—a land utilization corporation or land bank to acquire needed land for community purposes
—a housing development corporation to construct new housing and rehabilitate old houses
—an urban education institute to retrain and retread insensitive teachers
—a career institute to train residents for the Model Cities jobs that would be created

—six communications centers where residents would have new educational avenues for developing communications skills and learn how to use films and videotapes to present their points of view and to increase their ability to make sounder decisions about public programs

—incubator plants in which businessmen could be taught managerial skills on the job.

April 1969

Two days before the revised plan was sent to HUD, the Nixon Administration announced new guidelines for Model Cities and stated that all applications from all the cities would be completely scrutinized to weed out "unwise and unnecessary proposals." Little did we realize that Philadelphia would be the first victim of those vague words!

May 1969

In late May, HUD wrote to the mayor that the city's plan had "unusually heavy reliance on new corporations," had "too heavy involvement [of the AWC] in these operating corporations," and had "insufficient involvement of the City . . . and established institutions." In other words, HUD objected to the plan's fundamental strategy of power redistribution as projected in the creation of new community corporations. HUD was placing its confidence in the same old-line institutions that have traditionally betrayed the community.

June 9, 1969

Completely negating our partnership, the Model Cities administrator responded to HUD's qualms about the AWC's power by chopping us right down to a strictly advisory role in all seven of the proposed corporations. Without consulting us, she unilaterally sent HUD a supplementary statement, which promised that the AWC would only be allowed to nominate one-third of the board of the new corporations; the remaining two-thirds would be chosen personally by her or by some other citizen groups chosen by her.

Late June 1969

HUD and the city must have assumed that we would accept their outrageous conditions, because they were still quite willing to sign off on the

AWC's new $540,000 contract for its next year of operating expenses. In their minds, one-half million dollars must have seemed like a pretty good price for selling out a community.

As you can see, the Model Cities administrator carried out the bidding of the power structure against her own people. As we got down to the June 30 deadline when our contract would run out once again, she ignored our appeals to restore our partnership agreements (and other contract issues she was trying to force on us). Using a "take it or leave it" attitude, she insisted that if we didn't cave in by June 30, then any contract we might agree to at a later date would not be made retroactive.

We searched our souls. A few of us *were* ready to be bought off for that dollar figure. Some of us argued sincerely that it was better to accept a drastically reduced role in the program than to chuck it all after two years of blood, sweat, and tears.

After much discussion, we voted overwhelmingly to refuse the unilateral contract terms. Instead, we decided to take both the city and HUD to court to demand that our right to participate meaningfully be restored.

July–August 1969

Completely ignoring our objections, HUD announced that it would award the city $25 million for the first action year. It promised $3.3 million for immediate use to mount those few proposed projects that HUD liked. It told the city to go back to the drawing boards for the remaining $21.5 million, because HUD wanted the whole community corporation strategy knocked out.

HUD allowed as how it might approve one corporation for the first year if the city could "justify not using existing institutions." But, in that event, HUD demanded two more blows against the AWC's power: that it not be allowed to nominate *any* of its own members to serve on the corporation's board, and that it not be allowed to nominate *any* of the board members after the first year of operation. In other words, even the city's drastic cut in the AWC's powers did not satisfy HUD. Incredible as it may seem, HUD demanded that the AWC be stripped of every shred of influence over any corporation that might be created.

To keep ourselves going, we again turned to the community. We launched a $10,000 drive and arranged to have our rent and telephone expenses drastically reduced. By August 15, we filed our court suit charging HUD and the city with illegally limiting our right to participate.

November 1969

The rest of our bitter story is also a matter of history. In November, the Eastern District Court of Pennsylvania dismissed our court suit on the incredible grounds that we lacked "standing to sue." Our lawyers were just as outraged as we by the injustice of the court's decision. They and other lawyers, from as far away as California, volunteered their services to help us file a legal appeal.

Until we lost our first round with the courts, the AWC was together, and the city was restrained from organizing its own co-opted citizens group to act as representatives of the model neighborhood. When the District Court handed down its negative decision, we were torn apart.

The five month hold-up had taken its toll and split the community into many factions. Our unpaid staff had, of course, taken other jobs. Even some of our faithful AWC supporters had given up, or they were saying that it was better to have a minor AWC role than no role at all.

December 1969 to the Present

The strongest of us refused to be beaten down. We decided to keep the AWC alive and to fight for our rights. By February, we and our lawyers had worked out the details of a legal appeal.

We are now waiting for the decision of the U.S. Court of Appeals and hoping against hope that it will make several findings on our lawsuit: (1) that the AWC, the official citizen structure of the Model Cities Program, does indeed have the right to sue HUD and the city to protect our basic rights; (2) that the Secretary of HUD had no right to require the city to change the basic strategy of its Model Cities plan just because that strategy didn't fit in with his limited wisdom about power and powerlessness; (3) that the city had no right to agree to HUD's appalling requirement without even consulting the AWC, which was the legally constituted citizen structure for the Model Cities Program.

By January 1970 the Model Cities administrator appointed a Citizens Advisory Committee, and we are sorry to say that even some of the AWC's top leaders agreed to serve on that plantation-type structure which (like the old days of Urban Renewal) can only advise, while the politicians decide. They are just names on a letterhead with no accountability to the community.

The city is now trying to turn each of the AWC hubs into neighborhood councils. It hopes to buy off each council with a lousy $10,000 or $12,000 contract if it will "participate in an advisory capacity." You won't believe us, but those stranglehold contracts actually say that: if HUD reduces or terminates its funds to the city, the councils' funds may be reduced or terminated by the city *"at its sole discretion"*; the "City may suspend or terminate payments" if the councils' required monthly reports "are incorrect or incomplete in *any* material respect"; the city may withhold payment if the council "is *unable* or unwilling to accept *any additional* conditions that may be provided by law, by executive order, by regulations, or *by other policy* announced by HUD or [the] City"; and, finally, "notwithstanding anything to the contrary contained herein, either party will have the right to terminate this contract upon thirty days written notice" (emphasis added).

So, temporarily, the short-sighted politicians have won. The innovative citizen-city hall balance of power is dead here, and we have returned to an insulting plantation model under which the masters are assumed to know best and the slaves are expected to obey meekly.

They think they have beat us down, and maybe they have cut the ground out from under what was called the Area Wide Council, but fools that they are, they forget what President John F. Kennedy once said about those who crush efforts at self-determination: "Those who make peaceful revolutions impossible make violent revolutions inevitable."

Lessons We've Learned

Now! Having told you what happened to us, you might ask what that means for other community groups in the country, who, like the AWC, are struggling to turn things around in their community. You might even want us to give you a list of do's and don't's based on what we have learned.

The truth is that such a list would really not help you. It might in fact be harmful, because each city is different; each state is different. Even the regional offices of each of the federal agencies are very different. What works best in Philadelphia might be disastrous strategy in Nashville.

So, instead of giving you advice, we will tell the major lessons *we* have learned here in North Philadelphia, and you can use them for your own purposes. Not as do's and don't's, but as checkpoints for analyzing your own political scene and for finding your own solutions.

Lesson Number One: No Matter What HUD Says, Model Cities Is First and Foremost a Politician's Game. Although the mountains of HUD guidelines and technical bulletins insist that Model Cities is a technical planning process, everyone but community people seem to know by now that it's really a political process.

Each of the federal agencies involved, like HEW, Labor, and OEO, has its political motives for either cooperating with or fighting against HUD. Each of the city officials has his own vested interests and political agendas. Similarly, the private agencies and businessmen are looking for their piece of the action to fatten their agency budgets or personal wallets.

HUD, the White House, City Hall, and the Congress are constantly bickering over their conflicting political agendas for Model Cities. On paper, however, they carefully maintain the fairy tale that if all the right local and federal power holders jump into the Model Cities bed together, they will live happily ever after doing good for the poor.

In reality, HUD has created a game called Model Cities. HUD's rules for the game give each of the traditional power holders a certain number of playing chips depending on their political clout. But the community is told to play the game with no chips at all. It is told to beg while everyone else bargains.

HUD knows that the power holders will bicker and barter over the division of the Model Cities pie. But the community is told to cool all conflict and confrontation. It should achieve its goals by advising power holders and watching the results.

Nuts! It's certainly true that the power structure is not monolithic, and that there are different sets of power holders with different sets of agendas. But it simply isn't possible for the powerless to change these agendas from a nonpolitical begging position. We must have bargaining power!

Though the Model Cities legislation gave the City Hall politicians final decision-making power, we managed to get them to agree to share some of that power with the community. We all knew that City Hall was the senior member of our "partnership." The important thing about the partnership was that it enabled the community to enter the Model Cities game with its own stack of chips. Those chips made it possible for us to bargain instead of beg.

Philadelphia's comprehensive plan testifies to just how different a Model Cities plan did emerge when the politicians were required to negotiate with the community instead of just trampling all over it.

Lesson Number Two: You Can't Trust City Hall or HUD.   That's what the Nixon Administration ignores when it pronounces from on high that the goal of citizen participation is to "build trust" between City Hall and the community.

It might be beautiful if City Hall and HUD were trustworthy. But our history testifies to the fact that we'd be fools to trust the politicians. We were cheated each time we let our legal guard down. We only succeeded when we insisted that the politicians live up to their promises, and when we demonstrated that we had some power.

All four Model City directors used us to achieve their own ends. Each was willing to negotiate with us when he assumed the job and had some important HUD deadline to meet. Right after that goal had been achieved, each tried to renege on the partnership arrangement by creating an outrageous crisis around the renewal of our contract. Though some of the staff of the city and federal agencies were clearly honest and helpful, most of them lied, equivocated, cheated, and distorted.

HUD itself has demonstrated that it can't be trusted. Its official guidelines admitted that existing institutions have historically failed the community. It said that the cities had to demonstrate willingness to innovate if they wanted the Model Cities money. It promised that Washington would not dictate the methods to be used because it wanted the cities to create their own strategies for social change. Though HUD never advocated community control as a strategy for institutional change, it officially endorsed power sharing with the citizens as an experimental strategy.

So what happens? We took those guidelines at face value and struggled to achieve power sharing with our city. We were one of the few communities in the country with a sufficient community power base to get the city to agree to our demands. HUD put its seal of approval on our agreement. Despite many attempts by the city to subvert it, we managed to hang in. Through thousands of hours of blood, sweat, and tears we managed to negotiate a plan which had some genuine promise for community renewal. The plan clearly articulated that the basic strategy for achieving lasting social change is to shift the balance of power between exploiter and exploited. The mayor approved and sent the plan to Washington. Then HUD, the Big White Father, violated that agreement by announcing that the new Administration (with its limited wisdom about inner-city communities) thought it was too risky for the mayor and wanted it changed! The mayor happily agreed and submitted a different strategy without even consulting us! And HUD claims not to understand why people like us don't trust them! Why people like us feel they use maximum feasible manipulation.

Lesson Number Three: Community Coalitions Need to Develop Their Own Agendas Instead of Constantly Reacting to the Agendas of Outside Forces.   If you allow yourself to be kept busy reacting to the government's short-term contract negotiations, unrealistic deadlines, and mountains of bureaucratic paper requirements, you get diverted from the really important task of initiating, refining, and acting on your community's agenda. You also can get diverted from keeping your own house in order.

The hubs, for example, in responding to all the real tasks of the AWC and the phony crises created by the city, got sidetracked from the job of expanding their power base in the neighborhood and representing that base. Since there are a limited number of hours in the week, community people need to guard those hours like dollars in the bank to make sure that the community's agenda is not shortchanged in the thousands of transactions.

Some of us believe that if we managed to stay closer to the ground, we could have mobilized enough community support to march by the thousands on City Hall and forced the mayor to tell HUD to keep its hands off a local plan that met all of HUD's legal requirements. (Some community groups have managed to pull this off.)

Maybe it's not possible, under a federal program, to keep such a community coalition of the most activist to the most conservative continually expanding and continually increasing its level of sophistication. Some of us still believe it is. But we'll never know what would have happened if we could have developed at our own pace with the support of the city and the federal government instead of their harassment.

Lesson Number Four: Community Organizations Must Have the Dollars to Hire Their own Staff Technicians, and Must Be Able to Direct That Staff and to Hold It Accountable.   We knew when we started that without our own staff of technicians we couldn't possibly keep up with all the legitimate and illegitimate agendas that they would be running on us. One of the surprising lessons we learned was that some of our own community staff could be co-opted by the powerholders or be moving without us on their own agendas.

We discovered that if we were not equipped to do our own thinking, we could easily become patsies for some of our own pro's. Today, we would place more emphasis on training for ourselves as community leaders and for our staff as technicians. In saying that, however, we want to emphasize that we don't mean the kind of patronizing gobbledygook that is usually passed out by the old-line educationists. We mean honest training that is designed with us and not for us. We mean trainers selected by us for their technical knowledge, their integrity, and their ability to relate to the community.

Lesson Number Five: You Can't Organize a Community Without "Deliverables."   By this we mean that community people are daily struggling with basic bread-and-butter survival issues for themselves and their families. Attempts to organize them around their mutual problems for their mutual gain are doomed unless they can see tangible results of their efforts.

The Model Cities planning process, which required great personal sacrifices in hopes of uncertain payoff 12 months later, was a poor vehicle for building and maintaining a representative community coalition. For a group like the AWC to successfully organize a community, we needed to be able to deliver concrete benefits that could demonstrate the value of sticking together, struggling together, and holding each other accountable, e.g., an AWC ombudsman who could have arranged immediate help to individuals with personal problems like evictions, lack of bail money, or a child's expulsion from school.

Some of us are ready to say that it is impossible to organize a community today under any federal program in light of their pacification motives, unrealistic deadlines, insensitive requirements, and phony guidelines. On the other hand, if a community group has to work with pennies, while the establishment manipulates our lives with millions, the community gets nowhere in terms of tangible benefits. So it would be senseless for community groups to adopt a hands-off position on all federal dollars. Frankly, we haven't got a solid answer to this problem of heads-they-win, tails-we-lose. We include it among our lessons, because we now know that it is a fundamental question to which all community people must try to find an answer.

Lesson Number Six: Don't Underestimate the Potential Support for the Community's Agenda from Sympathetic People Outside the Community. During AWC's four contract crises, we learned that our struggle had considerable meaning to some people outside the community.

For example, some of the staff of the city agencies and some of the HUD and OEO people were real swingers who helped us time after time. Some of them told us inside information that gave us the upper hand in negotiating with their agencies. Some of them worked with us at night and on weekends giving us great technical help on our program ideas and showing us how to use some of the laws already on the books to achieve our priority agendas.

During the first crises some of the professionals working for the city Planning Commission were so outraged by the mayor's position that they actually contributed money from their own pockets to help us keep the AWC alive.

Some of our own AWC staff wrote checks as big as $100, $250, or $500 to help other staff deal with the payless paydays. Contributions were given by university people, Black churches, white churches, denominational offices, and the local chapter of the National Association of Intergroup Relations Officials.

Similarly, some of the press and elected officials turned out to be powerful allies. Community groups should systematically identify and encourage these political, technical, and financial allies.

Lesson Number Seven: Be Prepared to Fight each Frustrating Step of the Way When You're Trying to Break New Ground. Here again, the establishment refuses to see what dehumanizing hoops we have to jump through every time we agree to play in their ballpark. Look what happened on just one simple AWC project.

After a meeting with our school superintendent (who is one of the most approachable officials in our city), he agreed that an AWC pupil parent attitude survey would be valuable to him in developing quality education. As soon as we left him and his close circle of associates who claimed to understand what AWC and the Black students were striving for, we ran into one roadblock after another. The survey was doomed before it began.

Our first step was to visit his research department, because its imput was essential. Talking to the top research man, we got a lot of stuff like, "I don't have the authority to let my staff help you." We had to trot back to the superintendent's office to get official clearance. Then we had to play tag with the research people. They took the position that we had developed our ideas about the survey too far to suit them. Once again, we had to go to the superintendent's office to force a decision that several research staff members were to spend at least two hours each week to help us do our thing and not theirs.

When the survey was finally ready for the neighborhood, the district superintendent objected, because she had not been informed. So we lost several more weeks until we realized what her hang-up was about and went back to the superintendent again. After she received his clearance letter, she agreed to cooperate.

Our next problem was that the school-community coordinators had not been informed and involved in the project. So some of them felt they shouldn't "be used this way." They were instructed by the local superintendent to cooperate with us. But some remained adamantly opposed to our efforts, and this affected the way they assisted in administering the survey.

When the survey was completed, we again had to return to the superintendent's office to negotiate for staff time to analyze the results, because this had not been specified earlier and had to be agreed to in writing. Here we ran into the ultimate absurdity—the question of who was going to pay for the computer cards, since there was allegedly no money in the school budget for this. Lord knows what would have happened to the project if a community person hadn't solved this hang-up by getting his employer to donate the damned computer cards.

We had to spend all this energy just to find out how many of our children and parents felt the way the Black students did when they complained about teachers who looked down their noses at them and acted as if their culture was crude, their speech wrong, their dancing sensual, and their families unacceptable.

Frustrating experiences like these with "sympathetic" agencies reinforced our thinking about community-controlled institutions as the most hopeful strategy for dealing with our daily victimization.

Our experiences with unsympathetic and antagonistic officials were even worse. They have convinced us that Model Cities is designed to deceive the community by pacifying our minds, our spirit, and our ambition.

Lesson Number Eight: Community People All Over the Country Need to Get Together to Create Our Own National Power Base to Force "Our" Government to Deal With Us Directly. We need to be able to communicate with each other, to teach each other, and to jointly pressure the government into creating honest community programs with straightforward guidelines.

We have already been in touch with community people from more than 20 other model neighborhoods and have been struggling for some time to get funds from the foundations and churches to create a National Citizens' Institute on Model Cities. Our struggles for money without strings have yet to pay off, but we'll get it somehow. In carrying out that struggle, we are mindful of what the Black abolitionist-scholar Frederick Douglass said more than 100 years ago:

> The whole history of progress of human liberty shows that all concessions yet made to her august claims have been born of earnest struggle . . . if there is no struggle, there is no progress.

Notes

1. "They" is the establishment, the manipulators of the status quo. "They" is a shifting collection whose changing identity will become clear in the next pages.

14

CITIZENSHIP AND PROFESSIONALISM IN PUBLIC ADMINISTRATION

Terry L. Cooper

In searching for the source of legitimacy for the public administrator in a democratic society I conclude that it is to be found in the role of citizen.[1] Public administrators are "professional citizens," or "citizen-administrators"; they are fiduciaries who are employed by the citizenry to work on their behalf. In the words of Walzer, public administrators are to be understood as "citizens in lieu of the rest of us."[2]

With this role definition in mind, I argue that the ethical obligations of the public administrator are to be derived from the obligations of citizenship in a democratic political community. These obligations include responsibility for establishing and maintaining horizontal relationships of authority with one's fellow citizens, seeking "power with" rather than "power over" the citizenry.[3] This attitude on the part of public administrators calls for engaging in activities which amount to an ongoing renewal and reaffirmation of the "social contract."[4] The public administrator is one who, in the language of our Puritan forebears, is responsible for assisting

Source: *Public Administration Review* 44(Special Issue, 1984): 143–149.

the rest of us in the "covenanting" process.[5] This use of the social contract metaphor and this allusion to the Puritan concept of covenanting are intended to refer to a regular readjustment or reconstruction of the mutual expectations of citizens in a democratic polity.

This "covenanting" or "social contracting" is an ongoing process which is carried out at all levels of government through the exercise of citizenship as the public office of the individual member of a democratic society. This office obligates one to look beyond his or her own particular personal interests in search of the larger common interest.[6]

The public administrator's role as citizen takes priority over less fundamental demands, such as organizational imperatives, pressure from politicians, or blind commitments to worthwhile values, such as efficiency, stability, orderliness, and timeliness.[7] Specific administrative tasks and duties are properly viewed as penultimate responsibilities. They must be carried out, but their modes of conduct should be ones which encourage participation in the political community and help to maintain the horizontal bonds of political authority. Ultimately, a public administrator's actions should reflect respect for the public office of citizenship for which he or she bears an obligation, which is prior to any other associated with public employment.

It is clear that this view of the public administrative role has some rather significant implications for an understanding of professionalism in public administration. Questions emerge, such as: Is this perspective compatible with professionalism? If so, what would professionalism mean? How would public administration education be affected?

These are important questions to which I will attempt some response. Before addressing them, however, it seems appropriate to outline briefly the citizenship role and its functions, and then to consider what is meant by professionalism in public administration. At that point, it should be possible to deal with the questions from some clearly understood points of reference.

Definitions of Citizenship

Since the terms "citizen" and "citizenship" are employed in a variety of ways with a range of meanings, from precise and limited to vague and broad, it is essential to establish some definitional boundaries. We might begin with very broad definitions of "citizenship" and "citizen" such as the following:

> Citizenship is the status and role which defines the authority and obligations of individual members of a community. This status and role may be formally codified in terms of qualifications, rights, and obligations by constitutions,

charters, and laws, or informally determined by values, tradition, and consensus. A citizen is one who qualifies for the status of citizenship as prescribed formally, or informally, by a particular community, and is encumbered with the obligations assigned to this role by that community.

This definition is so broad in scope that it requires more detailed distinctions within its boundaries if it is to be useful for our purposes. Recent essays by Richard Flathman and T. J. Lowi provide two dimensions of citizenship with establish more specific definitional reference points. Each of these dimensions can be viewed in terms of its polar extremes, and/or in terms of continua between those poles.

The first of these dimensions has to do with the distribution of authority. Flathman deals with authority in terms of high and low views of citizenship.[8] High definitions of citizenship are those which assume wide distribution of authority and describe citizens as peers who share equally in the exercise of authority. Low citizenship assumes a hierarchical distribution of authority with only a limited claim provided for the individual citizen. Flathman associates the high view with Aristotle and Rousseau, together with current authors such as Walzer, Arendt, Thompson, and Barber who argue from a similar perspective. The low view is identified with Hobbes and those such as Michael Oakeshott who currently share his basic position on authority. Flathman also associates the 20th century "democratic elitists" with this perspective.[9]

Lowi deals with the extent to which the citizenship role is defined by law, on the one hand, or by less formal influences, such as values, norms, traditions, culture, and religion on the other.[10] The terms which he uses to identify the poles of this dimension are "legal citizenship" and "ethical citizenship." "Legal citizenship" is prescribed and defined in terms of qualifications, rights, and obligations by constitutions and statutes. It is related to particular governmental jurisdictions. Citizenship, in this sense, is a purely political status and role.

"Ethical citizenship" involves a much broader definition of the role, which includes the social and economic aspects of life as well as the political. Citizenship, from this perspective, has to do with membership in a community—any community. These communities include, but are not limited to, political communities. Ethical citizenship is a role in neighborhoods and voluntary associations, as well as governmental jurisdictions such as cities and nations. The qualifications, rights, and obligations of citizenship, understood in this way, are defined and prescribed by the values, norms, traditions, and culture of any given community or by consensus among members of the community in specific instances.

Table 14.1 depicts the results of relating the four poles of the two dimensions of citizenship to each other. Four types of citizenship can then be

TABLE 14.1 Definition of Citizenship

	Legal	Ethical
High	Membership in a government jurisdiction Membership status, rights, and obligations legally defined Obligations limited to governmental arena Authority shared among members by law Extensive participation provided by law	Membership in any community, including, but not limited to, governmental jurisdictions Membership status, rights, and obligation defined by values, norms, tradition, and culture Obligations include political, social, and economic arenas Authority shared among members by custom, tradition, and consensus Extensive participation provided by custom, tradition, and consensus
Low	Membership in a government jurisdiction Membership status, rights, and obligations legally defined Obligations limited to governmental arena Authority hierarchically distributed by law Minimal participation provided by law	Membership in any community, including, but not limited to, governmental jurisdictions Membership status, rights, and obligation defined by values, norms, tradition, and culture Obligations include political, social, and economic arenas Authority heirarchically distributed by custom, tradition, and consensus Minimal participation provided by custom, tradition, and consensus

identified: high legal, low legal, high ethical, and low ethical. This simple typology provides us with a useful conceptual chart for clarifying how "citizenship" is used by various authors and what is implied by their particular usage. Flathman, for example, deals primarily with the legal dimension of citizenship. His concern is with the problems of adopting either a high legal or a low legal view of citizenship. He leans toward the high perspective with a shared exercise of political authority and insists that the citizenship role be narrowly confined to the political realm.

However, the ethical dimension of citizenship becomes the fundamental focus for some other scholarly treatments of the concepts. For example, William Mosher's preface and opening chapter in *Introduction to Responsible Citizenship* assumes a high ethical understanding of citizenship. Mosher explains that the citizenship course at the Maxwell School during the 1930s and 1940s, from which his book evolved, began by defining citizenship "largely with respect to politics and government." However, "in the course of time," according to Mosher, "the citizen was considered to be man in society."[11] In his introductory chapter, Mosher identifies two characteristics of a good citizen which fit this high ethical perspective of citizenship: (1) "Sensitiveness to the Social Rights and Needs of Others" and (2) "Capacity of Independent Thinking and Critical Evaluation." In a summary statement, he argues that "Acceptance of the predominance of human values in all situations and under all circumstances is a primary characteristic of the thoughtful citizen."[12]

And, of course, in the literature there are treatments of citizenship which focus on the interaction or blending of the types. These more complex variations on the four simple types in Table 14.1 indicate, of course, that in reality there are continua among the types with a range of gradations. Although the full development of these continua is not of prime importance for this particular essay, a few illustrative examples may be helpful in suggesting some of the permutations that are possible.

One such perspective is Norton Long's discussion of the relationship between "legal constitutions" and "ethical constitutions."[13] Building upon the Aristotelian assumption that a consensus about the nature of the good life is more fundamental than the legal structures of a polity, Long argues that the legal constitutions of the United States must be "interpreted by the ethical constitution that informs it." Effective citizenship, by his line of argument, is the result of this process of interaction between the ethical and the legal dimensions of citizenship.

Paul Sniderman's research on citizens and the attitudes they hold toward government led him to some conclusions about the nature of citizenship in democratic society which are a complex blending of the types. He assigns primary importance to factors which I have identified with Lowi's ethical dimension, but his exclusive concern is with the governmental arena. He does not view citizenship in the broad fashion associated with the ethical types in Table 14.1, but neither are the legal definitions of citizenship the exclusive considerations in his study.

In treating this hybrid type, which suggests a continuum between the legal and ethical types, Sniderman argues that the existence of a "civil temper," coupled with certain attitudes and values concerning the nature of political authority and allegiance owed to government, are the critical factors in the working out of the citizenship role in the United States. He is concerned with the citizenship role established by laws, but he views these "ethical" components of the role, rather than any legal provisos, as critical in shaping the forms of citizenship in this country.

The two major role types which emerged from Sniderman's field research are the "supportive citizen" and the "committed citizen."[14] The latter tends to be passive, acquiescent, and compliant in the face of hierarchical governmental authority, while the former is far more likely to resist, criticize, question, and insist on sharing the authority of government. In this way, Sniderman's work also suggests the continuum which exists between the high and low types of citizenship in Table 14.1.

Robert Salisbury views citizenship in the broadest sense, consistent with the ethical types in Table 14.1, but does not ignore the legal bases of citizenship.[15] Salisbury's view is similar to Long's in that he views both the ethical and the legal components as essential, but he gives greater weight to the former.

Salisbury argues that citizenship in any community requires at least some minimum degree of formal rules, laws, or agreements to establish peer status among the members. In some communities, such as the U.S. Congress, there are also elaborate systems of rules for distributing specific responsibilities, granting conditional authority, and establishing procedures. However, according to Salisbury, these formal, legal definitions are never sufficient, even when fully elaborated. They merely provide a foundation or framework for "the moral community" with its informal norms and values, such as "civic commitment" and "loyalty." Salisbury's emphasis on equality of status among citizens, and the necessity for active citizenship identify him with the high view. These commitments, coupled with the significance which he attributes to the ethical dimensions, locate him somewhere in the high ethical category. However, Salisbury's view of the formal legal aspects of citizenship as the essential structures within which ethical citizenship emerges, once again, suggests a continuum between the legal and ethical types. It is not possible to determine on the basis of Salisbury's article whether it is a continuum between high ethical and high legal or high ethical and low legal.

This application of the conceptual matrix in Table 14.1 to the works of Flathman, Mosher, Long, Sniderman, and Salisbury has been presented to illustrate its usefulness in clarifying what particular authors intend by the term citizenship. However, beyond that function as an analytical device for dealing with the literature, this matrix should be of value in orienting one's own concerns and commitments. It should help one to specify the dimensions of citizenship one wants to address, the streams of literature which are most relevant, and the critical issues which need to be engaged.

Legal and Ethical Citizenship in the United States

With these broad definitional types before us, I wish to indicate that the primary concern of this essay is with the ethical dimensions of citizenship and that my own commitment lies somewhere in the high ethical category. However, my position also evidences the existence of a more complex continuum than is portrayed in Table 14.1. It is a continuum which extends between the high ethical and low legal types of citizenship. That is, I recognize that the legal constitutional definition of citizenship is one which distributes authority in a limited hierarchical fashion. That was the intent of the framers of the Constitution and their reasons for doing so are set out in the *Federalist Papers*.[16] Their preference for a limited exercise of authority by the citizenry resulted in the structure of our representative government with its limited franchise, indirect election of the Senate and president, and the dependence of local governments upon the states.

Some of these constitutional provisions have been subsequently amended, and statutory action has created more extensive opportunities for citizens to more directly participate in government. Thus, our legal definitions of the status of citizens are not as low as originally stated, but still fall generally into that category.

This relatively low legal framework for citizenship has also provided us with a weak formal tradition of citizenship in the United States, as I argued in the previous paper mentioned at the beginning of this essay.[17] The founders did not distribute authority on an egalitarian fashion, nor did they articulate the functions and obligations of citizenship in much detail. The emphasis of the Constitution is more upon rights than obligations. The *rights* to vote and hold assemblies freely are established, but nothing is said about any *obligations* to participate in the electoral process or to engage in public discussion of issues. While one might argue that obedience to the law is certainly an obligation, that obligation is imposed upon everyone—citizens, resident aliens, and tourists alike. Obedience to the law is not distinctly associated with citizenship.

In spite of this weak formal approach to citizenship there has been a rather lively American tradition of ethical citizenship. From the covenantal tradition of the early Puritan communities with their styles of participatory self-governance, the New England town meetings, the experience of forming voluntary associations, which captured the attention of de Tocqueville,[18] and the cooperative establishment of frontier settlements, there has emerged a set of values, customs, beliefs, principles, and theories which provide the substance for ethical citizenship. In the founding years it was informed by the participatory democratic thought of Jefferson and the egalitarian philosophy which he put forth in the Declaration of Independence. And it has been further inspired by certain strains of the Judeo-Christian tradition which have been expressed politically and economically from time to time in movements such as the "Social Gospel" led by Walter Rauschenbusch.[19] The participatory dimension of ethical citizenship has found expression in the abolitionist movement, the populist movement, the labor union movement, the feminist movement, the civil rights movement, the environmental movement, the neighborhood movement, and the anti-tax movement.

All of these perspectives, ideas, experiences, and activities represent a continuing stream in American history which has functioned as a counterpoint to the formal definition of citizenship. They have tended to encourage more active participation in political, social, and economic affairs. They have motivated citizens to assume greater obligations for collective life, and they have provided experience in the sharing of responsibility. Without this multifaceted tradition of ethical citizenship, the nation would have lacked political and social dynamism. It has been the source of the motivation to collaborate, build, and maintain the common good.

The ethical dimensions of citizenship tradition have regularly given rise to changes in the legal definitions of citizenship. The franchise has been extended to nonwhites and women, slavery has been abolished, civil rights have been expanded, the right to equal employment opportunities has been established, and citizen participation in public policy making has been mandated. These changes, based on law, would never have taken place without the sense of obligation and the insistence upon active participation in governance which has been embodied in the tradition of ethical citizenship. It has been the driving force behind the democratization of the relatively elitist form of government provided in the Constitution and the elitist society of the founding era.

On the other hand, I must acknowledge that while the participatory aspect of our tradition of ethical citizenship has enhanced our legal definition of citizenship it has produced mixed results. The emergence and growth of the very interest groups which demand and generally receive greater participation in the political process has not always been accompanied by a broad sense of obligation for the common good. In an expanding economy, and with the blessing of pluralist theory, unfettered competition for power and resources has been pursued by interest groups and tolerated by the political community. This quest for the satisfaction of particular interests must be balanced with the more cooperative and communal strains of our heritages of ethical citizenship. The exercise of citizenship as the public office of the individual must carry with it an obligation to consider individual and group interests in the context of larger social and community interests.

It is not the legal definitions of citizenship that are of concern here because they are not of major consequence for conduct. It is the ethical dimension of citizenship that warrants our primary attention at this time in public administration. It is the values, norms, and traditions that encourage the sharing of authority and active participation in collective life that are essential. They transcend governmental jurisdictions and extend across political, social, and economic realms. It is essential that public administrators identify with this perspective if democratization is to continue. Public administrators, as key agents in the administrative state, play a critical role. They may actively and intentionally encourage democratic government, or they may subvert it, consciously or otherwise. Their professional identity and self-understanding will be crucial in moving them in one direction or the other.

If citizenship is the appropriate normative basis for the public administrative role,[20] it is the view of citizenship which is characterized above as the high ethical type which should inform and shape the professional identity and role of public administrators.

Professionalism in Public Administration

What are the implications of these proposals for the professionalism of public administrators? That depends on what is meant by the term "professionalism." It is not very fruitful to begin with the construction of an deal type of professionalism to which we compare ourselves. Rather, it is better to examine first the phenomena which have been associated with professionalism in public administration, and then to consider the values inherent in those phenomena. We then need to ask whether those values are consistent with those associated with citizenship in a democratic society. If not, we need to ask what shape professionalism should assume in order to be consistent with those values.

Beginning in that fashion, if we mean by professionalism something akin to the drive for neutrality, order, efficiency, control, standardization, and quantification which characterized the Progressive era of public administration and much of our history since, then there are serious problems, indeed. While organizations like the Bureau of Municipal Research in New York contributed a great deal to the rationalization of government, their efforts, and others of a similar nature, have also tended to subvert active citizenship.

Although Progressive reforms were typically advanced under the banner of a citizenship movement, with journals such as *The Efficient Citizen*,[21] the long-term result was not one of enhancing the control and participation of the citizenry.[22] It was rather the strengthening of an emerging class of technically-oriented administrators who were committed to the development of a scientific approach to public administration, as suggested by Wilson[23] and others. What those reformers failed to foresee was the impossibility of maintaining the subordination of "expert," "professional" administrators to the politicians in a modern industrial state. The power of technical expertise and specialized knowledge, the complexity of the problems to be faced, and the scale of government have tended to crowd out both the citizenry and their would-be representatives. Single-minded attempts at furthering this kind of professionalism among public administrators cannot but continue to erode the ethical dimensions of citizenship.

Technical expertise, rational approaches to problem solving, and specialized knowledge are not to be eschewed, but they must not provide the
norms for the professional identity of the public administrator. Otherwise,
we reinforce the role of the politically passive citizen who views government as a provider of public services, on the one hand, and the role of the
professional administrator who views the citizen as a consumer, on the
other.

It was this "consumer" image of the citizenry, with its deprivation of political responsibility for government, which emerged as one of the central
concerns of the bicentennial conference of the Center for the Study of Federalism. In commenting on the deliberations at that conference, Daniel
Elazar observed:

> Particularly in a republic and most particularly in a democratic republic, those
> who share in the polity cannot be less than citizens if the polity itself is to sur-
> vive in its chosen form. Consumers, at most, pick and choose among goods
> offered them by others, in whose offering they have no real share. How differ-
> ent such a course is from that of citizens who must share in determining the
> activities of the government as well as in utilizing its products.[24]

Again, it is not that the expertise of public administrators as providers of
public goods and services should be shunned or dismissed. Rather, it is that
expertise and the capacity for achieving efficient operations of the bureaucracy must not provide the fundamental norms for the public administrator's relationship to the citizenry. As Norton Long has argued, we must not
"substitute a market with consumers for a polity with citizens."[25] This is
precisely the risk in identifying professionalism in public administration
with technical expertise and efficiency.[26]

Rosenbloom cautions against adopting the traditional goals of professionalized public administration in the United States for similar reasons.
He identifies the tradition of professionalism in the late 19th and 20th centuries with values which were derived from Wilson's famous essay, the scientific management school, and the movement for scientific principles of
public administration.[27] He argues that these values were efficiency, economy, and effectiveness—"the trinity for the professional bureaucrat."
Rosenbloom further maintains that at some point "orthodox public administration" adopted "the greatest good of the greatest number" as its definition of the public interest because this principle was most consistent
with its professional values.

However laudable these values and this principle may be when applied
conditionally, according to Rosenbloom, when employed unconditionally,
they present a threat to the rights of the citizenry. Rosenbloom correctly insists that this perspective is at odds with the values and principles of the
U.S. Constitution which "places no premium on efficiency, economy, or

even effectiveness in a programmatic sense." Rather the Constitution places limits on majoritarianism and sets a high value on liberty, individual freedom, and "moderately representative government." He concludes that "constitutional values simply do not mesh well with the values of professionalized public administration."

What is the source of this conflict or tension? It is the lack of a normative base for the public administrative role which would properly condition the influence of that trinity of values which Rosenbloom attributes to traditional professionalism in public administration. These are penultimate values for democratic government which must always be measured against the more ultimate values associated with citizenship. Efficiency must never be allowed to displace the right and the obligation of the citizenry to debate the issues and influence the formation of public policy. Effectiveness of particular programs and policies should always be viewed in terms of their positive and negative impacts on the ability of citizens to secure and maintain self-governance. Economy should never be the justification for actions which threaten the common good. The application of "the greatest good of the greatest number" should never be allowed to jeopardize the constitutional guarantees of a minority.

An understanding of professionalism in public administration which is appropriate for a democratic society should be one which is gounded in what is described earlier in this paper as a high ethical view of citizenship. We should identify ourselves first with the citizenry in their sharing of authority and their right and obligation to participate in the affairs of the political community. We should begin to identify the meaning of professionalism in public administration from this normative base. We should not do it for the self-serving instrumental reasons which are so typical of "professional" activities in many fields. I recognize the problems of poor professional image and indiscriminate attacks upon the public services by unscrupulous politicians.[28] However, these are insufficient justifications to move ahead on the subject of professionalism. These are expedient reasons which will be so perceived by the people. These are problems which are only symptomatic of the extent to which we have a deeper problem of the legitimacy of the public administrative role.

Why then should we be concerned with professionalism, and why should we begin from the perspective of citizenship? My answer to the first question is that we should be concerned with that problem of legitimacy. And that means we should be clear about what we "profess," or "avow publicly."[29] We need to be accountable for the core values that guide the exercise of our role. We will achieve that not by measuring ourselves against the plethora of generic definitions of professionalism nor by working our way down the "laundry lists" of professional attributes, but by clarifying the source of our authority, toward what end we exercise that authority, and in what status we do so.

We should begin our redefinition of professionalism from an understanding of citizenship because that is where the clarification of our role in a democratic society leads. The source of our authority is the citizenry. We are employed to exercise that authority on their behalf. We do so as one of them; we can never divest ourselves of our own status as members of the political community with obligations for its well-being. A search for a redefined professionalism in public administration necessarily requires an exploration of what it means to be a citizen/administrator.

Public Administration Education

If this image of the public administrator as a professional citizen is to be pursued, public administration education will have to be a critical component of any strategy for moving in that direction. What we offer as a formal definition of professionalism should be supported by our curricula. The courses we offer, the requirements we establish, and the allocation of scarce time among competing topics reflect the *de facto* normative definition of professionalism just as surely as a budget reveals the actual mission of an organization.

Under the assumptions that the leading academic programs in the nation represent the dominant educational emphases of the field, I have attempted to review their curriculum outlines in order to assess the current state of affairs in a general fashion. Eight of the top 10 schools in the Morgan and Meier reputational survey of master's degree programs in public administration were selected for this purpose.[30] Their bulletins and catalogs of courses were then reviewed and compared with two lists, one consisting of topics related to technical expertise and the other composed of topics dealing with citizenship in a democracy.[31] The result of this review was so unsurprising that it is not really necessary to belabor the obvious. The great weight of all of the curricula of these programs appears to lie in topics associated with technical expertise. The real question is whether any course-length treatment of citizenship related topics is provided at all.

If public administration is moving toward greater concern for professional gatekeeping (credentials, licensing, accreditation, standards), it is essential that we deal explicitly and overtly with those priorities before we create machinery to implement and enforce them.

David Rosenbloom has maintained that "professionalism requires an understanding of constitutionalism." He insists that "public bureaucrats who interact with people must learn to understand, respect, and protect the constitutional rights of those individuals."[32] This would be only a beginning, albeit a significant one. The value base for professionalism in public administration should include constitutional theory and history, along with other topics listed which are essential in order to "understand, respect, and protect" the rights of the citizenry, but also to be responsive to their preferences and able to work constructively with their conflicting demands.

Technical expertise, competence in specialized fields, and the ability to employ the best available scientific methods are unquestionably also essential for modern public administration. However, they will better serve the purposes of democratic government if employed by men and women who view themselves first as citizens in a political community, who are obligated to wield their expertise on behalf of their fellow citizens and under their sovereignty.

Notes

1. Terry L. Cooper, "Citizenship in an Age of Scarcity: A Normative Essay on Ethics for Public Administrators," in *Politics and Administration: Woodrow Wilson and Contemporary Public Administration,* James Bowman and Jack Rabin, eds. (New York: Marcel Dekker, forthcoming).

2. Michael Walzer, *Obligations: Essays on Disobedience, War and Citizenship* (Cambridge, Mass.: Harvard University Press, 1970), p. 216.

3. Mary Parker Follett, *Dynamic Administration: The Collected Papers of Mary Parker Follett,* Henry C. Metcalf and L. Urwick, eds., (New York: Harper and Brothers, 1940), pp. 101–106.

4. The term "social contract" is used metaphorically here and is not intended to suggest a dependence upon social contract theories.

5. Lawrence A. Scaff, "Citizenship in America: Theories of the Founding," in *The Non-Lockean Roots of American Democratic Thought,* J. Chaudhuri, ed. (Tucson: University of Arizona Press, 1977); Michael Walzer, *The Revolution of the Saints: A Study in Origins of Radical Politics* (New York: Atheneum, 1970); John Wise, "A Vindication of the Government of New England Churches," in *Colonial American Writing,* Roy Harvey Pearce, ed. (New York: Rinehart, 1950).

6. Samuel Walker McCall, *The Liberty of Citizenship* (New Haven: Yale University Press, 1915), pp. 17, 19; J. G. A. Pocock, *Politics, Language, and Time* (New York: Atheneum, 1971), pp. 86–87; Robert Pranger, *The Eclipse of Citizenship: Power and Participation in Contemporary Politics* (New York: Holt, Rinehart and Winston, 1968), p. 92; Walzer, *Obligations, op. cit.*

7. Herbert J. Spiro, *Responsibility in Government: Theory and Practice* (New York: Van Nostrand, 1969), p. 101.

8. Richard Flathman, "Citizenship and Authority: A Chastened View of Citizenship," *News for Teachers of Political Science* (Summer 1981).

9. Flathman, *ibid.,* cites Schumpeter, Berelson, and Lipset among others.

10. Theodore J. Lowi, "The Two Cities of Norton Long," in *Cities Without Citizens,* Benjamin R. Schuster, ed. (Philadelphia: Center for the Study of Federalism, 1981).

11. William E. Mosher, ed., *Introduction to Responsible Citizenship* (New York: Henry Holt and Company, 1941), p. iv.

12. *Ibid.,* pp. 4–7.

13. Norton E. Long, "Cities Without Citizens," in *Cities Without Citizens,* pp. 7–8.

14. Paul Sniderman, *A Question of Loyalty* (Berkeley: University of California Press, 1981), pp. 1–46.

15. Robert H. Salisbury, "On Cities and Citizens," in *Cities Without Citizens,* pp. 22–29.

16. See especially No. 10.

17. Cooper, "Citizenship in an Age of Scarcity."

18. Alexis de Tocqueville, *Democracy in America* (New York: New American Library, 1956).

19. Walter Rauschenbusch, *A Theology for the Social Gospel* (New York: Abingdon Press, 1945).

20. Cooper, "Citizenship in an Age of Scarcity," see summary at beginning of this essay.

21. Lawrence Joseph O'Toole, *The Concept of Participation in the Literature of American Public Administration: A Study of the Orthodoxy of Reform,* unpublished doctoral dissertation, Syracuse University, 1975, pp. 207–218.

22. Samuel P, Hays, "The Politics of Reform in Municipal Government in the Progressive Era," *Pacific Northwest Quarterly* (October 1964).

23. Woodrow Wilson, "The Study of Administration," *Political Science Quarterly* (June 1887).

24. Daniel J. Elazar, "Is Federalism Compatible with Prefectorial Administration?" *Publius* (Spring 1976), p. 3.

25. Norton Long, "The Three Citizenships," *Publius* (Spring 1976), p. 21.

26. This concern for the consumer image of the citizenry emerged again in *Publius* (Spring 1981). See especially pp. 21, 49, 52–53.

27. David H. Rosenbloom, "Constitutionalism and Public Bureaucrats," *The Bureaucrat* (Fall 1982), p. 54.

28. Jack Rabin, "The Profession of Public Administration," *The Bureaucrat* (Winter 1981–82), p. 11.

29. *Webster's New World Dictionary,* Second College Edition, 1970.

30. David R. Morgan and Kenneth J. Meier, "Reputations and Productivity Among U.S. Public Administration and Public Affairs Programs," *Public Administration Review* (November/December 1981), p. 669.

31. Although they were requested, materials were not received from Georgia and Princeton.

32. Rosenbloom, "Constitutionalism and Public Bureaucrats," p. 55.

15

CITIZENSHIP AND SERVICE DELIVERY: THE PROMISE OF COPRODUCTION

Charles H. Levine

One of the latent functions of the great taxpayer's revolt of 1978 is that it taught and continues to teach students of public administration many lessons. California's Proposition 13, in particular, has had a sobering effect on the theory and practice of public administration.

While many explanations have been offered for the passage of Proposition 13 and similar taxing and spending limits in other states and localities,[1] the rationale developed by Kirlin is one of most persuasive:[2] During the late 1960s and throughout the 1970s, the intricately complex political and administrative structure of the public sector became hopelessly beyond the reach of the average citizen through the traditional formal mechanisms of political participation—voting, parties, and interest groups. Taxing and spending referendums like Proposition 13 gave these alienated

[1] I wish to acknowledge the assistance of Barbara H. Seekins, a graduate student at the University of Kansas, and the thoughtful comments on an earlier draft of this paper by Glenn Fisher of Wichita State University and Paul Schumaker and Elaine B. Sharp of the University of Kansas.

Source: *Public Administration Review* 44(Special Issue, 1984); 178–187.

people an opportunity to express their frustration on a grand issue of public policy while also allowing them the opportunity to act on their disaffection by becoming "idiots" in the original Greek sense of the word, meaning someone indifferent to his duties as a citizen. If citizens could not understand or effect their government, then limiting it and ignoring it became a rational response.

The linkage between citizens and their government has become strained over the past two decades. At a minimum, citizens function as legitimizers of government "to transform power relations into authority relations."[3] In the United States, this legitimacy has eroded substantially under the strain of Vietnam, Watergate, and a host of factors like urbanization, governmental fragmentation, and rapid spatial mobility.[4] While there is little indication that diffuse support for the values that underpin democratic institutions has eroded significantly, confidence in the institutions of our government and for the people who occupy positions in those institutions has declined dramatically.

The contemporary crisis of public confidence in the institutions and leaders of American society is without parallel in this century. Lipset and Schneider capture the significance of this "confidence gap" in the conclusion of their recent extensive analysis of 45 years of public opinion research:

> Although we have pointed to evidence that Americans retain their faith in their social system, it would be wrong not to indicate our belief that the situation is much more brittle than it was at the end of the 1920s, just before the Great Depression, or in 1965, immediately preceding the unrest occasioned by the Vietnam War and the outbreak of racial tension. These two troubled eras, each of which resulted in a decline of faith in institutions, followed periods of high legitimacy. The United States enters the 1980s, however, with a lower reserve of confidence in the ability of its institutional leaders to deal with the problems of the polity, the society, and the economy than at any time in this century. As a result of the strains produced by the experiences of the last fifteen years, our institutional structure is less resilient than in the past. Should the 1980s be characterized by a major crisis, the outcome could very well be substantial support for movements seeking to change the system in a fundamental way. Serious setbacks in the economy or in foreign policy, accompanied by a failure of leadership, would raise greater risks of a loss of legitimacy now than at any time in this century. Although the evidence on the surface seems reassuring, there are disturbing signs of deep and serious discontent.[5]

The decline in trust and support for public administrators has followed this general trend: in the polls, public employees and public agencies are both held in low regard by the American people. Allegations that bureaucrats are generally lazy, untrustworthy, wasteful, and power hungry are widely accepted as fact. The paradox of this situation is that when citizens are asked to evaluate their concrete experiences with public agencies and public employees, they do so in a much more favorable light.

The explanation for this nearly inverse relationship between what Americans believe about their government's poor performance and the satisfaction they report in their day-to-day dealings with government has been fueled by a popular anti-government myth deeply rooted in our culture. According to Goodsell:

> A myth can be so grand only because it is somehow useful [to the enemies of government] . . . bureaucracy as an enemy is very dependable because it is never defeated and hence never disappears—thus never terminating its availability as an enemy. In addition, bureaucracy's imputed association with huge size, impersonalness, and mysterious technology, plus its connection with the sovereign power of the state make it particularly onimous and hence as a target of hatred. . . .
>
> . . . Americans' habitual suspicion of government and corresponding commitment to capitalism make public bureaucracy particularly exploitable: a bureaucratic America stands as the antithesis of a self-reliant, free, and entrepreneurial America. Unfortunate departures from this romantic vision can be blamed on bureaucracy.[6]

The antipathy toward bureaucracy is so pervasive and deeply rooted in our political culture that we cannot realistically begin any discussion of public administration and citizenship without accepting it as a given and perhaps even as a framework that conditions all possible relationships between citizens and the state in the United States. Within this framework, the strategy of "aggressive professionalism" that has characterized public administration for most of the past two decades must be judged as futile, misguided at best, and downright absurd at worst. Although there are numerous examples of excellence and success, relying on neutral competence as a defense against critics and political spoilsmen by sealing off more and more of the technical core of public agencies merely provides more ammunition for critics who charge public administration with being self-serving and unresponsive. Past attempts to remedy this problem by increasing citizen participation largely failed because of the reluctance of "bureaucrat-professionals" to incorporate "citizen-amateurs" on anything more than a marginal basis in agency operations and policy making. Such arrangements usually collapsed or simply limped along under the weight of widespread citizen apathy and indifference.[7] As a consequence, in the 1980s we find public agencies and public administrators beleaguered by diffuse hostility in the citizenry, vulnerable to increased tinkering by elected officials, and beset by financial stringency.

Fiscal Stress and Service Delivery Alternatives

Fiscal stress is an overlay on the anti-government/bureaucracy framework that conditions the relationship between citizenship and public administration. Combining the two sets of constraints highlights two persistent problems of public administration:

1. How can a government build support for taxation to finance public service when citizens do not trust government to produce appropriate services?
2. And, how can governments provide appropriate services if citizens are unwilling to pay for them through collective mechanisms like taxation?

If the answer to both these questions is "it can't," then we can only expect a starved public sector producing low-quality services. But the situation is more complex than that. Until recently, revenues produced through all sorts of indirect means like intergovernmental grants, income tax "bracket creep," and other "fiscal illusions" have provided revenues even when political support for government has been eroding.[8] By the 1980s, however, taxing and spending limitations, tax cuts, and other devices like tax-indexing have reduced the capacity of these mechanisms to produce funds automatically. The link between public support and resources is now more tightly coupled. As a result, either governments somehow are able to develop a new appreciation for the public provision of services or they must find some other way to provide services. In the solution to this dilemma lies a way out of the problems of building a collective appreciation for the public provision of services and, at the same time, rekindling, at least in a small way, citizenship.

In their struggle to cope with fiscal stress, governments have chosen a number of avenues to lighten their financial load. The specific tactics are familiar to those who have concerned themselves with alternative methods of delivering services. They include:

A. Privatizing service delivery
   1. Contracting with a private for-profit firm
   2. Franchising services to a private firm
   3. Vouchers
   4. User fees and charges to ration demand for services
   5. Shedding service responsibility to a private firm or non-profit organization

B. Intergovernmentalizing service delivery arrangements
    1. Shedding services to another unit of government or authority
    2. Sharing service responsibility
    3. Sharing functions like data processing, planning, and communications

C. Improving operating productivity
    1. Methods to monitor performance
    2. Methods to maximize output per dollar
    3. Methods to improve financial decision making
    4. Methods to track costs
    5. Methods to monitor and manage contracts

D. Deprofessionalizing bureaucracies
    1. Civilianizing sworn personnel
    2. Using volunteers and paraprofessionals
    3. Using reserves and auxiliaries

E. Devolving service responsibility
    1. Neighborhood organization of service delivery
    2. Self-help
    3. Coproduction
    4. Public/private partnerships to solve community problems.

It is important to recognize that for the most part debates over the value of these alternatives have been conducted almost exclusively on the basis of narrow economic and political criteria; i.e., how much money will be saved and how feasible will they be to implement in a political environment composed of people with strong stakes in the *status quo?*[9] Generally ignored in attempts to evaluate these alternatives are their potential contributions to improving citizenship including: (1) citizen trust in government; (2) citizen efficacy; and (3) a shared conception of the "common good." In other words, their contributions to resolving the gap between disaffected citizens and their government are disregarded.

At the heart of the citizenship issue is the stake citizens have in their community, its government, and its policies. As Norton Long observed well before our current crisis:

> Perhaps the first task of securing citizenship is the development of the sense of *moi commun*. There have to be citizens who feel responsible and they have to have something to feel responsible for. There must be quite literally a public thing with which they identify and which they are concerned to support.... Responsibility for something one takes no active part in is difficult to arouse and maintain.[10]

If we accept Long's notion of responsibility as the key to citizen trust in government, efficacy, and a shared conception of the common good, how do the service delivery alternatives governments are now considering and pursuing stack up? And, just as importantly, how do they contribute to reconciling the growing gap between citizens and public employees?

The most radical of these strategies, *privatizing public services,* gives great glee to those who criticize public agencies for failing to meet market tests of efficiency and responsiveness. They argue that if institutional arrangements for the provision of public services are organized along market lines, the consumers of these services will be better off because they will be receiving goods and services that take advantage of the efficiencies derived from competition.[11] Even where government is a monopoly supplier, it can reap efficiencies through the internal economies derived from the bidding of competitive suppliers. In the ideal world of the privatizers, almost everything government does can be put out for bids from vehicle maintenance in the police department to the actual delivery of patrol and security services. Better yet, from the viewpoint of the advocates of privatization, is the situation where governments merely provide a competitive environment where private firms supply services to consumers either with or without a formal contract. In such an arrangement, a city government, for example, can consist "of three persons: the city manager, the city attorney, and a secretary. Their main job [is] administering the contracts under which the various public services [are] provided."[12]

What is the role of the citizen and citizenship in this model? Put simply, citizens are consumers, buying privatized services just as they would buy any other service provided by the private sector. The rights and duties of a citizen in this arrangement would be restricted to buying services and voting in a government that directly provided few services. The high citizenship of Pericles, Aristotle, and Rousseau that requires citizens to be active members of a self-governing community is excused by the advocates of privatization as irrelevant in an age of rational, self-centered private interests.[13] Indeed, privatization affirms the contemporary view of citizenship as passive and legalistic and also the Lockean notion that government is a machine for the furtherance of one's private interests; civic consciousness and commitment are neither something worthwhile in themselves nor part of a citizen's responsibility.[14] This attitude is wholly consistent with the view of the privatizers that the citizen ought to be a consumer, a voter, and perhaps a member of interest groups, nothing more. Public-spirited action has no place in this scheme.

In a similar vein, *intergovernmentalizing* service delivery adds little to providing a structure to support citizenship. Shedding service responsibility to such arrangements simply makes government more complex and more difficult for citizens to comprehend.[15] And, to the extent that local services are transferred to either higher, larger, or more fragmented units of government like the states or special districts, they are likely to be administered by units of government where local interests have difficulty aggregating their influence and accessing decision makers.

The improvement of *operating productivity* has similar drawbacks from the viewpoint of providing citizens an opportunity and incentive to participate in government. Improving the productivity of government operations usually means tightening decision rules, applying technical rationality, and bounding out environmental turbulence—including politics and citizens. By rationalizing the services of government agencies to the most efficient level possible under monopoly conditions, this approach attempts to replicate the efficiencies of the market without market mechanisms. However, governments pursuing the productivity panacea will likely discover that after a few noteworthy gains, diminishing returns will set in fairly rapidly and services are bound to deteriorate as budgets contract. Furthermore, there is no place for citizens in this closed, mechanistic conception of public service delivery, except for their indirect role in setting the levels of services through voting and interest group participation and their direct role as service consumers.

More hope is offered by the other two clusters of alternatives—deprofessionalizing bureaucracies and devolving service responsibility. The growing *deprofessionalization* of public bureaucracies is being caused by the need to reduce the high cost of personnel. Examples include civilianizing positions previously occupied by sworn personnel and the use of paraprofessional, volunteer, part-time, reserve, and auxiliary employees. These tactics contribute to saving money on salaries, fringe benefits, and pension costs.

It should be recognized that deprofessionalization runs counter to the trend toward greater professionalization of public employees through specialized selection, education, training, equipment, and technologies. The development of a professional identity and status for public employees has been a mixed blessing. Although professionalization has allowed public employees to claim a legitimate right to define proper conduct with respect to matters concerned in their work, it has also had a perverse outcome: It has promoted the mystification of public work and, consequently, citizen confusion and alienation. In the case of police, for example, Menke, White, and Carey argue:

> We believe police professionalism has at least two consequences that go to the heart of the principles that underlie our society's form of democratic social organization. These consequences include the mystification of the issues of crime and disorder and mystification of the issue surrounding the right of the state (through its agents) to intervene in the lives of the citizenry.[16]

The ethos of professionalism has become so vital to the defense and legitimization of public organizations, their mission, and their decision rules that even when volunteers, civilians, and reserves are vital to meet demand, or simply to save money, they are usually incorporated into the organization with substantial resistance on the part of the full-time staff. Most often they are segregated into special units and treated as marginal employees so as not to "contaminate the professionalism" of the regular staff. Even where this separation breaks down under the most severe conditions of fiscal stress, it usually occurs with great reluctance on the part of managers and often with substantial concessions granted to unionized employees.

An even more promising development for citizenship is the alternative of *devolving service responsibility* to neighborhood organizations, individual service consumers, and public/private partnerships. Some of these activities can be lumped together under the label of "coproduction"; i.e., the joint provision of public services by public agencies and service consumers. The most common example is the carrying out of garbage to the curb rather than having a collector cart it from behind the house. Other examples include parent participation in the educational process by helping their children with homework and the voluntary organization of recreation programs by participants using facilities provided by a local government. Not only is coproduction widespread in our society, it is becoming more so as budgets (and public employee numbers) decline. As Nathan Glazer recently argued:

> A greater degree of voluntarism and of self-help can do a great deal to provide for needs and services that, if provided through the state, require a heavy burden of taxation, high deficits, and a variety of unpleasant and increasingly dangerous economic developments. Certainly the role of the welfare state is still crucial. But it must more and more ponder partnerships with the variety of voluntary, market, nonstatutory organizations and mechanisms that we find in each society. Beyond that, the welfare states must ponder the possibility that their own actions undermine these mechanisms. One thing in any case is clear: the problems the welfare state now confronts—economic, fiscal, social, psychological and political—can not be dealt with by further growth along the lines of the 1950's and 1960's.[17]

Perhaps the most significant thing about Glazer's observation is that he sees voluntarism, self-help, and coproduction as more than a financial panacea for fiscally strapped governments. Indeed, he sees these arrangements as mechanisms for a more continuous day-to-day involvement of individuals and neighborhoods in government. He argues that in a society that has more widespread affluence and education than ever before, the prospects for the successful devolution of service responsibility to citizens from the state increase, and with it a concomitant improvement in the relationship between the public employee and the citizen as they come to share more service and decision-making responsibility.

But despite these optimistic prospects, voluntarism, self-help, and coproduction arrangements by themselves are no guarantee that overall citizen competence and commitment to the common good will be improved. Activities like taking out the garbage, helping one's child with homework, or even serving on a neighborhood patrol will not by themselves necessarily improve a citizen's desire to take an active part in the community. Nevertheless, they are a potential wedge into improved citizenship that is qualitatively superior to the other four alternatives. For example, the private provision of services cannot possibly lead to better citizens—only smarter consumers—while coproduction lays the foundation for a positive relationship between government and citizens by making citizens an integral part of the service delivery process. Through these experiences citizens may build both competence and a broader perspective, a vision of the community and of what it can and should become. As Sheldon Wolin has observed:

> The specialized roles assigned the individual, or adopted by him are not a full substitute for citizenship because citizenship provides what other roles cannot, namely an integrative experience which brings together the multiple role-activities of the contemporary person and demands that the separate roles be surveyed from a more general point of view.[18]

The question remains, however, how does one design a system that builds a sense of community responsibility on the foundation of resident involvement in service delivery when that involvement is predicated on narrow self-interest? Some of the answer is provided in the next section of this paper by looking at an example of one such arrangement, community-based crime prevention groups. Before proceeding, the following table of alternative service delivery arrangements, strategies, and citizen roles summarizes the argument so far.

Community-Based Crime Prevention Groups

Communities always have been concerned about crime. Where effective law enforcement was not developed, citizens have always found ways of apprehending criminals and preventing crime. Citizen activity in modern law enforcement includes activities which can be performed by individuals or groups with or without the assistance or knowledge of the police. In the 1980s, these activities have become a very important deterrent to criminal activities. Yin argues, for example, that "community efforts, far from being a supplementary resource, may actually be the essence of successful crime prevention activities."[19]

TABLE 15.1   Service Delivery Arrangements, Strategies, and Citizen Roles

Alternative Service Delivery Arrangements	Dominant Strategy	Citizen Role
(1) Professionalized Bureaucracy	Specialization	Client
(2) Privatized Service Delivery	Contracting Out/User Fees	Consumer
(3) Intergovernmental Service Delivery Arrangements	Shedding and Sharing Service Responsibility	Client
(4) Improved Operating Productivity	Maximization of Output	Client
(5) Deprofessionalized Bureaucracies	Use of Paraprofessionals/ Civilianization	Marginal Employee
(6) Devolved Service Responsibility	Coproduction	Coproducer

As one might expect, there is a wide variety of citizen activity in crime prevention in the United States today. These activities can be roughly divided according to whether they are performed by individuals or groups.[20] Individual activities involve a number of target hardening activities, such as installing locks and alarms. Group activities include education projects and activities which facilitate reporting.[21] Educational projects are aimed at making the public more knowledgeable about crime. Activities include attempts to encourage witness reporting, group presentation projects, membership projects, and home presentation projects about home security and the reporting of suspicious activities. The theory behind these activities is that just being made aware of the scope and magnitude of crime will motivate people to become more involved in activities associated with bringing about its reduction. Educational activities may or may not be provided by law enforcement personnel and may take place in conjunction with other group activities not directly related to law enforcement.

Activities to facilitate reporting provide a means for residents to actually report any information related to criminal activity. These activities include two basic forms: stationary and active. Examples of stationary activities are whistle-stop projects, radio watch projects, and special telephone line projects. Whistle-stop projects involve a whistle alert system used by witnesses and victims of crime. Radio watch projects use people with access to two-way radios and a dispatcher to make crime reporting easier for individuals. Special telephone line projects facilitate anonymous reporting of criminal activities. Active reporting activities include various building and neighborhood patrol programs.

There are a number of important benefits to be derived from these citizen involvement programs. First, resource contraints can often restrict police to providing only arrest and investigation functions. Citizen involvement can supplement these core functions and, in doing so, can extend their role from crime prevention to the actual provision of law enforcement services as well. Second, if citizen groups provide better crime reporting information and are willing to testify, it becomes easier to bring individuals to trial. Finally, and perhaps most importantly, activities that reduce the opportunity to commit crime have been shown to aid the development of a neighborhood's sense of community.[22]

Despite these benefits, there are also a number of problems associated with citizen crime prevention programs. For example, Yin and his colleagues found that groups were susceptible to vigilante behavior when members were recruited on the basis of social compatibility with other patrol members or when group activity became particularly dull. However, one of their conclusions was that vigilantism was only occasionally present in resident patrols, and vigilante behavior can be dealt with through open membership drives and the development of activities to avoid prolonged boredom.[23]

Another problem is "crime displacement" which may occur when a program is successful in preventing crime in an area. Criminals may then move to an area without as successful a crime prevention program or to an area without any program. Crime displacement can be prevented if all areas of a city, or the country for that matter, implement effective crime prevention programs.

A third problem is that of program maintenance. Pomerleau has observed that: "a most significant problem with volunteer citizen groups . . . is the maintenance of enthusiasm and active participation."[24] As an example, one frequently given reason for quitting a crime prevention group is boredom, implying that decreased crime provides little to report and little to do. Maintaining community-based crime prevention projects is, therefore, a serious problem for a community and suggests an important avenue toward the development of responsible citizens.

Getting citizens to participate in an organization in the first place is substantially the same problem as that involved in maintaining that participation over time. Five conditions appear to be minimally necessary for the successful development and maintenance of community-based crime prevention groups: skills, incentives, independence, variety, and cooperation.

Though *skills* are usually recognized as important they are sometimes passed over lightly because they are so basic. For example, there are several important skills involved in reporting a crime or suspicious activity. First, the observer must be familiar with the area involved (e.g., be able to recognize a neighbor's car). Second, the observer must have a definition of crime or suspicious activity to apply to each situation (e.g., an unfamiliar car or van moving slowly through the neighborhood). Third, the reporter must know where to call. And finally, the observer must be able to provide as much information as is available to the police or group dispatcher (e.g., description, color, and license number of vehicle). The police can be particularly helpful in providing training or training materials related to these reporting skills.

Communications skills, while similar to reporting skills, also include the ability to converse with other group members. Salem found that these skills are usually acquired through previous organizational experiences.[25] If this is the case, the longer an individual is an active member of a group, the more likely the skills that person needs will develop.

Leadership skills allow members to direct the group themselves. Experience has shown that dependence on a single individual as a leader can cause a serious problem if the leader leaves the group.[26] The lack of a replacement may cause the group to disband. While it may be important to have a group leader it may be even more important that a number of members learn leadership skills. This may be accomplished if leadership roles, e.g., chairing meetings, rotate among members of the group.

Finally, some of the technical skills necessary to community-based crime prevention activities are obvious, e.g., the operation of two-way radios or the selection of security locks, and some are less obvious, e.g., first aid or auto safety. In any case, the police can play an important part in providing this technical know-how and assistance.

Long recognized as important for maintaining group solidarity, *incentives* provide the motivation to participate in group activities.[27] In her analysis of citizen participation, Arnstein has observed that you cannot organize a community without such "deliverables."[28]

Monetary incentives include direct and indirect rewards. Direct monetary incentives include payments for salaries of staff, payments for attending meetings or as awards for other participation, and the reimbursement for expenses, such as gas, phone calls, and postage. Indirect monetary incentives include such things as tax credits for "volunteer work" or free day care for the children of participants during activities.[29]

Feedback, the contact with group members by other members or people outside the group to let members know how well they are doing, is an important source of nonmonetary incentive for maintaining organizations. Such things as police reports summarizing calls and the results of those calls or an awards ceremony to recognize outstanding accomplishments are examples of feedback. Praise for a job well done on a day-to-day basis is also an important type of feedback. The importance of the police in providing positive feedback to group members cannot be overstressed. Even the tone of voice of the police dispatcher or the response time of an officer answering a member's report can have an effect on a member's participation.

Independence relates to the actual operations of the program and is not meant to imply that there should be lack of contact with police or a larger neighborhood organization, for example. There are three areas of program operations which relate to independence. First, overdependence on an individual member or group of individuals can cause problems when that individual or group is no longer associated with the program and no one else knows what to do. This would include dependence on professional organizers or the police if they helped organize the program. Second, overdependence on outside financial assistance can cause instability. A program which has come to depend on financial assistance (e.g., employed permanent staff) can be destroyed if that funding is eliminated. Finally, dependence on a single issue or some crisis to keep the group organized can threaten program maintenance. While crime is a great issue for getting people organized, it is a poor one for keeping them organized. Instead, getting people together to get to know each other and then making crime prevention one activity of many the group undertakes likely would be a better mechanism for building and maintaining a crime prevention group than a short-term crime crisis.

Variety of task, membership, and funding also are very important aspects in the maintenance of crime prevention groups. Members from various backgrounds bring different attitudes and experiences which can add to the group and can reduce the likelihood of vigilantism. Similarly, the greater number of activities the group undertakes will enhance the probability of attracting and retaining members. There is a fundamental tradeoff between size and variety, however. While a small group is likely to enhance the development of participation and group solidarity, it may die of its own success (e.g., if the threat of crime declines). A wider variety of activities may be necessary to sustain and stabilize the group, but this may cause the size of the group to increase and, subsequently, decrease group solidarity.[30] Somewhere during the process of growth and development a balance between the costs and the benefits of small size and diverse functions will have to be found to maintain long-term group effectiveness and solidarity.[31]

Finally, if funding is necessary, it should be attained from a variety of sources to protect the organization from cutoffs and cutbacks from any one source. Similarly, a group's nonmonetary sources of support, e.g., the media and police professionals, also should vary for the same reasons.

Cooperation is an important factor for program maintenance at several levels: with police; between members; and with other groups and organizations. Cooperation between police and private groups and the idea of sharing responsibilities is especially helpful in avoiding police resistance to a community-based crime prevention effort.[32] Similarly, the composition of the group is likely to be especially critical to fostering cooperation. Neighborhood unity or sense of community is likely to be enhanced as members

TABLE 15.2 Program Failure: Some Causes and Solutions.[33]

Causes	Solutions
reporting inconvenient; takes too much time; don't want to bother police; difficulties with police	simplify reporting; pamphlets on what to report; limit work hours; support from police, positive attitude
fear of involvement	anonymous reporting
no official recognition; no support from police, neighborhood, members, other organizations	awards, media coverage, ID cards; faster response times by police; community involvement
novelty wears off; lost interest; don't think important; nothing to do	other activities; other affiliations; increased responsibilities; show successes
it's not my job; that's what police are for	offer tax credits for participation
loss of community pride; apathy; not important; not seen as effective; no longer need; loss of police support; no sense of security	develop community support, sense of community, neighborhood unity; contact members frequently; show success; support of and by policy
boredom; lost interest	include other issues; redevelop goals
members do not have time, money for gas, phones, access, etc.	seek contributions; decrease amount of work by each member; environmental changes
not well organized; internal conflict; negative purpose	other affiliations; simplify activities; develop multipurpose, non-crime activity

get to know each other. The convergence of social interaction with shared territory, according to Sundeen, is "likely to contribute to the cohesiveness and solidarity of the community marked by gemeinschaft-like social relations among its members, such as mutual aid, cooperation, and wholistic ties. . . ."[34]

To summarize the issues involved in the organization and maintenance of community-based crime prevention groups, Table 15.2 lists some frequently given causes for program failure and proposes some solutions.

The Promise of Coproduction

Three questions immediately arise about the feasibility of the coproduction concept. The first concerns the utility of using the example of community-based crime prevention groups to discuss the linkage between coproduction and citizenship; that is, how generalizable is this example to other services that are not so central to citizens lives or so crisis prone? Second, what are the equity considerations that likely will arise from such administrative reforms? And, third, how does a narrow citizen-based, service-providing group promote the development of such attributes of citizenship as trust in government, citizen efficacy, and a concern for the common good?

Generalizability

Granted, crime and the fear of criminals are more likely to promote citizen interest and involvement than most any other collective problem. Until recently, the fear of crime was strong enough to encourage a steadily growing supply of funds for personnel and equipment for enhanced police protection in nearly every city in the country. Now with funds tight and crime rates high, citizens have stepped into the breech to provide even more support in the form of service coproduction. But crime is not unique in promoting citizen involvement. Enough examples exist of citizens taking and sharing responsibility for service delivery in areas like education, recreation, and social services to suggest that the phenomenon is widespread and deeply engrained in our civil culture.[35]

The challenge for public administrators and elected officials is to recognize the depth and value of these activities and to develop institutional arrangements that allow them to flourish. Before this occurs, however, there will have to be a change of mindsets on the part of most public officials. As Sharp has argued:

> The crucial point about the coproduction concept is that it highlights a different understanding of urban service delivery, and of productivity improvement, from that incorporated in the dominant model [i.e., public administrators produce services, citizens consume them]. Here, the assumption is not that government officials perform for citizens, and therefore bear total responsibility for productivity improvements or the lack thereof; rather, the emphasis is upon service delivery as a joint venture, involving both citizens and government agents.[36]

This change of mindsets will not be an easy transition for most public officials, or for that matter, for most citizens. At first, the coproduction concept will strike cords of an older notion anathema to public officials—"community control." Community control connotes a movement to remove authority from professionals and give it to neighborhood-based organizations and with it control over public agencies. Insofar as the advocates of coproduction promise to produce these results, they cannot expect to be met with anything other than fierce resistance by public officials who guard their authority jealously. A more moderate—and politically feasible—version of production involves sharing responsibility and authority in service delivery arrangements where the basic authority of public officials over the definition of what constitutes professional staff responsibility is protected and citizen groups work with officials to tailor services to neighborhood needs.

Equity

Coproduction has obvious implications for the equitable distribution of government burdens and benefits. By getting citizens to share some of the burden (in time, money, and effort) of delivering and receiving services, demand for services is likely to decline and along with it, cost. However, where agencies and neighborhoods compete for fair shares of a city's budget and services, there may be resistance to neighborhood assumption of coproduction responsibilities on the grounds that it constitutes a form of double taxation. This is especially likely to occur in communities where some neighborhoods are involved in coproduction and others are not.

The equity problem also can be compounded by social and economic stratification. As Rosentraub and Sharp observe:

> Wealthier, better-educated, or nonminority citizens may be more willing to engage in coproduction activities. To the extent that coproduction raises the quality of services received, it may exacerbate gaps between the advantaged and disadvantaged classes.[37]

Obviously, the capacity of the people in a neighborhood to carry the costs of assuming a greater proportion of service delivery responsibility will be an important consideration in achieving viable coproduction arrangements. When inequities in burdens and benefits are too great in a community, coproduction likely will fail as a means of delivering adequate services. If such serious inequality problems arise, the classic centralization/decentralization cycle described by Herbert Kaufman will occur:

> Decentralization will soon be followed by disparities in practices among the numerous small units, brought on by differences in human and financial resources, that will engender demands for central intervention to restore equality and balance and concerted action.[38]

Bridges to Citizenship

The answer to the question of how well coproduction arrangements serve to help revitalize citizenship lies in the strength of the bridge between gov-

ernment and citizens. At a minimum, such a bridge needs three strands: innovation, participation, and loyalty.

Successful coproduction must involve experimentation and *innovation*
in the methods used for making decisions and delivering services. For such
an arrangement to work best a community has to develop a supporting
structure for an "experimenting policy"; i.e., a political and administrative
climate where citizens, public employees, and public officials are willing to
try new methods of delivering traditional public services. Without these innovations, governments are likely to fall back on the limited strategy of
trying to tighten their traditional methods of delivering services in order to
improve productivity. Experimentation, on the other hand, promotes
"learning by doing," where both citizens and public employees learn more
about services—and one another—by participating in joint problem solving and service delivery efforts.[39] In such settings, a process of mutual adjustment occurs. According to Whitaker, both the citizen and the public administrator "share responsibility for deciding what action to take.
Moreover, each accords legitimacy to the responsibility of the other. The
citizen coproducer is not a 'client' in the sense that he or she is not a sup-
plicant seeking the favor of the agency."[40]

This kind of relationship stands at odds with the traditional inclination of
public administrators to keep the *participation* of citizens in agency operations at arms length. The warning should be clear: If the use of citizens in
service delivery is treated as a marginal activity by public agencies, then we
should not expect coproduction to be a very effective instrument for improving the competence or commitment of citizens. In contrast, if agencies
can find ways of integrating citizens in their core decision making and service delivery procedures, the likelihood of building lasting attachments will
improve. In such cases, the knowledge of citizens about services and service
costs will expand, the responsiveness, respect, and appreciation of citizens
and professionals to one another will grow, and at least a marginal improvement in citizens' commitment to their community will occur. At a
minimum, such changes promise to contribute to arresting the serious erosion of popular support for the institutions of government and their leaders.

The final critical strand in the bridge between coproduction and citizenship is the capacity of a service delivery arrangement to build in citizens a
loyalty to place, neighbors, and their community. Loyalty develops
through face-to-face contact and an investment of energy in the improvement of neighborhoods and communities. Volunteer programs like "adopt
a park," "friends of the library," and citizen patrols cannot help but contribute to building loyalty. "Sweat equity" in producing a service or maintaining a physical space promises to build commitment and a more cohesive view of the neighborhood and citizens' role in it.

In sum, the prospects for enhanced citizenship through citizen participation in coproduction arrangements are generally favorable. Where the conditions for coproduction are most favorable (e.g., in homogeneous communities with residential propinquity), we can expect it to flourish—and citizenship to grow. Where conditions are less favorable (e.g., highly stratified communities with scattered housing), other avenues will have to be found to promote *civitas*.[41]

Conclusion

Those who believe that citizenship, civic virtue, and "public service" should be an important part of our national culture should be distressed that these features of democracy have come to be regarded as mere myths in a polity that increasingly rewards narrow self-interest. Even those who accept this condition as a natural outgrowth of the characteristics of modern life, should be disturbed by our failure to reconcile the growing gap between the roles of citizens and public employees.

For those who wish a more communitarian arrangement of their civic life, coproduction promises a beginning that can be built upon, once working with public employees and with neighbors becomes habitual and an integral part of everyday life. Once this occurs, the prospects for a revitalization of a communitarian spirit rise as they experience the satisfaction of jointly solving problems.

For the public administrator the lessons are clear: The strategy of coproduction promises to be a powerful tool for resolving fiscal stress and an auspicious start on the road to restoring the trust and support of citizens for their public institutions.

Notes

1. See David O. Sears and Jack Citrin, *Tax Revolt: Something for Nothing in California* (Cambridge, Mass.: Harvard University Press, 1983), especially ch. 3.

2. See John J. Kirlin, *The Political Economy of Fiscal Limits* (Lexington, Mass.: D.C. Heath, 1982), p. 10 and ch. 6.

3. Robert A. Dahl, *Who Governs? Democracy and Power in an American City* (New Haven, Conn.: Yale University Press, 1961), p. 133.

4. See Richard Dagger, "Metropolis, Memory and Citizenship," *American Journal of Political Science*, vol. 25, no. 4 (November 1981), pp. 715–737.

5. Seymour Martin Lipset and William Schneider, *Confidence Gap: Business, Labor, and Government in the Public Mind* (New York: The Free Press, 1983), pp. 411–412.

6. Charles T. Goodsell, *The Case for Bureaucracy: A Public Administration Polemic* (Chatham, N.J.: Chatham House Publishers, 1983), pp. 144–146.

7. See Advisory Commission on Intergovernmental Relations, *Citizen Participation in the American Federal System* (Washington, D.C.: U.S. Government Printing Office, 1979).

8. See John Shannon, "The Great Slowdown in State and Local Spending in the United States: 1976–1984" (Washington, D.C.: Advisory Commission on Intergovernmental Relations, 1981).

9. See, for example, Robert Poole, Jr., "Objections to Privatization," *Policy Review,* no. 24 (Spring 1983), pp. 105–119; and Martha A. Shulman, "Alternative Approaches for Delivering Public Services," *Urban Data Service Reports,* vol. 14, no. 10 (Washington, D.C.: International City Management Association, October 1982).

10. Norton E. Long, "An Institutional Framework for the Development of Responsible Citizenship," in Charles Press, ed., *The Polity* (Chicago: Rand McNally, 1962), p. 184.

11. See E. S. Savas, *Privatizing the Public Sector: How to Shrink Government* (Chatham, N.J.: Chatham House, 1982).

12. Robert W. Poole, Jr., *Cutting Back City Hall* (New York: Universe Books, 1980), p. 194.

13. See Richard Flathman, "Citizenship and Authority: A Chastened View of Citizenship," *News for Teachers of Political Science,* no. 30 (Summer 1981), pp. 9–19.

14. See. Michael Walzer, *Obligations: Essays on Disobedience, War and Citizenship* (New York: Simon and Schuster, 1971); and C. B. Macpherson, *The Life and Times of Liberal Democracy* (Oxford, England: Oxford University Press, 1977).

15. See Edward K. Hamilton, "On Non-Constitutional Management of a Constitutional Problem," *Daedalus,* vol. 107 (1978), pp. 111–128.

16. Ben A. Menke, Mervin F. White, and William L. Carey, "Police Professionalization: Pursuit of Excellence or Political Power," in Jack R. Greene, ed., *Managing Police Work: Issues and Analysis* (Beverly Hills, Calif.: Sage Publications, 1982), p. 98.

17. Nathan Glazer, "Toward a Self-Service Society?" *The Public Interest,* no. 70 (Winter 1983), pp. 89–90.

18. Sheldon Wolin, *Politics and Vision: Continuity and Innovation in Western Political Thought* (Boston: Little, Brown, 1960), p. 434.

19. Cited in J. T. Duncan, *Citizen Crime Prevention Tactics: A Literature Review and Selected Bibliography* (Washington, D.C.: U.S. Government Printing Office, 1980), p. 4.

20. For discussions of this approach see: Frances E. Pennell, "Collective vs. Private Strategies for Coping with Crime: The Consequences for Citizen Perceptions of Crime, Attitudes Toward the Police and Neighboring Activity," *Journal of Voluntary Action Research,* vol. 7, nos. 1–2 (1978), pp. 59–74; Stephen L. Percy, "Conceptualizing and Measuring Citizen Co-Production of Community Safety," *Policy Studies Journal,* vol. 7 (1978), pp. 486–493; and Richard R. Rich, "Voluntary Action and Public Services: An Introduction to the Special Issue," *Journal of Voluntary Action Research,* vol. 7, nos. 1–2 (1978), pp. 4–14.

21. See L. Bickman, P. J. Lavrakas, S. K. Green, N. North-Walker, J. Edwards, S. Borkowski, S. Shane-Dubois, and J. Wuerth, *Citizen Crime Reporting Projects—*

National Evaluation Program—Phase 1 Summary Report (Washington, D.C.: National Institute of Justice, 1976).

22. See, for example, George J. Washnis, *Citizen Involvement in Crime Prevention* (Lexington, Mass.: D.C. Heath, 1976).

23. R. K. Yin, M. E. Vogel, J. M. Chaiken, and D. R. Both, *Patrolling the Neighborhood Beat: Residents and Residential Security* (Santa Monica, Calif.: Rand, 1976).

24. Donald D. Pomerleau, "Crime Prevention," in Bernard L. Garmire, ed., *Local Government Police Management* (Washington, D.C.: International City Management Association, 1977), p. 261.

25. Greta W. Salem, "Maintaining Participation in Community Organizations," *Journal of Voluntary Action Research,* vol. 7, nos. 3–4 (1978), pp. 18–27.

26. See Howard W. Hallman, *Neighborhood Control of Public Programs* (New York: Praeger, 1970).

27. See, for example, James Q. Wilson, *Political Organizations* (New York: Basic Books, 1973), especially ch. 3.

28. Sherry Arnstein, "Maximum Feasible Manipulation," *Public Administration Review,* vol. 32 (September 1972), pp. 377–390.

29. See G. T. Marx and D. Archer, "Citizen Involvement in the Law Enforcement Process," *American Behavioral Scientist,* vol. 15, no. 1 (1971), pp. 52–72.

30. See R. Nanett, "From the Top Down: Government Promoted Citizen Participation," *Journal of Voluntary Action Research,* vol. 9, nos. 1–4 (1980), pp. 149–162.

31. For more on this problem, see Mancur Olson, Jr., *The Logic of Collective Action* (Cambridge, Mass.: Harvard University Press, 1965).

32. See Mark H. Moore and George L. Kelling, "To Serve and Protect: Learning from Police History," *The Public Interest,* no. 70 (Winter 1983), pp. 66–90.

33. An earlier version of this table was developed in Barbara H. Seekins, "Maintaining Community-Based Citizen Crime Prevention Groups," field project report, M.P.A. program, University of Kansas, Lawrence, Kan., 1975, p. 28.

34. Richard A. Sundeen, "Coproduction and Communities: Implications for Local Administrators," unpublished paper, School of Public Administration, University of Southern California, Los Angeles, Calif., 1982; see also Fred Dubow and Aaron Podolefsky, "Citizen Participation in Community Crime Prevention," *Human Organization,* vol. 41, no. 4 (Winter 1982).

35. See Gordon P. Whitaker, "Coproduction: Citizen Participation in Service Delivery," *Public Administration Review,* vol. 40, no. 3 (May/June 1980), pp. 240–246.

36. Elaine B. Sharp, "Toward a New Understanding of Urban Services and Citizen Participation: The Coproduction Concept," *Midwest Review of Public Administration,* vol. 14, no. 2 (June 1980), p. 111.

37. Mark S. Rosentraub and Elaine B. Sharp, "Consumers as Producers of Social Services: Coproduction and the Level of Social Services," *Southern Review of Public Administration,* vol. 4 (March 1981), p. 517; see also Jeffrey L. Brudney and Robert E. England, "Toward a Definition of the Coproduction Concept," *Public Administration Review,* vol. 43, no. 1 (January/February 1983), pp. 59–65.

38. Herbert Kaufman, "Administrative Decentralization and Political Power," *Public Administration Review,* vol. 29, no. 1 (January/February 1969), p. 11.

39. See John Dewey, *Logic: The Theory of Inquiry* (New York: Henry Holt and Co., 1938).

40. Whitaker, "Coproduction," p. 244.

41. For a discusion of the civic education route to citizenship, see H. George Frederickson, "The Recovery of Civicism in Public Administration," *Public Administration Review,* vol. 42, no. 6 (November/December 1982), pp. 501–508.

16

THE QUESTION OF PARTICIPATION: TOWARD AUTHENTIC PUBLIC PARTICIPATION IN PUBLIC ADMINISTRATION

Cheryl Simrell King
Kathryn M. Feltey
Bridget O'Neill Susel

The appropriate role of the public in public administration has been an active and ongoing area of inquiry, experimentation, revolution, and controversy since the birth of this nation. The contemporary movement to examine the role of the public in the process of administrative decision making has come about in response to problems in the latter half of this century and as a result of concern on the part of citizens, administrators, and politicians over citizen discouragement and apathy (Box, 1996; Putnam, 1995; Timney, 1996; Thomas, 1995). As both citizens and their leaders

Source: *Public Administration Review* 58(1998): 317–326.

Methodology

The research reported here follows a grounded theory model of research (Strauss and Corbin, 1990) and is based on interviews with subject matter experts and focus group discussions among citizens and public administrators in northeast Ohio. We used qualitative techniques because of our desire for depth in addressing the question of how to make participation efforts more effective for both citizens and administrators. We also wanted to allow issues we may not have considered to emerge from the research.

Subject matter experts are individuals we identified as knowledgeable about participation, either through their research or practice. We conducted hour-long telephone interviews with five subject matter experts; one interview was conducted in person. Subject matter experts include two organizers who are currently engaged in extensive participation projects, one for the Environmental Protection Agency and one for the city of Dayton, Ohio; two former executives from national foundations that focus on increasing the links between citizens and government; a public participation practitioner currently working in nuclear waste cleanuup in Idaho; and one established scholar in the field.

In the interviews the subject matter experts talked about the meaning of participation, identified the key components of successful participation efforts, addressed the issue of decline in participation, suggested ways to bolster citizen involvement in civic processes, and discussed key theories guiding research and practice in participation. We used the results of the interviews to shape the discussion guidelines for the focused group discussions.

The focus groups included three types of participants in public administration: nonelected administrators in local government, activists, and citizens who had participated in at least one public process or event during the previous year. A type of snowball sampling helped us identify group participants. The first few participants were identified through our personal and professional networks; we asked them to recommend other potential participants. Surprisingly, given this technique, our participants were fairly diverse with regard to their experiences and perspectives.

The activists and citizens were similar in terms of their interest in, and commitment to, participation. They differed in that the activists were formally tied to organizations that represent citizen interests and had higher levels of participation than ordinary citizens because of their organization's mission and goals. Citizens who did not participate in public processes were not represented in the focus group discussions.

We convened seven groups in three communities in northeast Ohio, chosen to represent the diversity of communities in the area (large city, medium city, rural/edge city). The focus groups ranged in size from six to eleven members, with three citizen-only groups, one administrator-only group, one activist-only group, and two groups of both activists and administrators. Participants were diverse with regard to demographic characteristics, the focus of their participation efforts, and the organizations they represented, although the administrators were all local (city or county). Participants in the groups responded to four general questions: What does public participation mean to you? What are the barriers to effective public participation? How can effective public partici-

pation be achieved, if at all? What advice do you have to give to people studying and attempting to practice effective public participation? Other topics and
questions emerged in each group. The facilitators guided the discussions but
did not control the direction of the conversations. The discussions lasted for
two hours and were recorded verbatim by a courtroom transcriber.

In the first stage of the analysis, we coded the transcribed interviews and
discussions individually, using a qualitative form of content analysis (see
Strauss and Corbin, 1990). In the second stage of analysis, we synthesized
the separate analyses, using a nominal group technique to create the categorical themes discussed in this paper.

It is important to note that, except for administrators, all participants in the
focus groups were active in public participation processes. We wanted people
involved to give us guidance on how these processes might be more effective.
Every group discussion turned, at some point, to the question of nonparticipation. Our participants had a great deal to say about nonparticipation. We have
incorporated their views of nonparticipation into the discussion.

have noticed, "participation through normal institutional channels has little impact on the substance of government politics" (Crosby, Kelly, and
Schaefer, 1986, 172).

Many citizens, administrators, and politicians are interested in increasing
public participation in public decisions. Efforts to do so are currently underway across the country. However, there is considerable evidence to suggest
that these efforts are not effective (Crosby, Kelly, and Schaefer, 1986; Kathlene and Martin, 1991; Kweit and Kweit, 1981, 1987; Parsons, 1990). Some
efforts appear to be ineffective because of poor planning or execution. Other
efforts may not work because administrative systems that are based upon expertise and professionalism leave little room for participatory processes
(deLeon, 1992; Fisher, 1993; Forester, 1989; White and McSwain, 1993).

The question of how to engender effective and satisfying participation
processes is the central issue in this research. Our findings indicate that effective, or authentic, public participation implies more than simply finding
the right tools and techniques for increasing public involvement in public
decisions. Authentic public participation, that is, participation that works
for all parties and stimulates interest and investment in both administrators and citizens, requires rethinking the underlying roles of, and relationships between, administrators and citizens.

In the first section of this article we examine the question of the necessity
or desirability of more effective participation by reviewing the literature in
U.S. public administration and identifying the relevant contemporary issues
for both administrators and citizens. The current model of the participation
process is presented and critiqued in the second section, using the concept
of authentic participation as a starting point for moving toward more effective participatory processes. We then turn to identifying the barriers to effective participation as seen by our research participants. Strategies for

overcoming the barriers are discussed, and implications for the practice of public administration and citizenship are suggested in the last section. Following a grounded theory model (Strauss and Corbin, 1990), this article is organized around the themes that emerged from the literature review, interviews, and focus group discussions (see the Methodology Box).

The Necessity or Desirability of More Effective Participation

The role of participation in public administration has historically been one of ambivalence. Although the political system in the United States is designed to reflect and engender an active citizenry, it is also designed to protect political and administrative processes from a too-active citizenry. It is within this context that participation in the administrative arena has traditionally been framed.

In recent times, interest in public participation in administrative decision making has increased as a result of a number of factors, not the least of which is that a citizenry with diminished trust in government is demanding more accountability from public officials (Parr and Gates, 1989). There is also a growing recognition on the part of administrators that decision making without public participation is ineffective. As Thomas indicates, "the new public involvement has transformed the work of public managers . . . public participation in the managerial process has become a fact of life. In the future, this may become the case for even more managers, since the public's demand for involvement does not seem to be abating" (1995, xi). Thomas suggests that under contemporary political and economic conditions, we can no longer not include the public in public decision making.

Paralleling the increased practitioner interest in public participation, contemporary theorists have increasingly focused on participation in their theories of the role, legitimacy, and definitions of the field in what some call "postmodern" times (Frederickson, 1982; Stivers, 1990; Cooper, 1991; Farmer, 1995; Fox and Miller, 1995; Wamsley and Wolf, 1996). In an attempt to find a way to bridge the problems of traditional models of public administration, some researchers call for shifts in the governance process. Stivers calls these changed relationships "active accountability":

> Administrative legitimacy requires active accountability to citizens, from whom the ends of government derive. Accountability, in turn, requires a shared framework for the interpretation of basic values, one that must be developed jointly by bureaucrats and citizens in real-world situations, rather than assumed. The legitimate administrative state, in other words, is one inhabited by active citizens (1990, 247).

Although there is theoretical and practical recognition that the public must be more involved in public decisions, many administrators are, at best, ambivalent about public involvement or, at worst, they find it problematic. In an increasingly global and chaotic world, administrators are grappling with issues that do not seem to have definitive solutions, while still trying to encourage public involvement (Kettering Foundation, 1989). The issues traditionally facing administrators, "the more malleable problems, the ones that could be attacked with common sense and ingenuity, have in recent decades given way to a different class of problems—'wicked problems'—with no solutions, only temporary and imperfect resolutions" (Fischer, 1993, 172). Administrators need guidance and help in addressing these "wicked problems" but find that the help they seek from citizens often creates new sets of problems. As a result, although many public administrators view close relationships with citizens as both necessary and desirable, most of them do not actively seek public involvement. If they do seek it, they do not use public input in making administrative decisions (as indicated by a 1989 study conducted by the Kettering Foundation). These administrators believe that greater citizen participation increases inefficiency because participation creates delays and increases red tape.

As the Kettering Foundation study shows, an "undeniable tension" exists between the public's right to greater involvement and the prerogative of public officials to act as administrative decision makers (1989, 12). Citizens report feeling isolated from public administrative processes. Although they care about the issues facing their communities and the nation, citizens feel "pushed out" of the public process (Kettering Foundation, 1991). Citizens mistrust public officials and administrators. National opinion polls show that citizens' distrust of government is on the rise: 43 percent of citizens reported a lack of trust in government in 1992 while 70 percent reported distrust in 1994 (cited in Tolchin, 1996, 6). This distrust often leads to citizen cynicism or what Mathews (1994) calls impotence and causes interest in participation to decline (Berman, 1997).

Some citizens feel their concerns will be heard only if they organize into groups and angrily protest administrative policy decisions (Timney, 1996). NIMBYs (Not In My Backyard groups) have challenged administrative decisions on a variety of different issues in recent years (Fischer, 1993; Kraft and Clary, 1991), creating no end of trouble for people trying to implement administrative decisions. Citizens involved in these protest groups are confrontational in their participatory efforts because they believe administrators operate within a "context of self-interest" and are not connected to the citizens (Kettering Foundation, 1991, 7).

The participants of our study, administrators, activists, and citizens alike, agreed that participation is necessary and desirable. One citizen told us that participation was "the necessary opportunity to be a part of something bigger than oneself, a part of our responsibility to our community." An activist said, "it is very important to have an opportunity to influence

FIGURE 16.1   Context of Conventional Participation

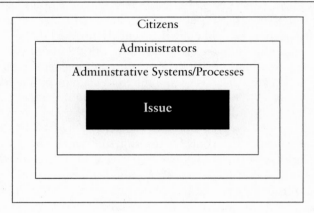

and to know that your influence has the potential to make a difference."
Administrators also stressed the centrality of input: "we *need* input," "we
don't make good decisions without it," "it is essential." Our research participants agreed that the main problem with participation as it is currently
practiced and framed is that it doesn't work. They believed that finding
better ways to engender participation will make it more meaningful for all
involved. Administrators recognize the need for participation, but they
cannot find ways to fit the public into decision-making processes. Citizens
believe that greater participation is needed, but they are rendered cynical
or apathetic by vacuous or false efforts to stimulate participation that ask
for, yet discount, public input. As a result, citizens find themselves moving
from potentially cooperative to confrontational situations that pit administrators against citizens in an adversarial way. Why are we in this paradoxical conundrum? One reason may be the way participation is currently
framed, the point to which we now turn.

How is Participation Currently Framed?

Public participation processes have four major components: (1) the issue or
situation; (2) the administrative structures, systems, and processes within
which participation takes place; (3) the administrators; and, (4) the citizens. Participation efforts are currently framed such that these components
are arrayed around the issue. The citizen is placed at the greatest distance
from the issue, the administrative structures and processes are the closest,
and the administrator is the agent between the structures and citizens, as
depicted in Figure 16.1.

In the context of conventional participation, the administrator controls the ability of the citizen to influence the situation or the process. The administrative structures and processes are the politically and socially constructed frameworks within which the administrator must operate. These frameworks give the administrator the authority to formulate decisions only after the issue has been defined. Thus, the administrator has no real power to redefine the issue or to alter administrative processes to allow for greater citizen involvement (Forester, 1989).

In the context of conventional participation the administrator plays the role of the expert. White and McSwain (1993) suggest that participation within this context is structured to maintain the centrality of the administrator while publicly presenting the administrator as representative, consultative, or participatory. The citizen becomes the "client" of the professional administrator, ill-equipped to question the professional's authority and technical knowledge. This process establishes what Fischer calls a "practitioner-client hierarchy" (1993, 165). In this falsely dualistic relationship, the administrator is separated from the "demands, needs, and values" of the people whom he or she is presumed to be serving (deLeon, 1992, 126).

Participation in this context is ineffective and conflictual, and it happens too late in the process, that is, after the issues have been framed and most decisions have been made. Therefore, rather than cooperating to decide how best to address issues, citizens are reactive and judgmental, often sabotaging administrators' best efforts. Administrators are territorial and parochial; they resist sharing information and rely on their technical and professional expertise to justify their role in administrative processes. Citizen participation is more symbolic than real (Arnstein, 1969). The power that citizens yield is aimed at blocking or redirecting administrative efforts rather than working as partners to define the issues, establish the parameters, develop methods of investigation, and select techniques for addressing problems.

Reframing Participation

As defined by the participants of our research, effective participation is participation that is real or authentic. Authentic participation is deep and continuous involvement in administrative processes with the potential for all involved to have an effect on the situation. An activist defined authentic participation as "the ability and the opportunity to have an impact on the decision-making process." According to an administrator, authentic participation is "on-going, active involvement, not a one-shot deal, not just pulling the lever . . . it needs to go out and reach out to every part of your community, however defined." An activist said that good participation has occurred when "people affected by the change are comfortable with the decision made." A citizen explained, "For me, when I change perceptions I know it's a success."

Both citizens and administrators in our study defined the key elements of authentic participation as focus, commitment, trust, and open and honest discussion. As an activist stated, "People need to know that their input is important and will be considered in making that decision." An administrator concurred, "I think one of the keys for effective participation at the citizen and neighborhood level is for decision makers to be interested; to really listen to what the needs are of the people." Another administrator talked about listening and trust: "The first step is to make it clear that you're going to be receptive to their comments. But also I think a critical second step to maintaining their trust is to demonstrate to them that they're being heard . . . and that their ideas are shaping whatever you're developing." To achieve all of this, according to a third administrator, citizens and administrators "need to have a partnership. We do that by being sensitive that other people do have an agenda . . . but everyone should gradually come together."

Authentic participation requires that administrators focus on both process and outcome. In this context, participation is an integral part of administration, rather than an add-on to existing practices. Authentic participation means that the public is part of the deliberation process from issue framing to decision making (Roberts, 1997). As a citizen indicated, "From the very beginning people need to be involved." An administrator told us, "If you go to the community with a totally preset agenda that doesn't work. Bringing people into the process too late does not work." An activist concurred, "I think that it is very important that individuals be given the opportunity, prior to the decision being made, to provide input. [Citizens must have] enough time to process that information. There is a lot of phony participation going on out there."

Addressing the limitations of current participatory efforts requires that public administrators become "interpretive mediators." They must move beyond the technical issue at hand by involving citizens in "dialectical exchange" (Fischer, 1993, 183) and by engaging with citizens in discourse (Fox and Miller, 1995), rather than simply getting citizens input. Then, the administrator becomes a cooperative participant, assisting citizens in examining their interests, working together with them to arrive at decisions, and engaging them in open and authentic deliberation.

A citizen offers a compelling summary of the tensions involved in public participation: "You have to get in there and ask their opinion. And they will tell you their opinion in the midst of telling you what a lousy job you are doing. And you have to be willing to deal with that, to put up with it. I think a lot of administrators, like us, don't like criticism. They'll, naturally,

FIGURE 16.2   Context of Authentic Participation

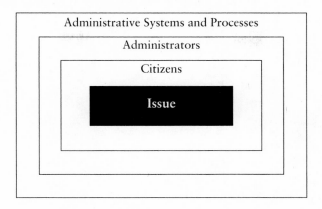

avoid it . . . and forget to go out in the field and get democracy." Getting democracy seems to lie at the core of why authentic participation is important. Engendering a discourse where all participants have an equal footing and where one group is not privileged over the other is at the heart of authentic participation (Habermas, 1975).

The context of authentic participation is very different from the context of conventional participation. Authentic participation places the citizen next to the issue and the administrative structures and processes furthest away. However, the administrator is still the bridge between the two, as depicted in Figure 16.2. Citizens are central and directly related to the issue; they have an immediate and equal opportunity to influence the processes and outcomes. The administrators' influence comes from their relationship with the citizenry as well as from their expertise and position. The administrative structures and processes are defined by the relationships and interactions of citizens and administrators.

Authentic participation moves the administrator away from a reliance on technical and expertise models of administration and toward meaningful participatory processes. Table 16.1 summarizes the key differences between unauthentic and authentic participation models. As an activist told us:

> Over the last year, the federal urban development people have put out some strict guidelines to encourage and mandate participation. And they don't know how to deal with the participation . . . they're intimidated . . . and they [are beginning to realize] that maybe we all can learn better ways of doing this. Their attitudes have always been: we know what's better for the neighborhoods. Maybe they're just beginning to realize that maybe citizens do know something. Maybe they do know what's best for the neighborhood and

TABLE 16.1 Comparison of Authentic and Unauthentic Participation

	Unauthentic Participation	Authentic Participation
Interaction style	Conflictual	Collaborative
Participation is sought	After the agenda is set and decisions are made	Early; before anything is set
Role of administrator	Expert technician/manager	Collaborative technician/governor
Administrative skills needed	Technical; managerial	Technical, interpersonal skills, discourse skills, facilitation skills
Role of citizen	Unequal participant	Equal partner
Citizenship skills needed	None	Civics, participation skills, discourse skills
Approach toward "other"	Mistrust	Trust
Administrative process	Static, invisible, closed	Dynamic, visible, open
Citizen options	Reactive	Proactive or reactive
Citizen output	Buy-in	Design
Administrator output	Decision	Process
Time to decision	Appears shorter and easier but often involves going back and "redoing" based upon citizen reaction	Appears longer and more onerous but usually doesn't require redoing because citizens have been involved throughout; may take less time to reach decisions than through traditional processes
Decision is made	By administrator/political and/or administrative processes perhaps in consultation with citizens	Emerges as a result of discourse; equal opportunity for all to enter the discourse and to influence the outcomes

they're in the process of trying to figure out how to balance what they've been doing all these years with the need for citizen participation.

Processes of authentic participation do not necessarily create more work for administrators. Authenticity does, however, require different kinds of work. In conventional processes, administrators often have to go back and redo projects that citizens block once decisions have been made. One administrator indicated:

> Why not get the citizens in and work these things out before we go with it? Actually, it may seem like it takes a little longer because, in the old way, we make a decision and run with it as far as we can; but then we have to run back and fix it. . . . There's always this arrogance that we know what the people need without their input—our system is set up to keep people away from the decision making.

Authentic participation involves citizens in the making of decisions instead of just judging. As one administrator told us, "There are two ways of participating: making, which includes doing something, and judgment. A lot of us go to meetings where we do nothing but judge. . . . It's the making and the doing that I think we're all wishing more citizens participated in."

Our research shows that the desire for participation is strong, and our participants recognize its importance. The next section examines the barriers to authentic participation.

Barriers to Authentic Participation

The focus group participants and subject matter experts agreed that participation methods and processes pose barriers to participation, but other factors do as well. Three categories of barriers were identified in our analyses: the nature of life in contemporary society, administrative processes, and current practices and techniques of participation.

The Nature of Life in Contemporary Society

The barriers stemming from the practical realities of daily life are tied to the social class position of citizens and include factors like transportation, time constraints, family structure, number of family members in the labor force, child care, and economic disadvantages. Some people express a desire to participate more fully in their communities, but the demands of day-to-day life get in the way. As one citizen said, "A lot of people are holding down two jobs and both people work in the family and are too tired . . . [from] trying to survive a day at a time."

The focus group members compared an idealized past where civic participation was common and visible, to the present, where it is nearly impossible to fit participation into an over-crowded schedule. The past was seen as a time of economic security with stable employment where participation in community life was a given. As one administrator explained, "At least in my grandparent's generation they weren't worried if Goodyear was going to be there. They knew they were. They were playing ball, going to Boy Scouts. Now . . . it's unusual if you have a bit of [worry-free] luxury in your life to participate."

According to the older members in the focus group, younger community members are not pursuing an activist tradition. It is a constant challenge to community activists to get younger citizens to participate. One activist said, "We're trying to replace people who were active in the block clubs with people who are from the young families to take over the reins of what the older citizens have been doing for years. That's a hard thing to do."

Citizens, administrators, and activists all agreed that participation is hindered by a lack of education, both informally within families and communities and formally in the schools. One administrator described how early childhood socialization prepared him for a life of participation:

> When I was a kid we would meet at the dinner table . . . and that was the place that almost without fail we'd get around to political and neighborhood and church goings on . . . that would be the basis for learning about and socializing into broader issues in the community. . . . The same thing was true for the neighborhoods. The adults used to gather on the front porches while their kids would play.

The demise of the neighborhood as an organizing and socializing system was described in the following way by one administrator: "People don't talk to each other anymore . . . the neighborhoods aren't neighborhoods . . . they used to be real tight-knit communities." Isolation from others is detrimental to participation.

One subject matter expert suggested that citizen participation is "abysmally low [because] we've taught people not to participate." However, he noted that even if people were invited to participate, "there is still the nature of citizen life itself, we are all very busy, perhaps too busy to participate." He warned against relying on standard indicators to draw conclusions about rates or levels of participation. Traditional participation indicators such as voting, attending civic meetings, or running for city council don't capture the cultural forms of participation that are more likely to involve younger members of the community. However, he also agreed that participatory values have not been reinforced in this "era of privatization and free market economy [where] individuals have a lot of economic pressures without much spare capital."

While day-to-day life keeps people from being more participatory and perhaps inculcates nonparticipatory attitudes and apathy, many of our research participants felt that current administrative processes are as much to blame for the lack of citizen participation.

Administrative Processes

The second set of barriers identified by our participants consists of those inherent in administrative processes themselves. These barriers are paradoxical. While most people define citizen participation as desirable, any participation seen as challenging the administrative status quo is blocked by the very administrators who desire more participatory processes. As one citizen lamented:

> Isn't it a shame [that] one of the obstacles in citizen participation seems to be government. . . . We're talking about grass-roots programs that work *despite* the government, [because they are able to] work around the officials. It seems to me that [elected officials and administrators] should all be wanting to get people to participate . . . not putting up barriers. They only want favorable participation . . . to keep the status quo.

An activist described the barriers in the process as follows:

> It seems to me that the political process gets in the way. You can do all the things that should be done, get the citizens together, get them involved, get input. But if the decision has already been made on a different level, it's all [window] dressing. And we have to get past that first. How do you do that when the political process has already made the decision which way it's going to go?

Citizens in our focus groups, like those included in other research, viewed communication in participatory processes as flowing one way—from the administrative professional to the citizen. Citizens in our project felt that information is usually managed, controlled, and manipulated, limiting their capacity to participate. As one citizen explained, "By the time we hear about issues it's too late to affect a decision." Another citizen concurred, "By the time we hear about the issues it is too late in the process. We might hear about it if we read the paper or if someone on your committee is on top of things enough to know what's going on." As a result, citizens talk about administrators as adversaries, as one citizen explained: "I think if we participate . . . we can sometimes beat the administrators to the gun.

Techniques of Participation

One of the most problematic administrative barriers is the techniques used in most participatory processes. As found in other research (Crosby,

Kelly, and Schaefer, 1986; Kathlene and Martin, 1991; Kweit and Kweit, 1981; 1987; Parsons, 1990), our focus group participants told us that most techniques used in current participation efforts are inadequate. The most ineffective technique is the public hearing. Public hearings do not work. Low attendance at public hearings is often construed as public apathy or silent approval of the status quo (Kathlene and Martin, 1991). In actuality, low attendance is more likely to be related to the structure of public hearings.

Administrators recognize that the structure of public hearings and public meetings prohibits meaningful exchange. As one administrator said, "The public hearing is not about communicating, it is about convincing." Another explained the limitations of public school board meetings, "When you go to a school board meeting, they get this egg timer, time to grab the microphone and speak. There's no follow-up. You don't even get to ask them questions. . . . There's no give and take." An activist suggested that the public hearing was window dressing, "We have these hearings so they can check off on their list that they've had their citizen participation. . . . It's participation out of the fear that they are going to look bad."

A major problem is the timing of public hearings. They are often held late in the process, when decisions have already been made. As one administrator explained, "I think public hearings are definitely too late. It's a formal process. Citizens know that. They know that and come to public hearings, but they know that it is already too late."

Other common methods of participation are citizen advisory councils, citizen panels, and public surveys (Crosby, et al., 1986; Kathlene and Martin, 1991; Parsons 1990). Limitations of councils and panels include biases in composition, particularly with regard to social class (Verba, et al., 1993). Surveys, on the other hand, document public opinions at one point in time (Kathlene and Martin, 1991) and do not allow for an interactive process or relationship between citizens and administrators.

Administrators in our project were clear that participation techniques need to be improved. One administrator pointed out: "We can't ignore the process of conducting a good meeting. There are many people who get turned off when [meetings aren't run well] . . . It could be a royal waste of my time and I resent that." Another administrator challenged all administrators:

> Look at alternative ways to get people involved. It isn't just if you can't come to the meeting, you can't be involved. That may be a very interesting challenge for us to think about. What other ways can people feel that they have some say in the process without having to leave their kids and get a baby-sitter and go to a meeting and so forth? Solving these problems may be a tremendous, innovative way to break down some of these barriers.

To move toward authentic participation administrators need to change many of their current practices. One change may be to go where the citizens are rather than asking citizens to come to them. As one administrator proposed, "So imagine if the councilman from your ward called you up and said, you know, I'm interested in meeting with a small group of your neighbors. Can I come to you rather than you coming here?" Another administrator concurred, "We've got to stop doing things the way we've always done them. We can't be having meetings during the daytime and expect people to come. We can't be doing things in a remote place and expect people to come at 8:00 at night. . . . We've got to go to them."

Accessibility is another important issue. As one administrator outlined, "Another effort in the community is grass-roots leadership. . . . Folks who have been historically excluded from processes of decision making about these scarce resources need to be increasingly included in the processes." Another administrator agreed, "In order to have true participation, those of us who have some authority have to be more active in bringing people who perceive themselves as excluded into the process."

Our research participants told us that they want authentic participation, but many barriers restrict participation. In the final section of this article we suggest how to overcome these barriers in order to move toward more authentic participatory processes.

Overcoming Barriers to Authentic Participation

As our findings indicate, people may be more willing to participate if they have a real opportunity to influence both administrative processes and outcomes. Shifting participatory techniques to more effective or authentic practices requires what deLeon (1992) identifies as a two-sided learning process. Both administrators and citizens need to learn.

In order to move toward authentic models, all three components of public participation—the administrative structures and processes, the administrators, and the citizens—must be addressed by those working in, and seeking to understand, public administration. Authenticity cannot be achieved by addressing problems in only one area. For example, citizen empowerment in the absence of administrative transformation is problematic. To develop processes that increase participation without changing the power relations between citizens and administrators is also problematic. Models of authentic participation must take a three-pronged approach, addressing all three components, seeking to (1) empower and educate community members, (2) re-educate administrators, and (3) enable administrative structures and processes. We discuss each of these objectives in the following sections. Table 16.2 provides a summary of practical actions that ad-

TABLE 16.2 Overcoming Barriers to Authentic Participation: Recommendations for Practice

Barriers	Objectives		
	Empowering and Educating Citizens	Re-educating Administrators	Enabling Administrative Systems and Processes
Realities of Daily Life	Talk with administrators; establish one-on-one relationships.	Take initiative to talk with citizens; establish one-on-one relationships.	Set up flexible meeting schedules; multiple opportunities.
	Pay attention.	Go out and get democracy.	Go to where people are (lunch hour, child care centers, schools, churches, laundry facilities, electronic, etc.).
	Talk to neighbors; form relationships with others in your area (interest or geographical).	Don't separate yourself from your job; you are a citizen also. Think about your life and plan participation efforts accordingly.	Use electronic resources (but don't rely only upon them).
	Strengthen local economies, emphasizing benefits to people versus the economy.	Be sure that projects are advertised so that people are informed (flyers in well-attended places, phone calls, mailings, etc.).	Provide on-site, free child-care; catered meals at a nominal charge for participants, free meals for disadvantaged participants.
	Create opportunities for people to interact with each other.		Seek diversity in representation.

(continues)

TABLE 16.2 Overcoming Barriers to Authentic Participation: Recommendations for Practice *(continued)*

	Objectives		
Barriers	*Empowering and Educating Citizens*	*Re-educating Administrators*	*Enabling Administrative Systems and Processes*
Administrative Systems and Processes	Teach citizens how to work within the system and to work with the system.	Begin to see citizenry as the fourth branch of government; one can't talk about governance and government without talking about citizens.	Allocate resources for participation efforts.
	Head off antigovernment sentiment by educating citizens about the necessity of government practices (red tape, etc.), assuming this is done in a good-faith effort to find ways to work more effectively with citizens.	Shift from majority focus of education on managerial skills to governance skills.	Reward administrators for participation efforts; change job descriptions; participation must be integral to job, not an add-on.
		Require continuing education credits for administrators that focus on innovations in practice.	Bring people in before agenda is set; create on-going project teams that follow project through to completion.
	Place more emphasis on civics and public participation in K-12 (add to 3Rs) as well as in higher education. Educate to participate.		Shift from emphasis on managerial roles of administration to governance roles.
Participation Techniques	Hold workshops with administrators that focus upon discourse skills, meeting skills, and research and statistics skills.	Infuse Master of Public Administration and undergrad curricula with training in the skills below; develop on-site training funded by agencies and local governments:	Change the way we meet and interact with each other and with citizens:
	Hold workshops and training opportunities with administrators prior to beginning project team work.	facilitation skills; team-building skills; organizational development skills; discourse skills; interpersonal skills.	many small meetings; roundtable discussions; outside facilitators; equal participants; no one privileged in group because of position, status, demographic characteristics, etc.
		Require these curriculum changes as part of NASPAA accreditation requirements.	Avoid one-shot techniques like surveys or biased techniques like boards or panels.

ministrators and citizens can take to overcome barriers to authentic participation in each of these areas.

Empowering and Educating Citizens

Empowering citizens means designing processes where citizens know that their participation has the potential to have an impact, where a representative range of citizens are included, and where there are visible outcomes. The central issue is one of access. According to one subject matter expert, "Creating opportunities for people to participate is the key. . . . It is all about access to skill building and to information."

The education of citizens should focus on teaching specific organizing and research skills. In addition, community members need leadership training. According to a subject matter expert, "democracy schools," much like the Citizenship Schools that fueled the civil rights movement in the South, should be established in local communities "to encourage people to see they can actually make a difference if they get involved." Another subject matter expert recommended learning centers "to provide continued education for elected officials and citizens alike."

Citizens and administrators must work as partners in the establishment of democracy schools or learning centers, and, according to one subject matter expert, "they should be learning the same skills." Educating people, according to one activist, "is having people feel confident and informed . . . directing their energies towards a specific goal instead of sitting there being angry with their situation. . . . Empowerment [comes from] education."

With a shared base of knowledge, citizens and administrators can work together from the very beginning when issues are being defined and framed. Citizens need to be involved from the beginning rather than brought in at the end when questions are already framed in ways that are not amenable to open decision making (e.g., the specific placement of a nuclear waste site versus the question of nuclear waste production and disposal as a community-based issue). In addition, citizens and administrators can work together to develop methods of investigation and select techniques for addressing problems.

Many of the realities of daily life that limit citizens' ability to be involved in public decisions seem almost too big for an administrator to change, especially at the local level. How can we change economies and habits of living that limit people's time, energy, and capacities to participate? Although it is difficult to address the major political, economic, and social issues that limit participation, participants in our research project told us that it is possible to chip away at these big issues. For example, some programs stimulate participation and reduce citizen alienation through the development of alternative economies. Summit County in northeastern Ohio is home of one of the first goods-exchange alternative economies that are now beginning to crop up across the country. People connect with one another through a program called "Summit Dollars," where both the currency and the products are services, hand-produced goods, or hours spent on a project. People barter and exchange their services and goods outside of the regular money economy. Not only are those involved benefitting from this program economically, but participants are also making connections and developing relationships that they may not have made without the program. As a result, alienation is decreasing and connections in the community are increasing.

Summit County also houses a successful program called SHARE, which brings together community members and corporate sponsors to provide $30.00 of groceries a month to each participant willing to pay a reduced amount for the food and donate two hours a month to a community effort. This program is interesting because it brings together participants across class, race, and other boundaries and gives people something tangible in return for their participation efforts. Although the decision to be connected rests with the individual, much can be done to address the barriers that discourage people from being more involved in public decision making.

Re-educating Administrators

Re-educating administrators means changing their roles from that of expert managers toward that of cooperative participants or partners. This task involves shifts at the personal level with regard to inter/intrapersonal skills (Denhardt and Aristigueta, 1996; Stivers, 1994), redefining the role of expertise in public administration, and changing the ways we educate and train public administrators.

Along with the traditional research, budgeting, and management skills that one normally learns in a graduate program in public administration, public administrators also need to be trained in process and interpersonal skills including communication, listening, team building, meeting facilitation, and self-knowledge. In their accreditation reviews public administration programs should be evaluated on the basis of their process-oriented curricula, much in the same way that the National Association of Schools of Public Affairs and Administration (NASPAA) currently evaluates content-oriented curricula.

Administrators need to examine their basic assumptions and practices regarding power. They need to become cooperative participants in the discourse, moving from a self-regarding intentionality where the goal is to protect self, promote self-interests, and hoard power, to a situation-regarding intentionality where power and community are grounded in the needs of the issue or situation (Fox and Miller, 1995). The motivation to do so is lacking, of course, when administrators are under pressure from their agencies and institutions to perform in certain ways that serve the institutions, rather than the citizenry. Therefore, examining the basic assumptions about power requires a significant shift in the mainstream values about what it is that administrators do. Administrators typically are expected to manage, not govern (Harmon, 1995; Wamsley, et al., 1990).

Enabling Administrative Structures and Processes

The most difficult things to change are the structures and processes of administration. To shift administrative structures is no small feat. This requires changing institutionalized habits and practices. Without real changes in how bureaucracies function, there will be little movement toward authentic participation and greater cynicism on the part of administrators and citizens. Public organizations must "not only democratize formal institutions and procedures, but also make room for nonbureaucratic discourse and organizational forms" (Tauxe, 1995, 489).

Most of the changes needed in administrative structures will originate with the people involved in administration. Systems and structures are nothing more than the habitual practices of the people involved in the system, or what Giddens (1984) calls recursive practices. If administrators change their practices and start working with citizens as partners, they will begin to shift the way administration is practiced at the microlevel. If changes are made at the microlevel, macrolevel administrative structures and processes will necessarily follow.

Administrators in our study made specific recommendations for changing microlevel practices (see Table 16.2 for examples). Experimenting with a variety of innovative microlevel techniques is a starting point for administrators as they grapple with the problem of how to increase the level of participation in their communities. Some changes must be made or else we risk continuing to hamper our work by practicing participation efforts that, according to a subject matter expert, "are inherently conflictual, discourage public participation, and yield silly outcomes." He added, "In a perfect world, if participation is sought at the first level of the decision rather than at the end, then citizens may be more likely to trust the experts and let them do their jobs. As it stands now, trust will never happen."

It is ironic that the obligation for facilitating change in citizens, administrators, and administrative practices falls on the shoulders of administrators. After all, the administrators have been doing it "wrong" all along. If we assume that a more authentic context of participation allows the administrator to act as facilitator, then it is the responsibility of the administrator to shape the participation process, starting as the initial change agent. It is essential that schools of public administration, as well as those in leadership positions in agencies, create environments within which these change agents can be successful. Such an environment requires appropriate levels of resources and changes in job descriptions for administrators.

We are asking a great deal of administrators and their agencies, but it is clear to us, based on our findings and participation efforts like those in cities such as Cleveland, Seattle, Dayton, and Phoenix (Crislip and Larson, 1994), that the potential is there. In addition, significant reorganization efforts in policy-making bodies, such as the U.S. Environment Protection Agency (King, Stivers, et al., 1998), indicate that it is possible to shift institutional systems so that the policy processes are amenable to collaborative work.

Authentic participation is possible. This study validates previous research, brings together the voices of the people involved in participation at the local level, and suggests a three-pronged approach toward authentic participation. Translating these recommendations into action requires that public administration practitioners and scholars address all three components at the same time, an essential strategy for shifting toward more authentic participation processes in public administration.

Acknowledgement

This article was funded by an inter-institutional grant from the Ohio Board of Regents' Urban University Program. The authors would like to thank Shannon O'Donnell Wolf and Brenda Cox for their assistance in the research. We are also grateful to our reviewers for their contributions.

References

Arnstein, S. (1969). "A Ladder of Citizen Participation." *Journal of the American Institute of Planners* 35: 216–224.

Berman, E. M. (1997). "Dealing with Cynical Citizens." *Public Administration Review* 57(2): 105–112.

Box, R. C. (1996). "The Institutional Legacy of Community Governance." *Administrative Theory and Praxis* 18(2): 84–100.

Cooper, T. L. (1991). *An Ethic of Citizenship for Public Administration*. Englewood Cliffs, NJ: Prentice-Hall.

Crislip, D. D., and C. E. Larson (1994). *Collaborative Leadership: How Citizens and Civic Leaders Can Make a Difference*. San Francisco: Jossey-Bass.

Crosby, N., J. M. Kelly, and P. Schaefer (1986). "Citizen Panels: A New Approach to Citizen Participation." *Public Administration Review* 46: 170–178.

deLeon, P. (1992). "The Democratization of the Policy Sciences." *Public Administration Review* 52: 125–129.

Denhardt, R. B., and M. D. Aristigueta (1996). "Developing Intrapersonal Skills." In J. Perry, ed. *Handbook of Public Administration*. 2nd ed. San Francisco: Jossey-Bass, 682–695.

Farmer, D. J. (1995). *The Language of Public Administration: Bureaucracy, Modernity, and Postmodernity.* University, AL: University of Alabama Press.

Fischer, F. (1993). "Citizen Participation and the Democratization of Policy Expertise: From Theoretical Inquiry to Practical Cases." *Policy Sciences* 26(3): 165–187.

Forester, J. (1989). *Planning in the Face of Power.* Berkeley: University of California Press.

Fox, C. J., and H. T. Miller (1995). *Postmodern Public Administration: Toward Discourse.* Thousand Oaks. CA: Sage.

Frederickson, H. G. (1982). "The Recovery of Civism in Public Administration." *Public Administration Review* 42: 501–508.

Giddens, A. (1984). *The Constitution of Society: Outline of the Theory of Structuration.* Berkeley: University of California Press.

Habermas, J. (1975). *Legitimation Crisis.* Boston, MA: Beacon Press.

Harmon, M. M. (1995). *Responsibility as Paradox: A Critique of Rational Discourse on Government.* Thousand Oaks, CA: Sage.

Kathlene, L., and J. A. Martin (1991). "Enhancing Citizen Participation: Panel Designs, Perspectives, and Policy Formation." *Journal of Policy Analysis and Management* 10(1): 46–63.

Kettering Foundation (1989). *The Public's Role in the Policy Process: A View from State and Local Policy Makers.* Dayton, OH: Kettering Foundation.

_____ (1991). *"Citizens and Politics: A View from Main Street America."* Report prepared for the Kettering Foundation by the Harwood Group. Dayton, OH: Kettering Foundation.

King, C. S., C. Stivers, et al. (1998). *Government Is Us: Public Administration in an Anti-government Era.* Thousand Oaks, CA: Sage.

Kraft, M., and B. B. Clary (1991). "Citizen Participation and the NIMBY Syndrome: Public Response to Radioactive Waste Disposal." *Western Political Quarterly* 44(2): 299–328.

Kweit, M. G., and R. W. Kweit (1981). *Implementing Citizen Participation in a Bureaucratic Society.* New York: Praeger.

_____ (1987). "Citizen Participation: Enduring Issues for the Next Century." *National Civic Review* 76: 191–198.

Mathews, D. (1994). *Politics for the People.* Urbana, IL: University of Illinois Press.

Parr, J., and C. Gates (1989). "Assessing Community Interest and Gathering Community Support." In International City Management Association, eds., *Partnerships in Local Governance: Effective Council-Manager Relations.* Washington, DC: International City Management Association.

Parsons, G. A. (1990). "Defining the Public Interest: Citizen Participation in Metropolitan and State Policy Making. *National Civic Review* 79: 118–131.

Putnam, R. D. (1995). "Bowling Alone: America's Declining Social Capital." *Journal of Democracy* 20(1): 65–78.

Roberts, N. (1997). "Public Deliberation: An Alternative Approach to Crafting Policy and Setting Direction." *Public Administration Review* 57(2): 124–132.

Stivers, C. (1990). "Active Citizenship and Public Administration." In G. L. Wamsley, R. N. Bacher, C. T. Goodsell, P. S. Kronenberg, J. A. Rohr, C. M. Stivers, O.

F. White, and J. F. Wolf, *Refounding Public Administration*. Thousand Oaks, CA: Sage, 246–273.

_____ (1994). "The Listening Bureaucrat: Responsiveness in Public Administration." *Public Administration Review* 54(4): 364–369.

Strauss, A. M., and J. L. Corbin (1990). *Basics of Qualitative Research: Grounded Theory Procedures and Techniques*. Thousand Oaks, CA: Sage.

Tauxe, C. S. (1995). "Marginalizing Public Participation in Local Planning: An Ethnographic Account." *Journal of the American Planning Association* 61(4): 471–481.

Thomas, J. C. (1995). *Public Participation in Public Decisions*. San Francisco: Jossey-Bass.

Timney, M. M. (1996). "Overcoming NIMBY: Using Citizen Participation Effectively." Paper presented at the 57th national conference of the American Society for Public Administration, Atlanta, GA.

Tolchin, S. J. (1996). *The Angry American: How Voter Rage is Changing the Nation*. Boulder, CO: Westview Press.

Verba, S., K. Schlozman, M. Brady, and N. H. Nie (1993). "Citizen Activity: Who Participates? What Do They Say?" *American Political Science Review* 87(2): 303–318.

Wamsley, G. L., and I. F. Wolf (1996). "Introduction: Can a High Modern Project Find Happiness in a Postmodern Era?" In G. L. Wamsley and J. F. Wolf, eds., *Refounding Democratic Public Administration: Modern Paradoxes, Postmodern Challenges*. Thousand Oaks, CA: Sage, 1–37.

Wamsley, G. L., R. N. Bacher, C. T. Goodsell, P. S. Kronenberg, J. A. Rohr, C. M. Stivers, O. F. White, and J. F. Wolf, (1990). *Refounding Public Administration*. Thousand Oaks, CA: Sage.

White, O. F., and C. J. McSwain (1993). "The Semiotic Way of Knowing and Public Administration." *Administrative Theory and Praxis* 15(1): 18–35.

Part Five

Professionalism in Public Administration

As we have seen in earlier sections, professionalism is an important theme in the study of administration. Beginning with Woodrow Wilson, many writers recognized the need for technically trained and dedicated career public servants. This theme was strengthened by Carl Friedrich's contention that professionalism was the principal element in assuring the accountability of public administrators (see introduction to the section on accountability). Since Friedrich, many writers—including many in this volume—have looked to professional knowledge and commitment as ways to temper bureaucratic power and ensure effective administration. Critics such as those in the previous section have warned that, by itself, professionalism is not enough to ensure that democracy is well served in the practice of administration—that more direct protections, such as the involvement of citizens in agency affairs, are necessary.

This section offers several perspectives on professional administration, ones that have shaped the debate on this topic over the years. The first article is "The Mind of the Career Man," by Fritz Morstein Marx (*Public Administration Review* 1960). Morstein Marx sharply poses a major dilemma of professionalism in administration: It creates a dual structure of responsibility. The goals of administrative professionals are not set by them, as is true for self-employed doctors and lawyers, but in the political process, by the people's representatives. Yet the administrator must also practice competently, according to professional standards. So the professional must find a way to direct his (or her) knowledge and skills toward politically established goals. In contrast to the position taken by Friedrich, Morstein Marx holds that the administrative professional is not free to substitute his own sense of the common good for the one embodied in political decisions. He observes: "The intricacies of the resulting relationship between the career man and his policy masters represent a key factor in the performance of public service."

The ensuing discussion raises many points that are still fresh today. For example, "it is in the nature of the expert to cherish what he knows." Therefore, in the author's view, administrators must take care not to isolate themselves in the cocoons of their specialized knowledge. They must also try to avoid the narrowness that can stem from viewing their own analyses and decision processes as rational and those of others, such as politicians, as corrupt. In addition, administrators need to take the broad view, and not let their specialized training limit them to seeing only select pieces of a situation. They must be "responsive as well as responsible" (see the essays on accountability in Part III) by developing a sense of integrity that enables them to act appropriately both in professional and political terms. Finally, administrators must cultivate public spirit that can "grow with thought and time into a guide toward the common good."

Richard C. Kearney and Chandan Sinha's essay, "Professionalism and Bureaucratic Responsiveness: Conflict or Compatibility?" (*PAR* 1988), explores in greater depth one of the issues raised by Morstein Marx: Does professionalism promote or hinder the form of responsiveness in which bureaucrats are primarily answerable to higher-ups in the agency chain of command (ultimately, through the appointed head, to an elected official)? We saw above that many writers on accountability, responsibility, and responsiveness have urged reliance on the administrator's "inner check," rooted in professional knowledge and dedication, rather than on external sources like the bureaucratic hierarchy or strict laws and regulations. Kearney and Sinha here argue that bureaucratic responsiveness and professionalism are not necessarily in conflict. Rather, professionalism may promote such responsiveness.

Kearney and Sinha observe that in contemporary American public administration there are two streams of professionalism. Organized professions, such as medicine, law, social work, librarianship, and many others have infiltrated public administration; in addition, administration itself has become professionalized. Citing Don K. Price's classic work, the authors note that a profession of public administration lacks several defining characteristics. Administrative professionals cannot determine entry standards, they cannot base practice on scientific knowledge alone, and no single specialized body of knowledge encompasses all of administrative work. Kearney and Sinha advocate a new model in which professional administration is linked both to science and to politics, interpreting each to the other. They conclude that professionalism and responsiveness are not at odds with one another. Rather professionalism encourages responsiveness because administrators will respond "neutrally and competently to competing interests," relying on professional norms and standards that promote the public interest, fairness, and other democratic values. (Compare this argument with the Rourke chapter in Part III, which also promotes the idea of neutral competence but suggests that politicians and the general public no longer trust administrators on this score.) "In a sense," they maintain, "the profession provides the professional administrator with a Rosetta Stone for deciphering and responding to various elements of the public interest." In addition, professionalism will temper some of the worst features of bureaucracy by working to decentralize authority. Finally, professionalism will facilitate interaction between the scientific and political communities.

The final article in this section is Beverly A. Cigler's "Public Administration and the Paradox of Professionalism" (*PAR* 1990). Cigler argues that the more public administrators have tried to professionalize their practice, the less political support they have been able to sustain. Observing that administration exists uneasily in a system of separated powers, Cigler notes that most administrative responsibilities are shared with other governmental and nongovernmental implementers. The more administrative agencies have to share responsibilities, the more difficult it is to hold them strictly accountable. Nor can administrators rely on command and control approaches; rather, they must manage strategically, negotiate, mediate conflict, bargain and persuade. In this more entrepreneurial context, bureaucratic legitimacy has to be sought within a patchwork system of checks on agency authority that often conflict with one another. In such a context, competent administration may not be enough to secure legitimacy. Instead, bureaucrats must convince clients and other constituencies of their ability to manage well. They must be "skilled at explaining their accomplishments." In addition, they must become more proactive in lobbying for the broad public interest, and seek ways to cultivate civic spirit among citizens. In other words, only by expanding their sense of their role beyond the conventional dictates of professional knowledge and norms do administrators have the potential to move beyond the "paradox of professionalism."

17

THE MIND OF
THE CAREER MAN

Fritz Morstein Marx

With all the vaunted occupational mobility in the United States, the popular image of the successful man still seems to favor the freely roaming jack-of-all-trades. But the realities of our civilization belie this popular image. It is a civilization that makes training and experience precious assets—in business as well as in other pursuits, not the least in government. If the modern history of American public administration is essentially the story of the rise of the professional spirit, the fundamental reason must be found in the same forces that have created our economic order. Industrial society clamors for more and more trained and experienced human beings. Indeed, it is a career society, for better or for worse.

Politics and Administration

Although increasingly common in most walks of life, the career man holds a particularly important place in the management of public affairs. His primary task is to provide the needed technical competence in administration.

NOTE: This paper is based on a talk presented at the organization meeting of the Association of Alumni of the School of Public Administration, University of Southern California.

Source: *Public Administration Review* 20(1960): 133–138.

In his entire performance, however, he must appreciate that the final decision in controversial matters is not likely to be one based on administrative criteria alone, but one reflecting value judgments that elected officeholders link with the will of the community. Under popular rule, a business that deals with the interest of the entire community, and with nothing else, must properly remain under the community's general direction.

Thus the management of public affairs is characterized by two functional structures. Its conduct is the joint yet divided responsibility of chosen representatives of the people, on the one hand, and of appointed administrative officials, on the other. The responsibility is joint in an ultimate sense, in the electorate's response to what government does or fails to do. In an immediate sense, however, the responsibility is divided. General responsibility for policy, together with responsibility for what is usually called political actions, falls to the chosen representatives of the public, lastly in the battle for reelection. Administrative responsibility—under disciplinary authority—must be borne by the appointed public servants. This extends to recommendations proffered to policy-makers as well as to the effectiveness of administrative operations.

To be in the service of the community lends stature to the career man in government. To fit himself into the dual structure of responsibility is his hardest assignment. He contributes his competence and his skill to the welfare of the community, but the specific goals toward which his work is being directed are not set by him. They are set by those who were lifted into power by the voters. He can reason with them, as a good adviser must at times; yet he is not free to substitute his own view of the common good for the policy commitments of his political superiors. On the contrary, he must accept the guidance embodied in these policy commitments. Although responsibility for policy and responsibility for administration are divided, they are hence also inseparable in certain ways. Only when the two are securely linked can it be said that government itself is responsible.

The intricacies of the resulting relationships between the career man and his policy masters represent a key factor in the performance of public service.

Inflexibility

Under democratic auspices, the most important standard of government is that the affairs of the people be administered in accordance with the people's preference. Those in whose hands the electorate has placed control over the political course will usually give closest attention to the effective attainment of policy ends. To them, administration is the vehicle meant to carry them to their goal, and with the least delay. By contrast, the career man, skilled in handling the vehicle, is much concerned with its proper use and its diligent care. He wants to do things "right"—that is, "right" from the expert's point of view. Quite like the policy-maker, he knows that the vehicle is indispensable for reaching the goal that has been set. Nor does he object to using the vehicle for getting there. But he is likely to insist that use of the vehicle in all particulars should conform to the judgment of the one who knows it best—his own.

Considering the reasons for the existence of the career man in government, this line of argument is not without some point. After all, he was trained to do his job, picked up priceless lessons in the school of experience, and is in many ways personally responsible for the condition of the administrative machinery. Policy-makers come and go, usually taking but negligible interest in the state of the machinery as it is passed on to their successors. Yet government itself is weakened when its administrative capability is impaired. In acting as the meticulous custodian of the means for accomplishing policy ends, the career man may well feel that he is safeguarding not only effective administration but also representative government, even the historic tenets of constitutional rule.

But it is in the nature of the expert to cherish what he knows, to worship at the altar of his own knowledge, and to smite both ignorance and heresy with inspired zeal. Unless he arouses himself to conquer this impulse, his world becomes self-contained and fixed. Things must be done the way he learned to do them. Procedures must be applied without revision because they have acquired sanctity with time. Precedents must be honored because departures would bring forth a tidal wave of discretionary determinations, engulfing his nice, dry microcosm. For each current question, the answer stalks forward from the past; and being the voice of the past, it must be accepted with reverence. Innovation becomes obnoxious.

All this is not entirely unnatural when the reputation of being an expert—rather than what he actually can do—is seen by the career man as his principal stock in trade. From such an angle, it will become emotionally necessary for him to spend more time showing himself right than exploring alternatives that may be more helpful in moving toward the government's goals. Policy-makers who come to him with fresh ideas or administrative suggestions will find him resentful and defensive. Is it not he to whom all worthwhile insights would occur first? If pressure develops toward new approaches in meeting emerging administrative needs, the one thing policy-makers can be sure to hear from him is a story of obstacles and difficulties.

Needless to say, when the career man thus settles in the cocoon of his superior knowledge, he disqualifies himself for a large part of his job. That part consists of showing policy-makers how to use the administrative machinery for carrying out their program. For imaginative use of this machinery, the career man is the most logical source of information. If he is not blocked by his own inflexibility, he will think ahead for the policy-makers, explain to them how to rely on administrative measures for gaining their objectives, indicate the most promising avenues of action, and take on his full share of duty as counselor in helping to define the strategy of government.

Narrowness

Inflexibility is perhaps a form of narrowness. But the evil of narrowness assails the career man also in other forms. It may feed upon his training, his social status, his functional isolation—and even upon his nonpolitical credo.

In the United States, educational preparation for public service has long been enmeshed in a tradition of vocational training. Even on the level of graduate study, great stress has been laid on the technology of public administration. Organization and procedures for program planning, budgetary control, position classification, management improvement and similar specialized fields of activity have tended to be at the center of attention.

One result has been that those entering government employment from the institutions of higher learning were generally able to find their way into productive work without much waste motion. To some degree, academic training sought to provide an equivalent to an otherwise necessary period of apprenticeship. The trained aspirants were made for the world of administration. For this very reason, however, they were far less well equipped to orient themselves in the larger political context. The world of the policy-maker seemed remote and perplexing. The relationship between political responsibility and administrative responsibility often remained obscure.

Nor is the normal social role of the career man an antidote to narrowness. Though "near the scene of exciting things," his participation in public affairs holds him to specified functions. His window is usually quite small. On the assembly line of government work, he is confined to particular operations. The completed institutional product may never appear plainly in his field of vision. Although he is its servant, the community at large lies toward the rim of his own life—a life dominated by his daily work, on the whole protected from political storms, predictable to a high degree, as neat and tidy as he wants it. In his privacy, he may be a walking encyclopedia on the compositions of Vivaldi, or a collector of ancient coins, or a writer of sonnets worthy of breaking into print. None of this, however, is likely to topple him from his middle-class island into the agitated seas about him.

Narrowness is also induced by the simple fact that the career man sits at his desk to do his job. Doing his job gives him plenty of worries. What comes to him on grounds of his competence cannot be passed on to policymakers. He has to do it: and the more there is of it, the less can he afford to stretch himself thin by looking at the business of government through the

policy-maker's glasses. In the chain of action, he is one link; and that is
what matters. He cannot—and should not—pretend to be the whole chain.
He does his best job by doing his job. He renders best account of himself
by sticking to his own knitting.

  Moreover, is it not true that undue involvement in policy matters ex-
poses the career man to the contagion of "politics"? As one of the peculiar-
ities inherited from the history of governmental reform in the United
States, he is particularly sensitive to the implications of the spoils system.
His professional rationality appears to him as the practice of virtue. Conversely, the political rationality of policy-makers seems somehow compromised by the shadow of vice. To the career man the choice is easy. His entire occupational background urges him to stay on his side, to remain
"clean."

  But even if it were the greatest honor to be called a politician, those engaged in the administrative arts would still be prompted to place themselves into their own compartment. Their ways of thought would continue
to be different from the ways of thought of policy-makers. Their intellectual processes would take different turns. Under conditions of party
change in government, the permanent cadre could not expect to last and at
the same time follow the policy-maker into the political arena. As the reverse of the coin, however, the career man is prone to withhold himself
from the thunderous issues of politics and to regard his nonpolitical status
as a toga of righteousness.

Specialization

It has sometimes been said that in the mushroom growth of specialization
the only "generalist" is the politician. No doubt the statement cannot be
taken literally. Too many representatives of the people owe too much to the
love they evoke at the headquarters of various special interests. As a matter
of fact, in the building of electoral support for political candidates it would
be bold to ignore the organized interests, with their capacity for delivering
votes or contributions—or both. But when the lawmaker, in his district, is
dependent on a considerable array of interests, or when he is called upon
to bring about a partial satisfaction of a whole string of special interests in
a legislative compromise—then he may well have to demonstrate his genius
as "generalist." Moreover, he is a generalist by talking the language of the
people, by trying to make general sense of the technical proposals advanced by specialists.

  In coping with this task, the policy-maker is usually glad to have help,
including the help of the career man—if it is available to him. Unfortunately, however, the career man, with dismal frequency, turns out to be a

specialist himself, or even a source of specialized pressure. This may be provoking, but it is hardly astonishing. Here again, the career man's behavior is simply evidence of his having come up in a career.

Way back when he started out on that career, he was instructed to knock at a door admitting only reasonably well specialized aspirants. In fact, knowing that much in advance, he prepared himself assiduously to pass muster at the entrance. Next, so that the marking would not wash off, he was accordingly "classified." And so on and up. At first, he would have liked to slip out of his classification and into another one, perhaps even a third or fourth. He soon discovered his error. Such shifts might make life richer, but in moving from one classification to another it was very easy to miss the occupational escalators.

Indeed, even in the broadest view, administration itself is a specialization. When he explains to the policy-maker which administrative steps might be most advantageous in a particular situation, and which steps should definitely not be taken, he is drawing upon his specialized knowledge. To the policy-maker, he is a specialist for that very reason. Unwittingly, he also may be expressing himself in highly specialized language. Although his jargon is perhaps not unfamiliar to the policy-maker, misunderstandings do creep in, sometimes with very disagreeable consequences—all because administration is something of a mystery to the outsider. Unless the career man succeeds in being his own interpreter, he may give the policy-maker the impression of living in a little box all by himself.

Specialization creates a preoccupation with pieces, be they segments or techniques or processes or functions. The piece, not the whole, becomes the center of gravity, absorbing the attention of the participants. To be pulled away from the special toward the general is resisted with all means. The monitor of the general aspect becomes the enemy. He must be kept out. Thus the spirit of specialization adds partition to partition, giving shelter to a fragmented functional kinship at the price of the larger unity. When the career man falls prey to this malady, he will readily convince himself that administrative responsibility and policy responsibility can never get together.

Integrity

Inflexibility, narrowness, specialization—these generate the kind of behavior that to the policy-maker will seem typically bureaucratic. They are influences that rise within the administrative setting, at work everywhere, as part of the occupational "facts of life." They can paralyze the free spirit, unless the career man is continuously on guard against them. It is not that these influences vanish before his good will or his devotion to duty. He needs to alert himself to their presence, to their persistence, and to their insidious effects. He must give combat in his own mind and fight the battle with his own personal resources.

In this struggle against the downward pull of his occupational environment, the career man is able to marshal great strength when he is guided by the counsel of integrity. Integrity demands more of him than not to steal. It goes beyond a conscious acceptance of the trust placed in him by both policy-makers and the public itself. It requires him to be responsive as well as responsible. But he is not to be a servile creature at the beck and call of those in power. In playing his public role, he must fully grasp its implications. True enough, it is for him to keep the wheels of administration going, to get things done, to render faithful support to the elected agents of the citizenry. But it is also his official duty so to shape his actions that they comply with the commands of law and the maxims of public ethics.

From this point of view, it cannot be a matter of indifference to the career man what influences impress themselves upon his mind. His mentality is too large a part of his effectiveness. Even though his attention is frequently diverted, he stands at a place where he can see more clearly than any one else how incessant is the drag of routine, the temptation of being busy by being busy, the push into a pointless self-sufficiency. If there are forces about him that make him a robot, running breathlessly in ever smaller circles, he alone is able to mount his defense. His integrity provides him with the stamina to resist being molded by his environment and instead to mold it on the pattern of his public purpose. Whether or not he does is a question which affects decisively the general quality of administration.

Integrity as well as inflexibility plead for the observance of ground rules that are to be respected. But inflexibility—as here discussed—has no motive except the egocentric joy of living behind blinders, of being self-serving, of staying put. Integrity rebels against such corruption of the mind in the management of public affairs. The career man's integrity must affirm the instrumental role of the machinery of administration—by conceiving of administration as the other half of policy, as the essential vehicle of political purpose.

Breadth

No element of the general public finds it easier to know its mind, to tell what it wants, and to go after it with tenacity than the special interest. By contrast, government comes nearest to fulfilling its fundamental obligations when it reflects broadly integrated interests. The dynamics of the special interest can best be appreciated as a spontaneous phenomenon of nature. It is a given thing, the embodiment of reality. By contrast, to achieve basic coherence in response to interest pressure is the result of insight and energy, contributed deliberately. The noblest task of government—and the most arduous—is to unite the community in widely inclusive programs. It may therefore be said that to govern is to move in breadth.

This carries an important implication for the career man. Knowing that the weight of convenience in his workaday existence draws him toward a narrow outlook, he must give special attention to marking out the dimensions of issues coming before him. He must search for ramifications and repercussions that remain hidden at first sight. Both when he advises policy-makers on program questions and when—on his own level—he determines policy himself, he must be willing to unravel the raw data patiently, to spot as many relevant aspects of the problem as possible, and to assess the likely effects of promising solutions. It is for him, looking at matters through the eyes of administrative experience, to see more than is shown.

In its most obvious significance, such orientation is simply a much needed therapy for the career man against the ill of narrowness. But the effect carries beyond the plane of his own occupational situation. By contributing breadth of point of view, he makes it easier for the policy-maker to shoulder the full burden of government. Policy-makers need a line of defense against the special pleader. Policy-makers also need impartial information on aspects of issues not likely to occur to them from the experience they gain as organizers and appraisers of community sentiment.

It is not necessary for the career man to appoint himself an eagle-eyed detective to identify the fingerprints of the special interest. All that is asked of him is that he lay before the policy-maker a complete analysis of the facts. Facts do not stop "raids upon the public treasury." But verified facts make it very difficult to deceive the public by exploiting its ignorance. The more the career man, as the spokesman of administrative impartiality, succeeds in bringing into the open all of the angles of an issue, the less it is likely that the policy-maker will be entrapped by special pleaders. The more closely circumscribed the career man's horizon because of his own specialized approach, the less sensitive his nose will be to the scent of the special interest.

Moreover, the "permanent cadre" is apt to be more concerned than policy-makers with the continuity of government as a going business. When it comes to consistency in the conduct of governmental functions, to the fundamental coherence of the total program, to observance of sound principle, the career man is often able to raise points which cannot safely be overlooked but escape notice on the political stage. Engrossed in the immediate, the policy-maker may even hate to concede such points. But the momentary involvements of policy-makers are overshadowed by the constant role of government—not only what it is today, but also what it will be tomorrow. In holding before the policy-maker the larger canvas, the career man provides an eminently constructive service even though he may not be graciously received.

Spirit

If the career man alert to his duties cannot always expect the applause of his political masters, he should nevertheless be able to earn at least their reluctant esteem. As his integrity is tested in the trials of the day, he has ample opportunity for demonstrating his service morality. But integrity can turn sour. It must have the support of spirit.

This is not simply to say that dispirited integrity is perhaps more a liability than an asset. In his relations with his associates as well as with policymakers, the career man cannot be blind to the factor of morale, including his own. He does not truly do his job if he habitually wears an expression of dejection or boredom, or seems lost to the cheerful word. Administration without energy is much less than half a loaf. And energy cannot be sustained without spirit.

But spirit is more important in a different sense—as public spirit. Public spirit is not what comes forth naturally in public offices. It is not an organic aspect of being in public employment. It has to be generated. It represents an achievement, the result of dedication as well as maturity.

No doubt public spirit is not a monopoly of those in the public service. It manifests itself not seldom as the quickening influence supplied by policymakers. Indeed, public spirit is the mark of the citizen—as he ought to be. But those who serve the public in the nature of their employment have a particular reason to cultivate public spirit.

When the career man consciously devotes himself to service, he must be able to displace within himself his private interests to the extent that these would be in the path of his public responsibilities. But that is only the first step. In addition, he must learn to recognize the difference between the public, as the generality of men, and the milling multitudes formed into many separate publics. By becoming subservient to any one public, he fails the general public. Above all, his public spirit should grow with thought and time into a guide toward the common good. Although the standard is exacting, it is the evidence of public spirit that signals the career man's real worth.

18

PROFESSIONALISM AND BUREAUCRATIC RESPONSIVENESS: CONFLICT OR COMPATIBILITY?

Richard C. Kearney
Chandan Sinha

The rise of professionalism in government has stirred some measure of fear and discomfort in the souls of those who reflect upon the relationship between public administration and American democracy. Luther Gulick (1936: 10) recognized the potential threat of professionalism, pithily remarking "caveamus expertum." Paul Appleby (1952: 145) proclaimed, "Perhaps there is no single problem in public administration of moment equal to the reconciliation of the increasing dependence upon experts with an enduring democratic reality." Later, in his influential book, *Democracy and the Public Service,* Frederick C. Mosher comprehensively described the origins and rise of the "professional state" and its negative implications for democracy.

Source: *Public Administration Review* 48(1988): 571–579.

In essence these and other scholars (e.g., Hummel, 1987; Piven and Cloward, 1971; Tullock, 1965) have been concerned that an increasingly professionalized public service tends to act in accordance with its own narrow self-interests, losing sight of its duty to respond to the public interest. In the process, the general public might be denied the opportunity for participation in democratic decision making. A self-serving, self-perpetuating bureaucracy would be the principal receptacle of power and knowledge, leading to a government of the technocrats, by the technocrats, and for the technocrats.

This paper does not claim that professionalism is a panacea for all the ills of bureaucracy. But it agrees with such notables as Aristotle, John Stuart Mill, Woodrow Wilson, and Max Weber that the preservation of a democratic system depends upon the competence of experts in government to preserve modern democracy.[1]

Following a discussion of the characteristics and nature of professionalism, Don K. Price's (1965) model of the four estates is reviewed and reconceptualized to demonstrate the increasing interpenetration of the "four estates," particularly the professions and administration. The reconceptualization emphasizes how the expanded role of the professional administrator has benefitted bureaucratic responsiveness.

After taking into account the principal criticisms of professionalism, its advantages are described. The conclusion is that when considered within the context of existing internal and external checks on administrative and professional discretion, professionalism does not preclude bureaucratic responsiveness. Dual streams of professionalism constitute not a threat to but a promise of bureaucratic responsiveness. Indeed, it is submitted that professionalism, in conjunction with other institutions, processes, and developments in public administration, strengthens bureaucratic responsiveness and helps to insure the survival of the democratic system.

Professionalism in Government

The term "profession" has many different definitions (e.g., Mosher and Stillman, 1977; Greenwood, 1957; Mosher, 1982; Riggs, 1982; Carr-Saunders and Wilson, 1983; Rabin, 1981). Moore (1970) offers one of the most useful definitions, owing to its comprehensiveness and operational specificity. He provides six characteristics of a profession: (1) The profession involves a full time occupation. (2) Requirements of membership include adherence to a set of normative and behavioral expectations, usually embodied in a code of ethics. (3) A professional organization is created to enhance and protect the "calling." (4) The profession possesses specialized knowledge based on education and training of exceptional duration. Such knowledge is recognized through formal credentials, advanced degrees, or certifications that differentiate one profession from others. (5) The profession has a service orientation; competent performance is related to client needs. (6) Members enjoy a degree of autonomy in decision making by virtue of their specialized knowledge, but they are restrained by responsibility.

Moore, as well as others (cited above) who have written on professionalism, agree that law, the clergy, medicine, and university teaching are the oldest "established" professions. More recently professionalized are such occupations as dentistry, architecture, and certified public accounting. In government, occupations generally accepted as professional include social work, teaching, librarianship, city planning and city management, the police, the military, foreign affairs, and educational administration (Mosher and Stillman, 1977). Other public service occupations may or may not be considered professions, depending upon how strictly one applies Moore's criteria.

Professionalization occurs in degrees. Occupations may be aligned along a continuum ranging from the non-professions to the established professions. Terminology such as "true profession" should be viewed as flawed and suspect, because the definition of profession is relative to time and space. For example, the professionalization of medical doctors took place over centuries. In medieval Europe carpenters were taken to be more professional than doctors, who were often viewed with superstitious suspicion and even loathing because they dissected corpses.

Andrew Jackson's purported belief in the simplicity of government administrative tasks (Crenson, 1975) has been debunked by the increasing complexity of modern government and the associated need for specialization. This is an important point with respect to professions in government. The percentage of professional, technical, and kindred (PTK) workers in federal government has grown steadily since the turn of the century. In late 1985 they comprised 58 percent of total federal civilian work force (excluding postal workers).[2] The great majority of top level federal executives today have graduate and/or professional degrees (Schmidt and Posner, 1986: 448). Seventy-five percent of them have scientific or professional backgrounds (Schott, 1976: 256). As Mosher (1982) has explained, government employs professionals at about twice the rate of the private sector. Indeed, members of all professions in American society are employed in at least one federal agency.

The professionalization of American government will not soon abate. Certain altered relationships within the work force have not received their share of scholarly attention, partly because the changes are only now being understood. Dual streams of professionalism have developed—the invasion of public administration by the professions, and the professionalization of the vocation of public administration. The convergence of the dual streams of administrative professionals and professional administrators has important implications for the future of American government that merit careful consideration by scholars and practitioners of public administration.

The Four Estates

The Spectrum from Truth to Power

A useful starting point for analyzing the continuing evolution of professionalism and its relationship to bureaucratic responsiveness is Don K. Price's (1965) model of the "four estates" and their position on the spectrum from truth to power. According to Price, American society is comprised of four estates: the scientific, the professional, the administrative, and the political. These estates fall along a continuum from truth, the domain of pure science, to power, the realm of pure politics. Truth is represented by knowledge, power by action, in a continuum from left to right.

Reasons for Reevaluation

Price argues that it is relatively easy to move from the left to the right of the spectrum, that is, from scientist to professional to administrator to politician. However, it is extremely difficult to move from the right to the left. The primary reason for this unidirectional mobility is that the estates in the left half of the spectrum are knowledge-intensive, requiring long years of training in specialized areas of study. But unidirectionality has not always characterized the spectrum. Thomas Jefferson developed much of his scientific expertise as an engineer, meteorologist, agronomist, paleontologist, and botanist while serving in the presidency. Obviously, the world is much more complex today.

Price's four estates do not exhibit clear-cut boundaries or hierarchy. They are somewhat arbitrary groupings "along a rather muddled spectrum" (Price, 1965: 192). Scientists and professionals are involved in policy formulation, initiation, and advocacy. Administrators use scientific knowledge and the professions for the purposes of their political superiors. In turn, the political superiors are pleased to be able to ground political decisions on scientific or professional consensus. Thus, there is considerable movement of individuals rightward across the spectrum and regularized inter-estate interaction and cooperation.

Price (1965: 122–125) emphasizes the importance of the professionals, who in his view serve as bridges between science and polities, between abstract knowledge and political action. Administrators are considered to be of less importance, except for the role of their professional training. The generalist administrator is *not* a professional (Price 1965: 133) for reasons that will be discussed below.

While Price's analysis of the four estates is insightful, its utility has been diminished by events of the past 20 years. A reconceptualization and refinement of the model is needed to represent the reality of the 1980s. The implicit linear property of the spectrum from science to politics no longer exists. The boundaries between estates, always fuzzy, have become more permeable as the estates have intermeshed and professionalism has flourished. Moreover, two of the estates—science and politics—have contracted.

One is hard pressed to find a "pure" science today. Laboratory research has been increasingly privatized (and, some would say, "truth" has been increasingly compromised) in the corporate search for new products and profits and the Defense Department's quest for practical weapons applications (Lambright and Teich, 1978). One is also hard pressed to find agreement among scientists on what constitutes "truth." The growing propensity of scientists to serve government and interest groups as policy advisors has been countered with increased skepticism by opposing interests and the general public who challenge the notion of "value free" science. Disagreements over scientific "facts" and their interpretation abound in public policy discussions. An obvious example is nuclear fission and its applications, including such questions as nuclear energy production, nuclear weaponry, "nuclear winter," and radioactive waste management.

The intrusion of politics into administration, which represents movement from right to left in Price's spectrum, has been an ill-kept secret for many years. Wilson's (1978) 1887 essay that first set forth the desirability of the politics/administration dichotomy was widely praised in theory but even more widely ignored in practice. Although it began much earlier, politicization of the federal bureaucracy through larger numbers of political appointments and other personnel strategies seems to have reached new heights during the 1970s and 1980s (Newland, 1987; Pfiffner, 1987). State and local merit systems also have experienced increased politicization.

The highest level of inter-estate crossfertilization involves professionals and administrators. The proliferation of administrative professionals has continued as predicted by Price and Mosher. This represents the conventional rightward movement from truth to power. However, Price and Mosher gave short shrift to the second stream in professionalization—the rise of professional administrators. Thus, there is the professional who has assumed an administrative post in a government organization—the administrative professional, who brings the values and knowledge of science and his/her profession into a broader, administrative sphere. There is also the professional administrator, trained in the field of public administration and public affairs and attuned to the vicissitudes of politics. The spectrum has further contracted due to the professionalization of politics, through the growing size and influence of executive, legislative, and judicial staffs.[3] In effect, all estates are drawing toward the professional sphere.

The Public Administration Profession

The professionalization of public administration is the most significant of these developments. It is a recent phenomenon in the United States, where a long heritage of spoils and other factors precluded the development of a professional administrative class. In the absence of a cadre of generalist administrators, the path was clear for scientists and professionals to move rightward along the spectrum into administration.

However, according to Price (1965: 133–134), administration cannot become a profession for three reasons: (1) Administrators cannot "determine the standards for entrance into their vocation. . . ." (2) Administrators cannot base their norms and standards on precise scientific knowledge. (3) The administrator's responsibilities extend beyond the confines of a single, specialized body of knowledge.

Price's conclusion deserves reconsideration. Professionalism is a term that should be defined relative to time and space. Choosing criteria to define a profession is a matter of judgment. Strictly applied, most definitions of professions would admit only the established ones such as law and medicine. Actually, however, a professional continuum exists, as Wilensky (1964) has described in his process model of professional development. A profession's position on the continuum may be determined by the number and extent of its professional attributes.

Price is correct in his assertion that schools of administration do not promulgate and enforce standards for entrance into a profession of administration. Public administrators are not "licensed." However, in some fields of public administration, such as city management, it is becoming increasingly difficult to find beginning employment without the Master of Public Administration (MPA) degree or its equivalent. A glance at the public administration positions advertised in professional magazines and newsletters (e.g., *Public Administration Times*) adds further credibility to the importance of the graduate degree in public administration.

With regard to basing standards on precise scientific knowledge, it must be recognized that the established profession of law is not founded on scientific facts. It is grounded in certain principles of ethics and behavior that have evolved over time, been codified into constitution and statute, and extended through court interpretation. Furthermore, professional administrators *have* become increasingly attuned to the utility of a scientific approach to management.

Public administration remains as much "art" as "science." But substantial elements of art exist in law and medicine as well. Waldo's (1975:

223–224) often quoted medical analogy points out the lack of a unified theory of sickness or health, the constantly changing medical technologies and theories, and the variety of competing paradigms in the "art" of medicine.

Price's third point regarding the extensive scope of administrative responsibilities is generally on target but not sufficiently salient to fatally flaw the argument in favor of the professionalization of administration. Public administration is inherently interdisciplinary; it cannot focus on a single aspect of man or society as do optometry or dentistry. Moreover, academicians and practitioners of public administration are developing a consensus on a common body of knowledge (Thai, 1983). The accreditation process for some 215 schools of public administration and public affairs that has been implemented by the National Association of Schools of Public Affairs and Administration (NASPAA) enforces a flexible, but coherent, core curriculum for the graduate degree in public administration. Meanwhile, just as subfield specializations have developed in established professions (e.g., surgery or ophthalmology in medicine), administrative specializations have emerged in government. These include personnel, labor relations, finance, purchasing, and training, in addition to more generalist administrative professions such as city and county management. As Leonard D. White said many years ago, the administrator:

> is a specialist . . . but not in the limited field of a profession or a science. His specialty is method rather than subject matter. He is a coordinator of knowledge rather than a researcher into the inner recesses of one of its branches" (quoted in Waldo, 1948: 95).

If one takes into account the increasing importance of the graduate degree in public administration, greater utilization of a scientific approach, the development of a subject matter core, accreditation activities by NASPAA, subfield specializations, and the Code of Ethics promulgated in 1984 by the American Society for Public Administration (ASPA) and compares these features with Moore's (1970) six-part definition of profession, it is apparent that public administration is an emerging profession.[4] It is also patently obvious that officials in NASPAA and ASPA intend to continue to promote the professionalization of public administration and the thinking of public administration as a profession.

The Spiralling of the Spectrum

The professionalization of public administration and the ongoing influx of professionals into administrative positions in the bureaucracy provide evidence of increased interaction between the estates. While the professional and administrative sectors have come together, pure science and politics at the extremes of the Price model have contracted. Science has become more professionalized and so has politics. The implication is that truth and power are drawing closer together with the increased scope of the professional sector in American society (see Wildavsky, 1979).

The increasing scope and pace of professionalism make it important to reconfigure Price's model. A graphic representation of the estates today would replace his linear configuration with four waved spirals, each representing an estate. Diminishing domains of science and politics are reflected by smaller spirals at either end of the model. Proximity of the spirals represents increasingly ambiguous boundaries between the estates and greater bidirectional movement among them.

As professionalization continues to grow and to penetrate the three other estates in government, a logical development would be the merger of the administrative estate into the professional. Professional administrators would serve as direct links between the scientific and the political estates. The combination of scientific background, bureaucratic skills, and political awareness would enable them to translate the political will to the scientists and scientific knowledge to the politicians. The question addressed in the remainder of this article is whether the growth of professionalism is benign or malignant.

What Is Wrong with Professionalism

The principal complaint about professions in government is that they hinder bureaucratic responsiveness. Each profession has its own world view, filtered through the education, experience, socialization, and specialized knowledge of its members. This world view may not be congruent with the "public interest." Critics hold that the professional bureaucracy often proceeds with its own notions of what is good for the people rather than seeking and responding to the interests and demands of the general public, agency clientele, or elected officials (Mosher, 1982; Hummel, 1987). Thus, the professional bureaucracies are "self perpetuating machines," not responsive to the public interest except as they, themselves, define it (Miewald, 1978: 52).

Mosher's (1982) treatment of the "professional state" is by no means alarmist. He raises salient issues related to professionalism and analyzes them objectively. However, other critics seemingly have confused the potential dangers of professionalism with those of bureaucracy generally. Professionalism is one of several targets of anti-bureaucratic diatribe in the academic literature and in the mass media (see Goodsell, 1983: 1–11). In these attacks bureaucracy is identified as the contemporary "devil" or *bete noir* in American society because of the almost incomprehensible size and complexity of government and its increasing visibility in people's daily lives (Kaufman, 1981: 6). When bureaucracy is examined for villains, the professions often are singled out for special opprobrium. Bureaucracy, it is said, is "out of control." It is further asserted that professional values and goals typically clash with, and ultimately displace, those of the organization. A related fear, revealed in the now dormant "New Public Administration" movement, is of a diabolical plot in which the cloak of professionalism is used to gain autonomy in a policy field, and then public power is employed for private purposes (see Marini, 1971).

Before presenting a rejoinder to the critics of professionalism, it is necessary to explore two key concepts: the public interest and bureaucratic responsiveness. They are closely related; the latter determines how closely bureaucratic activities and decisions coincide with the former.

The Public Interest

If, as Walter Lippman (1955: 42) suggested, "the public interest may be presumed to be what men would choose if they saw clearly, thought rationally, acted disinterestedly, and benevolently," then only rarely would it be identified. There are many competing interests, each subject to various interpretations (see Schick, 1975: 153) and typically ill-defined, poorly articulated, and difficult to measure or prioritize. Yet government agencies must strive to avoid the abuse of power by considering and balancing multiple, conflicting interests within the confines of the law (Meier, 1987: 118).

The professionalization of administration has strengthened the capacity for bureaucratic responsiveness to the public interest, however defined, because the four estates exist within the all encompassing society. Their members—whether scientists, professionals, administrators, or politicians—are also citizens. This conclusion leads to three propositions. First, neither professional bureaucrats nor bureaucrat professionals are divorced from the public interest. Second, it is likely that the aggregate interests of the members of the bureaucracy are the same as the "public" interest. Third, if they comprehend the popular will—indeed, if they are a part of it—then it is reasonable to suppose that the bureaucrats will readily respond to it.

Bureaucratic Responsiveness

Like the public interest, the concept of bureaucratic responsiveness is somewhat nebulous. Two types of individual administrative responsibility have been described: *objective* and *subjective* (see Mosher, 1982: 9–11). A recognized danger, of course, is that objective responsibility may diverge from subjective responsibility because of competing interests.

A third type of responsibility is not widely recognized: *professional* responsibility. It has two dimensions: (1) the professional's dedication to and confidence in his/her expert knowledge and skills, and (2) the utilization of that knowledge and those skills in accordance with certain standards and norms set forth by the profession in the context of what Friedrich (1935: 38) referred to as the "fellowship of science." The detractors of professionalism underscore the first and ignore the second. However, where specialized knowledge may lead a public administrator to adopt a particular method or to take a certain course of action, professional norms or standards help to place the behavior within the context of the public interest. This represents an important advantage of professionalism in government.

What is Right with Professionalism

There are four principal advantages of professionalism in government. First, it promotes bureaucratic responsibility and accountability through professional norms and standards that guide administrators' behaviors and provide democratic decision rules for allocating public goods and services. Second, it serves as an antidote to the common ailments of bureaucracy. Third, professionalism aids cooperation and understanding between the scientific and political estates. Finally, it provides an important source of intrinsic motivation for professional employees. Each of these advantages is discussed below.

Inculcation of professional responsibility and accountability in public administration has been encouraged by the merger of the professional and administrative estates. Professional responsibility consolidates objective and subjective responsibility. By helping to bridge the gap between them, it promotes accountability for work behavior, guides the sense of personal duty, and helps resolve conflicts between objective and subjective demands. More importantly, professional responsibility encourages bureaucratic responsiveness. The professional administrator is inclined to respond neutrally and competently to competing interests by applying expert knowledge and skills in accordance with professional norms and standards. In a sense, the profession provides the professional administrator with a Rosetta Stone for deciphering and responding to various elements of the public interest. Professional accountability as embodied in norms and standards also serves as an inner check on an administrator's behavior (Gaus, 1936). When joined with a code of ethics or conduct and the oath of office, professionalism establishes a value system that serves as a frame of reference for decision making (Stewart, 1985: 490) and creates a special form of social control conducive to bureaucratic responsiveness.

The professional standards that serve as the basis for allocative decisions for public goods and services stress democratic norms, with equal treatment for all citizens in like circumstances. Extensive empirical evidence of equity in the practical application of professional knowledge and expertise may be found in the urban service delivery literature (see Goodsell, 1983: 44–48).

A second advantage of professionalism is that it serves as an antidote to many of the commonly recognized dysfunctions of bureaucracy, particularly those related to the demands of hierarchy, the threat of oligarchy, and the restrictions of an oppressive organizational culture (Denhardt, 1981). In broad terms, professions make public bureaucracy more democratic (Mintzberg, 1979: 371). They create a dual system of authority in bureaucracies, with allegiance both to the organization and to the profession (Etzioni, 1959). In the words of Redford (1969: 159), authority "is less a power to command than to coordinate" in organizations that are highly dependent on the activities of internal groups of experts. The decentralization of authority inherent in a professional bureaucracy is especially beneficial in non-routine work environments, where the tendency towards bureaucratic inertia and attachment to the status quo can be overcome by the professional's ability to exercise independent judgment and to be innovative and creative in problem solving (Benveniste, 1983: 241).

The third advantage of professionalism is its facilitation of interaction between the scientific and political estates. Due to enhanced interdependence and increased proximity, actors within the estates are better able to understand their respective needs, strengths, and weaknesses, and to form mutual expectations accordingly. In this regard, recall President Kennedy's and the nation's aspirations to reach the moon and the willingness and ability of the professionals in bureaucracies at the National Aeronautics and Space Administration (NASA) and in other organizations to respond to it.

A fourth advantage of professionalism in government is that it serves as a prime source of intrinsic motivation for professional employees. The decision-making authority of the professional, joined with professional status and the possibilities of collegial recognition for a job well done, provide an auxiliary incentive system. This is particularly important in maintaining morale and serving as a countervailing force in an era of "bureaucrat-bashing" and poor monetary remuneration. Even in better times, however, intrinsic, non-monetary considerations appear to be superior motivators for professional employees (see Gabris, 1986).

How can society insure that professional bureaucracies, with their decentralized authority system, auxiliary incentive system, and distinctive sense of professional responsibility, will institutionalize and represent the same values and goals as the organizations within which they are ensconced? In other words, do professional values and goals tend to displace those of the organization? This is an important question that merits attention.

Misplaced Fears

Apprehension about professional domination of a government agency's values and goals contrary to the public interest is misplaced for five reasons. First, professional and organizational values and goals do not necessarily conflict. Also, members of a profession do not hold homogeneous values. Third, the professional bureaucracies are representative of broader society. Fourth, there is no monopoly on specialized knowledge and expertise. Finally, there are numerous political checks on bureaucratic activities. Each reason is treated below.

Although agencies in which professional and organizational values and goals are identical and in harmony with the public interest are difficult to find in the "real world" of bureaucracy, professional values do not exist in splendid isolation (see Bartol, 1979). Typically, professional and organizational values and goals have evolved and interbred over time. Also, both sets of values and goals, by definition, exist to serve the public.

In the public sector, professional values and goals are less likely to conflict with those of the organization than in the private sector because public service professions are characterized by less professional autonomy and lower levels of self-regulation (Yeager, Rabin, and Vocino, 1982). In addition, the expertise of public service professions typically includes broad "knowledge about the organizational and institutional setting in which the profession is practiced in government" (Rainey and Backoff, 1982: 325).

This presents a paradox. The very features that cause public administration to fall short of the established professions facilitate bureaucratic responsiveness. Public administrators tend to be committed less strongly to their separate professions but more strongly to their employer and to the broader institutions and processes of American government. In fact, the principal danger is not that the values and goals of professionals will displace those of the public organization, but that public service professions may be overly attentive to organizational values and goals which may not be congruent with the public interest (see Perrow, 1986: 159–164).

The second reason that professionals do not necessarily dominate a government agency's values and goals is that members of a profession do not have homogeneous values—they are not of one mind (e.g., Bucher and Stelling, 1980; Thompson, 1956; Guy, 1985). Professionals often differ in their interpretations of professional values and goals. Depending on the issue under consideration, nonprofessional variables such as personality traits, personal stakes, standards of conduct, or position in the hierarchy may become more salient in decision making (Redford, 1969: 44–53; Guy, 1985: 9).

The third counterweight to professional domination of public bureaucracy is representative bureaucracy. Heterogeneous decision-making preferences among members of a profession working in the same organization reflect diversity in geographical origin, family status, income, sex, race, and religion (Mosher, 1982: 15). Representative bureaucracy thus implies professions in government whose memberships broadly mirror society and thereby strengthen bureaucratic responsiveness. Clearly, certain biases are reflected in professional membership, but by no means is the attainment of professional standing restricted any longer to the well-born or well-heeled white male (see Rainey and Backoff, 1982: 327–329). Indeed, the professions are becoming increasingly "democratized" in membership characteristics. The claims for representative bureaucracy may have been exaggerated in some quarters (see Meier, 1987: 180–184), but the generally representative nature of American bureaucracy does appear to aid responsiveness to the general public (Saltzstein, 1983; Meier, 1984; Goodsell, 1983: 84–88).

The fourth factor that attenuates professional domination of an organization's value and goal systems is that few, if any, professions continue to hold monopolies on specialized knowledge and expertise (Kaufman, 1981). Competition and rivalry between professions occurs within individual government organizations and across professional bureaucracies. Professional claims to specialized knowledge are also challenged by nongovernmental actors. These include research groups, clientele organizations, citizen advisory boards, public interest groups, consulting firms, academic experts, unions and employee associations, and subject matter experts in the media, all of whom are capable of disputing professional expertise in various forums (Kaufman, 1981: 6).

Fifth, and finally, the American system of government has numerous formal, political checks on professional and bureaucratic discretion. These include executive, legislative, and judicial structures and processes that have been written on widely in the literature of public administration (e.g., Peters, 1984).

None of these five factors stands alone as an impregnable fortress against the irresponsible or illegal exercise of administrative power, for ". . . even under the best arrangements a considerable margin of irresponsible conduct of administrative activities is inevitable" (Friedrich, 1940: 3). However, taken together and conjoined with the internal checks on bureaucratic behavior outlined earlier, these factors offer important incentives for professionals in government to behave responsibly and responsively. All things considered, the advantages of professionalism considerably outweigh the alternative of government by amateurs. This assertion attains increasing significance as the scope of professionalization in government broadens and the pace quickens.

Conclusion

Mosher (1982: 236–240) placed his hope for a solution to the profession-alism/bureaucratic responsiveness conundrum in education. He urged universities to make the professions safe for democracy by preparing students from all disciplines for public service and by conducting appropriate (especially interdisciplinary) research in the social sciences.

Mosher's prescription is essentially on target: this complex age demands reconciliation of professionalism and bureaucratic responsiveness, and professional education in administration may facilitate that. Existing government structures and processes already help guide a bureaucracy dominated by professionals toward behavior responsive to the public interest. As the four estates continue to intermesh, the professionalization of public administration can serve as an additional factor to insure responsiveness, especially as a greater number of individuals with graduate degrees in public administration and public affairs enters the public service.[5] Professional public administrators enhance bureaucratic responsiveness by providing a greatly needed coordinating role within and between bureaucracies and competing professions. Professional public administrators are special assets to their respective organizations because their graduate training "provides them with a breadth of view, an understanding of the approaches, modes of analysis, and paradigms of other disciplines and professions and social-ization to more comprehensive, 'public interest' norms . . . " (Schott, 1976: 258; also see Nalbandian and Edwards, 1983).

To become truly effective, professional administrators require a working knowledge of the various professions which they are responsible for coordinating. Administrative professionals, for their part, must broaden their outlook beyond the narrow confines of their erstwhile profession to a comprehension of the general interests and purposes in American society. This may necessitate formal training in public administration through degree programs or, more feasibly, through staff training. Both groups of administrators are becoming generalists of a sort, better prepared to "reach for unifying themes in the plural voices of the general public" (Cleveland, 1985: 7).

The expansion of the professions in government is both inevitable and desirable in an increasingly complex, technological society. The fears voiced about the invasion of bureaucracy by professionals and the doubts cast at the professionalization of public administration are largely echoes and shadows from the past. As the spiral contracts and truth and power draw closer together with the merging of the estates into the professions, conflict gives way to compatibility. With the increasing recognition that all problems have their scientific and political dimensions, inter-estate cooperation seems inexorable. The professional administrator is destined to play a critical role in inter-estate interaction leading to the realization of common purposes and to the elusive public interest.

Notes

An earlier version of this paper was presented at the Southwest Political Science Association meeting, Dallas, Texas, March 1987. The authors extend their appreciation to Brian Fry, Steven Hays, Kathy Morgan, Lori Joye, and the anonymous reviewers for *PAR*.

1. See Barry V. Smith, "The Costs of Participation and the Role of Bureaucracy in a Democracy," paper presented at the 1987 meeting of the Southwestern Political Science Association, Dallas, Texas.

2. U.S. Office of Personnel Management, *Occupational Survey*, obtained October 31, 1985, via telephone.

3. Members of these enlarged political staffs do not always fit Moore's definition of "professional," indicating perhaps that society's definition of the concept is broadening.

4. This is a reasonable conclusion if one examines other professional "checklists" as well (see Riggs, 1982; Gillespie, 1981; Kline, 1981).

5. The number of graduate public administration degrees annually awarded grew rapidly from 1973 (N = 2,403) to 1981 (N = 6,736). Since 1981, the number has averaged around 6,250 per year. Approximately 55 percent of those graduates accepted positions at some level of government (NASPAA, 1986). According to a recent study by Lewis (1987), only a law degree is more valuable than the MPA in terms of civil service grade and pay. Lewis also finds that the number of MPA degree holders in the federal bureaucracy is growing at a much higher rate than other fields.

References

Paul Appleby, *Morality and Administration in Democratic Government* (Baton Rouge: Louisiana State University Press, 1952).

Kathryn M. Bartol, "Professionalism as a Predictor of Organizational Commitment, Role Stress, and Turnover: A Multidimensional Approach," *Academy of Management Journal,* vol. 22 (December 1979), pp. 815–821.

Guy Benveniste, *Bureaucracy,* 2d ed. (San Francisco: Boyd and Fraser Publishing Co., 1983).

R. Bucher and J. Stelling, "Characteristics of Professional Organizations," in R. L. Blankenship, ed., *Colleagues in Organizations* (Huntington, NY: Robert E. Kreiger Publishing Co., 1980).

A. M. Carr-Saunders and P. A. Wilson, *The Professions* (New York: Oxford University Press, 1983).

Harland Cleveland, *The Knowledge Executive: Leadership in an Information Society* (New York: E. P. Dutton, 1985).

Mathew A. Crenson, *The Federal Machine* (Baltimore: Johns Hopkins University Press, 1975).

Robert B. Denhardt, "Toward a Critical Theory of Public Organization," *Public Administration Review,* vol. 41 (November/December 1981), pp. 628–635.

Amitai Etzioni, "Authority Structure and Organizational Effectiveness," *Administrative Science Quarterly,* vol. 4 (1959), pp. 43–67.

Herman Finer, "Administrative Responsibility in Democratic Government," *Public Administration Review,* vol. 1 (Summer 1941), pp. 335–350.

Carl J. Friedrich, "Public Policy and the Nature of Administrative Responsibility," *Public Policy,* vol. 1 (1940), pp. 3–24.

———, "Responsible Government Service Under the American Constitution," in *Problems of the American Public Service* (New York: no publisher listed, 1935).

Gerald Gabris, "Why Merit Pay Plans Are Not Working: A Search for Alternative Pay Plans in the Public Sector—A Symposium," Part 1, *Review of Public Personnel Administration,* vol. 7 (Fall 1986), pp. 1–89.

John M. Gaus, "The Responsibility of Public Administrators," *The Frontiers of Public Administration* (Chicago: Chicago University Press, 1936).

Bonnie J. Gillespie, "Professionalism in the Latter Part of the Twentieth Century," *Southern Review of Public Administration,* vol. 5 (Fall 1981), pp. 370–391.

Charles T. Goodsell, *The Case for Bureaucracy: A Public Administration Polemic* (Chatham, NJ: Chatham House Publishers, 1983).

Ernest Greenwood, "Attributes of a Profession," *Social Work,* vol. 2 (July 1957), pp. 45–55.

Luther Gulick, "Notes on the Theory of Organization," in Luther Gulick and Lyndall Urwick, eds., *Papers on the Science of Administration* (New York: Institute of Public Administration, 1936).

Mary E. Guy, *Professionals in Organizations: Debunking a Myth* (New York: Praeger, 1985).

Ralph P. Hummel, *The Bureaucratic Experience,* 3d ed. (New York: St. Martin's Press, 1987).

Herbert Kaufman, "Fear of Bureaucracy: A Raging Pandemic," *Public Administration Review,* vol. 41 (January/February 1981), pp. 1–9.

Elliot H. Kline, "To Be a Professional," *Southern Review of Public Administration,* vol. 5 (Fall 1981), pp. 258–281.

Henry W. Lambright and Albert H. Teich, "Scientists and Government: A Case of Professional Ambivalence," *Public Administration Review,* vol. 38 (March/April 1978), pp. 133–139.

G. B. Lewis, "How Much Is an MPA Worth? Public Administration Education and Federal Career Success," *International Journal of Public Administration,* vol. 9, no. 4 (1987), pp. 397–415.

Walter Lippman, *Essays in Public Philosophy* (Boston: Little, Brown, 1955).

Frank Marini, ed., *Toward a New Public Administration: The Minnowbrook Perspective* (Seranton, PA: Chandler Publishing Co., 1971).

Kenneth J. Meier, "Teachers, Students and Discrimination," *Journal of Politics,* vol. 46 (February 1984), pp. 252–263.

Kenneth J. Meier, *Politics and the Bureaucracy,* 2d ed. (Monterey, CA: Brooks-Cole, 1987).

Robert D. Miewald, *Public Administration: A Critical Perspective* (New York: McGraw-Hill, 1978).

Henry Mintzberg, *The Structuring of Organizations* (Englewood Cliffs, NJ: Prentice-Hall, 1979).

W. E. Moore, *The Professions: Roles and Rules* (New York: Russell Sage Foundation, 1970).

Frederick C. Mosher, *Democracy and the Public Service*, 2d ed. (New York: Oxford University Press, 1982).

Frederick C. Mosher and Richard Stillman, "The Professions in Government," *Public Administration Review*, vol. 37 (November/December 1977), pp. 631–632.

John Nalbandian and J. Terry Edwards, "The Values of Public Administrators," *Review of Public Personnel Administration*, vol. 4 (Fall 1983), pp. 114–127.

National Association of Schools of Public Affairs and Administration, *Programs in Public Affairs and Administration: 1986 Directory* (Washington: NASPAA, 1986).

Chester A. Newland, "Public Executives: Imperium, Sacerdotium, Collegium? Bicentennial Leadership Challenges," *Public Administration Review*, vol. 47 (January/February 1987), pp. 45–56.

Charles Perrow, *Complex Organizations: A Critical Essay*, 3d ed. (New York: Random House, 1986).

B. Guy Peters, *The Politics of Bureaucracy*, 2d ed. (New York: Longman, 1984).

Frances Fox Piven and Richard A. Cloward, *Regulating the Poor* (New York: Random House, 1971).

James P. Pfiffner, "Political Appointees and Career Executives: The Democracy–Bureaucracy Nexus in the Third Century," *Public Administration Review*, vol. 47 (January/February 1987), pp. 57–65.

Don K. Price. "1984 and Beyond: Social Engineering or Political Values," in Frederick C. Mosher, ed., *American Public Administration: Past, Present, Future* (University: University of Alabama Press, 1965), pp. 233–252.

Don K. Price, *The Scientific Estate* (Cambridge, MA: Harvard University Press, 1965).

Jack Rabin, "The Profession of Public Administration," *The Bureaucrat*, vol. 10, no. 4 (1981), pp. 10–12.

Hal G. Rainey and Robert W. Backoff, "Professionals in Public Organizations: Organizational Environment and Incentives," *American Review of Public Administration*, vol. 16 (Winter 1982), pp. 319–336.

Emmette Redford, *The Administrative State* (New York: Oxford University Press, 1969).

Richard R. Riggs, "The Professionalization of the Public Service: A Roadmap for the 1980s and Beyond," *American Review of Public Administration*, vol. 16 (Winter 1982), pp. 349–369.

David H. Rosenbloom, "Public Service Professionalism and Constitutionalism," *Review of Public Personnel Administration*, vol. 1 (Spring 1983), pp. 51–59.

Grace Hall Saltzstein, "Personnel Directors and Female Employment Representation," *Social Science Quarterly*, vol. 64 (December 1983), pp. 734–746.

Allen Schick, "The Trauma of Politics: Public Administration in the Sixties," in Frederick C. Mosher, ed., *American Public Administration: Past, Present, Future* (University: University of Alabama Press, 1975), pp. 142–180.

Warren H. Schmidt and Barry Z. Posner, "Values and Expectations of Federal Service Executives," *Public Administration Review,* vol. 46 (September/October 1986), pp. 447–454.

Richard L. Schott, "Public Administration as a Profession: Problems and Prospects," *Public Administration Review,* vol. 36 (May/June 1976), pp. 253–259.

Debra Stewart, "Ethics and the Profession of Public Administration." *Public Administration Quarterly,* vol. 8 (Winter 1985), pp. 487–495.

Khi V. Thai, "Public Administration: A Professional Education." *Review of Public Personnel Administration,* vol. 3 (Spring 1983), pp. 35–50.

James S. Thompson, "Authority and Power in Identical Organizations." *American Journal of Sociology,* vol. 62 (November 1956), pp. 290–301.

Gordon Tullock, *The Politics of Bureaucracy* (Washington: Public Affairs Press, 1965).

U.S. Bureau of the Census, *Statistical Abstract of the United States* (Washington: U.S. Government Printing Office, 1986).

Dwight Waldo, "Education for Public Administration in the Seventies," in Frederick C. Mosher, ed., *American Public Administration: Past, Present, Future* (University: University of Alabama Press, 1975), pp. 181–232.

———, *The Administrative State* (New York: Ronald Press, 1948).

Aaron Wildavsky, *Speaking Truth to Power* (Boston: Little, Brown, 1979).

Harold L. Wilensky, "The Professionalization of Everyone," *American Journal of Sociology,* vol. 70 (September 1964), pp. 137–158.

Woodrow Wilson, "The Study of Administration," in Jay M. Shafritz and Albert C. Hyde, eds., *Classics of Public Administration* (Oak Park, IL: Moore Publishing Co., 1978), pp. 3–16.

Samuel J. Yeager, Jack Rabin, and Thomas Vocino, "Professional Values of Public Servants in the United States." *American Review of Public Administration,* vol. 16 (Winter 1982), pp. 402–411.

19

PUBLIC ADMINISTRATION AND THE PARADOX OF PROFESSIONALIZATION

Beverly A. Cigler

In the fiftieth anniversary year of the *Public Administration Review,* this essay examines the "practice" of public administration.[1] Since Americans seldom build monuments to bureaucrats or construct museums to house their work, choices among laws, events, trends, and individuals for examination are disputable.[2] Moreover, no attempt is made here to generalize about the relevant social, economic, cultural, geographic, and historical variables across all levels, sizes, and types of governments or their bureaucratic units.[3]

The Paradox of Professionalization

As government programs grew and bureaucratic responsibilities expanded over the last 50 years, the professionalization of permanent career bureaucrats at all levels has increased significantly. The 1960 census documented that American governments were the principal employers of professionals, with 36 percent of all "professional, technical, and kindred" U.S. workers

Source: *Public Administration Review* 50(1990): 637–657.

employed directly by government. About one-third of all government employees were engaged in professional and technical pursuits by 1960.[4]
Nearly one-third of today's public workforce claims professional or technical expertise in an identifiable and specialized occupation that minimally
requires a college degree and affords a lifetime career opportunity.[5]

In 1977, the U.S. Civil Service Commission reported that about 93 percent of those in the national government's general schedule grades 16
through 18 had a bachelor's degree, 63.4 percent had a master's degree,
and 24.4 percent had a doctorate.[6] By 1983, fifty-five percent of all federal
civilian employees had some college training and 16 percent had completed
some postgraduate work.

Nearly 22,000 had PhDs, over 150,000 had masters degrees, and more
than 15,500 were attorneys. The number of engineers on the federal payroll increased by more than 50 percent (to nearly 100,000) over the previous 20 years and computer specialists increased by 600 percent (to nearly
50,000).[7] The popular image of the federal government is one of acres of
clerks processing piles of forms. According to Levine, however, the federal
workforce is approaching the structure of a research and development
firm.[8]

Beginning in the early 1950s, state and local bureaucracies began to
grow faster than their national counterpart. Subnational governments became professionalized by hiring teachers, social workers, planners, engineers, and city managers to fight city decay, to guide suburban growth, and
to attend to the service needs of baby boomers. Averages of more than
200,000 new government employees per year between 1951 and 1960 expanded government's size and expertise.

Between 1960 and 1980, new national government programs further
stimulated subnational government growth and professionalization. Annual employment increases averaged more than 300,000 per year.[9] Today, a
little more than 17 percent of the government workforce is employed by
the national government; the states employ nearly a fourth of government
employees; and the key direct service providers, local governments, employ
the rest.[10]

As the professionalization of permanent career bureaucrats at all levels
increased significantly, bureaucracy's acceptance by its clients—citizens
and political elites alike—decreased. The loss of respect associated with
this "paradox of professionalization" is arguably the most important factor facing the public service today.

American public bureaucracy has experienced more than a decade of
sustained criticism.[11] Bureaucracy bashing became effective politics and
was a central theme for the presidential election victories of Nixon,
Carter, and Reagan, although it was not a factor in the Bush election.
What was once just an image problem for the national bureaucracy has

evolved into morale, recruitment, and retention problems[12] that ultimately affect government employees at all levels and the quality of services offered to citizens.

A recent survey of former members of the Senior Executive Service (SES) highlights the problems of today's public service. These people claim they exited government primarily for monetary and job dissatisfaction reasons. Fifty-seven percent cited dissatisfaction over an SES pay cap—the single most commonly mentioned reason. The nonmonetary issues given for SES resignations and retirements are striking: 47 percent cited recent criticism of federal workers; 46 percent said they no longer enjoyed what should be the most rewarding and challenging jobs in the public sector; 44 percent left because of perceived politicization (i.e., greater numbers and importance of political appointees at lower agency levels and increased direction by the White House); and 42 percent lamented the failure to use their knowledge and skills appropriately.[13]

Other data suggest a similar erosion of the human resource base (i.e., the skills, morale, and commitment of the workforce) of the technical, scientific, and managerial corps that make up the bulk of the federal career service. It has been argued that this erosion increased in the early 1980s.[14] There is less evidence, however, of sustained bureaucrat bashing at the state and local levels or of a significant erosion of their human resource base.

The tremendous growth in the size and scope of government programs is traced in this article.[15] The key focus, however, is on the changes in other actors and processes—Congress, the President, intergovernmental relations, interest groups, the general public—that affect the paradox of professionalization. Explanations for the loss of respect for bureaucracy are the decline of trust in government itself, the sweeping transformation of government spawned by growth, and the seemingly unending attempts at reform. Several trends which may diminish the paradox of professionalization are also noted to suggest the possibility of a brighter future for American public bureaucracy.

Growth and Transformation of Government Programs

What government in the United States does in both absolute and relative terms has changed substantially over the last 50 years. Government expenditures as a portion of the total economy were 20 percent in 1941, rising to 40 percent during World War Two. After a slight decline after the war, combined expenditures of local, state, and national governments climbed toward 35 percent of the Gross National Product (GNP).[16]

Empirical research that tests competing models of public sector growth has not yielded substantial agreement on the reasons for government growth, largely due to methodological drawbacks.[17] "Responsive government explanations" attribute changes in public sector size to natural economic and technological processes and/or public preferences. Examples are Wagner's Law, which links growth to increased industrialization, economic affluence, and population growth, and the Party Control Explanation, which links new government programs to voter preferences for liberal, usually Democratic, candidates.

"Excessive government explanations" of public sector growth reject the assumption of neutrality by government institutions in determining public sector size. The Fiscal Illusion Model, for example, argues that government reliance on revenue collection types that hide the costs of providing public goods cause citizens to underestimate the costs of goods and services and to demand more than they would otherwise. The Bureau Voting Model judges government employees and agencies to be self-interested political actors who desire to increase government spending for their own well-being. The Intergovernmental Grants Model, used to assess the effects of the influx of federal grants on the size of state governments, is another excessive government explanation.[18]

Wagner's Law provides the best explanation of United States national government growth from 1948 to 1979.[19] Tremendous social, economic, cultural, demographic, and technological changes transformed the United States from an industrial to a service-oriented and information-producing economy that became increasingly merged as one part of a global economy. Long an urban nation, the United States became a suburban nation by the 1970s and a Sunbelt nation by the 1980s. The service delivery bureaucracy increased to meet the demands of an affluent and mobile society.

In contrast, bureau voting and intergovernmental grant explanations are well supported empirically at the state government level, with Wagner's Law supported only modestly.[20] Dovetailing with this conclusion is the fact that 20 percent of all federal domestic spending still is in the form of grants-in-aid to state and local governments.[21] State government growth has significant implications for the overall growth of the public sector and appears to drive overall public sector growth. The number of federal employees has been relatively constant since 1945; state and local governments have experienced significant increases in numbers of government employees. Thus, it is not a large federal bureaucracy that depicts recent decades of government growth, but the dollars and rules that emanate from Washington to American states and communities. This is increasingly important as "new federalisms" transfer additional responsibilities to subnational governments.

To focus only on the growth of the national government and its intergovernmental aid programs, however, neglects the full sweep of the transformation that has occurred in government across the last 50 years. Public responsibilities are carried out by a complex combination of private sector and state and local entities—states, cities, counties, industrial corporations, nonprofit organizations, banks, hospitals, and others.[22] The national government still establishes priorities and generates funding, but service delivery and program operation are the responsibility of nonfederal third parties.

A proliferation of instruments is used to carry out national objectives—grants, direct loans and loan guarantees, interest subsidies, social regulation, tax expenditures, government corporations, price supports, entry restrictions, and a host of privatization strategies (e.g., contracting out, vouchers, franchises).[23] For example, the total amount of direct loans and loan guarantees outstanding in 1986 was more than two-thirds the size of the regular federal budget for that year.[24] While federal expenditures increased twelvefold in actual dollars and fourfold in inflation-adjusted dollars between 1950 and 1978, federal employment barely increased by 50 percent.[25]

Decline of Trust in Government and Loss of Respect for Bureaucracy

Government programs, then, have not simply grown; they have expanded and changed their form. In turn, government's role in society has changed. Recovery from the Great Depression (1929–1939) expanded the national government's role from referee among competing interests and service provider to that of overall guarantor of economic security. This concept was embodied in the Full Employment Act of 1946, which announced a government responsibility to "promote maximum employment, production, and purchasing power."[26]

Hundreds of federal programs were enacted with bipartisan support between 1964 and 1975, beginning with President Johnson's War on Poverty and extending through the New Federalism of President Nixon. The Great Society promoted social betterment as well as economic gain as government's purpose.[27] Cradle to grave programs were created, and significant increases in existing programs occurred. Categorical grant-in-aid programs proliferated, altering intergovernmental and public-private sector relations. The civil rights movement expanded dramatically and, with later causes such as consumer and environmental protection and worker health and safety, altered government's regulatory role. Economic competition heightened, and individuals were protected in an attempt to define the public interest, all at great financial cost. Today, the pervasiveness of government programs appears before the "cradle" (abortion) and after the "grave" (survivor's benefits).

Public sector expansion means that more Americans now move more money, provide more services, and enforce more regulations than ever before.[28] Redistribution, entitlement, and protection of the disadvantaged, however, engender more conflict than promises of general economic security. The controversies and *perceived* disappointments that engulfed programs on behalf of the less advantaged, along with events such as urban riots and the Vietnam War contributed to the growing loss of trust in government's ability to solve substantive problems in the 1970s and 1980s.[29] In 1978, only 30 percent of the public said they trusted Washington to "do what is right" all or most of the time, compared to 76 percent in 1964. Public perception of government officials' competence during the same period fell from 69 percent to 41 percent. The rise in political mistrust occurred in all demographic, partisan, and ideological subgroups of society, fueling such events as the tax revolt in California.[30]

The decline of trust in government was exacerbated by the development of social programs without a coherent welfare-state philosophy,[31] best indicated by the rapid passage of the Great Society legislation after President Kennedy's assassination. The features that made grant programs politically appealing (e.g., lenient matching fund requirements) reduced their potential effectiveness as the national government feuded with state and local officials about other conditions of aid (i.e., civil rights requirements) geared to achieve national objectives.

Subnational governments had the power and the will to resist national priorities. From a national perspective, policies and programs were fragmented, complex, and difficult to manage.[32] From a subnational view, grants did not reduce resource disparities, and grantsmanship absorbed valuable resources.[33] Social policies had expanded, but not necessarily in efficient or equitable ways. The lack of national agreement on the problems of the 1960s and the complexity of "solutions" contributed to the decline of trust in government that had evolved to cut across ideological and party lines, levels of government, elites, and average citizens.

President John F. Kennedy's election had marked a pinnacle in the call to public service. Americans were urged: "ask not what your country can do for you. Ask what you can do for your country."[34] President Johnson's initial programs marked the high point of American confidence in government's ability to solve society's problems—a confidence that had grown since the New Deal. After the Vietnam War, urban unrest, and the difficulties in achieving the Great Society, Earth Day in 1970 brought a brief sense of the same excitement. Throughout the decades, government careers had been perceived primarily as exciting and challenging.

After a decade of governmental institutional reforms in the 1970s, conservative complaints about an enlarged public sector gained support in the 1980s. President Reagan and his privatization policies increased the attack on government and its bureaucracies. In marked contrast to the words of President Kennedy, Ronald Reagan's election victories in 1980 and 1984 encouraged him to assert that "government is not the solution to our problem. Government is the problem."[35] That orientation to the role of government, and the related bureaucrat-bashing and anti-welfare and anti-tax rhetoric, symbolized the paradox of professionalization. Permanent career bureaucrats at all levels had reached high levels of professionalization, but bureaucracy's acceptance by its clients—including the President—had decreased significantly. The problems of today's public service, then, can be understood only within the larger problem of a general decline of trust in government itself.

Modes of Governance in Earlier Eras

Conflict and perceptions about programs and events alone cannot explain the decline of respect for bureaucracy. More fundamental is the understanding that, as government programs change, expand, and alter their form, so do relationships among governmental and nongovernmental actors change. Conflicts among government branches, levels of government, and governmental and nongovernmental actors instigated rapid institutional reforms in the United States, beginning in the 1970s. Many of these reforms were coercive, not cooperative, in their impacts on bureaucracy at all levels. In addition, the reforms were not based on a coherent framework, philosophy, or theoretical design for ordering what bureaucracy does at any level of government.

Writing about the Progressive era, Weibe referred to the "search for order."[36] The post–1960s "search for order" is a key focus of this article. The next section reflects on the relationships among key actors in the political system in earlier decades—when government mobilized the nation for dealing with industrialization, a Great Depression, the "New Deal," World War Two, and its aftermath. Such recollections set the stage for understanding the current modes of governance discussed later.[37]

The Lingering Spirit of the Progressive Era

The notion that *public authority* was necessary to set standards and to control private interests was one legacy of the Progressive Era's assault on corruption and inefficiency. Government was deemed to be an *independent* source of positive change. *Public–private sector cooperation* occurred at all levels. Examples are the municipal research bureaus—early think tanks—that worked for the cause of good government and the cooperative spirit between the public and private sectors when nuclear war was a concern in the 1950s. Cooperative agreements were used to carry out programs, but public authority remained with government.

A *collaborative sharing of powers* between the President and Congress engendered public trust at times when critical issues required compromise.

Both branches learned valuable lessons when President Franklin D. Roosevelt attempted to enlarge the Supreme Court and to implement the Brownlow proposals in 1937. Congress rejected both initially; only later did the two branches compromise to enact a major executive branch reorganization that facilitated presidential leadership.[38]

Interbranch cooperation was also highlighted by the Administrative Procedures Act (1946) and the regulatory form that was predominant in the development of the administrative state, the independent regulatory commission. The latter blends powers among government branches and, by design, is not based on the separation of powers. At the local level, the proliferation of city manager governments merged legislative and executive functions. *Interbranch and intergovernmental cooperation* characterized the enactment of the Great Society programs and initial expansion of intergovernmental programs under Democratic and Republican Administrations.

In earlier eras, key *leaders were few, respected, and visible* and, generally, reflected the dominant thinking *and* practice about the shaping of government. For example, all three of Franklin D. Roosevelt's (FDR) appointees to the 1937 Committee on Administrative Management (the Brownlow Committee)—Louis Brownlow, Charles E. Merriam, and Luther Gulick—were well known prior to their appointments. They helped found the American Society for Public Administration (ASPA) and promoted the Progressive philosophy of administrative management.

The Brownlow report dealt "with the problem of administrative management from the overall point of view." The Brownlow Committee stressed the idea of the *President as the singular leader*—"the center of energy, direction, and administrative management."[39] This laid the groundwork for giving the President reorganization authority, consolidating various line agencies and regulatory commissions into cabinet-level departments, transforming some administrative functions, and establishing the Executive Office of the President. Its companion report advanced the need for unity of command and a limited span of control, both aids to a strong chief executive.[40]

The Hoover Commissions (1947–1949 and 1953–1955), as well as President Nixon's Ash Council (1970), promoted the *President as a strong manager* by calling for a streamlined executive branch with fewer functional departments, attention to coordination and integration, and sufficiently staffed central managerial agencies to promote the President's institutional interests. As such, these commissions demonstrated the longevity of the good government principles.[41]

Advocates of a strong presidency also endorsed the *role of chief legislator for the President*, without much worry about an imperial presidency or gross abuses of power. In 1947, for example, Louis Brownlow claimed that "during the whole history of the thirty-two presidents, not one has been recreant to his high trust—not one has used his power to aggrandize himself at the expense of our settled institutions."[42]

There was a long-standing skepticism of legislatures, which, since the Progressive Era, were viewed as captured by utility companies, railroads, and political parties. Clear organizational lines of authority that insulated the bureaucracy from partisan political control and used the civil service as a buffer from elected officials and interest groups were stressed.

Throughout the period of government growth, the core technical functions of good management—budgeting, personnel, and other command and control functions—were key concerns of public bureaucracy. Faith in the scientific method and the linking of government management to advances in the corporate world (e.g., use of city managers, recruitment of business people to government) helped order the day.

Congress and the President granted broad delegations of authority to bureaucracy in the belief that bureaucratic autonomy was important for getting the tasks of government accomplished. A faith in experts, led to the expectation of bureaucracy as the solution to problems. The public service was a partner in the various cycles of public policy—with elected officials and the private sector, across all levels of government.

Clientelism was also a part of the governance process, serving to strengthen the policy and representativeness role of the bureaucracy.[43] FDR's New Deal was fueled, in part, by nearly 60 new agencies and 100,000 employees exempted from the merit system by Congress in the first two years of the New Deal. Staff members were selected on the basis of policy orientation and commitment, not necessarily only technical competence.[44] Citizens were also prominent in the policy formulation process, although not the bureaucratic implementation phase. Initiatives and referenda, for example, were popular at the local level.

The Failed Search for Order

Relationships among and between governmental and nongovernmental actors who affect public policy and service delivery have changed tremendously since the 1960s. This section discusses significant realities of government structure and organization that generally have been overlooked or underplayed when reforms to guide these relations occur. The argument is that this neglect has resulted in a failed "search for order"[45] which hampers the conduct of government's responsibilities and fuels the paradox of professionalization.

This argument dovetails with Rourke's recent observation that the myth of the all powerful bureaucracy since World War Two has overshadowed concern with the overwhelming opposition to bureaucracy and power. Rourke suggests that concern with how career officials have usurped the power of traditional government should be of less concern today than how the executive, legislative, and judicial branches have modified to cope with the threat of bureaucratic dominance. In essence, the rapid growth of the national bureaucracy since 1930 unwittingly served to trigger new ways by which other institutions and actors have met the challenge,[46] often with negative effects on bureaucrats and bureaucracy.

From Constitutional Ambiguity to Shared Authority

Public bureaucracy has always had uncertain legal standing in a system of governance in which democratic political institutions preceded the establishment of administrative ones. The U.S. Constitution barely hints at the existence of administrative agencies and does little to clarify their relationship to the President, Congress, and Supreme Court.[47] The operational difficulties of the separation of powers system lead to the necessity for shared authority and responsibilities that are easily blurred.

Most political activity is nonpartisan, involving the actions of individuals and groups to influence the allocation of resources to determine who gets what, how, and when, as Harold Lasswell wrote.[48] This means that bureaucrats and bureaucratic agencies must develop political skills and build independent political bases to pursue their goals—the iron triangle or subgovernments, with their "capture" capabilities, most prominent in the 1950s.[49]

Today, bureaucracy's dilemma is more complicated since much of its discretion over the use of public authority and the spending of public funds is *shared* with a host of governmental *and* nongovernmental implementers within the service delivery system.[50] The growth of the administrative state means that most of what is done by bureaucracy is interorganizational, with a great variety of organizations loosely linked by the implementation process. These implementing structures are the "new" institutions through which service delivery occurs.[51]

The multiplicity of U.S. governmental units suggests that fragmentation is the best descriptor of the system in which administrators work. Nearly 500,000 elected officials preside over 83,000 units of government. At the local level, the multiple governments and governmental units, which possess varying amounts of autonomy, include many overlapping jurisdictions that share authority.[52] This can offer citizens opportunities for participation and guarantees against excessive powers by a single agency or level of government, but the multiplicity poses difficult challenges for public administrators who must respond to simultaneous calls for economy, efficiency, effectiveness, equity and responsiveness.

Two ramifications of a highly fragmented public service bureaucracy that shares public authority are particularly important. First, the more that government administrators are required to share program authority with other actors—especially nongovernmental entities—the more difficult it is to hold them to standards of public and managerial accountability.[53] Second, public administrators cannot rely solely on the command and control strategies associated with core administrative functions such as personnel management and agency budgeting. The skills needed to deal with fragmented government and shared public authority include the abilities to think, plan, and manage strategically; to negotiate and mediate conflict among diverse actors and across sectors; to bargain and persuade; and to develop entrepreneurial abilities.[54]

Reforms Locked in Time

Most governmental reform efforts deal with internal management practices within a level of government. For example, the first Hoover Commission is especially important for its impact on recruitment practices, training and rewards; the second for contributing to the idea of a senior civil service. The Civil Service Reform Act of 1978 and President Carter's Reorganization Plan Number 2 placed major elements of the national personnel function under presidential control and created a separate senior service. Other reforms since the 1960s have been more piecemeal in nature, emphasizing process, not structure. Examples are Planning-Programming-Budgeting Systems (PPBS), zero-based budgeting (ZBB), management by objectives (MBO), regulatory impact analyses, and strategic planning.

The demand for reform of government structures in a system designed with competing values (fragmented structures that increase participation versus the need for accountability and efficiency) is unrelenting. Prescriptively, the response to governmental fragmentation has usually been hierarchical integration, with the call for a strong chief executive as the major thrust of reform at the national level. The most recent examples are President Reagan's proposals for organizing the national government in the direction of greater presidential control and streamlined governmental operations.

The Reagan Administration's management practices have been criticized, however, for further weakening the administrative capacity of the permanent federal workforce. The emergence of administratively intrusive bureaus and offices staffed by political appointees in the Executive Office of the President was achieved along with a change in attitude toward career bureaucrats. Career public servants are regularly cast in adversary roles, especially in the budgetary and planning functions in which they once served as partners. The traditional rewards of government service that stem from involvement of public servants in the policy process are lessened. Less allegiance by careerists to agency missions—due to the indifference of being thrust into service as an army of implementers—results in indifference that harms organizational effectiveness. In addition, national government executive branch reform proposals are no longer guided by a discernible set of principles or common purposes, when compared to the traditional public administration emphasis on legal authority and organizational structure.[55]

Another recent wave of reform calls for government to modify service delivery practices in line with a market-based economy. Rather than a focus on internal management practices, this reform suggests a reduction in governmental influence over private economic decisions and the devolution or privatization of many public goods and services. President Reagan's Private Sector Survey on Cost Control (the Grace Commission) rejected the distinctiveness of the public sector. An earlier example of state and local government reforms in this category is the notion of a loaned executive task force.[56]

Since privatization usually does not eliminate the need for ultimate governmental accountability, any failure to integrate the goals, values, and incentives of governmental agencies or units into the third sector organization risks failure. Privatization is important, but it should be done by examining the full gamut of alternative service delivery strategies and the central role that the public service has within the world of interconnections that defines third party government.

Reform attempts often overlook intergovernmental fragmentation and shared authority in the democratic and intergovernmental system which shapes bureaucracy's key role: deliverer of public services. Reforms tend to ignore fragmentation or treat it in a perjorative way in a search for *the* way to mend *the* system. Despite their influence, governmental reorganizations may be locked in time and the problems of the moment.

Additional political realities, such as divided government, increased policy activism by more groups, and the rise of legislative entrepreneurs and more competition among state and local governments, have led to piecemeal reforms that, collectively, erode administrative autonomy and morale, as well as public confidence in government's ability to solve problems. The next two sections of this article examine these additional political realities and their effects on bureaucracy.

Sources of Energy, Direction, and Management

Divided Government

Not one but many sources of governmental energy, direction, and management characteristically function in the United States. The resulting dynamics are exceedingly complex. Prescriptions for a strong executive, either of a managerial or a policy nature, overlook an electoral reality recently pointed out by Sundquist.[57] In the 36 years from 1955 through 1990, the national government has been divided between the parties for 24 years—two-thirds of the period. In contrast, in the 58 years from 1897 through 1954, the United States experienced a President and Congress from different parties during only eight years (14 percent of the time)—all in the last half of a presidential term. As Sundquist notes, the national "coalition government" of today is not voluntarily entered into by the coalition members; it is forced upon them. Political parties cannot be relied upon to bring cohesion and unity to interbranch rivalries by forging a common bond to serve government as a whole. The trend since the 1960s at the state level has also been toward divided party government due to candidate-centered campaigns, split-ticket voting, the resurgence of the Republican Party in some southern states, and Democratic victories in some traditionally Republican northern states. In addition, at the subnational level, decentralized political parties, government fragmentation, and shared authority work against centralizing options.

Multi-Centered Policy Dominance

The President and executive branch no longer have a monopoly on information. Congress is a remarkably different institution today than it was in the past. It has a large staff, strong service units (e.g., U.S. General Accounting Office, Congressional Budget Office, Congressional Research Service), empowered subcommittees, a new budget process, and a more assertive membership.[58] The more decentralized Congress and more active investigative media today interact with a professionalized bureaucracy and educated voters who possess relatively little party loyalty and no shared consensus on major policy initiatives.

The iron triangles that seemed to dominate the policy process in many respects in the past gave way in the 1970s in many policy areas to a more open, fluid, and temporary process. The new policy triangles consist of shifting coalitions of policy entrepreneurs, experts, and the media.[59] Today's leaders are many and not necessarily prominent or visible. When specialized knowledge holds centerstage, influence is possessed by whoever defines problems, suggests programs, and persuades policy makers.

Since World War Two, the proliferation of research "think tanks," consultants, and other information-producing agents has thrust public administration into the midst of an information explosion, especially in domestic policy areas.[60] The Brookings Institution, founded in 1927, and the American Enterprise Institute for Public Policy Research (AEI), developed after World War Two, along with the Heritage Foundation, the Urban Institute,

RAND, and Battelle are among the best known of the nearly 100 public policy research organizations in Washington, DC. Most of these organizations have a domestic policy focus; a notable exception is the Center for Strategic and International Studies (CSIS).

The Rise of the Legislative Entrepreneur

After achieving recognition as a collegial institution in the 1960s and early 1970s, Congress began to be described as decentralized, chaotic, fragmented, and unworkable in the late 1970s.[61] The flood of complex and polarizing issues brought to Congress by a larger, more heterogeneous electorate and a greater number and variety of organized interest groups possessing strong organizational capacity[62] molded a new breed of national legislator. This individual, less dependent on parties and known for policy activism, is best characterized as an independent entrepreneur who champions causes and demonstrates responsiveness to various constituencies.

Political entrepreneurship also occurs in state and local legislative bodies, although it is more difficult to develop due to the difficulties of building the capacity to achieve policy dominance. Press coverage is less than in Washington, as are the personalized resources (e.g., staff size, computers) of would-be policy entrepreneurs. Careerism is not as persistent.[63]

The Entrepreneurial State

Perhaps more important than subnational institutional entrepreneurs at this juncture is the notion of the entrepreneurial state. Eisinger uses the term to refer to the demand-oriented entrepreneurial process in which individual American states and communities develop industrial policies in which investment and production decisions are led by government rather than the private sector. This reality has led to more governmental competition, not cooperation, at the subnational level. A truly competitive, decentralized government might result in overall responsiveness to citizen preferences, incentives for government to become efficient and to provide quality services at lowest costs, slow public-sector growth, and policy innovation. Competitive federalism, of course, requires new ways of thinking about service delivery and the skills needed for effective government.[64]

Control of Bureaucracy

Questions about bureaucratic legitimacy have little to do with inadequate knowledge or outmoded technology. The levels of expertise held by most administrators today are greater than at any time in history. Former faith in experts, however, has evolved to a "control" of experts by the multiplicity of actors in the governance system. Use of techniques to ensure such core public-service values as accountability among experts has been abandoned in place of a patchwork of "checks" that lack flexibility and innovation and that often work at odds with each other. This compounds the ability to deal with problems—further eroding good will among governmental branches and levels and adversely affecting public confidence and public employee morale.

Legislative Controls

An increase has occurred in congressional oversight—especially formal primary hearings—in the last two decades. Traditional bureaucratic pathologies—clientelism, incrementalism, arbitrariness, imperialism, and parochialism—have been addressed largely by *generic* controls of a coercive nature.[65] No doubt, some of this so-called micromanagement is the result of Congress seeking oversight over governmental programs perceived to be receiving inadequate executive branch scrutiny (e.g., the Department of Housing and Urban Development after the 1989 scandals). Some actions are responses to real or perceived abuses of presidential power (e.g., Iran-Contra) or bureaucratic power.

Intrusive checks on the national bureaucracy have created new bureaucratic pathologies, however. According to Gormley, these are: beancounting (the focus on outputs, not outcomes); proceduralism (adoption of uniform procedures to avoid charges of arbitrariness and unfairness); avoidance—even when action is appropriate, to avoid raising suspicions; particularism (deviation from general rules to benefit particular people, organizations, or governmental units; and defeatism (avoidance of public interest goals in the face of tighter controls and insults).[66] It must be acknowledged, in addition, that many of the checks on bureaucracy (e.g., regulatory impact analysis, new budgeting techniques) also contribute to increased professionalization.

Citizen Controls

A new emphasis on the "public" in public management means that citizens play key roles in the policy implementation process. New congressional requirements placed on bureaucracies facilitate citizen participation in regulatory policy after the legislation has passed. Participants are primarily middle and upper class individuals and groups who form broad and diffuse constituencies for environmental, consumer, and other causes, as well as coalitions born of expediency, not of any shared vision of a good society. The new citizen participation is marked by less interest in formal representation and more interest in tangible results than was citizen participation in the 1960s.[67]

Presidential Control

When the Bureau of the Budget was reorganized as the Office of Management and Budget (OMB) in 1970, much of the leverage within OMB shifted from career civil servants to political appointees.[68] The familiar executive control perspective was espoused by President Reagan, but it did not accept a legitimate policy role for the public service. This dovetailed with the broader goal of reducing the size and activism of government itself at all levels. Top-down budgeting strategies, political oversight, and regulatory control further politicized OMB.

The Reagan Administration was also accused of thwarting the intent of the Civil Service Reform Act of 1978. The appointment of a partisan political director of the U.S. Office of Personnel Management (OPM), for example, led to an abrupt reduction in OPM's workforce by nearly 20 percent (followed later by deeper cuts) but an increase from 12 to 34 in the number of political appointees. Examples of methods used to take away decision-making power from senior-level careerists were the threatened use of sanctions on agency officials who did not follow administration policies, such as the Senior Executive Service (SES); maximum use of reductions-in-force (RIFs); greater use of political appointees at both higher and lower levels in agencies; ideological litmus tests for important bureaucratic positions; and the politicized OMB which emphasized political oversight and regulatory control.[69] Presidential loyalty appeared, at times, to be more important than responsibility to the law.

Executive–Legislative Branch Relations and the Rule of Law

The new unwritten law guiding interbranch relations is, in many respects, self-interest. This contrasts with the ideal of a search for reasonableness under a rule of law.[70] Congressional response to the Bay of Pigs, Watergate, Vietnam, Abscam, nagging deficits, Iran-Contra, the 1988 HUD Scandal (U.S. Department of Housing and Urban Development) and other abuses at the top have led to a barrage of attacks on power, arrogance, inefficiency, and ineffectiveness in the political system. After some bipartisan efforts that led to a tax cut, a defense buildup, and domestic aid retrenchment in the first six years of the Reagan presidency, cooperation ended abruptly when Congress was circumvented by Iran-Contra.

The national bureaucracy had developed an image problem by the end of the 1960s when the apparently iron triangles and capture of government agencies by special interests led to a questioning of overall system integrity and public service. Since most citizens today may not differentiate between elected and appointed, permanent public servants when they think of government or bureaucracy, "the bureaucracy" is also blamed for the misdeeds of political appointees and elected officials. No longer considered a partner in solving problems, the policy activism role of the national bureaucracy has been downgraded to a compliance role.

State and Local Officials' Decline of Trust in the National Government

It took more than general public dissatisfaction to cause a decline of trust in big government. The net effect of intrusive conditions of aid, unfunded mandates, and regulatory federalism has been to extend bureaucracy's image problem beyond the general public to state and local elected officials and some careerists.

The federal government's response to the problems of growing complexity within the intergovernmental system is often perceived to be more coercive than cooperative, although there are many exceptions. Between 1965 and 1980, attempts at coordination and cooperation included Councils of Government, A–95 Review, Integrated Grants, Federal Regional Councils, Interagency Coordinating Councils, Annual Arrangements, and Joint Funding Projects. The politics of problems dominated the agendas of Presidents Kennedy and Johnson, however, not the politics of intergovernmental structure.

Much of President Nixon's New Federalism dealt positively with intergovernmental concerns in an attempt to return power to state and local governments. New block grants, general revenue sharing, grant consolidation, and program devolution in several functional areas are examples of forward-looking approaches. The domination of foreign policy in the early Nixon years (e.g., Vietnam) and, later, Watergate, led to mixed congressional reaction and results, however.

The premise behind President Reagan's New Federalism, in contrast to that of President Nixon, was a skepticism of governmental activism at all levels in domestic affairs due to a philosophical rejection of "social engineering."[71] Because the Reagan proposals did not have a strong organizing principle beyond reduced spending, proposals were often inconsistent and incoherent. The "Reagan Revolution" has been relabeled as a Reagan Redirection. Congressional resistance to many program cuts, buttressed by strong, well-established interest groups, often dominated. After the Iran-Contra disclosure in November 1986, acrimony between the President and Congress resulted in traded victories on federalism issues.[72]

Dismantling the Intergovernmental Management Structure

President Reagan's intergovernmental approach included a relatively successful dismantling of the intergovernmental management structure that had developed over previous decades. Executive Order 12372 introduced a new set of rules by which civil servants were to communicate and coordinate with each other in the intergovernmental system. Funding for regional planning and coordination was reduced. OMB's intergovernmental role shifted from grants management to regulatory relief and political oversight. Existing intergovernmental activities were conducted by fewer staff and many positions in intergovernmental affairs offices in executive agencies were abolished.[73]

Changes in the *structure* of intergovernmental interaction and service delivery disrupted the operating culture among public bureaucracies across levels of government. This, in turn, changed patterns of communication and interaction, and altered the established modes of governmental service delivery. The effective integration of the system had begun to falter in the late 1970s when state legislatures imposed their political goals on the national programs that their states administered. For example, 26 states increased their oversight of federal grant funds in 1978 and 1979.[74] The unending waves of new presidencies and new federalisms make it difficult for implementing structures (i.e., intergovernmental service delivery bureaucracies) to achieve integration and coordination.

The dismantling of the formal mechanisms of intergovernmental management came at the same time that the national government increased its sharing of authority with third parties. That less concern with systematic design of consultation and cooperation techniques for program implementation occurred simultaneously with the growing complexity of service delivery systems further fueled state and local officials' concern with intergovernmental relations.

Regulatory Federalism

The Reagan years were not all devolution, decentralization, and dismantling. Many actions of the national government make it difficult for subnational governments, especially the states, to assume new responsibilities. There has been a dramatic increase in regulatory federalism, a centralizing force in intergovernmental relations. National regulation is no longer tied only to specific industries or problems. Regulation of state and local public governments is an important policy tool in such areas as civil rights, environmental and consumer protection, the health and safety of workers, energy conservation, and so forth.

National governmental regulations include direct orders or mandates, cross-cutting requirements, crossover sanctions, and partial preemptions.[75] National funding for administration and oversight in many areas is often perceived to be at odds with state and local priorities and inconsistent with the concept of intergovernmental partnership. State and local officials perceive a lack of consultation in the design of national programs that undermines their roles as program innovators in the American political system.[76]

Congress has increased its use of broad authority (e.g., the commerce and supremacy clauses of the Constitution) to preempt state and local laws and ordinances. Examples are the Airline Deregulation Act of 1978 (which disallows state and local government regulation of the routes, rates, or services of air carriers), the Motor Carrier Act of 1980, and the Bus Regulatory Reform Act of 1982, deregulating the trucking and busing industries, respectively. New direct orders, backed by civil or criminal penalties, are still not common but have increased. Most notable is the extension of the Fair Labor Standards Act to state and local government employees, which was upheld by the U.S. Supreme Court in *Garcia* v. *San Antonio Metropolitan Transit Authority.*

While it appeared for a time during the 1970s that the states would be allowed greater freedom from federal regulation and taxation, the federal courts have also reasserted federal dominance.[77] Fears about limitations on the Tenth Amendment have been so intense that the National Governors' Association has proposed limiting such powers over state and local government through the constitutional amendment process. The U.S. Advisory Commission on Intergovernmental Relations (ACIR) has proposed discussions on constitutional reform for the purpose of reinvigorating federalism.[78]

A Renewed Search for Order

This article has suggested that modes of governance in the United States and relationships among and between governmental and nongovernmental actors have changed significantly over the last 50 years. Government is no longer viewed as an independent source of change but is thought of as an obstacle to significant change. It is difficult to attract people to public service when the economic and political spheres are not considered separate and distinct human endeavors—and when the pay is better elsewhere.

Public administrators are perceived to be self-interested actors in the political system. Governments lobby government and states are told to enter the political arena to settle disputes. Government competes with other sellers of services in a pricing system that is wary of governmental monopoly. Accountability is often far removed from service provision. Prior concern with agency capture seems less threatening when compared to government sharing its *authority* with nongovernmental actors.

Public policies and management reforms are piecemeal and largely born of expediency. Management reforms are often coercive, with process separated from structure. No coherent view of government's role or rationale for bureaucratic activity and no consensus on national needs or priorities has evolved. American political parties are not the organizing links they once were. Bureaucracy is more professionalized than it ever was, but it is appreciated less. Professionals are fragmented across fields and micro-managed agencies. The intergovernmental lobby is adept but spatially fragmented.

Traditionally, the President has been a source of hope who elicits and crystallizes a new national purpose. But, as Reich has argued, no one leader now provides alternative visions of what is desirable or possible, to stimulate deliberation, to provide premises, and to broaden the range of possible responses.[79] Divided government, legislative and state and local governmental entrepreneurship, policy triangles (especially the growing influence of think-tanks), and other political realities make the vision of the singular leader seem unlikely to occur.

Effective leadership is the key to coalition building, but interbranch, intergovernmental, popular democracy, and intersectoral fears have developed a policy-making system in which power is not simply dispersed but nearly diffused. Individual and institutional responsibility is, thus, easily avoided. Where power exists, it seems to be abused more than in the past. Today's leaders are numerous and diverse—legislators, executives, judges, professionals, researchers, subnational governments, business groups, Democrats and Republicans, liberals and conservatives. When everyone is in charge, there is a feeling that no one is in charge.

Actors and institutions have changed, as have public perceptions of them, and no situation is ever ideal. Today's political realities, however, offer exciting prospects for new directions of governance and for a reversal of the paradox of professionalization. Some of the most important trends are discussed below.

Opportunities for Policy Leadership and the Power of Public Ideas

Coincident with the rise of new policy triangles based on expertise in the early 1970s, interest group lobbying also grew rapidly. While special interests are powerful, policy specialists have been able to match that power, on occasion. Good ideas matter and can sometimes offset the power of numbers and money. The ideas of experts, promoted by the media, can stimulate policy change by altering the way policy makers see the world, their priorities, and their orientations to commitment and advocacy. Government is part of the information age and can play an increasingly facilitative role. The opportunities for those who serve the public to move organizations—or the nation—in new directions are increasing.

Leaders do not act alone; they move in concert with political trends. Leadership to create new possibilities for society will occur, in the future, in different ways than in years past because more actors are in the policy system. Increased concern with the "public" in public management means that more sides to every argument are voiced. Decentralized policy activism can produce exciting ideas. The sheer density of administrative competence, moreover, can make a difference in changing organizations. Transforming leaders, who challenge citizens to realize their highest moral potential in political activity, and transactional leaders, who can rearrange societal interests without creating a new system of politics, will both be needed in the 1990s and may come from many quarters.[80]

Opportunities for Facilitative Management

Multicentered policy dominance, the multiplicity of governments, and the realities of governmental fragmentation highlight the need not only for political leadership but also for facilitative styles of management (e.g., council-manager government). A vast array of new types of formal and informal governance structures are emerging that, collectively, deal with the problems of achieving "coordination without hierarchy" and "order without design."[81] The intergovernmental management system has, in many respects, shifted from the vertical domination of the national government to horizontal relations among local and state governments.[82] Since the 1950s, economic conditions and public spending, as well as legal and regulatory changes, have led to more shared objectives among many organizations.

As states and communities define their roles, determine benefits from cooperation, and seek democratic outcomes, organizational leaders and state and local professionals with clear vision and facilitative skills have formed intercommunity partnerships, public-private partnerships, interstate compacts, and other mechanisms for experimentation and implementation. At the same time, a more competitive federalism with opposite and rival interests is also emerging, especially in the area of economic development. It may be that partnerships and cooperative sharing and competition can exist side by side to strengthen the overall American system of government. Informal channels among and between actors at different levels and in different organizations and governments may lead to linked webs of interdependence that prove effective and durable as instruments for service delivery. Rationality, flexibility, and the representation of varied interests may be advanced along with efficiency, effectiveness, and accountability if many of the decentralized, informal organizational arrangements in existence are scrutinized and compared to traditional centralized, formal arrangements for achieving coordination in the policy system.

Minnesota's STEP (Strive Toward Excellence in Performance) Program, which promotes managerial innovation is a process for change that has spawned dozens of innovative initiatives.[83] Governmental units are rethinking their missions and their service provision, increasing relations with clients, constituents, and those that represent them (legislatures). Recognition is growing that some partnerships are necessary because government, communities, and businesses cannot all solve problems by themselves. Resources are scarce and managerial information and service problems are common. Leadership for the new networks that govern is emerging rapidly.[84]

New tools of management—proxy advocates, ombudspersons, mediators—are being used to deal with complex adversarial, collaborative, and adjudicative relationships among individuals and groups.[85] Demands for increased governmental efficiency and effectiveness translate to the necessity to develop new and better ways to ensure managerial and governmental accountability. This is especially the case with governmental service delivery which is likely to continue to separate provision from production of services.[86] Increased citizen activism thrusts elected officials into more policy activist roles, necessitating greater public administrator skills to do the public's business.

State Resurgence and a Reshaping of Fiscal Relations

Between the 1950s and the 1970s, state governments not only reformed their structures and processes[87] but were transformed by court decisions on reapportionment (e.g., *Baker* v. *Carr*), which reduced the rural-urban imbalance of state legislatures, and the enactment of national civil rights laws,[88] which made it acceptable to think about a serious state role. As state modernization continued into the 1980s, general public and political elite support for an increased state role also developed.

The philosophy and programs of the Reagan presidency quickened the pace of devolutionary domestic policies. This fueled the states' resurgence by redirecting intergovernmental fiscal policy. After being bypassed for decades, the states demonstrated their improved management capabilities when offered the opportunity to administer block grants. Overreaction by state governments to the 1981–1982 recession resulted in tax raising efforts that left them with strong finances just as federal aid retrenchment policies began to be felt. Budget driven federalism, especially federal aid cuts and their "fend-for-yourself" effects at the state and local levels also instigated cutback management and productivity improvement.[89]

The clearest intergovernmental fiscal trend is that federal aid as a percentage of state and local government revenue continues to decline. In 1966, of every dollar of state and local government revenue 13.5 cents came from the federal government; in 1978—the year in which federal aid peaked—the federal share soared to 18.7 cents; in 1988, it dropped back to 13.6 cents. Devolution, disengagement, and decremental budgeting in the Reagan era had dramatic effects.[90] Other aspects of budget driven federalism—the zero-sum dynamic of the Gramm-Rudman-Hollings constraints, the effects of the 1986 tax reform, and continuing federal deficits—also indicate federal fiscal retreat.[91]

Subnational governments, however, must respond to a staggering array of traditional responsibilities and new demands and generally cannot borrow their way out of problems. Just as many state programs of the 1920s were models for the national government's New Deal programs, states in the 1970s and 1980s increased their management capacity and revenues to become the engines of innovation for such policies as education, welfare, and the environment.[92] New roles were forged in state-local and state-local-private relations.[93] State courts took on a new activism, exhibiting more liberalism by expanding tort law, the rights of injured parties, and individual rights in general.[94] The intergovernmental lobby grew in skills as did the nation's capacity to understand intergovernmental affairs.[95]

Moreover, there is little evidence that public service morale in state bureaucracies matches the negative federal experience. Little Volcker Commissions have not proliferated, although some have emerged (e.g., Illinois and Ohio). New York, the first state in the nation to produce a comprehensive public sector workforce plan, reports a serious and growing workforce crisis, but it is one with origins in long-term changes in the labor force and the nature of work.[96]

New public demands for state action seem endless—product liability, the right to die, teenage pregnancy, surrogate motherhood, pay equity, homelessness, acquired immune deficiency syndrome (AIDS), drugs in the schools, the medically indigent, etc. are the newest issues. The states have become domestic policy innovators in such areas as environmental and natural resources policy, economic development, health care and human services, education, business and insurance regulation.[97] States have the relative luxury, compared to the national government, of experimenting with service delivery options. Successes can be kept and failures discarded with minimal risk.

Emerging Analytical Consensus on Governmental Sorting Out and Policy

The states have proven to be more responsive than the federal government in some policy areas and more cooperative with their local governments than in the past. One result is an emerging analytical consensus within the new policy triangles that is producing leadership in the direction of a sorting out of governmental functions across the intergovernmental system.[98] The work of the ACIR is especially important in this regard. Moreover, discussions about a realignment of state-local relationships is now timely. Officials are examining key and separate elements of governmental responsibility: which level performs a particular function, which controls performance, and which pays the costs.

Rather than focusing only on privatization alternatives, a comprehensive look at what government does and the many ways things can be done is proceeding. New forms of intergovernmental cooperation are especially popular (e.g., joint purchasing, circuit riders). In addition, Executive Order 12612, "Federalism," (26 October 1987) mandates that national agencies take into account federalism principles and policy-making criteria in the formulation and implementation of agency policies.

In several policy areas, a consensus is emerging to move toward significant policy changes. Recent examples are found in the areas of deregulation and tax reform[99] and, perhaps, re-regulation. Earlier policy shifts in civil rights and the Great Society programs occurred via a general societal consensus toward new programs. Bottom-up approaches for developing a policy consensus in selected areas are gaining ground. The National Conference on Social Welfare (1985) is a good example of collaborative thinking about important, comprehensive policy initiatives.

Recognition of "Subjective Expertise"

Bureaucracy will continue to professionalize. Witness the "Green Books" of the city management profession or the "Blue Book"—*Governmental Accounting, Auditing and Finance Reporting,* a milestone for state and local government reporting. Note the seriousness of the ethics revolution and the activities of such professional associations as the American Society for Public Administration (ASPA) and the National Association of Schools of Public Affairs and Administration (NASPAA), with its standards for accreditation of graduate programs. Consider, also, the proliferation of professional training programs, such as the Certified Public Manager programs in many states, and other support for professionals such as the Academy for State and Local Government or the Coalition to Improve Management in State and Local Government.

Public administrators rarely receive positive recognition, however. When Americans think of such projects as the moon landing, they credit science. Few are aware, for example, of the incredibly complex management challenge required of James E. Webb, Administrator of the National Aeronautics and Space Administration (NASA) in the 1960s, to harness the talent of many fields in a large-scale research and management undertaking.[100]

Interestingly, however, the professional bureaucracy at all levels has become aware that managing well is not enough to halt negative public perceptions of bureaucratic performance. The extension of the Volcker Commission to devise strategies for implementation of its recommendations is a key example, as are the brochures now produced by city managers and state agency officials that depict the work of their organizations in lay language for mass distribution.

Being able to convince others that one has managed well may be as critical as competent administration itself. A professional's expertise is not simply a factor of objective attributes—the accumulation of training, education, and measurable experience. The psychological, or subjective, dimension of expertise or professionalism is evident when public and elected official acceptance of professionals is considered. The paradox of professionalization must be examined from the vantage points of bureaucracy's clients.[101] This dovetails with studies of leadership that find that communication—inside and outside of the organization—is essential for success. Vision and hard work are not enough; leaders must be skilled at explaining their accomplishments to their clients.[102]

The Vitality of Local Governments

A 1989 ACIR national poll on public perceptions asked which government level spends money the most wisely, which responds best to needs, and which has the most honest officials and needs more power. Local governments were rated highest by citizens on all factors and received at least twice as many favorable responses as the national government on each item. The states were ranked second in responsiveness and spending decisions. The national government ranked last on all items except for honesty, for which it ranked slightly higher than state government.[103]

The paradox of professionalization appears to be driven by the reactions to the national government and its bureaucracy. At the local level, citizens are more likely to experience well-run government that facilitates collaborative civic authority and coordinated, institutionalized administration. This is the case especially for council-manager government in its attempt to practice transformational politics through professionally expert administration that offers relatively neutral access and responsiveness.[104] The ideals of council-manager government—a legacy of an earlier "search for reasonableness" are fundamental, according to Newland, for understanding how ideals can meet practice in American governance.

Civic Duty and Obligation as the Costs of Freedom

Stahl recently argued the need to educate the public that business should behave more like government! The reality of subjective expertise suggests that one way to address the paradox of professionalization is for public administrators themselves to be more proactive in lobbying for the broad public interest.[105] Public administrators are beginning to take the lead in arguing that the United States cannot afford the option of operating without government or without investing in its operations.[106] The Volcker Commission, ASPA, NASPAA, NAPA, the Academy for State and Local Government, and other organizations are helping to educate the nation that the business of government is business—and much more. In addition, the Volcker Commission and NAPA, especially, are making recommendations about the restoration of civic values and respect for law.

Without a triggering event to test citizenship, finding ways to kindle a new spirit of civic duty and obligation is difficult. There are signs, however, of an emerging regional citizenship due to problems that spill over community boundaries, such as solid and toxic waste disposal. For the first time in many years, the case for a national volunteer service is receiving attention. Similar efforts already exist in some communities and statewide (Maryland).

As trust in government is rebuilt, respect for the people who serve in it may grow. The diversity of all opinions on all sides of the current political spectrum increases opportunities for public discussion about what is good for society. From it, civic discovery and workable policy options may emerge. Supreme Court Justice Oliver Wendell Holmes once said, "I like to pay taxes. With them, I buy civilization." The paradox of professionalization must be addressed in multiple ways; the cultivation of an educated citizenry—one that can think critically and draw reasoned conclusions about why they should pay taxes—may be a key.

Notes

The author thanks her brother, Allan J. Cigler for his help and encouragement and Phillip J. Cooper and anonymous reviewers for their helpful comments.

1. Dwight Waldo suggests using capital letters to designate the academic field of Public Administration and lower case to designate public administration practice. See Dwight Waldo, *The Administrative State: A Study of the Political Theory of American Public Administration* (New York: Ronald Press, 1948) and the 2d. ed. (Holmes and Meier, 1984). Here, the emphasis is on public administration practice, and lower case is used throughout. However, the assumption is that no strict dichotomy separates theory and practice and that the issues discussed will help guide academic discourse and research also.

2. Useful references that assess laws, trends, and events are Frederick C. Mosher, ed., *Basic Documents of American Public Administration, 1976–1950* (New York: Holmes & Meier Publishers, Inc., 1976); Richard J. Stillman II, ed., *Basic Documents of American Public Administration Since 1950* (New York: Holmes & Meier, 1982); and Melvin I. Urofsky, ed., *Documents of American Constitutional & Legal History: The Age of Industrialization to the Present,* vol. 2 (New York: Alfred A. Knopf, 1989).

3. On such matters, readers can consult relevant chapters in James L. Perry, ed., *Handbook of Public Administration* (San Francisco, CA: Jossey-Bass, 1989); Ralph Clark Chandler, ed., *A Centennial History of the American Administrative State* (New York: Macmillan, 1987); Jack Rabin, ed., *Handbook of Public Administra-*

tion (New York: Marcel Dekker, Inc., 1989); and Naomi Lynn and Aaron Wildavsky, eds., *Public Administration: The State of the Discipline* (Chatham, NJ: Chatham House Publishers, 1990).

4. Frederick C. Mosher, *Democracy and the Public Service* (New York: Oxford University Press, 1968), p. 103.

5. Donald G. Hodges and Robert F. Durant, "The Professional State Revisited: Twixt Scylla and Charybdis?" *Public Administration Review,* vol. 49 (September/October 1989), pp. 474–485.

6. U.S. Civil Service Commission, *Executive Personnel in the Federal Service* (Washington: U.S. Civil Service Commission, 1977).

7. Howard Rosen, *Servants of the People: The Uncertain Future of the Federal Civil Service* (Salt Lake City, UT: Olympus Publishing Company, 1985), pp. 13–30; Kathy Sawyer, "Uncle Sam's New Look: A Workforce in Transition From Clerks to Technocrats," *The Washington Post* (4 August 1980), pp. A1 and A7; and Charles H. Levine, "The Federal Government in the Year 2000: Administrative Legacies of the Reagan Years," *Public Administration Review,* vol. 46 (May/June 1986), pp. 195–206.

8. Levine, "The Federal Government in the Year 2000," *supra,* p. 198.

9. Larry Sabato, *Goodbye to Goodtime Charlie: The American Governor Transformed,* 2d. ed. (Washington: Congressional Quarterly Press, Inc., 1983) and Thomas J. Anton, *American Federalism & Public Policy: How the System Works* (New York: Random House, Inc., 1989).

10. U.S. Advisory Commission on Intergovernmental Relations, *Significant Features of Fiscal Federalism, 1985–86* (Washington: ACIR, 1986), p. 132; U.S. Office of Management and Budget, *Special Analysis, Budget of the United States Government, Fiscal Year 1989* (Washington: U.S. Government Printing Office, 1988), pp. 1–11.

11. Charles T. Goodsell, *The Case for Bureaucracy* (Chatham, NJ: Chatham House Publishers, 1983 and 1985).

12. See the Report of The National Commission on the Public Service, *Leadership for America: Rebuilding the Public Service* (Washington: National Commission on the Public Service, 1989) and its four task force reports; Charles H. Levine and Rosslyn S. Kleeman, "The Quiet Crisis of the Civil Service: The Federal Personnel System at the Crossroads," Occasional Paper (Washington: The National Academy of Public Administration, 1988); U.S. General Accounting Office, *The Public Service: Issues Affecting Its Quality, Effectiveness, Integrity and Stewardship* (Washington: GAO, June 1989); Carolyn Ban, "The Crisis of Morale and Federal Senior Executives," *Public Productivity Review,* no. 43 (Fall 1987), pp. 31–49; and Twentieth Century Fund, *The Government's Managers: Report of the Twentieth Century Fund Task Force on the Senior Executive Service* (New York: Priority Press, 1987).

13. U.S. Merit Systems Protection Board, *The Senior Executive Service: Views of Former Federal Executives* (Washington: U.S. Merit Systems Protection Board, October 1989).

14. Edie N. Goldenberg, "The Permanent Government in an Era of Retrenchment and Redirection," in Lester M. Salamon and Michael S. Lund, eds., *The Reagan Presidency and the Governing of America* (Washington: The Urban Institute,

1985), pp. 381–404; Charles H. Levine, "Retrenchment, Human Resource Erosion and the Role of the Personnel Manager," *Public Personnel Management,* vol. 13 (Fall 1984), pp. 249–263; and Levine, "The Federal Government in the Year 2000," p. 200.

15. No strict 50-year boundaries are used for this discussion in the *PAR's* fiftieth year due to the important legacies of the Progressive Era and the New Deal period.

16. Anton, *American Federalism & Public Policy, supra,* p. 41; and Vincent Ostrom, Robert Bish, and Elinor Ostrom, *Local Government in the United States* (San Francisco: Institute for Contemporary Studies, 1989).

17. Examples of this literature include: William Niskanen, *Bureaucracy and Representative Government* (Chicago: Aldine, 1971); Thomas E. Borcherding, ed., *Budgets and Bureaucrats: The Sources of Government Growth* (Durham, NC: Duke University Press, 1977); William D. Berry and David Lowery, *Understanding United States Government Growth: An Empirical Analysis of the Postwar Era* (New York: Praeger, 1987); James C. Garand. "Explaining Government Growth in the U.S. States," *American Political Science Review,* vol. 82 (September 1988), pp. 837–849; and James G. Garand, "Measuring Government Size in the American States: Implications for Testing Models of Government Growth," *Social Science Quarterly,* vol. 70 (June 1989), pp. 487–496. Also see: Thomas J. Anton, "Intergovernmental Change in the United States: An Assessment of the Literature," in Trudi C. Miller, ed., *Public Sector Performance: A Conceptual Turning Point* (Baltimore, MD: The Johns Hopkins University Press, 1984), pp. 15–64; and Richard Rose, "The Growth of Government Organizations: Do We Count the Number or Weigh the Programs?" in Colin Campbell, S.J., and B. Guy Peters, eds., *Organizing Governance, Governing Organizations* (Pittsburgh, PA: University of Pittsburgh Press, 1988), pp. 99–128.

18. David Lowery and William Berry, "The Growth of Government in the United States: An Empirical Assessment of Competing Explanations," *American Journal of Political Science,* vol. 27 (November 1983), pp. 665–694.

19. *Idem.*

20. Garand, "Explaining Government Growth in the U.S. States," *supra,* pp. 837–849.

21. Lester M. Salamon, ed., *Beyond Privatization: The Tools of Government Action* (Washington: The Urban Institute Press, 1989), p. 5. The original source is the U.S. Office of Management and Budget (OMB), *Special Analysis, Budget of the United States Government, Fiscal year 1989* (Washington: OMB, 1988), p. H–20.

22. For early explorations of this argument, see Lester M. Salamon, "Rethinking Public Management: Third-Party Government and the Changing Forms of Government Action," *Public Policy,* vol. 29 (Summer 1981), pp. 255–275; Frederick C. Mosher, "The Changing Responsibilities and Tactics of the Federal Government," *Public Administration Review,* vol. 40 (November/December 1980), pp. 540–548; and Lloyd D. Musolf and Harold Seidman, "The Blurred Boundaries of Public Administration," *Public Administration Review,* vol. 40 (March/April 1980), pp. 124–130.

23. Salamon, *Beyond Privatization, supra.* Also see Donald F. Kettl, *Government By Proxy: Mis(?) Managing Federal Programs* (Washington: Congressional Quar-

terly Press, 1988), and Harold Seidman, "The Quasi World of the Federal Government," *The Brookings Review* (Summer 1988), pp. 23–27.

24. Salamon, *Beyond Privatization, supra,* p. 5. The original source is the U.S. Office of Management and Budget (OMB), *Special Analysis, Budget of the United States Government, Fiscal Year 1989* (Washington: OMB, 1988), pp. F–16 and F–21.

25. Salamon, *Beyond Privatization, supra,* p. 10.

26. The Full Employment Act only assured "maximum" employment. The wording was changed after its original introduction, conveying the controversy surrounding the concept.

27. See David A. Rochefort, *American Social Welfare Policy: Dynamics of Formulation and Change* (Boulder, CO: Westview Press, 1986), and John E. Schwartz, *America's Hidden Success: A Reassessment of Twenty Years of Public Policy* (New York: W. W. Norton, 1983).

28. Francis E. Rourke, "Bureaucracy in the American Constitutional Order," *Political Science Quarterly,* vol. 102 (Summer 1987), pp. 217–232.

29. Good summaries of the decline in trust in government are found in Arnold Meltsner, ed., *Politics and the Oval Office* (San Francisco: Institute of Contemporary Studies, 1981), and David O. Sears and Jack Citrin, *Tax Revolt: Something for Nothing in California* (Cambridge, MA and London, England: Harvard University Press, 1982).

30. Jack Citrin, "Comment: The Political Relevance of Trust in Government," *American Political Science Review,* vol. 67 (September 1974), pp. 973–987.

31. See: Harold L. Wilensky, *The New Corporatism, Centralization and the Welfare State* (Beverly Hills, CA: Sage Publications, 1976), and Harold L. Wilensky, *The Welfare State and Equality: Structural and Ideological Roots of Public Expenditures* (Berkeley: University of California Press, 1975).

32. Jeffrey L. Pressman and Aaron Wildavsky, *Implementation* (Berkeley: University of California Press, 1973); Martha Derthick, *The Influence of Federal Grants* (Cambridge, MA: Harvard University Press, 1970); Daniel A. Mazmanian and Paul A. Sabatier, *Implementation and Public Policy* (Glenview, IL: Scott, Foresman, 1983); and Helen Ingram, "Policy Implementation Through Bargaining: The Case of Federal Grants-in-Aid," *Public Policy,* vol. 25 (Fall 1977), pp. 499–526.

33. David B. Robertson and Dennis R. Judd, *The Development of American Public Policy: The Structure of Policy Restraint* (Glenview, IL: Scott, Foresman and Company, 1989), p. 157.

34. "Inaugural Address of President John F. Kennedy," 20 January 1961.

35. "Inaugural Address of President Ronald Reagan," 23 January 1981.

36. Robert Wiebe, *The Search for Order, 1877–1920* (New York: Hill & Wang, 1967).

37. Other sources on the Progressive and Post-Progressive periods include Richard Hofstadter, *The Age of Reform* (New York: Alfred A. Knopf, 1956); Stephen Skowronek, *Building a New American State: The Expansion of National Administrative Capacities, 1877–1920* (Cambridge, England: Cambridge University Press, 1982); James A. Stever, *The End of Public Administration: Problems of the Profession in the Post-Progressive Era* (Dobbs Ferry, NY: Transnational Publishers, Inc., 1988); Dennis R. Judd, *The Politics of American Cities: Private Power*

and Public Policy, 2d. ed. (Boston: Little, Brown and Company, 1984); Samuel P. Hays, "The Politics of Reform in Municipal Government in the Progressive Era," in Daniel N. Gordon, ed., *Readings in Social Change and Urban Politics* (Englewood Cliffs, NJ: Prentice-Hall, 1973), pp. 107–127; and George E. Mowry, *The Era of Theodore Roosevelt, 1900–1912* (New York: Harper & Row, 1958). Jeffrey R. Henig, "Political Ideas and Political Interests in Education Reform," paper presented at the annual meetings of the American Political Science Association, Atlanta, GA, 1989, was especially helpful as the argument presented here developed.

38. See Louis Fisher, *The Politics of Shared Power: Congress and the Executive,* 2d. ed. (Washington: Congressional Quarterly, Inc., 1987); Chester A. Newland, "Shared Responsibility and the Rule of Law," *The Bureaucrat,* vol. 18 (Spring 1989), pp. 37–42; and, especially, Chester A. Newland, *Public Administration and Community: Realism in the Practice of Ideals* (McLean, VA: Public Administration Service, November 1984).

39. U.S. President's Committee on Administrative Management, *Report With Special Studies* (Washington: U.S. Government Printing Office, 1937).

40. See Luther Gulick and Lyndall Urwick, eds., *Papers on the Science of Administration* (New York: Institute of Public Administration, 1937), especially Gulick's "Notes on the Theory of Organization," pp. 1–45. For an examination of the reforms produced by the Brownlow reports, see James Fesler, "The Brownlow Committee Fifty Years Later," *Public Administration Review,* vol. 47 (July/August 1987), pp. 291–295. The antecedent to the Brownlow reports were earlier studies devoted to state and local government reforms to enhance executive powers.

41. U.S. Commission on the Organization of the Executive Branch of Government, *The Hoover Commission Report* (New York: Macmillan Co., 1949), and U.S. Office of Management and Budget, *Papers Relating to the President's Departmental Reorganization Program* (Washington: U.S. Government Printing Office, 1970). Also see Harvey C. Mansfield, "Federal Executive Reorganizations: 30 Years of Experience," *Public Administration Review,* vol. 29 (July/August 1979), pp. 332–345. Little Hoover Commissions at state and local levels in the 1950s–1960s produced numerous reports. Local reform efforts then and later often attempted to create metropolitan governments and city-county consolidations. Since 1942, for example, more than 90,000 local school districts have been abolished through consolidations. During the same period, the number of special districts has increased threefold.

42. See Louis Brownlow, *The President and the Presidency* (Chicago: Public Administration Service, 1949). This is a compilation of lectures given in 1947. Also see James L. Sundquist, "Needed: A Political Theory for the New Era of Coalition Government in the United States," *Political Science Quarterly,* vol. 103 (Winter 1988–89), pp. 613–635.

43. See James Q. Wilson, "The Rise of the Bureaucratic State," *The Public Interest,* vol. 41 (Fall 1975), pp. 77–103.

44. The percentage of federal employees covered by the merit system dropped from about 80 percent in 1932 to 60.5 percent in 1936. See Paul P. Van Riper, *History of the United States Civil Service* (Evanston, IL: Row, Peterson, 1958) and Newland, "Shared Responsibility," *supra,* pp. 37–42.

45. Wiebe, *The Search for Order, supra.*

46. Rourke, "Bureaucracy in the American Constitutional Order," 1987. Also see Steven D. Stehr, "Top Bureaucrats and the Distribution of Influence in Reagan's Executive Branch," paper delivered at the annual meeting of the American Political Science Association, Atlanta, Georgia (1989).

47. See Michael Nelson, "A Short, Ironic History of American National Bureaucracy," *Journal of Politics,* vol. 44 (August 1982), pp. 747–778; John Rohr, *To Run a Constitution: The Legitimacy of the Administrative State* (Lawrence: University Press of Kansas, 1986); and Wilson, "The Rise of the Bureaucratic State," 1975.

48. Harold Lasswell, *Politics: Who Gets What, When, How* (Cleveland, OH: Meridian Books, 1958).

49. See Douglas Cater, *Power in Washington* (New York: Vintage Books, 1965) and Herbert A. Stein, "The Washington Economics Industry," *Washington Bedtime Stories: The Politics of Money and Jobs* (New York: The Free Press, 1986).

50. See Salamon, *supra.*

51. More than 60 percent of nonprofit organizations (excluding hospitals and higher education institutions) were created between 1960 and 1984 according to Lester M. Salamon, "Nonprofit Organizations: The Lost Opportunity," in John L. Palmer and Isabel V. Sawhill, eds., *The Reagan Record* (Cambridge, MA: Ballinger, 1984), pp. 261–285. Taking contributions made by the national, state, and local governments into account, the nonprofit sector may derive more than 40 percent of its revenues from government sources.

52. In addition to the national government and 50 states, there are 83,166 local governments. Of these, 38,938 are general-purpose local governments—3,042 counties, 19,205 municipalities, 16,691 townships. The remainder (more than half of the total) are limited-purpose local governments, including 14,741 school districts and 29,487 special districts. There are more than 17,281,000 full-time and part-time government employees, including 3,091,000 federal government civilian employees and 14,191,000 state and local employees. See U.S. Bureau of the Census, *Census of Governments* (Washington: U.S. Government Printing Office, 1987).

53. Beverly A. Cigler, "County Contracting: Reconciling the Accountability and Information Paradoxes," *Public Administration Quarterly,* vol. 14 (Winter 1991).

54. Beverly A. Cigler, "Trends Affecting Local Administrators," in Perry, ed., *The Handbook of Public Administration, supra,* pp. 40–53.

55. See Michael G. Hansen and Charles H. Levine, "The Centralization-Decentralization Tug-of-War in the New Executive Branch," in S. J. Colin Campbell and B. Guy Peters, eds., *Organizing Governance and Governing Organizations* (Pittsburgh, PA: University of Pittsburgh Press, 1989), pp. 255–282, and Ronald C. Moe, "Traditional Organizational Principles and the Managerial Presidency: From Phoenix to Ashes," *Public Administration Review,* vol. 50 (March/April 1990), pp. 129–140.

56. See President's Private Sector Survey on Cost Control, *War on Waste* (New York: Macmillan, 1984). Discussion of the activities and recommendations of the Grace Commission are found in J. Peter Grace, *Burning Money* (New York: Macmillan, 1985); W. Bartley Hildreth and Rodger P. Hildreth, "The Business of Public Management," *Public Productivity Review,* vol. 12 (Spring 1989), pp. 303–321; Charles T. Goodsell, "The Grace Commission: Seeking for the Whole

People?" *Public Administration Review,* vol. 44 (May/June 1984), pp. 196–204; Congressional Budget Office and General Accounting Office, *Analysis of the Grace Commission's Major Proposals for Cost Control* (Washington: U.S. Government Printing Office, 28 February 1984); and Comptroller General of the United States, *Compendium of GAO's Views on the Cost Savings Proposals of the Grace Commission* (Washington: U.S. General Accounting Office, 9 February 1985), GAO/OCG–81–1. Also see Henry C. Dolive, "Loaned Executives—Those Other Resources," *Public Administration Review,* vol. 47 (September/October 1987), pp. 441–445.

57. Sundquist, "Needed: A Political Theory," *supra,* pp. 613–635, and Alan Rosenthal, *Governors & Legislatures: Contending Powers* (Washington: Congressional Quarterly Inc., 1990), pp. 55–56.

58. See Roger H. Davidson and Walter J. Oleszek, *Congress Against Itself* (Bloomington: Indiana University Press, 1977); Steven S. Smith and Christopher J. Deering, *Committees in Congress* (Washington: Congressional Quarterly Press, Inc., 1984); and Steven S. Smith, *Call To Order: Floor Politics in the House and Senate* (Washington: The Brookings Institution, 1989).

59. On policy triangles, see Martha Derthick and Paul Quirk, *The Politics of Deregulation* (Washington: The Brookings Institution, 1985); Robert B. Reich, ed., *The Power of Public Ideas* (Cambridge, MA: Ballinger Publishing Company, 1988); and Steven Kelman, *Making Public Policy: A Hopeful View of American Government* (New York: Basic Books, 1987). On issue networks, see Hugh Heclo, "Issue Networks and the Executive Establishment," in Anthony King, ed., *The New American Political System* (Washington: American Enterprise Institute, 1978), pp. 87–124.

60. On today's "think tanks" see Gregg Easterbrook, "Ideas Move Nations," *The Atlantic Monthly,* vol. 257 (January 1986), pp. 66–80; Larry Van Dyne, "Idea Power," *The Washingtonian,* vol. 21 (April 1985), pp. 102–165; and R. Kent Weaver, "The Changing World of Think Tanks," *PS: Political Science & Politics,* vol. 22 (September 1989), pp. 563–578.

61. Smith, *The Call to Order, supra.*

62. John Chubb, *Interest Groups and the Bureaucracy* (Palo Alto, CA: Stanford University Press, 1983); Kay Lehman Schlozman and John R. Tierney, *Organized Interests and American Democracy* (New York: Harper & Row, 1986); Larry J. Sabato, *PAC Power: Inside the World of Political Action Committees* (New York: W.W. Norton, 1984); and Burdett A. Loomis and Allan J. Cigler, "Introduction: The Changing Nature of Interest Group Politics," in Allan J. Cigler and Burdett A. Loomis, eds., *Interest Group Politics,* 2d. ed. (Washington: Congressional Quarterly, Inc., 1986), pp. 1–26.

63. Burdett Loomis, *The New American Politician* (New York: Basic Books, 1988) and Alan Rosenthal, "The Legislative Institution: Transformed and at Risk," in Carl E. Van Horn, ed., *The State of the States* (Washington: Congressional Quarterly Press, Inc., 1989), pp. 69–101.

64. Peter K. Eisinger, *The Rise of the Entrepreneurial State: State and Local Economic Development Policy in the United States* (Madison: University of Wisconsin Press, 1988). Also see Thomas R. Dye, *American Federalism: Competition Among Governments* (Lexington, MA: Lexington Books, 1990) and John Shannon and

James Edwin Kee, "The Rise of Competitive Federalism," *Public Budgeting & Finance,* vol. 9 (Winter 1989), pp. 5–20.

65. See Joel D. Aberbach, *Keeping a Watchful Eye: The Politics of Congressional Oversight* (Washington: Brookings Institution, 1990). Also see Judith E. Gruber, *Controlling Bureaucracies* (Berkeley and Los Angeles: University of California Press, 1987); Bernard Rosen, *Holding Government Bureaucracies Accountable,* 2d. ed. (New York: Praeger Publishers, 1989); and John P. Burke, *Bureaucratic Responsibility* (Baltimore, MD: The Johns Hopkins University Press, 1986). The listing of "traditional bureaucratic pathologies" is from William T. Gormley, Jr., *Taming the Bureaucracy: Muscles, Prayers, and Other Strategies* (Princeton, NJ: Princeton University Press, 1989).

66. Gormley, *ibid.*

67. U.S. Advisory Commission on Intergovernmental Relations, *In Brief: Citizen Participation in the American Federal System* (Washington: U.S. Government Printing Office, 1979).

68. Steven J. Wayne, *The Legislative Presidency* (New York: Harper & Row, 1978), pp. 70–100; Fisher, *Shared Authority, supra,* p. 46.

69. See Richard P. Nathan, *The Administrative Presidency* (New York: John Wiley & Sons, 1983); Edward P. Fuchs, *Presidents, Management, and Regulation* (Englewood Cliffs, NJ: Prentice-Hall, 1988); Richard W. Waterman, *Presidential Influence and the Administrative State* (Knoxville: University of Tennessee Press, 1989); Bernard Rosen, "Crises in the U.S. Civil Service," *Public Administration Review,* vol. 46 (May/June 1986), pp. 207–214; Bernard Rosen, "Uncertainty in the Senior Executive Service," *Public Administration Review,* vol. 41 (March/April 1981), pp. 203–212; Chester A. Newland, "A Midterm Appraisal—The Reagan Presidency: Limited Government and Political Administration, *Public Administration Review,* vol. 43 (January/February, 1983), pp. 1–21; Peter M. Benda and Charles H. Levine, "Reagan and the Bureaucracy: The Bequest, the Promise, and the Legacy," in Charles O. Jones, ed., *The Reagan Legacy: Promise and Performance* (Chatham, NJ: Chatham House Publishers, Inc., 1988), pp. 102–142; and James P. Pfiffner, "Political Appointees and Career Executives," *Public Administration Review,* vol. 47 (January/February 1987), pp. 57–65.

70. For a significant statement of this argument, see Newland, *Public Administration and Community, supra.*

71. See Timothy Conlan, *New Federalism: Intergovernmental Reform for Nixon to Reagan* (Washington: The Brookings Institution, 1988).

72. See Richard P. Nathan, Fred C. Doolittle, and Associates, *Reagan and the States* (Princeton, NJ: Princeton University Press, 1987), and Michael A. Pagano and Ann O'M. Bowman, "The State of American Federalism—1988–1989," *Publius,* vol. 19 (Summer 1989), pp. 1–18. An example of congressional-presidential intergovernmental strife is the federal Civil Rights Restoration Act, approved in March 1988 over President Reagan's veto. The law extends federal antidiscrimination laws to all activities of an entity receiving funds and was a direct repeal of the controversial Supreme Court ruling, *Grove City College* v. *Bell,* 104 S. Ct. 1211 (1984).

73. See George Gordon and Irene Fraser, "Out With the Old, In With the New: The New Federalism, Intergovernmental Coordination, and Executive Order

12372," *Publius,* vol. 14 (Summer 1984), pp. 31–48, and James A. Stever and Lewis G. Bender, "An Organizational-Administrative View of Federalism," in Lewis G. Bender and James A. Stever, eds., *Administering the New Federalism* (Boulder, CO: Westview Press, 1986), pp. 3–14.

74. National Conference of State Legislatures, *A Legislative Guide to Oversight of Federal Funds* (Denver, CO: NCSL, 1980); James E. Skok, "Federal Funds and State Legislatures: Executive-Legislative Conflict," *Public Administration Review,* vol. 40 (November/December 1980), pp. 561–567.

75. See U.S. Advisory Commission on Intergovernmental Relations, *Regulatory Federalism: Policy, Process, Impact, and Reform,* A–95 (Washington: U.S. Government Printing Office, 1984), p. 8; U.S. Office of Management and Budget, *Managing Federal Assistance in the 1980s, Working Papers,* vol. 1 (Washington: U.S. Government Printing Office, 1980); and Harold Seidman and Robert Gilmour, *Politics, Position, and Power: From the Positive to the Regulatory State,* 4th ed. (New York: Oxford University Press, 1986).

76. J. W. Moore, "Mandates Without Money," *National Journal,* vol. 18 (4 October 1986), pp. 2367–2370, and on state mandates, Kathleen Sylvester, "The Mandate Blues," *Governing,* vol. 2 (September 1989), pp. 26–30. Also see Michael Fix, Daphne A. Kenyon, eds., *Coping with Mandates: What are the Alternatives?* (Washington: The Urban Institute Press, 1990), and Michael J. Rich, "Distributive Politics and the Allocation of Federal Grants," *American Political Science Review,* vol. 83 (March 1989), pp. 193–213.

77. See *South Dakota v. Dole,* 483 U.S. 203 (1987); *South Carolina v. Baker,* 485 U.S. 505 (1985); and *Garcia v. San Antonio Metropolitan Transit Authority,* 469 U.S. 528 (1985). Also see Robert L. Bland and Li-Khan Chen, "Taxable Municipal Bonds: State and Local Governments Confront the Tax-Exempt Limitation Movement, *Public Administration Review,* vol. 50 (January/February 1990), pp. 42–48.

78. See U.S. Advisory Commission on Intergovernmental Relations, *Is Constitutional Reform Necessary to Reinvigorate Federalism? A Roundtable Discussion* M–154 (Washington: ACIR, November 1987) and the special issue on "The Disappearing 10th Amendment," *Journal of State Government,* vol. 62 (January/February 1989), pp. 3–55.

79. Reich, *The Power of Public Ideas,* 1988. Especially helpful is Jeffrey R. Henig, "Political Ideas and Political Interests," *supra.*

80. See Jameson W. Doig and Erwin C. Hargrove, eds., *Leadership and Innovation* (Baltimore, MD: The Johns Hopkins University Press, 1987); James MacGregor Burns, *Leadership* (New York: Harper & Row, 1978), pp. 18–23; and Bryan D. Jones, ed., *Leadership and Politics* (Lawrence, KA: The University of Kansas Press, 1989).

81. Important references are Donald Chisholm, *Coordination Without Hierarchy: Informal Structures in Multiorganizational Systems* (Berkeley, CA: University of California Press, 1989); Martha S. Feldman, *Order Without Design: Information Production and Policy Making* (Stanford, CA: Stanford University Press, 1989); and Robert W. Gage and Myrna P. Mandell, eds., *Strategies for Managing Intergovernmental Policies and Networks* (New York: Praeger, 1990).

82. A good overview is Deil S. Wright, "Federalism, Intergovernmental Relations, and Intergovernmental Management: Historical Reflections and Conceptual Comparisons," *Public Administration Review,* vol. 50 (March/April, 1990), pp. 168–178.

83. On the STEP program, see Sandra J. Hale and Mary M. Williams, *Managing Change: A Guide to Producing Innovation From Within* (Washington: The Urban Institute Press, 1989). Recent reviews of other innovations are Harry P. Hatry, Kenneth P. Voytek, and Allen E. Holmes, *Building Innovation Into Program Reviews: Analysis of Service Delivery Alternatives* (Washington: The Urban Institute Press, 1989) and Joan W. Allen, Keon S. Chi, Kevin A. Devlin, Mark Fall, Harry P. Hatry, and Wayne Masterman, *The Private Sector in State Service Delivery* (Washington: The Urban Institute Press, 1989).

84. Gage and Mandell, *Strategies for Managing Intergovernmental Policies and Networks, supra.*

85. Gormley, *Taming the Bureaucracy, supra,* discusses new forms of interest representation. Karen M. Hult and Charles Walcott, *Governing Public Organizations: Politics, Structures, and Institutional Design* (Pacific Grove, CA: Brooks/Cole Publishing Company, 1990) examine new types of governance networks.

86. The classic work is Ted Kolderie, "The Two Different Concepts of Privatization," *Public Administration Review,* vol. 46 (July/August 1986), pp. 285–291.

87. Nearly 40 states ratified new constitutions or significantly amended existing ones since the 1960s. Nearly two dozen states have had comprehensive reorganizations since 1965 and the others have been partially reorganized. Governorships are held by more qualified individuals who can hold longer terms of office and succeed themselves. Ballots for statewide offices have been shortened, giving governors more appointive powers and visibility. Gubernatorial budgetary, veto, and removal powers have been increased. Legislatures have practically been rebuilt from scratch, with more capable people and adequate staffing, streamlined rules, and stronger conflict of interest statutes. There has been statewide unification of court systems and increases in administrative capacity. State bureaucracies have grown in size and professionalism. See Van Horn, *The State of the States, supra,* pp. 3–4; Sabato, *Goodbye to Goodtime Charlie, supra;* and U.S. Advisory Commission on Intergovernmental Relations, *The Question of State Government Capability* (Washington: ACIR, 1985), number A–98.

88. See Martha Derthick, "American Federalism: Madison's 'Middle Ground' in the 1980s," *Public Administration Review,* vol. 47 (January/February 1978), pp. 66–74, on "the end of southern exceptionalism"—the argument that integration in the South has created a situation in which a growing role for the states can at last begin to be discussed on its merits. On the rise of the states, see Ann O'M. Bowman and Richard C. Kearney, *The Resurgence of the States* (Englewood Cliffs, NJ: Prentice-Hall, 1986), and Nathan, Doolittle, and Associates, *Reagan and the States, supra.*

89. See John Shannon, "The Return to Fend-for-Yourself Federalism: The Reagan Mark," *Intergovernmental Perspective,* vol. 13 (Summer/Fall 1987), pp. 34–37, and Theodore H. Poister and Gregory Streib, "Management Tools in Mu-

nicipal Government: Trends Over the Past Decade," *Public Administration Review,* vol. 49 (May/June 1989), pp. 240–248.

90. Robert D. Reischauer, "Fiscal Federalism in the 1980s: Dismantling or Rationalizing the Great Society," in Marshall Kaplan and Peggy L. Cucuti, eds., *The Great Society and Its Legacy,* (Durham, NC: Duke University Press, 1986), p. 179.

91. See Aaron Wildavsky, *The New Politics of the Budgetary Process* (Glenview, IL: Scott, Foresman, 1988), and Donald F. Kettl, "Expansion and Protection in the Budgetary Process," *Public Administration Review,* vol. 49 (May/June 1989), pp. 231–239.

92. See Richard P. Nathan and J. R. Lago, "Intergovernmental Relations in the Reagan Era," *Public Budgeting and Finance,* vol. 8 (Fall 1988), pp. 15–29 and Carl E. Van Horn, "The Quiet Revolution," in Van Horn, *The State of the States, supra,* pp. 1–13.

93. See William G. Colman, *State and Local Government and Public-Private Partnerships: A Policy Issues Handbook* (New York: Greenwood Press, 1989); Robert Agranoff, "Managing Intergovernmental Processes," in Perry, *Handbook of Public Administration, supra,* pp. 131–147; and Gage and Mandell, *Strategies for Managing Intergovernmental Policies and Networks, supra.*

94. See John Kincaid, "The New Judicial Federalism," *The Journal of State Government,* vol. 61 (September/October, 1988), pp. 163–169.

95. Charles H. Levine and James A. Thurber, "Reagan and the Intergovernmental Lobby: Iron Triangles, Cozy Subsystems, and Political Conflict," in Cigler and Loomis, *Interest Group Politics, supra,* pp. 202–220. Also see Donald C. Menzel, "Collecting, Conveying, and Convincing: The Three C's of Local Government Interest Groups," *Public Administration Review,* vol. 50 (May/June 1990), pp. 401–405.

96. Civil Service Commission, *New York State Work Force Plan* (Albany, NY: New York State Department of Civil Service, 1989).

97. Van Horn, *The State of the States, supra,* pp. 1–13.

98. Paul E. Peterson, Barry G. Rabe, and Kenneth K. Wong, *When Federalism Works* (Washington: The Brookings Institution, 1986). Also see Paul R. Schulman, "The Politics of 'Ideational Policy,'" *Journal of Politics,* vol. 50 (May 1988), pp. 213–291.

99. Derthick and Quirk, *The Politics of Deregulation, supra;* Timothy J. Conlan, Margaret T. Wrightson, and David R. Beam, *Taxing Choices: The Politics of Tax Reform* (Washington: Congressional Quarterly Press, 1989).

100. Elmer B. Staats, "James E. Webb: Space Age Manager," in Robert L. Haught, *Giants in Management* (Washington: National Academy of Public Administration, 1985).

101. Beverly A. Cigler, "Mandated Expertise: Consultants and Local Capacity-Building," *Urban Affairs Papers,* vol. 2 (Fall 1980), pp. 32–42 and Beverly A. Cigler, "A Proposal to Increase Professionalism," "Newsletter: ASPA Section for Professional & Organizational Development," (Winter 1985), pp. 5–7 discuss the notion of subjective expertise as an attribute of professionalism.

102. Doig and Hargrove, *Leadership and Innovation,* 1987; Mark A. Abramson, "The Leadership Factor," *Public Administration Review,* vol. 49 (November/December 1989), pp. 562–565.

103. U.S. Advisory Commission on Intergovernmental Relations, *Changing Public Attitudes on Government and Taxes: 1989* (Washington: ACIR, 1989).

104. Chester A. Newland, "The Future of Council-Manager Government," in H. George Frederickson, ed., *Ideal & Practice in Council-Manager Government* (Washington: International City Management Association, 1989), pp. 257–273. Also see James H. Svara, *Official Leadership in the City* (NY: Oxford University Press, 1990).

105. James R. Carr, ed., "The Changing Public Service: Looking Back . . . Moving Forward . . . ," *Public Administration Review,* vol. 50 (March/April 1990), pp. 199–209.

106. Charles A. Bowsher, "The Emerging Crisis: The Disinvestment of Government," (Washington: National Academy of Public Administration, 2 December 1988).

Part Six

Bureaucracy

This section presents three views on bureaucracy. As earlier sections demonstrated, bureaucracy has been a central theme in the study of administration. At the most fundamental level, the presence of organized hierarchies is problematic within the framework of democratic government. The key features of bureaucracy include rules, official duties, a chain of command, systematic record-keeping, trained personnel, and an emphasis on efficiency. (The classic statement of the bureaucratic model is Max Weber, "Bureaucracy" [1922]. Interested readers should consult the original essay rather than various anthologized versions, most of which leave out important aspects of Weber's discussion.) In contrast, democracy is defined by elements such as inclusiveness, equality, and freedom. Thus attempts by bureaucrats to streamline administrative processes are continually checked by the need to defend bureaucratic action in terms of democratic values. The existence of "red tape" is testimony to the conflict between bureaucracy and democracy. (Compare Karl's essay in Part I on this point.) Often tedious and inefficient purchasing and hiring rules, for example, are in place not primarily to improve administrative rationality but to make these processes more open, fair, and inclusive. In a similar way, measures that mandate citizen involvement in administrative affairs aim not to make administration more efficient but to make it more democratic. Given this tension, bureaucrats find themselves having constantly to make judgments about how to balance these two sets of values. The articles presented here critique from fresh perspectives some of the premises on which the bureaucratic model is based. All offer alternatives to the classic bureaucratic model. In doing so, they offer readers the opportunity to gain useful distance from "administration as usual."

The first essay takes a starkly different approach to studying bureaucracy from the classic Weberian view. Orion F. White, Jr.'s "The Dialectical

393

Organization," appeared in *Public Administration Review* in 1969. He calls for a radically new understanding, one that will enable bureaucracies to respond more effectively to a continuing problem: relationships between administrative agencies and their clients. In White's view, this problem is not solved by efficient management. Rather it stems from the existing view of the relationship, which sees clients primarily as irrational children and administrators as rational adults. White argues that administrative behavior is neither as rational nor as efficient as this picture suggests. By implication, he calls into question Weber's model. He urges a different, "dialectical" way of thinking about bureaucracies and their clients.

For a dialectical—i.e. oppositional—view, White looks to nonbureaucratic organizations, where commitment to impersonal, efficient service is replaced by personal involvement with clients, and administrators never give up on anyone and try their best to make a difference. In this framework the relationship between client and administrator is one between equals instead of being based on an adult–child, or therapeutic, model. The goal is not to *restructure* the client but to *facilitate* the client's negotiational effectiveness. The administrative structure necessary to support such a relationship is nonhierarchical. Roles are fluid, and diverse perspectives are accommodated. White maintains that while implementing such a model in large-scale public organizations raises difficult tactical questions, its relevancy to issues of effective democratic government is greater now than ever. More than thirty years after this essay was published, readers may still ponder whether its dialectical view holds greater promise than exclusive reliance on the bureaucratic model when it comes to addressing issues of citizen disaffection from government raised in previous sections of this book.

In 1976, a groundbreaking essay by Robert B. Denhardt and Jan Perkins appeared in *PAR*. "The Coming Death of Administrative Man" argues that feminist organization theory offers a radical alternative to conventional understandings of bureaucracy and the place of the "administrative man" in it. Weberian bureaucratic theory conceives of the organization as a rational structure for the accomplishment of work. "Administrative man" accepts organizational goals as his own; he forms the habit of cooperating with others to do whatever it takes to accomplish these goals. Administrative man, in other words, becomes an instrument—a means to organizational ends. Hierarchical directives govern his behavior, and the pressure to conform is strong. The world of administrative man is "efficient but also joyless."

In contrast, feminist theory offers a more hopeful vision of the organization. Feminists emphasize fluid, temporary structures in which process is as important as tasks and the personal development of members takes precedence over efficiency. Unlike administrative man, whose work life requires full commitment of his time and energy, feminist theory views organization members as having other dimensions to their lives, especially marriage and family. Feminists argue that hierarchical authority is unnecessary to the achievement of goals and restricts members' personal growth. Therefore they seek more egalitarian and flexible organizational forms. Denhardt and Perkins conclude with this question: How will bureaucracies be affected by the entry of increasing numbers of women administrators? The authors argue that the presence of more women will not necessarily lead to more flexibility and equality in organizational life. Feminists and those who share their views must work actively to reduce levels of hierarchy and domination. Given the significant growth in percentages of women in government bureaucracies over the quarter-century since the article was written, readers may want to consider whether and in what ways bureaucracies have changed as a result.

The final contribution to this section is David Lowery's "A Bureaucratic-Centered Image of Governance: The Founders' Thought in Modern Perspective," which appeared in the *Journal of Public Administration Research and Theory* in 1993. In reflecting on bureaucratic power, Lowery takes us back to the views of the American founders. Opposing the conventional view, he suggests that administration was quite important to the architects of the American system. But the founders' thought about administration (or bureaucracy) was essentially grounded in political rather than organizational theory; thus their perspective seems alien in modern eyes.

Lowery examines four aspects of the founders' thinking and its implications: (1) their view of administration as a threat to individual liberty; (2) their views on the source of this threat; (3) the extent to which their views can be transposed to the analysis of modern bureaucracy; and (4) what this new sort of analysis might contribute to contemporary research.

The founders feared the potential of bureaucracy to interfere in the private lives of citizens and to upset the carefully drawn constitutional system of checks and balances. The sources of the threat lay in administrative monopoly over crucial information, in the selfish personal motives of administrators, in the propensity for what we now call "pork barrel politics" (serving individual constituents instead of the general good), and in excessive legislative control over administrative agencies. Lowery argues that despite changes in the context and differences from modern analyses, the founders' views are still salient. Reflection on their arguments makes clear the danger of separating the study of bureaucracy from larger political theories. Lowery calls for more rigorous research into the workings of bureaucracy than the "anecdotal" form on which the founders relied. His analysis points up important differences between political and organizational theories of public administration. Like the other two authors in this section, he suggests that the study of administration requires attention to both perspectives.

20

The Dialectical Organization: an Alternative to Bureaucracy

Orion F. White, Jr.

One of the more interesting aspects of the early development of public administration in the United States was the extent to which sociological factors apparently affected the prescriptions and principles of which its literature was composed. Faced with the task of making a secure role for themselves in the American academic, governmental, and societal structure, writers of the early public administration literature hardly felt impelled to notice or to dwell in their work on the less attractive aspects of administration in the governmental process. As a consequence of this shading in the early perspective, however, a literature was produced which explicitly disavowed but nonetheless contained significant ideological

The author wishes to acknowledge the invaluable help given him by Buford Farris and Richard A. Brymer of Wesley Community Centers, San Antonio, Texas, and by Gideon Sjoberg in carrying out the research reported here.
Source: *Public Administration Review* 29(1969): 32–42.

premises.[1] This ideological bent was characterized by the tendency to see administration as the solution—a remedy which is only technically problematical and without side effects—to most problems of government.

This picture of administration—through the early teachings, the successes of the reform movement, and the widespread adoption of the city-manager form of government—has been widely distributed both through academia and the general public.[2]

This strain of thinking probably is still the dominant one in the established centers of public administrative study in the United States. However, there is quite definitely a tangent of thought which is moving out from the established core. Political scientists and sociologists have begun to raise questions about the operation of administrative structures in and on government and society.[3] It seems odd that the field of public administration itself has not evidenced a general awareness of the rumblings of change that are being heard in the public and from some intellectuals—especially in light of the fact that in its early days as a discipline it prompted a radical governmental reform movement. There does appear to be some cognizance of the increasing criticism of government administration, but there is little orientation toward change in the sense of reaction to broader problems.

What is the problem of administration which is creating the public and intellectual reaction alluded to above? In a general sense, it is the way in which *people* are being treated by administrative systems: it is the problem of "clientele bureaucracies." The other aspects of the problem of formal bureaucratic organization—the problems of effective operation, capacity to plan effectively, and that of making job roles compatible with the healthy human personality—have been and are being given extensive attention by scholars in the general areas of administration, organization theory, and management, but little attention has been turned to the problem of understanding and improving the relations between organizations and their clients. It is not surprising that this is the case, however, since traditionally the client was viewed as demanding only "efficiency," defined in the same sense that administrators defined it. Hence the problem of effective clientele relations was seen as essentially a problem in effective "management."

Two Models of Client Relations: Adults and Children

In order to understand fully the nature of the complaints about the treatment of clients in current administrative institutions, and in turn what can be done to meet these complaints, it is helpful to examine the question of what forms clientele relations can take.

The client-organization relation has not been a major theoretical concern of those interested in bureaucratic organizations and administration. However, one particularly relevant analysis does exist and it can be em-

ployed as an outline of a framework.[4] Basing an analysis on some sugges-
tive data gathered by Alvin Gouldner, Victor Thompson conceptualized
client-organization relations in terms of the maturity of personality
brought to the relationship by the client. While he is definitely aware of the
pathology of bureaucratic personality and structure, Thompson depicts
much of the concern about "red tape" and other problems as stemming
from excessive "childishness" in some clients. Thompson's perspective provides a useful basis for a dichotomous analysis of the problematic aspects
of organization-client relations. Viewed at the one extreme, the client's
posture *vis-a-vis* the organization with which he is interacting could be
seen as essentially "childlike," while at the other extreme, essentially
"adult."

The Client as Child

Though admittedly a somewhat artificial schema, the child's psychological
makeup can be viewed in terms of five closely related aspects: (1) a feeling
of powerlessness, (2) inability to abstract well and consequent tendency to
personalize all relationships, (3) inability to cathect energy in future
goals—i.e., to delay gratification of wants he seeks to satisfy, (4) inability
to take the role of the other and hence to see the point in explaining or accounting for his behavior, and (5) an expectation that his needs will be met
without his having to pay a price for the gratifications.

   When confronted with the demands of a formal organization, the childlike client will find much that clashes with his personality. Because he feels
powerless, he is somewhat afraid and suspicious of authoritative administrative institutions; his propensity to personalize all his relationships pre-
vents him from understanding, much less accepting, the impersonal operation of formal organizations; his inability to tolerate delayed gratification
causes him to become irritated at time-consuming formalities; and his expectation of reward without price leads him to resent the demands which
organizations inevitably make on recipients of their services or goods. It is
such clients—ones who carry childlike orientations to their organizational
relations—who in large part define the "problem of bureaucracy."

The Client as Adult

In contrast, for the segment of clients which could be termed "adult," no
such problem exists. The "adult client" finds that his basic personality in-
clinations coincide with the patterns of operation of formal organization.
As an adult, he feels no relative power deprivation and hence no fear of
powerful institutions. He is able to assume an impersonal attitude toward
others when the occasion demands (probably most often in his own job

role) and is thereby able to "understand" when organizations treat him in an impersonal fashion. The adult, since he understands the instrumental nature of the economic relationship and is able to distinguish it from the love relation, realizes both that he must by necessity pay for what he gets and most likely will have to wait for it in addition. As an adult he is proba-bly able to achieve self-insight by assuming an "objective" posture toward his own personality structure. He sees that important segments of his self are obscure even to him. Hence he finds little offense in even somewhat personal organizational probing.

The current criticism of the way administrative bureaucracies are operat-ing on clients in general fits the pattern of objections outlined in the client-as-child model, indicating that the Gouldner-Thompson analysis is still ac-curate. The charges against administrative structures as they are popularly framed are that they are too powerful, inhumanly impersonal, rather slow in acting (or, more often, simply do not help people at all), pry too far and too often into individuals' lives, and exact too heavy a price from individu-als through the use of rules. Viewed from this perspective, the problem of bureaucracy can be viewed as a form of clash between generations, in that demands are being made that clients be treated in a more personal, child-like fashion by formal organizations.

Two Comments on the Adult World Of Organizations

In regard to the question of what justification there is for a serious re-sponse to demands from "childlike" clients, it is enlightening to examine two central tenets of traditional administrative structure: the concept of "policy rationality" and the "efficiency criterion." These mainly are the principles which define and justify the "adult" nature of administrative or-ganizations, hence weaknesses in these tenets must be considered as right-ful openings for arguments that the nature of such organizations be altered or transformed.

Regardless of whether or not the concept of rationality, to begin with, can adequately comprehend the reality of the process by which public goals are transformed into administrative action, it serves a useful purpose if it can be shown that it provides a basis for organizational coherence through systemization of policy.

However, Gideon Sjoberg, Richard Brymer, and Buford Farris have re-cently drawn attention to the striking and undeniable point that bureau-cracies do not hold to truly systemized, rational policy.[5] Rather, they en-force policy differentially in response to pressures by clients and in accord with the clients' social class position. Just as is the case of children and adults in actuality, where parents enforce rules of behavior on their chil-dren which they violate themselves, "childlike" lower-class clients are forced to conform to rules and to patterns of treatment which "adult" middle-class clients are able to avoid.

Hence, the "rational" policy or rule is in many cases the "best way to do it" (or, as is often claimed, "the only way") mainly for those who lack the resources required to pressure the organization into using another and less onerous "best way" in their particular case. This inconsistency in rational policy application, when coupled with the related fact that rational policy is not "rational," but is actually based in large part on a less than comprehensive survey of possibilities thought out through only a political logic, should serve as substantial grounds for challenge of this concept as a basis of defense for traditional organizational structure.[6]

Just as with the rationality principle, so can the "efficiency" criterion be critically examined in light of its ideological aspect. What has tended to be obscured in discussions of organizational efficiency—because the dominant concern has been with how to measure and maximize it—is the fact that the criterion of efficiency itself is but a technical version of the classic and fundamental political question of order versus freedom. The degree of efficiency with which an organization works its way on a client is simply a lower-level framing of the question of how much freedom the client wishes or may have to yield in the name of the general order. Efficiency as an idea and operational standard is subject to political definition.

It thus appears that two basic tenets of traditional administration cannot serve as effective defenses for it. A helpful method for moving away from the traditional conceptualization might be to view the problem "dialectically." Rather than aim toward "balance," the dialectically formulated objective would be reversal of past patterns. By so doing, a picture could perhaps be drawn of an organization which could meet even the most extreme shift in its client environment.

Dimensions of a Dialectical Analysis of Bureaucratic Organizational Structure

In order to carry out this type of analysis most effectively here, observational data from a case study of a small clientele-centered organization will be presented.[7] These data are directly relevant in that the organization is attempting to operate with a structure that is antithetical to the traditional bureaucratic type. Hence its experience provides both a concrete example of what a counter-bureaucratic model of organization would be like and what problems might be encountered in attempting to implement such a model in practice.

The agency to be analyzed is a private, church-related social service agency which operates in a low-income area of San Antonio, Texas. It has roots going back to 1909, but was officially constituted in its present form in 1958. While the agency is church related, it is definitely ecumenical in its approach to social service work. Policy control over the agency is carried out through a board of directors, which has authority to make policy and develop procedures for the agency consistent with the general guidelines of the national division in the church which governs such agencies. The great bulk of its sizable annual funds comes from church sources and the United Fund, but some money is received from membership and service fees, and from agency projects. With a staff of approximately 32 (at the beginning of the study), the agency maintains three separate neighborhood centers, which during fiscal years 1965–66 served 3,000 individuals (or approximately 1,200 families) through groups, special services, clinic programs, and home visiting.

In addition to carrying out such programs as building neighborhood organization, and maintaining a clinic and kindergarten, the agency has been carrying out a delinquency control program, and is involved officially in the "war on poverty." It supervises a day-care center financed with poverty funds, is involved in a Neighborhood Youth Corps program, and supervises a VISTA program. While the agency is firmly implanted in its environment and enjoys close ties to the neighborhoods it serves (some agency workers were involved in agency programs as children), it is by no means stagnant or fixed in its outlook or its actual operation. It is attempting a basic innovation in social work style, and along with this change in style have gone fundamental alterations in organization structure. The unorthodox patterns can be catalogued as in the areas of clientele interactions, administrative structure, organizational ideology, and the staff's "organizational mentality."

Dimension I: Client Relations

The nature of the interaction of client and organization is for the most part defined by the particular structural arrangements characteristic of the organization, since these not only impose formal constraints on the interaction, but also tend to shape its more subtle, informal aspects, as Merton showed when he detailed the structural sources of the bureaucratic personality and how this affects interactions with clients.[8] With the traditional bureaucratic organizational structure, relations to clients are quite definitely circumscribed in several ways.

The whole tenor of the interaction is set, in the first place, by the fact that the client is viewed as a subordinate to the bureaucrat.[9] The hierarchical pattern of authority in which the bureaucrat functions is simply extended into the client relation. This means, in addition, that the same process by which responsibility, or as Victor Thompson put it, "blamability," is transmitted from the powerful top to the weaker bottom levels of the hierarchy works on the client.[10] This means that the client is blamed or held responsible for the failure of the bureaucracy to treat or remedy his problems.

Second, just as the bureaucrat's role is specialized, so is his interaction with the client segmental—he relates to the client not as a total person, but as a specific type of problem or in terms of one part of a general problem.

Third, because bureaucratic structures are legitimate or authoritative, they usually represent and advocate the status quo to the client. Most social service organizations have traditionally stressed helping the client "adjust" to his life situation, rather than working for rearrangement of the social structure which is causing the client's problem.

Fourth, even though the client-oriented bureaucrat's task is the quite intimate one of helping effect a personal adjustment, he must carry out his interaction with the client in an impersonal fashion because he operates from a fixed role definition, the purpose of which is to insure "objectivity" and "impartiality" in his treatment of clients.

Fifth, because the bureaucrat operates under the norm of efficiency, he can invest his and his organization's resources in the client in only a qualified fashion. That is, if the client appears to require more resources or "input" for treatment than the solution of his case represents as a unit of organizational "output," he simply will not be treated. To treat him would be "inefficient."

The type of client relation which is dialectically opposite to the bureaucratic type is obvious and easily describable in terms of the five characteristics mentioned above. The opposite of the client-as-subordinate framework of bureaucratic organizations is the client-as-peer as the basic posture of the professional-client interaction. Instead of viewing the client segmentally as a "problem" or part of a problem, he would be viewed in terms of a "gestalt" type perspective as a total person. Rather than advocating the current social order to the client, the nonbureaucrat professional would, at least, be *willing* to solve the client's problem by removing its more general causes in society if this were the course of action indicated. A personal involvement rather than an objective-instrumental type relation would be characteristic of the nonbureaucratic client relation—perhaps at the expense of impartiality or bureaucratic "fairness." There would be a willingness, last, to keep on attempting to help clients—even supposedly helpless cases. The commitment to client service would be unequivocal.

Client Interaction

These conditions of client interaction are being realized in the Wesley agency. Instead of allowing the consideration of the structural integrity of the agency to dictate the mode of client interaction, the agency's conceptualization of the proper client-organization interaction prevails and the administrative structure is fitted to this. This conceptualization is based upon or derives primarily from two sources: a theologically founded service orientation and the new theory of social work practice which has been developed in the agency. The agency sees definite implications in its theological base for service to clients. As it is stated in personnel orientation materials discussing the service orientation, these implications are:

1. Service is not at a distance—it means personal involvement with people.
2. No person or problem is beyond our concern or attention. In fact, we are obligated to seek out the "outcasts."
3. Our motivation for service cannot be the possibility of success or any other condition that might be associated with the receiver of the service. We can never really give up on a person.
4. Our own interests or personal feelings are not of any importance as we serve. We may not personally like the person.
5. We must individually assume that we are responsible when others do not live up to their responsibility, and thus try our best to make a difference.

This explicitly stated orientation supports in obvious ways the dialectically defined client relation sketched earlier: in particular the personal involvement and disregard for "efficiency" (traditionally defined) in the helping relation are clearly supported by the agency's theological base. Also, the personal involvement with the client means that he will be viewed as a total person rather than segmentally.

The other major source of the unorthodox client orientation, as noted above, is the theory of social work style developed in the agency. In broad terms, the Wesley agency theory of social work stresses mutual conciliation of all parts of a social problem situation. Hence it differs from the classical clinical style, which stresses a therapeutic role for the social worker through which a psychic rearrangement or restructuring of the individual client is effected. These excerpts from one document stating the Wesley agency theory summarize the points relevant to the present discussion:

> [Our] outlook involves a responsiveness to all of the perspectives of all participants involved in the social work process. It is assumed that all social processes involve the interaction of participants having similar and dissimilar perspectives. The social worker . . . is responsible for transcending these perspectives, and this transcendent ideology becomes the perspective to which he is accountable. However . . . the social worker may have to be more partisan in favor of the perspective of those having an unequal power position such as the poor. The goal of the social worker is a consensus or a "concord" of

equals rather than a peaceful arrangement based on inequality. . . . [The] worker would help equalize the power positions of the participants before working on an agreement between different or conflicting perspectives.

The ultimate objective of this type of social work is to enable the client to represent himself as an equal in the process of working out a concord between himself and community institutions. Hence the goal is not to subordinate the client, but to elevate him to a position of equal power and negotiational effectiveness. On the other hand, workers must interact with representatives of community institutions in an effort to build good will or "credit" with them which can then be used to the benefit of the client. Also, an effort is made to alter the institutions' view of their lower-class clients.

Orienting professional workers toward clients in this fashion has created some problems for the agency, however. As has often been noted, a great deal of strain is introduced into the service role when a person who has undergone long and arduous professional education and training must relate to his client as a peer and thereby allow him, for example, to judge the success of the professional's effort to help him. A much more comfortable position for the professional is to utilize his organizational position, social status, and educational superioriy to hold the client in a subordinate posture. Group work in the agency, where the social worker plays the role of leader adorned with obvious physical and symbolic status indicators, tends to be favored over individual work with problem cases "out in the neighborhood," where clients are confronted more on a peer basis and where the worker is responsible to the client, and not to his "profession," its organizations, nor to "professional knowledge."

Further, it is highly frustrating to work on really tough cases, with little hope of success and no possibility of simply "giving up." In addition, there is a tendency to avoid necessary efforts at building "credit" with the representatives of community institutions. These people often hold a higher status position than the workers, and sometimes regard them as nuisances. The agency must keep reinfusing its professionals with its conceptualization of clientele relations, so as to combat the inevitable tendency to slip back into the more secure bureaucratic posture.

Since the objective of the agency's style is to enable clients to fend for themselves before community institutions, its successes often turn out to have the quality of a double-edged sword. Since the agency is itself a community institution which is highly visible, it is often confronted with effective criticism from its own, successfully helped clients. While these attacks are problems for the agency, however, what they mean is that the agency is constantly forced to reevaluate its operations and change itself in the direction dictated by client needs as these become apparent. This is in effect a "dialectical administrative process," in that the agency is held constantly responsive to contradictions between itself and client needs.

A further problem is the one of resources. This difficulty has two essential aspects. On the one hand, given the unqualified commitment to all clients, a shortage of worker resources is virtually inevitable. One reaction to this is overwork on the part of the personnel—a problem which the organization must take explicit action against. The other aspect of this problem is maintaining a sufficient input of resources from the agency's supporting environment. Since the agency is committed to active social change where it seems necessary—especially in raising the power position of the lower class—it lives in danger of criticism from representatives of the status quo in the community. This criticism can result in threats or actual sanctioning of the agency. It possesses a major defense in this regard, however, in its theologically based operating philosophy. It can employ powerful and widely shared symbols from this philosophy in rationalizing its actions to its environment.

In spite of these problems, the agency's relations with its clients must be considered effective at least as far as current observations indicate. It has scored some striking successes with extremely hard cases—such as with an individual who at one point committed violent physical aggression against an agency social worker, but who through persistent personal involvement by the worker was developed into a stable, highly effective personality. In one other case, a young male was successfully reinstated in school after having been expelled from five different schools and dropped as a "case" by other welfare agencies. He was considered "hopeless" and public school officials stated flatly that they would never readmit him.

The religious base of the agency no doubt plays a part in its success in having its social workers relate to clients in the problematical, unorthodox fashion described. However, not all the staff have the same religious affiliation as the agency and not all are religious in the conventional sense. The conceptualization of the client relationship probably is generally a workable one, if the other aspects of an organization are such that the unorthodox client relationship is supported, and can yield distinctive success in some hard cases.

Dimension II: Administrative Structure

The traditional bureaucratic administrative structure possesses two central characteristics which are most relevant to the analysis here. The more basic of these two is the principle of hierarchy, which entails strictly defined roles articulated in terms of layers of authority. Policy is set at the top of the hierarchy and transmitted down through rules and close authoritative supervision which insures that the rules are followed. Categories of decisions, decision points, and decision criteria are all closely defined, and the most rule-bound of roles are those at the bottom of the hierarchy—where the client is met. In addition, bureaucratic structures promote a cohesive (*vis-à-vis* the environment) and homogeneous social structure. Conformity to a comprehensive and rather strictly defined set of norms is a primary characteristic of bureaucracies. (Because these norms are primarily middle class, bureaucratic organizations often find that they can neither understand nor communicate with lower-class clients.)[11]

In direct contrast to this type of administrative structure would be one where the basic principle of organization would be nonhierarchical—where roles are allocated authority functionally and equally, and where authority relations are thereby lateral instead of vertical. Hence at all levels roles would not be strictly defined, but would be fluid according to functional necessity. Also, policy would be set in a "balance of power" fashion by laterally related groups instead of "at the top." Instead of homogeneity, heterogeneity would prevail and be supported administratively in the organization. Conformity, in fact, would not be possible because there would be no predominant personnel "style" such as there is in a bureaucratic organization.

These are the administrative conditions which exist at the Wesley agency. Policy within the agency is fluid and is set, as an agency document notes, by "several bodies [executive staff, area staff, total program staff, and total staff] to insure flexibility and some balance of power within the staff." The two areas of policy not subject to change by the staff are those regarding alcoholic beverages and games of chance. Staff relations are explicitly designed on a principle of "non-dominance"—i.e., of not allowing individuals to possess or develop truly authoritative positions in the agency. Supervisory or management positions are periodically assigned by total staff decision, and in addition, the agency operates with overlapping administrative roles, so that one person may be over another in one functional area but under him in another area. While there are job descriptions, these are general in nature. No specific constraints except those relating to housekeeping activities (reports, records, etc.) are defined for the various roles. Also, except for such guidance as can be obtained from the agency's social work theory, few criteria for defining duties and effective role performance exist.

Heterogeneity is markedly evident in the organization, since it is only by maintaining a direct organizational cognizance of various perspectives and individual styles that the agency feels it can truly be responsive to its clients. Variety of three types is evident in the agency personnel: social class, personality, and service skill and style. Whereas bureaucratic agencies would not easily tolerate personnel who exhibited lower social class behavior patterns, such persons are valued staff people at the Wesley agency. By maintaining some lower social class personnel on the staff, the agency cannot readily develop a monolithic, class-based orientation. Heterogeneity in personality type and in service skills and style also help in this regard, in that a broad range of individuals and social service situations can be effectively communicated about and reacted to by the agency, and it is hence not forced by organizational necessity to define some persons or situations as "impossible" for it to handle.

The primary problem arising from use of this type of administrative structure is its "expense." Because of the rather unstructured, heterogeneous, and egalitarian nature of the agency, much flexibility and freedom of communication is obtained. At the same time, the efficient conflict-dampening and ambiguity-relieving effects of hierarchy are absent, and other more costly administrative techniques must be employed by the agency director as a substitute. A continuing socialization effort must be carried on in the agency. Through this process it is hoped that the staff will introject new norms which will supplant the culturally dominant norms of bureaucratic job structure which they had internalized.

This helps ease anxieties in a situation where duties, decision criteria, evaluation criteria, and a means for measuring output per unit of time are absent. Also, administrative supports for this same purpose must be provided. Salary is allocated by need and is not used as a technique of reward and punishment. The evaluation process is highly private and two-way and sanctions are not brought into play. Job tenure in the agency as far as possible is insured. Further difficulties are created by the regular conflicts and dissensions in the staff which arise out of its heterogeneous composition. Personality frictions, disputes over priorities of skills, and social class-based conflicts in viewpoint occur and must be combatted through a resocialization effort and through administrative support for whichever perspective in the dispute appears to be in the weaker position. These conflicts, it should be noted, are "valued" in the agency for the constant stimulus to evaluate which they provide. Hence the point of the administrative effort to contain them is not to smooth them out through human relations techniques, but rather to structure them so that they will be productive rather than destructive.[12]

In spite of the fact the agency employs an administrative structure which fosters diversity and dissent, and which creates anxieties among its personnel, it functions rather well administratively. It is quite organized in its internal procedures and so far even rather intense conflicts among the staff have been effectively mediated. Further, the problem appears to be lessening as the resocialization efforts led by the agency director continue.

Dimension III: Organizational Ideology

One way of conceptualizing organizational ideologies is in terms of an Apollonian-Dionysian continuum.[13] Norman O. Brown has characterized the human ego in such terms in order to denote the contrast between individuals who are unable to confront the reality of death and hence are oriented toward moderation and longevity—these he calls Apollonians after the Greek god of moderation, Apollo—rather than toward using themselves up in the process of life, as those people do who through a stronger ego are able to confront death without fear—these he calls "Dionysians" after the Greek god of the full life, Dionysius.[14]

There is a counterpart to this analogy at the organizational level. The traditional bureaucratic form of organization is clearly Apollonian in nature, in that it stresses first and above all self-preservation as an organizational structure—even at the complete expense of its goals. The numerous studies which document the phenomenon of goal succession in bureaucratic organizations bear this point out.[15] In contrast would be the nonbureaucratic organization form, which stresses first in a Dionysian fashion, the attainment of its purposes or goal.

It is possible to see from evidence already presented that Wesley agency's ideology at least approximates the nonbureaucratic Dionysian type. The heavy commitment to client service—even to the extent of actively working for changes in currently dominant community institutions—is one indicator of this, since activity of this sort could result in serious attack on the agency. More directly to the point, however, is the agency's position in regard to the involvement of staff or its neighborhood organizations in controversial issues or political issues. Each individual's or organization's civil right to participate in a controversial issue is supported explicitly in the agency. The decision of whether or not to participate is left up to the worker, and the agency will support him, even though his own differentiation of his agency and individual roles in the controversy is not accepted by the public. One such instance has occurred and it very nearly resulted in the effective destruction of the agency as it is presently constituted.

The only problem that exists because of the agency's Dionysian organizational ideology exists as a matter of definition. From the agency's own point of view, its willingness to spend itself in the service of its goal is natural and proper. It is only from a more Apollonian perspective that such a disposition could be faulted.

Dimension IV: Organizational Mentality

Herbert A. Shepard has effectively characterized the "mentality" of traditional bureaucratic structures as "primary" in nature.[16] At the individual level, the primary mentality, as Shepard puts it:

> sees himself as separated from the rest of the world by his skin. . . . To provide what his internal environment needs . . . he must compete with other in-

dividuals for the scarce resources available in the external environment. Other individuals are at best instrumental to him in the satisfaction of his needs.[17]

This is, obviously, the mentality of the classical "economic man" and, indeed, of human nature itself as it has been defined by the most of psychology and our dominant socializing institutions.

The primary mentality is reflected in traditional organization structure in that it is built on the assumption that relations between people are threatful, competitive, and mutually exploitative. Cooperation and order must therefore be effected by coercion and compromise through a pyramidal structure of formal power. Individuals bargain across the levels of this pyramid as best they can and "win-and-lose" (go up, down, or stay put in the hierarchy) according to their skill in this competition. Organizational life in this situation has been aptly called "antagonistic cooperation," and the dysfunctional consequences it produces are many and serious.[18] The structure of most organizations, however, affirms the view of reality represented in the primary mentality, and thereby gives it the nature of a self fulfilling prophecy. Hence it appears that the only way to exact an organizational effort from people is through coercion and compromise.

In contrast to this type of mentality is the "secondary" type. Briefly, in Shepard's words:

> [The] secondary mentality assumes that individuals can have more than instrumental meaning for one another. . . . [It] assumes that personal development, well being, self actualization are the products of authentic, non-exploitive interpersonal relations. . . . [This] means that the provision of the consumables needed for physical well-being can be accomplished through collaboration, and their distribution determined on a consensual basis. . . . The commitment of members of collaboration–consensus systems is to one another's growth, and to superordinate goals on which their growth in part depends.[19]

It should be clear from what has been said already about the Wesley agency that it must at least approximate the secondary mentality among its staff. The heavy emphasis on consensual decision in policy formulation and resource allocation and the nonhierarchial staff relationships indicates this. Further, while there is conflict, it is carried out for the most part through open, genuine confrontation about problems.

Most indicative, however, of the "secondary" nature of the organizational mentality of the agency is its intense commitment to the superordinate goal of service and the principle of existential responsibility which it espouses. Instead of attempting to avoid or shunt away responsibility in the way a primary mentality would in its attempt to win the organizational game of dominance he constantly plays, Wesley agency staff assumes a generalized existential responsibility for what happens in the agency. Each individual must be committed to the principle of shouldering whatever burden he sees must be shouldered in order to make the agency effective in its goal attainment effort without regard for the question of whether or not he is directly to "blame" for creating or for solving the problem.

It is probably by virtue of the fact that the staff is rather theologically oriented that they evidence secondary mentality traits to the extent that they do. At any rate, it is no doubt through a secondary mentality perspective and behavior patterns that the unorthodox structure of the agency functions so well. This apparent fact makes the organization type represented in the agency seem all the more feasible; since, as Shepard describes, people can be trained into the secondary mentality.

Wesley Agency as a Dialectical Organization

It is possible to see from the above description of a nonbureaucratic client organization that a central difference between the bureaucratic and nonbureaucratic types is the process by which client needs are defined. Every aspect of the bureaucratic type dictates that clients will be analyzed as subordinates by the organization and their problems will be organizationally diagnosed. It is largely because of this fact alone that bureaucratic organizations become unresponsive to their clients. Traditional definitions of problems and solutions to these become crystallized in rigid policies and rules which inevitably lose their relevance over time. Because of the highly fluid nature of Wesley agency's organizational structure, however, and in addition its commitment to clients, this does not occur. Instead, as client demands change and inconsistencies between these and the agency develop, a new synthesis of agency operations and client demands is achieved through the fluxional internal decision process of the agency. Because this is a dialectical process, the nonbureaucratic organization type described here could be called the "dialectical organization."

Toward a Dialectical Political System

Transferring the experience of this small, private, and church-related agency into the arena of large-scale government and politics raises many large and complicated questions, but making the effort to answer these questions may become of critical importance to the effective continued functioning of our political system. It is interesting and instructive in this regard to view the United States Supreme Court in its recent history as performing a dialectical role. What it has done recently is react to inconsistencies in the structure of the American legal system by altering it in ways which reflect a personal, immediate, and human concern with the clients of the legal system and other institutions. Because it has worked out a contemporary synthesis of individual and system needs, it probably has saved the system from some mighty strains that would have originated from the unresolved inconsistencies.

The reverse of this trend appears to be occurring, however, in our public administrative institutions—probably in large part because of the ongoing influence of traditional patterns of administrative thinking. Instead of moving toward responsive, flexible, and human modes of operation, they are becoming more and more mechanical. There seems to be little possibility that the Court can take cognizance of the problem, hence it seems imperative that students of the administrative process set themselves at the task. The opportunity seems to be at hand to recall the heritage of radical reform out of which the study of administration grew. Certainly, the relevance and immediacy of the administrative process to effective democratic government is as great now as it was then.

Notes

1. See Dwight Waldo, *The Study of Public Administration* (New York: Random House, 1955), and his *The Administrative State: A Study of the Political Theory of American Public Administration* (New York: The Ronald Press, 1948).

2. For a discussion which suggests the nature of this impact in regard to city-manager government for cities, see "Leadership and Decision-making in Manager Cities, a Symposium" *Public Administration Review,* Summer 1958, pp. 208–230.

3. The classic traditional work on this line of argument is Charles S. Hyneman's *Bureaucracy and Democracy* (New York: Harper and Brothers, 1950). More recent statements include James Q. Wilson, "The Bureaucracy Problem," *The Public Interest,* Winter 1967, pp. 3–9; Robert Presthus, "University Bosses: The Executive Conquest of Academia," *The New Republic,* February 20, 1965, pp. 20–24; Sheldon S. Wolin, *Politics and Vision* (Boston: Little, Brown and Company, 1960), pp. 352–434; William W. Boyer, *Bureaucracy on Trial* (Indianapolis: Bobbs-Merrill Company, 1964). Also, see Gabriel Almond and Sidney Verba, *The Civic Culture* (Boston: Little, Brown and Company, 1963), for data relating to the American attitude toward bureaucracy. Also, the work of Warren Bennis is relevant in this regard. See Warren Bennis, "Beyond Bureaucracy," *Trans-action,* July–August 1965, pp. 31–35. Recent widespread discussion of the possibility of establishing an "ombudsman" system in the United States also indicates the type of concern described here.

4. Victor A. Thompson, *Modern Organization* (New York: Alfred A. Knopf, 1965), pp. 170–177; Alvin W. Gouldner, "Red Tape as a Social Problem," in Robert K. Merton (ed.), *Reader in Bureaucracy* (New York: The Free Press, 1952), pp. 410–418.

5. Gideon Sjoberg, Richard A. Brymer, and Buford Farris, "Bureaucracy and the Lower Class," *Sociology and Social Research,* April 1966, pp. 325–337. It should be noted, also, that Weber himself made only a qualified claim for the rationality of

bureaucratic structure, saying that it possesses a "formal" as opposed to "substantive" rationality. See Bertram M. Gross, *The Managing of Organizations: The Administrative Struggle* (New York: The Free Press of Glencoe, 1964), p. 142.

6. A major critique of the idea of a synoptic rationality is Charles Lindblom's *The Intelligence of Democracy: Decision-Making Through Mutual Adjustment* (New York: The Free Press, 1965).

7. The author entered the agency as a "research consultant" and maintained access for 16 months. Data were obtained from agency documents, lengthy unstructured interviews with the director and other personnel, and through direct observation.

8. Robert K. Merton, "Bureaucratic Structure and Personality," in Robert K. Merton (ed.), *op. cit.*, pp. 361–371.

9. Gideon Sjoberg, Richard A. Brymer, and Buford Farris, *op. cit.*

10. Victor A. Thompson, *op, cit.*, pp. 129–137.

11. Gideon Sjoberg, Richard A. Brymer, and Buford Farris, *op cit.*

12. The "power equalization" which has been effected in this agency is therefore unlike the commonly discussed pattern. See George Strauss, "Some Notes on Power-Equalization," in Harold J. Leavitt (ed.), *The Social Science of Organizations* (Englewood Cliffs, N.J.: Prentice-Hall, Inc., 1963), pp. 39–84.

13. This typology is developed fully in another paper: "Organization Structure and Political Process—From an Apollonian to a Dionysian Politics," forthcoming in a book of original papers edited by J. W. Dyson.

14. Norman O. Brown, *Life Against Death: The Psychoanalytic Meaning of History* (New York: Vintage Books, 1959).

15. David L. Sills, "The Succession of Goals," in Amitai Etzioni (ed.), *Complex Organizations* (New York: Holt, Rinehart, and Winston, Inc., 1961), pp. 146–159.

16. Herbert A. Shepard, "Changing Interpersonal and Intergroup Relationships in Organizations," in James G. March (ed.), *Handbook of Organizations* (Chicago: Rand McNally and Company, 1965), pp. 1115–1143.

17. *Ibid.*, p. 1118.

18. *Ibid.*, pp. 1122–1124.

19. *Ibid.*, pp. 1127–1128.

21

THE COMING DEATH OF
ADMINISTRATIVE MAN

Robert B. Denhardt
Jan Perkins

Contemporary theories of organization are largely theories about men in organizations, by men, and for men. For this reason, it should not be surprising (nor considered coincidental) that the key paradigmatic commitment of organizational analysis is expressed by the concept of administrative *man*. Nor should it be surprising that the behavior of most organizational practitioners is well characterized by this idea. Administrative *man* provides not only a starting point from which all major components of the rational model of organization flow, but also a model for the culturally dominant version of how people in organizations should act.

In marked contrast to this view of organizational life, some feminist theorists are developing alternative models of organization, based primarily on their experience in the women's movement. Both women's rights groups and radical feminists are experimenting with new patterns of group activity which substantially depart from the rational model of administration. In this article, we will ask how these new patterns may affect the way individ-

Source: *Public Administration Review* 36(1976): 379–384.

uals think about and consequently behave in complex organizations. After describing the concept of administrative *man*, we will focus on alternative theories of organization developed in the women's movement. We will then consider the implications of these ideas for the future of organizations.

Concept of Administrative Man

The concept of administrative *man* can be traced to a series of writings appearing in the late '40s and early '50s, involving most prominently the organization theorist, Herbert Simon. In his now class work, *Administrative Behavior*, Simon suggests that "the theory of administration is concerned with how an organization should be constructed and operated in order to accomplish its work efficiently."[1] Since the skills, values, and knowledge of the individual organizational member are limited, these attributes become the scarce means which must be maximized to attain organizational ends. When this occurs, the "bounded rationality" of the single organizational member is transcended by the rationality involved in the efficient utilization of organizational resources. "The 'administrative man' takes his place alongside the classical 'economic man'."[2]

In the organization's pursuit of rationality, administrative *man* is hardly an active participant. By accepting the goals of the organization as his own, administrative *man* loses his distinctiveness and becomes an instrument to be used in the pursuit of organizational rationality. In a passage from *Public Administration,* Simon et al. describe administrative *man* in terms more reminiscent of organization man:

> Administrative man accepts the organization goals as the value premises of his decisions, is particularly sensitive and reactive to the influences upon him of the other members of his organization, forms stable expectations regarding his own role in relation to others and the roles of others in relation to him, and has high morale in regard to the organization's goals. What is perhaps most remarkable and unique about administrative man is that the organizational influences do not merely cause him to do certain specific things (e.g., putting out a forest fire, if that is his job), but induce in him a habit pattern of doing *whatever* things are appropriate to carry out in cooperation with others the organization goals. *He develops habits of cooperative behavior* (emphasis added).[3]

Indeed, such patterns of behavior are absolutely essential in order for rationality to be achieved by social institutions. "Since these institutions largely determine the mental sets of the participants, they largely set the conditions for the exercise of docility, and hence of rationality in human society."[4]

Having chosen to emphasize the rational achievement of purpose. Simon is led inevitably to an instrumental view of the organizational member. As Dahl and Lindblom point out,

A bias in favor of a deliberate adaptation of organizational means to ends requires that human relationships be viewed as instrumental means to the prescribed goals of organization not as sources of direct prime goal achievement. Joy, love, friendship, pity, and affection must all be curbed—unless they happen to foster the prescribed goals of the organization. . . .[5]

As we will see, this depersonalization of the organizational member is in considerable contrast to much contemporary feminist thought.

The means-end dilemma faced by administrative *man* suggests another component of the rational view of organization, the inevitability of hierarchy. As Simon points out, "Ends themselves, however, are often merely instrumental to more final objectives."[6] These intermediate levels become ends with reference to levels below, but means with reference to levels above. Following this chain, one is forced to conclude that the only sensible way of ordering the complex process of achieving goals is through a hierarchical structure in which various sub-units contribute their limited goals as means toward the ultimate goal of the total organization. As Vincent Ostrom notes in *The Intellectual Crisis in Public Administration*, Simon chose to confine his analysis to organizations in action rather than to develop a broader theory of rational choice. In doing so, he was forced to focus primarily on institutions "characterized by hierarchical ordering."[7]

From the top of the resulting organizational hierarchy flow the directives that govern the behavior of administrative *man*. Simply put, "the values and objectives that guide individual decisions . . . are usually imposed in the individual by the exercise of authority."[8] Authority is basically a relationship between a superior and a subordinate in which it is expected that the superior will issue directives which will be followed by the subordinate under normal circumstances. In Simon's formulation, orders are accepted only when they fall within the individual's "zone of acceptance." However, when one recalls that administrative *man* develops "habits of cooperative behavior," which greatly expand the zone, this hardly presents a serious problem.

The rational organization requires that individuals accept (1) a view of organization as a method or instrument for achieving rational efficiency, and (2) patterns of superior domination through hierarchical patterns of authority. In the world of administrative *man,* these elements have assumed the proportions of "cultural traits," adopted through a process of social learning at an early age.[9] Indeed, the pressure to conform to the standards of the rational model is so strong that the concept of administrative *man* is no longer an abstraction helpful in developing a theory of rational choice, but is now a model for the behavior of people in complex organizations. We are all socialized to adopt the character of administrative *man,* efficient but also joyless.

More Hopeful Alternatives

In contrast to the dismal picture of administrative *man* drawn by the rational theory of organization, certain elements of the current women's movement are developing more hopeful alternatives. While differences are apparent in the way in which divergent feminist groups conceptualize the primary problem confronting women, there are developing similarities in approaches to organization. In this section, we will discuss the emerging organizational concerns of two types of feminist groups, women's rights feminists and radical feminists. Women's rights feminists, probably comprising a majority of women in the movement, are those seeking expansion of women's rights within the existing social structure. Radical feminists, on the other hand, see the social structure itself as the problem and thus are seeking radical alteration of the system.

National *women's rights* organizations with local chapters such as the National Organization for Women, National Women's Political Caucus, and Women's Equity Action League accept "the basic structure of the society and social relationships, but (seek) to improve the status of women through legal, economic, and political means."[10] For example, NOW has as its original and stated goal to "take action to bring women into full participation in the mainstream of American society *now*, exercising all the privileges and responsibilities thereof in truly equal partnership with men."[11] Accordingly, little is considered wrong with current institutions beyond the fact that women are excluded from them.

The formal structure of NOW consists of a well-defined hierarchy of authority, with a national board at the top and statewide organizations serving as bridges from the national level to the local chapters. National NOW has written rules, by laws procedures, and membership dues requirements which are to be followed by all state and local NOW organizations. On the local level, like the national, a complex division of labor with specified job assignments is found; for instance, most local chapters have the positions of president, membership chairperson, treasurer, fund-raiser, and anywhere from one to 15 task force chairpersons.

Although the formal structure is fairly traditional, increasingly the top leadership and local chapters are informally adopting an anti-authoritarian stance, with aspirations of a participatory ideal. The developing ideal is that

> all participants should be able to express their personal needs and to develop their individual talents in a sympathetic social environment. . . . Implicitly and explicitly such members adopt a consensus model of decision-making in contrast to the adversary model of the "male world".[12]

In this view, leaders are considered facilitators, persons with special talents in helping the group reach decisions. All members have the responsibility to fully participate in the process and let the leader know their feelings. Conversely, the officers must "learn to grasp the sense of a meeting and to present this in a way that emphasizes everyone's responsibility."[13] NOW has adopted consciousness raising as a means to bring its members into active participation of the organization.

The *radical feminist* branch of the women's movement consists of local or regional feminist groups, such as Female Liberation in Boston, the N.Y. Radical Feminists, Redstockings, and WITCH. Radical feminists see their mission as going to the root of social phenomena to criticize and to seek changes in power relationships and social institutions. Radical feminists may agree to the need for some reforms sought by women's rights groups, but reforms are not considered the ultimate solution. Indeed, some feel that to accept reform constitutes the greatest danger for the feminist movement, for to engage in reform is to accept the present structure and risk being co-opted by it, thereby preventing in the future fundamental change in the structure.[14] Furthermore, by accepting reform and thus an immediate increase in opportunities for participation in economic and political institutions, many radical feminists fear that women end up trading off positive aspects of the traditional female role for less attractive aspects of the male role.[15]

Female Liberation of Boston, a radical feminist group, has articulated its struggle with these issues in its quarterly, *The Second Wave*. In one issue of the magazine its members discussed the organization's split into two groups: socialist feminists and radical feminists. The root difference was the socialist emphasis upon end product as opposed to the radical insistence on the "importance of process-consciousness."[16] The socialists contended that so-called personal change must wait until "after the revolution"; the other group argued that if feminists are not developing new ways of relating to each other and the world around them along the way then there will be no revolution.

> If we have not developed new forms, the same types of structure will supplant the old with only a change in content. That is no revolution. Power must be shared, not controlled by a few at the top of the pyramid.[17]

Female Liberation began to understand that work on interpersonal relations and projects go together, with one enhancing the other, and that women "have been conditioned to be receptive to each others' needs and feelings, and we must *not* lose this quality."[18] The group felt that a major difficulty in its organization was equalizing the desire to be a supportive group for its members, with the goal of bringing about social change in the environment. "We recognize that the integration of internal and external, or personal and political, is a classic problem in our schizoid society and that the attempt itself is revolutionary."[19] Indeed the foundation of their feminism has been the integration of "male and female" principles: female-principle qualities of inner growth and nurturing and male-principle qualities of action and outreach (not to be confused with women and men).[20]

In their third year, Female Liberation found that the division of labor issue was central, so they set out to (1) uncover the covert informal structure and examine its destructive effects, (2) discover why they had drifted into that structure, and (3) develop an alternative structure and the means to get there.[21] They found that although they held the ideal of collective effort, their process was in fact not collective. Secondly, the process was found to be physically and emotionally oppressive to the person in charge, while the interrelationships of the staff were not enhanced. They felt that because they had all been socialized to operate in hierarchical structures they naturally fell into that pattern. Consequently, the organization periodically consciously evaluated its efforts in light of its ideology and goals.

Basis for Challenge

The organizational challenges posed by the women's groups described in the preceding section go to the heart of the rational theory of organization—the concept of administrative *man*. Specifically, parts of the women's movement extol alternative values which contrast sharply with the traditional concerns for (1) organization as a method for achieving rational efficiency, and (2) superior domination through hierarchical patterns of authority. In this section, we will examine the basis for this challenge, suggesting that these alternatives may eventually help change the way we think about organizations and the way we behave as members of organizations.

As noted earlier, the traditional view of organization as a method for achieving rational efficiency leads directly to an instrumental conception of the organizational member. To the extent that the organization is conceived as devoted to the efficient utilization of resources, including human resources, the individual organizational member is simply a tool in the organizational process, not a part of the process itself. The focus of administrative *man* is on the completion of tasks (e.g., putting out the forest fire); therefore, he needs little involvement in the process of determining organizational operations.

A significant challenge to this view is coming from radical feminists in their insistence upon fluid, temporary structures in which process is as important as tasks. Emphasis in these groups is upon consensual decision making for the purpose of enhancing both creativity and group solidarity.[22]

Personal development of members' skills and insights is aided by the flexible structure of feminist groups. This concept of self-realization, developing full human potential both intellectually and emotionally,[23] is clearly inconsistent with the bureaucratic emphasis upon task efficiency. Radical feminists believe that it is only after members feel they have had an opportunity to develop their personal ideology and understand the views of others that they can effectively work towards common goals. Indeed, once a goal is formulated, tasks are then divided upon the basis of skill and interest in the particular situation.

The rational view of organization suggests that it is only through his participation in organized endeavor that administrative *man* can approximate full rationality. "The rational individual is, and must be, an organized and institutionalized individual."[24] The rationality of the organizational member is not defined in terms of the full range of the individual's interests, but only in terms of a contribution to the accomplishment of organizational purpose. The notion of rationality does not extend to the individual's life-work outside the organization. The direction for administrative *man* is clear—full rationality requires complete commitment to the pursuit of organizational goals.

This degree of commitment is unacceptable to feminists who wish to balance various life interests. Women participating in the workforce are more conscious of the competing demands of marriage and family than previously had been the case among male workers.[25] Traditionally career success for men has meant that if conflict arose between work and family roles, the conflict would be resolved in favor of work.[26] Career in this sense connotes a demanding, pre-ordained life pattern, to which everything else is subordinated. Success for men has been traditionally measured in terms of upward mobility, status, and monetary rewards; there have been no predetermined standards against which to measure "success" for women if one removes marriage and motherhood as role indicators. A number of new strategies are aimed at developing a new concept of increased occupational flexibility, through part-time work, flexible work hours, longer leaves of absence without pay, educational leaves, and alternative retirement options.[27]

The feminist challenge to the second major theme suggested by administrative *man* is even more explicit; it argues that superior domination through hierarchical patterns of authority is not essential to the achievement of important goals but in fact is restrictive of the growth of the group and its individual members. All feminists agree that women should have the right to control their own lives, which necessarily precludes continued male domination. The issue is carried further by radical feminists in their stance that domination by males should not simply be replaced by domination by leaders. Where women's rights feminists largely operate within formal hierarchical organizations, some (e.g., NOW) have recently adopted more flexible and egalitarian forms at the local level. All along most radical feminist groups have sought equality of members within an anti-elitist structure.

As the notion of superior domination relates to the more general issue of power, feminists are struggling with what they see as the root of their oppression. Women's rights feminists feel that if they are given a significant amount of power, particularly in economic and political institutions, then the essential problems facing women will generally be solved. Radical feminists too realize that feminist visions can only be obtained if women gain some control or power in society. The problem as they see it is to redefine power so that there is not simply a substitution of a female elite for the present male elite, a situation which would still maintain the oppression of men and most women. Such a redefinition of power would include such questions as the following:

> What kind of organizations must [feminists] develop to support a different kind of power and decision making? Must women dominate or might it be possible to share power with men once [women] have obtained it? Will a feminist society have leaders at all? If so, how will they be chosen? Is it possible to envision a society in which there is not power, where there are no leaders? Are women ready to work collectively? With men?[28]

One response is the belief that it is impossible to significantly develop one's own ideology and personhood if one accepts the authority of leaders and thereby abdicates personal responsibility. Operationalization of this strategy has sometimes led to "structureless" and "leaderless" groups, with structurelessness "a natural reaction against the overstructured society" in which feminists find themselves.[29] Others have found that the informal structure allows formation of elites, who have, in effect, control over the group and exclude other members from participation in decision making.[30] However, effectiveness in achieving group goals is undermined where there is no structure within which expectations can become explicit and egalitarian decisions can be made.

This is not to say that traditional organizational forms are being adopted by radical feminist groups. Indeed these groups are finding that "temporary" structures are often best suited to their needs. These structures usually last "only as long as the activity and then dissolve, leaving no permanent leaders or organizational apparatus."[31] Another form of structuring to accomplish goals is through focusing of certain groups on particular problems.[32] For example, there may be one group conducting classes on women's history and another one teaching self-defense within one particular region or locality. Similarly, other groups (such as the Michigan Women's Liberation Coalition) are experimenting with the use of coalitions which serve to provide flexible coordination of groups and activities while preserving the autonomy of members. The structure is nonhierarchical—one of diffused leadership and responsibility.[33]

Potential Impact

The feminist challenge to the concept of administrative *man* has not yet been fully articulated; however, the basic elements of that challenge are clear. In contrast to the dependence of administrative *man* on a view of organization as a method for achieving rational efficiency, a growing number of feminists view group activity as also valuable in terms of personal growth and are therefore interested in *both* task and process. In such a view, the inevitable passivity and impersonality of administrative *man* is replaced by activity and self-disclosure on the part of the organizational member. In contrast to the traditional domination of administrative *man* through hierarchical systems of authority, feminists are experimenting with alternative forms of organizational structure and alternative patterns of leadership. The emphasis in such experiments is on the development of individual capacities as well as feminist ideology in a more open and supportive environment.

We can anticipate that feminist theories of organization will continue to be refined and more clearly articulated, especially as they are consistent with and encouraged by other organizational humanists.[34] However, it remains an open question as to whether such theories will have any major impact on the structure of public and private organizations in the future. Increasing numbers of women will be entering such organizations in the coming years; however, larger numbers of women in these organizations will not in itself bring about the demise of administrative *man*. As noted earlier, there are powerful social forces which act to maintain the existing model of organization. Women entering traditionally structured organizations will be subject to substantial pressures to adopt the model of administrative *man;* they may be socialized into traditional patterns of behavior.

In order for alternative beliefs to develop in traditional organizations, it will be necessary for feminists to counter the pressures to conform. For those feminists who are willing to undertake this task, several activities may be useful. Among these, feminists must develop appropriate systems of support among others in the organization for the purpose of sharing information, mutually resolving emerging difficulties, and aiding one another in resisting the forces of socialization. A related activity is the formation of consciousness-raising groups, which encourage independent thinking concerning the central issues of feminist thought. Consciousness-raising activities may bring about changes in the way women view themselves, developing new images which may deviate from the traditional view of organizational life. Such groups could develop a close connection between personal development and organizational change.

The key to the potential impact of feminist thinking on organizations of the future may finally come in the radical feminist rejection of the notion of superior domination—either by men or other elites—and their adoption of the concept of the authority of personal experience.[35] Rejecting the traditional acceptance of "expert" opinions, ideology, or structure, radical feminists believe they must develop an ideology and a structure from their experience of being female in a male-dominated society. They are therefore unwilling to give up personal responsibility for their own actions by submitting to the authority of some accepted theory or structure. To the extent that individuals follow this admonition and accept personal responsibility for their actions, even in the face of powerful pressures to conform to the model of administrative *man*, we may expect more and more people to become aware of the values of a feminist and ultimately humanist organization. And we may expect the coming death of administrative *man*.

Notes

1. Herbert A. Simon, *Administrative Behavior* (New York: The Free Press, 2nd ed., 1966), p. 38.

2. *Ibid.*, p. 39.

3. Herbert A. Simon, Donald W. Smithburg, and Victor A. Thompson, *Public Administration* (New York: Alfred A. Knopf, 1950), p. 82.

4. Simon, *op. cit.*, p. 104.

5. *Ibid.*, p. 252.

6. *Ibid.*, p. 62.

7. Vincent Ostrom, *The Intellectual Crisis in American Public Administration* (University, Ala.: University of Alabama Press, 1974), p. 46.

8. Simon, *Administrative Behavior, op. cit.*, p. 198.

9. See Herbert G. Wilcox, "The Cultural Trait of Hierarchy in Middle Class Children," *Public Administration Review,* Vol. 28 (May/June 1968), pp. 222–235; and Robert B. Denhardt, "Bureaucratic Socialization and Organizational Accommodation," *Administrative Science Quarterly,* Vol. 13 (December 1968), pp. 441–450.

10. Barbara Bovee Polk, "Women's Liberation: Movement for Equality," in Constantina Safilios-Rothschild (ed.), *Toward a Sociology of Women* (Xerox Corp., 1972), p. 321.

11. Nancy Reeves, *Womankind* (Chicago: Aldine Publishing Co., 1973). p. 119.

12. Maren Lockwood Carden, *The New Feminist Movement* (New York: Russell Sage Foundation, 1974), p. 128.

13. *Ibid.*, p. 129.

14. Jo Freeman, *The Politics of Women's Liberation* (New York: David McKay Co., 1975). p. 241.

15. See Jessie Bernard, *Women and the Public Interest* (Chicago: Aldine Publishing Co., 1971), p. 41; and Caroline Bird's "old feminists," in *Born Female* (New York: McKay, 1970), p. 161.

16. "From Us," *The Second Wave,* Vol. 2, No. 2, p. 2.

17. *Ibid.*

18. *Ibid.*

19. "From Us," *The Second Wave,* Vol. 2, No. 4, p. 2.

20. Linda Thurston, "On Male and Female Principle," *The Second Wave,* Vol. 1, No. 2.

21. "From Us," *The Second Wave,* Vol. 3, No. 1, p. 2.

22. See Reeves, *op. cit.,* p. 182; and Alice Rossi, "Sex Equality: The Beginnings of Ideology," in Safilios-Rothschild, *op. cit.,* p. 352.

23. Carden, *op. cit.,* p. 86.

24. Simon, *Administrative Behavior, op. cit.,* p. 102.

25. See Rhona Rapoport and Robert N. Rapoport, "The Dual-Career Family: A Variant Pattern and Social Change," in Safilios-Rothschild, *op. cit.,* p. 236.

26. Bernard, *op. cit.,* p. 192; also see Philip Slater, *The Pursuit of Loneliness* (Boston: Beacon Press, 1971), p. 73.

27. Constantina Safilios-Rothschild, *Women and Social Policy* (Englewood Cliffs, N.J.: Prentice-Hall, Inc., 1974), p. 73.

28. Jane Dolkart and Nancy Hartsock, "Feminist Visions of the Future," *Quest,* Vol. II, No. 1 (Summer 1975), p. 6.

29. Joreen (Jo Freeman). "The Tyranny of Structurelessness," in Anne Kordt, Ellen Levine, and Anita Rapone (eds.), *Radical Feminism* (New York: New York Times Book Co., 1973), p. 285.

30. *Ibid.*

31. Polk, *op. cit.,* p. 329.

32. Carden, *op. cit.,* p. 73.

33. Polk, *op. cit.,* p. 326.

34. Wendell L. French and Cecil H. Bell, *Organization Development* (Englewood Cliffs, N.J.: Prentice-Hall, Inc., 1973), pp. 65–66.

35. Carden, *op. cit.,* p. 86.

22

A BUREAUCRATIC-CENTERED IMAGE OF GOVERNANCE: THE FOUNDERS' THOUGHT IN MODERN PERSPECTIVE

David Lowery

Bureaucratic Power and the Republican Synthesis

Larry B. Hill (1991) recently outlined in this journal an agenda for a research program using a "bureaucratic-centered image of governance." Its focus, he suggested, must concern the role of bureaucratic power in the American governance process. The centrality of this issue to public administration should be self-evident. Yet, Hill is quite correct in noting that it remains curiously understudied. Or rather, as he demonstrates in his review of twenty metaphors commonly used in the literature, public administration is inundated with multiple conflicting and contradictory images of bureaucratic power, images that are used all too uncritically. This article contributes to clarifying this research program by examining several political images of bureaucracy during America's formative period.

Source: *Journal of Public Administration Research and Theory* 3 (1993): 182–208.

This may seem an odd departure point, given that the usual texts say little about the founders' views on administration (e.g., Stillman 1987, 266–68; Yates 1982, 2–4). Except for White's (1948, 12–14) casting of Hamilton as an early incarnation of Luther Gulick and Ostrom's (1974) and Rohr's (1986) Madisonian interpretation of the founders' understanding of bureaucracy, this lack of attention is taken as evidence that the era's bureaucracy was so rudimentary as to deserve little comment (Stillman 1987, 29). Thus, James Q. Wilson (1975, 77) noted that "the great political and constitutional struggles were not over the power of the administrative apparatus, but over the power of the President, of Congress, and of the states." Accordingly, most essays on bureaucratic power assume, implicitly or explicitly, that it is a recent issue (e.g., Fiorina 1977, 82; Fesler and Kettl 1991, 1–3; Nachmias and Rosenbloom 1980, 38–68; Gormley 1989, 7; Gruber 1987, 1–7; Yates 1982; Stillman 1987, 29; Rourke 1984, 1; Meier 1979, xvii). Even the few works focusing on earlier periods (e.g., Skowronek 1982; Crenson 1975) fail to touch upon the eighteenth century.

The central argument of this article is that this conventional wisdom is wrong. Administration, however rudimentary it might have been, was quite important to the founders. As just stated, this is not an entirely new argument (e.g., Rohr 1986; Ostrom 1974; White 1948), even if it is a minority perspective. We argue further, however, that the founders thought about bureaucracy very differently than do thinkers today. Indeed, we argue, elements of their analysis of bureaucracy are so grounded in classical political thinking that the analysis remains irrecoverably alien to the modern literatures.

We explore these issues by examining three works: Bernard Bailyn's *The Ideological Origins of the American Revolution* (1967), Gordon S. Wood's *The Creation of the American Republic: 1776–1787* (1969), and Lance Banning's *The Jeffersonian Persuasion: Evolution of a Party Ideology* (1978). These works trace the varied strains of American Whiggism from 1760 until 1800. They do this by consciously using the same method, by relying on the political pamphlets of the day, and by focusing on consecutive periods of time.

These three works make up the canon of the Republican synthesis, a highly influential interpretation of the revolutionary and postrevolutionary period. In contrast to traditional historiography, which views the founders' thinking as essentially modern, the Republican synthesis claims that Whiggism—a broadly consistent ideology with roots in classical political thought—both guided the founders' understanding of political events and governed their design of public institutions (Lienesch 1988, 4–8).

This claim is still highly controversial among historians, and, as Lienesch (p. 7) has suggested, "The truth lies somewhere in between." Indeed, because the founders' thinking about bureaucracy includes both classical and modern elements, one must carefully distinguish those of their arguments that are relevant to modern discourse on administrative power from others with few contemporary counterparts.

Before beginning, however, two caveats are in order. First, bureaucracy is not central to Bailyn's, G. S. Wood's, or Banning's work. In developing their thesis on the pervasive influence on the founders of classical thought, however, Republican synthesis authors raise a number of issues about bureaucratic power. It is these secondary or supporting issues that are of interest here. Accordingly, our reading of these works is inevitably selective and partial, suiting our present purposes rather than, necessarily, their authors'. Substantively—and following Hill's (1991, 253–67) characterization of the bureaucratic-centered image of governance—this means that we have positioned administrators in the center of the political system as an initial act of faith and then asked what evidence Bailyn, G. S. Wood, and Banning offer about the role of bureaucratic power in the founders' thought.

Second, liberties are also taken with the concept of bureaucracy. Scholars from White (1948) to Wilson (1989, 376) and social commentators from Tocqueville to Marx (Skowronek 1982, 5–8) are obviously correct in asserting that the administrative function was very limited in the United States of the eighteenth century. And what administrative arrangements existed were hardly "bureaucratic" in a Weberian sense. Despite this, our use of the term "bureaucracy" here is not inappropriate. The focus of the founders' concerns—the carrying out of recognizable administrative tasks by subordinate officers—was similar to present-day concerns. More importantly, the political actions they feared from government officers closely parallels how contemporary scholars think about bureaucratic power. For these reasons, as well as for convenience, the term bureaucracy is employed.

The analysis proceeds in four steps. First, we examine the touchstone of the founders' political analysis—the preservation of liberty in a world governed by self-interest—and how they viewed bureaucracy as the "substance" of the threat to liberty. Second, we review their several and sequential diagnoses of the "source" of the administrative threat to liberty or who was wielding the bureaucratic stick. Third, we evaluate the founders' thought by distinguishing those components of their analysis that fit well with modern perspectives on bureaucracy from others that are essentially classical. Finally, we consider what this analysis can tell us about our present-day research program.

The Founders, Liberty, and Bureaucracy

The essential classicism of the founders' thought lies in their conception of liberty and the difficulties involved in preserving it. We consider the fragile nature of liberty first, and then we give a more detailed consideration to how bureaucracy entailed the substance of the threat to liberty.

The Fragile Nature of Liberty

To Bailyn, G. S. Wood, and Banning, the Whig philosophy that motivated the founders as they moved through rebellion to nation-building was internally consistent, sophisticated, and yet compellingly simple. To the colonial thinkers, as G. S. Wood (1969, 18) suggests, "politics was nothing more than a perpetual battle between the passions of the rulers, whether one or the few, and the united interests of the people—an opposition that was both inevitable and proportional."

To the English Whigs of the seventeenth century and their American descendants of the next, virtue had little role in this battle. Rather, they saw pervasive and inherent self-interest generating omnipresent threats to liberty as the tensions between rulers and ruled were played out (Bailyn 1967, 60; G. S. Wood 1969, 429; Banning 1978, 47). The most obvious threat, of course, was tyranny. Yet, as G. S. Wood notes (p. 23), "the people, like the rulers, could abuse their power; such a perversion of liberty was called licentiousness or anarchy."

Given these poles, individual liberty could be protected, according to the Whigs, only through a balance of self-interests such that power checked power so as to control inevitable corruption, a common theme in discussions of the design of the Federal Constitution (Dahl 1956; Ostrom 1971). As G. S. Wood (1969, 24) notes, "Public liberty was the combining of each man's individual liberty into a collective governmental authority, the institutionalization of the people's personal liberty, making public or political liberty equivalent to democracy or government by the people themselves." And to the Whig political philosophers, the English constitution prior to the 1760s provided the ideal model of a balanced preservation of public or political liberty.

Given their view of the self-interest basis of politics, however, they recognized that such solutions are by their very nature extremely fragile, and may readily collapse into tyranny. As Banning suggests,

The theory of mixed government arose from a concern for temporal stability, and it was grounded in assumptions that induced its proponents to anticipate disturbance of the balance upon which liberty must rest . . . Balances could not grow stronger. An equilibrium could be altered only for the worse. Accordingly, the crucial task for friends of liberty in balanced states would be to keep a constant vigil, to concentrate on frequent efforts to restore an always fragile, always threatened system (1978, 48).

The tenuous nature of balance, and, therefore, liberty, meant that citizens must be ever vigilant in its defense.

One important implication of such vigilance is that citizens must be attentive to even the smallest and seemingly innocuous threats to liberty or even anticipate such hazards before they occur. For if the balance of interests that preserves liberty is so fragile, then even such minor movements toward tyranny could lead to far more severe compromises of liberty. G. S. Wood captured this fear of small portents of tyranny in his review of the writings of the colonial pamphleteers, from whom he freely quotes:

> In a variety of metaphors the colonists sought to express their understanding of how the rulers, possessing their own "peculiar purposes," slyly used the historical process. Every one of their acts of usurpation was "like a small spark [that] if not extinguished in the beginning will soon gain ground and at last blaze out into an irresistible Flame"; or it was "like the rollings of mighty waters over the breach of ancient mounds—slow and unalarming at the beginning; rapid and terrible in the current; a deluge and devastation at the end"; or it was like "a spot, a speck of decay, however small the limb on which it appears, and however remote it may seem from the vitals," that would grow and corrupt "till at length the inattentive people are compelled to perceive the heaviness of their burthens," usually, however, too late for the people to resist . . . All history was therefore an object lesson in the power of the seemingly insignificant (1969, 38).

Thus the founders' philosophy led them inexorably toward reacting strongly to even the smallest perceived threats to liberty, a disproportioning of stimulus and response that is a hallmark of Whiggish thought.

This ready anticipation of liberty's imminent demise and the attendant responsibility to act in its defense, even to extremes, on even the smallest cause seems to have little counterpart in the justifications offered in contemporary debates over governance. Yet it is a critical part of the founders' thought, for it helps to account for what may appear to be an anomaly in the central argument of this article. That is, why would the founders have a very well-developed assessment of the problem of administrative control in the absence of even the most rudimentary administrative apparatus? The answer lies in Whiggish thought, which stressed the dangers of even the tiniest, most remote encroachments on liberty. Even at the time, this hair-trigger propensity to act on the basis of the smallest of perceived injustices set colonial political philosophers-practitioners apart. As G. S. Wood has noted:

> Where the people of other countries had invoked principles only after they had endured an "actual grievance," the Americans, said Burke, were anticipating their grievances and resorting to principles even before they actually

suffered. "They auger misgovernment at a distance and snuff the approach of tyranny in every tainted breeze." The crucial question in the colonists' minds, wrote John Dickinson in 1768, was "not, what evil has actually attended particular measures—but, what evil, in the nature of things, is likely to attend them" (1969, 5).

While perhaps unusual, the ready anticipation and reaction by the colonists to even the slightest tipping in the balance of interests that preserved liberty makes much of their revolutionary fervor understandable.

To this point, the familiar outlines of the Whiggish view of politics have been sketched. What is missing, however, is some description of the specific transgressions that the colonists used to justify rebellion in defense of their traditional liberties as Englishmen. It is here that one finds the beginnings of the founders' thoughts about and fears of bureaucracy.

Bureaucracy as the Substance of the Threat to Liberty

While we will argue below that the colonists and, later, the new citizens of the United States held varied views about who used bureaucracy to undermine liberty, they all agreed that the administrative branch was the immediate agent of tyranny. Simply put, kings or parliamentarians could do little on their own that directly encroached on citizens' liberty. The bureaucracy—or rather, its prebureaucratic antecedent—was the inevitable instrument of tyranny. Even James Q. Wilson (1975, 101), despite his conclusion that administration was a peripheral concern to the founders, has noted that "Except for the issue of taxation, which raised for the colonists major issues of representation, almost all of the complaints involved the abuse of administrative power." Thus the substantive vehicle of tyranny must be administration.

Just what was it about bureaucracy that was so abhorrent? Today's common complaint about inefficiency was not central to Whig thinkers. Certainly, there were many unflattering descriptions of ministerial officers— "baneful harpies," "parasitic officeholders," "base-spirited wretches," or "born with long claws like eagles" (Bailyn 1967, 102–3)—that equal in virulence anything uttered by Howard Jarvis (1979) two centuries later. And the inefficiencies of legislative administration under the Articles of Confederation were often noted in their justifications of the new constitution (Nelson 1982, 750–51). But because efficiency only has meaning in reference to an accepted goal, an indictment of inefficiency still implies that a legitimate purpose is being served. Instead, the Whigs challenged the legitimacy of the goals of the ministries. This raised their critique of bureaucracy to the level of the political, making it something more than a standard charge about bureaucratic foot-dragging (Wilson 1975, 80).

To Whigs, the political danger of bureaucracy was twofold. The first was the direct loss of individual liberty through interference with the personal affairs of citizens via the agency of administrative action. Whether through the undermining rights of private property by the Stamp Act or the challenge posed to freedom of the press and freedom of expression by the Alien and Sedition Laws, the Whigs' concern was for individual liberty (G. S. Wood 1969, 21).

Bureaucracy also posed a second, indirect hazard through its potential for disturbing the always-fragile checks and balances essential to the preservation of political liberty. If administrative officers used their resources so as to capture their nominal political superiors, or if a faction of superiors could deploy the resources of the bureaucracy so as to usurp their colleagues' independence, the unbalanced system would deteriorate inevitably into tyranny (G. S. Wood 1969, 407). Such perils were especially real to the Whigs, given their assumption that the fragility of balance made the slide into tyranny a very short and slippery slope (p. 24).

Bernard Bailyn's review of the political pamphlets of the revolutionary period places great emphasis on their authors' concern that the many new administrative officials being imposed on the colonies prior to the revolt were agents of tyranny. He reviews (1967, 103) the colonists' comments on the Townshend Duties, the Navigation Laws, the Sugar Act of 1764, and the American Board of Customs Officials established in 1767, all of which greatly expanded the number of customs officials. He concludes that, "all of these developments could be seen to have provided for an 'almost incredible number of inferior officers,' most of whom the colonists believed to be 'wretches . . . of such infamous characters that the merchants cannot possibly think their interests safe under their care.'" These infringements on liberty through excessive administration were compounded by later impositions, including that terror—the standing army imposed on the colonists via the Quartering Act (Bailyn 1967, 119). To the colonists, this constituted nothing less than a plan to deprive them of their liberties (G. S. Wood 1969, 42).

Gordon Wood's review of the period under the Articles of Confederation illustrates well Nelson's (1982, 751) first irony of American bureaucracy: that the revolt against the old administrative order planted the seeds for the new administrative order. Wood (1969, 149) notes that "The American emasculation of their governors lay at the heart of their constitutional reforms of 1776. . . . The changes they made were momentous, with implications for the nature of magisterial authority that they did not foresee." In short, they only shifted control of the magistrates from executives or the magistrates themselves to legislators.

Thus, Wood (1969, 155) writes, the new constitution "intensified legislative domination of the other parts of government. The Revolutionary constitution-makers released and institutionalized what had previously been varied and often confused and thwarted attempts by the legislatures to assume magisterial responsibilities." But it was not democratic licentiousness or anarchy—problems arising from a deficiency of administrative control—that need be feared most in this situation, although this was a theme tapped by the Federalists (G. S. Wood 1969, 432). Rather, as Wood (pp. 403–13) forcefully argues, it was the use by the legislature of the administrative branch to either directly diminish liberty by abusing traditional rights, especially those of minorities, or to undermine the separation of powers and popular control and thus indirectly make tyranny more likely. In either case, those we now call bureaucrats became the substantive agents of tyranny.

Lance Banning has found much the same in his interpretation of the political pamphlets written during the period between Washington's and Jefferson's inaugurations. Again, administrative officials were the necessary agents of tyranny, although now they operated under wholly domestic control. Banning, seeing the same underlying critique on the part of Republicans of the Federalist plan for a national bank, concluded (1978, 148) that "the opposition to a national bank derived from the same British traditions. William Maclay immediately identified the bank as 'an aristocratic engine' and 'a machine for the mischievous purposes of bad ministers.'" Even more directly damaging to liberty, "the Alien and Sedition Laws established, in Jefferson's expression, a veritable 'reign of witches' in the United States" (Banning 1978, 255). The substance of the threat to liberty—the arm of tyranny—was an active government in the form of, at least potentially, an all too extensive bureaucracy.

In all three analyses, what we now call bureaucracy is necessarily the agent of tyranny. Government must appoint subordinate officers to accomplish its varied tasks. But these same officers endanger liberty. As Madison noted in 1788 (Meyers 1973, 62), "The appointment to offices is, of all the functions of Republican & perhaps every other form of Government, the most difficult to guard against abuse." But while the founders concurred that the administrative branch constituted the substance of government's threat to liberty, they disagreed sharply about the ultimate source of the threat.

Three Views of the Source of Bureaucracy's Threat

The Whig pamphleteers developed three alternative hypotheses about who actually wields the power of the administrative branch against the peoples' liberties. While there were occasions when two or even all three dangers were perceived simultaneously, such as the accrediting of the infringemenets on liberty during the 1760s to the king by some and to his ministers by others, these hypotheses generally reflect the major oppositions in the revolutionary and postrevolutionary periods: the Traditional Whig view that justified revolution; the position of the Federalists as they criticized and then abandoned the Articles of Confederation; and the view of Jeffersonian Republicans as they opposed the policies of the Federalist presidents.

The Traditional Whig Diagnosis

Traditional Whigs had some initial difficulty in specifying the source of bureaucratic tyranny. Until quite late in the rebellion, according to Bailyn (1967, 122), the colonists were unprepared and unwilling to challenge the king or Parliament directly by accusing them either of willfully planning the demise of liberty. Such an attack would be inconsistent with their conception of the rebellion as a defense of their traditional liberties as Englishmen. But if the king and Parliament were not to blame for their troubles, then who was? Bailyn's interpretation points directly to the bureaucracy as not only the substance of tyranny, but the source as well:

> The most common explanation [for the tyrannical acts imposed on the colonists], however—an explanation that rose from the deepest sources of British political culture, that was a part of the very structure of British political thought—located "the spring and cause of all the distresses and complaints of the people in England or in America" in "a kind of fourth power that the constitution knows nothing of, or has not been provided against." This "overruling arbitrary power, which absolutely controls the King, Lords, and Commons," was composed, it was said, of the "ministers and favorites" of the King; who, in defiance of God and man alike, "extend their usurped authority infinitely too far," and, throwing off the balance of the constitution, make their "despotic will" the authority of the nation (1967, 124–25).

In modern terms, the colonists were arguing that bureaucrats had subverted the other arms of government for their own all-too-often nefarious purposes.

From where did such power derive? Given the Whigs' acceptance of the inherent nature of self-interest and its attendant potential to undermine liberty, it is not surprising that they believed that administrative officers might seek to impose tyrannical rule for their own benefit. But the incentives inherent in self-interest need not necessarily give rise to tyranny; an agent of tyranny must have also the capacity to exercise that self-interest. The administrative officials who were the villains in the colonists' reconstruction of the plot against their liberties had no independent basis of power as did the king, Lords, or Commons. Or did they? In terms that we will see are fully reflected in the modern critique of bureaucracy, two sources of bureaucratic influence and power were noted by the pamphleteers.

The first was the administrators' power of information and advice, which was viewed as misguiding the king, who was still absolved of personal culpability in the colonists' troubles. As Bailyn (1967, 125) quotes the Whig pamphleteers, "This 'junto of courtiers and state-jobbers,' these 'court-locusts,' whispering in the royal ear, 'instill in the King's mind a divine right of authority to command his subjects' at the same time as they advance their 'detestable scheme' by misinforming and misleading the people." At another juncture, Bailyn (p. 99) writes, "For from whom had the false information and evil advice come that had so misled the English government? From officials in the colonies, said John Adams, said Oxenbridge Thatcher, James Otis, and Stephen Hopkins—from officials bent on overthrowing the constituted forms of government in order to satisfy their own lust for power, and not likely to relent in their passion." Thus, long before Niskanen (1971), the colonists developed a theory of tyranny founded on control of information by administrative officials.

The second mechanism used by administrators to subvert liberty addressed the legislative branch. The Whigs argued that the ministerial officials subverted Parliament by intertwining the personal self-interest of the members of Parliament with that of the ministries. This was especially evident for the quintessential aggrandizing agency of the day—the military. Banning notes that

> It posed more distant dangers because it was already part of a design by the ministry intended to control all parts of government and reduce the balanced constitution to a sham. Parliament was filled with army officers and others who held government posts or pensions. These pensioners and placemen would not jeopardize their livelihoods by voting against the wishes of the crown. Through them, accordingly, the ministry found a way to weaken the resistance of the other parts of government to its designs. Rather than encroach directly on the powers of the Commons or the Lords, it would determine their decisions (1978, 49–50).

The corruption of parliamentary rule by bureaucracy even extended to elections. As Banning (p. 59) summarized the case for rebellion, "Growing revenues and higher taxes make it possible for ministers to create a horde of officers, who fill the Parliament and exercise a rising influence on elections." Thus it became impossible for Parliament to defend liberty, having been trapped by the ministries in conflicts of interests. And while the mechanisms of intertwining interests have changed, the same general argument underlies some contemporary analyses of bureaucratic influence on Congress (e.g., Arnold 1979).

With ample indirect means to subvert the English government, bureaucrats did not need to have their hands directly on the levers of authority. To the colonial Whigs, "the balance of the constitution had been thrown off by a gluttonous ministry usurping the prerogatives of the crown and systematically corrupting the independence of the Commons" (Bailyn 1967, 130). Bureaucracy, then, was both the substance and the source of tyranny. Thus, notes Bailyn (p. 126), "the formal address of the first Continental Congress to the people of Great Britain dilated on 'the ministerial plan to enslave us.'" And, he continues, "The second Congress justified its actions by reference to 'the rapid progress of a tyrannical ministry'" (p. 126).

The Federalist Diagnosis

With the success of the revolution, the new nation was no longer subject to the whims of ministers who had the ear of a pliant king. But critics of the new government almost immediately diagnosed a new threat to liberty in the form of excessive democracy. To Federalist critics of the Articles of Confederation, the bureaucracy was being used by the state and national legislatures to undermine liberty in at least three ways.

First, legislators used their authority over administrative decisions providing localized benefits in a manner designed to circumvent effective democratic control. Legislative control of localized benefits—what we now call pork barrel—posed a threat because it provided the essential tool for those least qualified to hold high office to gain election. As G. S. Wood (1969, 477) quotes the Federalist pamphleteers, "Everywhere 'Specious, interested designing men,' 'men, respectable neither for their property, their virtue, nor their abilities,' were taking a lead in public affairs that they had never quite had before, courting 'the suffrages of the people by tantalizing them with improper indulgences.'" To the Federalists, Wood suggests (p. 501), legislative control of allocative decisions undermined republican government so that "'Instead of choosing men for their abilities, integrity and patriotism,' the people seemed too prone to 'act from some mean, interested, or capricious motive.' They 'choose a man because he will vote for a new town, or a new county, or in favor of a memorial.'" Thus, long before Fiorina (1977) discussed the problems of pork barrel, the Federalists decried the practice.

A second and related target of the Federalist critics addressed what is now known as "casework," or interference in administrative decisions to provide relief to individual constituents. As G. S. Wood (1969, 408) quotes the Federalists, "The people 'have been taught to consider an application to the legislature as a shorter and more certain mode of obtaining relief from hardships and losses, than the usual process of law,'" so that, he suggests, "The Revolution . . . served to accentuate the medieval court-like character of the American legislatures." So great had this tendency become, suggests Wood (p. 408), that the political meaning of grievances was redefined as "simply 'hardships that will always arise from the operation of the general laws,' or 'even the misdeeds of particular officers, or private men, for which there is an easy legal remedy,' or sometimes even 'inconveniences' growing out of the negligence of the sufferer himself." In such an environment, suggest Federalist and contemporary critics (e.g., Fiorina 1977) alike, more fundamental issues of politics are neglected.

In part, Federalist attention to the pernicious effects of pork barrel and casework reflected concerns about the class roots of legislators as well as those being provided public beneficence and relief. But to the Federalists, excessive social mobility could arise only because legislators had the power through their direct control of administrative decisions to seduce the populace away from responsibly exercising their duties as citizens. The result, they argued, was a democratic system too attentive to narrow and localized interests rather then to the broader, society-wide interests that must be protected if liberty is to be preserved (G. S. Wood 1969, 510–11).

A third mechanism generated even greater anxiety among the Whig opponents of the Articles of Confederation. Excessive legislative control over administrative (as well as judicial) appointments, they argued, necessarily undermines the always delicate balance of interests essential for effective preservation of liberty. As G. S. Wood (p. 407) notes, "The appointing authority which in most constitutions had been granted to the assemblies had become the principal source of division and factions in the states." To the Federalists, this posed an even more serious danger than legislative corruption of the law through pork barrel and casework, as it constituted in Madison's terms (p. 407), "drawing all power into its [the legislature's] impetuous vortex." This, of course, was for Whigs the very definition of tyranny.

Legislative control of bureaucracy, charged the Federalists, resulted in capricious, mercurial, and fickle policy. Even worse, it jeopardized the balance required of a vigilant defense of liberty and emancipated legislators from effective popular control. These dangers were so severe, they said, that they necessitated reconsidering some of the basic lessons of the revolution. As Hamilton suggested, "We have been taught to reprobate the danger of influence in the British government, without duly reflecting how far it was necessary to support good government" (G. S. Wood 1969, 551). To that end, the Federalists concluded that "The proper cure . . . for corruption in the Legislature was to take from it the power of appointing to offices" (p. 551).

The Republican Diagnosis

Under the new Constitution, having established agencies independent of any king's ministers and secure from the excesses of a run-away legislature, who now might employ the administrative branch as an agent of tyranny?

The answer—from Jefferson and his rising "Republican" faction—was the executive, which had always posed a special hazard in Whig thinking (Banning 1978, 55–56). Banning marks the speech of William Branch Giles in the Second Congress as one of the earliest challenges to the Federalists from an emerging Republican ideology: "All representative governments," he said, "display a natural tendency to degenerate from Republicanism to Monarchy" (pp. 163–64).

And it was no accident that the bureaucracy again served as the focus of Whiggish opposition. For although the agent controlling the bureaucracy had changed, the essential argument of the Republicans was the same as that used by Traditional Whigs and by the Federalists. As Banning notes, the Republicans

> seized the only intellectual grounds for such an opposition that had proven tenable in Anglo-American politics. With remarkably little revision of the premises relating to the methods of subverting legislative independence, Giles was able to invoke the traditional rhetoric of eighteenth century oppositions to charge the Federalist administration with a deliberate attempt to undermine the constitutional structure that guaranteed liberty and democracy. With little change, the whole apocalyptic ideology seemed to apply (1978, 164).

The Republican diagnosis was merely the latest evolution in Whig ideology.

How might the Federalists use the new national administration to subvert democracy in what would in all but name become a monarchy? While the preeminent source of tyranny was the executive, the nascent bureaucracy was assigned its own satisfyingly villainous, albeit supporting, role. To the Republican critics (Banning 1978, 151), the few but growing number of bureaucratic administrators were nothing more than a "mercenary corps of adventurers" whose self-interest would lead them to be far more loyal to an aggrandizing executive than to the liberties of the people. If not chief conspirators, bureaucratic administrators were still compliant henchmen.

And what was the executive's interest in this malign collaboration? To Jefferson's partisans, it was nothing less than employing the bureaucracy to undermine the checks and balances protecting public liberty. Hamilton, through control of the Treasury Department, was surely the archpriest of the monarchist conspiracy. In a New York *Journal* article cited by Banning (1978, 151), for example, one Republican critic asked: "Could Hamilton have in view 'a political increase of salaries and multiplication of offices to give a ministerial strength to party and political energy to a confederation which must destroy the states or be destroyed?'"

The Republicans' charges were more inclusive than a narrow antipathy to Hamilton, however. In arguing for a reduction in the diplomatic corps, for instance, John Nicholas claimed that "appointments had been used by the executive to reward its followers in Congress, establishing a 'thirst for office' and a commitment to 'executive infallibility' that tended to 'produce a union and consolidation' of different parts of the government and to 'destroy the Constitution'" (Banning 1978, 248). To Republicans, the government had become an executive patronage engine, alternatively corrupting or ignoring Congress, charges echoed, in part, two centuries later in Nathan's (1983) analysis of White House personnel policy under Presidents Nixon and Reagan.

Even more alarming, the president as commander-in-chief might use the military—again, the Whigs' most dreaded bureaucracy—to undermine both personal and public liberty, charges repeated in the present time in Schlesinger's (1973) indictment of the imperial presidency. This scenario seemed to be realized on the occasion of the neutrality crises starting in 1795. The Republican critique of the military build-up hinged, in part, on the tendency of war governments to make dependents of citizens, and thus allies in its designs on liberty. As Banning (1978, 261–62) summarizes the Republicans' assertions: "War increased the proportion of the nation intimately connected with the government in power, turning independent merchants into war contractors, creating military officers, and requiring an enlargement of the civil establishment."

But the danger of war was potentially far more direct, for it "required an increase in the size of the regular army, and every Anglo-American knew that standing armies were the classic instruments of liberticide" (Banning 1978, 262). Further, "Wars permitted the repression of domestic opposition," given reality by the Alien and Sedition Laws, "and turned the people's minds away from their domestic discontents" (p. 261).

In sum, the founders offered three distinct diagnoses of how bureaucracy might be used to place liberty in jeopardy, diagnoses that were pitted against each other sequentially as they moved from rebellion to Jefferson's election in 1800. Moreover, specific aspects of their argument, at least on face, seem to foreshadow elements of the modern critique of bureaucracy. Now we turn to considering how deep these similarities really are.

The Contemporary Literature from the Founders' Perspective

Two questions were raised at the beginning of this article. The first concerned the applicability of a "bureaucratic-centered image of governance" to American political thought during the late eighteenth century. Clearly, reading the three core works of the Republican synthesis through this lens necessitates revising the conventional assessment of the founders. What we now call bureaucracy was very important to their sequential diagnoses of problems of governance. Bureaucracy comprised the substance of the threat to liberty to all three Whig perspectives, even as they differed over specifying who controlled bureaucracy or what institution comprised the underlying threat to liberty.

But what of our second question on the contemporary relevance of the founders' thought? Does their thinking shed light on the present, highly contentious literature on bureaucratic power? In general, Lienesch (1988) is correct in arguing that, even on issues with a surface resonance with those addressed by the founders, modern political discourse remains distinctive. Therefore, the convergence and divergence between the founders' view of bureaucracy and our own must be mapped with care.

The Nature of Bureaucracy's Threat to Liberty

The key difference between the founders' perspective and that of the contemporary literature on bureaucratic power concerns not the list of ills inherent in administrative authority but the context within which the analysis is set. The founders viewed liberty as fragile, with the slope from liberty to tyranny particularly short and slippery. As Lienesch (1988, 64) has noted, "In republican political thought, the earliest and most enduring theme has been the idea of revolution. Its origins lay in a theory of cyclical renewal. . . . Their readings of classical history suggested that the ancient republics had followed a continuous cycle of founding, corruption, and reform." Given self-interest, tyranny was virtually inevitable to the founders.

This changed with the institutionalization of the new American regime after the election of Jefferson. Having discovered a new political science, the founders claimed to have established a government with such a flexible but rigorous balance that the old cycle of founding, corruption, and reform had been abolished. The new regime would continue in perpetuity, thereby obviating the need for the older Whig psychology of vigilant skepticism (Lienesch 1988, 159–83). This revision of the Whig idea of revolution has several implications for American political thought, including our thinking about bureaucracy.

The key implication concerns the responsibilities of citizenship. The Whig citizen was always on guard, always suspicious of government. After 1800, however, such suspicion was unfounded, and administrative officers were to be considered agents of the citizenry. This invoked a far more passive model of citizenship than that provided by Whiggism. As Lienesch (p. 179) notes, "In effect, the new psychology stipulated that from that time, heroic politics existed only in the past, the duty of Americans being to revere the founders, remembering their illustrious deeds, applauding their magnificent government, and cherishing their hallowed constitution."

In stark contrast to classical notions of citizenship, the inhabitants of the new nation were to turn their attention away from politics and government. "From that time on," Lienesch (p. 183) suggests, "Constitutional citizens would bear at least some of the attributes of modern liberalism, considering it their primary responsibility to act in the private realm, pursuing their individual interests and thereby building the country's economy." Liberal detachment replaced Whig cynicism.

This reinterpretation of citizenship influenced the literature on public bureaucracy in at least three ways. First, the focus of modern critiques of bureaucracy generally is not on liberty, but on some other value that takes for granted the political legitimacy, if not always the wisdom, of government action. That most commonly invoked by approaches founded on a liberal model of citizenship (Galston 1982 and 1988) is efficiency, which, although understood quite differently, serves as the evaluative criterion for public administration (Fesler and Kettl 1991, 43–44), policy analysis (Jenkins-Smith 1990, 20; Weimer and Vining 1989, 397), and parts of the public choice interpretation (Ostrom 1974, 50). Alternatively, critiques predicated on a communitarian understanding of citizenship (Barber 1984; Elkins 1987) tend to posit some form of self-actualization as a core value (e.g., Dvorin and Simmons 1972; Lewis 1977; Hummel 1977). Still other criteria are given priority and, thereby, equally superseding liberty in the many extant critiques of public bureaucracy (Jackson 1983, 7; Stillman 1991, 214).

This does not mean that the value of liberty disappeared by any means, or that government action is always presumed to be prudent, as is fully evident in the public choice critique of bureaucracy (e.g., Buchanan 1975). In many literatures, the essential "politicalness" of the founders' concern for liberty is functionally replaced by attention to the more modern issues of political control and accountability (e.g., Knott and Miller 1987). But these proxies are mere shadows of the founders' regard for liberty and the omnipresent perils posed to it by administrative bureaucracy. That is, accountability, like efficiency, presumes the legitimacy of the governmental principal to whom the administrative agents are held accountable. And even the public choice literature focuses more often on efficiency as a core value than on political control.

Second, the demise of the Whig model of citizenship as skeptical guardian altered as well the burden of proof required to demonstrate bureaucratic abuse. To the founders, given their theory of fragility, even the smallest encroachment on liberty could signal its collapse into tyranny. Thus the evidence required to invoke a defense of liberty was limited to citing a few examples of tyranny or even precursors to tyranny. In effect, the fragility corollary short-circuited modern rules of inference. With the reconceptualization of 1800, however, the Constitution was presumed to be sufficiently robust so as to be able to withstand isolated threats. Therefore, much more than a telling example of abuse of power is required of contemporary critiques of bureaucracy.

Once the short, slippery slope of the Whigs is transmuted into an infinite plain, modern rules of inference must govern evidence about bureaucratic abuses. Simply put, case studies—the modern analog of the pamphleteer's anecdote—are no longer sufficient to draw inferences about the regime as a whole, which is presumed to function generally in accord with the designers' intentions. Unlike the founders, students of government today would consider it invalid to generalize from Robert Moses' empire building (Caro 1975) to an indictment of the Constitution. While still important for narrow purposes, such "cases" carry far less general meaning when stripped of the ancillary idea of fragility. To launch a general critique or analysis of bureaucracy power, one must now effectively sample from the whole domain of public administrative activity to build an indictment.

Obviously, very little of this has been done. This is especially evident in the empirical literature on control of bureaucratic outputs (Weingast 1984; Weingast and Moran 1983; Wood and Waterman 1991; Moe 1982 and 1985; B. D. Wood 1988, 1990, and 1992; Eisner and Meier 1990), which relies exclusively on case studies on one or a small handful of regulatory agencies. Perhaps only Kaufman's work (1976; 1985, 141–51) constitutes a serious effort to struggle with the difficulties of defining the appropriate universe. Therefore, we have yet to fully accommodate ourselves to this implication of transiting from the founders' classical perspective to our own world view.

Still, this shift in the rules of inference may have influenced us in unexpected ways. The paradox of the founders' anxieties arising in a prebureaucratic world was a function of their concern for even small portents of tyranny. This does not however, explain why recent analyses of administrative power typically ignore the founders, assuming that the problem of bureaucracy originated in the twentieth century. The answer may lie in retroactively applying modern, standard rules of inference when reading the founders. By modern rules, the rudimentary state of administration at the end of the eighteenth century is sufficient by itself to have circumvented the political dangers of bureaucracy. One might then reason that their founders' fears must have been exaggerated and that their comments on administrative bureaucracy, therefore, can be dismissed as mere chaff obscuring their real concerns. If so, our prevailing wisdom that the founders had little to say about bureaucracy may be due to a blind spot imposed by modern rules of inference coupled with a failure to appreciate the classical context of their political writings.

Third, even when evidence of bureaucratic abuse is forthcoming, the actions available to citizens are now sharply delimited. To the founders, a few examples were sufficient to fully justify rebellion. As Lienesch (1988, 65) has noted, "The cyclical theory implied a politics of resignation and rebellion. Radical republicanism, assuming both declension and revision, combined long periods of waiting with short bursts of protest." Direct linkages between example and revolution have not disappeared entirely, as fully illustrated in Howard Jarvis's (1979) rhetoric of the tax revolt. But such rhetoric is nearly absent in the scholarly literature on bureaucratic power. Political legitimacy is now rarely questioned. Therefore, specific, narrow, and precise reform, not rebellion, is the appropriate action in response to contemporary evidence of administrative abuse of discretion (e.g., Knott and Miller 1987).

In effect, the founders' analysis of bureaucracy rested on a conceptual schema radically different from our own. Theirs was a classical point of view, while our modern perspective results in part from their reconceptualizing the revolution from being only the latest in a cycle of rebellions into a definitive break with the past. Crucially, this content lends meaning to our facts about bureaucracy. Once the Whig model of citizenship is excised, critiques of bureaucracy necessarily take on a very different relationship to the larger body of political discourse, one that is more isolated, peripheral, and self-contained. No longer do examples of real or anticipated bureaucratic abuses constitute an indictment of an entire regime. Therefore, it is not unreasonable to conclude that administrative power was even more important to the founders' understanding of politics than it is to our own.

The Source of Bureaucracy's Threat to Liberty

If the context of the founders' assessment of bureaucracy was fundamentally different from modern perspectives, the instruments of administrative power with which they were concerned strike modern sensibilities as familiar. In the Traditional Whig, Federalist, and Republican interpretations of the source of the bureaucratic threat, one sees a ready foreshadowing of administrative control of information and the selective allocation of resources to seduce nominal superiors. There also were charges of legislative misuse of agencies through casework, pork barrel, and appointments to subvert democratic control of elected representatives. In addition, the Republicans claimed the Federalists misused the bureaucracy to circumvent control by Congress and by the electorate. In each case, we identified the modern literature to which mechanism of abuse cited by Bailyn, G. S. Wood, or Banning can be linked. Even the tone of the modern analyses, though not their relatively colorless language, matches that of the pamphleteers in its emphasis on corruption.

It is not, however, these similarities with the modern literatures on bureaucracy that are most striking. Rather, most notable is how utterly different the founders' and modern arguments are in their organization. The founders' diagnoses are tightly melded into a series of three great oppositions so that a prevailing interpretation is pitted against an alternative: loyalist vs. Traditional Whig, Traditional Whig vs. Federalist, and Federalist vs. Republican. How one answered the query of who controlled the bureaucracy clearly defined one's position along this continuum of disagreements.

The recent literature, in contrast, evidences little coherent structure. As fully illustrated by Hill's (1991) examination of twenty metaphors commonly used to understand bureaucratic power, all three perspectives survive contemporaneously. Within nearly the same decade, Ostrom (1974) and Niskanen (1971) decried bureaucratic independence, while Schlesinger (1973), Nathan (1983), and Fisher (1975) denounced executive dominance. At the same time, Fiorina (1977), Weingast and Marshall (1988), and McCubbins and Schwartz (1984) posited a congressional dominance model of the bureaucracy.

Nearly the same pattern emerges if one limits review to empirical analyses of similar types of agencies by authors employing a common paradigmatic approach. Thus, analysts working within the "New Institutionalism" paradigm (Moe 1984) have generalized findings on one or a handful of regulatory agencies to the conclusion that Congress (Weingast 1984; Weingast and Moran 1983), the president (B. D. Wood 1990; Wood and Waterman 1991; Moe 1982), or the bureaucracy (B. D. Wood 1988 and 1992; Eisner and Meier 1990) controls agency outputs.

That both patterns represent disorganization is evident in the failure to contrast these competing positions with each other. Even on the rare occasions when an analyst finds evidence of congressional, presidential, and bureaucratic influence of agency policy (Moe 1985) or when one perspective is used to challenge another (Moe 1987), the resulting analysis is politely ignored by all parties as somehow embarrassing.

Can one freely ignore the vast differences among the assumptions and empirical findings evident in the contemporary literature? Or should they be organized into open disputes as did the founders? In part, there is less need for this today than there was for the founders. To the extent that the modern literature restricts itself to case studies and limits generalizations to the case at hand, all three perspectives can coexist. Bureaucratic, executive, and legislative control of bureaucracy might be valid concurrently in all their various shadings for different parts of the government. For intellectual consistency, one might desire at most, as Durant (1991, 473–74) has suggested, a "contingency theory of bureaucratic influence" to help explain why one agency differs from another. But our need for consistency is less compelling than it was for the founders. Since the focus of the modern literature is narrow, precise, and specific reform rather than the global legitimization of rebellion, there is little intellectual compulsion to reach an overarching judgment about who controls bureaucracy.

On the other hand, many proposed reforms are not agency specific, but speak to broader remedies that assume that administrative abuse is noncontingent—revision of White House control of personnel policy or the budget, a presidential line-item veto, term limitations, and so on. When assessing these more generic proposals, one cannot blithely adopt just any position on the question of who controls the bureaucracy. Whether a line-item veto is appropriate or not, for example, depends a great deal on whether the predominant source of a bureaucracy's abuse is the bureaucracy itself, Congress, or the president. In such circumstances, our failure to critically contrast the several hypotheses about who controls bureaucracy begs an essential premise of the analysis.

The fact that we do not regularly test these vastly different assumptions about who controls the bureaucracy is perhaps the single greatest failing of the contemporary literature. Indeed, except for Moe's (1985 and 1987) work, almost the only such debate recently is the Rourke (1991) and Durant (1991) exchange in this journal, and this was inconclusive given their mutual failure to define the universe of agencies about which they were making inferences. This failing was not evident in the founders' discourse. While their conception of citizenship obviated any need to sample from the full domain of administrative activities in order to draw meaningful inferences, they quite directly and sequentially confronted the several hypotheses about who controlled the bureaucracy.

Developing a Bureau-Centered Research Program

Our review of the founders' analysis of bureaucracy via the Republican synthesis yields two conclusions. Contrary to conventional wisdom, administrative power was central to their understanding of the necessity for revolution and then their design of a new government. We earlier quoted James Q. Wilson (1975, 77) as concluding that "The great political and constitutional struggles were not over the power of the administrative apparatus, but over the power of the President, of Congress, and of the states." Perhaps a more accurate characterization of the extended debate encompassing the three great oppositions is that, in a most fundamental sense, it was a contest over who would wield the power inherent in the administrative apparatus. What would come to be "the bureaucracy" was necessarily the agent of tyranny to the founders, a view that accords well with modern analyses. Even the specific institutional sources diagnosed sequentially as the loci of the bureaucracy problem match well the answers offered by contemporary scholars.

At the same time, however, the larger context within which the founders' understanding of bureaucracy was embedded was quite different from the present context. Informed as it was by classical thought, the pamphleteers employed criteria for evaluating administrative abuses, presumptions about the legitimacy of government activity, a burden of proof for action against the government, and a menu of actions citizens might invoke that diverges sharply from those of modern interpretations of the problem of bureaucratic power. The same facts, the same causes, the same motivations would have very different implications for the founders than for us. While important analogues remain, their thinking about administrative bureaucracy does not fit into the contemporary literature very easily. No matter how one strains to find Luther Gulick within Alexander Hamilton (White 1948) or to see Vincent Ostrom transfiguring James Madison (Ostrom 1974), the founders' perspective and our world-views diverge too sharply to identify clear lines of intellectual descent. There will always be a divide between the classical Whig and the present understanding of the problem of bureaucracy.

What does this analysis say about the larger concern for developing a research program based on a bureaucratic-centered image of governance? At a minimum, the inability to fit the founders' thinking neatly into the modern literature point to the generalizability of Hill's (1991) approach. The model also works well in a setting very different from the present, even one that was prebureaucratic in any modern sense. Importantly, the approach illuminates important similarities and differences between the two generations' understandings of the political problem of administration. These become stark when bureaucracy is, metaphorically, placed at the center of government and one asks: What is the problem of bureaucracy, and who controls it? And, most importantly, a modern research program can learn from the founders' creative struggles with the political power of bureaucracy even while their construction of the problem differs considerably from ours. Indeed, three attributes of the founders' mode of analysis merit attention.

First, this analysis demonstrates that interpretation of the problem of bureaucracy cannot be separated from the larger political theories governing a society. The founders' theory of bureaucracy was intimately linked with and derived power from their Whig philosophy. It is the more general theories about citizenship and the nature of political motivations that set the crucial context within which one interprets "facts" about the behavior of administrators. Such theories establish the criteria by which to assess administrative success and failure, and they specify whether bureaucracy poses a central or peripheral problem for a community. Therefore, a bureaucratic-centered research program must connect to the broader currents of political thought to be interpretable.

Second, the Whig conception of the fragile nature of liberty necessitated trip-wire criteria for justifying revolution. Heroic political action could be justified on even the slimmest evidence. Lacking a Whig conception of politics, today's requirements for inference are more rigorous. Justifying major reform today, much less rebellion, requires a broader sampling of the universe of administrative activity, not simply a few examples. It is also clear, however, that the evidentiary standards operative today are more similar to those of the founders than they are to our hypothetical sample. As seen in the Rourke (1991) and Durant (1991) debate, we still employ anecdote as the foundation of even the broadest claims. This would be fine if we too operated under a Whig conception of politics. Since we do not, developing and employing such a sample constitute important opportunities to be exploited by our research program.

Third, the founders did not shy away from contrasting competing images of who controlled bureaucracy. For them, avoiding the issue would constitute not intellectual tolerance but begging one of the essential conundrums of self-government. That we shun this issue today—or, at best, occasionally toss anecdotes and regulatory case studies back and forth—is obviously problematic. Again, defining the domain of relevant administrative activity and developing a means to sample from it would contribute to resolving this question. While research may never specify who controls bureaucracy in any absolute sense, developing agreed-upon comparative assessments across agencies, governments, and time is conceptually viable and would move the research program forward considerably.

Developing such measures and even defining the appropriate universe from which to sample will be extraordinarily difficult and controversial. But until this is accomplished, we will be in the paradoxical situation of employing modern conceptions of politics while using "classical" methods of analysis. These methods were appropriate for the founders and were fully justified within their understanding of politics. Given modern conceptions of politics, using their more relaxed analytic methods is inappropriate. Until we elaborate and reconcile the methods, substantive foci, and the broader theoretical context of our research program on bureaucratic politics, it will approach that outlined by the Republican synthesis in neither intellectual rigor nor consistency.

References

Arnold, R. Douglas.
1979   *Congress and the Bureaucracy.* New Haven, Conn.: Yale University Press.
Bailyn, Bernard.
1967   *The Ideological Origins of the American Revolution.* Cambridge, Mass.: Belknap and Harvard University Press.
Banning, Lance.
1978   *The Jeffersonian Persuasion, Evolution of a Party Ideology.* Ithaca, N.Y.: Cornell University Press.
Barber, Benjamin.
1984   *Strong Democracy.* Berkeley: University of California Press.

Buchanan, James M.
1975   *The Limits of Liberty.* Chicago: University of Chicago Press.

Caro, Robert.
1973   *The Power Broker: Robert Moses and the Fall of New York.* New York: Vintage.

Crenson, Matthew A.
1975   *The Federal Machine: Beginnings of Bureaucracy in Jacksonian America.* Baltimore: Johns Hopkins University Press.

Dahl, Robert A.
1956   *A Preface to Democratic Theory.* Chicago: University of Chicago Press.

Durant, Robert F.
1991   "Whither Bureaucratic Influence?: A Cautionary Note." *Journal of Public Administration Research and Theory* 1:461–76.

Dvorin, Eugene P., and Simmons, Robert H.
1972   *From Amoral to Humane Bureaucracy.* San Francisco: Canfield.

Eisner, Marc Allen, and Meier, Kenneth J.
1990   "Presidential Control versus Bureaucratic Power: Explaining the Reagan Revolution." *American Journal of Political Science* 34:269–87.

Elkin, Stephen.
1987   *City and Regime in the American Republic.* Chicago: University of Chicago Press.

Fesler, James W., and Kettl, Donald F.
1991   *The Politics of the Administrative Process.* Chatham, N.J.: Chatham House.

Fiorina, Morris P.
1977   *Congress: Keystone of the Washington Establishment.* New Haven, Conn.: Yale University Press.

Fisher, Louis.
1975   *Presidential Spending Power.* Princeton, N.J.: Princeton University Press.

Galston, William A.
1982   "Defending Liberalism." *American Political Science Review* 76:621–29.
1958   "Liberal Virtues." *American Political Science Review* 52:1277–92.

Gormley, William T., Jr.
1989   *Taming the Bureaucracy: Muscles, Prayers, and Other Strategies.* Princeton, N.J.: Princeton University Press.

Gruber, Judith E.
1987   *Controlling Bureaucracies: Dilemmas in Democratic Governance.* Berkeley: University of California Press.

Hill, Larry B.
1991   "Who Governs the American Administrative State? A Bureaucratic-Centered Image of Governance." *Journal of Public Administration Research and Theory* 1:261–94.

Hummel, Ralph P.
1977   *The Bureaucratic Experience.* New York: St. Martin's.

Jackson, P.M.
1983   *The Political Economy of Bureaucracy.* Totowa, N.J.: Barnes and Noble.
Jarvis, Howard.
1979   *I'm Mad as Hell.* New York: Times Books.
Jenkins-Smith, Hank C.
1990   *Democratic Politics and Policy Analysis.* Pacific Grove, Calif.: Brooks/Cole.
Kaufman, Herbert.
1976   *Are Government Organizations Immortal?* Washington, D.C.: Brookings.
1985   *Time, Chance, and Organizations.* Chatham, N.J.: Chatham House.
Knott, Jack H., and Miller, Gary J.
1987   *Reforming Bureaucracy: The Politics of Institutional Choice.* Englewood Cliffs, N.J.: Prentice-Hall.
Lewis, Eugene.
1977   *American Politics in a Bureaucratic Age: Citizens, Constituents, Clients and Victims.* Cambridge, Mass.: Winthrop.
Lienesch, Michael.
1988   *New Order of the Ages: Time, the Constitution, and the Making of Modern American Political Thought.* Princeton, N.J.: Princeton University Press.
McCubbins, Mathew D., and Schwartz, Thomas.
1984   "Congressional Oversight Overlooked: Police Patrols versus Fire Alarms." *American Journal of Political Science* 28:165–79.
Meier, Kenneth J.
1979   *Politics and the Bureaucracy.* North Scituate, Mass.: Duxbury.
Meyers, Marvin.
1973   *The Mind of the Founder: Sources of the Political Thought of James Madison.* Indianapolis: Bobbs-Merrill.
Moe, Terry M.
1982   "Regulatory Performance and Presidential Administration." *American Journal of Public Administration* 26:197–224.
1984   "The New Economics of Organization." *American Journal of Political Science* 28:739–77.
1985   "Control and Feedback in Economic Regulation: The Case of the NLRB." *American Political Science Review* 79:1094–116.
1987   "An Assessment of the Positive Theory of Congressional Dominance." *Legislative Studies Quarterly* 12:475–620.
Nachmias, David, and Rosenbloom, David H.
1980   *Bureaucratic Government USA.* New York: St. Martin's.
Nathan, Richard P.
1983   *The Administrative Presidency.* New York: John Wiley and Sons.
Nelson, Michael.
1982   "The Short, Ironic History of American National Bureaucracy." *Journal of Politics* 44:747–78.

Niskanen, William A., Jr.
1971   *Bureaucracy and Representative Government.* Chicago: Aldine and Atherton.

Ostrom, Vincent.
1971   *The Political Theory of the Compound Republic.* Blacksburg, Va.: Center for Study of Public Choice.
1974   *The Intellectual Crisis in American Public Administration.* University: University of Alabama Press.

Rohr, John A.
1986   *To Run a Constitution, The Legitimacy of the Administrative State.* Lawrence: University Press of Kansas.

Rourke, Francis. E.
1984   *Bureaucracy, Politics, and Public Policy,* 3d ed. Boston: Little, Brown.
1991   "American Bureaucracy in a Changing Political Setting." *Journal of Public Administration Research and Theory* 1:111–130.

Schlesinger, Arthur M., Jr.
1973   *The Imperial Presidency.* Boston: Houghton Mifflin.

Skowronek, Stephen.
1982   *Building the American State: The Expansion of National Administrative Capacities, 1877–1920.* Cambridge: Cambridge University Press.

Stillman, Richard J. II.
1987   *The American Bureaucracy.* Chicago: Nelson-Hall.
1991   *Preface to Public Administration: A Search for Themes and Directions.* New York: St. Martin's.

Weimer, David L., and Vining, Aidan R.
1989   *Policy Analysis: Concepts and Practice.* Englewood Cliffs, N.J.: Prentice-Hall.

Weingast, Barry R.
1984   "The Congressional-Bureaucratic System, A Principal-Agent Perspective." *Public Choice* 44:147–91.

Weingast, Barry R., and Marshall, William J.
1988   "The Industrial Organization of Congress; or, Why Legislatures, Like Firms, Are Not Organized as Markets." *Journal of Political Economy* 96:132–63.

Weingast, Barry R., and Moran, Mark J.
1983   "Bureaucratic Discretion or Congressional Control? Regulatory Policy-making by the Federal Trade Commission." *Journal of Political Economy* 91:765–800.

White, Leonard. D.
1948   *The Federalists.* New York: Macmillan.

Wilson, James Q.
1975   "The Rise of the Bureaucratic State." *Public Interest* 41:77–103.
1989   *Bureaucracy: What Government Agencies Do and Why They Do It.* New York: Basic Books.

Wood, B. Dan.
1988   "Principals, Bureaucrats, and Responsiveness in Clean Air Enforcements." *American Political Science Review* 82:213–34.
1990   "Does Politics Make a Difference at the EEOC?" *American Journal of Political Science* 34:503–30.
1992   "Modeling Federal Implementation as a System: The Clean Air Case." *American Journal of Political Science* 36:40–67.

Wood, B. Dan, and Waterman, Richard W.
1991   "The Dynamics of Political Control of the Bureaucracy." *American Political Science Review* 85:801–27.

Wood, Gordon S.
1969   *The Creation of the American Republic: 1776–1787*. New York: W.W. Norton.

Yates, Douglas.
1982   *Bureaucratic Democracy*. Cambridge, Mass.: Harvard University Press.

Part Seven

Leadership

This final section reflects on various dimensions of the individual administrator's place in the overall scheme of governance. The extent to which administrators (at least the ones in key positions) ought to be "leaders" has been at issue since the beginnings of the field in the early twentieth century. Woodrow Wilson, for example, argued that administrators ought to take pro-active steps to implement policies established by legislatures; but he also relied on administrators' neutral competence to justify their exercise of authority. Over the years, debate has sought to balance these two elements.

The notion of administrative discretion (that is, administrators do not just blindly follow orders, but instead have to use their judgment) implies that administrators' actions are based both on the specifics in law and regulation and on their own sense of what is appropriate to the situation. Perspectives that emphasize discretion tend to turn to ideas of authority and leadership to shape views of how administrators ought to behave. In contrast, the idea of neutral competence attempts to constrain the exercise of discretion by seating it within the confines of the objectivity thought to be instilled by technical training. Perspectives that emphasize neutrality lend themselves less well to ideas about leadership. In the neutrality framework, phrases like "on tap but not on top" and "a passion for anonymity" suggest selfless service rather than pro-active discretion. Particularly in recent years, faith in neutral competence has waned and more attention has been turned to questions such as: If administrators are (at least in some situations) "leaders," what does this appropriately entail? What sort of leader should an administrator aim to be?

Robert Presthus's essay, "Authority in Organizations" (*Public Administration Review* 1960), argues that, in order to be effective, administrative leaders must understand how to exercise authority, that is, how to get sub-ordinates to carry out their orders, a question first raised in Chester I. Barnard's classic *The Functions of the Executive* (1938). Presthus observes that authority cannot simply be imposed from above; it must be viewed by subordinates as legitimate or valid. There are four bases for legitimacy: technical expertise, formal role, rapport, and a generalized deference to authority. To the extent that executives rely on rapport rather than technical or formal elements, they seek to create a work climate that fosters buy-in on the part of subordinates. In this respect they are not just authority figures but leaders. Presthus comments: "We know that executives rarely fail for lack of technical skill but rather for inadequate personal relations." He concludes that authority grows out of a "dynamic, reciprocal relationship between leaders and led." From this perspective, while the exercise of administrative leadership could potentially constitute a threat to bureaucratic rationality, it can also reinforce chain of command authority by encouraging subordinates to accede freely to orders from their superiors.

The next essay, Anders Richter's "The Existentialist Executive" (*PAR* 1970) has the flavor of the time during which it was written, the late 1960s. This was an era in which it was easy to conclude, as Richter does, that conservatism was dead and a revolution was in progress. Yet the questions raised in his argument have long-lasting relevance. Richter argues that "rather than looking to given standards of value and behavior, the new executive will be forced to rely on his self-created norms and interests in coping with a world of change." He sees the position of the administrator as fundamentally existential: Administrators must act without the guaranteed help of unquestioned values; therefore administrative action is ambiguous and often anxiety-producing. Administrators must choose, not knowing what the results of their choices may be. They must take risks. And they must tolerate difference, rather than try to impose conformity. A sense of personal responsibility for their actions is what will enable administrators to influence the entire "moral tone" of their organizations.

David C. Korten's "The Management of Social Transformation" appeared in *PAR* in 1981. Anticipating the dialogue on globalism that, two decades later, has become pervasive, Korten draws our attention to world-wide economic, political, and environment changes, ones that transcend national boundaries. He contrasts two paradigms of societal development, the open or "cowboy" model and the closed or "spaceship" model. The contrast between them has important implications for leadership. In the cowboy economy, growth and progress are emphasized, leading to capital- and energy-intensive investments that do little to increase employment and that compete with the informal sector. The spaceship economy recognizes inevitable resource limits and emphasizes sustainability rather than growth. To adapt to the spaceship economy, Korten suggests that we must replace reliance on scientific knowledge, analysis, "blueprints" for grand schemes, and linear thinking with what he calls social knowledge, which relies on synthesis, gradual learning, tentative solutions and frequent feedback. In this new paradigm, which demands new forms of organizational leadership, "the management of social learning involves linking knowledge, power, and people in ways which simultaneously generate new knowledge, new benefits, and new action potentials . . . the facilitation by top management of local level experimentation." Leaders must replace command and control with capacity building, professionalization with mutual self-help.

The big challenge for bureaucratic agencies in the new paradigm, according to Korten, will be to build in a capacity for innovative learning: to give priority to systems over projects, innovation over compliance, and self-monitoring over formal planning and evaluation. Organizational leaders will not only have to be visionaries but able to translate this new global vision into actions that little by little transform whole systems.

The last view of leadership brings our attention from the global to the most down-to-earth, day to day actions that make for good leadership. In "Leadership: Arranging the Chairs—Reflections on the Lessons of Neely Gardner," which appeared in 1992 in *Public Administration Quarterly*, Camille Cates Barnett offers an admiring and affectionate remembrance of one of public administration's most fertile and creative minds. Neely Gardner, associated for many years with the University of Southern California, formulated a model of "action training and research" for public administration, one that was widely disseminated and used in public agencies across the country and predated many subsequent participatory approaches to orgnaizational change (see Gardner 1974).

Barnett's portrait looks behind the action research model at Gardner's own use of it. From her observations of Gardner in action, she derives a model of leadership based not only on action research principles but their formulator's own behavior. Some of the lessons she believes Gardner's approach teaches us: Know who all the stakeholders are. Pay attention to the psychological contract between you and those you are leading. Listen first, then move to set directions. Analyze the factors that are promoting or getting in the way of change. To sum up, she argues, action research offers a model of nonlinear, intuitive, participative and democratic leadership. Barnett concludes that leadership is stewardship, not just being in charge but setting the example, respecting others, and aiming for significance in addition to success. As Neely Gardner taught, leadership lies in creating a facilitative environment ("arranging the chairs"), focusing energy, and taking care of people.

23

AUTHORITY IN ORGANIZATIONS

Robert V. Presthus

The concept of authority provides a useful tool to help us understand organizational behavior because it asks and suggests answers to the question of how the organization achieves its objectives. How are the energies of its members directed along desired channels? While organizations are designed to gain certain large ends, they must enlist instruments of motivation and direction to overcome the individual goals of their members. Authority is a crucial element in this equation, particularly if it is defined to include the ideas of reward and reciprocity.

One view of the relations between organizational leaders and their followers assumes that compliance with authority is in some way rewarding to the individual and that each participant plays an active role in defining and accepting authority—not merely in some idealistic sense but in operational terms. This might be called a "transactional" view of authority.[1] Organizational behavior, in this view, consists of individual bargaining. But it is not bargaining in the static sense of equilibrium theory, which explains participation as the result of a rough balance between the individual's contributions to the organization and the psychic and economic compensations he receives in return. This theory implies that the organization and the individual independently decide what kinds of concessions

NOTE: This essay is a revised version of a chapter in Sidney Mailick and Edward Van Nes (eds.), *Organization and Administrative Theory* (Prentice-Hall, 1960).
   Source: *Public Administration Review* 20(1960): 86–91.

each is willing to make in sharing authority or in determining the work contract. In the transactional view, the individual is intrinsically involved in the authority process. One can have equilibrium in an organization without having this kind of reciprocity among individuals at different levels in the hierarchy.

What Authority Is

Authority can be defined as the capacity to evoke compliance in others. We are here concerned with formal organizations as systems in which interpersonal relations are structured in terms of the prescribed authority of the actors. Of course positions of authority develop even in so-called informal organization, as William F. Whyte and others have shown.[2]

One major proposition of the transactional view of authority is that it is reciprocal. This idea stems in part from the psychological theory of perception, which tells us that reality is not some fixed entity but is defined by each individual's perception; it is relative. The way B defines the cues he has received from A determines their meaning for him and his reply. How close B comes to A's intended meaning depends on chance and how many related values A and B share, as well as how precisely they express themselves. Individuals impute different meanings to the same situations, reflecting their own personality structures.

Authority, too, is not a static, immutable quality that some people have while others do not. Rather, it is a subtle *interrelationship* whose consequences are defined by everyone concerned. The process is reciprocal because each actor tries to anticipate the reaction of all participants before he acts. A gaming process occurs in which each actor asks himself, "If I do this, what will X's reaction be, and in turn, what will my response to his assumed reaction be?"

In organizations, one's perceptions of the authority enjoyed by others as well as by oneself is thus a critical variable. Experimental evidence supports this conclusion: As Lippitt found:

1. a group member is more likely to accept direct attempts to influence him from a person he defines as powerful, and
2. the average group member will tend to initiate deferential, approval-seeking behavior toward persons seen as more powerful than himself.[3]

We may conclude that in the highly structured authority system of the typical big organization such reactions to authority are especially likely. This proposition will be developed further after the process of validating authority is considered.

The Legitimation Process

The process by which authority is accepted may be called legitimation, which is roughly synonymous with "sanctioned" or "validated." It usually occurs when the individual is integrated into a society or a group, when he accepts its norms and values.

That authority must be legitimated is explicit in Barnard's conclusion that it can rarely be imposed from above but becomes viable only through the acceptance of those exposed to it.[4] Obviously, the social context including the mission and traditions of the organization, its program, the relative influence of the actors, and the way each behaves affects the process of legitimation. However, the *specific conditions* under which authority will be accepted or rejected remain to be isolated by careful research. Superficially, we can assume that in highly disciplined organizations such as the Marine Corps, the legitimation process becomes virtually automatic, reflecting the Corps' traditions, volunteer character, and the high degree of commitment among its members. Turning to the other end of the continuum, the university or the research organization, the process becomes highly diffused and unstructured, with professional values competing for legitimation with hierarchical authority.[5]

Personality is another variable that affects legitimation. One suspects that in most cases it reinforces legitimation as a result of the socialization process mentioned above. A recent study[6] illustrates the effects of this element. Personality tests[7] were given 54 male university students to determine their attitudes toward authority. Then the students were asked to perform a simple task, with the instruction that they could stop whenever they wished. However, when the student did stop, the researcher immediately asked, "Don't you want to do some more?" Some gave in to what the researcher seemed to want and continued; others refused to go on. By and large, the personality tests of those who went on revealed a general tendency to accept authority, and vice versa.

Such variations in the legitimation process in different organizations and among different individuals complicate its analysis. Moreover, the values of the observer also interfere. As Herbert Simon concludes, "Authority that is viewed as legitimate is not felt as coercion or manipulation, either by the man who exercises it or by the man who accepts it. Hence, the scientist who wishes to deal with issues of manipulation that are sometimes raised in human relations research must be aware of his own attitudes of legitimacy. . . . If he regards the area of legitimate authority as narrow, many practices will appear to him coercive or manipulative that would not seem so with a broader criterion of legitimacy."[8]

These variations are further complicated by the fact that authority has several bases of legitimation. While authority may appear to rest upon his formal role, an executive's reliance upon this formal position for legitimation of his leadership is usually a confession of weakness. Authority seems more likely to be a contingent grant, received initially as part of formal position but requiring nourishment from other kinds of legitimation as well.

Four Bases of Legitimation

Four bases of legitimation may be suggested: technical expertise, formal role, rapport, and a generalized deference to authority. They are, of course, intermixed in most situations. Each ramifies the other, although the relative weight of each varies among types of organizations. My purpose here is not an exhaustive analysis of each basis of legitimation but rather a brief, exploratory outline which may be useful in conceptualizing authority in an operating situation.

Legitimation by Expertise

For a variety of historical and cultural reasons technical skill and professional attitudes are perhaps the most pervasive criteria for validating authority in the United States, i.e., many persons accept the authority of competent persons simply because they are competent. In this country, equality of opportunity has always been an ideal; ability to do the job has been widely accepted as the only moral basis for selection. Our pragmatic approach to getting a job done, never impeded by a rigid class system, reinforces this moral conviction.

Respect for the superior's expertise as a source of validating his authority is particularly effective where his expertise is the same as that of his subordinate's, only greater. This source of legitimation has been strengthened by specialization, which, in turn, has been reinforced by the professionalization process.[9]

Legitimation by Formal Position

There are some indications that formal role is becoming more significant as a basis for the legitimation of authority. In big organizations, authority is structured to insure control by limiting information, centralizing initiative, restricting access to decision-making centers, and generally controlling the behavioral alternatives of members. The formal allocation of authority is also reinforced by various psychological inducements, including status symbols, rewards, and sanctions. Such differential allocations of status, income, and authority have important objectives and consequences other than as personal rewards for loyal and effective service. They provide a battery of cues or signals for the entire organization; they provide the framework for personal transactions; they communicate appropriate behavior and dramatize its consequences. In brief, such signals define and reinforce authority.

In addition to these structural and psychological instruments, the traditions and the mission of the organization are important conditioning factors. Business organizations exhibit a high potential for validating authority mainly in terms of hierarchy; military organizations are similar, although there is some evidence that technical expertise is assuming a larger role as warfare and weapons become more scientific and complex.[10] There is also some evidence that the great size and specialization of modern organizations are forcing a greater reliance upon legitimation by formal role, even in research and educational organizations where legitimation by expertise has been traditional. The bureaucratization of research which attends the huge grants of government and the big foundations provides some evidence.[11]

Still, in most organizations a conflict usually exists between formal position and expertise as bases for authority. In organizations with many functional areas this conflict is aggravated because the generalist at the top can rarely be expert in more than one or two functional areas. Thus he will be denied the legitimation of expertise by those in other fields. He may also experience conflict between his generalist role and his identification with a functional area. In universities, for example, it is well known that the department which represents the substantive field of an incoming president is bound to rise. When the inevitable occurs, other departments emphasize legitimation by expertise in an effort to buttress their claims for equality.

We can safely conclude that the problems of authority are aggravated by the tendency of individuals to validate authority on the basis of competence in their own fields and to thus look to different reference groups for models for their own behavior. This condition has important consequences for loyalty to the organization, acceptance of its rules and traditions, and for the direction of professional energy. Gouldner has divided individuals into two role types, "cosmopolitans" and "locals," according to the bases upon which they grant authority.[12] As the term suggests, "cosmopolitans" have an outward orientation; their major loyalty and energy are directed toward their profession, and their activities are aimed at gaining national prominence in their field. "Locals," on the other hand, are oriented toward the organization with which they happen to be associated; they express great loyalty toward it, accept its major values, justify its policies, and expect to carve out a career within it.

Authority that attempts to rely solely upon formal role is thus challenged by the conflicting values and assumptions of the groups that comprise large organizations. Legitimation by expertise suffers from a similar conflict as each self-conscious group strives to make its own skills and values supreme. Both the size and specialization of modern organizations aggravate this conflict. Indeed, one could probably construct a useful "index of anticipated conflict" on the basis of the number of discrete functional groups contained within a given organization.

The resulting stalemate among conflicting professions results in a power vacuum which the generalist soon fills, again reinforcing the hierarchical basis of authority. Thus, in the main, modern organizations are controlled by generalists, reflecting their monopoly of information and initiative, extended tenure allowing freedom for tactical maneuver, control of procedural and judicial matters within the organization, absence of any legitimate, internal opposition (the common one-party system) to the "official" policies enanciated by leaders, and mastery over external relations with other elites.[13]

Legitimation by Rapport

Democratic political theory, the conflicts between generalists and specialists, and, one fears, the desire to rationalize human personality in the service of management, have combined to emphasize human relations in organization. This emphasis also serves to blunt the impersonality and routinization of big organization. Authority, then, often will be legitimated on the basis of interpersonal skill and the work climate that executives and supervisors maintain. This process may be called legitimation by rapport. Our bureaucratically inclined economy reinforces this mechanism by standardizing work conditions, pay, and career opportunities. Sympathetic human relations tend to become the major distinction among jobs. As a result, expert and hierarchical criteria of legitimation are challenged by the warm personality of the boss. Research supports this proposition. We know that executives rarely fail for lack of technical skill but rather for inadequate personal relations. More important, the acceptance of authority has been shown to be positively related to affection for the person exercising it:

1. The amount of influence or authority that a leader *attempts* to exert increases with increased acceptance of him by the recipients;
2. The leader's actual influence over the group increases with increasing acceptance of him as a person.[14]

The same study verified the existence of legitimation by expertise. The more one's subordinates recognized him as an expert in their own specialized field, the more effective he was. Influence was also positively related to the formal role of leader.

The administrator, then, not only must be aware of these several bases of legitimation, he also must accommodate himself to the particular basis that an individual or a group seems most likely to use in validating his authority in a given situation.

Legitimation by a Generalized Deference to Authority

Individual needs for security often result in a generalized deference to authority. Indeed, one is tempted to suggest that other sources of legitimation are often used as rationalizations for this form of legitimation. This deference, which often reflects distorted perceptions of authority, seems to fall in the category of nonrational behavior, or at least it seems less rational than legitimations based upon objective indexes such as technical skill and formal position. However, definitions of rationality must rest upon an explicit statement of the objectives sought. If an individual derives security and less strained interpersonal relations by deterring to authority, his behavior is rational from his standpoint.

This basis of legitimation assumes that individual behavior in complex organizations may usefully be conceptualized as a series of reactions to authority. Its theoretical framework reflects Harry Stack Sullivan's view that personality is the result of an individual's characteristic mode of accommodating to authority figures over a long period of time. His belief that anxiety-reduction is the basic mechanism in such accommodations is also accepted here: "I believe it fairly safe to say that anybody and everybody devotes much of his lifetime and a great deal of his energy to . . . avoiding more anxiety than he already has, and if possible, to getting rid of some of this anxiety."[15]

Sullivan also insists that anxiety is the major factor in learning by both children and adults. They learn to trade approval and the resulting reduction of anxiety for conformity with authority. We thus assume that individual reactions to organizational authority are a form of learning. Moreover, as in all learning, the mechanisms of perception and reinforcement are operating. Complex organizations, then, may be regarded as educational institutions whose systems of authority, status, and goals provide clear stimuli for their members.[16]

Pavlov was among the first to note that anxious people acquire conditioned responses with unusual speed. Eysenck reports a study in which normal individuals required 25 repetitions of a nonsense syllable accompanied by a buzzer before a conditioned response was established, while anxiety neurotics required only 8 repetitions.[17] Research on the effects of different anxiety loadings would require further specification of organizational role types in terms of their reactions to authority. It seems reasonable to assume that a certain amount of anxiety is conducive to organizational socialization, while too heavy a load may result in dysfunctional reactions to authority.[18]

These considerations suggest some limitations of the "permissive" concept of authority which holds that subordinates play the major role in legitimating organizational authority. Basically, this concept seems to overstate the amount of discretion enjoyed by the recipient of a superior's order. It underestimates the disparities in power between any given individual and the organization's leaders. But more important, it neglects the behavioral effect of a lifetime of learned deference to authority and the psychological gains attending such behavior. If Sullivan is correct, the individual is trained from infancy to defer to the authority of parents, teachers, executives, and leaders of various kinds. He develops over time a *generalized* deference to authority, based upon such socialization and its compensations.

Legitimation by deference appears exceptionally compelling in an organizational milieu where the location of authority and the symbols that define it are clear. Unlike many groups, big organizations are authoritative milieux: influence—evoking compliance without the backing of sanctions—is not really the primary ingredient in interpersonal affairs. As Wright Mills says, organizations are systems of roles graded by authority. Titles, income, accessibility, size and decor of office, secretarial buffers, and degree of supervision are the stimuli that validate such authority. They provide cues that define interpersonal relations, limit alternatives, and inhibit spontaneity. The degree to which authority is institutionalized is suggested by the fact that whereas the individuals who occupy the formal roles may change, the *system* of authority relationships persists, again reinforcing deference toward the holder of the formal position.

It is a safe generalization, too, that most individuals tend to accept group judgments in return for the psychic satisfaction of being in the majority and winning the group's approval.[19] Organizations are composed of a congeries of such groups and subhierarchies, each bound together by authority, mission, and interest to form a microcosm of the larger system. Each has its own power structure in which its leaders enjoy considerable discretion in dealing with their own subordinates although they are often nonleaders when viewed from a larger perspective.[20] This devolution of power has important consequences for legitimation. Discipline is insured since the life chances of those in each group are determined largely by the representations made on their behalf by their leaders. Organizational authority is transmitted downward by the subleaders, reinforcing their own authority and status by the opportunity to demonstrate the loyalty and dispatch with which they carry out higher policy.

Role conflict may occur here between the leader's personal and his organizational role. He simultaneously must promote the larger goals of the organization yet maintain equilibrium in his group by defending those group objectives which are not the same as the organization's. He will sometimes be caught between the conflicting demands of hierarchy and technical skill: here, his own identification with a professional field may aggravate such conflicts, making it more difficult to meet the organizational claims implicit in his formal position.[21] For example, formal budget requirements which seem to impede the work of a research group may nevertheless be important to the goal of the larger organization. At other times conflicting goals or policies within the larger organization make role conflict almost certain. This problem is nicely demonstrated in prison administration where rehabilitation and custodial goals may be pursued in the same prison at the same time, resulting in role conflict among those dealing directly with the prisoners.[22] But where the organization's policies are consistent, we may safely assume that its groups will often play an active role in legitimating them, particularly when their leaders have been "sold" on their rationality.

Conclusions

In sum, authority seems to grow out of a dynamic, reciprocal relationship between leader and led, in which the values, perceptions, and skills of followers play a critical role in defining and legitimating the authority of organizational leaders. Acceptance of authority rests essentially upon four interlocking bases: the technical expertise of the leader; his formal role or position in the organization's hierarchy; his rapport with subordinates or his ability to mediate their individual needs for security and recognition; and the subordinates' generalized deference toward authority, reflecting in turn the process of socialization.

Notes

1. This conception of authority is similar to Barnard's permissive concept, but it incorporates more limitations on the individual's influence over those who exercise authority, and it attempts to set down the bases upon which authority will be accepted. C. I. Barnard, *Functions of the Executive* (Harvard University Press, 1938).

2. Whyte, *Street Corner Society* (University of Chicago, 1958, revised edition). Those interested in field research will find Whyte's appendix on the research methods used in this study fascinating.

3. R. Lippitt, N. Polansky, and S. Rosen, "The Dynamics of Power," 5 *Human Relations* 44–50 (No. 1, 1952).

4. *Op. cit.,* pp. 163–169.

5. N. Kaplan, "The Role of the Research Administrator," 4 *Administrative Science Quarterly* 20–42 (June, 1959).

6. J. Block and J. Block, "An Interpersonal Experiment on Reactions to Authority," 5 *Human Relations* 91–98 (1952).

7. Both thematic apperception tests and the Berkeley ethnocentrism scale were used.

8. "Authority" in C. Arensberg (ed.), *Research in Industrial Human Relations* (Harper & Brothers, 1957), p. 106. Simon posits four bases for accepting authority: confidence (technical skill); social approval; sanctions; and legitimation. Legitimation is thus used in a different, and more restricted sense than here.

9. For an inquiry into this problem see Robert V. Presthus, "The Social Bases of Organization," 38 *Social Forces* 103–109 (December, 1959).

10. See Morris Janowitz, "Changes in Organizational Authority: The Military Establishment," 3 *Administrative Science Quarterly* 473–103 (March, 1939).

11. C. Wright Mills, *The Sociological Imagination* (Oxford University Press, 1959); Dwight MacDonald, *The Ford Foundation* (Reynal & Co., 1956).

12. A. Gouldner, "Cosmopolitans and Locals: Toward an Analysis of Latent Social Roles," 2 *Administrative Science Quarterly* 281–306; 440–480 (December, 1957, March, 1958).

13. Robert Michels, *Political Parties: A Study of Oligarchical Tendencies in Modern Democracy* (The Free Press, 1949).

14. R. P. French and R. Snyder, "Leadership and Interpersonal Power," in D. Cartwright (ed.), *Studies in Social Power* (University of Michigan Institute for Social Research, 1959), pp. 118–149.

15. "Tensions, Interpersonal and International" in H. Cantril (ed.), *Tensions That Cause Wars* (University of Illinois, 1930), p. 95.

16. For a detailed analysis of organizational behavior in a psychological context, see my forthcoming *The Organizational Society*.

17. H. J. Eysenck, *The Psychology of Politics* (Praeger, 1954), pp. 260–261; O. H. Mowrer, "Anxiety Reduction and Learning," 27 *Journal of Experimental Psychology* 497–516 (1940).

18. See footnotes 3 and 6; T. Leary, *Interpersonal Diagnosis of Personality* (Ronald Press Co., 1957).

19. See, for example, the well-known experiments of Sherif and Asch, reported in M. Sherif, *Outline of Social Psychology* (Harper & Brothers, 1952) and S. E. Asch, *Social Psychology* (Prentice-Hall, 1952).

20. E. Stotland, "Peer Groups and Reactions to Power Figures," in D. Cartwright (ed.), *Studies in Social Power*, pp. 53–68; W. G. Bennis and H. A. Shepard, "A Theory of Group Development," 9 *Human Relations* 415–437 (November, 1956).

21. A. Etzioni, "Authority Structure and Organizational Effectiveness," 4 *Administrative Science Quarterly* 43–67 (June, 1959).

22. D. R. Cressey, "Contradictory Directives in Complex Organizations," *Ibid.*, pp. 1–19.

24

THE EXISTENTIALIST EXECUTIVE

Anders Richter

The debacle of the Vietnam War has manifested a number of massive and startling effects, including the fall of the Johnson government four years after its great affirmation of power, a systemic weakening of the American economy, aggravation of the hostility of our Negro and poor citizens, and alienation of the best part of our youth. Now it has become apparent that these are not temporary fissures in the body politic, but that we are in a process of rapid change heralding the demise of American conservatism which, since 1898, has so successfully maintained the power and prosperity of a "have" nation. The revelations of the war—a supine Congress, a leadership incapable of change in ideology or behavior, indeed, all of the "Emperor-has-no-clothes" phenomena—have indicated a probability that this process will be revolutionary in character.

Revolution from the Top

A most remarkable figment of the present sociopolitical situation is that, if it comes, the revolution well may be from the top. It may be a peaceful revolution of the bureaucracy, in time to forestall a violent revolution from the bottom. I was moved to this surmise during eight weeks as a student execu-

Source: *Public Administration Review* 30(1970): 415–422.

464

tive at the Federal Executive Institute in Charlottesville, Virginia. In this gentlemanly ambience, successive classes of middleclass, middle-aged federal executives are steeped in a heady brew of iconoclastic portents. Though no solutions are prescribed, it is suggested that more temporary organizations will be created to deal with the problems of a rapidly changing environment. I concluded that traditional institutions, such as religion and family, will provide less support for normative choices, and that even the most basic values will be challenged in a fluid society. Rather than looking to given standards of value and behavior, the new executive will be forced to rely on his self-created norms and interests in coping with a world of change. It will follow that the personal responsibilities thus imposed will cause him to experience anxiety about himself and his actions. Though perhaps not intended, and though doubtless pragmatically derived, these notions nevertheless bear a close resemblance to those of existentialism.

In reading the existentialist literature 15 years after its first vogue in America, I discovered that one can descend in a line from the seminal philosophies through what is called both existential and humanistic psychology, directly into management texts. To do so is to take a plunge in obscure terms: *Dasein*—phenomenology—self-actualizing—eupsychian—proactivert. *Dasein* is interesting for its compound meaning: *Da,* meaning there, in this context referring to the human psyche, with *sein,* or being, which in German has the active meaning of becoming, posits the elemental detachment-involvement enigma (or absurdity) of human existence. One first wonders, what does the word existentialism mean? Sartre's classical definition, the cryptic "Existence precedes essence," is not very helpful for the bureaucrat. For the philosopher, it proposes subjectivity as the point of departure to experience and knowledge. The world is deduced from consciousness—is revealed in the play of light which is consciousness. Existence lies outside consciousness, while the human subject, itself in a state of "there-being," forms concepts about the world only through experience. The field between thought and the outside world is where the individual maneuvers in personal venture and experience. It is an area of fundamental ambiguity, where confusion reigns as to what is endogenous and what exogenous. This ambiguity, known to existentialists as the human condition, is inescapable; it is best met with the ancient and humanistic dogma "Know Thyself."

The reason our existential age is one of anxiety is that it is possible for man to suddenly and shudderingly perceive himself as object. He can die, and he is subject to chance. Existentialists call this a feeling of contingency. Religion is man's attempt to escape his contingency, but it won't wash: Nietzsche killed God in 1884. No matter: latter-day existentialists offer a positive antidote to despair. They say that consciousness is not passive, but is intentional—that it seeks out experience, as it were, and thus gives meaning to our percepts of the world. Our ability to do this is our inner freedom. Most of us, however, reject this freedom quite stringently, and allow our everyday consciousness to present the world to us in familiar stereotype. But insights, intuitions of our freedom and power, intrude continuously to tell us that our everyday consciousness is a deceiver. Moments of encompassing clarity, common though unpredictable, reveal the true nature of consciousness, as do psychedelic experiences which may be induced. They are called peak experiences by humanistic psychologists.

According to the existential psychiatrist Rollo May, man's psyche exhibits a decisive attitude toward existence. This allows the existentialists another striking cliche, i.e., decision precedes knowledge. That is, commitment is a necessary prerequisite for seeing the truth. "The points of commitment and decision are those where the dichotomy between being subject and object is overcome in the unity of readiness for action."[1]

Action

Now we have arrived at something the executive can grasp: the notion of action. In truth, existentialism, which is life view rather than doctrine, is the most activist of all philosophies. Sartre himself writes that "man is nothing else but what he makes of himself."[2] The key is man's conscious intentionality, for this is what commits him to action, and his actions determine what he is, his being. People (as opposed to machines) are uniquely self-activating; that is, they initiate the getting of knowledge from their environments, which knowledge leads to immediate and suitable actions. Where we fear to know, we fear to act, as with those Germans who chose to be ignorant of the Nazi persecutions of the Jews.

Men of action have long been our acknowledged leaders. In his appraisal of the leaders of antiquity, Machiavelli remarked that "they owed nothing to fortune but the opportunity which gave them matter to be shaped into what form they thought fit."[3] The ideal for modern public administration is leadership which assumes the responsibility of changing organizations through action, and which maintains the welfare of society by remaining considerate of the purposes and behavior of others.

The conscious separation from what exists and self-projection toward what is intended give the existentialists a definition of man's freedom. Such liberty is the indispensable condition of all action. It is not a property of human nature in the sense that I can excuse my actions as determined by human nature. Nor can I find religious sanctions for my actions if God is a cop-out and does not exist. Freedom, in short, is absolutely individual and unfettered. It thus bestows an awesome responsibility. Man is responsible for what he is, and determines what he is by his actions. This is difficult enough, but Sartre goes further, and says that when a man is responsible for himself, he is thereby responsible for all men. The doctrine of personal responsibility is inherently fraught with danger to the state, and while occasionally it is expounded by a disestablishmentarian such as Thoreau, it rarely finds its way into proclamations of government. One landmark exception was the determination of war guilt made by the Nuremberg Tribunal. "The official position of Defendants, whether as heads of State, or responsible officials in Government departments, shall not be considered as freeing them from responsibility, or mitigating punishment. . . . The fact that the Defendant acted pursuant to order of his Government or of a superior shall not free him from responsibility. . . ."[4] This is the stuff of existentialism, and of arresting significance to every executive engaged in execution of the United States war policy for Vietnam.

Choice

Throughout the existentialist literature, there is a dominant theme: choice. All leaders know the anguish of choice; Sartre gives the example of a military officer accepting responsibility for an attack—a responsibility to himself and to others which cannot be evaded. Failure to act is also choice, and the officer may choose to be a coward. That is, he is choosing his own being. There is no compulsion; if a man fails to act one way it is because he prefers certain other values, such as conformity or the good opinions of others. It is no good for Eichmann to say that he was not responsible for his acts; every administrator is fully responsible, for if he is passive it is because he has chosen passivity. The confrontation with choice is a never-ending, existential process. Choice and consciousness are one and the same thing.

What is the nature of choice? Optimism: even in times of the darkest uncertainty, our choices are the best that seem possible. And at those times when his goal beckons clearly, man is most enterprising and resourceful. Open-mindedness: the existentialist executive must be prepared to alter his choices as he receives fresh information from his environment. Empathy: on the basis of our own subjective feelings of making choices, we also impute choices to others. Finally, choice has the quality of altering the personality of the chooser. Observers of management frequently have discerned significant changes of behavior as a consequence of individuals making decisions. This has been marked especially within teams organized for so-called project systems, where involvement in decision making has resulted in personal commitments which produce high yields of output.

The management term for choice is decision making. A decision is required when something is blocking the intentionality of the administrator or the purposeful activity of the organization. Choices then must be made among different ways of dealing with the blockage. According to the management specialist Bertram Gross: "An important decision is invariably a huge cluster of sequential choices in which the earlier choices help determine the alternatives available."[5] He then contends that this can lead to a synergistic creativity, because the sequential steps lead to the formulation of significant new questions, which in turn create new and productive alternatives for the decision maker.

Are we federal executives conscious of our freedom to choose? The existential novelist Colin Wilson believes that all men would engage in more creative acts of conscious freedom if they were more aware of their elemental intentionality. Because of laziness and passivity, we submerge our freedom in the unconscious. We are then too secure, we become bored, and lose our sense of action. We make a habit of limited perception. We establish a high threshold of indifference to protect ourselves from disturbing events in our environment; but this is a fallacy, for the environment acting inexorably on man is a myth. As Sartre says: "The environment can act on the subject only to the exact extent that he comprehends it; that is, transforms it into a situation."[6]

The federal bureaucrat finds many excuses for his rejection of choice. He is uncomfortable with intentionality, and lacks even good ordinary language to deal with organizational purposes; hence, the glittering generalities in which official purposes are typically phrased. The true purposes of the organization often are submerged beneath what management analysts call code observance. This is most pronounced in hierarchical organizations, where the code seems to require different behavior from individuals at different levels. Code compliance is manifested in either a grim or a bland, but always a tenacious, attachment to the system. The watchwords cooperation, extended to support of the status quo, and feasibility are invoked repeatedly to stifle deviant action. In recent years, still another excuse has succored the passive bureaucrat; the myth that man is a creature of technology. But the Great Blackout of 1965 was caused by man's inaction, not by technology. Seymour Melman argues that political interests, not technical requirements, have determined the character of our military establishment as well as the very design of its weapons: "A most important demonstration of the socially determined nature of technology was the decision by the United States in 1961 to build an overkill force of over 1,000 intercontinental ballistic missiles."[7]

Perhaps the most persistent bureaucratic cop-out is the old Pendleton Act principle about elected officials making policy, while appointed officials only execute. The appointed agency head who is an energetic policy maker, but who cannot translate his decisions into action through an inert career (i.e., Civil Service-protected) management, is in a familiar Washington pickle. Increasingly common is the converse situation, in which an activist middle-level manager is frustrated in his desire to execute a legislated program by the repressive forces of Congress or his agency superiors. One augury of the bureaucratic revolution is that Nader obtains much of his evidence of program failure from individuals engaged in program execution. It is reasonable to suppose that federal executives soon will attempt their own Nader-style identifications of breakdowns and will seek political support for their remedial actions.

Objectivity

A behavior of choice imposes on its practitioners a sense of objectivity—a more or less exact appreciation of where-I-am-now and how-I-can-get-where-I-am-going. This requires a certain discipline in viewing one's impulses from above. It requires, also, a hardnosed acceptance of the fact that one is the way one acts. For example, Sartre tells us that there is no such thing as a cowardly constitution;[8] a man makes himself a coward by his acts, and is fully responsible for his cowardice. For the individual, objectivity means an understanding of the consequences of one's behavior; for the organization, it means a critical examination of its culture, that is, the values and processes which have been created and are maintained in its environment. No organization can isolate itself, for its very members are individuals drawn from the environment who impose their values on the organization.

The enemy of true reality is ultrapracticality. The managerial class has long given its homage to pragmatism; the method of prior formulation, recurrent testing, and optimal decision making. Such scientism is inevitably impersonal, because models formulated for testing cannot encompass the complexities of people problems which, accordingly, are considered unprofessional. Hence, large-scale organizations tend to lose, both inside and outside, their rapport with people—that is, their objectivity. Those who would uphold people interests are dismissed as utopians, while decision making is delegated to experts. Alas, how often have these experts—be they highway engineers, economists, or geopoliticians—made the wrong choices? The expert's refuge and security is in rationalism. When threatened by the chaotic world-as-it-is, he defines his terms, states his assumptions, applies his rigorous logic, and sticks by his conclusions through the thin of aloof superiority and the thick of catastrophic failure. Thus has it been with Vietnam, both in the high reaches of the National Security Council and in the hamlets, where the second looey, entrapped at the end of someone else's logic train, could rationalize that "we had to destroy that village in order to save it." The old Whiteheadian aphorism is ever apt: "Life is larger than logic."

Following a book of rules may result in the most bizarre irrationalities because it suppresses recognition of nonroutine problems. It is irrational, also, to believe that administrators can conduct their affairs in the same manner that scientists conduct research. Indeed, there is much hogwash even concerning the infallibility of the scientific-technological process, in which there is at all times a good deal of magic. In physics, Heisenberg's uncertainty principle has demonstrated a fundamental limit to our ability to know or predict the world of matter; while in mathematics, queen of the sciences and the very fount of rationalism, Godel's upsetting theorem has presented us with ultimate conditions of absolute insolubility. Man cannot escape his finitude, or give over his problems to a giant computing machine.

The words of Gross are especially useful in laying the myth of administrative rationality:

> Because of its multidimensionality, there are few administrators capable of considering the rationality of an organization's entire purpose pattern. . . . Moreover, no matter what elements they may be concerned with, most administrators develop a personal style of comparative weighting among desirability, feasibility, and consistency. . . . When there are enough administrators in an organization to provide complementary representation for these various dimensions of reality, the conditions are ripe for the synthesis of these limited approaches into a broader pattern of rational action. Such a synthesis usually comes, it may be added, not in technical documents or in policy conferences *but in the heat of action itself.*[9]

I have added the italics, because this culminating phrase is purely existential.

A behavior of choice requires further of the executive a willingness to take risks which is endowed, in many cases, by a sense of commitment— but not of commitment to the organization. Bailey, after questioning two dozen company presidents, found them remarkably disposed to put their jobs on the line in support of important decisions.[10] Moreover, this readiness to accept consequences seemed to give the presidents an inner serenity, as if it were an ultimate safety valve allowing them to labor over critical problems free of anxiety for their personal futures. Less and less, in the society of American organizations, do professionals and executives see their careers in terms of one firm or agency. And, in choosing to join or leave an organization, the existentialist executive is more and more governed by the values and purposes upheld by the organization.

Yet a host of federal bureaucrats remain limited in their freedom to make choices by devotion to job security. Indeed, many of our bureaucratic evils—conformity, flight from conflict, code observance, the myth that administrators do not make policy—may be rooted in the fear of job loss. An entrenched system of legislated tenure allows the career administrator in the federal government to be secure in his job and in his passivity; he may raise higher the safe walls of everyday consciousness. It means, further, that he is pseudo-separated from the consequences of his acts. By bland non-compliance and inaction, or through cynicism, the federal bureaucrat can and does subvert changes promoted by political appointees, thus mindlessly and free of risk perpetuating his habit of routine and boredom. Yet in so doing, he paradoxically subverts his own standard of nonauthority for policy making; for, even as the existentialists say, he cannot evade the responsibility of his choices: by demolishing policy, he makes policy.

Authenticity

Perhaps the prime quality of a behavior of choice is what the existentialists call authenticity. Wilson writes that "authenticity is to be driven by a deep sense of purpose," in awareness of "a standard of values external to everyday human consciousness."[11] In more homely terms, it is behaving the way you are, in place of posing in a role. It means getting rid of irrelevant emotional garbage which, in Freudian context, is usually associated with the past; existentialists start with the here-and-now. It means honesty about one's self, and directness with others. Authenticity is telling it like it is. The management analysts Beatrice and Sydney Rome have derived, from their Leviathan methodology, a description of the authentic organization:

> A hierarchical organization in short, like an individual person, is "authentic" to the extent that, throughout its leadership, it accepts its finitude, uncertainty, and contingency; realizes its capacity for responsibility and choice: acknowledges guilt and errors; fulfills its creative managerial potential for flexible planning, growth, and . . . policy formation; and responsibly participates in the wider community.[12]

The psychologist Abraham Maslow refers to "living by illusions" as a sickness which is widely shared.[13] One cannot live in Washington. D.C., without feeling depressed by the prevailing phoniness of federal officialdom. There is an essential arrogance in bureaucratic behavior (though frequently its actors attempt to mask it with servilities to "the taxpayer"), for what often provides administrators with feelings of importance is their provision of services, not the need of others for them. In truth, the inauthentic bureaucrat is a pitiable hypocrite. According to the psychologist Hubert Bonner:

> In him the anxiety which is the lot of all of us is a function not of his awareness of life's imperfectibility or of the awesomeness of human choice but of the fear that others will see through his counterfeit choice. . . . He cannot choose or make decisions, for these entail risk regarding the unpredictable future.[14]

The present aspect of Washington is bleak, but the situation is ripe for the revolution from the top. That the contemporary literature of management is suffused with existentialism is only an indication of the historical forces which presently favor rapid change. According to Sartre's interpreter, H. J. Blackham:

> When there is prevailing confidence in established values and authorities, the primordial, absolute, and solitary responsibility of the individual is regarded either as a meaningless platitude or as a dangerous thought: in less settled times, it may come vividly home to some as a sharp and searching truth.[15]

These are less settled times. The nation is imperiled. Those who scoff at the suggestion of violent social revolution are retreating from the signs. Much more are we threatened with the extinction of our species.

> The assumed inevitability, probability or possibility of a third world war has become a guilding principle for the operations of a very considerable number of members of directorates, top managers, bureaucrats, and trade union leaders. This possibility is so much taken for granted that people who talk about the necessity for peace or disarmament are looked upon with a suspicion. . . .[16]

The fact that Gross wrote this in 1964 is itself cause for hope, because it seems less true today. A grand abstraction, such as peace, gains strength in the polity when its relationship to survival is so immediate. It is a truism that the citizenry become concerned about government to a greater degree when the state fails to serve basic human needs. The challenge of survival is not for the United States Congress, which has lost its republican character and abdicated its responsibility to curb a reckless Executive. In such an institutional vacuum, an enlightened class of federal administrators may achieve a new estate. The federal establishment must descend into the hands of gifted generalists whose expertise resides in the ability to improvise in the presence of a superb new technology. We must discover proactive administrators who possess the objectivity with which to make responsible choices. The fact is, existentialism emphasizes many human qualities which can be identified with traditional virtues, which is further cause for optimism. Energy, the characteristic of the man of action: honesty; sense of responsibility; committedness—such attributes are not likely to be rejected by the conventional ethics of the American public.

Even more will an existentialist revolution in government appeal to the present young generation who are the coming executive class. Young men and women, in an increasing degree, reject money as the measure of achievement. Many young intellectuals will reject academia for its inability to act, or because of its corruption of scholarly prerogatives with opportunism. Many will continue to choose the professions, but many more than in the part will go where the action is, into government, the arena of greatest confrontation with problems of moment and opportunity for effective action. They will bring with them a strong infusion of existentialist values—most emphatically a commitment to action, a readiness to accept the consequences of their acts, and an abhorrence of phoniness. These qualities are evident in today's campus rebels, and they will be the motive forces for the revolution of the bureaucracy.

The prospect of our government in the hands of such innerdirected administrators may be disquieting for the average American. What saving social ethic is present to curb these self-actualizing choice makers? Ernest Hemingway is said to have remarked that "morality is what you feel good about after you've done it, and immorality is what you feel bad about after you've done it." Does the ethic of existentialist choice reduce to that?

Tolerance

Existentialism is not a prescriptive behavior for the individual, nor is it a social doctrine. Tolerance, following choice, is a second keystone of existentialism. The existentialists are not dedicated to conversion; they only seek liberation of the individual by showing him his essential freedom and by eliminating the poison of moralism. The concept of Moral Law is inimical to existentialism, for that way lies coercion and the evil of dictatorism. "Indeed," writes May, "compulsive and rigid moralism arises in given persons precisely as the result of a lack of sense of being."[17] If, instead, man is aware of his elemental purposiveness, he instinctively acts in protest against the present and its values. He especially rejects the value of social conformity, which often is no more than a false mode of self-esteem. This emphatically does not mean, however, that existentialism is unlimited self-gratification (which is, in the final analysis, like moralism conducive to personal aggrandizement and tyranny). Existential philosophy is explicitly attentive to the freedom of others. Sartre writes:

> in wanting freedom, we discover that it depends entirely on the freedom of others, and that the freedom of others depends on ours. . . . Consequently, when, in all honesty, I've recognized that man is a being in whom existence precedes essence, that he is a free being who, in various circumstances, can only want his freedom. I have at the same time recognized that I can only want the freedom of others.[18]

Philosophically, an individual's freedom is limited by his condition as an object to others. Simone de Beauvoir states it thus: "to be free is not to have the power to do anything you like; it is to be able to surpass the given toward an open future; the existence of others as a freedom defines my situation and is even the condition of my own freedom."[19] Yet—and this is the critical paradox—recognition of the freedom of others does not in itself limit one's own freedom. The limitations are present in the given interpersonal condition; they are not imposed by others as prohibitions, and every man is free to realize himself through his experience.

The existentialist executive makes his own choices, and at the highest level this has been seen as the "terrible isolation" of the American presidency. But, in the process, various and contending interests are weighted. Gross writes that one of the great virtues of making choices is that, in the act, "a magic common denominator is somehow or other found that cuts across all the pro's and con's. . . ."[20] The usual means of resolving conflict through decision making is not by relying on compromise alone, but by widening the agenda of attention to encompass a new basis for the solution. For this reason the generalist, better than the expert, will fill the role of proactive administrator, a role which requires a broad perspective toward life and a varied acquaintance with the total environment. Some assurance has been obtained from empirical studies of proactive people which show, according to Maslow, that they are "quite spontaneously identified with the human species, with other people," and that they are "especially concerned with duty, with responsibility," and "with a kind of intrinsic ethics or morality which they do not learn by precept. . . . These characteristics appear as a by-product of their personalities, as an epiphenomenon. It would appear that it is not necessary to teach these virtues."[21] If this is true, then Hemingway's definition of morality, though illogical because it assumes moral people, may be applicable to existentialist administrators.

In respect to organizations, the Romes tested their hypothesis that "authentic organizations" are more effective than others in system performance. "On the basis of evidence," they wrote, "it appears that our hypothesis . . . has received preliminary but vivid experimental corroboration."[22]

Every person within an organization is responsible for his own choices. Personal responsibility is, however, multidirectional. The nexus of personal responsibilities and behavior is the determinant of moral tone throughout the organization. It is a huge leap of understanding to think that federal executives may literally preserve the planet by discarding pseudo-attitudes and phony behavior—as a beginning, at least. The existential proactivert will readily believe it, and act on it.

Notes

1. Rollo May (co-ed.), *Existence: A New Dimension in Psychiatry and Psychology* (New York: Basic Books, 1958). p. 88.

2. Jean-Paul Sartre, *Existentialism and Human Emotions* (New York: Philosophical Library, 1957), p. 15.

3. Niccolo Machiavelli, *The Prince* (Oxford: Oxford University Press, 1906), chapter VI.

4. *Trial of the Major War Criminals before the International Military Tribunal,* (Nuremberg: International Military Tribunal, 1947). Volume 1. pp. 223–224.

5. Bertram M. Gross, *The Managing of Organizations* (Glencoe: The Free Press, 1964), p. 764.

6. Sartre, *op. cit.,* p. 77.

7. Seymour Melman, "Who Decides Technology?" *Columbia University Forum* (Winter 1968).

8. Sartre, *op. cit.,* p. 34.

9. Gross, *op. cit.,* p. 757.

10. Joseph C. Bailey, "Clues for Success in the President's Job." *Harvard Business Review,* 1967.

11. Colin Wilson, *Introduction to the New Existentialism* (Boston: Houghton, Mitflin and Co., 1967), p. 153.

12. Beatrice and Sydney Rome, "Humanistic Research on Large Social Organizations." in James F. T. Bugental (ed.), *Challenges of Humanistic Psychology* (New York: McGraw Hill and Co., 1967). p. 185.

13. Abraham Maslow, *Toward a Psychology of Being* (New York: D. Van Nostrand Co., 2nd edition. 1968), p. 16.

14. Hubert Bonner, "The Proactive Personality," in James F. T. Bugental, *op. cit.,* p. 64.

15. H. J. Blackham. *Six Existentialist Thinkers* (London: Routledge and Kegan Paul, 1952). p. 155.

16. Gross, *op. cit.,* p. 87.

17. May, *op. cit.,* p. 45.

18. Sartre, *op. cit.,* pp. 45–46.

19. Simone de Beauvoir, *The Ethics of Ambiguity* (New York: Philosophical Library, 1948), p. 91.

20. Gross, *op. cit.,* p. 531.

21. Abraham Maslow, "Power Relationships and Personal Development," in A. Kornhauser (ed.), *Problems of Power in American Democracy* (Detroit: Wayne State University Press, 1957).

22. Rome and Rome, *op. cit.,* p. 192.

25

THE MANAGEMENT OF
SOCIAL TRANSFORMATION

David C. Korten

Human societies around the globe are experiencing a growing sense of crisis as economic growth rates decline, inflation soars, environmental deterioration accelerates, the gap between rich and poor persists, and continued rapid population growth increases the pressures on already strained systems. In the process the legitimacy of many of society's institutions is increasingly called into question. Many of these problems transcend national boundaries and political ideologies.[1]

The central issues are poverty, ecology, and the inability of present human institutions to provide a decent livelihood for all of human kind in a manner which both sustains fragile ecosystems and allows for continued growth of the human spirit. The failures transcend political philosophy, revealing themselves in both capitalistic and socialistic systems. No nation, rich or poor, escapes the realities which call for attention to the issues of social transformation. The high income, industrialized nations face the reality that the spatial distribution of their populations, the structure of their productive systems, and their patterns and levels of material consumption are dependent on the extravagant exploitation of non-renewable resources

Source: *Public Administration Review* 41(1981): 609–618.

at levels which are unsustainable in a finite world even in the relatively short run.

The low income, pre-industrial nations face poverty as their dominant social reality. Rapid population growth, the struggle for survival, and the quest for development place increasing strain on fragile ecosystems, destroying croplands and watersheds on which the livelihoods of both present and future generations depend. Generally such nations are committed by national policy to achieving social transformations intended to alleviate these conditions. Yet, the tragic irony is that the models of transformation chosen, with few exceptions, have been based on the experience and structures of the presently industrialized nations, models which are in themselves unsustainable. To the extent that pre-industrial nations remain committed to such models they are engaged in a quest which over the long term is futile, even self-defeating, no matter how successful they may be in obtaining greater resource transfers from the wealthier nations.

The partially industrialized nations face the dilemmas of both the industrial and the pre-industrialized nations. They have affluent, modernized sectors built on models of questionable sustainability while simultaneously facing the reality that major portions of their populations live in dehumanizing poverty with little realistic prospect for achieving the advancement they increasingly come to see as a basic human right.

The modernization of human society has been accompanied by a sharp dichotomization of the individual's public and private lives. "Public life" is that portion in which decisions are dominated by what Berger and Neuhaus have labeled megastructures, which include the modern state, the large economic conglomerates of both capitalist and socialist enterprise, big labor, and the governmental bureaucracies that administer major sectors of society's affairs. Massive and impersonal they seem to take on a life of their own that transcends human will, revealing a need to suppress individuality, initiative, and creative innovation in the interest of bureaucratic convenience. Both individual and societal needs become subverted to institutional need—the servant becomes the master. The individual becomes increasingly dependent for a sense of uniqueness and personal significance on what remains as his or her "private life," the "unorganized" sector in which he is free to organize his life around particular needs and preferences which are the basis of individuality.[2]

The alienation growing out of a sense of powerlessness in the face of the dominance of one's life by unresponsive megastructures is revealed even in traditionally democratic societies in the loss of confidence in once revered institutions. While representative democracy continues to provide protection against the more visibly oppressive forms of tyranny, it is insufficient, especially given the power of these megastructures, to provide the individual with a sense of meaningful participation in decisions important to his or her life. An individual vote, as important as it is, hardly expresses the richness of individual preferences and is a poor substitute for more direct participation of the type possible only in community level forums.

The Directions of Social Transformation

Numerous individuals and institutions are searching for new visions of the post-industrial society based on structures which meet the criteria of sustainability, equity, well-being, and participation. Toffler, among others, argues that the sustainable post-industrial society will be based on exploitation of the one resource that is inexhaustible—information and the human capacity for creative imagination.[3] The structures of its social institutions must be designed with the intent of gaining fullest advantage of the potentials of this resource. This is basic not only to sustainable and equitable material well-being, but to the non-material advancement of human kind as well.

Toward the end of rehumanizing society, Berger and Neuhaus suggest policy actions to strengthen the role of intermediate, human scale institutions such as the family, the neighborhood, the self-managing work group, the voluntary association, which perform a mediating role between individual and megastructure, providing a source of personal support and recognition, and facilitating local problem solving and creative innovation.[4] Stobes argues that ultimately, even most problems of global scope can be resolved only through creative local action.

> Many of the most successful efforts to solve global problems already take place at the local level. In the United States, home gardeners stretch their food budgets by up to 10 percent; in some socialist countries, private-plot agriculture provides one-quarter of many families' income. Self-help housing saves American homeowners one-quarter to one-half on construction costs and in the developing world, provides millions of homes. Self-health care cuts hospital admissions in half for some chronic illnesses, while basic preventive health measures reduce the incidence of coronary heart disease and cancer in industrial countries and of dysentery and parasitic infections in the Third World. Simple housing design changes that adapt homes to climate conditions reduce heating bills by 50 percent in industrial countries. Solar energy provides much of the power for Chinese villages. All these initiatives are decentralized and participatory. Their successes are the product of direct action by individuals and communities.[5]

One key to the sustainable society is to reestablish the individual's lost sense of intimacy with and responsibility for his or her local community and its natural environment.

The answer rests not in abolishing society's megastructures since they are basic to the functioning of any modern society. Rather it rests in substantially reforming them, in loosening central control and strengthening the feedback systems that increase potentials for self-direction and direct participation at local levels in ways consistent with the well-being of the larger society. It will be necessary to move beyond more primitive forms of bureaucratic organization, able only to control or to substitute for local level action, to substantially more sophisticated forms which can work to strengthen capacities for creative local self-help action and self-control. Though most calls for greater reliance on local level solutions to global problems look to such action as a substitute for bureaucratic action, it is neither so easy to dismiss their stifling regulatory power or to achieve effective problem solving on the scale required without access to their massive resources. As concluded in the introduction to a recent series of studies on bureaucracy:

> Although many critically important problems face us today, most of the problems as well as proposals for their solutions are defined and shaped in bureaucratic organizations. . . . Our capacity to understand and modify bureaucracy in the present decade will greatly determine our capacity to solve our problems and thus shape the decades to come.[6]

The Search for a New Paradigm to Guide Human Advancement

The progress of the era of human evolution from which the world is now emerging was guided by a powerful paradigm, a product largely of Western thought and experience, which shaped the dominant images of the nature and direction of societal development, dictated the definition of the problems to which policy attention was directed, and spawned sophisticated methodologies for guiding human choice in directions consistent with its underlying premises. Harman has summarized the dominant characteristics of this paradigm as follows:

- Development and application of scientific method; wedding of scientific and technological advance
- Industrialization through organization and division of labor; machine replacement of human labor
- Acquisitive materialism; work ethic; economic-man image; belief in unlimited material progress and in technological and economic growth
- Man seeking control over nature; positivistic theory of knowledge: manipulative rationality as a dominant theme

- Individual responsibility for own destiny; freedom and equality as
  fundamental rights; nihilistic value perspective, individual
  determination of the "good"; society as an aggregation of
  individuals pursuing their own interests.[7]

This paradigm for all its limitations has been an important driving force
in the advancement of human society. But the very progress which it
spawned has resulted in important changes in the human reality such that
the paradigm itself has become a threat rather than a guide to further human advancement. Harman delineates new factors which render the old
paradigm obsolete:

- Interconnectedness, so that laissez-faire approaches are less
  workable
- Reduction of geographical and entrepreneurial frontier
  opportunities
- Approaching limits of natural recycling capabilities
- A sharpened dichotomy between "employed" and "unemployed"
  through gradual elimination of the informal sector, placing
  excessive demands on the formal sector for job creation
- Substantial advances in the living standards of a fraction of the
  population, highlighting the gap between rich and poor and
  creating expectations which exceed the limits of the system
- Transition from a basic condition of labor scarcity to one of job
  scarcity
- Approaching limits of some resources
- Faustian powers of technology and industrialization that have
  reached the point where they can have a major impact on the
  physical, technological, sociopolitical, and psychological
  environment.[8]

The persistence of the old paradigm, even in the face of accumulating evidence of its limitations, is a reflection of the extent to which it has become
embedded not only in individual value systems and institutional structures,
but also in the available frameworks and methodologies which dominate
problem identification and solution processes at both individual and institutional levels.[9] While progress has been made in articulating alternative
value systems, and in demonstrating new lifestyles and technologies, these
have only marginally influenced the dominant decision-making frameworks and methodologies. Little attention has been given to the formulation, testing, and institutionalization of operational alternatives based on a
fundamental reorientation in perspective dictated by the new human reality. Two dimensions of this reorientation in paradigm are of particular im-

portance. One involves the distinction between scientific knowledge and social knowledge. In both, the orientation of the industrial era paradigm has been largely a product of Western thought and experience. The new orientations are likely to be more consonant with the traditions of Eastern thought and experience which tend toward a more holistic view of life and a search for a harmonious relationship between man and nature.

Open-System Economics Versus Closed-System Economics

This deals with a distinction between two fundamentally different ways of viewing the design and performance of society's production-consumption systems, first introduced by Boulding in a now classic paper.[10]

Open-System Economics. In open-system economics the environment of the economic system is treated as an "externality," i.e., external to the analysis on which decisions are based. Though recognizing the role of scarcity value in pricing, the "real" cost of resource inputs to the economic system is presumed to be only the costs incurred in their extraction. Similarly the costs of waste disposal are also externalized. Wastes are simply dumped into the environment, which is presumed to dispose of them costlessly. Thus Boulding's apt and colorful label:

> The "cowboy economy," the cowboy being symbolic of the illimitable plains and also associated with reckless, exploitative romantic, and violent behavior, which is characteristic of open [economic-systems] societies. . . . In the cowboy economy, consumption is regarded as a good thing and production likewise; and the success of the economy is measured by the amount of the throughput from the "factors of production," a part of which, at any rate, is extracted from the reservoirs of raw materials and non-economic objects, and another part of which is output into reservoirs of pollution.[11]

The primary criterion for measuring the performance of the open-systems economy is the level of total throughput, essentially what is measured as Gross National Product—a presumed surrogate for human well-being. Consistent with the frontier mentality, the open-system economy operates according to the principle of survival of the fittest. Rather than presuming a common destiny, it involves what Garret Hardin has characterized as "lifeboat ethics," which divides the world into survivors and non-survivors, and sees first to maintaining the comfort and security of the survivors.

The models of open-system economics dominate the tools of economic analysis and decision making, keeping the focus of development efforts on the expansion of the modern economy while externalizing environmental and social costs and significantly discounting the future. The results for developing countries are especially tragic as the logic of open-system economics creates a substantial bias toward capital and energy intensive investments which hold no prospect of providing for the employment needs of rapidly growing populations[12] and are in addition likely to be competitive with the informal sector on which the vast majority of the population depends for its livelihood.[13] There is a special irony in the bias toward displacement of the informal sector, as among the main characteristics of the informal sector is the substitution of human labor for energy and capital and a reliance on recycling as a primary source of raw materials.[14] The planning methods of open-systems economics also create biases toward urban concentrations which can be sustained only through intensive and increasingly costly energy subsidies,[15] costs which are also largely externalized in the investment calculations of open-systems economics.

Successful as open-systems economics has been in guiding the development of powerful industrial giants and in providing an unprecedented material quality of life for a substantial minority of the world's population, it has become evident that this success has been dependent on energy and ecosystems subsidies, the limits of which have nearly been reached.[16]

Closed-System Economics. The basic conceptual frame of reference of closed-system economics is best presented by Boulding's analogy of the spaceship.[17] Aside from the input of solar energy, it is a closed system which contains all resources which will be available during the course of its journey. Disposal outside the spaceship's boundaries permanently reduces the resources available for reuse and is not undertaken lightly. The measure of life-support system performance is the state of the bodies and minds of the ship's inhabitants, not the rate of throughput. Key goals in system design are to minimize the levels of production and consumption necessary to maintain the desired states of physical and mental health. Thus throughput is minimized to reduce energy expenditures and carefully regulated so as not to exceed the capacity of recycling systems to return wastes to useful resource stocks.

The sustainability of post-industrial society depends on learning to live in balance with the natural life-support systems of planet earth. Movement toward such a balance will require a new economics based on what Boulding calls "spaceman" economics. This suggests: (1) new models for the design of closed production-consumption systems in which wastes and discards are the primary inputs for new production; and (2) decision tools which lead to more direct assessment of choices in terms of their impact on natural resource stocks (including natural recycling capacity) and contributions to human well-being, rather than their contribution to increased throughput.

Scientific Knowledge Versus Social Knowledge

This distinction deals with alternative ways of perceiving the nature of knowledge, in particular the processes by which knowledge is generated and utilized. The central problem is the presumption that the frames of reference and methodologies which have contributed so substantially to the technological advance of human society are equally relevant to the solution of its social problem.[18]

Scientific Knowledge. The methods of modern Western science have been based on a process of analytic reductionism which proceeds by reducing complex problems into component parts for individual study, isolating causality through experimental and quasi-experimental methods, placing the researcher in the role of objective observer, and limiting inquiry to those effects which are observable and measurable. The underlying presumption is of a universe that works according to mechanical (nonpurposive) principles of behavior. Continuous preoccupation with the refinement of methodologies for isolating causality makes the creation of scientific knowledge a highly self-conscious process. The generation of scientific knowledge is presumed to be quite separate from and to take place prior to its application.

In its application, the relationships or laws discovered through scientific inquiry are applied to the design of deterministic or machine like systems designed to amplify human behavior. The design of such systems is engineered by specialists who assume the posture of external manipulators of physical phenomena. Where value choices are involved the concern at the design stage is only with instrumental values or efficiency criteria.[19]

This paradigm has in recent years been transferred from the realm of the physical sciences to that of social problem solving, forming the basis of what Wildavsky refers to as the "intellectual cognition" school of public policy.[20] Its underlying approach to complex social problems, such as changing women's roles, leads to their being broken down into discrete components and reduced to questions such as: Would the investment of public funds in day care be cost-effective? Defined in such terms the problems seem mainly to involve a matter of technical computation, an appropriate assignment for a technical analyst located at levels of the bureaucracy far removed from the people to whose needs the analysis is directed. The analyst is charged with refining the definition of the problem, identifying action alternatives such as whether to provide subsidies for private day care centers or maintain a system of publicly managed centers, estimating the costs and benefits of each alternative action, arriving at a preferred solution, and preparing an implementation plan—all before any action begins. The process is not much different than that involved in designing a bridge or other physical structure. Once the plan is prepared the responsibility of the planner ends, and action is turned over to an implementing agency—in the social realm usually a government bureaucracy—which is supposed to act faithfully according to the blueprint provided by the planner.[21]

But when so applied in the social realm the scientific knowledge paradigm has proven less than adequate[22]—perhaps in part because of the complexity and interdependence of the phenomena involved and in part because human behavior involves both values and purpose—complicating features not found in most machines.[23] Indeed the substantial preoccupation with attempting to transfer the scientific knowledge paradigm from the physical to the social realm may be a major contributor to the frustrating lack of success being experienced by human societies around the globe in coming to grips with what Botkin *et al.* refer to as the "human gap"—the gap between the growing complexity of human society and our ability to cope with it.[24]

Furthermore, by the implicit presumption of value consensus on efficiency criteria where the social reality is one of diverse values and interests, implementation of policies which are the product of such a planning process leads to a necessary reliance on essentially coercive measures to achieve bottom-up compliance with top-down direction, contributing to alienation and stifling the creative local initiative on which the real solutions to complex social problems usually depend.[25]

In the developing countries the application of the scientific knowledge paradigm is manifested in widely accepted development management methodologies which attempt to reduce social problem solving to the preparation by technicians, often foreigners on short-term assignment, of project blueprints. One result of the methodology is the virtual exclusion from meaningful participation in the decision making by those who will be responsible for implementation, to say nothing of the local people who are the presumed beneficiaries. The almost inevitable result is programs which are poorly executed and ill-suited to the needs of the intended beneficiaries.[26] Still another consequence of the methodology, as manifest in both developed and developing countries, is a tendency to treat every social problem as a problem in the allocation of public funds, even where the problem is predominantly organizational rather than financial in nature, as in the day care example noted above.[27]

Social Knowledge. The concepts and methods underlying the development and application of knowledge of social systems must reflect the special nature of those systems. These include their continuously changing, internal relationships; the difficulties of observing, measuring, and categorizing social behavior; the purposive nature of human choice making; and the importance and diversity of individual human value preferences. A social system is not a simple summation of its parts and its variables cannot be isolated for individual study without substantial loss of information essential to understanding the whole. Thus the insights which can be gained from breaking a social problem down into its component parts are seldom as useful as those which emerge by trying to understand the parts in terms of their relationship to the larger systemic context—a synthetic process basically the antithesis of the reductionist analytic methods of conventional science. Efforts to break social problems into distinct components for separate treatment are likely to result in treating symptoms rather than underlying causes.

The application of social knowledge is further complicated by the reality that the instruments as well as the ends of social action are themselves social systems, ill-defined, purposeful and resistant to manipulation. Scientific knowledge transfers with comparative ease from scientific papers and the heads of experts to blueprint drawings which are the guides to action in manipulation of the physical world. But the usable blueprints for social action are not found on pieces of paper. They are found deeply imbedded in the value systems and structures of the action taking agency. This is the only truly useful social knowledge, as it represents potentials for institutional action. Until social knowledge is translated into this form it does not represent a usable potential. And it does not transfer easily from scientific papers and the heads of individual experts to these institutional "blueprints." The latter are the products of the collective experience of the organization and its members in dealing with innumerable real life problems and in adjusting to new contingencies as they arise. They are not easily changed, except through the long painful process of acquiring and assimilating new experience—a process of *social learning*.

It is through such social learning processes that useful social knowledge is both acquired and applied—simultaneously. It is a process in which the social specialist can perform an important facilitating role, but in which he or she is seldom the central actor.

The key to social learning is not analytical method, but organizational process; and the central methodological concern is not with the isolation of variables or the control of bureaucratic deviations from centrally defined blueprints, but with effectively engaging the necessary participation of system members in contributing to the collective knowledge of the system and in generating policy choices out of what Wildavsky refers to as a *social interaction* process.[28] The more complex the problem and the greater the number of value perspectives brought to bear, the greater the need for localized solutions and for value innovations, both of which call for broadly based participation in decision processes. The social knowledge paradigm leads quite naturally to a search for system structures which facilitate local level decision making through exchange and bargaining processes involving many minds, structures able to gain full advantage of the creative potentials of the system's many members.

In applying the concept of social learning to the problem of social transformation it is important to address the distinction made by Botkin *et al.* between *maintenance learning* and *innovative learning*.[29] The former is the common everyday learning in which most social systems are continuously engaged—a process which is largely unconscious and accommodated by the normal management systems of a healthy organization. It involves learning within the framework of an established paradigm. Social transformation, however, calls for innovative learning which is directed to creating new values, structures, and problem formulations. The mechanisms for managing such learning are rarely incorporated into the structures of large organizations. Yet it is the ability to manage such learning in innumerable individual institutions as a conscious purposeful activity which human society desperately needs in order to negotiate successfully the transformation to a post-industrial form.

The barriers to development of such capacity are substantial. First the large bureaucracies and related organizing structures—the megastructures—that dominate life in modern society and which must be the focal points for innovative social learning have become so large and powerful in their own right that they seem almost to have taken on lives of their own, unresponsive to human redirection. Second the methodologies for managing innovative social learning as a conscious process in such institutions are poorly developed and the skills relevant to their development and application are in short supply.

The paradigm which guides the creation and utilization of scientific knowledge places great value on order, precision, and external manipulation and control. The management methods which are an outgrowth of this paradigm place great value on these same attributes, especially preplanning, order, quantification, and external control.

Social learning is by nature a messy, even chaotic process in which error and unpredicted outcomes are routine. Central management can facilitate and structure the learning process to set its general direction and accelerate its progress. It can even anticipate that as learning progresses, error rates will fall and predictions improve, but efforts to eliminate error or to lay stress on detailed preplanning and central control would presume both existing knowledge and a capacity to utilize it that seldom exist in the social realm and would eliminate the very learning on which effective action depends.[30]

Thus, the methods for managing social learning must emphasize central facilitation over central control, performance monitoring and self-correction over preplanning, and reflect a tolerance for the ambiguity and uncertainty which are inherent in the social learning process. Similarly they should encourage local initiative and self-control, suggesting a substantial emphasis on strengthening information systems which provide local level performance feedback.[31] The purpose here is not to detail the nature of the management systems involved, but rather to make clear that the management style and methods involved bear little resemblance to those which are an outgrowth of the scientific paradigm. To speak of managing learning processes does not imply central authoritarian direction and detailed pre-planning!

Conceptually the management of social learning involves linking knowledge, power, and people in ways which simultaneously generate new knowledge, new benefits, and new action potentials as integral outcomes of a single process. Operationally it involves the facilitation by top management of local level experimentation as a basis for gradual evolution of agency policies, structures, and management systems.[32]

If the objective is *innovative* learning then it may be assumed that:

- Top management must take a central role in the design of the experimentation, in monitoring the details of its progress, and in assessing its implications for the larger organization.
- The experimentation must be designed to explore the potentials of fundamentally redefined agency purposes and modes of operation.
- One or more key members of top management must have specific responsibility for building the agency's capacity to act on the potentials so identified.
- Major attention must be focused on the changes in organizational values, structures, and management systems required to support desired changes in field level operations.

A Capacity-Building Strategy

The capacity to manage social learning is itself a form of social knowledge which is created through social problem solving and which is not easily transmitted through textbooks or conventional training. The key to its formation is to encourage a growing number of experiments in innovative social learning through facilitating the formation of what for the sake of convenience will be referred to as *social learning clusters*. Each such cluster would include the major public or private operating agency in which a learning process is centered and a group of supporting knowledge resource institutions.

Then to encourage the reflection, exchange, and documentation that is crucial to making social learning a fully conscious process and to speeding its advance it is desirable that knowledge resource institutions involved in a variety of social learning clusters be formed into *social learning networks*. While the primary purpose of such networks would be to facilitate the exchange of experience gained through the cluster involvements of their members, secondary outputs would include: (1) a continually growing understanding of the unique nature and requirements of the role of the knowledge resource institution in facilitating social learning; and (2) contributions to the building of a more formalized body of knowledge and method which, while no substitute for firsthand experience, would make the process of acquiring such experience easier for others.

There are, thus, two somewhat separable activities involved. One is the formation and facilitation of social learning clusters. The other is the formation and facilitation of social learning networks. The former, to the extent that external intervention and support is required, can be substantially facilitated by interested and sympathetic donor organizations with permanent in-country staff and the ability to make facilitating grants to the action agency involved. Unfortunately it is a role which requires a greater level of in-country staff input, intellectual credibility, and funding flexibility than most important donors are at present able to provide. The Ford Foundation has provided one prototype for the type of staffing patterns and funding style required. Presumably other interested donors could develop their own capacities to facilitate the formation and operating of such social learning clusters if they chose to do so.

The second of the two major activities, the formation and facilitation of social learning networks, might proceed more or less as follows:

- Identify a number of priority topics on which there is need for rapid advance in social knowledge of direct relevance to the management of social transformation.
- For each priority topic, form a social learning network comprised of individuals and institutions which are already engaged in social learning clusters or which exhibit substantial potential for participating in the formation of such clusters.
- Facilitate periodic exchange of experience between members of such networks to strengthen their ability to contribute to their respective or prospective social learning clusters.
- Support activities carried out within the context of each individual network which lead to the documentation, comparative study, and dissemination of the social learning cluster experiences through publication, training, and advisory activities.
- As the capacity-building process gains momentum, facilitate exchanges between networks and form new networks as new needs and opportunities are identified.

One prototype for the formation of such networks might be the Management Institutes Working Group on Social Development which was formed by four leading Third World management institutes in 1977 to facilitate the sharing of their experiences directed to developing new management technologies appropriate to the special requirements of social development.[33] This network has helped strengthen the work on social development management at each of the member institutes while also contributing to the broader recognition that new styles of development action depend on achieving significant changes in the structures and modes of operation of governmental bureaucracies that are achieved only through the sustained commitments of top level leadership. The experience of this group suggests that each network should have its own governing structure to ensure that it remains responsive to the interests of its members. At the same time each should have its own coordinator whose role would involve helping the network members arrive at a synthesis of their individual experiences to shape a shared intellectual agenda and to facilitate the publication and broader dissemination of the experience being generated. This individual must be able to at once provide intellectual leadership within the network and yet remain highly sensitive to the interests of the individual participants.

Four priority topics are suggested as the basis around which to form the initial learning networks.

- Planning Methods for a Closed-System Economics
- Mutual Self-Help Approaches to Social Services
- Community Level Management of Natural Resources
- Bureaucratic Reorientation.

The question of whether individual networks should include both developed and developing country participation and whether more than one network might be formed for a given topic might be left open for the moment. Since there are likely advantages in limiting the size of individual networks, consideration might over time be given to forming regional networks around a given topic, linked together by a global network which brings together the leading institutions in each of the regional networks.

The substance of each topic area is elaborated below. Each is shaped by the framework of the new paradigm based on concepts of closed-systems economics and innovative social learning. Each will stress the themes of sustainability, equity, human well-being, and participation. Given the power of the old paradigm and the ease of slipping back into its general frame of reference, the presentation of each topic includes a cautionary note on the more likely pitfalls which this effort should take care to avoid, especially in its early stages.

Planning Methods for a Closed-System Economics

The outdated and increasing dysfunctional frameworks of open-system "cowboy" economics are likely to continue to dominate decision making until the theoretical and methodological basis of an alternative closed-system "spaceman" economics becomes well established. Support for the development and application, through a social learning process, of planning tools based on an alternative economics should receive a high priority. A learning network should be formed of individuals and institutions pioneering the development of such tools within an applied context, i.e., within an agency which is seeking to integrate their use into its own decision processes.

Of major interest would be development planning systems which lead to fundamentally reshaping the definition of the development problems on the part of government agencies and others. One example would be the work of the Joint Centre for Environmental Sciences at the University of Canterbury, New Zealand which is working with a number of government ministries on energy accounting methods for assessing the net energy implications of alternative schemes for developing unused agricultural and forestry lands. They were able to demonstrate that one proposed scheme to introduce an export crop would have required a substantial net energy subsidy just for the production, and that an alternative cropping use would result in a substantial net energy contribution through a more efficient biological conversion of solar energy. Another example is the collaborative effort being planned by USAID and the Philippines' National Economic Development Authority to develop capabilities for substantially new approaches to provincial and regional level development planning which emphasize support for the self-help development efforts of major poverty groups. The planning methods involved would center on the identification of major categories of poor households classified by the characteristics of their survival strategies in relationship to their access to and use of local land and water resources, and identifying potential opportunities for enhancing the returns to the households from their own self-help efforts through increased access to resources, new technologies, and new forms of social organization. Major attention would be given to ways in which the poor themselves can take a more active and effective role in the equitable, productive, and sustainable management of local resources, building from rather than attempting to displace the "informal" or "unorganized" economy.[34]

In general, the planning systems of interest would attempt to highlight relationships between human needs, available resources, net energy flows, and alternative production systems. They would draw attention to opportunities for self-help initiatives, for local governance, for small-scale, worker-owned and/or controlled production units, for recycling, for using waste products as resource inputs to new industries, for developing local sources of renewable energy generation and reduction in energy subsidy requirements, and for managing natural resource systems in ways which gain full advantage from them while sustaining their long-term productive potential. They would facilitate the examination of alternative production systems and population distribution patterns in terms of their net energy implications and their compatibility with natural ecological processes.

Efforts to tinker at the margins with the decision-making tools of the open-system paradigm such as internalizing certain pollution costs into cost benefit analysis do not reflect the fundamental departures ultimately required and probably should not occupy the attention of this network, nor should theoretical exercises in how to allocate pollution costs. In general approaches which seek to address these complex problems *mainly* in terms of investment choices and the comparison of economic costs against economic benefits are holdovers from the old paradigm—distractions from the more fundamental innovative learning which the problem demands.[35]

Mutual Self-Help Approaches to Social Services

Modernization has been accompanied by a trend toward professionalizing, centralizing, and publicly funding an ever growing number of activities which once were the province of the individual, the family, and the community—from health care, home building, and neighborhood renewal to day care and care of the elderly. The financial and managerial burdens of this approach to meeting basic human needs are proving too much even for the most wealthy of nations, to say nothing of the depersonalization, inefficiency, and general ineffectiveness of many such programs. But reversing the trend is not a simple matter. Modernization and increased education and mobility have had a substantial impact on the family and community relationships on which traditional mutual self-help activities were traditionally based and on the level and quality of the services demanded. New mutual self-help arrangements must reflect the realities of these changes and come to terms with the constraints imposed by professional and bureaucratic monopolies and the complex web of governmental regulations which sustain them.

Substantial experimentation is taking place within contemporary settings, as extensively documented by Stokes[36] and others, directed to the creation of new mutual self-help arrangements to meet needs for mental and physical health care, family planning, home building, neighborhood rehabilitation, dispute settlement, child care, transportation, even agricultural research within the more modern social context. In general, the experiments which should be of interest are those designed to function largely under individual or local level control with only minimal governmental regulation and partial subsidy—though quite possibly with governmental encouragement and technical support. It is suggested that this network *not* be concerned with schemes where the central feature is the use of those paraprofessionals who work largely as extensions of centralized, professionalized service delivery agencies. Generally these are mainly efforts to tinker at the margins of the old paradigm without reducing the dependency creating power monopoly of the megastructures which supervise and fund them. Ivan Illich refers to it as the "colonization of the informal sector."[37]

At the other end of the spectrum are the truly spontaneous small-scale local initiatives which are nearly infinite in their number and variety. Such efforts are of substantial value and represent the cutting edge of the transformation. But their study is of limited utility unless it results in the generation of social knowledge imbedded in the structures of an agency able to act on it. Thus, the persons invited to participate in this network should generally be those who are collaborating in a social learning process centered in a large public or private agency concerned with developing its own capacity to facilitate the development of such local initiatives on a significant scale.

Emerging insights into a number of issues might result from the exchanges of such a network. What can be said about the differing requirements of different types of activities and the appropriate ways of organizing to address them? If services are self-financing how can access by the poorer members of the community be assured without creating dependence? What measures provide some assurance of quality and a maintenance of minimum community standards without resorting to formalized, depersonalized regulation that stifles the individual initiative being sought? What is the appropriate role of the agency which seeks to stimulate such mutual self-help initiatives? How can necessary community commitment be mobilized? What are the characteristics of communities in which such efforts are relatively easy as compared to those where they are relatively difficult? How can the relevant characteristics be identified and what responses are appropriate given various sets of circumstances?

Community Level Management of Natural Resources

While closely related to the topic of mutual self-help approaches to social services, the community level management of natural resources involves complex issues relating to asset control, benefits allocation, adaptation of technology to microenvironments, and preservation of productive potentials that seem to merit specialized attention. This network would share experiences in developing individual and community capability to manage natural resource systems: land, water, energy, air, and waste management. The focus would be on approaches designed to achieve equitable, intensified, and sustainable use of natural resources. Programs relating to the local management of fishing grounds, irrigation, household water, soil erosion, grazing lands, cropping systems innovations, forests, renewable energy sources, etc. would all be of interest here. In the urban setting it might include programs aimed at increasing food self-sufficiency through use of backyards, city lots, rooftops and balconies for intensive home gardening. Of particular concern would be issues relating to organization for resource management to obtain an effective balance between individual initiative, collective control, and incentives for resource conservation.

This is an area in which it is easy to slip into concern for strictly technical issues abstracted from social reality—theoretical water use efficiencies of alternative schemes of irrigation water distribution, or the comparative biologic and economic benefits of alternative cropping systems. The sharing of strictly technical information is *not* an appropriate function of this network. Nor should it concern itself with isolated local experiences any more than should the network on mutual self-help social services. Rather it should be comprised of people working within the setting of a larger agency concerned with the efforts to achieve in real life settings an improved configuration between local social structures, technologies, and microenvironments which result in productive, equitable, and sustainable production systems. The interest is not in identifying replicable models— local conditions are likely to be sufficiently diverse that replicability of models is a false god. Rather the concern is with developing frameworks for understanding the dynamics of the system involved and the processes by which combinations appropriate to any given local setting can best be worked out.

Bureaucratic Reorientation

From a management perspective the central challenge of social transformation is how to build into large bureaucratic organizations a capacity for innovative learning leading to a fundamental reorientation in their purposes and modes of operation.[38] While all of the other learning networks proposed would to some extent be concerned with this issue, the others would be more concerned with the ends of bureaucratic reorientation: What is the agency in question trying to learn to do by way of strengthening particular kinds of community level, action-taking capabilities. The bureaucratic reorientation network would focus specifically on management of the innovative social-learning process—its organization, change strategies, and the types of internal policies, organizational structures, procedures, personnel skills and values toward which the agency must evolve. One of this network's concerns would be with identifying and articulating the implications of alternative ways of linking knowledge resource institutions into the process.

For reasons of simplicity the discussion of social-learning clusters has so far been presented as if such clusters would always be centered in individual agencies of government, generally with line functions, and concerned with the reorientation of the internal structures of such agencies. But the needs for innovative social learning extend beyond these relatively straightforward situations. For example, there will be a need to learn how to plan and coordinate development actions across a number of line agencies within a defined geographical area. This will involve planning bodies, local governments, and political bodies. How can these be joined into a learning process leading to the alteration of their roles and relationships in ways consistent with a development process based on closed-systems economics and social-learning approaches to policy formulation? How to address such complicating realities would be included among the concerns of this network. While the problem of achieving effective community input to the development decision process would be a natural concern of all networks, it would be a particular interest of the bureaucratic reorientation network.

The bureaucratic reorientation network would not address the more conventional concerns of development and public administration. It would, for example, give priority to the management of systems over the management of projects, to innovation over compliance, and to methodologies for continuous self-monitoring and rapid self-correction over formalized planning and evaluation methodologies.

*   *   *

The management of social transformation calls for radical departures from commonly accepted approaches, concepts, and methods of operation. There are able and committed people all around the world who recognize the need and who are capable of breaking with old assumptions and reaching for new approaches, both within major action agencies and strong knowledge resource institutions. But they generally work in institutional settings which reinforce only those behaviors consistent with the old paradigm. They remain largely isolated from one another and may lack frameworks for translating into action that which they think is needed. When they attempt to act within the system in ways consistent with their sense of the new reality they face formidable obstacles.

The proposed effort to facilitate the formation of social-learning clusters and networks is in part an effort to form a larger action coalition *within* the system, linking together such individuals in a collective commitment to appropriate action and providing them with an enlarged mutual support system able to lend legitimacy to their efforts and to facilitate the more rapid emergence of the operational concepts and methodologies needed to translate their good intentions into effective action. This proposal sketches the bare outlines of such an effort. The details can only emerge out of the social learning process itself, a product of an ever expanding circle of creative minds addressing a shared concern with the context of their individual local realities.

Notes

1. This article is based on a paper prepared for the United Nations University (UNU) at the request of its rector, Dr. Soedjatmoko, as a contribution to a proposed UNU program in the management of social transformation. The views expressed are those of the author.

2. Peter L. Berger and Richard John Neuhaus, *To Empower People: The Role of Mediating Structures in Public Policy* (Washington, D.C.: American Enterprise Institute for Public Policy Research, 1977), pp. 2–3.

3. Alvin Toffler, *The Third Wave* (New York: William Morrow and Company, Inc., 1980), p. 368; and Kenneth E. Boulding, "The Economics of the Coming Spaceship Earth." *Environmental Quality in a Growing Economy* (Baltimore: Johns Hopkins Press, 1966) as reprinted in Herman E. Daly (ed.), *Toward a Steady-State Economy* (San Francisco: W. H. Freeman and Company), pp. 121–132.

4. *Op. cit.*

5. Bruce Stokes, "Local Responses to Global Problems: A Key to Meeting Basic Human Needs," *Worldwatch Paper 17,* Worldwatch Institute, 1776 Massachusetts Avenue, N.W., Washington, D.C. 20036, February 1978.

6. W. Boyd Littrell, "Bureaucracy in the Eighties: Introduction." *The Journal of Applied Behavioral Science,* Vol. 16. No. 3, July-September (1980), p. 263.

7. Willis W. Harman, "Key Choices of the Next Two Decades," *A Look at Business in 1990: A Summary of the White House Conference on the Industrial World Ahead* (Washington, D.C.: U.S. Government Printing Office. 1972).

8. *Idem.*

9. See Elizabeth Dodson Gray, *Why the Green Nigger: ReMything Genesis* (Wellesley, Mass.: Roundtable Press, 1979).

10. Boulding, *op. cit.*

11. *Idem.*

12. Kathleen Newland, "City Limits: Emerging Constraints on Urban Growth," *Worldwatch Paper 38,* Worldwatch Institute, 1776 Massachusetts Avenue, N.W., Washington. D.C. 20036, August 1980.

13. George Carner, "Survival, Interdependence, and Competition Among the Rural Poor," Paper presented at the Philippine Sociological Society's 1980 National Convention. November 27–28, 1980 at the Faculty Center Hall, University of the Philippines, Diliman, Quezon City. Forthcoming in *Asian Survey.*

14. Newland, *op. cit.;* and Kathleen Newland, "Global Employment and Economic Justice: The Policy Challenge." *Worldwatch Paper 28.* Worldwatch Institute, 1776 Massachusetts Avenue, N.W., Washington, D.C. 20036, April 1979.

15. Newland, "City Limits," *op. cit.*

16. Robert Fuller, "Inflation: The Rising Cost of Living on a Small Planet," *Worldwatch Paper 34,* Worldwatch Institute, 1776 Massachusetts Avenue, N.W., Washington, D.C. 20036, January 1980.

17. Use of the term *closed-system* requires some qualification in this context. "Highly-bounded" or "relatively closed" might be technically more correct, though awkward, expressions. Using to the fullest the solar energy input to the system

would most likely be a central concern in closed-system economics. Closed-systems economics is also likely to be oriented toward regional and local self-sufficiency to reduce the energy costs of transportation. But here again the system will be closed only in comparative, not in absolute terms.

18. The following discussion of this problem has been substantially influenced by Russell L. Ackoff, *Redesigning the Future: A Systems Approach to Societal Problems* (New York: John Wiley & Sons, 1974); Edgar S. Dunn, Jr., *Economic and Social Development: A Process of Social Learning* (Baltimore: The Johns Hopkins Press, 1971); J. Friedmann and G. Abonyi, "Social Learning: A Model for Policy Research," *Environment and Planning,* Vol. 8, 1976, pp. 927–940; John Friedmann and Barclay Hudson, "Knowledge and Action: A Guide to Planning Theory," *AIP Journal,* January 1974, pp. 2–16; John D. Steinbruner, *The Cybernetic Theory of Decision: New Dimensions of Political Analysis* (Princeton, N.J.: Princeton University Press, 1974); Aaron Wildavsky, *Speaking Truth to Power: The Art and Craft of Policy Analysis* (Boston: Little, Brown and Company, 1980), and the writing and lectures of Willis Harman. While it might be argued that the model of scientific knowledge presented below is an idealized view not reflected in the reality of the physical sciences, it remains the ideal which the social sciences have tended to take as their standard.

19. Dunn, *op. cit.,* pp. 240–41.

20. Wildavsky, *op. cit.*

21. Policy analysts of the intellectual cognition school have come to focus attention on the reality that bureaucracies seldom act so faithfully, leading to the development of a field of study called "implementation analysis" which starts from exactly the opposite assumption, i.e., that bureaucracies are totally perverse in their orientation and are intent on defeating the intentions of the policy makers. Eugene Bardach, *The Implementation Game: What Happens After a Bill Becomes Law* (Cambridge, Mass.: MIT Press, 1977) caricatures this perspective in this volume which is described on its cover as revealing "the strategies employed by bureaucracies to impede enactment of new laws" and offering guidance to policy planners on how "to design against these problems for more game-proof legislation."

22. Wildavsky, *op. cit.,* p. 8, makes the categorical statement that this type of planning ". . . has failed everywhere it has been tried." It calls for predictive and computational capabilities which simply do not exist.

23. Dunn, *op. cit.,* p. 238, observes that: "the distinctive thing about the social process is that mankind, as individuals and as groups, is capable of *behavior directed to changing behavior.* Change [in social system behavior] is not purely stochastic, but includes a purposive element."

24. James W. Botkin, Mahdi Elmandjra, and Mircea Malitza, *No Limits to Learning: Bridging the Human Gap* (Oxford: Pergamon Press, 1979), p. 6.

25. Etzioni as cited by Friedmann and Hudson, *op. cit.,* p. 10.

26. For further discussion of the limitations of blueprint planning see David C. Korten, "Community Organization and Rural Development: A Learning Process Approach," *Public Administration Review,* Vol. 40, No. 5, September/October (1980), pp. 480–5, 1.

27. For an excellent analysis of these issues in relation to the day care problem see Richard R. Nelson, *The Moon and the Ghetto: An Essay on Public Policy Analysis* (New York: W. W. Norton & Company, Inc., 1977), pp. 81–104.

28. *Op. cit.*

29. *Op. cit.*

30. For further discussion of the role of error in social learning see Donald N. Michael, *On Learning to Plan—and Planning to Learn* (San Francisco: Jossey-Bass Publishers, 1973), pp. 131–143; and D. Korten, *op. cit.*, pp. 498–499.

31. The choice of variables on which feedback is provided is obviously of critical importance in shaping the way in which problems are defined at the local level. The issues involved go beyond the scope of this paper, however.

32. For a case example demonstrating the application of this approach within the Philippine National Irrigation Administration and illustrating the methods employed see Korten, *op. cit.*; Benjamin U. Bagadion and Frances F. Korten, "Developing Viable Irrigators' Associations: Lessons from Small Scale Irrigation Development in the Philippines," *Agricultural Administration*, Vol. 7, 1980, pp. 273–287; and Frances F. Korten, "Building National Capacity to Develop Water Users' Associations: Experience From the Philippines," Ford Foundation, Manila. Paper prepared for World Bank Sociological Workshop, Washington, D.C. July 27, 1981. To appear as a World Bank Staff Paper.

33. David C. Korten, "The Management Institutes Working Group on Social Development," Working Paper of the Management Institutes Working Group on Social Development, The Asian Institute of Management, Makati, Philippines, 1981.

34. For further discussion of this and other applications of people-centered planning methods see David C. Korten, "Social Development: Putting People First," in David C. Korten and Felipe B. Alfonso (eds.), *Bureaucracy and the Poor: Closing the Gap* (Singapore: McGraw-Hill, 1981), pp. 201–221.

35. There is no intention to imply here that conventional economic considerations can be ignored in decision making under the new paradigm—quite the contrary. Such choices must meet the standard of economic viability, but the tools required for such assessments are already well developed. This is not the area in which innovative learning is needed.

36. *Op. cit.*

37. Ivan Illich, "The New Frontier for Arrogance: Colonization of the Informal Sector," *International Development Review,* Vol. XXII, No. 2–3, 1980, pp. 96–101.

38. The argument for and the concept of bureaucratic reorientation is developed in greater detail in David C. Korten and Norman T. Uphoff, "Bureaucratic Reorientation for Rural Development," unpublished paper available from the Center for International Studies, Cornell University, Ithaca, New York, April 1980.

26

LEADERSHIP: ARRANGING THE CHAIRS—REFLECTIONS ON THE LESSONS OF NEELY GARDNER

Camille Cates Barnett

Introduction

In the middle of a department head retreat, I returned to the empty meeting room to find our facilitator Neely Gardner arranging the chairs.

"Neely, you shouldn't be doing that! Here, let me help. Shall I get someone in here to do that?"

"No, Camille, it's my job. You see," he said with a wry look, "It's one of the most important things I do: arrange the chairs."

I thought he must be joking. He was not. Even when Neely joked, he was not joking.

At that time, he explained something about the theory of physical arrangement determining perspective, communication, and behavior patterns. To this day, I never enter a room or host a meeting without checking the physical arrangement. It goes with my other permanent addictions from Neely—flip charts and index cards.

Source: *Public Administration Quarterly* 16(1992): 180–188.

But this memory of Neely stays with me for other reasons. My mind's eye can still see Neely arranging those chairs, gently teaching me my most important lesson about leadership: a person with power can act with humility.

Neely's understanding of power was the opposite of most of what I had been taught until then. Neely believed a person gained power by empowering others, not by controlling them. Neely taught me that leaders are facilitators.

Neely's arranging those chairs taught me another lesson: complex systems are changed by small interventions. Those leverage points are not found rationally but by intuition. Neely taught me that changing organizations requires one to think differently. A fundamental shift of mind allows one to see order emerging from chaos.

Action Training, Research as Leadership Theory

Action Training and Research (AT&R) was a favorite theory and practice for Neely. When he taught it to me, I never considered it a theory of *training*; it always seemed to be a theory of *leadership*. Listen to Neely summarize in four sentences a complete theory of leadership. It also happens to be his theory of AT&R (Gardner, 1974:107):

> [P]eople are more likely to change if they participate in exploring the reasons for, and means of, change. Human beings are goal centered and will behave in a way consistent with achieving goals. Participative leadership is effective in setting the stage for creativity, productivity, and innovation. The action training and research process releases the interpersonal energies that are stifled in most authority-bound systems.

I have spent the 20 years since Neely taught me this finding ways to make it work in cities. It is a leadership theory that can bring both success and significance.

AT&R is simple and straightforward. As Neely (1978:92) describes it:

> The practice is for individuals interested in engaging in change to embark on a VOYAGE OF DISCOVERY together (1) estimating the situation, (2) defining the problems and opportunities, and (3) undertaking a mutually satisfactory course of action.

Neely's strategy for change is also a strategy for leadership. The values of his strategy are the values of a superb leader (*Ibid.*):

> [B]ring people together rather than divide them; lead to cooperation rather than opposition; and help to promote a sense of community and trust.

So much of what I actually *do* when I assume responsibility for a new organization is based on the AT&R model Neely described.

Phase 1: Orientation

Identify the clients. All the clients. The real clients.

Make sure they know your values. As Neely (1974:108) said, "My own bias is toward helping create a situation in which we consciously move toward individual freedom and effectiveness."

When I became City Manager of Austin, Texas, my first client was the city council who hired me. Once hired, my clients expanded to include citizens of Austin, the news media, several interest groups, the executives, and the workforce as a whole. Balancing the expectations of these clients first requires that all the clients are identified.

As I entered the city and the organization, I spoke consistently of two values: service and leadership. These words were the basis of all of my speeches to community groups, my introduction of myself to the department directors, and my interviews with the news media. I paid attention to the response. The reaction and resonance made me feel I was in the right place.

Phase 2: Contract Setting

Pay attention to the psychological contract. ". . . [M]odel and elicit effective and authentic communication" (Gardner, 1974:108).

One of my first acts with my new council was to change a communications rule of my predecessors. No longer were council members barred from speaking directly with department directors. Everything no longer has to go through the city manager's office. Directors and council members now understand each other's perspective and information is easier to get and to give. That change in communication continues to improve understanding and build trust.

Recognizing that my first day on the job would be covered by the media and could be a symbolic statement of values, I focused on communications. My first meeting was with department directors introducing myself. That first day I also met for lunch with firefighters, with the city manager office staff, with the Mayor, and the news media. None of the images were behind a desk; all the photos were of a manager reaching out, communicating, and listening.

In my first weeks on the job, I met with each executive and council member individually, toured city facilities, met city employees, held a one-day management retreat, and spoke to community groups.

I have not consciously thought about the psychological contract for some time, but I realize on reflection how much it governs my entry into an organization. The implicit deal I was making was: "I will be open with you if you will do the same with me. I can help you, but you must also help me."

Phase 3: Reconnaissance

Enter an organization with an attitude of ignorance.

Neely turned ignorance into both an asset and a strategy. This notion that ignorance was valuable because you have no preconceived answers is a freeing one for me. Ignorance as a strategy compels you to listen. As a theory of leadership, recognizing ignorance keeps the leader in balance and empowers those led. Neely taught me to keep my eyes and ears open and my mouth shut.

For the first several months on the job, I resisted the inevitable questions and dangerous temptations to give my views on various local issues. Instead, with both the city council and the city executives, I used Neely's (1974:109) magic three questions:

What is going well in the organization that should not be changed?
What are the abrasive or problem areas that should be examined?
If you could change the organization with "a stroke of the pen," what would you do?

These questions were some of the first I asked when new to this organization and I still ask them. A year into the job, I used a variation of the three questions to ask all the directors and assistant directors to evaluate me. Using the ubiquitous index cards, I asked them: "What am I doing that helps you that you want me to *keep* doing? What am I doing that gets in the way that you want me to *stop* doing? What would help you that I can *start* doing?

The notion of leadership embodied in the reconnaissance phase of AT&R is both subtle and dramatic. The leader is not assumed to be the one who knows the most. The leader sets the direction *after* listening to those in the organization and those served in the organization. Neely's lesson for leaders is that they must be learners.

Neely was ahead of his time. What he said, wrote, taught, and did decades ago is now the popular press. I smiled last year and thought of Neely when I read this in *Fortune Magazine* (1989:48):

Forget your old, tired ideas about leadership. The most successful corporation of the 1990's will be something called a learning organization, a consummately adaptive enterprise with workers freed to think for themselves, to identify problems and opportunities, and to go after them. In such an organization, the leader will ensure that everyone has the resources and power to make swift day-to-day decisions. Faced with challenges we can guess at now, he or she will set the overall direction for the enterprise, after listening to a thousand voices from within the company and without. In this sense, the leader will have to be the best learner of them all.

Neely taught leaders to thing differently about their job.

Phases 4 and 5: Problems, Opportunities, and Goals

The listening of the reconnaissance phase provides Problem and Opportunity Identification (Phase 4) and Goals or Aspirations (Phase 5).

In Austin, the active listening I did led me to conceptualize 3 goals: 1) focus on customer service: 2) invest in the workforce; and 3) live within our means. These 3 goals were first presented to the council in the first budget presented by the new city manager. These 3 goals have since become the foundation for our Management Plan, our city's one-page statement of goals for the year. These 3 goals now also form the departmental annual business plans and the basis for each individual executive's performance plan and performance evaluation. These goals ring true and are helping this organization change not because I was so smart but because I listened.

Phase 6: Analysis

One of Neely's favorite forms of Analysis is the Lewin-inspired force field analysis. It is a simple method to identify forces *driving* toward the change and forces *restraining* the change.

The lesson from force field analysis is that it is often easier to remove an obstacle rather than to overcome it. Using analysis as a strategy for leadership has also taught me to be less impulsive, to value research, and to check assumptions.

Phases 7–12: Plan, Act, and Evaluate

The last phases of the AT&R model are to develop a plan, act on it, and evaluate it. Experimentation (Phase 7) is followed by Results Analysis (Phase 8), Program Design (Phase 9), Program Implementation (Phase 10), Evaluation and Feedback (Phase 11), and Rc-Cycle (Phase 12).

The problem with describing this model is that it begins to sound linear, sequential, rational, reductionistic, and boring. Neely tries to describe an essentially intuitive, right-brain, nonlinear approach to organizations in the popular language of his time. The result is that his description of his methods are sometimes different from my observations of his methods.

My observation of Neely's theory and methods were that they were experimental, participative, and iterative. The theory fits most of what actually goes on in organizational change. The model is more of a spiral than a line. Neely was describing a paradigm shift. It is difficult to use the language from one paradigm to describe another paradigm. Perhaps it is as Thomas S. Kuhn said: "Communication across the revolutionary divide is inevitably partial" (quoted in Gleick, 1987:241).

Neely's insight is not that any sequential, linear process cam change an organization, but that a simple process applied to a complex system will uncover the basic order in the chaos. The analogy with scientists in chaos research seems appropriate for Neely's work with organizational theory (Gleick, 1987:266):

> It reflected the faith of these scientists that order was so deeply ingrained in apparent disorder that it would find a way of expressing itself even to experimenters who did not know which physical variables to measure or who were not able to measure variables directly . . .

Neely taught that "organic" organizations were healthier than "mechanistic" bureaucracies. He had faith in this new metaphor for organizations because he trusted some force or order or pattern he perceived in those systems. He also understood the relationship of the leader and the organization that reminds me again of scientists studying chaos (Gleick, 1987:24):

> Nonlinearity means the act of playing the game has a way of changing the rules . . .

A leader is never separate from an organization; each changes the other. Action Training and Research is a nonlinear, intuitive, participative approach to leading and changing organizations.

Participative Leadership

Neely also recognized that, because his theory is simple and straightforward, some will reject it. Action Training and Research is not a theory and practice of leadership that is elitist. It is inclusive and democratic. It is leadership for the many, not the few. In a master understatement, Neely (1978:92) says:

> It is difficult for some people to believe that the act of participating, influencing and serving can bring about a commitment and the feeling of community necessary to solve the problems that face us.

Neely understood something he never fully articulated. He understood that participation was a leverage point that could fundamentally change complex systems. He understood a primary leadership task to be empowering people. He trusted the underlying patterns in organizations, the health in chaos. He understood that nonlinearity in feedback processes serves to regulate and control, to keep the system on track (Gleick, 1987:292):

> What has become clear to me as I have used Neely's theory and practice is surprising.

My first surprise was: "I thought I would be in charge!" It took a while to realize that city management is an oxymoron. Being chief executive officer of a billion dollar municipal corporation does not mean a glamorous lifestyle among the power brokers of the land. It does not mean grateful people happily following your wise orders.

It means something much more important. It means I have the opportunity to learn what real leadership is all about. What Neely taught me is that we are all connected, and a true leader reminds us of that. What has become clear to me is that leadership is stewardship. Real leaders are not just successful. They leave behind something of significance.

The ancient Athenians understood this notion of the leader's legacy of significance. The last line of the Oath of the Athenian City State read: "We will transmit this city not only not less, but greater, better and more beautiful than it was transmitted to us."

What has also become clear to me is that leadership is by example. Who we are and what we do speak louder than anything we say or anything that is said about us. We are all role models, whether we realize it or not. What has become clear to me is that complex organizations are not managed by systems of control but by systems of values. Organizations based on respect for the individual breed creativity and joy. It is the little things that happen between people that make a great family, a great organization or a great city. It is creating an environment that nurtures the quality of those interactions that makes a great leader.

What has become clear to me is that the underbelly of power is interdependence. A leader's power comes from an abiding respect for connections, not dominance. What has become clear to me is something beyond success. It is not enough to achieve. It is not enough to be recognized. Some leaders never succeed according to society's standards. And some of our most important leaders are never recognized.

A leader does more than succeed; he does work of significance. Significance comes from your values. Doing what you really care for. Something that captures your imagination and ignites your passion. Something you would give your life for because that is what we are all doing. Little by little, day by day, we are giving our lives for something. Significance is born from a sense of stewardship, a sense of connection. The significance, the power of a leader is known by the values he/she personifies and by the beauty he/she leaves behind.

Neely's Challenge

As I reread much of what Neely left behind, I was arrested by the following passage, a challenge to all of us now leading cities (Gardner, 1978:92):

> Most persons engaged in the business of managing our cities know full well that knowledge, skill and resources exist which should enable us to solve many vexing and troublesome urban problems. Despite this technical capability, these problems are not being solved—indeed, may never be solved—because people had not developed agreement and commitment to the solutions. It is also generally accepted that for many of the problems we face there are a whole range of viable options available for their solution. Any of these solutions might lead to a more desirable state than that which presently exists because we are fiddling while the city deteriorates.

Neely cared what happened. He cared particularly about government, organizations, and leaders who did not do their jobs. His response was to show how. He changed organizations and taught people.

Neely was a model of a learning leader. He melded theory and practice. He managed me like I would like to manage others—by not *managing*; he *led*. It never crossed my mind that he did not care. He believed in people.

He taught me to think differently: to empower others; to see patterns, not just events; to trust my intuition; to find the order in chaos; to do what I really cared about.

Leadership for Neely was in the arranging of the chairs: create the environment; focus the energy; facilitate the interaction; take care of the people.

Thank you, Neely.

References

Dumaine, Brian (1989). "What the Leaders of Tomorrow See." *Fortune Magazine* (July 3).

Gardner, Neely (1974). "Action Training and Research: Something Old and Something New." *Public Administration Review* (March):103–112.

_____ (1978). "The Law of the Other Guy's 'Thing'," in *Cases in Public Administration: Narratives in Administrative Problems*. Boston: Holbrook Press.

Gleick, James (1987). *Chaos*. New York: Viking Penguin.

EDITOR'S REFERENCES

Barnard, Chester I. 1938. *The Functions of the Executive*. Cambridge, MA: Harvard University Press.

Cooke, Jacob E., ed. 1961. *The Federalist*. Middletown, CT: Wesleyan University Press.

Finer, Herman. 1941. Administrative responsibility in democratic government. *Public Administration Review* 1 (Summer): 335–350.

Friedrich, Carl Joachim. 1940. Public policy and the nature of administrative responsibility. In *Public Policy: A Yearbook of the Graduate School of Public Administration, Harvard University*, eds. C. J. Friedrich and Edward S. Mason. Cambridge, MA: Harvard University Press, 3–24.

Gardner, Neely. 1974. Action training and research: Something old and something new. *Public Administration Review* 34(2): 106–115.

Gulick, Luther, and Lyndall Urwick. 1937. *Papers on the Science of Administration*. New York: Institute of Public Administration.

Sayre, Wallace. 1950. Trends of a decade in administrative values. *Public Administration Review* 10(1): 1–9.

Schachter, Hindy Lauer. 1998. *Reinventing Government or Reinventing Ourselves*. Albany, NY: State University of New York Press.

Stivers, Camilla. 2000. *Bureau Men, Settlement Women: Constructing Public Administration in the Progressive Era*. Lawrence, KS: University Press of Kansas.

Waldo, Dwight. 1948. *The Administrative State*. New York: Ronald Press.

Weber, Max. 1968 (1922). Bureaucracy. In Max Weber, *Economy and Society*, Vol. 3, eds. Guenther Roth and Claus Wittich. New York: Bedminster Press, 956–1005.

Wilson, Woodrow. 1887. The study of administration. *Political Science Quarterly* 2(2): 197–222.

ABOUT THE EDITOR

Camilla Stivers is Albert A. Levin Professor of Urban Studies and Public Service at Cleveland State University and associate editor of *Public Administration Review.* For nearly two decades she was a manager in nonprofit and public organizations. She is the author of *Bureau Men, Settlement Women: Constructing Public Administration in the Progressive Era* and *Gender Images in Public Administration: Legitimacy and the Administrative State.*

INDEX

509